Why Do You Need This New Edition?

If you're wondering why you should buy this new edition of *American Government* here are six good reasons!

1. **New Chapter Openers** have been added to each chapter of the book. These discussions present the latest political developments at the outset of each chapter, framing the discussion for each chapter's content.
2. **New presentation of Learning Objectives.** Each chapter now contains a "What We Will Learn" section in which each objective is phrased as a question, and the "What We Learned" summary at the end of each chapter is now framed in the form of answers to the questions that were posed at the beginning of the chapter.
3. **New advice on how to succeed in college** is now included throughout the book via a text message learning tip feature.
4. **Several chapters have been reorganized for greater clarity to students**. Chapters 1, 2, and 5 have been reorganized and sections have been re-titled to further enhance student understanding of key concepts in American politics.
5. **A discussion of the 24-hour news cycle** has been added to Chapter 6 along with a new chapter opener on the decline of the newspaper business and its possible impact on the quality of democracy in the United States.
6. **Chapter 9 contains discussions of new concepts.** This chapter now covers the concepts of issue ownership and the invisible primary. There is also a new discussion of the proposed reform of the Electoral College through the adoption of an interstate compact.

PEARSON STUDY EDITION

American Government

POLICY AND POLITICS

Eleventh Edition

NEAL TANNAHILL
Houston Community College

Pearson
Boston Columbus Indianapolis New York San Francisco Upper Saddle River
Amsterdam Cape Town Dubai London Madrid Milan Munich Paris Montreal Toronto
Delhi Mexico City São Paulo Sydney Hong Kong Seoul Singapore Taipei Tokyo

Executive Editor: Reid Hester
Associate Development Editor: Donna Garnier
Senior Media Producer: Stefanie Liebman
Senior Marketing Manager: Lindsey Prudhomme
Production Manager: Bob Ginsberg
Project Coordination, Text Design, and Electronic Page Makeup: S4Carlisle Publishing Services
Cover Design Manager/Cover Designer: John Callahan
Cover Photo: Inmagine/Aspireimages
Senior Manufacturing Buyer: Roy L. Pickering, Jr.
Printer and Binder: RR Donnelley & Sons Company/Crawfordsville
Cover Printer: RR Donnelley & Sons Company/Crawfordsville

Credits and acknowledgments borrowed from other sources and reproduced, with permission, in this textbook appear on the appropriate page within text or on page 533.

Library of Congress Cataloging-in-Publication Data
Tannahill, R. Neal, date.–
American government: policy and politics / Neal Tannahill.—11th ed.
p. cm.
Includes index.
ISBN-13: 978-0-205-21055-8
ISBN-10: 0-205-21055-4
1. United States—Politics and government—Textbooks. I. Title.
JK276.T35 2012
320.473—dc22
2011008392

10 9 8 7 6 5 4 3 2 1—DOC—14 13 12 11

www.pearsonhighered.com

ISBN 10: 0-205-21055-4
ISBN 13: 978-0-205-21055-8

Brief Contents

Contents

To the Instructor

New to This Edition

This edition has been revised throughout to reflect recent political developments from the last two years, including the 2010 midterm elections. In addition to updating the data in tables and figures, below are some of the specifics on what's new in each chapter:

Introduction The approach to the policymaking process has been updated and enhanced with the addition of the concepts of policy legitimation and policy change to the policymaking framework. Some definitions of terms have been revised as well.

Chapter 1 A new chapter opener focuses on the Arizona immigration law. The sections in the chapter have been rearranged and re-titled to provide for a more clear presentation to students. The concepts of socialism and mixed economy have been added to the section that discusses capitalism.

Chapter 2 A new chapter opener examines the interplay between the Constitution and politics by looking at the effort by Democrats in Congress to expand the State Children's Health Insurance Program (SCHIP). As in Chapter 1, sections within the chapter have been rearranged and re-titled for clarity.

Chapter 3 A new chapter opener discusses Race to the Top, the educational reform initiative of the Obama administration. A new discussion of nullification and state efforts to nullify healthcare reform has been added.

Chapter 4 A new chapter opener focuses on public attitudes toward abortion. A new Around the World feature on survey research in Afghanistan has been added, and the section on political philosophy has been re-written for greater clarity.

Chapter 5 A new chapter opener looks at the Tea Party movement, and the chapter has been reorganized for greater clarity.

Chapter 6 A new chapter opener discusses the decline of the newspaper business and its possible impact on the quality of democracy in the United States. Discussions of several new concepts have been added to this chapter, including the 24-hour news cycle.

Chapter 7 A new chapter opener discusses the impact of recent Supreme Court decisions on campaign finance restrictions on political campaigns, including the emergence of Super PACs.

Chapter 8 A new chapter opener examines the decision of Republican Governor Charlie Crist to run for the U.S. Senate as an independent because he was apparently too moderate to win the Republican primary. The definition of a political party has been revised to reflect the notion that power is an end in itself.

Chapter 9 A new chapter opener surveys the results of the 2010 midterm election and discusses their effect on national policymaking and redistricting. New concepts covered in this chapter include issue ownership and the invisible primary. There is also a new discussion of the proposed reform of the Electoral College through the adoption of an interstate compact.

Chapter 10 A new chapter opener traces the enactment of healthcare reform to illustrate the legislative process. The Around the World feature now focuses on healthcare in Canada, and the section on the filibuster has been updated to discuss its ubiquity in the modern Senate.

Chapter 11 A new chapter opener discusses the war in Afghanistan and the decision that President Obama made to add troops while, at the same time, declare a timetable for a future withdrawal.

Chapter 12 A new chapter opener focuses on the decision of the Obama administration to address climate change through the regulatory process rather than the legislative process. This chapter also includes a new Around the World feature on the response of the Egyptian government to the swine flu scare.

Chapter 13 A new chapter opener focuses on the role of Justice Anthony Kennedy as the swing vote on a closely divided Supreme Court.

Chapter 14 A new chapter opener focuses on the federal deficit and the growth of the national debt. The Around the World feature now spotlights the debt crisis in Greece, and an overview of the new healthcare reform legislation has also been added.

Chapter 15 A new chapter opener describes the recent decision of the U.S. Supreme Court that life in prison without the possibility of parole for juvenile offenders constitutes cruel and unusual punishment under the Eighth Amendment. This chapter also contains a new section on gun rights that focuses on recent Supreme Court rulings on the meaning of the Second Amendment.

Chapter 16 A new chapter opener examines the legal challenge against Proposition 8 in California.

Chapter 17 The chapter opener has been revised to focus solely on the Iranian nuclear program. The chapter now includes a discussion of new approaches taken by the Obama administration to foreign and defense policy, and a section has been added on the dilemma posed to American policymakers by the democratic movement in Egypt.

The eleventh edition has also been enhanced pedagogically to provide for a more dynamic teaching and learning experience. Each chapter now opens with a "What We Will Learn" section in which each objective is phrased as a question, and the "What We Learned" summary at the end of each chapter is now framed in the form of answers to the questions that were posed at the beginning of the chapter.

Finally, each chapter includes a text message learning tip—good advice to students on how to succeed in college.

Approach and Features of This Book

My experience as a classroom teacher has taught me that a textbook needs to work well for both students and faculty. Students prefer a text that is interesting, easy to read, and designed for effective study. Faculty members want a textbook with solid scholarship, thorough coverage of the subject, and features that support effective teaching. I have written *American Government* to address all of these goals.

The underlying premise of my writing is that many students are unfamiliar with American culture and ignorant of the basic principles of American government and politics. I teach at a large urban community college with a diverse student population that includes many international students and students who are first-generation Americans. I recognize that these students have not had the decades of immersion in American culture that I have had. References that may be obvious to me, such as the mention of FDR or the use of a baseball analogy, may flummox them. I also write with the knowledge that many students, even some native-born Americans, do not know the basics of American government. When I first began teaching, I assumed that students already knew how bills become law, how presidents are chosen, how the courts operate, and so forth, but I soon learned that I was mistaken.

I believe that an American government textbook should address the major policy controversies of the day in order to be interesting and relevant to students and instructors as well. For example, how better to introduce the legislative process than to explain it through an examination of the battle over the enactment of healthcare reform? My goal is for students to understand course materials by relating them to the major events and critical policy issues of the day.

A good textbook should show students how to become participants in their own government. The quality of American democracy depends on citizen participation. For example, the 2008 presidential election produced a revival of political interest in young people across the nation, giving faculty an opening in the classroom to help students develop real understanding of the democratic process. My goal is for this textbook to be an ally in that endeavor.

A good textbook should introduce students to the discipline of political science. Although I do not expect many of my students to major in political science, I believe that all students should recognize and appreciate the difference between scholarship and advocacy. I expose students to as much political science research as possible and expect them to be able to relate political science concepts to current political developments and controversies.

A good textbook should stress skills. Introductory American government classes should be about more than just description. I want students to be able to use the Internet, read graphs and charts, identify points of view, and apply scholarly concepts to contemporary events. In my class, students gain experience reading, writing, speaking, researching, and thinking critically. Those are skills that assist students throughout their academic and professional careers.

Finally, a good textbook should be a learning guide for students and a teaching resource for instructors. This textbook includes a number of features that will benefit both students and faculty:

- **What We Will Learn** Each chapter begins with a list of learning objectives posed in question form. The questions help students organize their study by identifying the most important points in the chapter. Instructors can use the questions to structure lectures and other classroom activities.
- **What We Have Learned** Each chapter ends with a brief summary organized around the questions with which the chapter began.
- **Key Terms** Words and phrases that have a specific meaning in the context of the subject matter appear in bold type, followed by a clear, straightforward definition. Each key term with its definition is also highlighted in the margin of the text.
- **Glossary** The glossary in the back of the textbook enables students to quickly review the definitions of key terms used in the text.
- **Getting Involved** This feature is a set of student projects that are designed to enable students to learn by doing, such as recording a weekly journal on the impact of government on their lives, volunteering at a local government office or nonprofit agency, or registering to vote. The activity for Chapter 2 is a service-learning project. Instructors may want to work with local governments and nonprofit organizations to identify possible placement opportunities for students. Many colleges have service-learning offices that can provide support for instructors and students. Furthermore, several Getting Involved activities, such as asking students to complete the paperwork to apply for financial aid or attending a meeting of a student organization, are designed to promote student retention in college.
- **What Is Your Opinion?** Each chapter includes a number of highlighted focus questions that ask students their opinions on some of the political controversies discussed in the text. The questions are designed to hold student interest as they read; some questions may also serve as the starting point for an interesting class discussion.
- **Around the World** I have included a short essay in each chapter on the government and politics of another nation. It is important that students recognize that other nations have different policy structures and may approach policy issues differently. The comparative approach gives students added insight into American government. Furthermore, the feature will help draw international students into the subject matter.
- **Practice Test Questions** I have written a set of multiple-choice questions for each chapter that is designed to allow students to assess their understanding of chapter content. I wrote the questions myself to ensure that they focus on the meat of the subject and that they challenge students to think critically about course topics. Although some questions are fairly straightforward, a good many of them require students to apply concepts to real world situations.

ACKNOWLEDGMENTS

Many persons contributed to the writing and production of this book. Reid Hester, Elizabeth Alimena, and Donna Garnier at Pearson Education gave me sympathetic and professional help from the beginning of my work on this edition to its completion.

I am grateful to my friends and colleagues among the government faculty at Houston Community College for their friendship and support. I have learned most of what I know about teaching from them. Finally, I want to recognize the people that are important to me personally, especially Anup Bodhe, Anderson Brandao, Jason Orr, Kim Galle, and Chris Marraudino.

NEAL TANNAHILL
neal.tannahill@hccs.edu or ntannahill@aol.com

To the Student

I designed this textbook with students in mind. I have been a member of the political science faculty at Houston Community College for more than 30 years, teaching hundreds of introductory American government classes, probably much like the one you are taking now. I have learned from experience that students want a textbook that is logically organized and easily read. Consequently, my primary goal as a textbook author is to write clearly. I want students to be able to understand every sentence, every paragraph, and every chapter without having to read them over and over again.

I also know that students want a textbook that is interesting. In order to catch and hold student interest, I have organized the textbook around the major policy controversies of today, including Arizona's immigration law, healthcare reform, and the war in Afghanistan. The text includes colorful features, graphs, and photographs selected not just to catch your attention but to enhance your understanding of course concepts.

Students want a textbook that will guide their study. To help with this, each chapter is framed with a set of *What We Will Learn* learning goals and *What We Have Learned* summaries to help students navigate the chapter and understand its main concepts. Other features include key terms, a glossary, a self-test for each chapter, and "Getting Involved."

I am proud to have the opportunity to be part of your education. If you have questions about the text or about American government, you can write to me at neal.tannahill@hccs.edu or ntannahill@aol.com. I hope to hear from you!

NEAL TANNAHILL

Introduction

Government, Politics, and the Policymaking Process

CHAPTER OUTLINE

Why Government Is Important

Government and Politics

The Policymaking Process
- The Context of Policymaking
- Agenda Setting
- Policy Formulation
- Policy Adoption
- Policy Legitimation
- Policy Implementation
- Policy Evaluation
- Policy Change

What We Have Learned

WHAT WE WILL LEARN

After studying the Introduction, students should be able to answer the following questions:

1. How does government affect the lives of individuals and society as a whole?
2. What is the difference between government and politics?
3. What are the stages of the policymaking process?

Americans with Disabilities Act (ADA) A federal law intended to end discrimination against persons with disabilities and to eliminate barriers preventing their full participation in American society through imposing a broad range of federal mandates.

The **Americans with Disabilities Act (ADA)** is a federal law designed to end discrimination against persons with disabilities and eliminate barriers to their full participation in American society. The ADA protects people with disabilities from discrimination in all employment practices, including hiring, firing, promotion, and compensation. The ADA does not force employers to hire unqualified individuals who happen to be disabled, but it does require companies to make "reasonable accommodation" for otherwise qualified job applicants or current employees who happen to be disabled unless the business can show that the accommodation would put an "undue hardship" on its operation. The ADA also requires that private businesses that are open to the public—such as restaurants, hotels, theaters, retail stores, funeral homes, healthcare offices, pharmacies, private schools, and day care centers—be accessible to persons with disabilities. Business owners may have to modify their premises or change their way of doing business so long as the necessary modifications or accommodations do not unduly burden the business or force business owners to fundamentally alter the nature of the goods or services they provide.[1]

Why Government Is Important

The ADA illustrates the importance of government. For millions of Americans with disabilities, the ADA offers the promise of opportunity to compete in the workplace without discrimination. It also guarantees these individuals access to restaurants, hotels, shops, and clinics. The ADA forces employers to review their employment practices to ensure compliance with the law and to take reasonable steps to accommodate the needs of workers and customers with disabilities. For society as a whole, the ADA gives millions of people with disabilities the opportunity to become full participants in the nation's economy, both as workers and consumers.

Government affects individual Americans through regulations, taxes, and services. Government regulates many aspects of daily life, either directly or indirectly. The government sets speed limits and other driving regulations, establishes a minimum age to purchase and consume alcoholic beverages, and determines the educational and technical qualifications required for practicing many occupations and professions. Government regulations affect the quality of air and water, gasoline mileage performance of automobiles, and working conditions in factories. In addition, regulation attempts to protect consumers from unsafe products, untested drugs, misleading package labels, and deceptive advertising.

Government services benefit all Americans. Public hospitals, schools, and transportation networks serve millions of people. Many college students receive financial aid and attend institutions that benefit from public funding. Government welfare programs assist millions of low-income families. Older people and many individuals with disabilities receive Social Security and Medicare benefits.

Gross domestic product (GDP) The value of goods and services produced by a nation's economy in a year, excluding transactions with foreign countries.

However, government regulations and services cost money. In 2010, federal, state, and local governments combined raised $3.6 trillion in taxes and fees, a figure representing 25 percent of the nation's **gross domestic product (GDP),** which is the value of goods and services produced by a nation's economy in a year, excluding transactions with foreign countries.[2] Workers pay income and payroll taxes on the wages they earn. Consumers pay sales taxes on retail purchases, as well as excise taxes on tobacco, alcohol, tires, gasoline, and other products. Homeowners and business owners pay property taxes on their homes and businesses.

Government not only touches the lives of individual Americans, but it also affects the nation's quality of life. Most people would not want to live, work, or run a business in a country without a fully functioning government. Government regulations and services help ensure safe neighborhoods, a healthy environment, an efficient transportation system, and an educated workforce. The tax system provides a mechanism for government to spread the cost of its operation over a broad range of individuals and groups in society. In times of emergency, such as a terrorist attack or a natural disaster, people turn to government to respond to the crisis, assist the victims, and rebuild damaged communities.

Studying American government is important because of its great impact on individuals and society. People who understand how government works will be better equipped to take advantage of the benefits and services government provides and more able to prepare themselves to live effectively under government regulation and taxation. Studying American government helps citizens understand how they can influence government policies through voting, participating in political organizations, and contacting public officials.

WHAT IS YOUR OPINION?

Do you favor a small government that provides relatively modest services but holds down taxes or an active government that provides more services but costs more?

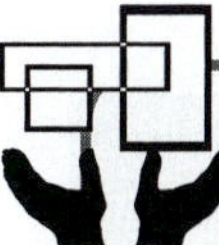

GETTING INVOLVED

Government and You

Government policies affect each of us every day in some ways that are obvious and in other ways that may not always be readily apparent. If a police officer stops you for speeding on your way to class, the government has touched you in a fashion that is direct and clear. In contrast, when you pick up a relative at the airport for a holiday visit, it may not occur to you that tax dollars paid to build the airport. An important goal of this course is for students to recognize the relevance of government to their own lives and to the life of their community. Your assignment is to keep a journal documenting the impact of government on your daily life, directly or indirectly, throughout the semester. Your instructor will grade your journal on the following criteria:

- **Number and frequency of entries.** Your journal must include at least four dated entries for each week of the course.
- **Evidence of growth in your understanding of American government.** As the course progresses, your journal entries should reveal a higher level of sophistication than do entries made in the first few weeks of the term.
- **Quality of journal entries.** Some of your entries should identify a connection to concepts discussed in your textbook or in the classroom. At least one entry a week should include a personal evaluation of the role of government, displaying evidence that you have thought critically about the role of government in your life and in society as a whole.

Government and Politics

Government The institution with authority to set policy for society.

Government and *politics* are distinct but closely related terms. **Government** is the institution with authority to set policy for society. Congress, the presidency, courts, and government agencies, such as the Social Security Administration (SSA) and the Food and Drug Administration (FDA), are all structures of American national government. Each state has a governor, legislature, court system, and administrative departments in addition to a series of local governments, such as municipalities, townships, counties, and school districts.

Politics The process that determines who shall occupy the roles of leadership in government and how the power of government shall be exercised.

Whereas government is an *institution*, politics is a *process*. One political scientist says that **politics** is the way in which decisions for a society are made and considered binding most of the time by most of the people.[3] Another scholar declares that the study of politics is "the attempt to explain the various ways in which power is exercised in the everyday world and how that power is used to allocate resources and benefits to some people and groups, and costs and burdens to other people and groups."[4] We could add a third definition: Politics is the process that determines who shall occupy the leadership roles in government and how the power of government shall be exercised.

Each of these definitions of politics emphasizes different aspects of the concept. Taken together, they highlight certain key elements of politics as well as the relationship between politics and government:

- Government and politics are entwined. The selection of government personnel and the adoption of government policies are political. The enactment of the ADA, for example, took place through the political process.

Politics is the process that determines who shall occupy the leadership roles in government and how the power of government shall be exercised.

- Politics is broader than government. In addition to the institutions of government and government officials, politics also involves individuals, groups, and organizations that are not officially part of the government, such as individual political activists, voters, the media, interest groups, political parties, and policy experts.
- Politics involves making decisions about the distribution of government benefits and the allocation of their costs.
- Politics is competitive. In American politics, individuals and groups compete with one another over the selection of the persons who will occupy government offices and over the policies government will enact and enforce.

The Policymaking Process

Public policy What government officials choose to do or not to do about public problems.

Government program A system of projects or services intended to meet a public need.

Policymaking process A logical sequence of activities affecting the development of public policies.

Public policy is what government officials choose to do or not to do about public problems. Government policies can take the form of laws, executive orders, administrative regulations, court decisions, or, in some cases, no action at all. The ADA, for example, is a law aimed at addressing the problem of access to buildings open to the general public and to employment opportunities for people with disabilities. Some public policies may take the form of government programs. A **government program** is a system of projects or services intended to meet a public need. For example, the Supplemental Nutrition Assistance Program (SNAP), which was formerly called the Food Stamps Program, was created to address the problem of hunger in America. In late 2010, more than 40 million people received SNAP benefits.[5]

The **policymaking process** is a logical sequence of activities affecting the development of public policies. It takes place within the context of American society and includes seven stages: agenda setting, policy formulation, policy adoption, policy legitimation, policy implementation, policy evaluation, and policy change.

The Context of Policymaking

The policymaking process takes place within a context of factors that determines the problems that government confronts, the set of policy alternatives that decision-makers are willing to consider, and the resources available to the government for addressing the problems. Political scientists Michael E. Craft and Scott R. Furlong identify several aspects of the context for policymaking in the United States:

- The social context, including the diversity of the nation's people, population growth, population movement within the United States, and immigration from abroad. The proportion of the population with disabilities or who have friends or family members with disabilities influences the policymaking process for disability rights because it determines the number of people who must be accommodated, as well as the potential strength of forces advocating disability rights.

- The economic context, including the strength of the nation's economy and the government's budgetary situation. The likelihood of the adoption of disability rights legislation is greater when the economy is strong than when it is weak because business and governments are better able to afford the architectural adjustments necessary for making facilities accessible during good economic times.
- The political context, including the strength of the two major parties and public opinion. The emergence of organized groups advocating disability rights was a key factor in the passage of the ADA. Furthermore, public opinion generally supported the goals of the disability rights movement.
- The governing context, including the constitutional system and the structures of government. Adoption of the ADA involved approval by both chambers of Congress and the president.
- The cultural context, including the political values of the nation and its people.[6]

Agenda Setting

Agenda setting The process through which issues become matters of public concern and government action.

Global warming The gradual warming of the Earth's atmosphere, reportedly caused by the burning of fossil fuels and industrial pollutants.

Agenda setting is the process through which problems become matters of public concern and government action. Agenda setting involves government officials and groups outside of the government competing to determine which problems government will address. Whereas some interests want to promote the consideration of certain issues, forces opposing change work to block discussion by denying that a problem exists or by arguing that the government either cannot or should not address it. Consider the controversy surrounding **global warming,** the gradual warming of Earth's atmosphere which is reportedly caused by the burning of fossil fuels and industrial pollutants. Many scientists believe that global warming is a threat to the planet which, if left unchecked, will lead to serious consequences for life in the United States and around the world. Environmentalists want the government to take action to reduce the greenhouse gas emissions that cause global warming. In contrast, people who oppose government efforts to address climate change are skeptical that it exists, doubt that it is caused by human action, and/or question the effectiveness of government actions to address the problem. They want government to take no action or minimal action.

Agenda setting not only identifies problems for government attention but also defines the nature of those problems, and therefore the eventual direction for a policy solution. Consider the issue of disability rights. During the debate in Congress on the ADA, spokespersons for advocacy groups for the disabled, such as the Disability Rights Education and Defense Fund (DREDF) and the Americans Disabled for Attendant Programs Today (ADAPT), noted that the employment rate for persons with severe disabilities was only 23 percent compared to an employment rate for adults without disabilities of nearly 80 percent.[7] The supporters of disability rights argued that discrimination or a lack of access to public facilities prevented many persons with disabilities from working. They proposed passage of federal legislation prohibiting discrimination against people with disabilities and ensuring access to business facilities as a solution to the problem. In contrast, business groups opposed government regulation. They denied that employment discrimination against people with disabilities was a major problem, suggesting instead that the employment rate for people with disabilities was low because many people with disabilities either cannot work or do not want to work. Furthermore, they said, individuals with disabilities who have few skills can make more money from government disability payments than they can earn in low-wage jobs.

Policy Formulation

Policy formulation The development of strategies for dealing with the problems on the policy agenda.

Policy formulation is the development of strategies for dealing with the problems on the policy agenda. Government officials as well as individuals and organizations outside of government, such as interest groups, political parties, policy experts, and the media, participate in policy formulation. The formulation of ADA legislation, for example, involved negotiations among members of Congress, executive branch officials, business interests, and advocacy groups for people with disabilities. Although most business groups supported the goals of the ADA, they were concerned that the law would require businesses to hire unqualified applicants or make extensive (and expensive) physical modifications in their facilities. Business owners also worried that the new law would subject them to lawsuits and the possibility of expensive jury settlements.

The ADA was a compromise between the supporters of people with disabilities and business interests. The advocacy groups succeeded in writing a broad definition of disability into the law. The ADA declares that an individual with a disability is "a person who has a physical or mental impairment that substantially limits one or more major life activities, a record of such an impairment, or is regarded as having such an impairment."[8] Major life activities include the ability of individuals to care for themselves, perform manual tasks, walk, see, hear, speak, breathe, learn, work, sit, stand, lift, and reach. Under the law, persons with learning disabilities, epilepsy, mental illness, muscular dystrophy, HIV infection, cancer, diabetes, mental retardation, alcoholism, and cosmetic disfigurement are all considered disabled.

Business groups succeeded in limiting the scope of the law. Although the ADA prohibits discrimination, it does not establish a quota system for hiring people with disabilities. It requires only that employers hire and promote qualified candidates without regard to disability. Furthermore, the ADA declares that a business need only make "reasonable accommodation" for employees and customers with disabilities that do not place an "undue hardship" on its operations.

Policy Adoption

Policy adoption The official decision of a government body to accept a particular policy and put it into effect.

Policy adoption is the official decision of a government body to accept a particular policy and put it into effect. The ADA, for example, was enacted through the legislative process. Congress passed the measure and the president signed it into law.

The ADA gives millions of people with disabilities the opportunity to become full participants in the nation's economy, both as workers and consumers.

Not all policies are drafted into formal legislation and adopted through the legislative process. Courts adopt policies when they decide cases. Government agencies, such as the Environmental Protection Agency (EPA), adopt policies by issuing regulations. The president can adopt a policy by issuing executive orders. Government officials also make policy when they decide either to take no action or continue policies already in place.

Policy Legitimation

Policy legitimation The actions taken by government officials and others to ensure that most citizens regard the policy as a legal and appropriate government response to a problem.

Policy legitimation refers to the actions taken by government officials and others to ensure that most citizens regard a policy as a legal and appropriate government response to a problem. For example, the president, congressional leaders from both political parties, and disability rights spokespersons helped to legitimize the ADA by celebrating its passage as a step toward fairness and equal opportunity for millions of Americans with disabilities. Although not everyone agreed with all the details of the ADA, the measure itself enjoyed broad support. In other words, the ADA was widely regarded as a legitimate use of government power. Not all policies enjoy such a high level of legitimacy. For example, nearly 40 years after *Roe v. Wade*, the Supreme Court decision that legalized abortion throughout the United States, the country's abortion policy remains illegitimate in the eyes of millions of Americans.

Policy Implementation

Policy implementation The stage of the policy process in which policies are carried out.

Policy implementation is the stage of the policy process in which policies are carried out. Implementation involves not just government officials but also individuals and groups outside of the government. Private businesses, individual with disabilities, the Equal Employment Opportunity Commission (EEOC), and the courts all participate in the implementation of the ADA. The law requires private businesses to take reasonable steps to accommodate employees and customers with disabilities. If individuals with disabilities believe they have suffered discrimination, the law allows them to file a lawsuit against the offending business and/or file a complaint with the EEOC. Penalties for violators can be as high as $110,000 for repeat offenders.[9] During 2010, the EEOC, which also hears charges of discrimination based on racial, ethnic, gender, and age, handled 25,165 complaints based on the ADA, more than a fourth of the total complaints filed with the agency.[10]

The implementation process often involves supplying details and interpretations of policy that are omitted, either intentionally or unintentionally, during policy formulation. The ADA, for example, requires businesses to make "reasonable accommodations" for employees and customers with disabilities that do not place an "undue hardship" on their operations. How these terms apply to hundreds of specific circumstances depends on their interpretation by the EEOC and the courts. The EEOC, for example, has ruled that employers may not refuse to hire people with disabilities because of concerns about their impact on health insurance costs.[11] More often than not, the courts have sided with employers, narrowing the scope of the ADA and making it difficult for individuals to prevail in disability discrimination lawsuits filed against businesses. Employers win more than 90 percent of the workplace discrimination cases filed under the ADA.[12]

Policy Evaluation

Policy evaluation The assessment of policy.

Policy evaluation is the assessment of policy. Is a policy working well? Is it achieving its goals? Are there unintended consequences? Is it cost effective? Evaluation studies show that the ADA has had a mixed impact:

- A survey of corporate executives found that the median cost of making the workplace more accessible was only $223 per individual with disabilities. Two-thirds of the executives surveyed reported that the ADA had not spawned an increase in lawsuits.[13]
- A majority of ADA complaints filed with the EEOC have involved issues that members of Congress did not discuss in drafting the law, such as back problems and psychological stress. Only 10 percent of the complaints have come from people with spinal cord injuries or other neurological problems—the conditions most frequently mentioned when the ADA was written.[14]
- Despite the ADA, the employment rate for people with disabilities has not improved.[15]

WHAT IS YOUR OPINION?

Has the ADA been a success or failure? What is the basis for your answer?

Policy Change

Policy change The modification of policy goals and means in light of new information or shifting political environments.

Policy change refers to the modification of policy goals and means in light of new information or shifting political environments. Policy change is frequently the result of policy evaluation. Programs that are successful may no longer be needed; unsuccessful programs may be eliminated because of their failure. Partially successful programs or programs with unintended negative consequences may be modified in hopes of improving their operation. Policies may also change when the political landscape changes. Programs adopted by Democratic Congresses and presidents may be revised when Congress and the presidency are in the hands of the Republicans and vice versa.

WHAT WE HAVE LEARNED

1. **How does government affect the lives of individuals and society as a whole?**
   Government affects individual Americans through regulations, taxes, and services. Government also influences the nation's quality of life.

2. **What is the difference between government and politics?**
   Government is the institution with authority to set policy for society. Politics is the process that determines who shall occupy the leadership roles in government and how the power of government shall be exercised. Although politics and government are intertwined, politics is broader than government. It involves the distribution of government benefits and the allocation of their costs. Politics is also competitive.

3. **What are the stages of the policymaking process?**
   The policymaking process is a logical sequence of activities affecting the development of public policies. The policymaking process takes place within a context of factors, including the social, economic, political, governing, and cultural contexts. It includes seven stages: agenda setting, policy formulation, policy adoption, policy legitimation, policy implementation, policy evaluation, and policy change.

KEY TERMS

agenda setting
Americans with Disabilities Act (ADA)
global warming
government
government program
gross domestic product (GDP)
policy adoption
policy change
policy evaluation
policy formulation
policy implementation
policy legitimation
policymaking process
politics
public policy

NOTES

1. Civil Rights Division, U.S. Department of Justice, "A Guide to Disability Rights Laws," September 2005, available at www.usdoj.gov.
2. Office of Management and Budget, "Total Government Receipts in Absolute Amounts and as a Percentage of GDP: 1948–2010," *The Budget for Fiscal Year 2012, Historical Tables*, available at www.omb.gov.
3. David Easton, "Political Science in the United States," in David Easton, John G. Gunnell, and Luigi Graziano, eds., *The Development of Political Science* (London: Routledge, 1991), p. 275.
4. Thomas A. Birkland, *An Introduction to the Policy Process: Theories, Concepts, and Models of Public Policy Making* (Armonk, NY: M.E. Sharpe, 2001), pp. 4–5.
5. Nutrition.gov, available at www.nutrition.gov.
6. Michael E. Craft and Scott R. Furlong, *Public Policy: Politics, Analysis, and Alternatives*, 3rd ed. (Washington, DC: CQ Press, 2010), pp. 10–15.
7. Jack M. McNeil, *Employment, Earnings, and Disability*, U.S. Bureau of the Census, 2000, available at www.census.gov.
8. Civil Rights Division, "A Guide to Disability Rights Laws."
9. U.S. Equal Employment Opportunity Commission, Department of Justice, Civil Rights Division, *The Americans with Disabilities Act: Questions and Answers*, available at www.usdoj.gov.
10. U.S. Equal Employment Opportunity Commission, "Charge Statistics FY 1997 through FY 2010," available at www.eeoc.gov.
11. U.S. Equal Employment Opportunity Commission, "Selected Enforcement Guidelines and Other Policy Documents on the ADA," available at www.eeoc.gov.
12. National Resource Center on AD/HD, "Workplace and Higher Education Issues," available at www.help4adhd.org.
13. Jill Smolowe, "Noble Aims, Mixed Results," *Time*, July 31, 1995, p. 55.
14. U.S. Equal Employment Opportunity Commission," available at www.eeoc.gov.
15. Samuel R. Bagenstos, *Law and the Contradictions of the Disability Rights Movement* (New Haven, CT: Yale University Press, 2009), pp. 116–123.

Chapter 1

A Changing America in a Changing World

CHAPTER OUTLINE

WHAT WE WILL LEARN

After studying Chapter 1, students should be able to answer the following questions:

1. How is the population of the United States described in terms of size, age distribution, growth rate, immigration (both legal and illegal), race and ethnicity, and geographic distribution?
2. How does the United States compare with other nations in terms of size, military might, economic strength, and cultural influence?
3. What is the global economy and how does it affect American workers?
4. What are the patterns of wealth, poverty, and healthcare insurance coverage in America, and how does the economic and health insurance status of families and individuals vary based on race, ethnicity, residence, region, and gender?
5. What are the most important elements of the political culture of the United States?

Arizona has enacted the nation's strictest and most controversial immigration law. The purpose of the measure is to identify, prosecute, and deport illegal immigrants. The law makes failure to carry immigration papers a crime for noncitizens and it empowers the police to stop individuals if they have a "reasonable suspicion" that the person may be undocumented. The measure makes "transporting and harboring" undocumented people a crime as well.

The Arizona law grew out of the frustration Arizona's residents felt regarding the federal government's failure to effectively address the issue of illegal immigration. Arizona is a border state with Mexico and consequently a gateway for illegal immigration. It has also become an avenue for narcotics smuggling. Many Arizonans worry that the drug violence south of the border may spill into their state.

Racial profiling The practice of a police officer targeting individuals as suspected criminals on the basis of their race or ethnicity.

The Arizona immigration measure unleashed a firestorm of controversy. President Obama criticized it, suggesting it was irresponsible, and some opponents demanded that conventions boycott Arizona.[1] Critics declared that the law was an invitation for **racial profiling,** which is the practice of a police officer targeting individuals as suspected criminals on the basis of their race or ethnicity. Furthermore, they warned that the law will undermine law enforcement in the state. Police will be distracted from their real work of fighting violent crime and undocumented immigrants will no longer feel comfortable reporting crimes or cooperating with authorities.[2]

The defenders of the law believe that it is a reasonable effort by a state to address a serious problem. They note that the requirement that noncitizens carry their immigration papers mirrors federal immigration laws. The police cannot stop people because of the color of their skin or their accent because Arizona Governor Jan Brewer has signed an executive order making it illegal to consider race and ethnicity in the measure's enforcement.[3]

The controversy over the Arizona immigration law introduces Chapter 1, which examines some of the important elements of the context for policymaking in the United States. The chapter begins with a profile of the nation's population, considering immigration, illegal immigration, and population diversity. It considers the United States' place in the world as well as the global economy. The chapter looks at the distribution of wealth, poverty, and healthcare. Finally, it discusses the political culture of the United States, focusing on democracy and capitalism.

The American People

Baby-boom generation The exceptionally large number of Americans born after the end of World War II.

The United States has more than 310 million people. Figure 1.1 traces the population growth rate of the United States since 1900. The nation's population increased rapidly in the early decades of the century before the Depression years of the 1930s, when the growth rate fell sharply. The population growth rate accelerated in the late 1940s and 1950s with the birth of the **baby-boom generation,** which refers to the exceptionally large number of Americans born after the end of World War II. Many American families delayed having children during the Great Depression in the 1930s and World War II in the early 1940s. After the war, the birthrate soared

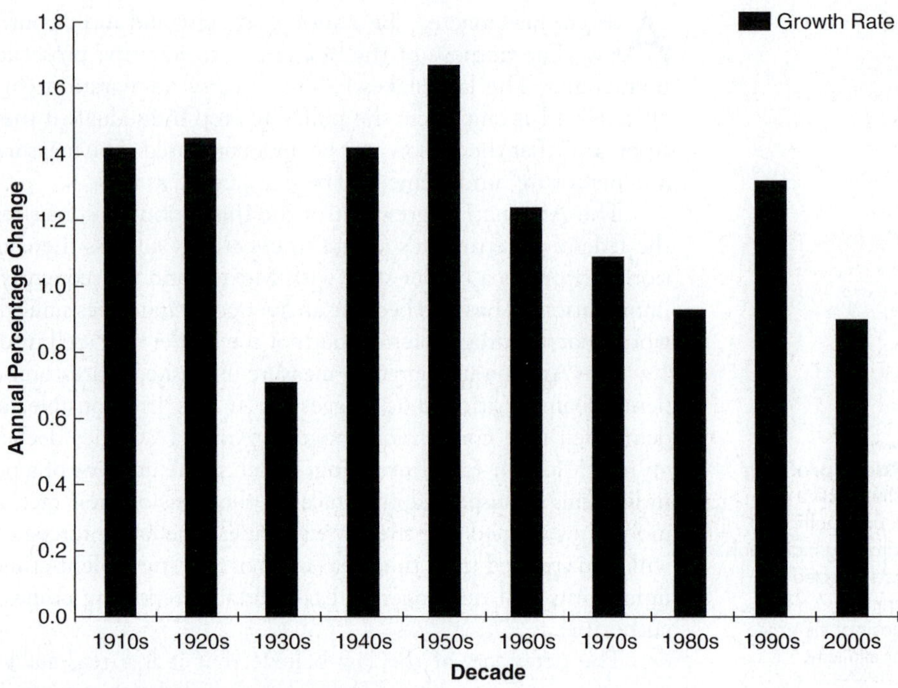

FIGURE 1.1 Average Annual Population Growth.
Source: U.S. Census Bureau.

because families reunited and people grew optimistic about the future. With the end of the baby boom in the early 1960s, the rate of population growth slowed in each subsequent decade until the 1990s, when the nation's population increased more rapidly than it had in any decade since the 1950s. Even though birthrates fell during the 1990s, the population growth rate climbed because of increased immigration. In contrast, the population grew at the slowest rate since the 1930s during the last decade. Demographers attributed the slower growth rate to falling birthrates among whites and a slowdown in immigration because of the economic downturn in 2008 and 2009.[4]

The U.S. population is aging. In 2009, 40 million Americans were age 65 and older.[5] The U.S. Census Bureau estimates that the number of older Americans will increase steadily for at least the next two decades. The number of people 65 years old or more will be 47 million in 2015, 55 million in 2020, and 64 million in 2025. As a percentage of the total population, the group of people 65 years and above will steadily increase from 13 percent in 2008 to 18 percent in 2025. While the older population is increasing rapidly, the number of people between 16 and 64 years of age, the prime working years, is growing slowly and actually falling as a percentage of the total population. Between 2010 and 2025, the number of people age 16 to 64 will fall from 66 percent to only 61 percent of the total population.[6]

Medicare A federal health insurance program for people 65 and older.

Medicaid A federal health insurance program for low-income persons, people with disabilities, and elderly people who are impoverished.

Social Security A federal pension and disability insurance program funded through a payroll tax on workers and their employers.

The aging of the population threatens the financial solvency of the government's major healthcare and pension programs—Medicare, Medicaid, and Social Security. Medicare and Medicaid are healthcare programs. **Medicare** is a federal health insurance program for people 65 and older. As the population ages, the number of people eligible for Medicare will climb and the cost of the program will grow. **Medicaid** is a federal health insurance program for low-income persons, people with disabilities, and elderly people who are impoverished. Although older people are a minority of Medicaid recipients, the cost of their healthcare is greater than it is for other groups of beneficiaries. **Social Security** is a federal pension and disability insurance program funded through a payroll tax on workers and their employers. Its costs will rise as more people reach retirement age and begin collecting benefits. Because the working age population is growing slowly, payroll tax revenues will be unable to keep up with program expenditures, forcing the government to cut benefits or find other revenue sources to fund the program.

The slow growth of the traditional working age population threatens the economy as well as the government's ability to raise sufficient revenue to cover the costs of Medicare, Medicaid, Social Security, and other government programs. Who will fill the jobs currently held by older Americans as they reach retirement age? Will many people age 65 and above decide to remain in the workforce beyond the traditional retirement age of 65? Will their places be taken by new waves of immigrants and their children?

Immigration

Immigrants constitute an eighth of the nation's population.[7] Whereas earlier waves of immigration to the United States were primarily from Europe, most recent immigrants immigrated from Latin America or Asia. The primary countries of origin for recent legal immigrants to the United States are, in order of importance, Mexico, Philippines, India, and China.

Illegal Immigration

In 2009, 11.1 million illegal immigrants lived in the United States, down from 12 million in 2007.[8] The undocumented population is evenly divided between people who entered the country legally on temporary visas, such as student visas and tourist visas, and people who crossed the border illegally. Mexico accounted for 60 percent of unauthorized immigrants in 2009. A fifth of illegal immigrants are from other Latin American countries, particularly Honduras, El Salvador, Guatemala, Nicaragua, and Brazil. The rest come from Canada, Europe, Asia, and Africa. Although undocumented immigrants are found in every region of the country, a majority of them live in the states of California, Texas, Florida, New York, Illinois, and New Jersey.[9]

People migrate to the United States primarily for economic reasons. The number of illegal immigrants in the United States declined in 2008–2009 because of a weak job market. Unauthorized workers account for 5.1 percent of the civilian workforce. They are concentrated in low-wage occupations such as farming, cleaning, construction, and food preparation. Although unauthorized workers in the United States earn only about half as much per person as do American citizens and permanent residents, they make substantially more money than they earned in their home countries.

Most undocumented immigrants live in families rather than alone as single adults. The ratio of men to women is 58 percent to 42 percent. Undocumented families include four million children who are U.S. citizens because they were born in the United States. Most unauthorized families live at or near the poverty level and lack health insurance.[10]

Illegal immigration is controversial. Critics charge that undocumented workers drive down wage rates for American citizens while overcrowding schools and hospital emergency rooms. They argue that unauthorized immigrants undermine the nation's cultural integrity because they create cultural enclaves that resemble their home countries instead of learning English and adopting the customs of the United States. The opponents of illegal immigration favor tighter border controls, strict enforcement of immigration laws, and punishment for American citizens who provide unauthorized immigrants with jobs, housing, healthcare, and other services.

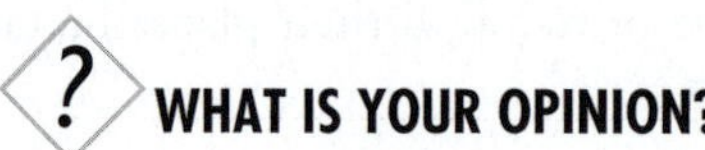

Should U.S. immigration policies favor people from countries that speak English?

In contrast, immigration advocates contend that the United States benefits from immigration, even illegal immigration. They argue that undocumented workers take jobs that citizens do not want and that they pay more in taxes than they receive in government services. An influx of hard-working, well-motivated manual workers enhances the competitiveness of American industry and provides additional jobs for citizens as managers. The defenders of immigration believe that today's immigrants enrich the nation's culture just as did earlier waves of immigrants from Great Britain, Germany, Ireland, Italy, and Poland. Furthermore, the proponents of immigration contend that most recent immigrants are quick to learn English and eager to become citizens so they can participate in the nation's political life. Immigration advocates believe that the United States should grant legal status to undocumented workers who have helped build the nation's economy while enacting a realistic immigration system to enable foreign workers to enter the country legally to find jobs.

Population Diversity

The United States is a multiracial/multiethnic society. The nation's population is 65 percent white, 16 percent Latino, 13 percent African American, 5 percent Asian American, and 1 percent American Indian or Alaska Native. Latinos are the fastest growing American ethnic group.[11] Because of continued immigration and relatively high birthrates for Latino women, demographers expect that the Latino population

Major agriculture producers say that they need immigrant labor to take positions that American citizens are unwilling to fill.

will continue to grow rapidly, increasing from 16 percent of the population in 2010 to 24 percent in 2050.[12]

Many Americans consider themselves biracial or multiracial. More than seven million people, 2.5 percent of the total population, classified themselves as biracial or multiracial in the 2000 Census.[13] In 2008, more than 8 percent of college freshmen identified with more than one racial/ethnic group.[14]

Sunbelt The Southern and Western regions of the United States.

Frostbelt The Northeastern and Midwestern regions of the United States.

The population of the United States has been shifting to the South and the West, the region known as the **Sunbelt,** and away from the Northeast and Midwest, the **Frostbelt.** In 1970, a majority of the nation's population, 52 percent, lived in the Frostbelt. The population has subsequently shifted steadily to the Sunbelt, which now holds a majority of the nation's population. The Sunbelt population is growing because of relatively higher birthrates in the region, immigration from abroad, and intrastate migration from the Frostbelt.

Population changes have affected the political balance in the U.S. House of Representatives. Because the Northeast and Midwest have lost population, they have lost seats in the House. New York and Ohio each lost two House seats while eight other states lost one seat each. In contrast, Texas gained four seats in Congress and Florida two. Six other states added one seat apiece. Sunbelt politicians have also dominated the race for the White House. Every elected president between John Kennedy from Massachusetts, who won office in 1960, and Barack Obama from Illinois, who won in 2008, was from the Sunbelt. Lyndon Johnson (1964) was from Texas, Richard Nixon (1968 and 1972) from California, Jimmy Carter (1976) from Georgia, Ronald Reagan (1980 and 1984) from California, George H. W. Bush (1988) from Texas,

Around the World

Immigration Policy and Politics in France

The government of France encouraged immigration after World War II to provide labor for postwar reconstruction. France experienced a postwar labor shortage because it suffered 600,000 casualties during the war. It also had the lowest birthrate in Europe between World War I and World War II. The steel, mining, and electric power industries in particular needed foreign workers to meet the postwar demand. Many foreign workers took jobs in service industries as well. Over the next 30 years, millions of foreign workers migrated to France. Sometimes they were joined by their families. Immigrants came to France from Southern Europe, especially Italy and Portugal, and from North Africa. Algeria, which had been a French colony prior to its independence in 1962, was the most important North African nation of origin.*

The presence of a large number of North African immigrants in France has been controversial. Some French see North Africans as a threat to social cohesion and even national security. North Africans, most of whom are Arab Muslims, are ethnically and culturally different from the French European majority, most of which is non-observant Catholic. Some French also consider North Africans a threat to national security because of the association of some European Islamic immigrants with 9/11 and other terrorist acts. Nonetheless, many European French reject anti-immigrant appeals because they believe that anti-immigrant sentiments contradict the fundamental principles of French democracy, which are *Liberté, Égalité, Fraternité* (liberty, equality, and brotherhood). They believe that France should embrace the cultural diversity of immigrant populations rather than forcing their assimilation.†

France has adopted a series of laws and regulations aimed at addressing the issue of non-European immigration. France has halted the immigration of non-European workers but continues to allow family reunification, which has increased the number of North Africans living in France. In order to reduce the size of the immigrant population, France has offered financial incentives to immigrants to return home, but the program has had little success. The country's leaders have threatened to fine employers who use illegal workers. France has also attempted to pressure North African immigrants to assimilate into French culture. A 2004 law, for example, bans headscarves from public schools, preventing Muslim girls from covering their heads.‡

QUESTIONS

1. How important is it for immigrants to adopt the culture of the majority of people in their new country?
2. Are Mexican immigrants in the United States as culturally different as North African immigrants in France?
3. Is opposition to non-European immigration in France (and the United States) racist?

* Christopher Rudolph, *National Security and Immigration: Policy Develops in the United States and Western Europe Since 1945* (Stanford, CA: Stanford University Press, 2006), pp. 126–142.

† Mari-Claude Blanc-Chaléard, "Old and New Migrants in France: Italians and Algerians," in Leo Lucassen, David Feldman, and Jochen Oltmer, eds., *Paths of Integration: Migrants in Western Europe (1880–2004)* (Amsterdam: Amsterdam University Press, 2006), p. 54.

‡ Alec G. Hargreaves, *Multi-Ethnic France: Immigration, Politics, Culture, and Society* (New York: Routledge, 2007), p. 201.

Bill Clinton (1992 and 1996) from Arkansas, and George W. Bush (2000 and 2004) from Texas.

The United States is an urban country. Census data show that 80 percent of the nation's people reside in metropolitan areas, with a majority of Americans living in urban centers of more than a million residents. Furthermore, metropolitan areas are growing more rapidly than non-metropolitan areas.

THE UNITED STATES AND THE WORLD

The United States is one of the largest countries in the world, both in terms of population and physical size. It is the third most populous country, after China and India, each of which has well over a billion people. In terms of land area, the United States ranks third, after Russia and China.[15]

Superpower A country powerful enough to influence events throughout the world.

Gross domestic product (GDP) The value of goods and services produced by a nation's economy in a year, excluding transactions with foreign countries.

Recession An economic slowdown characterized by declining economic output and rising unemployment.

Per capita Per person.

Standard of living A term that refers to the goods and services affordable by and available to the residents of a nation.

Developing countries Nations with relatively low levels of per capita income.

The United States is the foremost nation in the world, militarily, economically, and culturally. Since the collapse of the Soviet Union in 1991, the United States has emerged as the world's only **superpower,** which is a country powerful enough to influence events throughout the world. The U.S. defense budget accounts for more than 40 percent of world military spending, and is more than seven times as much as China, the second place country, spends on its military.[16]

The United States is also the foremost economic power with the world's largest and most productive economy. The **gross domestic product (GDP)** is the value of goods and services produced by a nation's economy in a year, excluding transactions with foreign countries. The U.S. GDP stood at $14.9 trillion in late 2010, substantially greater than that of China ($5.9 trillion) and Japan ($5.5 trillion).[17] With only 4.6 percent of the world's population, the United States generates 23.6 percent of the world's economic output.[18]

Although the United States has the world's largest economy, it does not have the fastest growing economy. Among the world's larger economies, both China and India are experiencing more rapid economic growth than the United States. In 2009, the Chinese economy grew by 9.1 percent; the economic growth rate for India was 5.7 percent. In contrast, the U.S. economy, locked in a severe recession, shrank by 2.6 percent.[19] (A **recession** is an economic slowdown characterized by declining economic output and rising unemployment.)

Figure 1.2 shows Gross National Income (GNI) **per capita** (per person) adjusted for purchasing power differences for China, Germany, Japan, Mexico, the United Kingdom, and the United States. Because the cost of goods and services varies from country to country, the same amount of money does not purchase the same quantity of goods and services from one nation to another. Adjusting GNI per capita to reflect differences in purchasing power is a good measure of a nation's **standard of living,** which refers to the goods and services affordable by and available to the residents of a nation. As the figure indicates, the average American enjoys greater purchasing power than people living in the other countries listed in the table. Americans are somewhat better off than people living in other industrialized countries, such as Germany, Japan, and the United Kingdom. Meanwhile, the standard of living in the United States is substantially higher than it is in Mexico and other **developing countries,** which are nations with relatively low levels of per capita income. Even though the rapidly growing Chinese economy is the second largest in the world after the United States, per capita purchasing power is relatively low in China because the nation has a huge population.

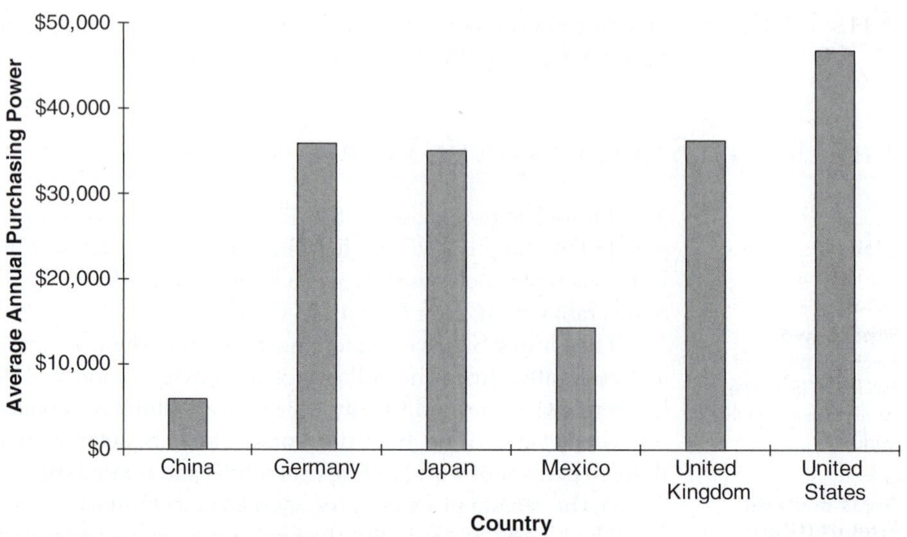

FIGURE 1.2 Per Capita Purchasing Power, 2008.
Source: U.S. Census Bureau, "Gross National Income per County (GNI):2000 and 2008," *2011 Statistical Abstract,* available at www.census.gov.

American culture permeates the world. American fashion, music, and entertainment are pervasive. People around the world eat at McDonald's restaurants, wear Levi jeans, drink Pepsi or Coke, and watch Hollywood movies.

American culture permeates the world.

The Global Economy

Global economy The integration of national economies into a world economic system in which companies compete worldwide for suppliers and markets.

North American Free Trade Agreement (NAFTA) An international accord among the United States, Mexico, and Canada to lower trade barriers among the three nations.

The United States emerged from World War II as the world's foremost economic power. With European and Asian competitors devastated by war, American companies dominated the domestic market and shipped manufactured goods around the globe. Millions of Americans with only a high school education found good-paying jobs working in steel mills or on automobile assembly lines.

Today, the United States is part of a **global economy,** which is the integration of national economies into a world economic system in which companies compete worldwide for suppliers and markets. International treaties and agreements, such as the **North American Free Trade Agreement (NAFTA),** have reduced the barriers to trade among the world's countries. NAFTA is an international accord among the United States, Mexico, and Canada to lower trade barriers among the three nations. The move toward free trade has allowed American companies to compete for business abroad, but it has also forced them to compete at home against overseas competitors.

Some American companies and workers have prospered in the global economy. American agriculture, major retailers such as Walmart, and the nation's biggest makers of automobiles and automobile parts have benefited from international trade. For example, although General Motors (GM) has been steadily losing market share in the United States to foreign competitors, it is doing very well abroad, especially in China where it has become that nation's leading automobile seller. In fact, GM now sells more cars in China than in the United States.[20] Companies that have lowered their cost of doing business through outsourcing or the use of modern technology have also done well. Their investors have profited from higher stock prices, and their managers and executives have reaped the reward in higher salaries and bonuses. Skilled workers who understand the latest technology in their fields and can operate the newest equipment are in high demand. This is especially true for workers who have the ability to adapt quickly as technology changes.

In contrast, international trade has been a disaster for workers in fields that have been unable to compete against low-wage competition from abroad. Less expensive transportation and communication systems make it possible to produce goods in areas of the world where production costs are low and then transport those goods to markets worldwide. How can an American manufacturer afford to pay $15 an hour to low-skill assembly workers in the United States if workers in Indonesia, China, or the Caribbean will do the same work for less than $2 an hour? The American firm must either move its production process to a country with lower wage costs or lose market share because it cannot compete. Since 1995, textile employment in the United States has fallen from 850,000 jobs to 120,000 as companies either go out of business or move their operations overseas where wage rates are lower.[21] American companies have also begun to cut costs by outsourcing information technology work and some business process functions to India, China, and Russia—countries that have a large number of college-educated workers that will work for much lower wages than their counterparts in the United States. While GM is reducing its workforce in the United States, it is hiring in China. Analysts estimate that wages and benefits per factory worker in China are about a tenth of what they are in the United States.

Walmart is the largest private employer in the United States.

GM plans to open a new factory in China within the next few years and may begin exporting vehicles from there to the United States.[22]

Low-skill, poorly educated American workers have also been damaged by technological change. Modern technology has enabled companies to replace low-skill workers with machines, generating the same output or more with fewer workers. Between 1979 and 2000, U.S. factory output nearly doubled even though the number of manufacturing jobs fell by more than two million. A quarter century ago, General Motors (GM) employed 454,000 workers to manufacture five million vehicles. Today, the GM payroll has shrunk to 75,000 employees and its sales are less than three million vehicles a year.[23] Even though the American workers who lose their jobs because of international trade and technological change usually find new positions, their new jobs typically pay less than their old jobs and often come without benefits.[24] In 1979, General Motors, Ford, and General Electric were the nation's largest employers; today, the companies employing the most workers are Walmart, McDonald's, and UPS.[25]

Wealth, Poverty, and Healthcare Coverage

Income Distribution

As the economy has changed, the gap between the rich and other income groups has widened. Table 1.1 shows the share of national income earned by each of five income groups, from the poorest fifth of American families through the wealthiest

TABLE 1.1 Share of National Income Received by Each Fifth of Families: 1980–2009

Year	Poorest Fifth	Second-Poorest Fifth	Third-Poorest Fifth	Fourth-Poorest Fifth	Wealthiest Fifth
1980	5.3%	11.6%	17.6%	24.4%	41.4%
1990	4.6	10.8	16.6	23.8	44.3
2000	4.3	9.8	15.5	22.8	47.4
2009	3.4	8.6	14.6	23.2	49.4

Source: U.S. Census Bureau, *2009 Statistical Abstract,* available at www.census.gov; U.S. Census Bureau, "Income and Earnings Summary Measures by Selected Characteristics: 2008 and 2009," *Income, Poverty, and Health Insurance Coverage in the United States: 2009,* available at www.census.gov.

fifth. Between 1980 and 2009, the proportion of national income received by the wealthiest fifth of the population increased from 41.4 percent to 50.3 percent. The rich got richer. In the meantime, the share of national income earned by the four other groups of families declined. In particular, the share of income earned by the poorest families fell by more than 35 percent, from 5.3 percent of the total in 1980 to 3.4 percent in 2009. The poor got poorer, at least relative to other income groups.

Economist Robert H. Frank attributes the growth of income inequality to changes in the economy and tax policy. Professor Frank says that the United States has a winner-take-all economy in which small differences in performance often translate into huge differences in economic reward. Corporate executives, sports stars, and well-known entertainers earn huge paychecks, many times greater than the earnings of ordinary workers, average athletes, and entertainers without star power. In the meantime, income tax cuts adopted during the Ronald Reagan and George W. Bush administrations significantly reduced income tax rates for upper-income earners, effectively shifting wealth toward the top of the income ladder.[26]

Household income in the United States varies, depending on race, ethnicity, residence, region, and gender. Whites and Asian Americans/Pacific Islanders are better off than Latinos and African Americans. In 2009, the median household income in the United States was $49,777. Asian American/Pacific Islander households had the highest average income—$65,469. The average income for white households was $54,461. In contrast, the average household income for African Americans and Latino households was significantly lower—$32,584 and $38,039, respectively. Incomes vary depending on whether families live in metropolitan or nonmetropolitan areas. The average household income for families living in metropolitan areas was higher than it was for families located outside big cities. Suburban households had higher incomes than families living in the inner city. Family incomes also differ based on region. Household income was lower in the South than it was in any other region of the country. Household income was highest in the Northeast. Income also varies by gender. In 2009, the average income of male full-time, year-round workers was $47,127 compared with $36,278 for women.[27]

Income differences among racial and ethnic groups, and between men and women, reflect disparities in education and training, social factors, and discrimination. As a group, Asian Americans and whites are better educated than African

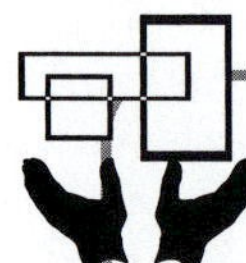

GETTING INVOLVED — A Changing Nation, Changing Communities

Data from the 2010 U.S. Census show that the United States is changing. Is your local community changing as well? Your assignment is to research the ways in which your community has changed by interviewing one or more people who have lived in the community for at least 15 or 20 years. They can be relatives, friends, coworkers, or fellow students. Your questions should cover the following topics:

- **Population change.** Has the population of the area grown? Have people immigrated to the community from other states or other nations? How has the racial/ethnic makeup of the population changed? Has the population as a whole grown younger or older?
- **Economic change.** Has the mix of businesses and industries changed? Have any major employers gone out of business? Are there new industries?
- **Cultural change.** Does the community have places of worship for religious faiths that are new to the area? Are there new types of restaurants? Do grocery stores carry different varieties of produce to match the tastes of new residents? Does the community celebrate different or additional holidays and festivals?

Take careful notes on what you are told because your instructor plans to organize a class discussion around the research that you and other students have completed. The instructor will ask students to relate the information they learned from their interviews and then analyze the impact of socioeconomic change on the policymaking process. Prepare for the discussion by considering the following questions: Would you expect different political issues to emerge today as compared with 20 years ago based on the changes that have taken place in your community? Do you think the capacity of government to respond to policy demands has changed? Would you expect that the community's standard for evaluating government performance has changed?

Americans and Latinos. Women often fall behind their male counterparts on the career ladder because many women leave the workforce for years to raise children. Jobs that are traditionally held by women, such as nursing and education, typically pay less than jobs that are traditionally held by men. Finally, many observers believe that the incomes of women and minorities lag behind those of white males because of employment discrimination.

Poverty

Poverty threshold The amount of money an individual or family needs to purchase basic necessities, such as food, clothing, healthcare, shelter, and transportation.

The government measures poverty on a subsistence basis. The **poverty threshold** is the amount of money an individual or family needs to purchase basic necessities, such as food, clothing, healthcare, shelter, and transportation. The actual dollar amount varies with family size and increases with inflation. In 2009, the official government poverty threshold was $22,050 for a family of four.[28] More than 43 million Americans—14.3 percent of the population—lived in poverty in 2009.[29]

Although the poverty rate for racial and ethnic minority groups and for families headed by women has declined over the last 50 years, it is still higher than it is for other groups. In 2009, the poverty rate for Latinos, African Americans, and Asian Americans stood at 25.3 percent, 25.8 percent, and 12.5 percent, respectively, compared with 9.4 percent for whites. Poverty also disproportionately affects children and families headed by women. Nearly 21 percent of the nation's children under age 18 lived in families that were poor in 2009. The poverty rate for families headed by women was 29.9 percent.[30]

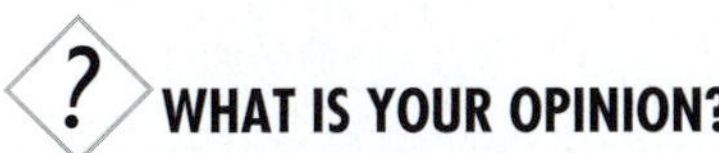

Should the government do more to reduce poverty?

Health Insurance Coverage

Nearly 51 million Americans, 16.7 percent of the population, lack health insurance coverage. African Americans (21.0 percent) and Latinos (32.4 percent) are more likely to be uninsured than are whites (12.0 percent) and Asians (17.2 percent). Insurance coverage also varies based on citizenship status. The uninsured rate for native-born Americans is 14.1 percent compared with a rate of 19 percent for naturalized citizens and 46 percent for noncitizens.[31]

For most Americans, health insurance coverage depends on employment or eligibility for government programs. Almost 60 percent of the population enjoys health insurance through their employers although that figure has been falling because some companies have dropped coverage for existing employees or have chosen not to offer coverage to new employees.[32] Government-funded health-insurance programs—Medicare, Medicaid, and military healthcare—cover about a fourth of the population. Most of the people who lack health insurance work in jobs that do not provide coverage. They have too much income to be eligible for Medicaid and are too young to qualify for Medicare. Without health insurance, they and their families must do without healthcare, pay for health services out of pocket, or go to hospital emergency rooms. They are more likely than the insured to postpone care for injury or illness, and to neglect preventive medical care, such as regular checkups and vaccinations. Meanwhile, a significant percentage of people filing bankruptcy or losing their homes to foreclosure do so because of catastrophic medical expenses.

Government officials estimate that the healthcare reform legislation passed in 2010 will cover an additional 30 million people when it is fully implemented in 2016.[33] The reform measure expands Medicaid to cover more low-income people, requires businesses with 50 or more employees to provide coverage, and gives tax breaks to small businesses to encourage them to cover their employees. The law requires uninsured people who earn too much to qualify for Medicaid to purchase their own health insurance with the help of a government subsidy, depending on their income level, or pay a penalty to the government.[34] Twenty-two million people will still lack insurance, including illegal immigrants (who are ineligible for healthcare reform), people who choose to pay the fine rather than purchase coverage, and people who qualify for Medicaid but fail to sign up for it.[35]

Political Culture

Political culture The widely held, deeply rooted political values of a society.

Political culture refers to the widely held, deeply rooted political values of a society. These values are important for the policymaking process because they define the terms of political debate and establish the range of acceptable policy options available to policymakers.

Democracy

Democracy A system of government in which ultimate political authority is vested in the people.

Attitudes toward democracy and capitalism constitute the core of America's political culture. A **democracy** is a system of government in which ultimate political authority is vested in the people. Political scientist Robert A. Dahl identifies eight criteria of democracy:

1. **The right to vote.** All or nearly all citizens enjoy the right to vote and have their votes counted equally. In the United States, every adult citizen has the right to vote except people who have lost their voting rights because they have been convicted of a serious crime. Significant restrictions on the right to vote are undemocratic. For example, Saudi Arabia held elections for the first time in 2006 to select members of municipal councils but only allowed men to cast ballots. Although holding an election is a step toward democracy, excluding women is undemocratic.
2. **The right to be elected.** Citizens have the right to compete for elective office, including people who oppose the policies of the current government. In 2007, Vietnam held elections for the National Assembly with 876 candidates competing for 500 positions. The election fell short of democracy, however, because all but two independent candidates were either members of the Communist Party or nominated by organizations affiliated with the party.[36]
3. **The right of political leaders to compete for support and votes.** Candidates have an opportunity to conduct campaigns in order to win support. If candidates cannot campaign, voters are unable to make informed choices. For example, the repressive military government of Myanmar (also known as Burma) has held political leader Aung San Suu Kyi under house arrest off and on since 1990 when her political party won a majority of seats in a parliamentary election.
4. **Free and fair elections.** All candidates compete under the same set of rules, without legal advantage or disadvantage. Democratic governments respect the outcomes of elections, peacefully stepping down from office and allowing opposition political parties and leaders to take power. Rigging election outcomes is undemocratic. International observers questioned the fairness of the 2009 Afghan national election because of widespread ballot-box stuffing, voter intimidation, ballot destruction, and ballots cast by phantom voters.[37]
5. **Freedom of association.** Citizens have the right to form political parties and organize groups. They can attend meetings, participate in political

rallies, and take part in peaceful demonstrations. In 2009, the government of Iran proved itself undemocratic because, when demonstrators took to the streets to protest the outcome of an election that they considered stolen, the government responded with violence, brutally suppressing the demonstrations and arresting protest leaders.

6. **Freedom of expression.** People living in a democracy have the right to express their political views without censorship or fear of government retaliation. Governments that jail their critics are not democracies. Chinese human rights activist, Liu Xiaobo, won the 2010 Nobel Peace Prize, but he was unable to travel to Oslo, Norway to accept the award because he was in a Chinese prison.
7. **Alternative sources of information.** The citizens in a democracy have access to information sources that are not controlled by the government. Elections cannot be free and fair if the only information voters have about government policies and candidates is information supplied and controlled by the government. In Russia, for example, the government has shut down or taken over all private television networks with a national reach. Journalists who dare to report information that contradicts the official government line face the danger of lawsuits, imprisonment, and even death.[38]
8. **Institutions for making public policies depend on votes and other expressions of citizen preference.** In a democracy, citizens elect policymakers. Free and fair elections are meaningless if military leaders or religious figures that do not answer to the voters are the real policymakers.[39] Saudi Arabia, despite its recent elections for municipal councils, is an **absolute monarchy,** which is a country ruled by one person, usually a king or queen. King Abdullah rules Saudi Arabia. In contrast, Great Britain is both a democracy and a constitutional monarchy. A **constitutional monarchy** is a country in which the powers of the ruler are limited to those granted under the constitution and the laws of the nation. The British monarch, Queen Elizabeth, is a tourist attraction rather than an actual ruler.

Absolute monarchy A country ruled by one person, usually a king or queen.

Constitutional monarchy A country in which the powers of the ruler are limited to those granted under the constitution and the laws of the nation.

Capitalism

Capitalism An economic system characterized by individual and corporate ownership of the means of production, and a market economy based on the supply and demand of goods and services.

Socialism An economic system characterized by governmental ownership of the means of production and control of the distribution of goods and services.

Capitalism is the other principal element of America's political culture. It is an economic system characterized by individual and corporate ownership of the means of production, and a market economy based on the supply and demand of goods and services. Under capitalism, businesses and industries are privately owned rather than controlled by the government. The marketplace, in which buyers and sellers freely exchange goods and services, determines what goods and services are produced, how they are produced, and for whom they are produced. The proponents of capitalism argue that it is good for consumers because businesses compete to provide quality goods and services at prices that consumers are willing to pay. They believe that capitalism promotes economic growth because only the most efficient business enterprises survive the competition of the marketplace.

The primary alternative to capitalism is **socialism,** which is an economic system characterized by governmental ownership of the means of production and control of the distribution of goods and services. In a socialist economy, the government owns and operates business and industry. It makes decisions about the production and distribution of goods and services in the public interest without regard for the profit motive. The proponents of socialism believe that it is a better system than capitalism because, they say, it prevents the unfair concentration of wealth and power in a small segment of society. In contrast, capitalists contend that socialism retards economic growth because economic decisions reflect the political biases of government bureaucrats rather than the law of supply and demand.

Mixed economy An economic system that combines private ownership with extensive governmental intervention.

Public sector Governmentally owned segment of the economy.

Private sector Privately owned segment of the economy.

The economy of the United States and that of other capitalist nations is best described as a **mixed economy,** which is an economic system that combines private ownership with extensive governmental intervention. Although most businesses and industry are in private hands, the government owns and operates some sectors of the economy and closely regulates others. The industries most frequently owned by the governments around the world are telecommunications, power, petroleum, railways, airports, airlines, public transport, healthcare, postal service, and sometimes banks. In the United States, the **public sector,** which is the government-owned segment of the economy, is relatively small. Nonetheless, the **private sector,** which is the privately owned segment of the economy, is closely regulated by the government through labor, safety and health, consumer, and environmental regulations.

In 2008–2009, the U.S. government temporarily increased the size of the public sector by becoming the controlling shareholder of General Motors and Chrysler (the automobile manufacturers), Freddie Mac and Fannie Mae (the two large mortgage companies), AIG (the giant insurance company), and several large Wall Street banks, including Citigroup, Bank of America, and Wells Fargo. The George W. Bush administration in late 2008 and the Obama administration in 2009 acted because they believed that the American economy, already in a severe recession, could not withstand the collapse of so many large and important companies. In other words, the government bailed out companies that were "too big to fail." Although the government promised to sell off its shares of the companies as soon as the firms became profitable again, critics charged that the bailouts put hundreds of billions of dollars of taxpayer money at risk. Furthermore, government ownership of the firms invariably raised the question of the role of political considerations in corporate decision making.[40]

WHAT WE HAVE LEARNED

1. **How is the population of the United States described in terms of size, age distribution, growth rate, immigration (both legal and illegal), race and ethnicity, and geographic distribution?**

The United States has more than 310 million people. The population grew rapidly in the post-World War II years with the birth of the baby-boom generation. Population growth rates subsequently fell before increasing in the 1990s, primarily because of immigration. The population grew at a somewhat slower rate in the first decade of the twenty-first century. Immigration, both legal and illegal, has added substantially to the nation's growth rate and to its diversity. Latinos are the largest and fastest growing minority group. A majority of Americans live in the Sunbelt. As a result, Sunbelt states now hold a majority of seats in the U.S. House of Representatives.

2. **How does the United States compare with other nations in terms of size, military might, economic strength, and cultural influence?**

   The United States is third among nations in land area and population, but it is the world's foremost military and economic power. With the collapse of the Soviet Union, the United States has emerged as the world's lone military superpower. It has the world's largest economy by far and, among large nations, the world's highest standard of living. It does not have, however, the world's fastest growing economy. Several nations, including China, have economies that are growing more rapidly. Meanwhile, American cultural influences are pervasive.

3. **What is the global economy and how does it affect American workers?**

   The global economy is the integration of national economies into a world economic system in which companies compete worldwide for suppliers and markets. It increases competition for companies and workers. Companies that are able to compete effectively do very well because their potential market has increased, whereas inefficient companies risk losing out to international competitors. Meanwhile, creative managers and highly skilled workers do well because their services are in demand, whereas low-skill American workers suffer a loss in wages in competition with low-skill workers around the globe who will work for less money.

4. **What are the patterns of wealth, poverty, and healthcare insurance coverage in America, and how does the economic and health insurance status of families and individuals vary based on race, ethnicity, residence, region, and gender?**

   As the economy has changed, the gap between the rich and the poor in the United States has widened. Whites and Asian Americans/Pacific Islanders are better off than Latinos and African Americans. They earn higher incomes and are less likely to be poor. People living in metropolitan areas earn more than people living outside metro areas. Suburban residents are more affluent than people living in the inner city. The South is the poorest region; the Northeast is the wealthiest. Families headed by women are worse off than other families. African Americans and Latinos are less likely than whites to have health insurance. Citizens are more likely than noncitizens to have health insurance as well. For most Americans, health insurance coverage depends on employment or eligibility for government programs, especially Medicare and Medicaid. Government officials estimate that the healthcare reform legislation passed in 2010 will cover an additional 30 million people when it is fully implemented in 2016.

5. **What are the most important elements of the political culture of the United States?**

   Attitudes toward democracy and capitalism constitute the core of America's political culture. A democracy is a system of government in which ultimate political authority is vested in the people. Professor Robert Dahl identifies eight criteria of democracy that focus on voting rights, fair election procedures, and freedom of expression and association. Capitalism is an economic system characterized by individual and corporate ownership of the means of production, and a market economy based on the supply and demand of goods and services. The primary alternative to capitalism is socialism, which is an economic system characterized by governmental ownership of the means of production and control of the distribution of goods and services. The economy of the United States and that of other capitalist nations is best described as a mixed economy, which is an economic system that combines private ownership with extensive governmental intervention. The public sector is relatively small in the United States, at least compared with the nations of Western Europe, but it increased in size—at least temporarily—in 2008–2009 when the government bailed out GM, Chrysler, Fannie Mae, Freddie Mac, AIG, and several big banks.

KEY TERMS

absolute monarchy
baby-boom generation
capitalism
constitutional monarchy
democracy
developing countries
Frostbelt
global economy
gross domestic product (GDP)
Medicaid
Medicare
mixed economy
North American Free Trade Agreement (NAFTA)
per capita
political culture
poverty threshold
private sector
public sector
racial profiling
recession
Social Security
socialism
standard of living
Sunbelt
superpower

NOTES

1. Randal C. Archibald, "Arizona Enacts Stringent Law on Immigration," *New York Times*, April 23, 2010, available at www.nytimes.com.
2. Jim Wallis, "Arizona's Immigration Bill Is a Social and Racial Sin," *Huffington Post*, April 21, 2010, available at www.huffingtonpost.com.
3. Kirk Adams, "The Truth Behind Arizona's Immigration Law," *Washington Post*, May 28, 2010, available at www.washingtonpost.com.
4. Sabrina Tavernise and Jeff Zeleny, "South and West See Large Gains in Latest Census," *New York Times*, December 21, 2010, available at www.nytimes.com.
5. U.S. Census Bureau, "Annual Estimates of the Resident Population by Sex and Age Groups for the United States: April 1, 2000 to July 1, 2009," available at www.census.gov.
6. U.S. Census Bureau, "Resident Population Projection by Sex and Age," *2010 Statistical Abstract*, available at www.census.gov.
7. U.S. Census Bureau, "Census Bureau Data Show Key Population Changes Across Nation," available at www.census.gov.
8. Jeffrey S. Passel and D'Vera Cohn, "U.S. Unauthorized Immigration Flows Are Down Sharply Since Mid-Decade," Pew Hispanic Center, September 1, 2010, available at http://pewhispanic.org.
9. U.S. Citizenship and Immigration Services (USCIS), *Fiscal Year 2008 Yearbook of Immigration Statistics*, available at http://uscis.gov/graphics/.
10. Ibid.
11. U.S. Census Bureau, *The Population Profile of the United States: 2010*, available at www.census.gov.
12. U.S. Census Bureau, "Projected Population of the United States, by Race and Hispanic Origin: 2000 to 2050," available at www.census.gov.
13. U.S. Census Bureau, "Population by Race, Including All Specific Combinations of Two Races, for the United States, 2000," available at www.census.gov.
14. Jennifer Hochschild and Vesla Mae Weaver, "'There's No One as Irish as Barack O'Bama': The Policy and Politics of American Multiracialism," *Perspectives on Politics* 8 (September 2010): 749.
15. U.S. Census Bureau, "Population by Country or Area: 1990–2010," *The 2010 Statistical Abstract*, available at www.census.gov.
16. Stockholm International Peace Research Institute, "Military Expenditure Data, 1999–2008," available at www.sipri.org.
17. Bureau of Economic Analysis, "National Income and Product Accounts," January 28, 2011, available at www.bea.gov.
18. Hiroko Tabuchi, "China Replaced Japan in 2010 as No. 2 Economy," *New York Times*, February 14, 2011, available at www.nytimes.com.
19. International Monetary Fund, "World Economic Outlook Database," available at www.imf.org.
20. David Barboza, "G.M. Eclipsed at Home, Soars to the Top in China," *New York Times*, July 22, 2010, available at www.nytimes.com.
21. Department of Labor, Bureau of Labor Statistics, "Textile Mills, 2009," available at www.bls.gov.
22. Bill Powell, "The Other GM," *Time*, June 1, 2009, p. 2.
23. Peter Whoriskey, "Revamped GM Loses $1.2 Billion," *Washington Post*, November 17, 2009, available at www.washingtonpost.com.
24. Michael Luo, "New Jobs Mean Lower Wages for Many," *New York Times*, August 31, 2010, available at www.nytimes.com.
25. Scott Burns, "Jobs and Benefits Are a la Carte Now," *Dallas Morning News*, May 18, 2004, available at www.dallasnews.com.

26. Robert H. Frank, "Income Inequality and the Protestant Ethic," in Victor Nee and Richard Swedberg, eds., *Capitalism* (Stanford, CA: Stanford University Press, 2007), pp. 73–79.
27. U.S. Census Bureau, *Income, Poverty, and Health Insurance Coverage in the United States: 2009*, available at www.census.gov.
28. U.S. Department of Health and Human Services, "2008 Annual Update of the HHS Poverty Guidelines," available at www.hhs.gov.
29. U.S. Census Bureau, *Income, Poverty, and Health Insurance Coverage in the United States: 2009*.
30. *Income, Poverty, and Health Insurance Coverage in the United States: 2009*.
31. Ibid.
32. Ibid.
33. "Experts Talk Healthcare Reform Impact," *Bloomberg Business Week*, March 22, 2010, available at www.businessweek.com.
34. Karen Tumulty and Kate Pickert with Alice Park, "America, The Doctor Will See You Now," *Time*, April 5, 2010, pp. 24–32.
35. Ezra Klein, "Who Is Left Uninsured by the Health-Care Reform Bill?" *Washington Post*, March 22, 2010, available at www.washingtonpost.com.
36. "Factbox: National Assembly Elections in Vietnam," May 17, 2007, available at www.reuters.com.
37. Joshua Partlow and Pamela Constable, "Accusations of Voter Fraud Multiply in Afghanistan," *Washington Post*, August 28, 2009, available at www.washingtonpost.com.
38. M. Steven Fish, *Democracy Derailed in Russia: The Failure of Open Politics* (New York: Cambridge University Press, 2005), p. 71.
39. Robert A. Dahl, *Polyarchy: Participation and Opposition* (New Haven, CT: Yale University Press, 1971), p. 3.
40. Steven Mufson, "The Reluctant Shareholder," *Washington Post National Weekly Edition*, May 4–10, 2009, p. 24.

Chapter 2

The American Constitution

CHAPTER OUTLINE

The Historical Background of the Constitution
- The Colonial Period
- The Articles of Confederation

The Philosophical Background of the Constitution

Representative Democracy

The Structures of Government
- Separation of Powers with Checks and Balances
- Bicameralism
- Federalism

Restrictions on the Power of Government
- Rule of Law
- Limited Government and the Bill of Rights

Constitutional Change
- Constitutional Amendments
- Practice and Experience
- Judicial Interpretation

The Constitution, Politics, and Public Policy

What We Have Learned

WHAT WE WILL LEARN

After studying Chapter 2, students should be able to answer the following questions:

1. Which historical events had the greatest influence on the development of the Constitution of 1787?
2. Which elements of American political thought had a significant impact on the development of the Constitution?
3. What sort of democracy does the Constitution create?
4. How does the Constitution divide political power among the structures of government?
5. How does the Constitution limit the power of government?
6. How does the Constitution change?
7. How does the Constitution affect the policymaking process?

State Children's Health Insurance Program (SCHIP) A federal program designed to provide health insurance to children from low-income families whose parents are not poor enough to qualify for Medicaid.

Medicaid A federal health insurance program for low-income persons, people with disabilities, and elderly people who are impoverished.

The **State Children's Health Insurance Program (SCHIP)** is a federal program designed to provide health insurance to children from low-income families whose parents are not poor enough to qualify for **Medicaid.** Although both Democrats and Republicans supported SCHIP when it was created, the effort to renew the program in 2008 proved controversial. Whereas Democrats favored expanding SCHIP eligibility to reduce the number of uninsured children, Republicans opposed the expansion as a backdoor attempt to enact government-run healthcare. Congress, which was controlled by Democrats, passed SCHIP expansion legislation in 2008, but Republican President George W. Bush vetoed the measure and Congress was unable to override the veto. In 2008, the political landscape changed with the election of Barack Obama, a proponent of expanding SCHIP. Congress quickly passed the expansion legislation in early 2009 and President Obama signed the measure into law.

The battle over SCHIP illustrates the interplay between the U.S. Constitution and contemporary politics. The Constitution establishes the roles officials play in the policy process, determines the powers they can exercise, and outlines the procedures for policy adoption. A measure cannot become law unless it passes both houses of Congress and the president signs it into law or allows it to become law without signature. If the president vetoes a bill, the Constitution provides that it can become law only if both houses of Congress vote to override the veto by a two-thirds margin. SCHIP expansion failed in 2008 because the president vetoed the measure and Congress was unable to override the veto. The measure became law in early 2009 because the election of Obama, a proponent of SCHIP expansion, as president changed the policymaking environment.

The Historical Background of the Constitution

Constitution The fundamental law by which a state or nation is organized and governed, and to which ordinary legislation must conform.

A **constitution** is the fundamental law by which a state or nation is organized and governed, and to which ordinary legislation must conform. It establishes the framework of government, assigns the powers and duties of government bodies, and defines the relationship between the people and their government. The U.S. Constitution, which is more than 220 years of age, is the oldest written national constitution still in effect in the world today.

The Americans who wrote the Constitution of 1787 had lived through two difficult periods: the late colonial period under British rule and the period under the government created by the Articles of Confederation. To a considerable degree, the Constitution was a reaction to these two experiences.

The Colonial Period

The American colonists were initially satisfied with their political relationship with Great Britain. Preoccupied with matters at home, the British authorities allowed the Americans a substantial measure of self-government. Each colony had a governor, appointed by the king, and a legislative assembly whose members were locally elected. The colonial assemblies could levy taxes, appropriate money, approve or reject the governor's appointments, and pass laws for their colony. Although the governor had the power to veto legislation, the assemblies exercised considerable leverage over the governor by virtue of their control of the budget. This **power of the purse,** which is the authority to raise and spend money, made the locally elected legislative assemblies the dominant bodies of colonial government.

Power of the purse The authority to raise and spend money.

After 1763, the British chose to reorganize their colonial system. The French and Indian War (1756–1763), in which the British and the Americans fought against the French and their Indian allies for control of North America, left the British with a sizable war debt. The British also faced the problem of governing Canada and enforcing treaties with the Indians, which limited westward expansion by the colonists.

British officials decided that the American colonists should pay part of the cost of defending and administering the empire in North America. The British imposed new taxes, such as the Sugar Act of 1764 and the Stamp Act of 1765, and attempted to crack down on smuggling to prevent colonists from avoiding customs taxes. To enforce their policies, the British increased the number of officials in North America and permanently stationed troops in the colonies. The Quartering Act required colonists to provide living quarters in their homes for British troops.

The Americans were outraged. Over the years, the colonists had grown accustomed to self-government and they were unwilling to surrender the privilege. They regarded the new policies as a violation of local traditions and an abridgment of their rights as British citizens. Before 1763, the only taxes the Americans paid to London were duties on trade, and the colonists interpreted the duties as measures to regulate commerce rather than taxes. Now, however, London attempted to impose levies that were clearly taxes. The Americans argued that as English citizens they could be taxed only by their own elected representatives and not by the British Parliament. No taxation without representation, they declared. This argument made no sense to the British. In their view, every member of Parliament represented every British citizen; it was irrelevant that no Americans sat in Parliament. The dispute over taxation and other issues worsened, leading eventually to revolution and American independence.

During the Revolutionary War, the American colonies became the United States, loosely allied under the leadership of the Continental Congress, which was a **unicameral** (one-house) **legislature** in which each state had a single vote. Although the Continental Congress had no official governing authority, it declared America's independence, raised an army, appointed George Washington commander-in-chief, coined money, and negotiated with foreign nations. The Continental Congress also drafted a plan for national union. This plan, known as the Articles of Confederation, went into effect in 1781, upon approval by the 13 states.

Unicameral legislature Legislature with one chamber.

The Articles of Confederation

The Articles of Confederation created a league of friendship, a "perpetual union" of states, with a unicameral congress. Although state legislatures could send as many as seven delegates to the Confederation Congress, each state possessed a single

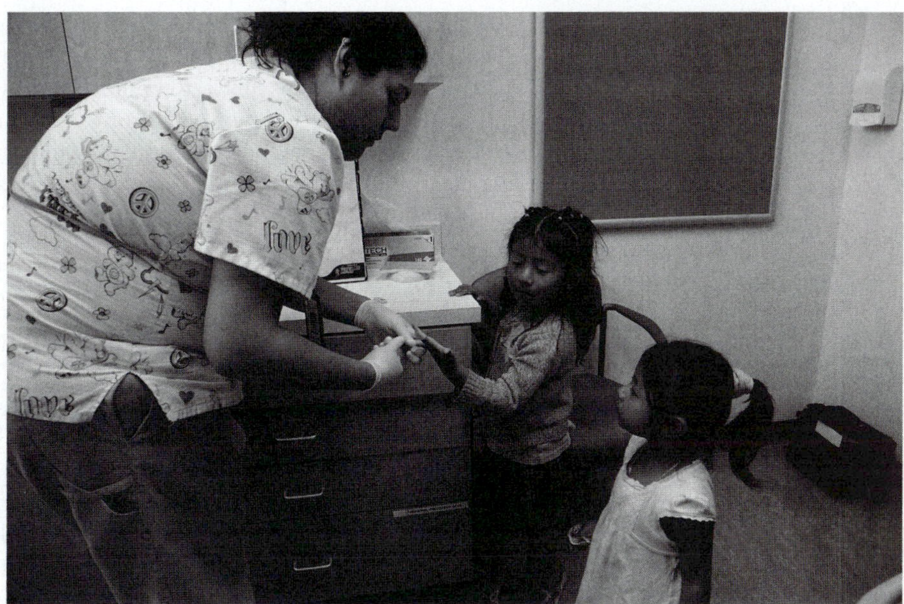

In early 2009, President Obama signed legislation to expand SCHIP eligibility.

vote, and nine states (of 13) had to approve decisions. Amending the Articles required unanimous approval of the states. The Articles provided for no independent national executive or national judiciary.

The states, rather than the Confederation government, were the primary units of government in the new nation. People considered themselves citizens of their states rather than citizens of the nation. Each of the 13 states had its own state constitution that established a framework for state government. These state constitutions typically provided for a **bicameral** (two-house) **legislature,** a governor, and a court system. Because Americans feared executive power as a source of tyranny, they adopted state constitutions that limited the powers of state governors, making legislatures the dominant branch of state government.[1]

Bicameral legislature Legislature with two chambers.

The Americans who wrote the Articles of Confederation were determined to create a government whose powers would be strictly limited. Having just freed themselves from British rule, they did not want to create a strong national government that might become as oppressive as the British colonial government. The Americans who wrote the Articles apparently went too far, however, because the Confederation proved too weak to deal effectively with the new nation's problems. It lacked the power to collect taxes from individuals, having to rely instead on contributions from the states. When state governments failed to pay—as many did—the confederation government was left without financial support. The Confederation also lacked authority to regulate commerce, prohibit states from printing worthless currency, enforce the provisions of the peace treaty with Great Britain, or even defend itself against rebellion. When small farmers in western Massachusetts engaged in an armed uprising against the government over debt and taxes in 1786–1787, the Confederation government failed to respond. After a private army finally crushed the insurrection, which was known as Shays' Rebellion after its leader, Daniel Shays, public opinion began to coalesce in favor of a stronger national government than the one provided by the Articles of Confederation. Attempts to amend the Articles to correct deficiencies failed because Rhode Island refused to agree and the amendment process required the unanimous consent of the states.

The Philosophical Background of the Constitution

The nation's founders were educated people who studied the important political writings of their day. The work of Englishman John Locke (1632–1704) was particularly influential. In his *Second Treatise on Government* (1689), Locke declared that people were born free and equal, and possessed certain natural rights, which were life, liberty, and property. Unfortunately, Locke said, evil people disrupt the good life by conspiring to deprive others of their life, liberty, or property. In order to protect their rights, people voluntarily join together to form governments. The power of government, then, stems from the consent of the governed, who entrust the government with responsibility for protecting their lives, liberty, and possessions. Should government fail in this task, Locke declared, the people have the right to revolt and institute a new government.

Americans drew three important principles from Locke's thought. First, Locke's theory of revolution offered the perfect theoretical rationale for the American Revolution. In the Declaration of Independence, which is reprinted in the Appendix of this text, the founders drew on Locke's thinking to justify independence from Great Britain. The Americans were justified in revolting against the King, the founders declared, because the King deprived them of their rights to "Life, Liberty, and the pursuit of Happiness." Thomas Jefferson, the principal author of the Declaration, substituted the phrase *pursuit of Happiness* for the word *property* in order to give the document a more idealistic tone. Second, Locke provided a theoretical basis for the creation of a national government that could be a positive force in society instead of just a necessary evil. According to Locke, the people create government in order to accomplish certain goals, that is, to protect life, liberty, and property from the dangers inherent in a state of nature. In theory, then, government can play an active, positive role in society. Third, Locke's concept of natural rights offered a theoretical foundation for limiting government authority over the individual. The **doctrine of natural rights** is the belief that individual rights transcend the power of government. People create government to protect their rights, not to abridge them. Locke's theory of natural rights provided a basis for a bill of rights, a constitutional document guaranteeing individual rights and liberties.

Doctrine of natural rights The belief that individual rights transcend the power of government.

Although the nation's founders frequently cited the works of European philosophers such as Locke, they did more than just apply the theories developed in Europe to the United States. They created a nation and wrote a Constitution based on American events, experiences, and ideas, citing European political philosophers selectively to reinforce what they already believed. Furthermore, the Americans were not afraid to disregard the advice of the political theorists when it did not fit their image of American political reality.[2]

The most important element of American political thought was the changing conception of the nature of politics and government. At the time of the Revolution, American political theorists believed that politics was a never-ending struggle between the people and the government. In their view, the people were virtuous and united in support of the public good, whereas the government, personified by the king, was corrupt and oppressive. After declaring their independence, the Americans knew that they needed a national government, but they did not want a strong one. The government established by the Articles of Confederation fit the bill nicely.

After a few years of independence, many Americans recognized that their understanding of the nature of the people and the role of government was mistaken. Rather than being united behind a common perception of the public good, society was composed of a variety of interests or factions, which opposed one another on a number of policy issues. Furthermore, practical political experience in the states demonstrated that the people were not so virtuous after all. When one faction gained control of the government of a particular state or locality, it would often use its power to enforce its will over opposing interests.

By 1787, many Americans had decided that a strong national government could play a positive role in society. First, the national government could reconcile the divergent concerns of various groups in society to produce policies designed to achieve the public good. A large nation, such as the United States, includes a wide range of interests competing for power. Although a particular group or faction might be strong enough to control the government in one state or a local area, no single group would be able to dominate nationwide. A strong national government would provide a forum in which groups would be able to reconcile their differences. The result would be policies that would be acceptable to a broad range of interests.

Second, a strong national government could protect individual liberty and property from the power of oppressive majorities. At the state or local level, a dominant faction could adopt policies designed to advance its own religious or economic interests at the expense of the minority. At the national level, however, no one group or faction would be powerful enough to enforce its will on the entire nation. Because every group held minority status in one state or another, it would be in each group's interest to protect minorities against the power of oppressive local majorities.[3] For example, the framers of the Constitution included a provision prohibiting a state-supported church because of the multiplicity of religious sects in America. Although many of the early American religious groups would have liked nothing better than to establish their faith as the official state religion, they lacked the power to achieve that goal. Consequently, they preferred an official government policy of religious freedom to risking the possibility that another religious group would gain official recognition.[4]

The framers of the Constitution included a provision prohibiting a state-supported church because of the multiplicity of religious sects in America. They preferred an official government policy of religious freedom to risking the possibility that another religious group would gain official recognition.

Representative Democracy

Democracy A system of government in which ultimate political authority is vested in the people.

Direct democracy A political system in which the citizens vote directly on matters of public concern.

Tyranny of the majority The abuse of the minority by the majority.

A **democracy** is a system of government in which the people hold ultimate political power. Although the framers of the Constitution favored a government that would answer to the people, they did not want to give too much power to majority opinion. The framers were particularly wary of **direct democracy,** a political system in which the citizens vote directly on matters of public concern. The framers of the Constitution worried that ordinary citizens lacked the information to make intelligent policy decisions. They feared that direct democracy would produce policies reflecting hasty, emotional decisions rather than well-considered judgments.

The framers also worried that direct democracy would enable a majority of the people to enact policies that would silence, disadvantage, or harm the minority point of view, thus producing a **tyranny of the majority,** the abuse of the minority by the majority. The danger of majority rule is that the majority may vote to adopt policies that unfairly disadvantage the minority. The challenge for the framers of the Constitution was to create a form of government that would provide for majority rule while protecting the rights and liberties of minorities.

Instead of a direct democracy, the framers created a **representative democracy** or **republic,** which is a political system in which citizens elect representatives to make policy decisions on their behalf. The framers believed that elected representatives would act as a buffer between the people and government policies. Representatives

Representative democracy or **republic** A political system in which citizens elect representatives to make policy decisions on their behalf.

would be more knowledgeable than ordinary citizens about policy issues. They would also be more likely than the general public to recognize the legitimate interests of different groups in society and seek policy compromises designed to accommodate those interests.

WHAT IS YOUR OPINION?

Assuming that modern technology would overcome any logistical problems, do you think the United States would be better off today with a direct democracy rather than a republic? Why or why not?

Supermajority A voting margin which is greater than a simple majority.

To further guard against the tyranny of the majority, the framers provided that some policy actions could be taken only with the consent of a **supermajority,** that is, a voting margin which is greater than a simple majority. Constitutional amendments must be proposed by two-thirds of the members of both the House and the Senate and ratified by three-fourths of the states. Treaties must be approved by two-thirds of the Senate. Presidential vetoes can only be overridden by a two-thirds vote of each chamber of Congress. Executive and judicial officials can be removed from office only by a two-thirds vote of the Senate. In each of these cases, a simple majority of 50 percent plus one does not prevail. Instead, policy actions require the support—or at least acceptance—of a supermajority of two-thirds or more.

The Structures of Government

Legislative power The power to make laws.

The Constitution creates a representative democracy that divides political power among the branches of government, between the chambers of Congress, and between the national government and the state governments.

Executive power The power to enforce laws.

Separation of Powers with Checks and Balances

Judicial power The power to interpret laws.

Separation of powers The division of political power among executive, legislative, and judicial branches of government.

The framers of the U.S. Constitution adopted separation of powers with checks and balances as a means for controlling the power of government. Although the roots of these concepts went back a century, their modern development was the work of Baron de Montesquieu, an eighteenth-century French political philosopher. Montesquieu identified three kinds of political power: the power to make laws (**legislative power**), enforce laws (**executive power**), and interpret laws (**judicial power**). Montesquieu warned against allowing one person or a single group of people from exercising all three powers because that person or group would become so powerful as to pose a threat to individual liberty. To protect freedom, Montesquieu advocated **separation of powers,** that is, the division of political power among executive, legislative, and judicial branches of government. He called for a system of checks and balances to prevent any one of the three branches from becoming too strong. **Checks and balances** refer to the overlapping of the powers of the branches of government, designed to ensure that public officials limit the authority of one another.

Checks and balances The overlapping of the powers of the branches of government, designed to ensure that public officials limit the authority of one another.

Federalist Papers Series of essays written by James Madison, Alexander Hamilton, and John Jay to advocate the ratification of the Constitution of 1787.

Factions Special interests who seek their own good at the expense of the common good.

James Madison was the principal architect of America's system of separation of powers with checks and balances. In fact, scholars sometimes refer to the nation's constitutional apparatus as the Madisonian system. Madison and two other proponents of the new constitution, Alexander Hamilton and John Jay, wrote a series of essays known as the ***Federalist Papers*** to advocate the ratification of the Constitution of 1787. In *The Federalist* No. 51, Madison identified two threats to liberty: (1) **factions,** which are special interests who seek their own good at the expense of the common good, and (2) the excessive concentration of political power in the hands of government officials. Madison's remedy for these dangers was the creation of a strong national government with separation of powers and checks and balances.

Madison believed that the nation needed a strong national government to control the power of factions. In this regard, Madison noted the advantage of a large nation with many diverse interests. At the local or state level, he said, a single faction might be powerful enough to dominate. It could unfairly force its will on the minority, creating a tyranny of the majority. Over the breadth of the entire nation, however, the narrow perspectives of that faction would be checked by the interests of other factions entrenched in other areas. A strong national government would provide an arena in which factions would counterbalance one another. National policies, therefore, would reflect compromise among a range of interests.

Madison also favored separation of powers with checks and balances as a means to control the power of government officials. Madison said that the goal of the system was "to divide and arrange the several offices [of government] in such a manner as that each may be a check on the other."[5] In this fashion, the selfish, private interests of officeholders would counterbalance each other to the public good. "Ambition," Madison wrote, "must be made to counteract ambition."[6]

James Madison is the principal architect of the U.S. Constitution, so much so that America's system of government is sometimes called the Madisonian system.

The Constitution contains an elaborate network of checks and balances. The executive branch, for example, checks the judicial branch through the president's power to appoint members of the Supreme Court and other federal courts. Congress, in turn, checks the president and the courts in that the Senate must confirm judicial appointments. Similarly, the Constitution declares that Congress has the authority to declare war, but it names the president commander-in-chief of the armed forces. The president negotiates treaties, but the Senate must ratify them.

Parliamentary system A system of government in which political power is concentrated in a legislative body and a cabinet headed by a prime minister.

Separation of powers with checks and balances creates tension among the branches of government because the framers of the Constitution refused to draw clear lines of authority among Congress, the president, and the judiciary. In fact, the phrase *separation of powers* is misleading. What really exists is a system in which separate institutions *share* power.[7] Friction is inevitable.

Parliament The British legislature.

Bicameralism

The framers of the Constitution expected the legislative branch to be the dominant institution of American national government because it was the most important branch of state governments. To prevent the national legislature from becoming too

Around the World — The British Parliamentary System

Most of the world's democracies are patterned after the British parliamentary system rather than the checks and balances system of the United States. A **parliamentary system** is a system of government in which political power is concentrated in a legislative body and a cabinet headed by a prime minister. The British legislature, which is called the **Parliament,** has two chambers, a House of Commons and a House of Lords. Real power is in the hands of the House of Commons, which is composed of 660 members elected from districts. The House of Lords, which includes the bishops of the Church of England and other members appointed for life by the king or queen, is now little more than a debating society with the power only to delay legislation, not defeat it.

British voters understand that when they vote for Parliament they are also choosing a government. At election time, each British political party presents the voters with a detailed set of policy proposals that it promises to implement if given the opportunity. Voters know that a vote for a particular parliamentary candidate is a vote for the policies offered by that candidate's political party. It is also a vote for the election of that party's leader as prime minister.

The primary check on the government in Great Britain is the electorate. The government must hold a new parliamentary election within five years, giving voters the opportunity to keep the current government in power or turn the government over to the opposition. In 2010, British voters ended 13 years of Labour Party rule, but failed to give the opposition Conservative Party enough seats for an outright majority. Subsequently, the Conservatives formed a coalition government with the smaller Liberal Party and Conservative leader David Cameron became prime minister.

QUESTIONS

1. Which political system is more responsive to citizen demands—the American or the British system?
2. Which political system is more likely to produce dramatic policy change?
3. Which political system is better equipped to protect the rights of minorities?

GETTING INVOLVED

Service Learning

Service learning is based on the concept that students can learn more about a subject through participation and experience, combined with traditional coursework, than they can through classroom instruction alone.

Use the following checklist to guide you through your service-learning project:

1. Identify a government office or agency that welcomes student volunteers. You may wish to begin with the mayor's office, school district, hospital district, or state legislator. They can give you referrals to agencies that deal with issues related to your career goals.
2. Call the agency or department that interests you and ask to speak to the volunteer coordinator. Explain that you are completing a service-learning project for your college and want to know about volunteer opportunities.
3. Note that your instructor will set the number of hours you should volunteer. Normally, students should expect to work from 20 to 40 hours over a semester to receive full benefit from the activity.
4. As you complete your assignment at the agency, ask the volunteer coordinator to provide you with documentation of the hours of your work to present to your instructor. You will be required to keep a reflective journal documenting your service. Journal entries should discuss your work on the project and your reaction to the experience, covering the following topics:
    1. What you did for the organization.
    2. What you thought of the organization, including the clients served, the work done, and the other employees or volunteers.
    3. How your experience relates to course materials.
    4. How your experience relates to topics in the news.

Write at least one journal entry for every two hours you spend at your placement. You will be evaluated on the amount of time you spent at your placement, the number and length of your journal entries, and the quality of your entries.

powerful, the framers divided Congress into two houses with different sizes, terms of office, responsibilities, and constituencies. The precise organization of America's bicameral Congress was the product of an agreement between large-state and small-state forces known as the Connecticut Compromise. Members of the House of Representatives would be chosen by direct popular election to serve two-year terms with the number of representatives from each state based on population. Each state would have two senators chosen by their state legislatures to serve six-year terms. The adoption of the Seventeenth Amendment in 1913 provided for direct popular election of senators.

The framers expected that the popularly elected House of Representatives would be constrained by a more conservative Senate. With a two-year term, members of the House would be closer to the people and more likely to act hastily in accordance with short-term popular sentiment. In contrast, senators, chosen by state legislatures and serving longer terms, would be insulated from popular pressures, thus enabling them to act more cautiously and put the national interest ahead of short-term political gain.[8]

Federalism

The Americans who gathered in Philadelphia in 1787 for the constitutional convention had lived under both a unitary system and a confederation. The British North American colonies were part of a **unitary government,** which is a governmental system in which political authority is concentrated in a single national government. The local colonial governments could constitutionally exercise only those powers specifically granted to them by the British parliament. The defenders of unitary government argue that it provides for consistent policy administration throughout a country and allows for efficient handling of nationwide problems. In contrast, the critics of unitary government say that it fails to permit sufficient local variation to accommodate differing local circumstances. American dissatisfaction with the policies of Britain's centralized administration led to the Revolution.

Unitary government A governmental system in which political authority is concentrated in a single national government.

The Articles of Confederation established a **confederation,** which is a league of nearly independent states, similar to the United Nations today. Under the confederation government, individual Americans were citizens of their respective states but not the national government. As a result, the government under the Articles lacked the authority to deal directly with individuals (to tax them, for example); it could deal only with the governments of the 13 states. The advantage of a confederation is that it allows states to cooperate without surrendering any of their basic powers. The disadvantage is that it provides for a weak central government, which proved the undoing of the confederation.

Confederation A league of nearly independent states, similar to the United Nations today.

The framers of the Constitution set out to establish a government that would be capable of effective administration but would not undermine the American tradition of local control. Their solution was to create a federation. A **federation** or **federal system** is a political system that divides power between a central government, with authority over the whole nation, and a series of state governments.

Federation or **federal system** A political system that divides power between a central government, with authority over the whole nation, and a series of state governments.

A federation is a compromise between unitary government and a confederation. In a unitary system, the national government is sovereign. **Sovereignty** is the authority of a state to exercise its legitimate powers within its boundaries, free from external interference. The powers of state and local governments (if they exist) are granted to them by the national government. In a confederation, the states are sovereign. The national government's authority flows from the states. In a federal system, the national (or federal) government and the state governments are both sovereign. They derive their authority not from one another but from the Constitution. Both levels of government act directly on the people through their officials and laws, both are supreme within their proper sphere of authority, and both must consent to constitutional change.

Sovereignty The authority of a state to exercise its legitimate powers within its boundaries, free from external interference.

Federalism offers several advantages. A federal system provides a means of political representation that can accommodate the diversity of American society. Individual Americans are citizens of their states and the nation as well, and participate in the selection of representatives to both levels of government. In a federal system, local interests shape local policy. The national government, meanwhile, is an arena in which local interests from different regions can check and balance one another, permitting the national interest to prevail.

Federalism can help protect against the tyranny of the majority. The federal system creates a series of overlapping state and district election systems that select members of Congress as well as the president. The federal election system gives minorities of all kinds—racial, ethnic, religious, regional, local, occupational, social, and sexual—the opportunity to be part of a majority because they may comprise the swing vote in a closely divided state or district. Consequently, they must be consulted; their interests must be considered.[9]

WHAT IS YOUR OPINION?

Which is the best form of government—a unitary government, a confederation, or a federal government?

Nonetheless, a federal system imposes certain disadvantages. Local variations confuse citizens and hinder business. Traveling Americans face different traffic laws in each state. People who move from one state to another must adapt to different laws regarding such matters as marriage, divorce, wills, and occupational licensing. A couple approved as foster parents in one state may have to go through the approval process again if they move to another state. Businesses must adjust to variations in tax laws and regulations. Federalism also sets the stage for conflict. American history is filled with examples of disputes between states and the national government. The dispute between the North and the South over extending slavery to the territories led to the Civil War. Issues such as the enforcement of federal environmental laws and the implementation of healthcare reform are contemporary examples of conflicts between states and the national government.

Restrictions on the Power of Government

The framers of the Constitution created a government whose powers over the individual would be limited.

Rule of law The constitutional principle that holds that the discretion of public officials in dealing with individuals is limited by the law.

Writ of *habeas corpus* A court order requiring that government authorities either release a person held in custody or demonstrate that the person is detained in accordance with law.

Rule of Law

The **rule of law** is the constitutional principle that holds that the discretion of public officials in dealing with individuals is limited by the law. The very existence of a written Constitution implies the rule of law, but certain constitutional provisions deserve special notice. In Article I, Section 9, the Constitution guarantees the privilege of the writ of *habeas corpus* except in cases of invasion, rebellion, or threat to public safety. A **writ of *habeas corpus*** is a court order requiring that government authorities either release a person held in custody or demonstrate that the person is detained in accordance with law. *Habeas corpus* is designed to prevent arbitrary arrest and imprisonment. The Constitution protects Americans from being held in custody by the government unless they are charged and convicted in accordance with the law.

WHAT IS YOUR OPINION?

Should the government be allowed to arrest American citizens and hold them without charges and without trial if it believes that they are involved in planning terrorist attacks against the United States?

Bill of attainder A law declaring a person or a group of persons guilty of a crime and providing for punishment without benefit of a judicial proceeding.

***ex post facto* law** A retroactive criminal statute that operates to the disadvantage of accused persons.

Due process of law The constitutional principle holding that government must follow fair and regular procedures in actions that could lead to an individual's suffering loss of life, liberty, or property.

The Constitution prohibits the passage of bills of attainder and *ex post facto* laws. A **bill of attainder** is a law declaring a person or a group of persons guilty of a crime and providing for punishment without benefit of a judicial proceeding. An ***ex post facto* law** is a retroactive criminal statute that operates to the disadvantage of accused persons. It makes a crime out of an act that was not illegal when it was committed.

Due process of law is the constitutional principle holding that the government must follow fair and regular procedures in actions that could lead to an individual's suffering loss of life, liberty, or property. In both the Fifth and Fourteenth Amendments, the Constitution provides that neither Congress (the Fifth Amendment) nor the states (the Fourteenth Amendment) may deprive any person of "life, liberty, or property, without due process of law." Due process of law generally protects individuals from the arbitrary actions of public officials. Before individuals may be imprisoned, fined, or executed, they must be given their day in court in accordance with law. Among other rights, the Constitution guarantees accused persons the right to a speedy, public trial by an impartial jury, the right to confront witnesses, and the right to legal counsel.

The Constitution guarantees accused persons the right to a speedy, public trial by an impartial jury, the right to confront witnesses, and the right to legal counsel.

Limited Government and the Bill of Rights

Limited government The constitutional principle that government does not have unrestricted authority over individuals.

Bill of Rights A constitutional document guaranteeing individual rights and liberties. The first ten amendments to the U.S. Constitution constitute the U.S. Bill of Rights.

Limited government is the constitutional principle that government does not have unrestricted authority over individuals. The government of the United States is not a dictatorship with absolute authority; its power is limited. Perhaps the most important constitutional restriction on the authority of government is the **Bill of Rights,** the first ten amendments to the Constitution.

The Bill of Rights was not part of the original Constitution because a majority of the framers of the Constitution believed that such a provision was unnecessary, redundant, useless, and possibly even dangerous. The framers thought that a bill of rights would be unnecessary because each state constitution had a bill of rights and the national government lacked sufficient power to threaten individual liberty. They considered a bill of rights redundant because the Constitution already contained a number of provisions designed to protect individual liberty, such as the prohibition against *ex post facto* laws and bills of attainder and the guarantee of due process of law. They thought that a bill of rights would be useless because they believed that a paper guarantee of individual liberty would mean little in the face of public pressure. Finally, the framers resisted the inclusion of a bill of rights in the Constitution because they worried that some rights might be inadvertently left out and that any right omitted from the document would be lost.[10]

Antifederalists Americans opposed to the ratification of the Constitution of 1787 because they thought it gave too much power to the national government.

Federalists Americans who supported the ratification of the Constitution of 1787.

The failure of the proposed Constitution to include a bill of rights became a political issue during the debate over ratification. After the Constitution was written in 1787, it still had to be approved (or ratified) by 9 of the 13 states. The **Antifederalists** were Americans opposed to the ratification of the Constitution of 1787 because they thought it gave too much power to the national government. They raised the issue of a bill of rights in hopes of defeating the Constitution and forcing the convening of a new constitutional convention. The **Federalists** were Americans who supported the ratification of the Constitution of 1787. Although most Federalists initially opposed inclusion of a bill of rights in the Constitution, they switched sides on the issue in order to secure ratification and prevent a new convention. They promised to add a bill of rights once the Constitution was ratified and the new government took office.[11]

The Federalists kept their promise. In 1789, the First Congress of the United States proposed 12 amendments, 10 of which were ratified by a sufficient number of states to become part of the Constitution by 1791. One of the rejected amendments, a provision requiring that a congressional pay raise could not go into effect before an intervening election took place, was finally ratified in 1992 to become the Twenty-seventh Amendment.

The authors of the Bill of Rights intended that it would apply only to the national government and not the states because the states already had bills of rights. The U.S. Constitution and the national Bill of Rights would protect individual rights against abuse by the national government, whereas state constitutions and state bills of rights would secure individual rights from infringement by state governments.

The Fourteenth Amendment, which was added to the Constitution immediately after the Civil War, provided the constitutional basis for applying the national Bill of Rights to the states. Congress proposed the Fourteenth Amendment in 1866 to protect the rights of the former slaves from infringement by state governments. The amendment defined U.S. citizenship, making it clear that all Americans are citizens of both the United States and the state in which they live. The amendment declared that state governments could not take life, liberty, or property without "due process of law," or deny to any person within their jurisdiction "equal protection of the laws." The Fourteenth Amendment also prohibited states from making laws abridging the "privileges or immunities" of citizens.

Selective incorporation of the Bill of Rights against the states The process through which the U.S. Supreme Court interpreted the Due Process Clause of the Fourteenth Amendment of the U.S. Constitution to apply most of the provisions of the national Bill of Rights to the states.

The Fourteenth Amendment did not play a major role in the protection of individual rights until the twentieth century. Initially, the Fourteenth Amendment had little impact on individual rights because the Supreme Court of the United States refused to interpret its provisions to protect individual rights. Not until the twentieth century did the Court begin the process known as the **selective incorporation of the Bill of Rights against the states.** This is the process through which the U.S. Supreme Court interpreted the Due Process Clause of the Fourteenth Amendment of the U.S. Constitution to apply most of the provisions of the national Bill of Rights to the states. Although the Supreme Court has never ruled that the Bill of Rights as a whole applies to the states, it has selectively held that virtually all of its key provisions apply against the states through the Due Process Clause of the Fourteenth Amendment. As a result, the national Bill of Rights now protects individual rights against infringement by both the national and state governments.

Constitutional Change

The Constitution has not just survived for more than 220 years—it has grown and matured with the nation, and still serves as the fundamental framework for policymaking. When the original document was written in 1787, the United States was a nation of only about four million people, most of which lived on farms and in small towns. Many Americans—slaves, women, and individuals without property—were denied full rights of participation in the policymaking process. Today, the country is dramatically changed, but the Constitution, with only 27 official amendments, endures as the centerpiece of policymaking.

The genius of the Constitution lies in its ability to adapt to changing times while maintaining adherence to basic principles. The Constitution is a brief, general document that is full of phrases that lack clear definition. The Eighth Amendment, for example, prohibits "cruel and unusual punishments." Article I, Section 8 gives Congress the power to regulate "commerce." Article II, Section 4 declares that the president may be impeached and removed from office for "treason, bribery, or other high crimes and misdemeanors." The Fourth Amendment prohibits "unreasonable searches and seizures." What do these terms mean? What punishments are *cruel and unusual*? What is *commerce*? What are *high crimes and misdemeanors*? Which searches and seizures are *reasonable* and which are *unreasonable*?

The Constitution is often vague, as the framers intended. They set down certain basic, fundamental principles, but omitted details in order to allow succeeding generations to supply specifics in light of their own experiences. The basic idea behind the concept of "cruel and unusual punishments," for example, is that government must not go too far in punishing criminals. The prohibition against "unreasonable searches and seizures" places limits on the police. Had the framers of the Constitution decided to spell out everything in detail, they would have produced a document far longer and less satisfactory than the one we have. Eventually, the nation would have outgrown it and either cast it aside or been forced to amend it repeatedly.

WHAT IS YOUR OPINION?

Is the Constitution too general? Would the nation be better served had the framers created a more specific document?

Constitutional Amendments

Constitutional amendment A formal, written change or addition to the nation's governing document.

A **constitutional amendment** is a formal, written change or addition to the nation's governing document. A major flaw of the Articles of Confederation was that the articles could be amended only by unanimous vote. In practice, correcting weaknesses in the document proved impossible because of the obstinacy of only one or a few states. In 1787, then, the Constitution's framers were careful to include a reasonable method of amendment that was difficult enough to preclude hasty, ill-conceived changes, but not impossible.

The Constitution provides two methods for proposing amendments and two methods for their ratification. An amendment can be proposed by either a two-thirds vote of each house of Congress or by a constitutional convention called by Congress upon petition by two-thirds of the states. The former method of proposal has been used many times: Congress proposed all 27 amendments that have been added to the Constitution. The convention procedure has never been used and no one knows for sure just how the process would work. Must state petitions be written in identical form? Could a state withdraw a petition after submitting it? Would Congress *have* to call a convention if the required number of states submitted petitions? Would the convention be limited to the subject identified in the petitions or could the convention rewrite the entire document? Because of these unanswered questions, many constitutional scholars are apprehensive about the possibility of a new constitutional convention.

After an amendment is proposed, either by Congress or convention, three-fourths of the states must ratify it. Ratification can be accomplished either by vote of the state legislatures or by specially called state conventions. The former method has been used successfully 26 times; the latter was used only once, to ratify the Twenty-first Amendment repealing Prohibition.

The road to constitutional amendment may be difficult, but a number of groups believe their cause is worth the effort. In the 1970s and early 1980s, the Equal Rights Amendment (ERA), which was a proposed amendment guaranteeing equality before the law, regardless of sex, passed Congress but fell three states short of ratification. In recent years, Congress has considered but failed to pass other proposed amendments dealing with such issues as prayer in schools, flag burning, term limitation, abortion, Electoral College reform, a balanced budget, and gay marriage.

WHAT IS YOUR OPINION?

Is amending the Constitution too difficult, too easy, or just right?

Practice and Experience

The Constitution has adapted to changing times through practice and experience. Consider the role of the presidency. The historical development of the office has given definition to the powers of the presidency beyond the scope of the office that was foreseen by the framers. Other elements of American government have developed despite slight mention in the Constitution. Even though the federal bureaucracy is barely discussed in the Constitution, its importance in American government has grown to the point that some observers refer to it as the fourth branch of government. Furthermore, some important contemporary features of American government are not mentioned at all in the Constitution, including the committee system in Congress, the president's cabinet, and the political party system. To an important extent, the meaning of the Constitution is found in its historical development over time as succeeding generations of Americans have addressed policy issues within its framework.

Judicial Interpretation

A final means of constitutional change is judicial interpretation. In fact, it may be no exaggeration to say that what counts most in constitutional law is the interpretation of the Constitution by the courts, particularly the U.S. Supreme Court, rather than the words of the document itself. Many phrases important to constitutional law are not even in the Constitution, including *war power*, *clear and present danger*, *separation of church and state*, *right of privacy*, *separate but equal*, and *police power*. These famous words appear not in the Constitution but in judicial opinions.

Judicial interpretation of the Constitution is inevitable because of the document's general nature. Many of the phrases of the Constitution are purposely ambiguous, requiring continuous reinterpretation and adaptation. Indeed, one constitutional scholar says that we have an unwritten constitution, whose history is the history of judicial interpretation.[12]

Judicial review The power of courts to declare unconstitutional the actions of the other branches and units of government.

The power of courts to declare unconstitutional the actions of the other branches and units of government is known as **judicial review.** Although the Constitution is silent about the power of judicial review, many historians believe that the founders expected the courts to exercise the authority. Ironically, the Supreme Court assumed the power of judicial review through constitutional interpretation, first holding an act of Congress unconstitutional in 1803 in the case of *Marbury v. Madison*.[13]

The case had its roots in the election of 1800 when President John Adams was defeated and his political party, the Federalist Party, lost its majority in Congress.

In the period between the election and the inauguration of the new president, Adams proceeded to nominate, and the Senate to confirm, the appointments of a number of loyal Federalists to serve in the judicial branch of government.

One of these judicial appointments went to William Marbury, who was named justice of the peace for the District of Columbia. President Adams signed and sealed Marbury's official commission on the day before he left office, but the secretary of state neglected to deliver the commission. When Thomas Jefferson, the newly elected president, took office, he ordered his secretary of state, James Madison, not to deliver the commission. Marbury subsequently sued, asking the Supreme Court to issue a writ of *mandamus* to order Madison to deliver the commission. A **writ of *mandamus*** is a court order directing a public official to perform a specific act or duty.

Writ of *mandamus* A court order directing a public official to perform a specific act or duty.

The case presented the Supreme Court with a dilemma. Chief Justice John Marshall and the other members of the Court were Federalists who would have liked nothing better than to blast the Jefferson administration and order Madison to deliver the commission. Had the Court done so, however, Jefferson would probably have defied the order. Marshall knew that defiance by the president would destroy the Court's prestige, but he also wanted to avoid ruling for the administration.

Judicial review provided Marshall and the Court a way out of their dilemma. Marshall used the Court's opinion to scold Jefferson and Madison for refusing to deliver the commission. Marbury was entitled to his commission, said Marshall, and a writ of *mandamus* was in order. Marshall ruled, however, that the Supreme Court lacked authority to issue the writ. Marshall pointed out that the Constitution lists the types of cases that may be tried before the Supreme Court in Article III, Section 2, and that the list does not include the power to issue writs of *mandamus* to federal officials. Congress had given the Court the authority to issue the writ legislatively in the Judiciary Act of 1789. Marshall held that Congress had no constitutional authority to expand the Court's **jurisdiction,** which is the authority of a court to hear a case. Therefore, the section of the Judiciary Act that gave the Court the power to issue writs of *mandamus* was unconstitutional. By this means, Marshall was able to attack Jefferson without giving the president the opportunity to defy the Court's authority.

Jurisdiction The authority of a court to hear a case.

The long-term significance of *Marbury v. Madison* is that it is the first case in which the Supreme Court exercised the power to hold acts of Congress unconstitutional. In his ruling, Marshall stated that the Constitution is the "fundamental and paramount law of the nation" and that it is the duty of the courts to interpret the law. "Thus," Marshall continued, "the particular phraseology of the Constitution of the United States confirms and strengthens the principle . . . that a law repugnant to the Constitution is void." Marshall concluded that in conflicts between the Constitution and acts of Congress, it was the Court's duty to enforce the Constitution by refusing to uphold the law.

Equal Protection Clause A provision found in the Fourteenth Amendment of the U.S. Constitution that declares that "No State shall . . . deny to any person within its jurisdiction the equal protection of the laws."

Judicial review is an instrument of constitutional change because the process involves constitutional interpretation. Professor Richard H. Fallon, Jr., says that today's justices interpret the Constitution in light of history, precedent (that is, earlier interpretations), and considerations of moral desirability and practical workability.[14] Consider the history of judicial interpretation of the **Equal Protection Clause,** which is the provision found in the Fourteenth Amendment of the U.S. Constitution that declares that "No State shall . . . deny to any person within its jurisdiction the equal protection of the laws." Historians believe that Congress proposed this phrase to safeguard the civil rights of former slaves and their offspring by requiring states to treat all of their residents equally under state law, regardless of race.

The U.S. Supreme Court's initial interpretation of the Equal Protection Clause came in 1896 in *Plessy v. Ferguson*. The case centered on the constitutionality of a Louisiana law that required racial segregation (separation) in passenger railcars. Could a state government prohibit African American travelers from sharing a railcar with white passengers without violating the Equal Protection Clause? The Supreme Court answered that it could as long as the accommodations were equal. "Separate but equal" facilities, said the Court, were sufficient to satisfy the requirements of the Fourteenth Amendment.[15] Almost 60 years later, the Supreme Court addressed a similar issue in the case of *Brown v. Board of Education of Topeka* (1954). The *Brown* case involved a constitutional challenge to state laws requiring or permitting racial segregation in public schools. Could a state government prohibit African American youngsters from sharing a school with white children without violating the Equal Protection Clause? In this case, the Supreme Court overruled *Plessy*, holding that the Equal Protection Clause of the Fourteenth Amendment prohibits state laws requiring racial segregation in public schools. The Court declared that "separate but equal" was a contradiction because the legal requirement of separation placed the stamp of inferiority on the black race.[16] And so the Constitution was changed, not through the adoption of a constitutional amendment (the wording of the Equal Protection Clause remained the same), but because of changing judicial interpretation.

The Constitution, Politics, and Public Policy

The U.S. Constitution affects the policymaking process by fragmenting political power. Separation of powers divides power at the national level among legislative, executive, and judicial branches. Bicameralism splits the legislative branch in two, dividing power between the House and Senate. Federalism distributes power between the national government and the states.

The fragmentation of political power in the United States produces slow, incremental change. Presidents need the cooperation of Congress to have their programs enacted. In turn, Congress has difficulty acting without presidential initiative or at least acquiescence. Both the president and Congress need the support of the bureaucracy if their policies are to be faithfully executed. Frequently, they require the cooperation of state and local officials as well. The courts, meanwhile, can reverse or delay policies adopted at other levels or by other branches of government. With so many steps and so many power centers involved in the policy process, change is usually slow in coming if it comes at all. When policy changes occur, they are generally incremental and gradual, reflecting compromise among the various political actors involved in the process.

The framers of the U.S. Constitution favored a system that would ensure deliberation and delay rather than precipitous action. They were cautious people, wary of rapid change and none too confident about the judgment of popular majorities. Consequently, they created a constitutional apparatus that would work slowly and be unlikely to produce dramatic upheavals in public policy. The founders feared that rapid, major change would too often produce more harm than good.

The Constitution promotes policy stability. The election of a new president or a change in control of Congress is unlikely to produce dramatic policy change because the Constitution works against dramatic change. A new president with bold new ideas must convince both houses of Congress that the policy ideas are wise and, if legal challenges arise, convince the federal courts that they are constitutional.

The framers of the Constitution wanted to ensure that the diversity of political interests in American society would be represented in the policy process. During the debates at the constitutional convention of 1787, one of the major issues was how best to protect the small states from large-state domination. In response to the controversy, the authors of the Constitution established a system that would provide opportunity for the varied groups and interests of American society to participate in policymaking. Today, many Americans still see this as a virtue.

Nonetheless, America's constitutional arrangements have their critics. The oldest complaint, first voiced by the Antifederalists, is that the Constitution favored the rich and wellborn over the interests of the common people. In the early twentieth century, historian Charles Beard echoed the position of the Antifederalists by arguing that the framers of the Constitution had been members of a small group of wealthy Americans who set out to preserve and enhance the economic and political opportunities of their class.[17] Although modern historians have refuted most of Beard's research, a number of contemporary observers nonetheless believe that the Constitution benefits special interests. The constitutional fragmentation of power that presents a range of forums in which different groups may be heard also provides a series of power centers that interest groups can control. Because of the complexity of the constitutional process, entrenched groups can frequently muster the influence to halt policy changes they consider unfavorable, sometimes overriding the wishes of a majority in Congress and the nation. The supermajority provisions in the Constitution allow a determined minority to block the will of the majority.

The most basic criticism of the Constitution is that it is a blueprint for political deadlock among the branches and units of government. By dividing government against itself, the founders ensured that all proposals for policy change must pass through a maze of power centers. The complexity of the arrangement not only slows the policymaking process but also gives most of the trump cards to the forces opposing whatever measure is under consideration. It is easier to defeat policy proposals than to pass them.

Professor James Sundquist believes that American history is filled with the failures of the system to respond effectively to policy crises. Consider the dilemma of the Vietnam War. Congress and the president were unable to agree either to withdraw American forces or do what was necessary to win the war. As a result, the nation was condemned to a half-in, half-out compromise policy that satisfied no one and, in the long run, proved disastrous. Sundquist says the same constitutional paralysis hindered the nation's ability to deal with secession in the 1860s, the Great Depression in the 1930s, and federal budget deficits of the 1980s.[18] Some political observers would add the war in Afghanistan, climate change, and, once again, the federal budget deficit to a current list of problems made insolvable by political gridlock.

Nonetheless, constitutional stalemate is not inevitable. Sundquist's list tells only half the story. The nation did eventually rise to the challenge of secession and preserved the Union. The constitutional deadlock over the Great Depression ended. The budget deficit of the 1980s was finally eliminated. Furthermore, we can point to national crises such as World War II and the Cuban Missile Crisis that the American government was able to address in a forthright, spirited manner, without constitutional gridlock.

Policy deadlocks are as much political as they are constitutional. The Constitution structures the policy process by setting the ground rules for policymaking. It does not dictate the outcome of the policy process. The failure of American government to resolve the Vietnam War reflected a lack of political consensus on a proper course of action rather than a constitutional breakdown.[19] The same can be said of the contemporary failure to end the war in Afghanistan, address climate change, or reduce the federal budget deficit.

Consider the controversy over SCHIP expansion. After the 2006 election, a majority of the members of the U.S. House and Senate favored expanding SCHIP coverage to include a larger number of low-income children, but the advocates of SCHIP expansion lacked sufficient numbers in Congress to override a presidential veto. Congress and the president deadlocked over whether to renew SCHIP without change or to enlarge eligibility to include more low-income families. The voters broke the deadlock in the 2008 election by returning a Democratic Congress and electing Barack Obama, an SCHIP expansion proponent, as president. In early 2009, Congress passed legislation to expand SCHIP and President Obama signed it into law.

WHAT IS YOUR OPINION?

Does the Constitution need to be rewritten for the twenty-first century? If so, how?

WHAT WE HAVE LEARNED

1. **Which historical events had the greatest influence on the development of the Constitution of 1787?**

   The framers of the U.S. Constitution of 1787 lived through two important historical periods that influenced their approach to constitutional development—the colonial era and the period under the Articles of Confederation. Initially, Americans were comfortable with colonial rule because London authorities allowed them considerable autonomy in running their own affairs. After the end of the French and Indian War in 1763, the king increased taxes to raise revenue to pay war debts and expanded the presence of British troops in the colonies. American outrage over these actions led to revolution and eventual independence. The experience made Americans wary of strong central authority. The first American constitution, the Articles of Confederation, created a confederation. The government established under the Articles proved too weak, however, and the stage was set for the constitutional convention of 1787.

2. **Which elements of American political thought had a significant impact on the development of the Constitution?**

The political theories of John Locke were important for the Americans who wrote the Declaration of Independence. Locke said that the power of government flows from the consent of the governed and that people form governments to protect their life, liberty, and property. If the government fails to do that, the people have the right to change governments. The framers embraced Locke's theory to justify their revolution. The Americans also developed their own political theories to match their unique circumstances. At the time of the Revolution, American political theorists believed that politics was a never-ending struggle between the people and the government. In their view, the people were virtuous and united in support of the public good. In contrast, the government, personified by the king, was corrupt and oppressive. After a few years of independence, many Americans recognized that society was composed of a variety of interests or factions, which opposed one another on a number of policy issues. A strong national government could reconcile the divergent concerns of various groups in society to produce policies designed to achieve the public good. A strong national government could protect individual liberty and property from the power of oppressive majorities.

3. **What sort of democracy does the Constitution create?**

The Constitution creates a representative democracy as opposed to a direct democracy. Citizens elect representatives to make policy on their behalf rather than making policy decisions directly, which, the framers feared, might lead to tyranny of the majority.

4. **How does the Constitution divide political power among the structures of government?**

Separation of powers is the division of the powers of government into legislative, executive, and judicial branches. The concept of checks and balances refers to the overlapping of the powers of the branches of government, which is designed to ensure that public officials limit the authority of one another. Federalism is the division of power between a national government and a series of state governments. It can be regarded as a compromise between the British unitary system and the confederation created by the Articles of Confederation. Bicameralism is the division of the legislative branch into two chambers, a House and a Senate. It too is designed to limit the power of government by dividing political authority.

5. **How does the Constitution limit the power of government?**

The rule of law is the concept that the discretion of public officials in dealing with individuals is limited by law. Public officials are not at liberty to jail their political enemies, and even the worst criminals are entitled to their day in court. Limited government is the constitutional principle that government does not have unrestricted authority over individuals. In particular, the Bill of Rights protects individual rights from the government, including freedom of speech, freedom of religion, and the like. It was not included in the original constitution, but added immediately. It initially applied only to the federal government, but the Supreme Court eventually incorporated most of its provisions to apply to the states.

6. **How does the Constitution change?**
The Constitution changes through amendment, experience, and judicial review. The Constitution has been amended a mere 27 times. Amendments must be proposed and ratified. Some elements of the Constitution have developed through practice and experience, such as the role of the president as commander-in-chief. Judicial review, which is the power of courts to declare unconstitutional the actions of the other branches and units of government, is another way the Constitution has changed.

7. **How does the Constitution affect the policy-making process?**
The U.S. Constitution fragments political power. Separation of powers divides national government among branches, bicameralism divides Congress into chambers, and federalism divides political power between a national government and a series of state governments. Political fragmentation produces slow, incremental change. It promotes stability and facilitates the representation of diverse interests. Although fragmentation can lead to political deadlock, the gridlock often reflects a lack of political consensus rather than constitutional failure.

KEY TERMS

Antifederalists
bicameral legislature
bill of attainder
Bill of Rights
checks and balances
confederation
constitution
constitutional amendment
democracy
direct democracy
doctrine of natural rights
due process of law
Equal Protection Clause
executive power
ex post facto law
factions
Federalist Papers
Federalists
federation *or* federal system
judicial power
judicial review
jurisdiction
legislative power
limited government
Medicaid
Parliament
parliamentary system
power of the purse
representative democracy *or* republic
rule of law
selective incorporation of the Bill of Rights against the states
separation of powers
sovereignty
State Children's Health Insurance Program (SCHIP)
supermajority
tyranny of the majority
unicameral legislature
unitary government
writ of *habeas corpus*
writ of *mandamus*

NOTES

1. Gordon S. Wood, *The Creation of the American Republic 1776–1787* (Chapel Hill, NC: University of North Carolina Press, 1969), pp. 131–148.
2. Donald S. Lutz, "The Changing View of the Founding and a New Perspective on American Political Theory," *Social Science Quarterly* 68 (December 1987): 669–686.
3. Wood, pp. 601–614.
4. Lutz, p. 677.
5. *The Federalist*, No. 51.
6. Ibid.
7. Richard Neustadt, *Presidential Power*, rev. ed. (New York: Wiley, 1976), p. 33.
8. Edward C. Carmines and Lawrence C. Dodd, "Bicameralism in Congress: The Changing Partnership," in Lawrence C. Dodd and Bruce I. Oppenheimer, eds., *Congress Reconsidered*, 3rd ed. (Washington, DC: Congressional Quarterly Press, 1985), pp. 414–436.
9. Robert A. Dahl, *A Preface to Democratic Theory*, expanded edition (Chicago, IL: University of Chicago Press, 2006), p. 137.
10. Paul Finkelman, "James Madison and the Bill of Rights: A Reluctant Paternity," in Gerhard Casper, Dennis J. Hutchison, and David Strauss, eds., *The Supreme Court Review* (Chicago, IL: University of Chicago Press, 1990), pp. 309–311.
11. Richard Labunski, *James Madison and the Struggle for the Bill of Rights* (New York: Oxford University Press, 2006), pp. 96–255.
12. Leonard Levy, *Judgments: Essays on American Constitutional History* (Chicago, IL: Quadrangle Books, 1972), p. 17.
13. *Marbury v. Madison*, 1 Cranch 137 (1803).
14. Richard H. Fallon, Jr., *The Dynamic Constitution: An Introduction to American Constitutional Law* (New York: Cambridge University Press, 2004), p. 193.
15. *Plessy v. Ferguson*, 163 U.S. 537 (1896).
16. *Brown v. Board of Education of Topeka*, 347 U.S. 483 (1954).
17. Charles A. Beard, *An Economic Interpretation of the Constitution of the United States* (New York: Macmillan, 1913).
18. James L. Sundquist, *Constitutional Reform and Effective Government*, rev. ed. (Washington, DC: Brookings Institution, 1986), pp. 5–6.
19. Peter F. Nardulli, "The Constitution and American Politics: A Developmental Perspective," in Peter F. Nardulli, ed., *The Constitution and American Political Development* (Chicago, IL: University of Chicago Press, 1992), p. 12.

Chapter 3

The Federal System

CHAPTER OUTLINE

The Powers of the National Government
- The Powers of the Legislative Branch
- The Powers of the Executive Branch
- The Powers of the Judicial Branch
- National Supremacy Clause
- Federal Preemption and Federal Mandates

The Role of States in the Federal System

The States' Rights/Strong National Government Debate

The Federal System and the Supreme Court

Federal Grant Programs
- Types of Federal Programs
- Grant Conditions

What We Have Learned

WHAT WE WILL LEARN

After studying Chapter 3, students should be able to answer the following questions:

1. What powers does the Constitution delegate to the national government?
2. What is the constitutional relationship of the states to one another and to the national government?
3. What are the arguments presented by each side in the debate between the advocates of states' rights and the supporters of national government supremacy?
4. What is the status of the federal system in light of *McCulloch v. Maryland* and recent Supreme Court rulings?
5. What are the different types of federal programs and what sort of restrictions does Congress place on the receipt of federal money?

Charter schools Publicly funded but privately managed schools that operate under the terms of a formal contract, or charter, with the state.

No Child Left Behind (NCLB) A federal law that requires state governments and local school districts to institute basic skills testing as a condition for receiving federal aid.

School Lunch Program A federal program that provides free or reduced-cost lunches to children from poor families.

The Obama administration is using federal money as an incentive for states to adopt educational reforms. When Congress passed the $787 billion Economic Recovery and Reinvestment Act of 2009, popularly known as the stimulus bill, it allocated $4.4 billion to the U.S. Department of Education to distribute to public schools. Secretary of Education Arne Duncan announced that the administration would use the money to fund an initiative called Race to the Top.[1] In order to qualify for money, states would have to adopt a set of reforms. First, states would have to ease limits on **charter schools,** which are publicly funded but privately managed schools that operate under the terms of a formal contract, or charter, with the state. Because charter schools are exempt from most state regulations, they have the freedom to adopt creative instructional approaches to help students learn.

Second, states must eliminate barriers to using student test scores for evaluating the performance of teachers and principals. Testing is now common practice in public schools because of **No Child Left Behind (NCLB),** which is a federal law that requires state governments and local school districts to institute basic skills testing as a condition for receiving federal aid. To qualify for Race to the Top money, states have to repeal state laws and regulations prohibiting the use of test scores in teacher and principal evaluation.

Third, states have to move toward common academic standards. Under NCLB, states must administer a set of basic skills tests and use the results to evaluate student and school performance, but they can choose their own testing instruments and set their own standards. States with weak school systems can adopt an easy test and set low passing standards. Common academic standards will expose low-performing school systems, creating pressure on school administrators and elected officials to improve. After all, no governor running for reelection wants to explain why the state's schools are among the worst in the country.[2]

Race to the Top continues the aggressive federal role in shaping public education policy taken by the George W. Bush administration with NCLB. Historically, state and local governments have been primarily responsible for making education policy. They operate the nation's public education system and provide more than 90 percent of the money.[3] The role of the federal government has been limited to funding certain targeted activities. Both NCLB and Race to the Top changed the relationship by making federal funding contingent on states adopting certain reforms involving basic skills testing, charter schools, and use of test scores in teacher evaluations.

The proponents of federal involvement in public education believe that federal resources can ensure access to a quality education for all the nation's children. Some states and school districts are too poor or perhaps unwilling to spend enough money to provide a quality education for all children, especially youngsters with special needs that are expensive to address. Federal money supports the education of children with disabilities and students with limited English proficiency. Federal dollars provide computers for schools in low-income areas and training for teachers. The **School Lunch Program** is a federal program that provides free or reduced-cost lunches to children from poor families.

The supporters of federal education policy argue that federal regulations improve the quality of education nationwide by setting standards for fairness and performance. Federal laws and regulations prohibit discrimination on account of race and ethnicity, and require school districts to educate all children, even students with severe learning disabilities. The federal government has compelled school districts to adopt policies designed to ensure safe and drug-free schools. NCLB requires states to administer basic skills tests to evaluate student and school performance. Race to the Top goes further by promoting charter schools, developing common academic standards nationwide, and linking teacher and principal evaluations to student performance.

The critics of federal involvement in public education question the wisdom of setting education policy in Washington, DC. Who is better positioned to understand the problems of local schools, they ask, federal bureaucrats or officials at the state and local level? Federal education programs may not address the needs of local school districts in the ways that local educators think are most effective. NCLB forces states to neglect their own education reform plans to concentrate instead on creating an intricate system of high-stakes basic skills testing. Race to the Top increases the importance of testing even more. With administrative careers, teacher assignments, and student promotions all depending on test results, principals and teachers have a strong incentive to drop everything else and concentrate on the test. Instead of learning to read, write, and do math, students will learn how to take multiple-choice exams to pass a particular test. The school may even pressure weak students to drop out of school before the test is administered in order to inflate school test scores.[4]

The controversy over the federal role in public education demonstrates the federal system's relevance to the policymaking process. The United States does not have just one set of policymaking institutions but literally thousands. In addition to the national government, 50 states and more than 80,000 local governments participate in the policymaking process. Many public policies reflect the interplay among the levels of government. Education policy, for example, reflects decisions made at the national, state, and local levels.

Federation or **federal system** A political system that divides power between a central government, with authority over the whole nation, and a series of state governments.

? WHAT IS YOUR OPINION?

If you were a state official, would you change state policies dealing with charter schools and teacher evaluations in order to qualify for Race to the Top money?

The Powers of the National Government

The United States has a federal system of government. A **federation** or **federal system** is a political system that divides power between a central government with authority over the whole nation and a series of state governments. The Constitution delegates certain powers to the national government while leaving other powers to the states.

No Child Left Behind (NCLB) is a federal law that requires state governments and local school districts to institute basic skills testing in reading and mathematics for students in grades three through eight and to use the results to assess school performance and track the progress of individual students.

Delegated or **enumerated powers** The powers explicitly granted to the national government by the Constitution.

The powers explicitly granted to the national government by the Constitution are known as the **delegated** or **enumerated powers.** The Constitution grants each branch of the national government certain powers. It gives the legislative branch the most extensive list of powers and the judicial branch the least extensive list.

The Powers of the Legislative Branch

Legislative power The power to make laws.

Power of the purse The authority to raise and spend money.

Tariffs Taxes on imported goods.

The Constitution vests the **legislative power,** the power to make laws, in Congress. In Article I, Section 8, the Constitution gives Congress broad legislative authority. Congress has the **power of the purse,** which is the authority to raise and spend money. Congress can levy taxes, including **tariffs,** which are taxes on imported goods, and **excise taxes,** which are levies assessed on the manufacture, transportation, sale, or consumption of a particular item or set of related items. The Constitution charges Congress with providing for the "common defense and general welfare." It authorizes Congress to borrow money and repay the nation's debt.

The Constitution also grants Congress the power to promote economic development. Congress can regulate commerce among the states and trade with other nations. It can coin money, enact laws governing bankruptcy, set standards for weights and measures, provide for the punishment of counterfeiters, create post offices and post roads, and establish rules for copyright and patent protection.

Excise taxes Taxes levied on the manufacture, transportation, sale, or consumption of a particular item or set of related items.

Implied powers Those powers of Congress not explicitly mentioned in the Constitution but derived by implication from the delegated powers.

The Constitution also gives Congress an important role in foreign affairs and the nation's defense. Congress can suppress insurrection and repel invasion. It can declare war, raise and support armies, and maintain a navy.

Article I, Section 8 concludes with the **Necessary and Proper Clause** or **Elastic Clause.** "[Congress shall have the power] to make all laws which shall be necessary and proper for carrying into execution the foregoing powers, and all other powers vested by this Constitution in the government of the United States, or in any department or office thereof." The Necessary and Proper Clause is the basis for much of the legislation passed by Congress because it gives Congress the means to exercise its delegated authority.

The Necessary and Proper Clause is the constitutional basis for the doctrine of implied powers. **Implied powers** are those powers of Congress not explicitly mentioned in the Constitution but derived by implication from the delegated powers. Because the Constitution explicitly grants Congress the authority to raise armies,

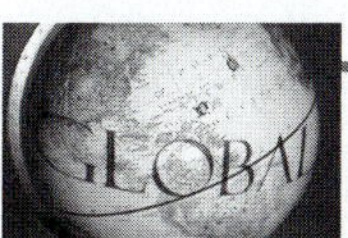

Around the World

Education Policy and Federalism in Germany

Germany established a federal system after World War II at the encouragement of the allied powers. Having fought two world wars against Germany, the allies wanted the Germans to create a political system that would disperse power among the national government and a series of states, rather than concentrate it in a central government. The German federal system divides power between a national government and 16 states called länder.*

Although the German Constitution grants the länder exclusive jurisdiction over education policy, the German public supports a uniform national approach to education. Unlike the American states, the länder are more accurately described as administrative units than historically or culturally distinct regions. Public opinion favors centralized education policymaking with a uniform national policy because German society is culturally homogeneous and the public wants the schools to promote national unity. The German public also believes that a consistent national educational policy promotes academic excellence, whereas educational diversity produces mediocrity.

The länder use the Standing Conference of Ministers of Culture (KMK) as a mechanism to circumvent the constitutionally required decentralization of educational policy. The KMK has negotiated an agreement to standardize the curriculum, establish uniform educational assessment criteria, and coordinate the timing and duration of the school year among the länder. Consequently, Germany has a uniform national education policy despite the constitutional requirement of decentralization.†

Questions

1. Would the German public favor or oppose an educational initiative such as No Child Left Behind? Why or why not?
2. Why do Americans, unlike the Germans, resist a national set of educational policies?
3. Do you believe states should be able to set their own education policies or should education policy be determined at the national level?

* Karen Adelberger, "Federalism and Its Discontents: Fiscal and Legislative Power-Sharing in Germany, 1948–1999," *Regional and Federal Studies* 11 (Summer 2000): 43–68.

† Jan Erk, *Explaining Federalism: State, Society and Congruence in Austria, Belgium, Canada, Germany, and Switzerland* (New York: Routledge, 2008), pp. 58–70.

Necessary and Proper Clause or **Elastic Clause** The Constitutional provision found in Article I, section 8, that declares that "[Congress shall have the power] to make all laws which shall be necessary and proper for carrying into execution the foregoing powers, and all other powers vested by this Constitution in the government of the United States, or in any department or office thereof." It is the basis for much of the legislation passed by Congress because it gives Congress the means to exercise its delegated authority.

Due Process Clause The constitutional provision that declares that no state shall "deprive any person of life, liberty, or property, without due process of law."

Equal Protection Clause A provision found in the Fourteenth Amendment of the U.S. Constitution that declares that "No State shall . . . deny to any person within its jurisdiction the equal protection of the laws."

the power to draft men and women into the armed forces would be an example of an implied power. The authority to draft is not explicitly granted as a delegated power, but it can be inferred as an action "necessary and proper" for carrying out one of the delegated powers—in this case, raising armies.

Several constitutional amendments expand the authority of Congress beyond those powers listed in Article I. The Fourteenth Amendment includes the Due Process and the Equal Protection Clauses. The **Due Process Clause** is the constitutional provision that declares that no state shall "deprive any person of life, liberty, or property, without due process of law." The **Equal Protection Clause** declares that "No State shall . . . deny to any person within its jurisdiction the equal protection of the laws." The amendment gives Congress the power to enforce both provisions through "appropriate legislation." Congress also has the power to enforce the Fifteenth Amendment, which declares that the rights of citizens to vote shall not be abridged on account of race, color, or previous condition of servitude. The Sixteenth Amendment grants Congress the authority to levy an income tax.

The Powers of the Executive Branch

The Constitution grants **executive power,** the power to enforce laws, to the president, declaring that the president should "take Care that Laws be faithfully executed." In Article II, the Constitution says that the president shall be commander-in-chief of the nation's armed forces. It states that the president may require reports from the heads of the executive departments, grant pardons and reprieves, make treaties with "the Advice and Consent" of the Senate, and appoint ambassadors, judges, and other officials. The president may also make policy recommendations to Congress, receive ambassadors, and convene special sessions of Congress.

The Powers of the Judicial Branch

The Constitution vests **judicial power,** the power to interpret laws, in a Supreme Court and whatever other federal courts Congress sees fit to create. In Article III, the Constitution declares that the judicial power extends to all cases arising under the Constitution, federal law, and treaties. The Constitution gives the Supreme Court of the United States the authority to try a limited range of cases, such as cases affecting ambassadors and cases in which a state is a party. The Constitution empowers Congress to determine the types of cases on which the Court may hear appeals.

National Supremacy Clause

The Constitution addresses the question of the relative power of the national and state governments in Article VI in a passage known as the **National Supremacy Clause.** This is the constitutional provision that declares that the Constitution

Executive power The power to enforce laws.

Judicial power The power to interpret laws.

National Supremacy Clause The constitutional provision that declares that the Constitution and laws of the United States take precedence over the constitutions and laws of the states.

Nullification A constitutional theory that gives an individual state the right to declare null and void any law passed by the U.S. Congress which the state deems unacceptable and unconstitutional.

Federal preemption of state authority An act of Congress adopting regulatory policies that overrule state policies in a particular regulatory area.

Federal mandate A legal requirement placed on a state or local government by the national government requiring certain policy actions.

and laws of the United States take precedence over the constitutions and laws of the states. In short, the National Supremacy Clause declares that the constitutional exercise of national power supersedes state action. The U.S. Constitution is superior to national law, state constitutions, and state laws. National law is superior to state constitutions and state laws.

Periodically in American history, state officials have asserted a state right of **nullification,** a constitutional theory that gives an individual state the right to declare null and void any law passed by the U.S. Congress which the state deems unacceptable and unconstitutional. Before the Civil War, for example, southern state officials argued that states could refuse to honor federal laws restricting slavery. In the 1950s, several southern states invoked the doctrine of nullification in an effort to block federal efforts to force the racial integration of southern schools and other facilities. Healthcare reform is the latest target of nullification efforts. A number of states have adopted measures aimed at blocking the implementation of healthcare reform within their borders. In 2010, for example, Arizona voters adopted an amendment to their state constitution barring any rules or regulations that would require state residents to participate in a healthcare system.

Despite the current interest in nullification, it has no legal basis. The American Civil War clearly established that national law is superior to state law. Constitutional scholars agree that state nullification contradicts the National Supremacy Clause as well as dozens of Supreme Court rulings.[5]

Federal Preemption and Federal Mandates

The federal laws and regulations that have the greatest impact on state and local policymaking take the form of federal preemption and federal mandates. Federal preemption *prevents* states from adopting their own policies in selected policy areas, whereas federal mandates *require* certain state policy actions. An act of Congress adopting regulatory policies that overrule state policies in a particular regulatory area is known as a **federal preemption of state authority.** Congress has passed more than a hundred laws preempting state regulation, including the preemption of state policies dealing with cellular phone rates, nuclear power safety, pension plans, automobile safety standards, and trucking rates.[6]

A **federal mandate** is a legal requirement placed on a state or local government by the national government requiring certain policy actions. The **Americans with Disabilities Act (ADA),** a federal law intended to end discrimination against persons with disabilities and to eliminate barriers preventing their full participation in American society, imposes a broad range of federal mandates. When a new building goes up or an old building undergoes a major renovation, it must be made accessible to people with disabilities, and accommodations must be made for employees with disabilities. Because of the ADA, colleges and universities typically provide special assistance to students with disabilities, such as sign-language interpreters for students who have hearing impairments and additional time to take exams for students with learning disabilities.[7]

Americans with Disabilities Act (ADA) A federal law intended to end discrimination against persons with disabilities and to eliminate barriers preventing their full participation in American society through imposing a broad range of federal mandates.

The School Lunch Program is a federal program that provides free or reduced-cost lunches to children from poor families.

The Role of States in the Federal System

Full Faith and Credit Clause The constitutional provision requiring that states recognize the official acts of other states, such as marriages, divorces, adoptions, court orders, and other legal decisions.

Defense of Marriage Act (DOMA) The federal law stipulating that each state may choose either to recognize or not recognize same-sex marriages performed in other states.

The Constitution defines the relationship of states with one another and with the national government. Article IV contains the **Full Faith and Credit Clause,** which is the constitutional provision requiring that states recognize the official acts of other states, such as marriages, divorces, adoptions, court orders, and other legal decisions. The constitutional meaning of the Full Faith and Credit Clause may soon be tested by the controversy over gay marriage. In 2004, the Massachusetts Supreme Court interpreted the state constitution of Massachusetts to hold that the state could not legally restrict the right of marriage to heterosexual couples. Several other states have since legalized same-sex marriage. Gay couples who marry in states where it is legal may move to other states and then ask their new home states to recognize their marriage under the Full Faith and Credit Clause. Consequently, the U.S. Supreme Court may eventually be asked to rule on the meaning of the Full Faith and Credit Clause and the constitutionality of the **Defense of Marriage Act (DOMA),** which is a federal law stipulating that each state may choose either to recognize or not recognize same-sex marriages performed in other states.

Article IV also addresses the concepts of privileges and immunities, as well as extradition. The **Privileges and Immunities Clause** is a constitutional provision prohibiting state governments from discriminating against the citizens of other states. This provision ensures that visitors to a state are accorded the same legal protection, travel rights, and property rights as a state's own citizens. The courts have held, however, that states may

Privileges and Immunities Clause The constitutional provision prohibiting state governments from discriminating against the citizens of other states.

Extradition The return from one state to another of a person accused of a crime.

Republic A political system in which citizens elect representatives to make policy decisions on their behalf.

Reserved or **residual powers** The powers of government left to the states.

Concurrent powers Those powers of government that are jointly exercised by the national government and state governments.

deny out-of-state residents certain privileges such as voting and paying lower tuition at state colleges and universities. **Extradition** is the return from one state to another of a person accused of a crime. A person charged with a crime in California who flees to Nevada, for example, could be extradited back to California.

The Constitution prohibits states from taking certain actions. States may not negotiate international treaties, form alliances with foreign countries, or engage in war unless they are invaded. States may not create their own currency or levy taxes on commerce with other states or foreign nations.

The Constitution includes a number of guarantees to the states. In Article IV, the Constitution declares that states may not be divided or consolidated without their permission. The Constitution also promises states defense against invasion, protection from domestic violence when requested, equal representation in the U.S. Senate, and a republican form of government. A **republic** is a representative democracy in which citizens elect representatives to make policy decisions on their behalf. The Eleventh Amendment prohibits foreign residents or the citizens of other states from suing a state in federal court.

The best-known constitutional guarantee given to the states is the Tenth Amendment: "The powers not delegated to the United States by the Constitution, nor prohibited by it to the states, are reserved to the states respectively, or to the people." This provision forms the basis for the doctrine of reserved or residual powers. The powers of the national government are enumerated in the Constitution—the delegated powers. According to the Tenth Amendment, the powers not delegated to the national government are reserved to the states or to the people. **Reserved** or **residual powers,** then, are the powers of government left to the states. In other words, the national government may exercise only those powers granted to it by the Constitution, whereas state governments possess all the powers not given to the national government, except those that are prohibited to the states by the Constitution.

This description of the federal system implies that the division of powers between the national government and the states resembles a layer cake, with each level of government exercising authority in its own sphere without overlap. In practice, however, the authority of the national government and the powers of the states overlap considerably. For example, both the states and the national government participate in education policymaking. The powers of government that are jointly exercised by the national government and state governments are known as **concurrent powers.** Both levels of government have authority to tax, spend, and regulate. Instead of a layer cake, the federal system today more closely resembles a marble cake with its overlapping textures.

The States' Rights/Strong National Government Debate

The supporters of states' rights and the proponents of national government supremacy have long debated the role of the states and the national government in the federal system. The doctrine of **states' rights** is an interpretation of the Constitution that favors limiting the federal government's authority while expanding the powers of the states. The advocates of states' rights believe that the Constitution is a compact among the states that restricts

States' rights An interpretation of the Constitution that favors limiting the authority of the federal government while expanding the powers of the states.

the national government to those powers explicitly granted to it by the Constitution, that is, to the delegated powers. They would question, for example, whether the federal government should be involved in public education at all. The advocates of states' rights argue that the scope of the implied powers should be strictly limited. Modern states' rights advocates oppose national healthcare reform, bailouts of struggling banks and other companies, and federal regulatory efforts designed to address climate change. In contrast, the supporters of national government supremacy contend that the Constitution is a compact among the people rather than the states. They note that the document begins with the following phrase: "We the people . . . ." The supporters of a strong national government believe that the implied powers should be construed broadly in order to further the interests of the people. The federal government has a role to play in public education, they say, because it has a duty to "promote the general Welfare." Modern advocates of a strong national government favor healthcare reform, federal efforts to manage economic growth, and regulatory actions designed to combat global warming.

The controversy over the respective roles of the national government and the states has also been argued on the basis of practical politics. States' rights advocates believe that local control makes for more efficient government because it permits a closer match between the services government provides and the policy preferences of constituents. Who should know better what public policies citizens favor—national officials or local officeholders? Furthermore, the supporters of states' rights believe that local control of public policy enhances the opportunity for citizen participation. State and local governments are closer to the people. If citizens disapprove of policy decisions, they can work to affect state policies and policymakers more effectively than they can influence policies and officeholders at the national level.

The supporters of a strong national government believe that national control makes for better public policy. Some problems such as healthcare, education reform, and climate change are too big and complex to be resolved at the state level because state governments may lack the financial resources or the political will to address the issues. State officials may be indifferent to environmental issues or unwilling to spend the money to expand access to healthcare. They may choose to discriminate against racial minorities or be indifferent to the plight of the poor. Only the federal government can supply the resources and the political will to achieve national goals.

WHAT IS YOUR OPINION?

Which side more closely reflects your point of view: the supporters of a strong national government or the advocates of states' rights?

The Federal System and the Supreme Court

Constitutional controversies about the relative powers of the states and the national government are a recurrent theme of American history. On several occasions, the U.S. Supreme Court has addressed federalism issues. The Court first dealt with the controversy over the relationship between the states and the national government in the famous case of *McCulloch v. Maryland* (1819).

Gay couples who marry in states where it is legal may move to other states and then ask their new home states to recognize their marriage under the Full Faith and Credit Clause.

In 1791, Congress chartered a national bank, the First Bank of the United States, amid great controversy. Thomas Jefferson, who was then secretary of state, opposed the bank because he believed that the Constitution did not authorize its creation. In contrast, Alexander Hamilton, who was secretary of the treasury, supported the bank. He argued that the action of Congress was justified as an exercise of authority reasonably *implied* by the delegated powers. Despite the controversy, no legal challenge to the bank arose, and it operated until its charter expired in 1811.

Congress chartered the Second Bank of the United States in 1816 and it too became the object of controversy, particularly in the West and South. Critics accused the bank of corruption and inefficiency. The most serious charge was that the bank was responsible for an economic downturn that ruined thousands of investors. Several states responded to the public outcry against the bank by adopting restrictions on it or levying heavy taxes against it. Maryland, for example, required payment of an annual tax of $15,000 on the bank's Baltimore branch, which, in those days, was a sum large enough to drive the bank out of business in the state. Of course, that was just what the Maryland legislature wanted. When James W. McCulloch, the bank's cashier, refused to pay the tax, Maryland sued. The case presented two important constitutional issues: (1) Does the national government have authority to charter a bank? And (2) Does a state have the power to tax an arm of the national government?

Chief Justice John Marshall wrote the unanimous opinion of the U.S. Supreme Court, answering both questions. First, the Court upheld the authority of Congress to charter a bank on the basis of the doctrine of implied powers. Marshall noted that although the Constitution does not specifically grant Congress the power to incorporate a bank, the Constitution does say that Congress may lay and collect taxes, borrow money, and raise and support armies. What if, Marshall asked, tax money collected in the North is needed in the South to support an army? The creation of a national bank to transport that money would be a "necessary and proper" step to that end. The power to charter the bank, Marshall held, was implied by the Necessary and Proper Clause.[8]

Second, the Court ruled that Maryland's tax was unconstitutional. The power to tax, said Marshall, is the power to destroy because a high tax can drive the object of the taxation out of existence. If Maryland or any state has the authority to tax an arm of the national government, it could effectively shut it down and that would be contrary to the nature of the federal union as stated in the National Supremacy Clause.

In sum, the Supreme Court's decision in *McCulloch v. Maryland* supported the position of those who favored national government supremacy. By giving broad scope to the doctrine of implied powers, the Court provided the national government with a vast source of power. By stressing the importance of the National Supremacy Clause, the Court denied states the right to interfere in the constitutional operations of the national government.

The Supreme Court has not always been as receptive to the exercise of federal power as it was in *McCulloch v. Maryland.* In 1857, a few years before the outbreak of the Civil War, the Court held that the national government lacked authority to regulate slavery in the territories in the infamous *Dred Scott* decision.[9] Similarly, in the early 1930s, the Supreme Court limited the power of the national government to respond to the Great Depression by striking down much of the New Deal as unconstitutional. The **New Deal** was a legislative package of reform measures proposed by President Franklin Roosevelt for dealing with the Great Depression. It involved the federal government more deeply in the nation's economy than ever before.

New Deal A legislative package of reform measures proposed by President Franklin Roosevelt for dealing with the Great Depression.

Both the Supreme Court's decision in *Dred Scott* and its anti-New Deal rulings were eventually reversed. Congress and the states overturned the *Dred Scott* decision by proposing and ratifying the Thirteenth, Fourteenth, and Fifteenth Amendments to the Constitution. The Supreme Court reversed itself in the late 1930s, eventually holding New Deal legislation constitutional. For half a century thereafter, the Supreme Court found few constitutional limitations on the exercise of federal power. If Congress could present a plausible constitutional basis for an action, the Court would uphold it as constitutional.

Congress took advantage of the Supreme Court's broad interpretation of the doctrine of implied powers to exercise authority in a wide range of policy areas. In particular, Congress made frequent use of the Commerce Clause to justify legislation. The **Commerce Clause** is the constitutional provision giving Congress authority to "regulate commerce . . . among the several states." Congress used the Commerce Clause as a basis for legislation dealing with such diverse subjects as child labor, agricultural price supports, and racial discrimination in public places. In each instance, Congress argued that the particular activity it sought to regulate was part of interstate commerce, which Congress is empowered to regulate; in each instance, the Supreme Court eventually accepted the argument.

Commerce Clause The constitutional provision giving Congress authority to "regulate commerce . . . among the several states."

In recent years, the Supreme Court has somewhat limited federal authority under the Commerce Clause, holding that Congress can only regulate economic activity that substantially affects interstate commerce. In 1995, the Supreme Court held that Congress had exceeded its constitutional authority when it enacted the Gun-Free School Zones Act of 1990, a federal law banning firearms within 1,000 feet of a school, because, the Court said, the possession of a firearm in the vicinity of a school does not meet the standard.[10] Similarly, in 2000, the Supreme Court overturned a provision in the federal Violence Against Women Act that gave the victims of sexual assault the right to sue their attackers for damages. Congress based its action on the Commerce Clause, but the Court ruled that violent crime is insufficiently connected to interstate commerce to justify Congress acting.[11] In contrast, in 2005, the Supreme Court upheld federal authority under the Commerce Clause to enforce the Controlled Substances Act (CSA) against individuals growing marijuana for their own personal medicinal use, even though the action was legal under state law. The Court distinguished this case from its other recent Commerce Clause rulings in that the sale, transportation, distribution, and use of marijuana is a significant part of interstate commerce, whereas possession of firearms near a school and violent crime are not.[12]

University of California students protest a 32 percent increase in tuition. Federal stimulus funds were insufficient to close the budget gap in California, forcing state officials to slash state spending and increase fees, including college and university tuition.

Federal Grant Programs

Federal grant program A program through which the national government gives money to state and local governments to spend in accordance with set standards and conditions.

A **federal grant program** is a program through which the national government gives money to state and local governments to spend in accordance with set standards and conditions. NCLB and Race to the Top are federal programs that deal with public education. Other federal programs address such policy areas as transportation, childhood nutrition, healthcare, public housing, vocational education, airport construction, hazardous waste disposal, job training, law enforcement, scientific research, neighborhood preservation, mental health, and substance abuse prevention and treatment. In 2010, the federal government gave $654 billion in grants to state and local governments, which made up 17.6 percent of federal outlays.[13]

Recession An economic slowdown characterized by declining economic output and rising unemployment.

Figure 3.1 graphs the allocation of federal grant money to state and local governments from 2000 through 2010. Federal funding levels increased steadily in the early years of the decade, leveled off in the middle years, and then rose dramatically in 2009 and 2010. Federal grant funding to state and local governments increased in the latter years of the decade because of the adoption of the federal stimulus act, the Economic Recovery and Reinvestment Act of 2009, which allocated billions of dollars to state and local governments to help them weather the recession. During the **recession,** an economic slowdown characterized by declining economic output and rising unemployment, revenues fell while the demand for services rose. Congress and the president provided state and local governments with billions of stimulus dollars in order to help them maintain services and avoid layoffs of state and local employees without increasing their taxes.

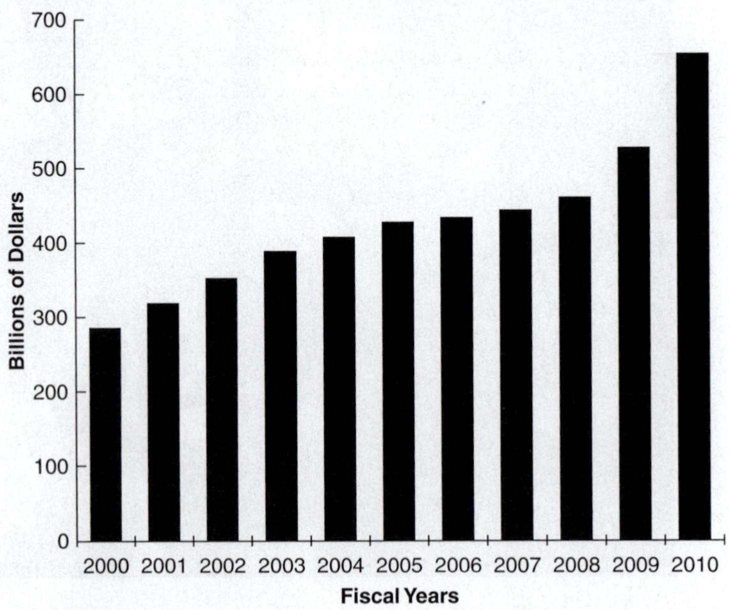

FIGURE 3.1 Federal Grants to State and Local Governments, 2000–2010.
Source: Office of Management and Budget.

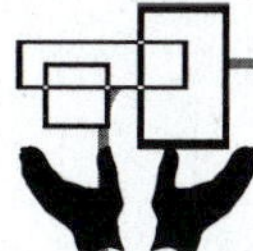

GETTING INVOLVED

Federal Programs and You

Federal grants and loans are important for students and the institutions they attend. Many students depend on federal financial aid to complete their degrees. Students need not repay grant money, but loans must be repaid. Pell Grants provide federal financial assistance to students based on their financial need. The amount of money that students can receive depends on the cost of their education and their available financial resources. Federal Family Education Loans (FFEL) and the Stafford Loan Program enable students to borrow money to attend college. Depending on their financial need, students may be eligible for subsidized federal loans, which do not begin assessing interest until recipients begin repayment.

Your assignment is to complete the paperwork to apply for federal financial aid. Visit your college's financial aid office or go to its website to obtain the appropriate documents. You may wish to attend a financial aid seminar to learn what aid is available and whether you are eligible. Complete the paperwork and submit the original or a copy to your instructor to document that you have completed the assignment.

Types of Federal Programs

Categorical grant program A federal grant program that provides funds to state and local governments for a narrowly defined purpose, such as removing asbestos from school buildings or acquiring land for outdoor recreation.

Block grant program A federal grant program that provides money for a program in a broad, general policy area, such as childcare or job training.

Federal programs come in a variety of forms.

Categorical and Block Grants A **categorical grant program** is a federal grant program that provides funds to state and local governments for a narrowly defined purpose, such as removing asbestos from school buildings or acquiring land for outdoor recreation. In this type of program, Congress allows state and local officials minimal discretion as to how the money is spent. Categorical grants comprise more than 90 percent of all federal grants and provide nearly 90 percent of federal grant money to state and local governments.[14] Most federal education programs are categorical grant programs.

A **block grant program** is a federal grant program that provides money for a program in a broad, general policy area, such as childcare or job training. State and local governments have more discretion in spending block grant funds than they have in spending categorical grant money. Nonetheless, Congress tends over time to attach conditions to the receipt of block grant money, thus reducing the flexibility of state and local officials. For example, Congress and the president originally created the Surface Transportation Program to give states a lump sum of money to spend on highways and other transportation projects in accordance with statewide objectives. Congress subsequently added restrictions, requiring that 10 percent of the funds must be used to improve the safety of state highways and that another 10 percent must be spent on transportation enhancement activities, such as hike and bike trails.

Officials at different levels of government hold contrasting views about categorical and block grants. Most state officeholders favor block grants because they allow states more discretion in implementation. In contrast, members of Congress usually prefer categorical grants because they enable Congress to exercise more control over implementation. Members of the U.S. House, in particular, favor categorical grants because they fund special projects that can be targeted to individual congressional districts.[15]

WHAT IS YOUR OPINION?

If you were a member of Congress, would you prefer block grants or categorical grants?

Project grant program A grant program that requires state and local governments to compete for available federal money.

Formula grant program A grant program that awards funding on the basis of a formula established by Congress.

Matching funds requirement A legislative provision that the national government will provide grant money for a particular activity only on condition that the state or local government involved supplies a certain percentage of the total money required for the project or program.

Supplemental Nutrition Assistance Program (SNAP) A federal program (once called the Food Stamp program) that provides vouchers to low-income families and individuals that can be used to purchase food from grocery stores.

Project and Formula Grants Federal grants differ in the criteria by which funding is awarded. A **project grant program** is a grant program that requires state and local governments to compete for available federal money. State and local governments make detailed grant applications which federal agencies evaluate in order to make funding decisions. The Department of Education, for example, administers project grants dealing with a range of educational initiatives, such as teacher training, math and science education, bilingual education, and preparing students for the demands of today's workforce. Public schools, colleges, and universities make application to the agency, which then decides which grant proposals merit funding.

A **formula grant program** is a grant program that awards funding on the basis of a formula established by Congress. In contrast to project grants, formula grants provide money for every state and/or locality that qualifies under the formula. The Community Development Program, for example, is a federal grant program that awards annual grants to cities and urban counties to implement a wide variety of community and economic development activities directed toward neighborhood revitalization, economic development, and the provision of improved community facilities and services. The program awards funds based on a formula that includes population, poverty, and overcrowded housing. Most formulas are based on state population with modifications designed to focus on areas of greater need, and to ensure that every state receives at least a minimal amount of money. Formula grants outnumber project grants by a four-to-one ratio. Most federal money is awarded through formula grants as well.

Grant Conditions

Federal grants usually come with conditions. A **matching funds requirement** is the legislative provision that the national government will provide grant money for a particular activity only on the condition that the state or local government involved supplies a certain percentage of the total money required for the project or program. For example, the federal government covers only 75 percent of the cost of highway construction projects, requiring states to provide a 25 percent match. About half of all federal grant programs require funding participation by the recipient. Even federal programs that do not mandate financial participation by state and local governments usually require contributions in-kind. The **Supplemental Nutrition Assistance Program (SNAP),** the new name for the old Food Stamp program, is a federal program that provides vouchers to low-income families and individuals that can be used to purchase food from grocery stores. Even though the national government covers the cost of food stamps, it requires that states administer the program.

Medicaid A federal health insurance program for low-income persons, people with disabilities, and elderly people who are impoverished.

Matching funds requirements sometimes force states and localities to devote ever-growing sums of money to particular programs. Consider the impact on state budgets of **Medicaid,** which is a federal program designed to provide health insurance coverage to low-income persons, people with disabilities, and elderly people who are impoverished. The federal government and the states split the cost of Medicaid, with the federal government picking up 50 to 80 percent of the cost, depending on a state's wealth. Because healthcare costs are rapidly rising, especially the cost of prescription drugs, Medicaid is the fastest growing item in most state budgets, accounting for 21 percent of state general fund expenditures.[16]

Congress also imposes mandates on recipients of federal funds. Some mandates apply to grant recipients in general. These include provisions in the area of equal rights, equal access for the disabled, environmental protection, historic preservation, and union wage rates for contractor personnel. Individual programs often have particular strings attached as well. In order to receive federal law enforcement grants, for example, states must collect data on sex offenders, include DNA samples, and prepare a statewide sex offender registry database.[17] Each of these requirements is an example of an **unfunded mandate,** which is a requirement imposed by Congress on state or local governments without providing federal funding to cover its cost. In 1995, Congress passed—and the president signed—the Unfunded Mandates Reform Act to curb the growth in unfunded mandates, but it has been ineffective.

Unfunded mandate A requirement imposed by Congress on state or local governments without providing federal funding to cover its cost.

Grant conditions and federal mandates impose substantial costs on state and local governments. The National Conference on State Legislatures estimates the annual cost of federal mandates to states at $30 billion.[18] The most expensive federal programs for states and localities are federally mandated special education programs, NCLB, and prescription drug costs for people eligible for both Medicare and Medicaid.

WHAT IS YOUR OPINION?

Do you think state officials should turn down federal money in order to avoid federal mandates?

WHAT WE HAVE LEARNED

1. **What powers does the Constitution delegate to the national government?**

   The Constitution specifically grants certain powers to the national government—the delegated powers. The list of powers given to the legislative branch is the most extensive. The Necessary and Proper Clause is the basis for the implied powers, which enable Congress to put its delegated powers into operation. The National Supremacy Clause declares that the national government is the dominant partner in the federal system. Some states' rights advocates assert a right of state nullification of federal action, but nullification has no basis in constitutional law. The federal laws and regulations that have the greatest impact on state and local policymaking take the form of federal preemption and federal mandates.

2. **What is the constitutional relationship of the states to one another and to the national government?**
The Full Faith and Credit Clause requires that states honor the official acts of other states, such as divorces and deeds. The Privileges and Immunities Clause prevents states from discriminating against the residents of other states. Extradition provides for the return of criminal suspects from one state to another. The Tenth Amendment says that the powers not granted to the national government are reserved to the states. In practice, both the national government and the states are involved in a broad range of policy areas.

3. **What are the arguments presented by each side in the debate between the advocates of states' rights and the supporters of national government supremacy?**
States' rights advocates want to limit the role of the federal government strictly to the delegated powers. They believe that local officials better understand local problems and know the policy preferences of local residents. In contrast, the advocates of national government supremacy believe that state governments may lack the financial resources and the will to tackle major national issues, such as healthcare and education reform.

4. **What is the status of the federal system in light of *McCulloch v. Maryland* and recent Supreme Court rulings?**
In *McCulloch v. Maryland*, the U.S. Supreme Court endorsed an expansive interpretation of the implied powers and stressed the importance of the National Supremacy Clause. In subsequent years, the Court has not always been a consistent proponent of national government authority. Beginning in the New Deal era, the Court adopted an expansive interpretation of federal power, especially under the Commerce Clause. In recent years, the Supreme Court has somewhat limited federal authority under the Commerce Clause, holding that Congress can only regulate economic activity that substantially affects interstate commerce.

5. **What are the different types of federal programs and what sort of restrictions does Congress place on the receipt of federal money?**
A federal grant program is a program through which the national government gives money to state and local governments to spend in accordance with set standards and conditions. Categorical grants provide money for fairly narrow purposes whereas block grants give state and local officials more discretion by providing money for a broad policy area. State and local governments submit proposals to compete for project grants; formula grants award funds based on a formula. Federal grants typically come with strings attached, including matching funds requirements and mandates.

KEY TERMS

Americans with Disabilities Act (ADA)
block grant program
categorical grant program
charter schools
Commerce Clause
concurrent powers
Defense of Marriage Act (DOMA)
delegated *or* enumerated powers
Due Process Clause
Equal Protection Clause
excise taxes
executive power
extradition
federal grant program
federal mandate
federal preemption of state authority
federal system *or* federation
formula grant program
Full Faith and Credit Clause
implied powers
judicial power
legislative power

matching funds requirement
Medicaid
National Supremacy Clause
Necessary and Proper Clause *or* Elastic Clause
New Deal
No Child Left Behind (NCLB)
nullification
power of the purse
Privileges and Immunities Clause
project grant program
recession
republic
reserved *or* residual powers
School Lunch Program
states' rights
Supplemental Nutrition Assistance Program (SNAP)
tariffs
unfunded mandate

NOTES

1. Gilbert Cruz, "Can Arne Duncan (And $5 Billion) Fix America's Schools?" *Time*, September 14, 2009, pp. 27–29.
2. Michael D. Shear and Nick Anderson, "A $4 Billion Push for Better Schools," *Washington Post National Weekly Edition*, August 3–9, 2009, pp. 12–13.
3. Claudia Wallis and Sonja Steptoe, "How to Fix No Child Left Behind," *Time*, June 4, 2007, p. 36.
4. Diana Jean Schemo, "Failing Schools Strain to Meet U.S. Standard," *New York Times*, October 16, 2007, available at www.nytimes.com.
5. Timothy S. Jost, "Can the States Nullify Health Care Reform?" *New England Journal of Medicine*, February 10, 2010, available at http://healthpolicyandreform.nejm.org.
6. Joseph F. Zimmerman, "The Nature and Political Significance of Preemption," *PS: Political Science & Politics*, July 2005, p. 361.
7. Josh Goodman, "The Costliest Ride," *Governing*, July 2009, pp. 50–52.
8. *McCulloch v. Maryland*, 4 Wheaton 316 (1819).
9. *Dred Scott v. Sandford*, 19 Howard 393 (1857).
10. *United States v. Lopez*, 514 U.S. 549 (1995).
11. *United States v. Morrison*, 529 U.S. 598 (2000).
12. *Gonzales v. Raich*, 545 U.S. 1 (2005).
13. Office of Management and Budget, "Summary Comparison of Total Outlays for Grants to State and Local Governments, 1940 to 2014," *The Budget for Fiscal Year 2011, Historical Tables*, available at www.whitehouse.gov/omb/budget.
14. Larry N. Gerston, *American Federalism: A Concise Introduction* (Armonk, NY: M.E. Sharpe, 2007), p. 69.
15. Frances E. Lee, "Bicameralism and Geographic Politics: Allocating Funds in the House and Senate," *Legislative Studies Quarterly* 29 (May 2004): 185–214.
16. National Association of State Budget Officers, "The Fiscal Survey of the States," June 2010, available at www.nasbo.org.
17. Paul Posner, "The Politics of Coercive Federalism in the Bush Era," *Publius: The Journal of Federalism* 37 (Summer 2007), p. 399.
18. National Conference of State Legislatures, available at www.ncls.org.

Chapter 4

Public Opinion

CHAPTER OUTLINE

WHAT WE WILL LEARN

After studying Chapter 4, students should be able to answer the following questions:

1. What is the process of political socialization and what role do the family, school, peer groups, religious institutions, the media, and genetics play in that process?
2. What is the theory of survey research and how do sampling, question wording, sequencing, phantom opinions, interviewer-respondent interaction, and timing affect survey research?
3. How well informed and interested are Americans in politics and government?
4. Do Americans support the principles of majority rule and minority rights, both in theory and in practice?
5. What does research on political trust indicate about public support for the American political system?
6. What does research on political efficacy indicate about the confidence people have that they can affect public policy?
7. Are Americans liberal or conservative?
8. To what extent does public opinion influence public policy?

Abortion is one of the most controversial issues in American politics. Abortion rights supporters emphasize a woman's right to control her own body. The decision to terminate a pregnancy should be made by a woman and her doctor, they say, not the government. In contrast, abortion opponents focus on the life of the unborn child. They believe that government should protect the fetus by prohibiting abortion, unless a woman's life is at risk.

Public opinion surveys consistently find that the public is closely and deeply divided over the issue. For more than a decade, the Gallup Poll has found that the percentage of people who call themselves pro-choice is almost equal to the percentage of people who say they are pro-life. When asked whether abortion should be legal under all circumstances, legal under certain circumstances, or illegal under all circumstances, a majority of Americans choose the "some circumstances" option with the rest of the survey respondents closely divided between those who say abortion should be "legal under all circumstances" and those who answer "illegal under all circumstances."[1] Furthermore, a candidate's position on abortion is an important consideration for most voters. According to the Gallup Poll, 13 percent of voters declare that they will vote only for those candidates who share their view of abortion. Another 49 percent say that a candidate's position on abortion is important but it is only one of a number of factors affecting the voting decision.[2]

The topic of abortion rights provides a good introduction to the study of public opinion by raising a number of questions:

- How do scholars measure public opinion on issues such as abortion rights? Are opinion surveys accurate, especially on controversial or complex subjects?
- Why do different groups of Americans hold different views on such topics as the issue of abortion rights? What factors account for the development of individual attitudes and beliefs?

GETTING INVOLVED

Family Politics

Political scientists believe that families play an important role in the socialization process. Politically active families typically raise children who become politically active adults. Families also pass along their party identification to their offspring, at least initially. How did your family impact your political socialization, particularly your level of political involvement and your party identification? Prepare to join a class discussion on this topic by taking the following steps:

1. Jot down some information about your own level of political involvement and party affiliation. Are you registered to vote? Are you a regular voter? Have you ever joined a political group or participated in a political campaign? How closely do you follow current events? Do you consider yourself a member of a political party? Have you always had the same party affiliation?
2. Speak with your parents or other members of your family and record your family's political involvement and party loyalties. Were your parents or the adults who raised you politically active? What was their political party allegiance?
3. Finally, consider the role your family played in your personal political socialization and be prepared to discuss the topic in class.

- What is the nature of public opinion in America? Does public opinion on issues such as abortion rights vary among different groups of Americans? Do people vary in the intensity with which they hold an opinion on a subject?
- Finally, to what extent does public opinion influence public policy?

WHAT IS YOUR OPINION?

Would you vote for a candidate with a different view on the issue of abortion if you agreed with the candidate on other issues?

Political Socialization

Political socialization The process whereby individuals acquire political knowledge, attitudes, and beliefs.

Individual attitudes about abortion and all other political issues are shaped through **political socialization,** which is the process whereby individuals acquire political knowledge, attitudes, and beliefs. Although socialization is a learning process, much of what individuals know and believe about politics and government does not come from formal classroom teaching but rather through informal learning that takes place throughout a lifetime. Filling out an income tax return, applying for a student loan, listening to talk radio, serving on a jury, helping a relative apply for permanent residency, and standing for the playing of the National Anthem at a sporting event are all opportunities for political socialization.

Abortion is one of the most controversial and emotional subjects in American politics.

Process of Socialization

Children recognize political figures and symbols before they understand political processes. When asked about government, youngsters mention the president, police officers, and firefighters. Although grade school students recognize political terms such as *Congress*, *political party*, and *democracy*, they do not understand their meaning. Most children think of Congress as a group of men and women who help the president. Many youngsters can name the political party their family supports, but they are unable to distinguish between the two major parties on issues. Even though most children declare democracy to be the best form of government, few understand the term's meaning.

Young children have a positive attitude toward the government and its symbols. They see police officers as friends and helpers, and tell researchers that the president is someone who is smarter and more honest than other people are. Most youngsters can also distinguish the American flag from the flags of other nations and say that it is their favorite.[3]

In adolescence, young people begin to resemble adults politically. They are able to separate individual roles from institutional roles, recognizing that it is possible to criticize the president, for example, while still supporting the office of the presidency. Procedures and processes such as voting and lawmaking are more visible and important to adolescents than they are for young children, and their general knowledge of the political process is more sophisticated.

Political events drive socialization during adolescence. For example, young people gain knowledge and develop political party attachments during a presidential election campaign. The more intense a particular political event is for an individual adolescent, the more enduring the political views. Major events such as the Civil War and the Great Depression made a lifelong impression on generations of Americans.[4]

Political socialization continues into adulthood although at a slower pace than during childhood or adolescence. Both attitudes and basic knowledge levels about politics and government crystallize during early adulthood and tend to persist with comparatively little change in the later years of life.[5] Nonetheless, as young adults enter the workforce, purchase homes, start families, change careers, and eventually retire, they may change their views on specific political issues.

Agents of Socialization

Agents of socialization Those factors that contribute to political socialization by shaping formal and informal learning.

The factors that contribute to political socialization by shaping formal and informal learning are known as **agents of socialization.** These factors affect the level, intensity, and direction of thoughts and actions about politics. In American society, the agents of socialization include the family, school, peer groups, religious institutions, and the media.

Family Children acquire certain attitudes and orientations toward politics from their families. Adults whose parents were politically active are more likely to be involved in politics themselves as compared with their peers whose parents were uninvolved in the political process. Voters are usually the children of voters.[6] Young people whose parents are politically knowledgeable are more likely to be well informed about government and politics than are children with uninformed parents.[7] Young people who discuss politics and current events with their parents are more knowledgeable about government and politics, and more committed to future voting than are other youth.[8]

Families influence the development of political party affiliation. As parents talk with one another and with their children, they are unconsciously constructing a family identity that can include a party identification.[9] The effectiveness of the political party identification transmission from parent to child is strongest when parental attitudes are consistent across time and between parents, and when parental convictions are strongly held. Parents who are strong Democrats or strong Republicans tend to raise children who have similar attachments.[10]

School The school is an important agent of political socialization. Civics classes enhance student knowledge of American government and politics, especially if the classes include discussions of current events. Coursework may lead students to watch news programs or read about current events online. Students taking civics classes may ask their parents more questions about political affairs than students not enrolled.[11] Furthermore, young people who volunteer to work in community organizations, perhaps as part of a high school course requirement, often develop a lifetime habit of civic engagement that includes participation in community organizations and voting.[12]

Schools teach patriotism. Historically, the public schools have trained the children of immigrants to be patriotic Americans and schools continue to play that role today. In the classroom, students pledge allegiance to the flag, sing patriotic songs, commemorate national holidays, and study the lives of national heroes, such as George Washington, Abraham Lincoln, and Martin Luther King, Jr. Schools provide students with opportunities to participate in extracurricular activities, including political clubs and student government organizations. Young people who learn participatory skills in school typically become participatory adults.[13]

WHAT IS YOUR OPINION?

What did you learn about American patriotic customs when you were in school? Did school activities make you feel proud to be living in the United States?

Schools also give young people firsthand experience working within a power structure. A school is a self-contained political system, with peers, authorities, rules, rewards, and punishments. Youngsters inevitably develop attitudes about authority and their roles as participants in the system. Schools are not democracies, of course; principals and teachers are often more interested in discipline than participation. Some scholars believe that the primary focus of schools on compliance with rules hinders the development of political participation skills. This phenomenon is particularly true of schools in low-income areas.[14]

Schools teach patriotism by engaging students in the rituals of American democracy, such as the pledge of allegiance.

The effects of college on political socialization are difficult to measure. Students who attend college differ politically from young people who do not continue their education beyond high school, but college-bound youngsters tend to vary from their peers even before they enter college. High school graduates who go to college are more knowledgeable and interested in politics and feel more capable of influencing the policy process than do young people who are not college-bound.[15] Nevertheless, college life does appear to loosen family ties as far as political attitudes are concerned. College can be a broadening experience because students are exposed to a greater variety of ideas and people than they were in high school. As a result, collegians are less likely to share their family's political views than are people who do not attend college.

Religious Institutions Churches, synagogues, mosques, and other religious institutions are important agents of political socialization for many Americans. Nearly two-thirds belong to a church, synagogue, or another religious body. Although the proportion of Americans who declare that they are religious has decreased since the 1950s, Americans are more religious than are the people in most other industrialized nations. According to the Gallup Poll, 65 percent of Americans report that they attend religious services once a week compared with 40 percent of Germans and 27 percent of people living in the United Kingdom.[16]

Personal involvement in religious organizations is associated with political participation. People who express strong religious commitment are more likely to vote than are people who lack a strong religious faith.[17] The association between religious activism and political activism is particularly important for African Americans.[18] Historically, the black church has been an important training ground for political leaders, including Dr. Martin Luther King, Jr., and Reverend Jesse Jackson.

Religious institutions may also foster the development of particular political attitudes. Even though people tend to join religious organizations that promote political beliefs that are similar to their own, churches, temples, and other religious bodies have an independent effect on political views.[19] This is particularly true for religious organizations that feature an intense commitment of faith and a belief in religion as a source of truth and community. Members of churches or other religious bodies who are accustomed to accepting the religious organization as the authoritative interpreter of the word of God often respect the political pronouncements of religious leaders as well.[20]

WHAT IS YOUR OPINION?

Should churches and other religious institutions take positions on political issues and candidates?

Peer Groups Personal communications among friends and coworkers help shape political attitudes and beliefs. Individuals who personally know someone who is gay or lesbian are more supportive of gay rights than are other people.[21] Interpersonal discussions are more important than the media in influencing voter decisions.[22] When adults change peer groups because of a new job or a move to a different city, their political views may change as well.[23]

The impact of a peer group on an individual's political views depends on the group's significance to the individual. People are more likely to share the values of a group that is important to them than they are those of a group that is less significant. Nonetheless, not all members of a group think alike. Many persons remain in a group even though they disagree with its values because they overlook the conflict. A study of conservative Christian churches found that nearly 40 percent of women members held feminist views that were contrary to the values of their church. The feminist women remained in the church despite the conflict because they perceived little or no connection between their religious beliefs and their political views.[24]

Media Media outlets are important agents of socialization. Political participation is closely associated with media usage, especially newspaper and newsmagazine readership. Nearly everyone who votes reads a newspaper and about half of regular voters read newsmagazines as well.

The most important media sources for political information in order of usage are local television news, newspapers, radio, evening network news, online news,

Fox News, CNN, and the morning network shows.[25] Young people who are frequent media users are more informed about politics and government than are young people who are less frequent users. They understand American government more clearly than less frequent media users and they are more supportive of American values, such as free speech.[26]

Political scientists believe that the media, especially television, determine the relative importance Americans attach to various national problems. In other words, the media help set the policy agenda. Television news stories influence the priorities Americans assign to various national problems.[27] Media reports also help define the criteria by which the public evaluates a president's performance. The more attention the media pay to a particular policy issue, the more the public incorporates what they know about that issue into their overall judgment of the president.[28]

Are Political Attitudes Genetically Transmitted?

Political scientists have begun to explore whether differences in political attitudes and beliefs have a genetic basis. Researchers comparing the political attitudes and ideologies of monozygotic (identical) and dizygotic (non-identical) twins in the United States and Australia have found a genetic basis for the way individuals respond to environmental conditions. Political similarities between parents and children may have as much or more to do with genetics than socialization. The scholars who conducted the research even suggest that the ideological division in American politics may have a genetic basis and they identify two distinct ideological orientations that reflect the interaction of genes and the environment. People with

Religious organizations are important agents of socialization for many Americans.

an absolutist orientation are suspicious of immigrants, yearn for strong leadership and national unity, and seek an unbending moral code. They favor swift and sure punishment for those who violate society's moral code, tolerate economic inequality, and hold a pessimistic view of human nature. In contrast, people with a contextualist orientation are tolerant of immigrants and seek a context-dependent rather than rule-dependent approach to proper social behavior. They dislike predetermined punishments for those who violate moral codes, distrust strong leaders, disapprove of economic inequality, and hold an optimistic view of human nature.[29]

Measuring Public Opinion

Survey research The measurement of public opinion.

Survey research, the measurement of public opinion, is a familiar part of the American scene. Businesses use market surveys to assess public tastes for their products and services. Political campaigns employ polls to plan strategy. Public officials use surveys to assess public understanding of problems and issues.[30] The media use opinion surveys to gauge public reaction to political events and assess the popularity of officeholders and candidates. Scholars rely on survey research as a tool for studying public opinion and political behavior.

Sampling

Universe The population researchers wish to study.

Sample A subset or part of a universe.

Margin of error (or sample error) A statistical term that refers to the accuracy of a survey.

Survey research enables scholars to examine the characteristics of a large group, the universe, by studying a subset of that group, a sample. In survey research, a **universe** is the population researchers wish to study. It may consist of all adult Americans, likely voters, Californians, or people who attend religious services regularly. A **sample** is a subset or part of a universe.

A properly chosen sample will reflect the universe within a given **margin of error** (or **sample error**), which is a statistical term that refers to the accuracy of a survey. The margin of error for a sample of 1,065 persons out of a universe of 500,000 or more is a plus or minus 3 percentage points, 95 percent of the time. Suppose that we know for a fact that 10 percent of all adults are left-handed. Sampling theory dictates that 95 percent of the time, a randomly selected sample of 1,065 people will include 7, 8, 9, 10, 11, 12, or 13 percent left-handers, that is, plus or minus 3 percentage points from the true proportion of left-handed people in the universe. Five percent of the randomly selected samples of 1,065 persons will produce an error that is greater than 3 percentage points. In other words, five samples out of a hundred will contain a proportion of left-handed people less than 7 percent or more than 13 percent.

The size of the margin of error depends on the sample size. Table 4.1 lists the margin of error for various sample sizes for a large universe. The margin of error decreases as the sample size increases and vice versa. The margin of error for samples of one hundred or fewer is so large as to make the survey meaningless. Researchers can reduce the margin of error by increasing the sample size but cannot eliminate it unless they survey every member of the universe. In practice, most professional survey research firms aim for a margin of error of plus or minus 3 to 4 percentage points.

TABLE 4.1 Margins of Error for a Universe Greater than 500,000

Margin of Error	Sample Size
+/− 4 percent	600
+/− 3 percent	1,065
+/− 2 percent	2,390
+/− 1 percent	9,425

Survey research is not exact. Because of the margin of error, a survey more closely resembles a shotgun than a rifle. Suppose a survey shows that Candidate X is leading Candidate Y by a 48 percent to 46 percent margin, while another survey indicates that Candidate Y is leading by 49 percent to 45 percent. The margin of error in each survey is a plus/minus 4 percentage points. Statistically, the surveys show the same result—support for the two candidates is within the margin of error. Neither candidate leads the other.

Statistical chance dictates that 5 percent of the samples taken will produce results that miss the true value by a margin greater than the margin of error. For example, even if two candidates are actually tied in voter support, an occasional sample will show one or the other with a lead greater than the margin of error. Over the course of an election campaign, surveys may show a good deal of relatively small voter movement between candidates with an occasional major shift in public support even if no actual change in voter support for the two candidates takes place.

To be an accurate reflection of a universe, a sample must be representative of the universe. If researchers are interested in the views of all Americans, a sample of a thousand people from Atlanta, a thousand women, or a thousand callers to a radio talk show would not likely be representative. An unrepresentative sample is a **biased sample,** that is, a sample that tends to produce results that do not reflect the true characteristics of the universe because it is unrepresentative of the universe. For example, radio talk programs present a distorted picture of public opinion because callers and listeners are disproportionately conservative Republican men with strong opinions on political issues.[31]

Biased sample A sample that tends to produce results that do not reflect the true characteristics of the universe because it is unrepresentative of the universe.

Internet polls are notoriously (and sometimes hilariously) unreliable because the sample consists of people who choose to participate, sometimes more than once. For example, *People* magazine once conducted an online poll to select the Most Beautiful Person of the Year. The editors at *People* expected that the winner would be a glamorous celebrity. When Howard Stern, a nationally syndicated radio talk show host, heard about the poll, he encouraged his listeners to vote for Hank, the Angry, Drunken Dwarf. Wrestling fans got into the act as well, flooding the *People* website with votes for Ric "Nature Boy" Flair, a professional wrestler. Hank, the Angry, Drunken Dwarf won the vote as *People*'s Most Beautiful Person and Flair finished second.[32]

A biased sample led to one of the most famous polling mistakes in history. During the 1920s and 1930s, a magazine called *Literary Digest* conducted presidential polls every four years. In 1936, the magazine mailed 10 million ballots to individuals whose names and addresses were taken from telephone directories and automobile registration lists across the country. About two million people responded. On that basis, *Literary Digest* predicted that Alf Landon, the Republican challenger, would defeat incumbent Democratic President Franklin Roosevelt by a resounding 57 percent to 43 percent margin. In fact, Roosevelt was reelected by the largest landslide in American history.

What went wrong? *Literary Digest*'s sample was unrepresentative of the universe of likely voters. In the midst of the Great Depression, most of the people who owned telephones and automobiles were middle- and upper-income folks, who tended to vote Republican. In contrast, many poor and working-class people could not afford cars and telephones and were not sampled by the poll. Most of them voted for Roosevelt.

Random sample An unbiased sample in which each member of a universe has an equal likelihood of being included.

Although nothing can guarantee a representative sample 100 percent of the time, the ideal approach is to employ a random sample. A **random sample** is a sample in which each member of a universe has an equal likelihood of being included; it is unbiased. If the universe were composed of the students at a particular college, researchers could select a random sample by picking every tenth or twentieth student from a master list. In contrast, taking a random sample of Roman Catholics or people who will vote in the next election is difficult because no master list exists. Identifying samples of likely voters is especially challenging for pollsters because people tend to overestimate the probability that they will cast a ballot. Surveys conducted before relatively low turnout elections are frequently inaccurate because pollsters are unable to separate voters from nonvoters.

National survey research firms generate samples using computerized systems to select a random set of telephone numbers. The researchers start with a list of all telephone exchanges in the United States along with an estimate of the number of households served by each exchange. A computer uses that information to create a master list of telephone numbers and then selects a random sample from the list. Because the computer is working from a list of possible numbers rather than actual telephone listings, people who have unlisted telephone numbers will be as likely to be included in the sample as will people with listed numbers. Survey researchers then use the list of numbers to conduct telephone interviews. To correct for the possible bias of including only those people in the survey who are usually home and answer their telephones, professional polling firms call back repeatedly at different times over several days. Once someone answers the telephone, the researchers do not necessarily interview the person who answered the phone. Instead, they ask for a list of all the adults in the household and then randomly select someone to interview, even if they have to call back at another time to find that person at home.

Many people refuse to participate in opinion polls. The response rate for major national surveys conducted over several days with callbacks to people who do not answer their phones initially is less than 30 to 40 percent. It is much less for snapshot polls taken overnight. Cell phones are another problem for survey researchers. Because wireless carriers often charge users by the minute, cell phone users are less likely to agree to participate than are people using landlines.[33] Scholars are particularly concerned that low response rates may make surveys inaccurate because the people who respond to surveys differ demographically from the people who refuse to participate. Researchers attempt to compensate for differential response rates by weighting their samples to add men, young adults, and other people whose demographic groups would otherwise be underrepresented in the sample.[34]

Question Wording

Even the best sample is worthless if survey questions are invalid. Questions that are confusing, oversimplified, or biased are unlikely to produce valid results. Consider the following survey questions:

1. Do you believe that waterboarding is torture and that the United States has a moral responsibility to not engage in or condone any form of torture? (a) Yes, (b) No (c) Unsure
2. Do you believe abortion should be legal? (a) Yes (b) No (c) No opinion
3. Should the Obama Administration step back from the rush to create "cap-and-trade" energy legislation that will cost jobs, harm future economic growth, and impose an estimated $1,761 new energy tax on America's families? (a) Yes (b) No (c) Not sure

Question 1 is confusing. The stem of the question raises at least two issues: whether waterboarding is torture and whether or not the United States should engage in or condone torture. How do people answer if they disagree with the first part and agree with the second part of the question or vice versa?

Question 2 is oversimplified. Many people believe that abortion should be legal under certain circumstances but illegal under others. The question, with its oversimplified answer alternatives, forces these people to misstate their views.

Biased question A survey question that produces results tilted to one side or another.

Question 3 is a **biased question,** which is a survey question that produces results tilted to one side or another. The question is clearly not a fair assessment of whether people favor or oppose cap-and-trade legislation. After all, who would be in favor of a program that costs jobs, hurts future economic growth, and imposes a high tax?

Subtle differences in question wording can affect survey responses. Consider the issue of abortion. Only 34 percent of the respondents to a CBS News/*New York Times* poll took a pro-choice stance when the pro-choice alternative was phrased as follows: "Abortion should be generally available to those who want it." Support for the pro-choice position grew to 55 percent in an NBC/*Wall Street Journal* survey in which the pro-choice alternative was written in different terms: "The choice of abortion should be left to the woman and her doctor." The NBC/*Wall Street Journal* question elicited a strong pro-choice response because its phrasing implied that the abortion decision, made in consultation with a doctor, was not taken lightly. In contrast, the wording of the CBS News/*New York Times* survey suggested that the choice of abortion could be made relatively lightly by "those who want it."[35]

? WHAT IS YOUR OPINION?

Should public officials use opinion surveys to determine what policies are most popular and then adopt those policies?

Question Sequencing

The order in which questions are asked can affect a survey's results because question sequence can determine the context within which respondents consider a question. For example, asking about presidential job performance following questions about a particular government policy affects the president's popularity depending on whether the policy is perceived as successful or unsuccessful. Professional researchers attempt to control for the impact of question sequencing by rotating the order in which questions are asked among survey respondents.[36]

Attitudes, Non-Attitudes, and Phantom Opinions

A survey sponsored by the *Washington Post* newspaper asked a national sample of Americans the following question: "Some people say the 1975 Public Affairs Act should be repealed. Do you agree or disagree that it should be repealed?" The survey found that 24 percent of the sample agreed that the act should be repealed, while 19 percent said that it should not be repealed. The other 57 percent had no opinion. Ironically, the people with no opinion were the best informed because the Public Affairs Act was a totally fictitious law. The survey researchers made it up in order to test how many respondents would express an opinion on an issue about which they obviously had no knowledge.[37]

Phantom opinions invalidate the results of survey research. Survey respondents make up responses to questions about which they have little or no information because they do not want to appear uninformed. Professional pollsters guard against distorting their poll results with uncommitted opinions by offering respondents a relatively painless opportunity to confess that they have not heard of an issue or do not have an opinion. Some survey researchers also ask respondents to indicate the intensity with which they hold their views and then take that intensity into account in interpreting the results of a survey.

Interviewer-Respondent Interaction

The race or gender of an interviewer can affect survey results when sensitive issues are involved because respondents sometimes attempt to say the right thing based on the interviewer's race or gender.[38] For example, a survey measuring racial attitudes found black respondents were considerably more likely to say that white people could be trusted when the interviewer was white than when an African American interviewer asked the same questions.[39] Similarly, women were much more likely to give pro-choice responses to questions about abortion to female interviewers than they were to male interviewers.[40]

Timing

Even the most carefully conducted survey is only a snapshot of public opinion on the day of the poll because public opinion can change. In March 1991, for example, immediately after the American victory in the First Gulf War, the Gallup Poll showed

Around the World — Survey Research in Afghanistan

If survey research is challenging under the best of conditions, consider how difficult it must be in a developing country at war. In the last few years, survey research firms have begun working in Afghanistan. International aid organizations, the U.S. government, and firms interested in marketing their products in Afghanistan are all willing to purchase survey research data on public opinion in Afghanistan, and professional polling firms are working to supply that demand.

Afghanistan has a large, diverse population with an illiteracy rate of nearly 50 percent. The population includes four major ethnic groups speaking different languages. A survey research firm consequently must hire a multiethnic, multilingual staff that includes both men and women. To build trust, interviewers should share the ethnic background of the person being interviewed and, of course, speak the same language. For cultural reasons in an Islamic country such as Afghanistan, women should interview women; men should interview men. Women interviewees are typically accompanied by a male family member, especially in rural areas.

Afghanistan is geographically large with few paved roads. Because of the war, travel is dangerous, especially in the southern part of the country near the Pakistani border. Survey research supervisors consequently need to review closely the survey data produced by field teams to avoid the possibility that contract workers simply make up the results rather than actually conduct the interviews.*

Despite the obstacles, survey research firms are already publishing the results of their work. In December 2010, for example, the Asia Foundation released the results of its annual survey of public opinion in Afghanistan. Nearly half of the respondents indicated that they believed that the country was headed in the right direction, an increase over the results of surveys taken in 2008 and 2009. Respondents cited improved security, construction and rebuilding, and opening schools for girls as reasons for their optimism. In contrast, Afghans who said that the country was going in the wrong direction identified problems with security, unemployment, and corruption as cause for their pessimism.†

QUESTIONS

1. Would you enjoy working for a survey research firm doing surveys in other countries? Why or why not?
2. Would it be appropriate in the United States for a survey research firm to match the racial/ethnic background of interviewers and interviewees?
3. How confident are you in the accuracy of surveys conducted in Afghanistan?

* Matthew Warshaw, "Starting from Scratch: Making Research a Reality in Afghanistan," available at www.publicopinionpros.norc.org.

† "Afghanistan in 2010: A Survey of the Afghan People," Asia Society, available at http://asiafoundation.org.

that the approval rating of President H. W. Bush was 89 percent. Many political observers predicted that the president would win reelection easily. By August 1992, however, Bush's popularity rating had fallen below 35 percent. Three months later, he was defeated for reelection.[41]

Using poll results to predict the future can be risky: ask Thomas E. Dewey. In 1948, Democratic President Harry Truman was running for election against Dewey, the Republican Party nominee. Throughout the summer and early fall, the polls showed Dewey well ahead and it was generally assumed that Dewey would win handily. Because the major polling firms stopped surveying voters more than a week

Harry Truman gets the last laugh. (*Source:* Photo Courtesy: Corbis/Bettmann).

before the election, they missed a late voter shift in favor of President Truman. Consequently, Truman's election victory was a surprise to many people, including the editors of the *Chicago Tribune* newspaper who rushed to press on election night with the famous headline: "Dewey Defeats Truman."

Political Knowledge and Interest

Public knowledge about and interest in politics and government has grown. Not long ago, survey research found that most Americans were poorly informed about politics and government. Although some Americans were quite knowledgeable about public affairs, a majority of the nation's adults could not accurately name their own representative in Congress or even one of the U.S. senators from their state. Most Americans were unable to identify the Bill of Rights. Less than a fifth could name the current chief justice of the United States.[42]

In contrast, recent surveys show that both political interest and knowledge are on the rise. The percentage of Americans who tell survey researchers that they follow the news about national politics very closely increased from 26 percent in 2000 to 43 percent in 2008. It jumped from 19 percent in 2001 to 36 percent in 2009.

(Political interest is typically higher in presidential election years such as 2000 and 2008 than it is in non-election years such as 2001 and 2009.) In addition to the 36 percent who indicated that they followed the national news very closely in 2009, another 42 percent declared that they followed the news somewhat closely. Only 6 percent said that they did not follow the news at all.[43]

Interested people are also knowledgeable people. According to a study conducted by the Pew Research Center in 2007, most Americans know which political party controlled Congress, could name the Speaker of the House, and could identify the two branches of Islam struggling for control of Iraq. The study found that 26 percent of respondents could answer all 10 of its political questions correctly, whereas only 14 percent could correctly answer three or fewer questions.[44]

Some groups of Americans are more interested and better informed than are other groups. As a group, men are more interested and knowledgeable than are women. Republicans are more interested and know more than do Democrats. Older Americans are better informed and more interested in politics than younger people. Men over 50 are the most knowledgeable and attentive segment of the population; younger women the least.[45]

Political interest and information affect political behavior and beliefs. Knowledgeable Americans are more likely to vote and more likely to cast an informed ballot than are the uninformed. Furthermore, knowledgeable respondents usually vote for candidates whose views on issues of importance to them coincide with their own. In contrast, there is almost no relationship between the political issues that low-knowledge voters say matter most to them and the issue positions of the candidates for whom they voted.[46]

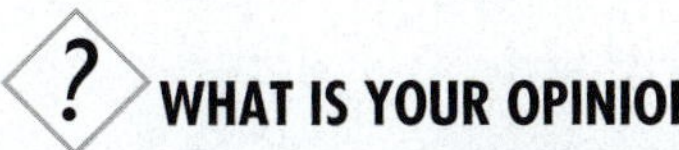

Are people who neglect to keep up with the news unpatriotic?

Support for Democratic Principles

Do Americans support the democratic principles of majority rule and minority rights? Political scientists have studied this question for decades. During the 1950s, Professor Samuel Stouffer conducted a major study to evaluate public opinion toward civil liberties and found a high level of intolerance toward persons with unpopular views. For example, only 27 percent of the persons interviewed in his sample would permit "an admitted communist" to make a speech.[47]

In 1960, political scientists James W. Prothro and C. W. Grigg published what has become a classic study on the subject of political tolerance. They conducted a survey in which respondents overwhelmingly endorsed the sentiment that public officials should be chosen by majority vote and that people whose opinions were in the minority should have the right to convince others of their views. When Prothro and Grigg asked about specific, concrete situations, however, they found dramatically less support for the practice of majority rule and minority rights. Many respondents said that a communist should not be allowed to take office, even if legally elected. Many persons also stated that atheists should not be allowed to speak publicly against religion.[48] In the years since the Prothro and Grigg study first appeared, other research has confirmed that Americans are more likely to endorse democratic principles in the abstract than in specific applications. One study even found that a majority of Americans opposed many of the specific guarantees of individual rights found in the Bill of Rights.[49]

A number of studies conducted in the 1970s concluded that Americans were growing more tolerant of political diversity. Using questions almost identical to those asked by Stouffer two decades earlier, political scientists found significantly larger percentages of Americans willing to tolerate atheists, socialists, and communists. Some scholars concluded that the trend toward greater tolerance reflected the views of a younger, more urban, and better-educated population.[50]

Subsequent research contradicted the conclusion that Americans have grown more accepting of political diversity. Although attitudes toward socialists, communists, and atheists have generally become more tolerant, many Americans express intolerant attitudes toward racists, persons advocating military rule in the United States, and, since 9/11, Muslims. Nearly a fifth of respondents told survey researchers that, because of security interests, the civil liberties of Muslims should be restricted; 17 percent said that it was acceptable to lock up Muslims just in case they were planning terrorist acts.[51] Americans are apparently no more tolerant of unpopular views today than they were in the 1950s. The difference is that the targets of intolerance have changed and the number of unpopular groups is less than it was 50 years ago.[52] Furthermore, some Americans do not feel free. More than half of fundamentalist

Americans favor civil liberties for groups they like; they oppose civil liberties for groups they dislike.

Christians and abortion rights opponents tell researchers that they believe that they cannot exercise full political freedom.[53]

Civil liberties The protection of the individual from the unrestricted power of government.

A number of political scientists believe that the general public has little understanding or concern for **civil liberties,** which is the protection of the individual from the unrestricted power of government. "[T]he only time many people consider . . . [civil liberties]," one scholar says, "is when they are being queried about it in public opinion surveys."[54] Consequently, people respond to questions about civil liberties based on their perception of a particular group's threat to society. In the 1950s, many Americans favored limiting free speech for communists because they feared communism. Americans today feel less threatened by communists than by racist groups such as the Ku Klux Klan or Islamic militants. When answering survey questions, then, they express more tolerance for communists than for members of the Klan.[55] In sum, Americans favor civil liberties for groups they like; they oppose civil liberties for groups they dislike.

WHAT IS YOUR OPINION?

Should a professor who believes that the United States "had it coming" on September 11, 2001, be allowed to teach at the university? Why or why not?

The apparent indifference of most Americans to civil liberties, at least as they apply to controversial groups, disturbs a number of observers. Tolerance for people of other races, ethnicities, religions, and political beliefs is an important underpinning for democracy.[56] Many political theorists believe that the maintenance of a free society requires a high degree of popular support for civil liberties. How, then, can we explain the stability of democracy in the United States in the face of research that has often found a lack of support for the fundamental principles of democracy?

Political scientists identify three factors accounting for the preservation of political freedom in the United States, despite the ambivalence and occasional hostility of many Americans to civil liberties. First, the Constitution protects individual rights. Although paper guarantees of individual freedom are not sufficient to ensure civil liberties, they provide an important legal foundation for individual rights. Second, Americans do not agree on the target groups to be suppressed. Some people believe that communists should be kept from expressing their views or holding public office, whereas others favor silencing Islamists or people who oppose abortion rights. Because Americans do not agree on which groups should be suppressed, they are unable to unite behind undemocratic public policies. Finally, a number of political scientists believe that the attitudes of the general public about civil liberties issues are not nearly as important as the views of **political elites,** who are persons that exercise a major influence on the policymaking process. Support for democratic principles in specific situations, not just in the abstract, is stronger among people who are politically active and well informed than it is among individuals who are politically uninvolved. Democracy endures because those who are most directly involved in policymaking—political elites—understand and support the principles of majority rule and minority rights.[57]

Political elites Persons that exercise a major influence on the policymaking process.

Political Trust and Political Legitimacy

Political legitimacy The popular acceptance of a government and its officials as rightful authorities in the exercise of power.

Many scholars believe that political trust is essential to political legitimacy in a democracy. **Political legitimacy** is the popular acceptance of a government and its officials as rightful authorities in the exercise of power. For the most part, democracy depends on the voluntary cooperation of its citizens rather than coercion. People pay taxes and obey laws because they accept the authority of the government. They seek political change through the electoral process and peacefully accept the outcomes of election contests because they recognize the decisions of the electoral process as binding. If a significant proportion of the population loses trust in the political system, the quality of democracy declines. Tax evasion and disrespect for the rule of law increase. The potential for a revolutionary change in the political order may develop. Political battles may be fought with bullets, not ballots.

Political scientists attempt to measure the level of political trust in society through a set of questions developed by the Center for Political Studies (CPS), which is a social science research unit housed at the University of Michigan. The questions probe the degree to which citizens believe that government leaders are honest (or crooked) and competent (or incompetent). One question asks, "How much of the time do you think you can trust the government in Washington to do what is right—just about always, most of the time, or only some of the time?" Another question reads, "Do you think that quite a few of the people running the government are a little crooked, not very many are, or do you think hardly any of them are crooked at all?"[58]

Political scientists average the answers to the questions to create a Trust Index. The index fell during the 1960s and 1970s, rose in the 1980s, fell again in the 1990s, increased dramatically after the terrorist attacks on September 11, 2001, and then dropped yet again. In 2010, only 22 percent of Americans told survey researchers that they trusted the government to do what is right just about always or most of the time, a record low.[59] The survey found that 56 percent of Americans were frustrated with the federal government; another 21 percent were angry. Only 19 percent answered that they were basically content with the government. Other surveys taken in 2010 indicated low levels of approval/high levels of disapproval for Congress and both major political parties.[60]

Political Efficacy

Political efficacy The extent to which individuals believe they can influence the policymaking process.

Political efficacy is the extent to which individuals believe they can influence the policymaking process. Political efficacy is related to participation. People who believe that they can affect government policies would logically be more inclined to participate politically than people who have no confidence in their ability to influence what government does.

Political scientists identify two components of this concept. **Internal political efficacy** is an individual's assessment of his or her personal ability to influence the policymaking process. The concept addresses a person's self-assessment of his or her

Internal political efficacy The assessment by an individual of his or her personal ability to influence the policymaking process.

knowledge of the political system and ability to communicate with political decision-makers. Scholars measure internal political efficacy by asking the following agree/disagree question: "Sometimes politics and government seem so complicated that a person like me can't really understand what's going on." Agreement with the statement indicates a low level of internal political efficacy and vice versa. In 2008, 68 percent agreed with the statement compared with 20 percent who disagreed.[61] Because internal political efficacy rose during the 1980s and 1990s, when voting turnout was in decline, most political scientists do not believe that the concept is related to voter participation. Low levels of internal political efficacy may explain why many Americans do not participate politically in other ways, but they apparently do not account for changes in voter participation rates.

External political efficacy The assessment of an individual's view of the government responsiveness government to his or her concerns.

External political efficacy refers to an individual's assessment of the government's responsiveness to his or her concerns. This concept deals with an individual's evaluation of the willingness of government officials to respond to the views of ordinary citizens. Political scientists have created a Government Responsiveness Index based on responses to questions such as the following: "Over the years, how much attention do you feel the government pays to what the people think when it decides what to do?" The index generally declined from the mid-1960s through the early 1980s, but it has subsequently increased.[62] Scholars believe that external political efficacy is associated with voter participation.[63]

Political Philosophy

Liberalism The political philosophy that favors the use of government power to foster the development of the individual and promote the welfare of society.

Conservatism The political philosophy that government power undermines the development of the individual and diminishes society as a whole.

Political right Conservatism.

In American politics, the terms *liberalism* and *conservatism* are often used to describe political philosophy. **Liberalism** is the political philosophy that favors the use of government power to foster the development of the individual and promote the welfare of society. Liberals believe that the government can (and should) advance social progress by promoting political equality, social justice, and economic prosperity. Liberals usually favor government regulation and high levels of government spending for social programs. Liberals value social and cultural diversity and defend the right of individual adult choice on issues such as access to abortion. In contrast, **conservatism** is the political philosophy that government power undermines the development of the individual and diminishes society as a whole. Conservatives argue that government regulations and social programs generally do harm rather than good. They believe charities, private businesses, and individuals can solve societal problems if the government will just leave them alone. Conservatives also believe that the government should defend the traditional values of society.

The terms *right* and *left* are also used to describe political ideology. In American politics, the **political right** refers to conservatism, the **political left** to liberalism. Similarly, **right wing** means conservative; **left wing** means liberal. The use of these terms comes from the traditional practice in European legislatures of seating members of liberal parties on the left side of the meeting hall, whereas members of conservative parties sit on the right side.

Political left
Liberalism.

Right wing
Conservative.

Left wing
Liberal.

Liberals and conservatives disagree about the government's capacity to solve problems. Although liberals and conservatives both acknowledge that the nation faces certain social problems, they disagree as to whether those problems can be best addressed by the government or private initiative. Liberals advocate government action to assist disadvantaged groups in society, such as the elderly, poor, minorities, and people with disabilities. They generally support such programs as Social Security, Medicare, welfare assistance for the poor, national health insurance, federal aid for education, and affirmative action programs for women and minorities. In contrast, conservatives argue that government, especially the national government, is too inefficient to solve the nation's social problems. They believe that government should reduce spending on social programs and cut taxes in order to promote economic growth, which, the conservatives argue, benefits everyone. As President Ronald Reagan once put it, "The best anti-poverty program is a job."

Liberals and conservatives disagree about the efficacy of government regulation. Liberals believe in the use of government power to regulate business in the public interest. They support environmental-protection laws to safeguard air and water quality, consumer-protection regulations to protect the buying public, occupational safety and health standards to ensure safe working conditions, and strict regulation of utilities to guarantee efficiency. Liberals are more likely than conservatives to endorse trade restrictions to protect American companies and workers from foreign competition. In contrast, conservatives warn that government regulations usually involve undue interference with the market economy. They believe that government regulations drive up the cost of doing business, increasing prices for consumers and lowering wage rates for workers. In this policy area, at least, conservatives agree with the motto: "The government that governs least governs best."

Global warming
The gradual warming of the Earth's atmosphere, reportedly caused by the burning of fossil fuels and industrial pollutants.

Consider the issue of the environment. Liberals value a clean environment even if it means sacrificing some economic growth. They advocate government regulation to ensure clean air and water. They favor government actions designed to respond to the threat of **global warming,** which is the gradual warming of Earth's atmosphere reportedly caused by the burning of fossil fuels and industrial pollutants. In contrast, conservatives want to proceed slowly in addressing environmental issues such as global warming to avoid negatively impacting economic growth. They prefer market-oriented solutions to the pollution problem rather than government mandates.

WHAT IS YOUR OPINION?

Do you consider yourself a liberal, conservative, or moderate?

However, conservatives and liberals trade positions on the role of government when it comes to social issues, such as pornography, gay and lesbian rights, abortion, school prayer, and women's rights. On these issues, conservatives favor a more active government, whereas liberals prefer less government involvement. Conservatives define social issues in terms of traditional family values. They regard pornography, gay and lesbian rights, abortion, assisted suicide, stem cell research, and the Supreme Court's refusal to allow government-mandated spoken prayer in public schoolrooms as direct assaults on God, family, and country. Conservatives generally support the rigorous enforcement of pornography laws, the adoption of a constitutional amendment against abortion, and the enactment of an amendment permitting school prayer. Conservatives oppose assisted suicide, most stem cell research, and laws protecting gay men and lesbians from discrimination. They also reject efforts to grant legal recognition to same-sex relationships.

In contrast, liberals believe that adults should be free to decide for themselves what books to read or films to watch. They hold that women should be allowed to pursue the career goals of their choice and should be treated equally with men under the law. Liberals believe that women should not be forced to bear unwanted children; gay men and lesbians should not suffer discrimination; and the government should not dictate prayers for children to recite in the public schools. They favor government support for stem cell research aimed at finding cures for disease.

Ironically, both liberals and conservatives criticize government. Liberals believe that government should act more aggressively to promote the democratic value of equality by helping disadvantaged individuals and groups gain economic and political power. Furthermore, when government does act, liberals say that it often favors the interests of the rich and powerful. In contrast, conservatives criticize government for undercutting capitalism by interfering with the efficient working of the free enterprise system, thus lowering economic productivity. Conservatives believe that government economic intervention hurts everyone, including the poor.

Although the terms *liberalism* and *conservatism* help define the contours of the policy debate in America, their usefulness is limited. The real-life differences between liberals and conservatives are often matters of degree and emphasis rather than dramatic contrast. Also, a number of policy issues, including many foreign policy issues, cannot easily be defined along liberal/conservative lines. Finally, few Americans are consistently liberal or conservative, with most people holding conservative views on some issues, liberal opinions on others.

Are Americans Liberal or Conservative?

More Americans self-identify as conservatives than as liberals. In 2010, the ratio of conservatives to liberals was 42 percent to 20 percent with another 35 percent declaring that their political views were moderate.[64] Nonetheless, political scientists caution about putting too much stock into self-appraisals of political philosophy because many Americans are unable to accurately define the terms *liberal* and *conservative*. Furthermore, relatively few Americans are consistently liberal or conservative on the full range of political issues. Table 4.2 displays the results of a series of recent Gallup Polls on a range of political issues. As the table indicates, the answer to the question whether Americans are conservative or liberal depends on the issue.

It is also unclear whether Americans are growing more liberal or more conservative. By a 39 percent to 18 percent margin Americans tell survey researchers that their views have been growing more conservative in recent years as opposed to more liberal, with another 42 percent indicating that their thinking has not changed. In looking at specific issues, however, polls show that whereas Americans have grown

TABLE 4.2 Are Americans Conservative or Liberal? Responses to Various Issues

Issue	Conservative Response	Liberal Response
Death penalty	Favor: 65%	Oppose: 31%
Environment	Economic growth is the top priority: 51%	Protecting the environment is the top priority: 42%
Gay rights	Gay/lesbian relations between consenting adults should not be legal: 40%	Gay/lesbian relations between consenting adults should be legal: 56%
Role of government	Government is doing too much: 57%	Government should do more: 38%
Gun control	Gun control laws should be less strict: 12%	Gun control laws should be more strict: 44%
Healthcare	Not the federal government's responsibility to ensure all Americans have healthcare: 50%	It is the federal government's responsibility to ensure all Americans have healthcare: 47%
Gay marriage	Should not be valid: 57%	Should be valid: 40%
Defense spending	Too little: 24%	Too much: 31%
Women allowed to hold combat jobs	Should not: 23%	Should: 74%
Options for saving Social Security	Better to curb benefits: 38%	Better to raise taxes: 53%
Income taxes you pay	Too high: 46%	About right: 48%
Taxes paid by upper-income groups	Too much: 13%	Too little: 60%
War in Afghanistan	Keep troops there until situation gets better: 48%	Set a timetable for withdrawal: 47%

Source: Gallup, various surveys, available at www.gallup.com.

Note: Percentages do not necessarily sum to 100 because of other alternatives, don't know responses, and no opinion responses.

more conservative on some issues, such as protecting the environment and gun control, they have become less conservative on other issues, such as immigration and tax rates. On still other issues, public positions have not changed.[65]

WHAT IS YOUR OPINION?

Do you consider yourself liberal, conservative, or middle of the road? Why?

Opinion Differences among Groups

Surveys show that political attitudes vary among individuals according to such factors as social class, race, and gender. For example, support for abortion rights is greatest among women, college graduates, young people, African Americans, higher income earners, Democrats, and people who lack a religious affiliation. In contrast, opposition to abortion rights is greatest among men, older adults, Republicans, people with relatively little formal education, lower-income groups, and regular church attenders.[66]

Social Class Lower-income persons are more liberal than middle- and upper-income people on some issues but more conservative on others. On social welfare issues, such as support for Medicare and Social Security, lower-income people tend to take more liberal positions than do middle- and upper-income Americans, apparently because they see themselves as beneficiaries of social welfare programs. Lower-income Americans are considerably more supportive of raising taxes on upper-income wage earners than are people in upper-income groups. In contrast, lower-income individuals are often more conservative than other income groups on such non-economic issues as abortion, teaching creation in public schools, and stem cell research.

In foreign policy matters, lower-income individuals are more isolationist than middle-income people, but also more supportive of the use of military force in dealing with other nations. Working-class people often oppose free trade, fearing the loss of jobs to international competition. In contrast, middle- and upper-income people have a more internationalist perspective; they tend to favor free trade, foreign aid, and negotiated settlements of disputes.[67]

Affirmative action programs Programs designed to ensure equal opportunities in employment and college admissions for racial minorities and women.

Race and Ethnicity African Americans and Latinos are more liberal than whites on economic issues, favoring activist government with strong job training and welfare programs. Members of both minority groups typically support **affirmative action programs,** which are programs designed to ensure equal opportunities in employment and college admissions for racial minorities and women. African Americans in particular perceive widespread racial discrimination in society and believe that it is the major reason that many African Americans have trouble finding good jobs and adequate housing. They want government to play an active role in the quest for racial equality. In contrast, many whites think that racism is a thing of the past.[68] When asked whether they believe that blacks have as good a chance as whites to get any kind of job for which they are qualified, 82 percent of whites and Hispanics agree with the statement compared with only 49 percent of blacks who agree.[69]

African Americans and Latinos are more conservative than whites on some social issues. Although African Americans and Latinos are less likely to support the death penalty than whites, they are more likely to hold conservative views than the general population on the issues of homosexual relations, gay marriage, and stem cell research. African American and Latino conservatism on these issues reflects relatively high rates of church attendance for both minority groups.[70]

Religious left Individuals who hold liberal views because of their religious beliefs.

Religious right Individuals who hold conservative views because of their religious beliefs.

Religion Many Americans participate in politics because of their religious faith. The **religious left** refers to individuals who hold liberal views because of their religious beliefs, whereas the phrase **religious right** refers to individuals who hold conservative views because of their religious beliefs. During the 1960s and early 1970s, many people supported civil rights for African Americans or opposed the Vietnam War because of religious principles. Today, poverty, peace, immigration, and the environment are important issues for religious liberals. Most members of the religious left are associated with mainline Protestant Christian churches, such as the Presbyterians, Episcopalians, and Church of Christ (Disciples), or with the Jewish faith. The religious left also includes Buddhists and many people who declare that they are "spiritual" but not associated with organized religion.[71] The most important political issues for the religious right are opposition to abortion, pornography, and gay and lesbian rights. Christian conservatives favor prayer in school and the right of parents to educate their children as they see fit. They support the wars in Iraq and Afghanistan, strongly back Israel, and hold negative views of Islam.[72] Christian conservatives tend to be associated with white evangelical Protestant churches, such as Assemblies of God and the Southern Baptist Convention.[73] Not all religious groups are firmly in the camp of the left or right, however. For example, although Roman Catholics oppose gay marriage, a position associated with the religious right, they also oppose the death penalty, support civil rights and immigrant rights, and favor government efforts to end poverty. The latter positions are typically associated with the religious left. Ironically, Roman Catholics are actually somewhat more supportive of abortion rights than are Protestants, despite the official opposition of the Catholic Church to abortion.[74]

In contemporary American politics, the religious right is more influential than the religious left. This development reflects the relative strength of the religious organizations associated with each cause. Whereas most mainline Protestant churches have been losing members for years, conservative evangelical churches have been growing. In the 1960s, twice as many white adults claimed membership in mainline Protestant denominations than were members of evangelical Protestant churches. Today, conservative evangelical Protestants outnumber members of mainline denominations. Furthermore, church attendance is higher among conservative evangelicals.[75]

Because of the growth of conservative Christian churches, active church participation is now associated with political conservatism. Among whites, the more

African Americans are relatively conservative on the issues of abortion and gay and lesbian rights, reflecting their high rates of church attendance.

actively involved people are with religious organizations, the more likely they are to hold conservative political views, and vice versa. For African Americans, the church is a basis for liberal activism on economic issues. Nonetheless, African Americans who are active church members hold more conservative views on social issues, such as abortion and gay marriage, than do African Americans who do not participate actively in a church.[76]

Generation Younger Americans are considerably more likely than middle-aged and older Americans to label themselves liberal.[77] They are more tolerant than older adults of ethnic, racial, and social diversity. They are also more sympathetic regarding affirmative action programs that aid minorities than are older people, and are more likely to favor gay and lesbian rights.[78] Despite conventional wisdom, studies find no evidence that people grow more conservative with age. Instead, age-related differences in political views reflect the impact of socializing events common to a generation. Younger Americans today, for example, came of age after the appearance of individual rights movements for African Americans, women, and homosexuals. In contrast, older people grew up at a time when African Americans were segregated, most women worked at home, and gay men and lesbians were in the closet. Differences in political views between generations may also represent different levels of education. Younger Americans may be more tolerant because they are better educated than previous generations.

Region Differences in political views among people from different geographical regions are fewer now than they once were, but they still exist. In general, people from the East and West coasts are more liberal than are people from the South, Midwest, or Rocky Mountain region. Although most regional differences can be explained by other factors such as class, race, and religion, some genuine regional variations based on unique cultural and historical factors may play a role in the political fabric of the nation. The South's lingering identification with the Old Confederacy is perhaps the most notable example of how history can affect the political thinking of a region.

Gender gap Differences in party identification and political attitudes between men and women.

Gender Men and women are different politically. The phrase **gender gap** refers to differences in party identification and political attitudes between men and women. For example, women are more likely than men to vote for Democratic candidates. They are more likely than men to favor government programs to provide healthcare and education, and to protect the environment. They are also more likely than men to support abortion rights and gay marriage. In addition, women are less tolerant of employment discrimination than are men.[79] Finally, women are less likely than men to favor increased defense spending and to believe that the wars in Afghanistan and Iraq are worth it.[80]

Public Opinion and Public Policy

Years ago, political scientist V. O. Key, Jr., introduced the concept of latent opinion to explain the relationship between public opinion and public policy. Latent opinion, he said, is not what voters think about an issue today, but what public opinion would be at election time if a political opponent made a public official's position on the issue the target of a campaign attack.[81] Elected officials make thousands of policy decisions. Except for a relatively few high profile actions, such as President George W. Bush ordering the American armed forces to attack Iraq, most of these decisions are invisible to the overwhelming majority of Americans. Nonetheless, public officials consider public opinion because they recognize that a future political opponent could raise the issue during an election campaign.

Contemporary political scientist James A. Stimson discusses the impact of public opinion on the decision-making calculus of public officials by introducing the concept of a **zone of acquiescence,** which is the range of policy options acceptable to the public on a particular issue. Stimson says that some policy options are too liberal to be acceptable to a majority of the public, whereas other options are too conservative. The zone of acquiescence encompasses those policy options that lie between the two extremes. The size of the zone varies from issue to issue and may change if public opinion grows more conservative or more liberal. Rational policymakers choose policy options within the zone of acquiescence; otherwise, they risk electoral defeat.[82]

Zone of acquiescence The range of policy options acceptable to the public on a particular issue.

The concept of a zone of acquiescence draws attention to a number of important points about the relationship between public opinion and public policy. First, public opinion does not dictate what government officials do so much as it limits the available policy options. On most issues, the zone of acquiescence is broad enough to include a number of policy options from which public officials may choose. Public opinion sets the range of acceptable alternatives, but it does not determine which options policymakers select. Other factors, including the influence of interest groups and political parties, come into play.

Second, the concept of a zone of acquiescence does not imply that policies are not controversial. The zone of acquiescence is based on majority preferences. For example, although abortion is legal in the United States, it remains controversial and many Americans find it totally unacceptable.

Third, the zone of acquiescence affects elected officials differently because they are chosen from different constituencies. A **constituency** is the district from which an officeholder is elected. **Constituents** are the people an officeholder represents. A member of Congress elected from a district where a majority of constituents are African American, for example, faces a more liberal zone of acquiescence on economic issues than does a representative whose constituents are mostly upper-income whites. The president, meanwhile, must deal with a nationwide constituency.

Constituency The district from which an officeholder is elected.

Constituents The people an officeholder represents.

Finally, the zone of acquiescence for a particular issue changes as public opinion changes. During the 1980s, public opinion grew more conservative on law and order issues such as the death penalty. Consequently, the range of acceptable policy options available to officials grew more conservative as well. States adopted laws giving harsher sentences to violent criminals and more states began implementing the death penalty. On other issues, such as gay and lesbian rights, public policy became more liberal as public opinion grew more liberal, especially in large urban areas whose residents were more likely to hold liberal views on the issue than people living in small towns and rural areas.[83] Policy positions that were not acceptable in the 1950s have now become acceptable.

WHAT WE HAVE LEARNED

1. **What is the process of political socialization and what role do the family, school, peer groups, religious institutions, the media, and genetics play in that process?**

   Political socialization is the process whereby individuals acquire political knowledge, attitudes, and beliefs. It begins in childhood and continues throughout the lifespan. The family, school, peer groups, religious institutions, and the media are all agents of socialization because they are the factors that contribute to political socialization by shaping formal and informal learning. For example, the family influences the initial development of political party affiliation. School civics classes enhance student knowledge of American government and politics. Schools also teach patriotism through patriotic rituals and symbols. Personal involvement in religious organizations is associated with political participation. Personal communications among friends and coworkers help shape political attitudes and beliefs. Political scientists believe that the media, especially television, determine the relative importance Americans attach to various national problems. Finally, political scientists have begun to explore whether differences in political attitudes and beliefs have a genetic basis.

2. **What is the theory of survey research and how do sampling, question wording, sequencing, phantom opinions, interviewer-respondent interaction, and timing affect survey research?**

   Survey research is based on the concept that a carefully drawn sample will allow a researcher to assess the characteristics of a universe within a given margin of error. To be an accurate reflection of a universe, a sample must be representative of the universe. Even a perfectly drawn sample is worthless if survey questions are confusing or biased. Question sequencing can influence survey results. People will sometimes profess to hold an opinion even when they do not just to keep from appearing uninformed. Sometimes the race or gender of the interviewer affects survey responses. Finally, even at its best, a survey is a snapshot of opinion on the day it is taken.

3. **How well informed and interested are Americans in politics and government?**

   Political knowledge and interest in politics have both increased over the last decade. Men, Republicans, and older Americans are generally more knowledgeable than women, Democrats, and young people. Knowledgeable Americans are more likely to vote and more likely to cast an informed ballot than are the uninformed.

4. **Do Americans support the principles of majority rule and minority rights, both in theory and in practice?**

   Research indicates that Americans overwhelmingly support democratic principles in the abstract, but show considerably less support when presented with concrete situations. Scholars identify a number of factors behind the persistence of democracy in America, including the phenomenon of political elites showing greater support for democratic principles in concrete situations than do Americans as a whole.

5. **What does research on political trust indicate about public support for the American political system?**

   Political scientists believe that trust is essential to political legitimacy in a democracy. Although data indicate declining trust in recent years, many scholars discount the data as more a measure of support for the current government rather than support for the political system.

6. What does research on political efficacy indicate about the confidence people have that they can affect public policy?

Political efficacy is the extent to which individuals believe they can influence the policymaking process. Internal political efficacy is the assessment by an individual of his or her personal ability to influence the policymaking process. External political efficacy refers to an individual's assessment of the responsiveness of government to his or her concerns. Scholars believe that the latter is associated with political participation.

7. Are Americans liberal or conservative?

Liberalism is the political philosophy that favors the use of government power to foster the development of the individual and promote the welfare of society. In contrast, conservatism is the political philosophy that government power undermines the development of the individual and diminishes society as a whole. More Americans self-identify as conservatives than as liberals. Nonetheless, political scientists caution about putting too much stock into self-appraisals of political philosophy because many Americans are unable to accurately define the terms *liberal* and *conservative*. Furthermore, relatively few Americans are consistently liberal or conservative on the full range of political issues. Surveys show that political attitudes vary among individuals according to such factors as social class, race, and gender. African Americans and Latinos are more liberal than whites on economic issues, for example, but more conservative on social issues, such as gay marriage.

8. To what extent does public opinion influence public policy?

Political scientist James A. Stimson discusses the impact of public opinion on the decision-making calculus of public officials by introducing the concept of a zone of acquiescence, which is the range of policy options acceptable to the public on a particular issue. Stimson says that some policy options are too liberal to be acceptable to a majority of the public, whereas other options are too conservative. Rational policymakers choose policy options within the zone of acquiescence; otherwise, they risk electoral defeat.

KEY TERMS

affirmative action programs
agents of socialization
biased question
biased sample
civil liberties
conservatism
constituency
constituents
external political efficacy
gender gap
global warming
internal political efficacy
left wing
liberalism
margin of error (or sample error)
political efficacy
political elites
political left
political legitimacy
political right
political socialization
random sample
religious left
religious right
right wing
sample
survey research
universe
zone of acquiescence

NOTES

1. Lydia Saad, "U.S. Abortion Attitudes Closely Divided," August 4, 2009, available at www.gallup.com.
2. "Abortion," at www.gallup.com.
3. Fred I. Greenstein, *Children and Politics* (New Haven, CT: Yale University Press, 1956).
4. David O. Sears and Nicholas A. Valentino, "Politics Matters: Political Events as Catalysts for Pre-adult Socialization," *American Political Science Review* 91 (March 1997): 45–65.
5. M. Kent Jennings, "Political Knowledge over Time and Across Generations," *Public Opinion Quarterly* 60 (Summer 1996): 228–252.
6. Eric Plutzer, "Becoming a Habitual Voter: Inertia, Resources, and Growth in Young Adulthood," *American Political Science Review* 96 (March 2002): 54.
7. Richard G. Niemi and Jane Junn, *Civic Education: What Makes Students Learn* (New Haven, CT: Yale University Press, 1998), p. 148.
8. Hugh McIntosh, Daniel Hart, and James Youniss, "The Influence of Family Political Discussion on Youth Civic Development: Which Parent Qualities Matter?" *PS: Political Science & Politics* 40 (July 2007): 495–499.
9. Cynthia Gordon, "Al Gore's Our Guy: Linguistically Constructing a Family Political Identity," *Discourse and Society* 15 (2004): 607–631.
10. M. Kent Jennings, Laura Stoker, and Jake Bowers, "Politics Across Generations: Family Transmission Reexamined," *Journal of Politics* 71 (April 2009): 782–799.
11. Niemi and Junn, *Civic Education*, p. 148.
12. Edward Metz and James Youniss, "A Demonstration That School-Based Required Service Does Not Deter—But Heightens—Volunteerism," *PS: Political Science & Politics* 36 (April 2003): 281–286.
13. Andolina, Jenkins, Zukin, and Keeter, "Habits from Home, Lessons from School: Influences on Youth Civic Engagement," pp. 278–279.
14. Edgar Lott, "Civic Education, Community Norms, and Political Indoctrination," *American Sociological Review* 28 (February 1963): 69–75.
15. Kenneth P. Langton, *Political Socialization* (New York: Oxford University Press, 1969), p. 116.
16. Steve Crabtree, "Religiosity Highest in World's Poorest Nations," August 31, 2010, available at www.gallup.com.
17. Paul R. Abrahamson, John H. Aldrich, and David W. Rohde, *Change and Continuity in the 2008 Elections* (Washington, DC: CQ Press, 2010), p. 97.
18. Frederick C. Harris, "Something Within: Religion as a Mobilizer of African American-Political Activism," *Journal of Politics* 56 (February 1994): 42–68.
19. Kenneth D. Wald, Dennis E. Owen, and Samuel S. Hill, Jr., "Churches as Political Communities," *American Political Science Review* 82 (June 1988): 531–548.
20. Kenneth D. Wald, Dennis E. Owen, and Samuel S. Hill, Jr., "Political Cohesion in Churches," *Journal of Politics* 52 (February 1990): 197–215.
21. Lymari Morales, "Knowing Someone Gay/Lesbian Affects Views of Gay Issues," May 29, 2009, available at www.gallup.com.
22. Paul Allen Beck, Russell J. Dalton, Steven Greene, and Robert Huckfeldt, "The Social Calculus of Voting: Interpersonal, Media, and Organizational Influences on Presidential Choices," *American Political Science Review* 96 (March 2002): 57–73.
23. Herbert P. Hyman, *Political Socialization* (Glencoe, IL: Free Press, 1959), pp. 109–115.
24. Clyde Wilcox, "Feminism and Anti-Feminism Among Evangelical Women," *Western Political Quarterly* 42 (March 1989): 147–160.
25. Doris A. Graber, *Mass Media and American Politics*, 7th ed. (Washington, DC: CQ Press, 2006), p. 4.
26. Ibid., p. 185.
27. Shanto Iyengar and Donald R. Kinder, *News That Matters: Television and American Opinion* (Chicago, IL: University of Chicago Press, 1987), pp. 112–113.
28. Jon A. Krosnick and Donald R. Kinder, "Altering the Foundations of Support for the President Through Priming," *American Political Science Review* 84 (June 1990): 497–512.
29. John R. Alford, Carolyn L. Funk, and John R. Hibbing, "Are Political Orientations Genetically Transmitted?" *American Political Science Review* 99 (May 2005): 153–167.
30. Jeffrey M. Stonecash, *Political Polling: Strategic Information in Campaigns* (Lanham, MD: Rowman & Littlefield, 2003), pp. 141–143.
31. Richard Morin, "Look Who's Talking," *Washington Post National Weekly Edition*, July 19–25, 1993, p. 37.
32. Richard Morin, "The Jokers Stacking the Deck," *Washington Post Nation Weekly Edition*, August 17, 1998, p. 42.
33. Megan Thee, "Cellphones Challenge Poll Sampling," *New York Times*, December 7, 2007, available at www.nytimes.com.
34. Herbert Asher, *Polling and the Public: What Every Citizen Should Know*, 6th ed. (Washington, DC: CQ Press, 2004), pp. 82–86.
35. Samantha Luks and Michael Salamone, "Abortion," in Nathaniel Persily, Jack Citrin, and Patrick J. Egan, eds., *Public Opinion and Constitutional Controversy* (New York: Oxford University Press, 2008), pp. 87–88.
36. Asher, *Polling and the Public*, p. 61.
37. Richard Morin, "What Informed Public Opinion?" *Washington Post National Weekly Edition*, April 10–16, 1995, p. 36.
38. Robert M. Worcester and Kully Kaur-Ballagan, "Who's Asking?" *Public Perspective*, May/June 2002, pp. 42–43.

39. Howard Schuman and Jean Converse, "The Effects of Black and White Interviewers on Black Response in 1968," *Public Opinion Quarterly* 35 (Spring 1971): 44–68; and Shirley Hatchett and Howard Schuman, "White Respondents and Race of Interviewer Effects," *Public Opinion Quarterly* 39 (Winter 1975): 523–528.
40. Asher, *Polling and the Public*, p. 96.
41. *Gallup Poll Monthly*, July 1992, pp. 8–9.
42. George H. Gallup, Jr., "How Many Americans Know U.S. History? Part I," October 21, 2003, available at www.gallup.com.
43. Lydia Saad, "More Americans Plugged into Political News," September 28, 2009, available at www.gallup.com.
44. Scott Keeter and Robert Suls, "Political Knowledge Update," Pew Research Center for the People & the Press, September 24, 2007, available at http://pewresearch.org.
45. Saad, "More Americans Plugged into Political News;" Keeter and Suls, "Political Knowledge Update."
46. Richard Morin, "Tuned Out, Turned Off," *Washington Post National Weekly Edition*, 5-11 February 1996, p. 7.
47. Samuel A. Stouffer, *Communism, Conformity, and Civil Liberties: A Cross Section of the Nation Speaks Its Mind* (Garden City, NY: Doubleday, 1955), pp. 28–42.
48. James W. Prothro and C. W. Grigg, "Fundamental Principles of Democracy: Bases of Agreement and Disagreement," *Journal of Politics* 22 (Spring 1960): 276–294.
49. Robert Chandler, *Public Opinion: Changing Attitudes on Contemporary Social and Political Issues*, A CBS News Reference Book (New York: R. R. Bowker, 1972), pp. 6–13.
50. Clyde Z. Nunn, Harry J. Crockett, Jr., and J. Allen Williams, Jr., *Tolerance for Nonconformity: A National Survey of Americans' Changing Commitment to Civil Liberties* (San Francisco, CA: Jossey-Bass, 1978); James A. Davis, "Communism, Conformity, Cohorts, and Categories: American Tolerance in 1954 and 1972–73," *American Journal of Sociology* 81 (November 1975): 491–513.
51. Council of American-Islamic Relations, "American Public Opinion Toward Islam and Muslims," 2006, available at www.cair.com.
52. Jeffrey J. Mondak and Mitchell S. Sanders, "Tolerance and Intolerance, 1976–1998," *American Journal of Political Science* 47 (July 2003): 492–502.
53. James L. Gibson, "Intolerance and Political Repression in the United States: A Half Century After McCarthyism," *American Journal of Political Science* 52 (January 2008), p. 105.
54. John Mueller, "Trends in Political Tolerance," *Public Opinion Quarterly* 52 (Spring 1988): 19.
55. Donald Philip Green and Lisa Michele Waxman, "Direct Threat and Political Tolerance," *Public Opinion Quarterly* 51 (Summer 1987): 149–165.
56. James L. Gibson, "Enigmas of Intolerance: Fifty Years After Stouffer's *Communism, Conformity, and Civil Liberties*," *Perspectives on Politics* 4 (March 2006): 21–34.
57. Dennis Chong, "How People Think, Reason, and Feel About Rights and Liberties," *American Journal of Political Science* 37 (August 1993): 867–899.
58. "The ANES Guide to Public Opinion and Electoral Behavior," available at www.electionstudies.org.
59. Pew Research Center for the People & the Press, "Public Trust in Government: 1958–2010," available at http://people-press.org.
60. Pew Research Center for the People & the Press, "Distrust, Discontent, Anger and Partisan Rancor," April 11, 2010, available at http://people-press.org.
61. "The ANES Guide to Public Opinion and Electoral Behavior," available at www.electionstudies.org.
62. Ibid.
63. Ruy A. Teixeira, *Why Americans Don't Vote: Turnout Decline in the United States 1960–1984* (New York: Greenwood Press, 1987), p. 78.
64. Lydia Saad, "In 2010, Conservatives Still Outnumber Moderates, Liberals," June 25, 2010, available at www.gallup.com.
65. Lydia Saad, "Special Report: Ideologically, Where Is the U.S. Moving," July 6, 2009, available at www.gallup.com.
66. Pew Research Center for the People & the Press, "Public Takes Conservative Turn on Gun Control, Abortion," available at http:/pewresearch.org.
67. Martin Gilens, "Preference Gaps and Inequality in Representation," *PS: Political Science & Politics* 42 (April 2009): 335–351.
68. Scott B. Blinder, "Dissonance Persists: Reproduction of Racial Attitudes Among Post-Civil Rights Cohorts of White Americans," *American Politics Research* 35 (May 2007): 299–335.
69. Frank Newport, "Little 'Obama Effect' on Views About Race Relations," October 29, 2009, available at www.gallup.com.
70. Frank Newport, "Blacks as Conservative as Republicans on Some Moral Issues," December 3, 2008, available at www.gallup.com.
71. Caryle Murphy and Alan Cooperman, "Seeking to Reclaim the Moral High Ground," *Washington Post National Weekly Edition*, May 29–June 4, 2006, p. 12.
72. Judy C. Baumgartner, Peter L. Francia, and Jonathan S. Morris, "A Clash of Civilizations: The Influence of Religion on Public Opinion of U.S. Foreign Policy in the Middle East," *Political Research Quarterly* 61 (June 2008): 171–179.
73. James L. Guth, John C. Green, Corwin E. Smith, and Margaret M. Poloma, "Pulpits and Politics: The Protestant Clergy in the 1988 Presidential Election," in Guth and Green, eds., *The Bible and the Ballot Box* (Boulder, CO: Westview Press, 1991), pp. 73–93.
74. Frank Newport and Lydia Saad, "Religion, Politics Inform Americans' Views on Abortion," April 3, 2006, available at www.gallup.com.

75. John C. Green and E. J. Dionne, Jr., "Religion and American Politics: More Secular, More Evangelical, or Both?" in Ruy Texiera, ed., *Red, Blue, and Purple America: The Future of Election Demographics* (Washington, DC: Brookings Institution Press, 2008), p. 206.
76. Frank Newport, "Religious Intensity Remains Powerful Predictor of Politics," December 11, 2009, available at www.gallup.com.
77. Lydia Saad, "'Conservatives' Are Single-Largest Ideological Group," June 15, 2009, available at www.gallup.com.
78. Amy Goldstein and Richard Morin, "The Squeaky Wheel Gets the Grease," *Washington Post National Weekly Edition*, October 28–November 3, 2002, p. 34.
79. Timur Kuran and Edward J. McCaffery, "Sex Differences in the Acceptability of Discrimination," *Political Research Quarterly* 61 (July 2008): 228–238.
80. Laurel Elder and Steven Greene, "The Myth of 'Security Moms' and 'Nascar Dads,' Parenthood, Political Stereotypes, and the 2004 Election," *Social Science Quarterly* 88 (March 2007), p. 11.
81. V. O. Key, Jr., *Public Opinion and American Democracy* (New York: Alfred Knopf, 1961), p. 499.
82. James A. Stimson, *Public Opinion in America: Moods, Cycles, and Swings* (Boulder, CO: Westview Press, 1991), pp. 19–21.
83. Kenneth D. Wald, James W. Button, and Barbara A. Rienzo, "The Politics of Gay Rights in American Communities: Explaining Antidiscrimination Ordinances and Policies," *American Journal of Political Science* 40 (November 1996): 1152–1178.

Chapter 5

Political Participation

CHAPTER OUTLINE

Forms of Participation

Explaining Participation
- Personal Resources
- Psychological Engagement
- Voter Mobilization
- Community Involvement

Trends in Voter Turnout

Participation Rates in Comparative Perspective

Patterns of Participation
- Income
- Age
- Race/Ethnicity
- Gender

Participation Bias

Increasing Voter Turnout

What We Have Learned

WHAT WE WILL LEARN

After studying Chapter 5, students should be able to answer the following questions:

1. What methods do individuals use to participate in the policy process and why are some methods used more frequently than others?
2. What are the most important factors influencing individual participation in the policy process?
3. How and why has voter turnout in presidential elections changed in recent elections?
4. How do voter participation rates in the United States compare and contrast with those in other democracies, and how do political scientists account for the differences?
5. What is the relationship between participation and the following factors: income, age, race/ethnicity, and gender?
6. How do the political and policy preferences of those people who participate compare and contrast with the preferences of adult Americans in general?
7. What are some of the proposed reforms aimed at increasing voter turnout and what is the likelihood of their effectiveness?

Tea Party movement A loose network of conservative activists organized to protest high taxes, excessive government spending, and big government in general.

The **Tea Party movement** is a loose network of conservative activists organized to protest high taxes, excessive government spending, and big government in general. The activists take their inspiration from the Boston Tea Party of 1773 when American colonists protested the British tax on tea by dumping three shiploads of tea into Boston Harbor. TEA is also an acronym for "taxed enough already." Tea Party activists have held rallies and organized demonstrations to oppose government bailouts, economic stimulus spending, deficit spending, environmental regulations, and healthcare reform. They became a significant political force during the 2010 election, backing conservative challengers against establishment-supported candidates in Republican primary elections. In the November general election, the energy of the Tea Party movement increased the turnout of conservative voters, helping the Republican Party capture a majority of seats in the U.S. House, reduce the size of the Democratic majority in the U.S. Senate, and win hundreds of seats in state legislatures around the nation.

The Tea Party movement is an example of a grassroots political organization because it is driven by community activists rather than national organizers. Although Freedom Works, a conservative advocacy group led by former Texas congressman Richard Armey, has provided some organizational support, the Tea Party movement has no professional staff, no official agenda, and no identifiable national leaders. Most of the organization's energy has come from local activists organized into hundreds of local groups who communicate with one another online, by e-mail, Twitter, and Facebook.[1]

Tea Party activism introduces this chapter on political participation. The chapter discusses voting and other forms of political participation in the United States. It examines why people participate and looks at patterns of participation. The chapter identifies recent trends in voter participation and compares turnout in the United States with participation rates in other democracies. It evaluates proposals for increasing participation and compares the policy perspectives of voters and nonvoters.

Forms of Participation

Political participation An activity that has the intent or effect of influencing government action.

Political participation is an activity that has the intent or effect of influencing government action. Voting is the most common form of political participation. Substantially more Americans tell survey researchers that they vote than claim to participate through any other type of political activity. More than three-fourths of the respondents to the American National Election Survey report casting ballots for president. (*Reported* turnout typically exceeds *actual* turnout because people do not want to admit to an interviewer that they neglected to vote.) In contrast, 48 percent said that they tried to influence people how to vote, 21 percent indicated that they wore political buttons or put bumper stickers on their cars, 13 percent contributed money to candidates or a party, 7 percent attended a political meeting, and 3 percent worked for a candidate or a party.[2]

Voting is the most common form of political participation.

Election turnout is closely related to the level of interest in a particular contest. Presidential races typically attract more voters on a percentage basis than other types of elections because of their high-profile nature. In contrast, voter turnout for congressional elections held in nonpresidential (midterm) election years rarely exceeds 40 percent of the voting eligible population. The voter participation rate in the 2010 midterm election was 42 percent. Even though that was the highest midterm election turnout since 1970, the figure was substantially less than the turnout in the presidential election years of 2004 and 2008, which exceeded 60 percent of eligible adults.[3]

People participate in election contests in ways other than voting. Individuals who want to do more for a candidate or political party than just casting a ballot take part in election campaigns. They contribute money, prepare campaign mailers, telephone potential voters, put up yard signs, and work the polls on Election Day.

Not all forms of political participation are election centered. People attempt to influence the policy process by contacting public officials. Surveys show that about one-third of Americans have contacted public officials, usually officials at the state or local level.[4] Many citizens write to their representatives in Congress, telephone state legislators, or appear in person before the local city council or school board. Sometimes people concerned about a particular issue or policy gather signatures on a petition to present to government officials.

Many Americans discuss government policies and politics on a regular basis. Two-thirds of a national sample report having informal conversations about politics at least several times a month. A fourth said that they had attended a formal or informal meeting in the past year to discuss a local, national, or international issue.

A similar number reported sending e-mail about policy issues several times a month or more.[5]

Americans also try to influence the policy process by joining or supporting interest groups. People interested in the reform of laws dealing with drunk driving join Mothers Against Drunk Driving (MADD) or Students Against Drunk Driving (SADD). Individuals concerned with animal rights contribute money to groups such as the American Society for the Prevention of Cruelty to Animals (ASPCA) or People for the Ethical Treatment of Animals (PETA). Opponents of gun control laws join the National Rifle Association (NRA).

Some Americans participate through unconventional political acts, such as protest demonstrations, sit-ins, or violence. Political movements, such as the Tea Party movement, often engage in protest demonstrations because they lack the organization to employ the political tactics typically associated with interest groups or political parties. A **political movement** is a group of people that wants to convince other citizens and/or government officials to take action on issues that are important to the group. Some individuals and groups resort to violence to further their political cause, including bombing federal buildings and shooting physicians who perform abortions.

Political movement A group of people that wants to convince other citizens and/or government officials to take action on issues that are important to the group.

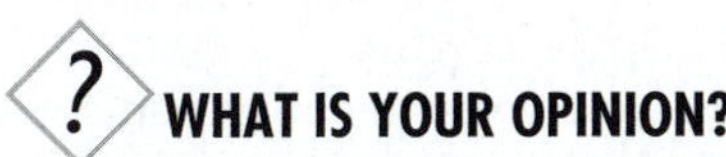

Is political violence ever justified?

Explaining Participation

The most important factors influencing individual participation are personal resources, psychological engagement, voter mobilization, and community involvement.[6]

Personal Resources

The personal resources most closely associated with political participation are time, money, and civic skills, such as communication skills and organizational ability. Each form of political activity requires a different configuration of resources. Some political activities take time; others require money; still others demand civic skills. People who want to contribute money to candidates and political parties must have financial resources. Individuals who work in campaigns or participate in political groups and activities must have both time and civic skills.[7] Participation rates are higher for activities that require relatively little time, few skills, and little or no expense. Voting is the most common form of political participation because it requires a relatively small amount of time and no expense. In contrast, relatively few people work in political campaigns or give money to candidates because those activities require significant amounts of time, civic skills, and money.

Psychological Engagement

People take part in the policymaking process when they are knowledgeable, interested, and have a strong sense of political efficacy. People participate in political campaigns for candidates and parties in whom they are interested, contact public officials over issues about which they are knowledgeable, and join political groups whose causes they support. Individuals who believe that a particular government policy affects their personal welfare are more likely to participate politically than would otherwise be expected. For example, lower-income Social Security recipients are more likely to participate on that issue than are upper-income recipients, probably because they are more dependent financially on their Social Security checks than are wealthier beneficiaries.[8] In contrast, people who are uninformed or disinterested in politics are usually uninvolved. Participation also depends on a sense of **political efficacy,** which is the extent to which individuals believe that they can influence the policymaking process. People are more likely to participate when they have confidence in their ability to affect the policy process and believe that policymakers are willing to accept their input.[9]

Political efficacy The extent to which individuals believe they can influence the policymaking process.

Voter Mobilization

Voter mobilization The process of motivating citizens to vote.

Political participation depends on **voter mobilization,** which is the process of motivating citizens to vote. Although some people are self-starters, the likelihood that individuals will vote, participate in an election campaign, join a political group, or engage in some other form of political participation increases if those individuals

Political demonstrations, such as this Tea Party protest, are a form of political participation.

are asked to participate.[10] The turnout of young voters, people age 18–29, increased from 16 million in 2000 to 20 million in 2004 to 23 million in 2008 primarily because organizations such as Rock the Vote and the New Voters Project worked to register young voters and get them to the polls.[11] Door-to-door and live telephone contacts (as opposed to recorded messages) increase the likelihood that individuals will go to the polls, especially if the contacts take place near Election Day.[12]

Community Involvement

Finally, people participate politically because of their involvement in the community. Individuals who have close community ties, such as home ownership and membership in community organizations, are more likely to participate than people without community ties. They regard voting and other forms of political participation as their civic duty because they can see the connection between participation and the quality of life in their community.[13]

Trends in Voter Turnout

Voting eligible population (VEP) The number of U.S. residents who are legally qualified to vote.

Voting age population (VAP) The number of U.S. residents who are 18 years of age or older.

Political scientists who study election participation measure voter turnout relative to the size of the **voting eligible population (VEP),** which is the number of U.S. residents who are legally qualified to vote. The VEP differs from the **voting age population (VAP),** which is the number of U.S. residents who are 18 years of age or older, because it excludes individuals who are ineligible to cast a ballot. In contrast to the VAP, the VEP does not include noncitizens, convicted criminals (depending on state law), and people who are mentally incapacitated.[14]

Figure 5.1 charts changes in presidential election turnout relative to the size of the VEP from 1964 through the 2008 election. More than 62 percent of the VEP cast ballots in the 1964 presidential election, capping a steady 36-year rise in voter turnout in the United States. For the next 30 years, voter participation rates generally fell, reaching a 70-year low in 1996 at 51.7 percent of the VEP. Election turnout subsequently rebounded, increasing to 54.2 percent in 2000, 60.3 percent in 2004, and 61.6 percent in 2008.

Recent presidential elections suggest that the United States is experiencing a voting revival. After years of declining or flat electoral participation rates, voter turnout has surged to a level not seen in nearly 40 years. The increase is the result of massive voter mobilization efforts coupled with high public interest in recent elections. The two major political parties, supported by their interest group allies, organized sophisticated get-out-the-vote (GOTV) campaigns in 2004 and 2008. Campaign volunteers and paid organizers have telephoned, mailed, e-mailed, or visited millions of potential voters, encouraging them to go to the polls. Exposure to intense campaign activity increases political engagement, especially among low-income voters, a group with typically low voter turnout rates.[15] In the meantime, hot-button issues such as wars in Iraq and Afghanistan, gay marriage, healthcare reform, taxes, and the economy have energized citizens to go to the polls. The percentage of Americans

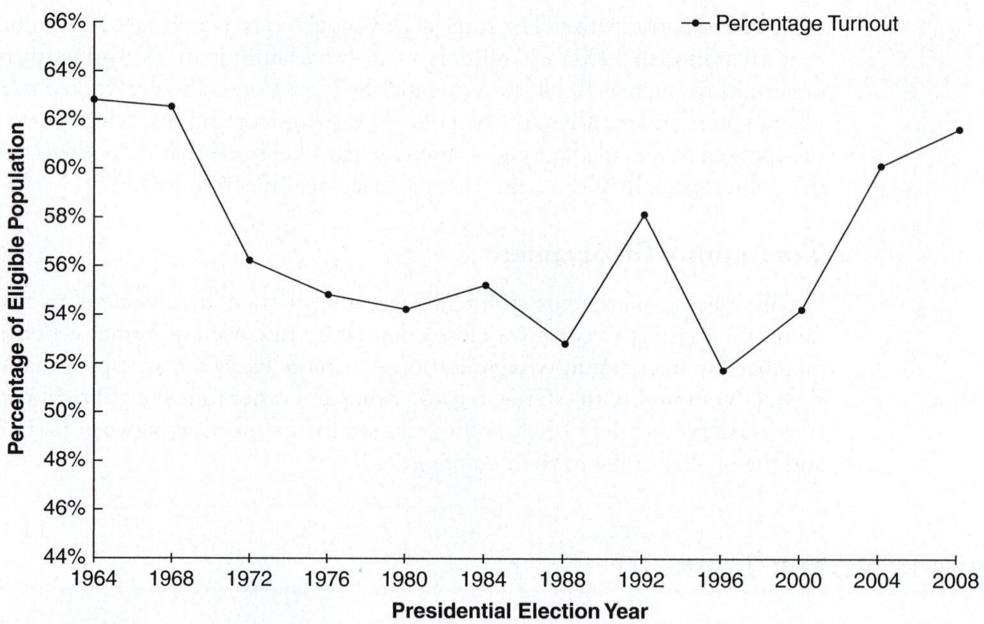

FIGURE 5.1 Voter Turnout 1964–2008.
Source: Vital Statistics in American Politics 2007–2008; Michael P. McDonald, U.S. Election Project.

who told survey researchers that they closely follow national political news increased from 26 percent in 2000 to 43 percent in 2008.[16] People who are psychologically engaged are more likely to vote than people who are not.

Participation Rates in Comparative Perspective

Voter turnout in the United States is relatively low compared with other established democracies. Table 5.1 displays the turnout rates in 21 selected democracies for their most recent national elections. As the table indicates, turnout ranges from a high of 95.2 percent in Australia to a low of 57.8 percent in India. The United States ranks eighteenth among the 21 countries in election turnout.

Political scientists identify three factors as primarily responsible for the United States having a lower voter turnout rate than most other established democracies. First, American election procedures are more cumbersome than they are in other countries. In most democracies, citizens are registered to vote automatically, but not in the United States. Before Americans can cast a ballot in most states, they must register to vote, usually no later than 30 days before an election. According to the U.S. Census Bureau, 29 percent of American citizens are not registered to vote.[17] American elections traditionally take place on Tuesday, whereas other countries declare a national holiday so citizens can vote without missing work or school. Moreover, the United States has more elections and more frequent elections than

TABLE 5.1 Voter Turnout in Comparison, Selected Democracies, Most Recent National Election

Country	Most RecentNational Election	Turnout
Australia	2007	95.2%
Belgium	2007	91.1
Denmark	2007	86.6
Iceland	2007	83.6
Austria	2008	81.2
Italy	2008	80.5
Netherlands	2006	80.4
Germany	2005	77.7
Norway	2005	77.4
Spain	2008	75.3
Greece	2007	74.1
Japan	2005	67.5
Ireland	2007	67.0
United Kingdom	2010	65.1
Finland	2007	65.0
Israel	2009	64.7
Portugal	2005	64.3
United States	2008	61.6
France	2007	60.4
Canada	2008	59.5
India	2004	57.8

Source: Institute for Democracy and Electoral Assistance, available at www.idea.int.

any other democracy. Many Americans, suffering from voter fatigue, stay home, especially for low-profile election contests in non-presidential election years.[18]

WHAT IS YOUR OPINION?

Should the United States reform its voting procedures to make it easier and more convenient for citizens to cast their ballots?

Second, voter participation rates in the United States are relatively low because the nation's political parties are relatively weak. Strong political parties enhance voter turnout by educating citizens about candidates and issues, stimulating interest in election outcomes, and mobilizing citizens to go to the polls. They recruit voters. Political scientist G. Bingham Powell, Jr., estimates that if American political parties were more centralized and had stronger ties to other social organizations, such as labor unions, religious bodies, and ethnic groups, then voter participation would rise by as much as 10 percent.[19] Labor unions in particular have an effect on voter turnout of low- and middle-income people.[20]

Finally, many citizens in the United States stay home from the polls because they do not perceive that elections have much effect on policy. The candidates who

Voter turnout surged in the 2004 and 2008 presidential elections.

Separation of powers The division of political power among executive, legislative, and judicial branches of government.

win elections may not be able to deliver on their promises because of **separation of powers,** which is the division of political authority among executive, legislative, and judicial branches of government. During the 2006 election campaign, Democratic congressional candidates called for the withdrawal of American combat forces from Iraq. Even though the Democratic Party captured majorities in both the House and Senate, it could not keep its promise, either because proposals to bring home the troops failed to pass both chambers of Congress or because President George W. Bush vetoed them.

Patterns of Participation

Participation rates vary among individuals based on such factors as income, age, race/ethnicity, and gender.

Income

Affluence and activity go together for every form of political participation. The higher the family income, the more likely a person will vote. According to the U.S. Census Bureau, the reported rate of voter turnout in 2008 for people in families earning more than $100,000 a year was 80 percent compared with a turnout rate for people with family incomes less than $30,000 of 54 percent.[21] The participation gap between high- and low-income groups is less for voting than it is for other types of participation, especially giving money to candidates and parties. A majority of citizens with incomes of $75,000 or more report making campaign contributions compared with only 6 percent of Americans with incomes under $15,000. In addition, 95 percent of major donors earn more than $100,000 a year.[22] People who are well-off financially are also more likely than low-income people to join organizations, contact public officials, and engage in political protests.[23]

Participation rates and income are associated because resources and psychological attachment rise with income. Obviously, people in higher income groups have more money to contribute to political causes. Because income and education are closely related, more affluent citizens are better informed about government and politics than are less wealthy individuals. They have better communication and organizational skills. Wealthy citizens are also more likely to have a relatively high level of political efficacy than less affluent people.

Compulsory voting The legal requirement that citizens participate in national elections.

Around the World — Compulsory Voting in Australia

Compulsory voting, which is the legal requirement that citizens participate in national elections, is a low-cost, efficient remedy to the problem of low turnout. Voter participation rates are almost 20 percent higher in nations with compulsory voting than they are in other democracies.* Almost everyone votes in Australia, a nation that has had compulsory voting since 1924. For example, voter turnout was 95 percent in the 2007 national election.†

The Australian Election Commission (AEC) enforces the nation's compulsory voting law. The AEC sends a "please explain" letter to people who fail to vote in a particular election. Election no-shows can either pay a fine or offer an explanation. If the AEC decides that the explanation is valid, it can waive the fine. The courts settle disputes between the AEC and individual nonvoters over the validity of excuses. The proportion of Australians fined for failing to vote never exceeds 1 percent of the electorate.‡

Political scientists believe that compulsory voting strengthens political parties in general and working class parties in particular. Because parties do not have to devote their resources to turning out the vote, they can focus on persuasion and conversion. Compulsory voting builds party loyalty among citizens who must regularly choose among party candidates. Survey research in Australia finds that most Australian voters express firm and longstanding commitments to a party. Compulsory voting also benefits political parties representing the working class relative to parties that reflect the interests of middle- and upper-income voters because lower-income people are less likely to vote than middle-income citizens.

QUESTIONS

1. Is nonvoting such an important problem that it needs a legal remedy?
2. Would you resent or appreciate a compulsory voting law that forced you to cast a ballot or face a fine?
3. Do you think that the United States will ever adopt compulsory voting? Why or why not?

* Mark N. Franklin, "Electoral Engineering and Cross-National Turnout Differences: What Role of Compulsory Voting?" *British Journal of Political Science* 29 (January 1999): 205.

† International Institute for Democracy and Electoral Assistance, "Voter Turnout," available at www.idea.int/vt/.

‡ M. Mackerras and I. McAllister, "Compulsory Voting, Party Stability, and Electoral Advantage in Australia," *Electoral Studies* 18 (June 1999): 217–233.

Age

Figure 5.2 graphs reported voter participation rates by age group in the 2008 presidential election. As the figure indicates, voter turnout is lowest for the youngest group. Younger adults have fewer resources and are less interested in the policy process than older adults. As adults mature, their incomes increase and their skills develop. Older adults establish roots in their communities that increase their interest and awareness of the political process. Consequently, participation increases with each successive age group, with the peak voting years coming between 65 and 74 years of age. After age 75, voter participation begins to decline because illness and infirmity force the elderly to reduce their involvement in the policy process.

Race/Ethnicity

Participation varies among racial and ethnic groups. Voter turnout is higher for whites and African Americans; lower for Latinos and Asian Americans. The voter turnout in 2008 was 66 percent of eligible voters for whites, 65 percent for African Americans, 50 percent for Latinos, and 48 percent for Asian Americans.[24] Although the overall voter turnout in 2008 was up only slightly from 2004, minority voter turnout increased substantially, especially African American turnout. Whereas the number of whites who voted in 2008 was roughly the same as it was in 2004, two million more African Americans, two million more Latinos, and 600,000 more Asian Americans participated in the 2008 election than took part in 2004. The historic

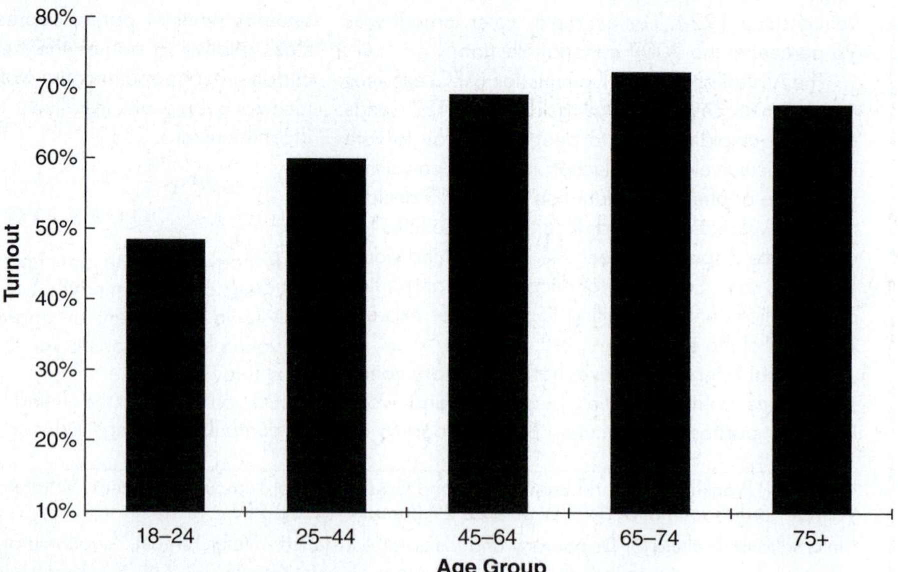

FIGURE 5.2 Voter Turnout by Age Group, 2008.
Source: U.S. Census Bureau.

candidacy of Barack Obama not only drew record numbers of African Americans to the polls but increased minority voter turnout in general.[25]

Many members of racial/ethnic minority groups are ineligible to vote either because they are not citizens or they are disqualified by criminal convictions. Only 8 percent of whites who were 18 years of age or older were unable to register and vote in 2008 because they were not citizens. The percentage of noncitizens among African Americans was 6 percent, compared with 33 percent for Asian Americans and 37 percent for Latinos.[26] Meanwhile, 5.3 million Americans are disqualified from voting because they are incarcerated or have prior criminal convictions. Eleven states permanently disfranchise individuals convicted of serious crimes. The policy of denying voting rights to criminal offenders disproportionately affects minority Americans, particularly African American males, 14 percent of whom are disfranchised because of criminal convictions.[27]

Racial/ethnic patterns of participation also reflect the importance of recruitment to political participation. We would expect that participation rates for African American and Latino citizens would be lower than participation rates for whites because of income and age differences. As a group, minority citizens are less affluent and younger than whites. Nonetheless, participation rates for African Americans exceed expectations because of the effectiveness of organizations in the African American community, such as churches and political groups, at mobilizing voters. Latino voter turnout, meanwhile, increases when Latino candidates are on the ballot.[28]

Minority voter turnout surged in 2008 because of the historic candidacy of Barack Obama.

Gender

Women are more likely to vote than men, but men are more likely than women to engage in many other forms of participation. In 2008, 66 percent of women who were eligible to vote reported that they cast ballots compared with 62 percent of eligible men.[29] Women are just as likely as men to participate in election campaigns, but they are less likely to contribute money to political campaigns, contact public officials, and join political organizations.[30]

These data reflect differences in resources and psychological engagement between men and women. Women have lower average incomes than do men. Income is closely associated with participation, especially forms of participation other than voting. Furthermore, surveys indicate that men are more informed about and interested in politics and government than women are, even when they have the same level of education.[31]

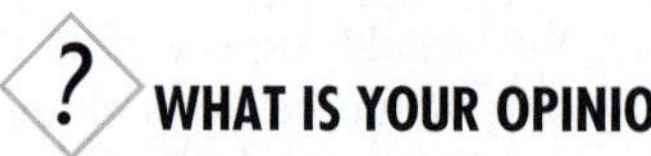

Does it really matter that Americans do not vote?

Participation Bias

Is participation biased in favor of some groups and against others? If everyone voted, would election outcomes change? Do those people who participate in campaigns, contact public officials, give money to candidates, and join political groups have issue preferences that are similar to all citizens? In short, does political participation bias public policy toward candidates and policy preferences that are not shared by Americans as a whole?

Conventional political wisdom holds that low election turnout helps the Republicans, whereas Democrats benefit from a large turnout. Young people, the unemployed, laborers, lower-income persons, individuals with relatively little formal education, people who are not married, Latinos, and people who seldom if ever attend religious services are disproportionately represented among nonvoters. Because surveys show that these groups of people tend to vote for Democratic candidates more frequently than they support Republicans, Democrats in Congress and state legislatures often favor reforming registration laws and other voting procedures to enhance voter turnout. For the same reason, Republican officials generally oppose election law reform.

Political science research sheds some light on the relationship between turnout and election outcomes. Low turnout helps the Republican Party because the groups of voters most likely to participate in a low turnout election tend to favor Republicans. Incumbent officeholders of either party also benefit from low turnout because the core voters who participate in low turnout elections are unlikely to support major change.[32] Increased turnout, meanwhile, typically advantages the Democratic Party. Nonetheless, political scientists are skeptical that near universal voter turnout would ensure victory for the Democrats.[33] Many nonvoters are disinterested and uninformed. Although surveys show that nonvoters are somewhat more likely to support the Democrats as the party best able to solve their problems, two-thirds of nonvoters (compared with half of voters) see no difference between parties and candidates on the issues.[34] Had every eligible voter gone to the polls in the presidential elections

Voting is a two-step process: registration and the actual vote itself.

held since 1992, Democrat Al Gore would probably have won the 2000 election, which was extremely close, and Democrat John Kerry might have won in 2004, another close race. None of the other elections were close enough for increased turnout to have made a difference in the outcome.[35]

Research does, however, show a bias in political attitudes. Political activists are more conservative than the population as a whole on economic issues. Compared with the general population, people who participate in the policy process are less likely to support government spending for public services, government help for minority groups, and programs to assist the poor. Individual campaign contributors tend to be more conservative and more Republican than the electorate as a whole.[36] Furthermore, African American and Latino activists are more conservative on economic issues than African Americans and Latinos as a group. In sum, political activity underrepresents those people who favor government programs for disadvantaged groups and overrepresents those who oppose them.[37] To the extent that elected officials respond to the demands of voters, public policies will be consistent with the interests of middle- and upper-income groups rather than the working class.

Interest group and political party activities contribute to the participation bias. In the nineteenth and early twentieth centuries, the nation's most important interest groups were large membership organizations that drew people from all strata of society, rich and poor alike. These groups advocated government policies that benefited people across class lines, such as Social Security, Medicare, public schools, and programs for war veterans. Since the middle of the twentieth century, large membership organizations, such as labor unions, have declined, whereas professionally managed advocacy groups composed mainly of middle- and upper-middle-class professionals have proliferated. These groups push middle-class agendas.[38] Political parties contribute to the imbalance in participation rates as well by targeting their campaigns at people with voting histories. With rare exceptions, political campaigns focus on turning out their core supporters rather than trying to expand the electorate.[39] The Internet has widened the participation gap as well because the overwhelming majority of

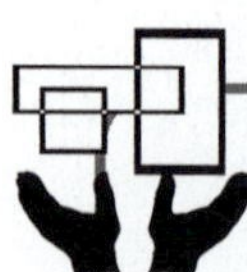

GETTING INVOLVED

Registering to Vote

Voting is a two-step process. Before Americans can vote, they must register. Registration is important because most people who register do subsequently vote. Your assignment is to learn how the voter registration process works in your state. You can obtain voter registration information from an office of county government, driver's license bureau, welfare office, and some public libraries. Complete the voter registration card and submit it to your instructor to document that you have done the assignment. This may be your opportunity to register to vote. If you are not eligible to vote (you might not yet be 18 or are not an American citizen) or are already a registered voter, write VOID or DO NOT PROCESS on the card.

political voices online have been white, upper-middle-class, highly educated professionals.[40]

Increasing Voter Turnout

Those observers who worry about low voter turnout favor the enactment of election-law reforms to enhance participation rates. The Government Accountability Office (GAO), an investigative arm of Congress, recommends the adoption of the following three election procedures: (1) Registration deadlines that fall on or close to Election Day; (2) toll-free telephone numbers to allow voters to request absentee ballots; and (3) increased use of mail balloting.[41] The state of Oregon has been using mail elections since the mid-1990s. Research indicates that mail elections have increased election participation by 10 percent.[42] Some states have also begun experimenting with Internet voting. Seven states allow same-day registration, which means that citizens can register to vote on Election Day.

National Voter Registration Act (NVRA) A federal law designed to make it easier for citizens to register to vote by requiring states to allow mail registration and provide an opportunity for people to register when applying for or renewing driver's licenses, as well as when visiting federal, state, or local agencies, such as welfare offices.

In 1993, Congress passed—and President Bill Clinton signed—the **National Voter Registration Act (NVRA),** which is also known as the Motor Voter Act. It is a federal law designed to make it easier for citizens to register to vote by requiring states to allow mail registration and provide an opportunity for people to register when applying for or renewing driver's licenses or when visiting federal, state, or local agencies, such as welfare offices. The law also prohibits states from removing names from the voter registration rolls merely for failure to vote.

Although the NVRA dramatically increased the number of people registered to vote, it did not increase voter turnout. The NVRA helped add 11.5 million people to the voter rolls between January 1995, when states were required to implement the law, and November 1996. Nonetheless, the voter turnout rate hit a 70-year low in 1996. "You may be able to spoon-feed someone and make it almost automatic to get them [sic] registered," said one election official, "but if it takes that much effort just to get them [sic] registered, how do you expect them [sic] to take the initiative to actually come out and vote?"[43]

Political science research indicates that voting has two stages: registration and the actual vote itself. The NVRA failed to increase voter turnout in 1996 because it affected only the ease with which people can register. It did not make anyone more interested in politics or better informed about candidates and issues. The NVRA did not increase political efficacy or strengthen the efforts of political parties and groups to draw citizens to the polls. Voter registration reform alone is not sufficient to increase citizen participation in the electoral process.[44]

Nonetheless, the NVRA may have set the stage for the substantial increase in voter turnout that began with the 2000 presidential election by making the job of voter mobilization easier for the political parties and their interest group allies. The NVRA increased the voter registration rates of groups that traditionally turn out in relatively low numbers, especially young people who tend to move frequently and often neglect to update their voter registration.[45] Consequently, the GOTV campaigns could focus on getting already registered people to the polls rather than having to spend valuable resources on extensive registration efforts.

WHAT WE HAVE LEARNED

1. **What methods do individuals use to participate in the policy process and why are some methods used more frequently than others?**

   Voting is the most common form of participation. People also participate in election campaigns, discuss politics and government with other people, contact public officials, join interest groups, take part in protest demonstrations, or engage in unconventional acts, sometimes including violence.

2. **What are the most important factors influencing individual participation in the policy process?**

   The most important factors influencing individual participation are personal resources, psychological engagement, voter mobilization, and community involvement. The personal resources most closely associated with political participation are time, money, and civic skills, such as communication skills and organizational ability. People take part in the policymaking process when they are knowledgeable, interested, and have a strong sense of political efficacy. Participation also depends on voter mobilization. Finally, people participate politically because of their involvement in the community.

3. **How and why has voter turnout in presidential elections changed in recent elections?**

   Political scientists who study election participation measure voter turnout relative to the size of the voting eligible population (VEP), which is the number of U.S. residents who are legally qualified to vote. Rates of voter participation fell from 1968 through the 1996 election, but they have subsequently rebounded because of sophisticated voter mobilization campaigns coupled with increased public interest.

4. **How do voter participation rates in the United States compare and contrast with those in other democracies, and how do political scientists account for the differences?**

   Voter participation rates in the United States are relatively low compared with turnout rates in many other democracies because American election procedures are relatively cumbersome, political parties and interest groups are relatively weak, and many citizens do not perceive that elections have much effect on public policy.

5. **What is the relationship between participation and the following factors: income, age, race/ethnicity, and gender?**

   Participation rates vary among individuals based on such factors as income, age, race/ethnicity, and gender. The higher the family income, the more likely a person will vote and participate in other ways. Voting participation increases with age until the latter years of life when participation declines because of ill health and infirmity. Voter participation rates are highest for whites and African Americans, but lower for Asian Americans and Latinos. Women are more likely to vote than men, but men are more likely to engage in other forms of participation.

6. **How do the political and policy preferences of those people who participate compare and contrast with the preferences of adult Americans in general?**

   Political activists are more conservative than the population as a whole on economic issues. Compared with the general population, people who participate in the policy process are less likely to support government spending for public services, government help for minority groups, and programs to assist the poor.

7. **What are some of the proposed reforms aimed at increasing voter turnout and what is the likelihood of their effectiveness?**

   Those observers who worry about low voter turnout favor the enactment of election-law reforms to enhance participation rates, including streamlined registration procedures, easy access to absentee ballots, and mail voting.

KEY TERMS

compulsory voting
National Voter Registration Act (NVRA)
political efficacy
political movement
political participation
separation of powers
Tea Party movement
voter mobilization
voting age population (VAP)
voting eligible population (VEP)

NOTES

1. Dan Eggen and Philip Rucker, "Loose Network of Activists Drives Reform Opposition," *Washington Post*, August 16, 2009, available at www.washingtonpost.com.
2. "The ANES Guide to Public Opinion and Electoral Behavior," available at www.electionstudies.org.
3. Michael P. McDonald, United States Election Project, available at http://elections.gmu.edu.
4. Sidney Verba, Kay Lehman Schlozman, and Henry E. Brady, *Voice and Equality: Civic Volunteerism in American Politics* (Cambridge, MA: Harvard University Press, 1995), p. 51.
5. Lawrence R. Jacobs, Fay Lomax Cook, and Michael X. Delli Carpini, *Talking Together: Public Deliberation and Political Participation in America* (Chicago, IL: University of Chicago Press, 2009), p. 37.
6. André Blais, *To Vote or Not to Vote?* (Pittsburgh, PA: University of Pittsburgh Press, 2000), pp. 12–13.
7. Henry E. Brady, Sidney Verba, and Kay Lehman Schlozman, "Beyond SES: A Resource Model of Political Participation," *American Political Science Review* 89 (June 1995), p. 3.
8. Andrea Louise Campbell, "Self-Interest, Social Security, and the Distinctive Participation Patterns of Senior Citizens," *American Political Science Review* 96 (September 2002): 565–574.
9. Verba, Schlozman, and Brady, *Voice and Equality: Civic Volunteerism in American Politics*, p. 354.
10. Thomas M. Holbrook and Scott D. McClurg, "The Mobilization of Core Supporters: Campaigns, Turnout, and Electoral Composition in the United States Presidential Elections," *American Journal of Political Science* 49 (October 2005): 689–703.
11. Kathleen Barr, "A Perfect Storm: The 2008 Youth Vote," in Dennis W. Johnson, ed., *Campaigning for President 2008: Strategy and Tactics, New Voices and New Techniques* (New York: Routledge, 2009), p. 106.
12. Melissa R. Michelson, Lisa García Bedolla, and Margaret A. McConnell, "Heeding the Call: The Effect of Targeted Two-Round Phone Banks on Voter Turnout," *Journal of Politics* 71 (October 2009): 1549–1563.
13. Blais, *To Vote or Not to Vote?* p. 13.
14. Michael P. McDonald, United States Election Project, available at http://elections.gmu.edu.
15. James G. Gimpel, Karen M. Kaufmann, and Shanna Pearson-Markowitz, "Battleground States Versus Blackout States: The Behavioral Implications of Modern Presidential Campaigns," *Journal of Politics* 69 (August 2007): 786–797.
16. Lydia Saad, "More Americans Plugged into Political News," September 28, 2009, available at www.gallup.com.
17. U.S. Census Bureau, "Voting and Registration in the Election of November 2008," available at www.census.gov.
18. Matthew J. Streb, *Rethinking American Democracy* (New York: Routledge, 2008), pp. 11–12.
19. G. Bingham Powell, Jr., "American Voter Turnout in Comparative Perspective," *American Political Science Review* 80 (March 1986): 17–43.
20. Jan E. Leighley and Jonathan Nagler, "Unions, Voter Turnout, and Class Bias in the U.S. Electorate, 1964–2004," *Journal of Politics* 69 (May 2007): 430–441.
21. U.S. Census Bureau, "Voting and Registration in the Election of November 2008," available at www.census.gov.
22. Campaign Finance Institute Task Force on Presidential Nomination Financing, *Participation, Competition, and Engagement: How to Revive and Improve Public Funding for Presidential Nomination Politics* (Washington, DC: Campaign Finance Institute, 2003), quoted in APSA Task Force Report, "American Democracy in an Age of Rising Inequality," *Perspectives on Politics* 2 (December 2004), p. 656.
23. APSA Task Force Report, "American Democracy in an Age of Rising Inequality," p. 656.
24. U.S. Census Bureau, "Voting and Registration in the Election of November 2008."
25. Sam Roberts, "2008 Surge in Black Voters Nearly Erased Racial Gap," *New York Times*, July 21, 2009, available at www.nytimes.com.
26. U.S. Census Bureau, "Voting and Registration in the Election of November 2008."
27. Jeff Manza and Christopher Uggen, *Locked Out: Felon Disenfranchisement and American Democracy* (New York: Oxford University Press, 2006), pp. 76–80.
28. Matt A. Barreto, "¡Sí Se Puede! Latino Candidates and the Mobilization of Latino Voters," *American Political Science Review* 101 (August 2007): 425–441.

29. U.S. Census Bureau, "Voting and Registration in the Election of November 2008."
30. Verba, Schlozman, and Brady, *Voice and Equality: Civic Volunteerism in American Politics*, p. 255.
31. Richard Morin, "Tuned Out, Turned Off," *Washington Post National Weekly Edition*, February 5–11, 1996, p. 6.
32. Thomas G. Hansford and Brad T. Gomez, "Estimating the Electoral Effects of Voter Turnout," *American Political Science Review* 104 (May 2010): 268–288.
33. Jack H. Nagel and John E. McNulty, "Partisan Effects of Voter Turnout in Presidential Elections," *American Politics Quarterly* 28 (July 2000): 408–429.
34. William Crotty, "Political Participation: Mapping the Terrain," in Crotty, ed., *Political Participation and American Democracy*, pp. 7–15.
35. John Sides, Eric Schickler, and Jack Citrin, "If Everyone Had Voted, Would Bubba and Dubya Have Won?" *Presidential Studies Quarterly* 38 (September 2008): 521–539.
36. Peter L. Francia, Rachel E. Goldberg, John C. Green, Paul S. Herrnson, and Clyde Wilcox, "Individual Donors in the 1996 Federal Elections," in John C. Green, ed., *Financing the 1996 Election* (Armonk, NY: M. E. Sharpe, 1999), p. 128.
37. Verba, Schlozman, and Brady, *Voice and Equality: Civic Volunteerism in American Politics*, pp. 475–493.
38. Theda Skocpol, *Diminished Democracy: From Membership to Management in American Civic Life* (Norman, OK: University of Oklahoma Press, 2003), pp. 6–13, 224–244.
39. APSA Task Force Report, "American Democracy in an Age of Rising Inequality," p. 657.
40. Matthew Hindman, *The Myth of Digital Democracy* (Princeton, NJ: Princeton University Press, 2009), pp. 141–142.
41. *Voting: Some Procedural Changes and Informational Activities Could Increase Turnout* (Washington, DC: General Accounting Office, 1990), p. 2.
42. Sean Richey, "Voting by Mail: Turnout and Institutional Reform in Oregon," *Social Sciences Quarterly* 89 (December 2008): 902–915.
43. Ronald D. Michaelson, Illinois State Board of Elections, quoted in Peter Baker, "An All-Time High for Ballot Box No-Shows," *Washington Post National Weekly Edition*, November 11–17, 1996, p. 11.
44. Michael D. Martinez and David Hill, "Did Motor Voter Work?" *American Politics Quarterly* 27 (July 1999): 296–315.
45. Cynthia Rugeley and Robert A. Jackson, "Getting on the Rolls: Analyzing the Effects of Lowered Barriers on Voter Registration," *State Politics and Policy Quarterly* 9 (Spring 2009): 56–78.

Chapter 6

The News Media

CHAPTER OUTLINE

WHAT WE WILL LEARN

After studying Chapter 6, students should be able to answer the following questions:

1. How are the news media changing?
2. What is the relationship between the government and the media?
3. How do the media cover the news and how do candidates and officeholders attempt to influence the tone and content of the coverage?
4. Are the media biased?
5. What role do the media play in the policymaking process?

The newspaper business is in trouble. During 2009, 139 newspapers ceased publishing, including such major daily papers as the *Rocky Mountain News* and the *Seattle Post-Intelligencer*.[1] The Chicago Tribune Company, owner of the *Chicago Tribune* and the *Los Angeles Times*, filed for bankruptcy in late 2008 in order to stay in business.[2] Many other papers were losing money.

Newspapers make their money from subscriptions and advertising revenue, and both are in decline. Newspaper circulation rates, which have been falling for 30 years, dropped by more than 10 percent in 2009.[3] Younger people in particular have been going online to find information for free. Although online newspaper readership has been growing, newspapers have had little success generating revenue online. Advertising revenue has fallen as well. Newspaper classified advertising has shrunk dramatically because of competition from free online alternatives, such as Craigslist. Revenue from other advertising, especially real estate and employment ads, has fallen as well because of the deep economic recession of 2008–2009.

Does the decline of the newspaper industry mean that Americans will have less information about their government or is it merely an indication that information sources are changing? Many experienced newspaper journalists worry that the trend is a threat to the quality of American democracy. Newspapers hold elected officials accountable by investigating what government does and reporting the results of their inquiries, good and bad, to the public. After all, it was two investigative reporters for the *Washington Post* newspaper, Bob Woodward and Carl Bernstein, who first uncovered **Watergate,** a scandal that involved the abuse of presidential power by President Richard Nixon and members of his administration that led to his resignation in 1974. Will freedom of the press mean anything, they ask, if the press goes out of business?[4]

Watergate
A scandal that involved the abuse of presidential power by President Richard Nixon and members of his administration that led to his resignation in 1974.

Not everyone agrees that the decline of the newspaper industry undermines the quality of American democracy. Some newspaper critics argue that investigative journalism of the Woodward and Bernstein variety is rare. Newspapers fill their pages with straightforward news stories, sports scores, and movie reviews, but relatively few investigative reports. On those rare occasions when a paper publishes an investigative report, the public is often indifferent.[5] Furthermore, the technologies that are making the old newspaper model of gathering and reporting the news obsolete are opening a new world of online journalism that is more robust than the old model. MySpace, Facebook, YouTube, Twitter, and other media allow online reporters, as well as citizen journalists, to provide readers with substantially more content than the traditional newspaper story, including links, videos, and reader comments.[6]

The decline of the traditional newspaper model of collecting and publishing the news introduces our discussion on the place of the media in the policymaking environment. The chapter begins by describing the news media in the United States and discussing how the media are changing. The chapter examines the relationship between the government and the media. It explores the way the media cover the news and the way candidates and officeholders attempt to shape that coverage. Finally, the chapter considers the question of media bias.

President Thomas Jefferson famously said, "Were it left to me to decide whether we should have a government without newspapers or newspapers without a government, I should not hesitate a moment to prefer the latter." What did he mean? Do you agree? Do you think that Jefferson would make the same statement today?

The Changing News Media Landscape

In contrast to much of the world, direct government ownership of media outlets in the United States is relatively limited. The federal government operates the Armed Forces Radio and Television Service, which provides news and entertainment to members of the U.S. armed forces worldwide. Many local governments, including cities, schools, and colleges, operate cable television stations. City governments may use their cable television channels to air city council meetings and other public service programming. Some colleges and universities operate radio stations.

Public Broadcasting Service (PBS) A nonprofit private corporation that is jointly owned by hundreds of member television stations throughout the United States.

National Public Radio (NPR) A nonprofit membership organization of radio stations.

The **Public Broadcasting Service (PBS)** and **National Public Radio (NPR)** are private nonprofit media services with public and private financial support. PBS is a nonprofit private corporation that is jointly owned by hundreds of member television stations throughout the United States; NPR is a nonprofit membership organization of radio stations. The **Corporation for Public Broadcasting** is a government agency chartered and funded by the U.S. government with the goal of promoting public broadcasting. It provides some funding for both PBS and NPR. Public radio and television stations also benefit from corporate donations and financial contributions from the general public. PBS and NPR regularly interrupt their programming to ask their viewers and listeners to pledge their financial support.

Corporation for Public Broadcasting A government agency chartered and funded by the U.S. government with the goal of promoting public broadcasting.

Print media Newspapers and magazines.

Broadcast media Television and radio.

Private businesses, often large corporations, own and operate most media outlets in the United States. Most **print media** (newspapers and magazines) and **broadcast media** (television and radio) outlets are part of large chains. Consolidation is an important trend in media ownership. The 10 largest newspaper groups control a majority of newspaper circulation in the nation. Most television stations belong to national networks, such as CBS, NBC, ABC, Fox, Univision, WB, or UPN. Clear Channel Communication and Cumulus Media own hundreds of radio stations, including many in the same city.[7] Cross-media ownership is common as well, in which one corporation owns several types of media. For example, the Tribune Company owns and operates 10 daily newspapers, 23 major-market television stations, several radio stations, and more than 50 websites.[8]

The media landscape is changing. Many mainstream media outlets, especially newspapers, newsmagazines, and the network evening news, have been in decline for years, at least in terms of circulation and ratings. Between 2001 and 2008, daily newspaper circulation fell by 13.5 percent; Sunday newspaper circulation dropped by 17.3 percent. As we noted in the opening section of the chapter, newspaper circulation fell by an additional 10 percent in 2009 alone. Circulation for the "big three" newsmagazines (*Time*, *Newsweek*, and *U.S. News*) is falling, with readership down by a third since 1994. In fact, one of the big three, *U.S. News*, ceased publishing as a weekly, converting instead to a monthly. Ratings for the network evening news and morning news shows are in a long decline as well. Over the past 25 years, the combined audience for the network evening news has fallen on average by a million viewers a year.[9] Before the emergence of cable television, the television news audience was concentrated among the major networks, all of whom broadcast their evening news during the same block of time. Television viewers

In 2009, President Barack Obama became the first president to appear on *The Tonight Show with Jay Leno*.

had no option but to watch the news because no other shows were available. When cable television came along, viewers who were not interested in the news turned to entertainment alternatives. Eventually, many news junkies turned away from the networks as well to watch cable news channels.[10]

New media A term used to refer to alternative media sources, such as the Internet, cable television, and satellite radio.

While traditional media sources are losing readers, listeners, and watchers, the **new media,** which is a term used to refer to alternative media sources, such as the Internet, cable television, and satellite radio, are growing in importance. Young people in particular are turning away from traditional media sources in favor of the new media.[11] Fox News, CNN, and MSNBC offer news coverage around the clock. Radio talk shows offer news and opinion much of the day. In the meantime, anyone with a computer can create a website or write a blog, post a YouTube video, sign up for a Twitter account, or create a Facebook page. Although online news sources vary considerably in quality and credibility, some of them have become important sources of information. The Matt Drudge website called the Drudge Report, for example, was the first media to break the news about the relationship between White House intern Monica Lewinsky and President Bill Clinton. Blogs in particular are important opinion outlets. In fact, liberal bloggers have become such an important source of opinion leadership in the Democratic Party that presidential candidates hired bloggers to write for their campaign websites during the 2008 election campaign.

Figure 6.1 shows the relative importance of news media sources in 2000 and 2008. As the figure shows, traditional media sources (newspapers, radio, and network

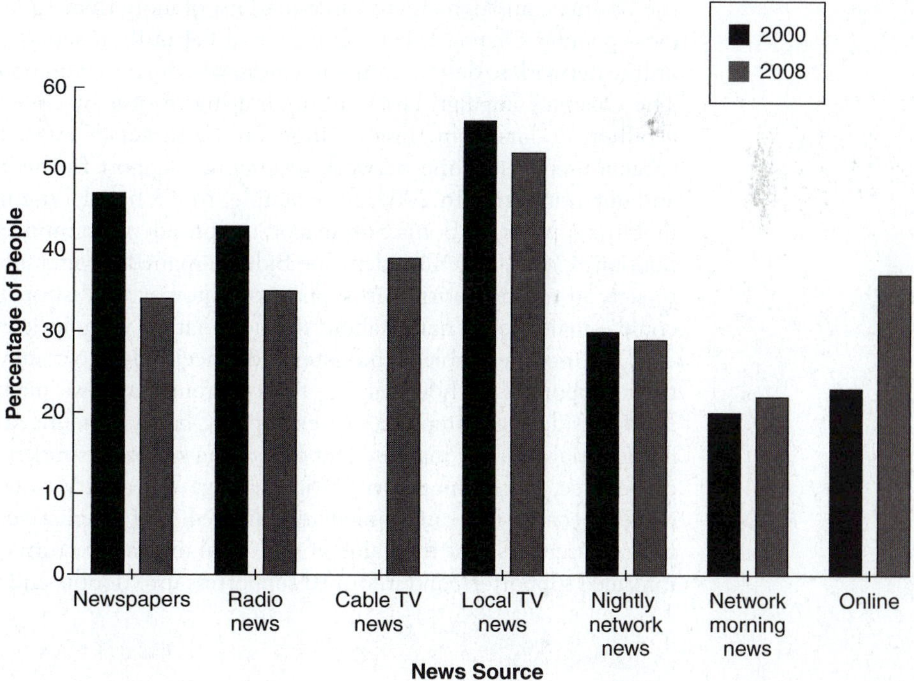

FIGURE 6.1 Media Sources for News.

TV) declined in importance over the period, whereas new media sources (cable TV and the Internet) grew in importance. In 2000, the most important news sources were local TV news, followed by newspapers and radio news. In 2008, local TV news continued to lead, but cable TV news and online news sources emerged as the second and third most important sources for news.

24-hour news cycle The round-the-clock reporting of news.

The emergence of the new media has helped produce the **24-hour news cycle,** which is the round-the-clock reporting of news. Before cable television and the Internet, a news story that broke during the night made the morning newspaper if information was available before the paper went to press. The network evening news and afternoon papers would then follow up with details and further developments. Major stories would develop in this fashion for days or even weeks. Today, however, cable television and the Internet allow for immediate reporting and continuous updating of a news story. Political developments that once came out over a number of days now unfold in a matter of hours.

Candidates and elected officials have adapted to the new media environment by using the Internet for communication and fundraising. Most candidates for office and most elected officials have a basic webpage with pictures, a biography, issue positions, and, for candidates, a fundraising link that accepts major credit cards. Technologically sophisticated candidates and officeholders go beyond a basic Internet site by utilizing the full array of social media, including Facebook, MySpace, YouTube, and Twitter.

No politician uses technology more effectively than Barack Obama. In 2008, the Obama campaign created an e-mail list of more than 13 million addresses. The most popular Obama Facebook page had 6.4 million supporters. Obama used his online network to deliver campaign messages, organize volunteers, and raise money. The Obama campaign broke all fundraising records by collecting more than half a billion dollars from three million online donors.[12] After becoming president, Obama used his online network to organize support for his legislative initiatives and appointments. In 2009, for example, the White House used its e-mail list to mobilize support for Sonia Sotomayor, the president's nominee to serve on the U.S. Supreme Court. Vice President Joe Biden e-mailed Obama supporters, asking them to sign an online petition in support of Sotomayor. Visitors to Obama's webpage could e-mail their senators about the nomination without leaving the site.[13]

Technology enables candidates and officeholders to communicate directly with their supporters without having to go through a news media filter. During the 2008 presidential campaign, for example, Obama announced his choice of a vice presidential running mate by text-messaging supporters rather than holding a press conference. Social media in particular have the ability to engage campaign supporters because they are immediate, targeted, and interactive. Political consultant Matt Glazer says that the value of the social media is to turn casual supporters into informed supporters, and informed supporters into donors and volunteers.[14]

Around the World

Government Control of the Media in Cuba

The government tightly manages the media in Cuba. The government owns the electronic media and controls its content. Foreign news agencies who wish to cover news stories in Cuba are forced to hire local journalists through government offices. Independent journalists are subject to harassment, detention, and physical attacks. Journalists found guilty of publishing anti-government propaganda or insulting government officials can be sentenced to long prison terms. According to Reporters Without Borders, an international nonprofit organization that advocates for freedom of the press, the Cuban government cracked down on the independent media in 2003, throwing 19 journalists in jail. Although Cuba recently released all but three of the imprisoned journalists, those who were freed were forced to leave the country immediately. Three other journalists, meanwhile, remain in prison in poor conditions.*

The Cuban government attempts to control Internet access by banning private Internet connections. As a result, less than 2 percent of the Cuban population has Internet access. People who want to surf the web or check their e-mail must go to Internet cafes, universities, or other public sites where their activities can be closely monitored. The computers in Internet cafes and hotels have software installed that alerts police whenever it spots "subversive" words. Cuban residents who write articles critical of the Cuban government for foreign websites are subject to 20-year prison terms.†

The U.S. government attempts to break the Cuban government's monopoly on information with Radio Martí, which broadcasts on shortwave and medium-wave transmitters from Miami, Florida. Miami's most popular Spanish-language AM radio station, which is powerful enough to be heard throughout Cuba, also carries an hour of news from Radio Martí each night at midnight. However, the Cuban government jams the shortwave and medium-wave Radio Martí broadcasts and the AM radio station in Havana as well, so the program's effectiveness is questionable.

Questions

1. Can a country be a democracy without a free press? Why or why not?
2. Is it ever appropriate for a government to manage the news media?
3. Should the United States continue to fund Radio Martí?

* "Press Freedom Index 2009," available at www.rsf.org.

† Ibid.

Government Regulation of the News Media

The U.S. Constitution guarantees freedom of the press. "Congress shall make no law," declares the First Amendment, "abridging the freedom of speech, or of the press." As a result, the news media enjoy broad freedom to report the news, even news that is critical of the government. The tradition of press freedom is so strong in the United States that even publicly funded media outlets are expected to operate without government interference. For example, Kenneth W. Tomlinson, the chair of the Corporation for Public Broadcasting, which provides some funding for PBS and NPR, was forced to resign over allegations that he was trying to influence the content of PBS programming.

The FCC and the Broadcast Media

Congress created the Federal Communications Commission (FCC) in 1939 to regulate the broadcast media using the public airwaves, which include VHF and UHF television and AM/FM radio. The Supreme Court has allowed government regulation of these media, despite the First Amendment, because the public airwaves spectrum is limited.[15] FCC regulation of broadcast frequency and transmission power ensures that stations do not interfere with one another. The FCC has no authority to regulate cable TV, satellite radio, or the Internet.

Equal-time rule An FCC regulation requiring broadcasters to provide an equivalent opportunity to opposing political candidates competing for the same office.

Some FCC regulations affect broadcast content. The **equal-time rule** is an FCC regulation requiring broadcasters to provide an equivalent opportunity to opposing political candidates competing for the same office. For example, if a television station gives Candidate A one minute of free airtime during primetime, then it must offer the equivalent opportunity to other candidates for the same office. The purpose of the equal-time rule is to prevent broadcasters from giving an unfair advantage to one candidate or a group of candidates. The rule does not apply to documentaries, interviews, newscasts, and news event coverage. The FCC exempts political debates from the rule as long as the media station itself is not hosting the debate. The equal-time rule also does not apply to paid campaign advertisements as long as the media outlet is willing to sell advertising time to all qualified candidates for an office.

Fairness Doctrine An FCC regulation requiring broadcasters to present controversial issues of public importance and to cover them in an honest, equal, and balanced manner.

Some media observers favor greater government regulation of the broadcast media. They want Congress or the FCC to reenact the **Fairness Doctrine,** which was an FCC regulation requiring broadcasters to present controversial issues of public importance and to cover them in an honest, equal, and balanced manner. The FCC repealed the Fairness Doctrine in 1987, arguing that it inhibited rather than enhanced public debate and that it appeared to violate the First Amendment. Congress passed legislation to restore the Fairness Doctrine, but President Ronald Reagan vetoed the measure and Congress was unable to override the veto. The proponents of the Fairness Doctrine believe that it is needed to provide for the public discussion of controversial issues and to ensure that all voices are heard. In contrast, critics of the Fairness Doctrine argue that it inhibits free speech because broadcasters sometimes will not discuss controversial political issues because they want to avoid having to provide free airtime for opposing views. Furthermore, they say, the Fairness Doctrine is unnecessary because the proliferation of media outlets, including Internet websites and blogs, ensures broad exposure to all sorts of competing points of view.

While the FCC has been reducing regulation of political views, it has adopted a more aggressive approach to regulating indecency. For example, the FCC fined CBS for Janet Jackson's "wardrobe malfunction" during the 2004 Super Bowl halftime show. Congress subsequently passed legislation to allow the FCC to impose fines as high as $325,000 for each violation of its decency standard.[16] Howard Stern, a radio talk show host famous for off-color remarks and sexual humor, moved his syndicated broadcast radio show to Sirius Satellite Radio to escape FCC scrutiny.

Reporters, Confidential Sources, and Criminal Prosecutions

Journalists frequently base their stories on information received from confidential sources, typically government officials who request that their identities be kept secret. Reporters honor the request because they know that their information sources will dry up if they cannot maintain their anonymity. The issue of confidential sources becomes especially troublesome if the reporter has information that may be relevant in a criminal prosecution or may impact national security. Journalists believe that the First Amendment shields reporters from being compelled to reveal their sources, but the courts have not agreed.[17] In 2005, for example, a federal judge ordered Judith Miller, a *New York Times* reporter, jailed for contempt of court for refusing to reveal her information source in the investigation of who illegally leaked the information that Valerie Plame was a covert Central Intelligence Agency (CIA) agent.

Shield law A statute that protects journalists from being forced to disclose confidential information in a legal proceeding.

A **shield law** is a statute that protects journalists from being forced to disclose confidential information in a legal proceeding. A majority of states have enacted shield laws but not the federal government.[18] The proponents of shield laws believe that they protect the public's right to know. Without shield laws, confidential sources would hesitate to reveal government inefficiency and corruption to reporters for fear that they will lose their jobs when their identities are revealed. In contrast, the opponents of shield laws argue that journalists should not be above the law. They should be required to appear in court and present evidence just like other citizens.

WHAT IS YOUR OPINION?

Do you favor the adoption of shield laws?

Covering the News

A major goal of news media outlets is to attract as large an audience as possible. Newspaper advertising rates depend on readership. Arbitron ratings of listeners determine advertising rates for radio stations; Nielsen ratings count television viewers. Online advertising rates depend on website traffic. Even nonprofit media outlets such as PBS and NPR want to attract a large audience to support their pledge drives.

Media outlets take different approaches to building an audience. Television networks, big city newspapers, and newsmagazines aim to attract a general audience. They cover mainstream news from a middle-of-the-road perspective with an eye to entertainment value by highlighting dramatic events and celebrities. Stories about Tiger Woods get more coverage than do in-depth analyses of budget policy. Reports on crime, traffic accidents, and severe weather dominate local news to the near exclusion of serious coverage of local policy issues. In contrast, other media outlets try to build a niche audience by targeting audiences based on political philosophy, issue focus, or religious values. Political activists can find a set of websites, blogs, radio talk shows, magazines, and television shows that reinforce their point of view.

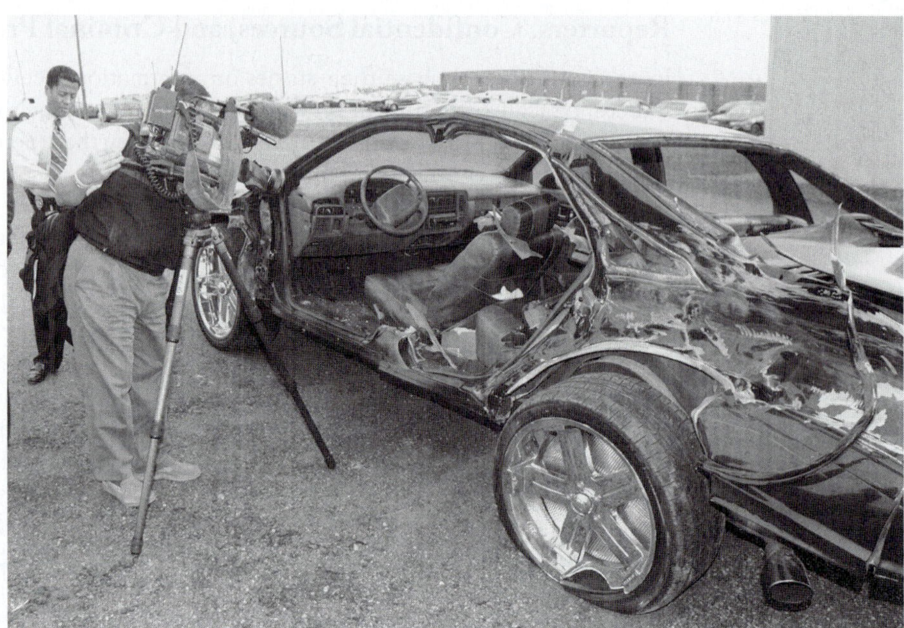

"If it bleeds, it leads." Reports on crime, traffic accidents, and severe weather dominate local news to the near exclusion of serious coverage of local policy issues.

Media consolidation impacts news coverage. Because of chain ownership, newspaper stories written for the *New York Times* or *Washington Post* may appear in local newspapers around the nation in identical form. In any given week, both *Time* and *Newsweek* may feature the same cover story. Meanwhile, local radio and television stations rely on network news feeds for national news. As a result, news outlets around the country tend to focus on the same handful of national stories each day, often told from the same perspective and sometimes in the same words. Because of staff reductions, local media outlets focus on national election coverage rather than state and local contests.[19]

Campaign organizations attempt to manage news coverage to present the candidates they favor in the most positive light. Indeed, the presidential campaigns of Reagan in 1980 and 1984 and George H. W. Bush in 1988 were the prototype of campaign control of news media coverage. The Reagan-Bush strategy, which most campaigns now attempt to copy, was based on several principles. First, campaign managers choose a single theme to emphasize each campaign day, such as crime, the environment, or defense. If the candidate and the members of the candidate's team address the same issue and only that issue, the news media will be more likely to focus on that issue in their daily campaign reports.

Second, the campaign selects an eye-catching visual backdrop for their candidate that reemphasizes the theme of the day, such as the Statue of Liberty, a retirement home, or a military base. In 1988, George H. W. Bush even staged a campaign event in a factory that made American flags. Campaign organizers try to ensure that everyone in the audience is friendly so that television images convey the impression of popular support. When President George W. Bush ran for reelection in 2004, he typically appeared at invitation-only rallies to ensure that news reports would be filled with pictures of smiling faces and cheering crowds.

Finally, campaign managers carefully brief the candidate to stick with the campaign script. Each speech includes one or two carefully worded phrases that can be used as sound bites on the evening news. A **sound bite** is a short phrase taken from a candidate's speech by the news media for use on newscasts. "Read my lips," said George H. W. Bush in 1988, "no new taxes." Candidates who lack discipline or who are prone to gaffes distract from their own message.

Sound bite A short phrase taken from a candidate's speech by the news media for use on newscasts.

Once in office, elected officials establish sophisticated communications operations to manage the news. President George W. Bush's communications operation had 63 full-time employees organized among the offices of communication, media affairs, speechwriting, global communications, press, and photography. Other communication employees worked in the offices of the vice president, first lady, and the National Security Council. Altogether, the Bush administration employed more than 300 people full-time to manage and support its communications operation.[20]

The Bush administration's communications strategy attempted to tie policy, politics, and communications together. Professor Bruce Miroff says that the Bush administration depicted the war in Iraq as if it were a professional wrestling match with the audience (the American people) watching the good guy (President Bush) overpower the bad guy (Saddam Hussein). President Bush declared victory on May 1, 2003, after landing in a jet on the deck of the aircraft carrier *Abraham Lincoln*. Bush, dressed in a green flight suit, used the aircraft carrier as a stage to announce that combat operations in Iraq were over. A large banner over the president's head proclaimed "Mission Accomplished."[21]

President Bush used an aircraft carrier as a backdrop to declare victory in the war in Iraq.

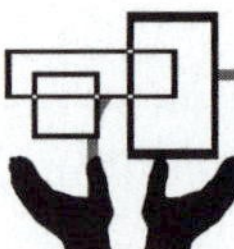

GETTING INVOLVED

News and Information Exposure

How varied are the online sources you visit for information and opinion? Your assignment is to create an annotated inventory of online sites in each of the following categories. For each entry, indicate the name of the site, give its URL, and describe it. Compare your list with those of your classmates to expand the breadth of sites you go to for news and political information:

- National news source that practices objective journalism;
- State and local news source that practices objective journalism;
- Political commentary, combining news and opinion; and
- Issue-oriented website that focuses on a particular issue, either objectively or subjectively.

President Obama used the media in an effort to shape the public debate over healthcare reform legislation by giving five back-to-back interviews on a single day to network correspondents. The interviews, which aired on CNN, NBC, ABC, CBS, and Univision on the same Sunday in September 2009, were remarkably similar with Obama making the same points, often in the same words, to each reporter. Obama's goal was to counter criticism of healthcare reform and build support for its adoption.[22]

However, candidates and officeholders do not always succeed in managing the media. The proliferation of media outlets along with the emergence of new communications technologies such as YouTube and blogging increase the likelihood that candidate bloopers will be caught on tape and broadcast widely. Events sometimes overwhelm an officeholder's communications strategy as well. Hurricane Katrina, for example, was a communications catastrophe for the George W. Bush administration. Rather than interrupt his vacation to address the crisis, President Bush left Secretary of Homeland Security Michael Chertoff in charge. While television viewers saw images of thousands of people stranded on roofs and huddled in the New Orleans Superdome, Chertoff declared his pleasure with the response of the federal government to the disaster. When President Bush finally arrived in the region, several days after the hurricane struck, his rhetoric seemed out of touch with the reality in New Orleans. "Brownie," he said to Federal Emergency Management Administration (FEMA) Director Michael Brown, "You're doing a heck of a job."[23]

Media Biases

Objective journalism is a style of news reporting that focuses on facts, rather than opinions, and presents all sides of controversial issues. Major newspapers, broadcast television news, and the major cable news networks pride themselves on their commitment to objective journalism. The trademark slogan for Fox News is "fair and balanced." Even though newspapers endorse candidates on their editorial page, the

Objective journalism A style of news reporting that focuses on facts rather than opinion, and presents all sides of controversial issues.

ideal of objective journalism is that candidate endorsements have no impact on the content or tone of their news coverage.

Nonetheless, most Americans believe that the media are biased. According to a 2009 survey conducted by the Pew Center for the People & the Press, 60 percent of Americans think that the press is politically biased. In addition, 63 percent believe that stories in the media are often inaccurate, 74 percent think that media stories tend to favor one side, and 74 percent say that the media are influenced by powerful people and organizations. People who identify with the Republican Party are more critical and less trusting of the media than are Democrats and independents.[24]

Research suggests that media sources may indeed play favorites. The network evening news, for example, treats Democratic candidates more favorably than it does Republicans. The Democratic candidate for president enjoyed more favorable coverage on the network evening news than the Republican candidate in three of the five presidential elections from 1998 through 2004. Coverage was balanced in the other two elections. In 2004, for example, 57 percent of the network news reports on Democratic presidential candidate John Kerry were positive compared with 37 percent of the news reports on President George W. Bush.[25] Similarly, a study of 2008 election coverage conducted by the Pew Research Center's Project on Excellence in Journalism found that press coverage of John McCain's presidential campaign was more negative than was coverage of the Obama campaign. The study, which examined campaign stories from 48 news outlets, categorized the tone of 57 percent of the stories on McCain as negative compared with 14 percent that were positive in tone and 29 percent that were neutral. In contrast, the tone of Obama coverage was more closely balanced between positive (36 percent), neutral (35 percent), and negative (29 percent) stories.[26]

Nonetheless, scholars have no evidence that news coverage affects election outcomes. Kerry lost the 2004 election, for example, despite receiving more favorable network news coverage than Bush. As we have noted, survey research indicates that many voters distrust the accuracy of media reports and suspect a media bias. If voters do not trust what the media have to say, they are unlikely to be swayed by bias. Furthermore, citizens have the opportunity to choose media sources that match their political predispositions. Whereas the main source of news for Democrats is CNN, most Republicans prefer Fox.[27] Similarly, blog readers gravitate toward websites that reflect their political beliefs, with few people reading both conservative and liberal blogs.[28]

Political science research has also identified media biases that are not based on party affiliation or political ideology. Research on Senate races has found that newspapers tend to slant the information on their news pages to favor the candidate endorsed by the paper on its editorial page, regardless of that candidate's party affiliation.[29] Furthermore, studies show that the press is biased against presidential and Congressional incumbents, without regard for party and ideology. An **incumbent** is a current officeholder. Presidents Reagan, Clinton, and George W. Bush all received news coverage that was less than 40 percent positive, more than 60 percent negative. Coverage of Congress is even harsher, with more than 80 percent of news stories taking a negative slant.[30] Media coverage of Congress typically focuses on

Incumbent Current officeholder.

conflict and controversy, personal ambition, and ethical lapses.[31] The press has grown increasingly negative. Since the 1960s, bad news has increased by a factor of three and is now the dominant theme of news coverage of national politics. Thirty years ago, press coverage of public affairs emphasized the words of newsmakers and stressed the positive. The press grew more critical during the 1970s as journalists began to counter the statements of government officials rather than just report them. By the late 1970s, the focus of the Washington, DC, press corps was **attack journalism,** which is an approach to news reporting in which journalists take an adversarial attitude toward candidates and elected officials. Reporters decided to critically examine the actions of newsmakers, countering the statements of public officials with the responses of their critics and adversaries.[32] Campaign coverage has grown negative as well. In 1960, 75 percent of press references to both major party presidential candidates (Richard Nixon and John Kennedy) were positive. In contrast, only 40 percent of references to the major party presidential candidates in 1992 (George H. W. Bush and Bill Clinton) were positive.[33]

Attack journalism An approach to news reporting in which journalists take an adversarial attitude toward candidates and elected officials.

WHAT IS YOUR OPINION?

Are the media too negative about government and public officials?

The Role of the Media in the Policymaking Process

Political scientists say that the press plays a **signaling role,** which is a term that refers to the accepted responsibility of the media to alert the public to important developments as they happen. The media may be unable to tell people what to think, but they generally succeed in telling people what to think about. In early 2007, the *Washington Post* published a series of stories about the poor quality of care injured service personnel had been receiving from Walter Reed Army Medical Center in Washington, DC. Other media outlets quickly picked up on the coverage, and the issue of medical care for Iraq war veterans soon rose to the forefront of the policy agenda. Several congressional committees held hearings on the issue, the Bush administration called for an investigation, and the Secretary of Defense removed the military commanders in charge of veterans' care at Walter Reed.

Signaling role A term that refers to the media's accepted responsibility to alert the public to important developments as they happen.

The media influence policymaking through **framing,** which is the process by which a communication source, such as a news organization, defines and constructs a political issue or public controversy. The way the media present an issue helps define the approaches that policymakers will take to its resolution. The vivid images of flooded homes and people seeking shelter in the New Orleans Superdome along with accounts of bureaucratic bungling ensured that policymakers would regard Hurricane Katrina as not just a natural disaster but also the failure of the government to respond effectively to a crisis.

Framing The process by which a communication source, such as a news organization, defines and constructs a political issue or public controversy.

WHAT WE HAVE LEARNED

1. **How are the news media changing?**
   Private businesses, often large corporations, own and operate most media sources in the United States. Many mainstream media outlets, especially newspapers, newsmagazines, and the network evening news, have been in decline for years, at least in terms of circulation and ratings. In contrast, the new media, which is a term used to refer to alternative media sources, such as the Internet, cable television, and satellite radio, are growing in importance.

2. **What is the relationship between the government and the media?**
   The Constitution guarantees freedom of the press. As a result, the news media enjoy considerable leeway to report the news, even news that is critical of the government. The FCC regulates the broadcast media, but not cable TV, satellite radio, or the Internet. A number of controversies have arisen over the relationship between government and the media, including the issue of whether reporters should be required to reveal the names of confidential sources to the government. Many states have adopted shield laws, which are statutes that protect journalists from being forced to disclose confidential information in a legal proceeding.

3. **How do the media cover the news and how do candidates and officeholders attempt to influence the tone and content of the coverage?**
   A major goal of news media outlets is to attract as large an audience as possible. The mainstream media seek to draw an audience by focusing on stories with entertainment value, such as crime stories and celebrity news. Other media outlets try to build a niche audience by targeting audiences based on political philosophy, issue focus, or religious values. Campaign organizations attempt to manage news coverage to present the candidates they favor in the most favorable light with sound bites and visual images all designed to support a theme of the day. Once in office, elected officials try to manipulate media coverage to build support for their policy initiatives and eventual reelection campaigns.

4. **Are the media biased?**
   Although major newspapers, broadcast television news, and the major cable news networks pride themselves on their commitment to objective journalism, most Americans believe that the media are biased. Research suggests that media sources may indeed play favorites, with the network evening news treating Democratic candidates more favorably than they do Republicans. Nonetheless, scholars have no evidence that news coverage affects election outcomes.

5. **What role do the media play in the policymaking process?**
   Political scientists say that the press plays a signaling role, which is a term that refers to the accepted responsibility of the media to alert the public to important developments as they happen. The media also influence the policymaking process through framing, which is the process by which a communication source, such as a news organization, defines and constructs a political issue or public controversy.

KEY TERMS

24-hour news cycle
attack journalism
broadcast media
Corporation for Public Broadcasting
equal-time rule
Fairness Doctrine
framing
incumbent

National Public Radio (NPR)
new media
objective journalism
print media
Public Broadcasting Service (PBS)
shield law
signaling role
sound bite
Watergate

NOTES

1. *Time*, December 28, 2009–January 4, 2010, p. 35.
2. "The State of the News Media 2010," available at www.stateofthenewsmedia.org.
3. Richard Perez-Pena, "U.S. Newspaper Circulation Falls 10%," *New York Times*, October 26, 2009, available at www.nytimes.com.
4. John Nichols and Robert W. McChesney, "The Death and Life of Great American Newspapers," *The Nation*, March 18, 2009, available at www.thenation.com.
5. Jack Shafer, "Democracy's Cheat Sheet?" *Slate*, March 27, 2009, available at www.slate.com.
6. Paul Gillin, "Journalism in a Wikified World," November 29, 2009, available at http://journalismethics.ca.
7. Project for Excellence in Journalism, available at www.stateofthenewsmedia.org.
8. "Annual Report," available at www.tribune.com.
9. "The State of the News Media 2009," available at www.stateofthenewsmedia.org.
10. Jeffrey E. Cohen, *The Presidency in the Era of 24-Hour News* (Princeton, NJ: Princeton University Press, 2008), pp. 135–166.
11. Pew Center for the People & the Press, available at http://people-press.org.
12. Jose Antonio Vargas, "Obama Raised Half a Billion Online," *Washington Post*, November 20, 2008, available at www.washingtonpost.com.
13. Elizabeth Gorman, "Obama Cashes in On-Line Political Capital for Sotomayor," ABC News, May 29, 2009, available at www.abcnews.com.
14. Quoted in *Texas Observer*, June 12, 2009, p. 15.
15. *Red Lion Broadcasting v. FCC*, 395 U.S. 367 (1969).
16. Broadcast Decency Enforcement Act of 2005, PL no. 109–235.
17. *Herbert v. Lando*, 441 U.S. 153 (1979).
18. Doris A. Graber, *Mass Media and American Politics*, 7th ed. (Washington, DC: CQ Press, 2006), p. 77.
19. Erika Franklin Fowler and Kenneth M. Goldstein, eds., "Free Media in Campaigns," in Stephen C. Craig, ed., *The Electoral Challenge: Theory Meets Practice* (Washington, DC: CQ Press, 2006), pp. 112–115.
20. Martha Joynt Kumar, "Managing the News: The Bush Communications Operation," in George C. Edwards III and Desmond S. King, eds., *The Polarized Presidency of George W. Bush* (New York: Oxford University Press, 2007), pp. 353–354.
21. Bruce Miroff, "The Presidential Spectacle," in Michael Nelson, ed., *The Presidency and the Political System*, 8th ed. (Washington, DC: CQ Press, 2006), p. 277.
22. Alessandra Stanley, "For President, Five Programs, One Message," *New York Times*, September 21, 2009, available at www.nytimes.com.
23. White House Press Release, "President Arrives in Alabama, Briefed on Hurricane Katrina," September 2, 2005, available at www.whitehouse.gov.
24. Pew Center for the People & the Press, "Press Accuracy Rating Hits Two Decade Low," September 13, 2009, available at http://people-press.org.
25. Farnsworth and Lichter, *The Nightly News Nightmare*, pp. 118–161.
26. Pew Research Center's Project for Excellence in Journalism, "How the Press Reported the 2008 Presidential Election," October 22, 2008, available at www.journalism.org.
27. Pew Center for the People & the Press, "Partisanship and Cable News Audiences," October 30, 2009, available at http://people-press.org.
28. Eric Lawrence, John Sides, and Henry Ferrell, "Self-Segregation or Deliberation? Blog Readership Participation and Polarization in American Politics," *Perspectives on Politics* 8 (March 2010): 141–157.
29. Kim Fridkin Kahn and Patrick J. Kenney, "The Slant of the News: How Editorial Endorsements Influence Campaign Coverage and Citizens' Views of Candidates," *American Political Science Review* 96 (June 2002): 381–394.
30. Stephen J. Farnsworth and S. Robert Lichter, *The Mediated Presidency: Television News and Presidential Governance* (Lanham, MD: Rowman & Littlefield Publishers, 2006), p. 41.
31. Michael L. Mezey, *Representative Democracy: Legislators and Their Constituents* (Lanham, MD: Rowman & Littlefield, 2008), pp. 170–172.
32. Thomas E. Patterson, "Bad News, Period," *PS: Political Science and Politics*, March 1996, pp. 17–20.
33. Elizabeth A. Skewes, *Message Control: How News Is Made on the Presidential Campaign Trail* (Lanham, MD: Rowman & Littlefield Publishers, 2007), p. 13.

Chapter 7

Interest Groups

CHAPTER OUTLINE

WHAT WE WILL LEARN

After studying Chapter 7, students should be able to answer the following questions:

1. Why do people join interest groups in spite of the free-rider barrier to group membership?
2. What types of interest groups are active in American politics and what are their goals?
3. What strategies and tactics do interest groups use to achieve their goals?
4. What factors determine the relative strength of interest groups?

National Rifle Association (NRA) An interest group organized to defend the rights of gun owners and defeat efforts at gun control.

The **National Rifle Association (NRA)** is one of the most successful interest groups in American politics. The NRA, which was organized to defend the rights of gun owners and defeat efforts at gun control, has largely succeeded in defining the gun debate in terms of the right to own, sell, and carry a weapon, as opposed to limiting criminal access to firearms. Instead of considering gun control legislation, the U.S. Congress and many states have focused instead on legislative measures to expand the rights of gun owners. In 2009, for example, Congress adopted legislation allowing people to carry loaded firearms into national parks and wildlife refuges. A number of state legislatures have passed gun measures as well. Florida recently adopted legislation giving people with concealed handgun permits the right to carry their weapon into the workplace. In Arizona, people with handgun permits can take their guns into bars and other establishments that serve alcohol. Several states are considering legislation to allow concealed handguns on college campuses.

The NRA is winning the gun control debate despite public opinion, which is divided over the issue. Most Americans believe that the Second Amendment to the Constitution guarantees an individual the right to own a gun. A Gallup Poll taken in 2008 found that 73 percent of respondents believe that the Second Amendment grants an individual the right to own a firearm, compared with 20 percent who think that the Constitution only guarantees the right of militia members to be armed.[1] Nonetheless, many Americans favor strict gun control regulations. According to a 2009 survey, 44 percent of Americans believe that gun control regulations should be made "more strict," compared with 12 percent who think they should be made "less strict." Another 43 percent of respondents favor keeping gun control laws as they are.[2]

Many members of the NRA believe passionately in a constitutional right to keep and bear arms.

The success of the NRA illustrates an important point about interest group politics: a relatively small group of people who are well organized and highly motivated have more political influence than a large group that is disorganized and disinterested. Gun rights enthusiasts as a group feel more strongly about the issue than do gun control advocates. Because ordinary citizens who favor gun control are less likely to base their voting decisions on the issue alone than are ordinary citizens opposed to gun control, the gun control side has less political power than gun rights forces. Furthermore, the NRA is far better organized than opposing groups. The Brady Campaign to Prevent Gun Violence, which is the largest gun control organization, is no match for the NRA in terms of money, membership, organization, and political influence.

The NRA's role in American politics introduces this chapter on interest groups. The chapter begins by considering why people join groups. It then identifies the various types of interest groups in American politics, discusses their political goals, and assesses their relative strengths. Finally, the chapter examines the tactics interest groups employ to achieve their goals and discusses the factors that affect the relative strength of groups.

Why People Join Groups

AARP (formerly known as the American Association of Retired Persons) An interest group representing the concerns of older Americans.

George and Inez Martinez are an older couple living in El Paso, Texas. They recently received a letter from AARP inviting them to join that organization. **AARP,** which was formerly known as the American Association of Retired Persons, is an interest group representing the concerns of older Americans. Mr. and Mrs. Martinez have heard of the AARP, approve of its work on behalf of older people, and note that annual AARP dues are relatively low. Nonetheless, why should Mr. and Mrs. Martinez join AARP? Surely, the few dollars they contribute in dues will be too little to have any appreciable effect on the fortunes of the organization. Furthermore, as senior citizens, Mr. and Mrs. Martinez stand to benefit from whatever legislative gains the AARP achieves whether or not they join the organization.

Free-rider barrier to group membership The concept that individuals will have little incentive to join a group and contribute resources to it if group's benefits go to members and nonmembers alike.

The situation facing Mr. and Mrs. Martinez illustrates what Professor Mancur Olson calls the **free-rider barrier to group membership,** which is the concept that individuals will have little incentive to join a group and contribute resources to it if the group's benefits go to members and nonmembers alike. Olson says that groups attempt to overcome the free-rider barrier by offering selective benefits that go only to group members.[3] The AARP, for example, provides members with a number of selective benefits, including the opportunity to purchase discounted dental, health, and long-term care insurance.

Political scientists identify three types of incentives individuals have for joining and participating in a group: (1) material, (2) solidary, and (3) purposive incentives, which are sometimes also called expressive incentives. Material incentives to group membership are tangible benefits that can be measured monetarily. For example, the NRA offers its members firearms training classes, life insurance for the families of police officers killed in the line of duty, gun-loss insurance, and discounts on car rentals, hotel reservations, and airline tickets. Solidary incentives to group membership are social benefits arising from association with other group members. The NRA has more than 10,000 state associations and local clubs. Members participate in training programs, clinics, and shooting tournaments. Purposive incentives to group membership are the rewards individuals find in working for a cause in which they believe. Many members of the NRA believe passionately in a constitutional right to keep and bear arms.[4] Some groups offer members one type of incentive to join, whereas other groups offer two types or all three kinds of incentives.

Types of Interest Groups

Interest group An organization of people who join together voluntarily on the basis of some interest they share for the purpose of influencing policy.

An **interest group** is an organization of people who join together voluntarily on the basis of some interest they share for the purpose of influencing policy. Sometimes the shared interest is economic. The National Milk Producers Federation, for example, promotes the economic interests of dairy farmers in dealings with the government. At other times, the interests that unite people involve morals, culture, and social values. Individuals concerned about government efforts to safeguard the environment may become involved in an environmental organization, such as the Sierra Club or Greenpeace.

Business Groups

Business groups are the most numerous—and probably the most potent—of America's interest groups. Although their voices are heard on virtually every major policy issue, business interests are especially concerned with tax laws, interest rates, environmental regulations, trade policy, labor laws, government contracts, and other matters that affect the way they conduct business.

Business interests attempt to influence public policy both as individual firms and through a variety of front organizations. Walmart, Exxon-Mobil, Citigroup, General Motors, Chevron, and other large firms are major players in national politics, aggressively promoting their particular interests with government officials. For example, energy companies, such as Exxon-Mobil, Chevron, and ConocoPhillips, favor offshore drilling but worry about the cost of environmental regulations imposed after the BP oil spill. Citigroup, Bank of America, and JP Morgan Chase are concerned with the implementation of financial regulatory reform legislation. The health insurance industry, for its part, focuses on the implementation of healthcare reform.

Chamber of Commerce A business federation representing the interests of more than 3 million businesses of all sizes, sectors, and regions.

Business interests join together across industry lines to promote pro-business public policies. The **Chamber of Commerce** is a business federation representing the interests of more than three million businesses of all sizes, sectors, and regions.[5] It has a national organization with headquarters in Washington, DC; organizations in every state; and chapters in thousands of cities throughout the nation. The National Federation of Independent Business (NFIB) is a federation representing the interests of small and independent businesses. In contrast, the Business Roundtable is an association of chief executive officers of major U.S. corporations.

Trade associations Organizations representing the interests of firms and professionals in the same general field.

Business groups work through **trade associations,** which are organizations representing the interests of firms and professionals in the same general field. Large financial institutions belong to the American Bankers Association. Other trade associations include the National Association of Manufacturers (NAM), National Restaurant Association, and the National Association of Wholesaler-Distributors.

Business groups are well positioned to influence policy. They are numerous, dispersed throughout the country, organized, and well funded. Small business owners and corporate executives are prominent figures in communities around the nation. They often know their member of Congress personally and understand how to articulate effectively their views to policymakers. Furthermore, business groups have funds to contribute to political causes. In 2010, business interests contributed more than $1.2 billion to candidates and political parties, substantially more than the $77 million given by organized labor.[6]

Labor Unions

Right-to-work laws Statutes that prohibit union membership as a condition of employment.

Organized labor is an important political force in America although it is not as powerful as it once was. More than a fourth of the civilian labor force belonged to a union in 1970 compared with only 12 percent in 2009.[7] The manufacturing industries in which unions have historically had their best organizing successes, such as automobile assembly and steel manufacturing, now employ significantly fewer workers than they did 40 years ago. More than 20 states have adopted **right-to-work laws,** which are statutes that prohibit union membership as a condition of employment.[8] Furthermore, many employers aggressively resist unionization. Walmart, the nation's

Walmart, the nation's biggest employer, has aggressively resisted efforts to unionize its workforce.

largest employer, has successfully fought off efforts to unionize its workforce. The unions that have had the most organizing success in recent years have been unions targeting public sector (government) employees and low-wage workers, such as janitors, agricultural workers, and people employed by nursing homes.

American Federation of Labor-Congress of Industrial Organizations (AFL-CIO) An American labor union federation.

The largest union group in the nation is the **American Federation of Labor-Congress of Industrial Organizations (AFL-CIO).** It is composed of 57 separate unions with a combined membership of 11.5 million. Some of the better known unions affiliated with the AFL-CIO are the American Federation of Teachers (AFT), American Postal Workers Union, International Brotherhood of Teamsters, United Mine Workers of America (UMWA), and the American Federation of State, County, and Municipal Employees (AFSCME).[9]

Frostbelt The Northeast and Midwest regions of the United States.

Sunbelt The Southern and Western regions of the United States.

Organized labor is strongest in the **Frostbelt** (the Northeast and Midwest) and weakest in the **Sunbelt** (the South and West). Unions are powerful in the large, industrialized states of the Northeast and Midwest. In Michigan, for example, the United Auto Workers (UAW) may be the state's single most potent political force. In most of the Frostbelt, labor is well organized and skilled at flexing its political muscle. In contrast, labor is not as well organized or as politically influential in the Sunbelt, the nation's fastest growing area. In many Sunbelt states, organized labor is hurt by anti-union laws and by a diverse and divided workforce, many of whose members are hostile to organized labor. Unionization in the South and Southwest has taken hold in only a few places.

Organized labor favors government policies aimed at making it easier for unions to organize. In particular, unions want Congress to pass the Employee Free Choice Act, which would allow the use of the card check method in union authorization elections. Under current law, workers form a union in a particular workplace by majority vote, usually by secret ballot. **Card check** is a method of union authorization that allows union organizers to collect employee signatures on authorization forms instead of holding a secret ballot election. Once a majority of worker signatures have been collected, the National Labor Relations Board (NLRB) certifies the union and the employer is forced to recognize it as the official representative of the workers. Organized labor favors card check because it makes it easier for workers to join a union. In contrast, business groups argue that card check denies workers their right to a secret ballot.

Card Check A method of union authorization that allows union organizers to collect employee signatures on authorization forms instead of holding a secret ballot election.

Organized labor supports programs and policies designed to improve the quality of life for working people and their families. Unions favor increasing the federal **minimum wage,** which is the lowest hourly wage that an employer can legally pay covered workers. They want the government to aggressively enforce workplace health and safety regulations, and to require the use of union labor and union wage scales on construction projects built with federal funds.

Minimum wage The lowest hourly wage that an employer can legally pay covered workers.

Conventional wisdom holds that organized labor and big business counterbalance each other, invariably taking opposing views on public policy issues. At times, that is the case. Management and labor generally disagree on labor-relations laws, occupational safety and health regulations, and minimum wage laws. At other times, however, big business and big labor find themselves on the same side in policy disputes. Labor leaders and business executives both favor higher defense spending, for example, because it means more defense contracts and more jobs. The United

Steelworkers and steel manufacturers join forces to push for import restrictions on foreign competition. Both business and labor oppose environmental regulations that could threaten the closing of offending plants and the loss of jobs.

Professional Associations

Doctors, lawyers, realtors, and other professionals form associations to advance their interests. Professional associations are influential because of the relatively high socioeconomic status of their membership. Professionals have the resources to make their voices heard, and they enjoy an added advantage because many elected officials come from the ranks of the professions, especially the legal profession.

American Medical Association (AMA) An interest group representing the concerns of physicians.

American Bar Association (ABA) An interest group representing the concerns of lawyers.

Professional associations are concerned with public policies that affect their members. The **American Medical Association (AMA),** an interest group representing the concerns of physicians, would like government to limit the amount of money judges and juries can award in medical malpractice lawsuits. The **American Bar Association (ABA),** a lawyers' group, opposes the AMA on the issue. Professional associations sometimes take stands on policy issues outside the immediate concerns of their membership, such as tax policy, defense spending, and the rights of women and minorities.

Agricultural Groups

Agricultural groups are influential on farm issues at the national level and in state legislatures in farming states. Farmers are knowledgeable about issues that affect them. They are organized and enjoy a favorable public image. Furthermore, agricultural interests are also business interests because much of agriculture has become agribusiness with all the advantages that business interests enjoy. The most important farm groups include the American Farm Bureau and the National Farmers Union. Associations representing farm interests related to a particular crop or commodity, such as the National Milk Producers Federation, are important as well.

National Association for the Advancement of Colored People (NAACP) An interest group organized to represent the concerns of African Americans.

In general, agricultural groups want government loan guarantees, crop subsidies, and the promotion of farm exports. Of course, each farm group has its own particular cause. Tobacco growers are concerned that government efforts to limit smoking will reduce demand for their products. Western cattle interests want to ensure continued low-cost access to public lands to graze their herds. Fruit and vegetable growers favor immigration policies designed to ensure a steady supply of farm workers.

League of United Latin American Citizens (LULAC) A Latino interest group.

American Indian Movement (AIM) A group representing the views of Native Americans.

Racial and Ethnic Minority Rights Groups

African Americans, Latinos, Asian Americans, Native Americans, and other racial and ethnic minority groups have created interest groups to promote their political causes. The **National Association for the Advancement of Colored People (NAACP)** is an interest group organized to represent the concerns of African Americans. The **League of United Latin American Citizens (LULAC)** is a Latino interest group. The **American Indian Movement (AIM)** is a group representing the views of Native Americans.

Around the World — Church and State in Mexico

Mexico is an overwhelmingly Catholic country. In 2000, 85 percent of the population told surveyors that they were Roman Catholic, compared with 4 percent who claimed to be Protestant, 4 percent who identified with another religion, and 6 percent who declared that they had no religious affiliation. Furthermore, most Mexicans are practicing Catholics. More than 40 percent of Mexican Catholics attend church on a weekly basis; another 20 percent attend at least once a month.*

Nonetheless, Mexico has a strong history of **anti-clericalism,** which is a movement that opposes the institutional power of religion and the church's involvement in all aspects of public and political life. Even though individual citizens enjoyed the right to worship as they pleased, the government restricted the power of the Catholic Church for years. The Mexican Constitution of 1917 established state superiority over religion. Clergy could neither vote nor criticize the government, its laws, or officials. The Constitution limited the role of the church in education. In addition, public education incorporated anti-church rhetoric in student lessons.†

The Mexican government suppressed the church in order to keep it from becoming a threat to state authority. Until recently, the Mexican government was semi-democratic at best. Although Mexico held regular elections, one political party, the Institutional Revolutionary Party (PRI), always won because it manipulated election laws and rigged the vote count to ensure the success of its candidates. Undemocratic governments attempt to restrict all sources of opposition. Government officials in Mexico regarded the Roman Catholic Church as a potential threat to their control because the overwhelming majority of Mexicans were practicing Catholics.

As Mexico has become more democratic, the government has eased restrictions on the church and its political involvement has grown. Although clergy are still prohibited from running for public office, they now enjoy the right to vote and can speak out on political issues as long as they do not oppose the laws of the country. As a result, the church has become an important interest group in Mexican politics.‡ It has addressed a number of political issues including the distribution of wealth, illicit drugs, and democratization. In particular, the church has criticized the government for not doing more to help the poor.§

QUESTIONS

1. Should churches take positions on political issues?
2. Do religious organizations play the role of interest groups in American politics?
3. Are interest groups essential to democratic development?

* Roderi Ai Camp, *Politics in Mexico: The Democratic Consolidation* (New York: Oxford University Press, 2007), p. 89.

† Roberto Blancarte, "Churches, Believers, and Democracy," in Andrew Selee and Jacqueline Peschard, *Mexico's Democratic Challenges: Politics, Government, and* Society (Stanford, CA: Stanford University Press, 2010), p. 291.

‡ Daniel C. Levy and Kathleen Bruhn, *Mexico: The Struggle for Democratic Development*, 2nd ed. (Berkeley, CA: University of California Press, 2006), pp. 123–124.

§ Camp, *Politics in Mexico*, p. 146.

Anti-clericalism A movement that opposes the institutional power of religion, as well as the church's involvement in all aspects of public and political life.

Racial and ethnic minority groups share the goals of equality before the law, representation in elective and appointive office, freedom from discrimination, and economic advancement. Minority groups are interested in the enforcement of laws against discrimination; the election and appointment of minorities to federal, state, and local offices; and the extension of government programs geared toward fighting poverty. Racial and ethnic minority groups generally support the enforcement of the Voting Rights Act and the implementation of affirmative

Voting Rights Act (VRA) A federal law designed to protect the voting rights of racial and ethnic minorities.

Affirmative action programs Programs designed to ensure equal opportunities in employment and college admissions for racial minorities and women.

action programs. The **Voting Rights Act (VRA)** is a federal law designed to protect the voting rights of racial and ethnic minorities. **Affirmative action programs** are programs designed to ensure equal opportunities in employment and college admissions for racial minorities and women. LULAC and other Latino rights organizations favor the adoption of immigration reforms that would allow longstanding undocumented workers the opportunity to work in the United States legally and eventually become citizens.

Organizations that represent the interests of racial and ethnic minorities are an important political force in most big cities and in states where minority populations are large enough to translate into political power. In addition, minorities, especially African Americans and Latinos, play an important role in national politics. Nonetheless, minority citizens, particularly Latinos, are underrepresented at the ballot box because of low voter turnout. Furthermore, the problems facing minority groups in America today—subtle discrimination, inadequate housing, substandard healthcare, malnutrition, poverty, and illiteracy—are particularly difficult to solve.

Religious Groups

Throughout American history, religious organizations have been actively involved in the policy process. Both the abolition (of slavery) and the prohibition (of alcoholic beverages) movements had strong religious overtones, as did the civil

Organizations that represent the interests of racial and ethnic minorities are an important force in most big cities and in states where minority populations are large enough to translate into political power.

rights and anti-Vietnam War movements of the 1960s and early 1970s. State aid to parochial schools has long been a cause dear to many members of the Roman Catholic Church, and Catholic organizations have been heavily involved in the fight against abortion. Jewish groups have likewise kept close watch over American policy toward Israel.

Religious right Individuals who hold conservative views because of their religious beliefs.

Religious left Individuals who hold liberal views because of their religious beliefs.

Today, the most active religiously oriented political groups are associated with the **religious right,** which refers to individuals who hold conservative views because of their religious beliefs. Focus on the Family, Family Research Council, and other conservative religious organizations are concerned with such causes as abortion, same-sex marriage, and prayer in school. Since the 2004 presidential election, religious liberals have begun organizing to counter the influence of the religious right. The **religious left,** which refers to people who hold liberal views because of their religious beliefs, has established a number of organizations and created websites. The religious left opposes the wars in Iraq and Afghanistan; however, they support immigration reform and the adoption of government programs to fight poverty and protect the environment.[10]

Citizen groups Organizations created to support government policies that they believe will benefit the public at large.

Common Cause A group organized to work for campaign finance reform and other good government causes.

Conservative Christian organizations have been more successful at the ballot box than they have in building influence in Washington, DC, because many Christian conservatives are uncomfortable with the policy compromises necessary to move legislation through Congress to passage.[11] Conservative Christian groups benefit from a core of highly committed supporters who can be mobilized to go to the polls and contact members of Congress over issues that are important to them, such as abortion and gay marriage. In 2004, for example, Christian conservatives turned out in large numbers in states that held referenda on the issue of gay marriage.[12] Similarly, the Roman Catholic Church and the Church of Jesus Christ of Latter Day Saints (LDS) led the successful effort to overturn gay marriage in California. Nonetheless, many conservative Christian activists are frustrated with the inability of Congress and the president to outlaw abortion and prohibit gay marriage through constitutional amendment.

Sierra Club An environmental organization.

American Civil Liberties Union (ACLU) A group organized to protect the rights of individuals as outlined in the U.S. Constitution.

WHAT IS YOUR OPINION?

Is it wrong for churches and other religious organizations to be politically involved?

Citizen, Advocacy, and Cause Groups

Citizen groups are organizations created to support government policies that they believe will benefit the public at large. For example, **Common Cause,** which calls itself "the citizen lobby," is a group organized to work for campaign finance reform and other good government causes. Other citizen groups include the **Sierra Club,** an environmental organization, and the **American Civil**

Advocacy groups Organizations created to seek benefits on behalf of groups of persons who are in some way incapacitated or otherwise unable to represent their own interests.

Cause groups Organizations whose members care intensely about a single issue or small group of related issues.

National Right to Life Committee A cause group that is opposed to abortion.

NARAL Pro-Choice America A cause group that supports abortion rights.

Club for Growth A cause group that favors a low tax and limited government agenda.

National Organization for Women (NOW) A group organized to promote women's rights.

Human Rights Campaign (HRC) A cause group formed to promote the cause of gay and lesbian rights.

Liberties Union (ACLU), a group organized to protect the rights of individuals as outlined in the U.S. Constitution.

Advocacy groups are organizations created to seek benefits on behalf of groups of persons who are in some way incapacitated or otherwise unable to represent their own interests. The Children's Defense Fund, for example, promotes the welfare of children. The Coalition for the Homeless is an organization that works on behalf of homeless persons. Other examples of advocacy groups include the Alzheimer's Association and the American Cancer Society.

Cause groups are organizations whose members care intensely about a single issue or small group of related issues. The **National Right to Life Committee** is a cause group opposed to abortion, whereas **NARAL Pro-Choice America** is a cause group that favors abortion rights. The **Club for Growth** is a cause group that favors a low tax and limited government agenda. Other cause groups include the NRA; AARP; **National Organization for Women (NOW),** a cause group organized to promote women's rights; and the **Human Rights Campaign (HRC),** a cause group formed to promote the cause of gay and lesbian rights.

Citizen, advocacy, and cause groups have achieved some victories in American politics. Many of these groups are expert at attracting media attention to their

Abortion opponents make their views known on the anniversary of the Supreme Court's decision in *Roe v. Wade*.

Mother's Against Drunk Driving (MADD) A cause group that supports the reform of laws dealing with drunk driving.

Social Security A federal pension and disability insurance program funded through a payroll tax on workers and their employers.

Medicare A federal health insurance program for people 65 and older.

issues by releasing research reports or conducting high-profile public demonstrations. Earth Day, for example, is an annual event designed to call attention to environmental concerns. The National Right to Life Committee holds a demonstration in Washington, DC, every year on the anniversary of *Roe v. Wade*, the Supreme Court decision that recognized that a woman's constitutional right to privacy includes the right to abortion during the first two trimesters of a pregnancy.

Many public policies reflect the policy values of citizen, advocacy, and cause groups. The Endangered Species Act, the Clean Air Act, and other pieces of environmental legislation are testimony to the effectiveness of the Sierra Club and other environmental organizations. **Mothers Against Drunk Driving (MADD),** a cause group that supports the reform of laws dealing with drunk driving, is the motivating force behind a successful effort to stiffen the nation's DWI laws. AARP is influential on policy issues affecting older Americans such as Social Security and Medicare. **Social Security** is a federal pension and disability insurance program funded through a payroll tax on workers and their employers. **Medicare** is a federally funded health insurance program for people age 65 and older.

Interest Group Strategies and Tactics

Interest groups employ a variety of tactics in an effort to achieve their goals.

Electioneering

Many interest groups seek policy influence by participating in the electoral process. A number of groups try to affect election outcomes by targeting enemies and endorsing friends. Each congressional election year, Friends of the Earth, an environmental group, targets for defeat a "Dirty Dozen," 12 members of Congress who voted consistently against the group's position on environmental legislation. The group publicizes its list in hopes that environmentally conscious citizens will vote against the representatives on the list. Other groups endorse candidates friendly to their cause. During the 2008 presidential campaign, the AFL-CIO and NARAL Pro-Choice America endorsed Democrat Barack Obama, whereas the NRA and the National Right to Life Committee threw their support behind Republican John McCain.

Some interest groups focus on educating their members and supporters about the merits of candidates. The AFL-CIO uses newsletters, phone banks, and rallies to encourage union members to support endorsed candidates. Many interest groups keep scorecards, showing how members of Congress voted on issues important to the group and assigning scores to senators and representatives indicating whether they are friend or foe. Groups hope that people sympathetic to group goals will consult the scorecards before deciding how to vote and for whom to contribute campaign contributions.

Groups with financial resources participate in the electoral process financially. Group members with high incomes give money to candidates and parties individually. In 2010, lawyers and law firms contributed $147 million to political candidates for Congress, with three-fourths of the money going to Democrats. Most lawyers and law firms backed Democratic candidates because they opposed Republican efforts to enact lawsuit reforms, which would limit the amount lawyers and their clients could recover in personal injury lawsuits. In contrast, oil and gas executives gave $58 million in campaign contributions, with 60 percent going to Republicans.[13] Energy executives generally favored Republican candidates because they agreed with Republican efforts to expand energy exploration and limit taxes on the industry.

Political action committee (PAC) An organization created to raise and distribute money in election campaigns.

Federal law requires that interest groups that want to contribute money directly to candidates must make their contributions through a **political action committee (PAC),** which is an organization created to raise and distribute money in election campaigns. Although organized labor created the first PACs in the 1940s, the modern PAC era did not begin until the 1970s, when Congress passed the Federal Election Campaign Act to reform campaign finance. Since the 1970s, the number of PACs active in American politics at the national level of government has grown from fewer than a thousand to more than 5,200.[14] The biggest spenders among PACs in the 2010 election were those associated with the National Association of Realtors, Honeywell International, AT&T, and the International Brotherhood of Electrical Workers.[15]

Interest groups follow different campaign funding strategies. Labor unions work to increase the number of members of Congress sympathetic to their point of view, usually Democrats.[16] In the 2010 election, PACs associated with organized labor made 83 percent of their contributions to Democratic candidates for Congress. Although most labor money goes to incumbent members of Congress, unions are willing to fund challengers and candidates for open seats who stand a reasonable chance of winning.[17]

Access The opportunity to communicate directly with legislators and other government officials in hopes of influencing the details of policy.

Many cause groups pursue strategies similar to those of organized labor in that they are primarily interested in increasing the number of elected officials who share their views. Although some cause groups work to elect friends and defeat enemies without regard for party affiliation, most groups are more closely associated with one party than the other. The bulk of NRA support goes to Republican Party candidates, for example, whereas most of the candidates backed by NOW are Democrats. Some cause groups aggressively fund challengers to incumbents who vote against their interests. Because groups such as the NRA and the National Right to Life Committee have narrow policy interests, they see little risk in working to defeat unfriendly incumbents.

Friendly incumbent rule A policy whereby an interest group will back any incumbent who is generally supportive of the group's policy preferences, without regard for the party or policy views of the challenger.

Business groups are more pragmatic than either organized labor or most cause groups and advocacy groups because they have broad policy interests. Business interests recognize that a public official who opposes them today on one issue may support them tomorrow on another issue. Business PACs contribute money to candidates with the goal of obtaining **access,** the opportunity to communicate directly with legislators and other government officials in hopes of influencing the details of policy. Many business-oriented PACs follow the **friendly incumbent rule,** a policy whereby an interest group will back any incumbent who is generally supportive of the group's policy preferences, without regard for the party or policy views of the challenger. A majority of corporate PAC money goes to incumbents, with most of the rest going to candidates for open seats. Because business-oriented groups favor incumbents, they tend to divide their contributions between the two political parties, despite the traditional alliance between business interests and the Republican Party.

Interest groups in general, not just business-oriented groups, tend to support incumbents. Most interest groups would rather give to a strong candidate who is only somewhat supportive of their cause than throw their money away on an almost certain loser who is completely behind the group's goals. Because incumbents win more often than challengers, especially in races for the U.S. House, most interest group money goes to them.

Bundling A procedure in which an interest group gathers checks from individual supporters made out to the campaigns of targeted candidates. The group then passes the checks along to the candidates.

Some interest groups funnel money to candidates they support through **bundling,** which is a procedure in which an interest group gathers checks from individual supporters made out to the campaigns of targeted candidates. The group then passes the checks along to the candidates. **EMILY's List,** a PAC whose goal is the election of pro-choice Democratic women to office, bundles money to give to Democratic women candidates who support abortion rights. The advantage of bundling for an interest group is that it allows the group to route more money to a candidate than it could legally contribute under its own name because the group is simply acting as a clearinghouse for checks written by hundreds of individuals.

EMILY's List A PAC whose goal is the election of pro-choice Democratic women to office.

527 Committee Organization created to influence the outcomes of elections by raising and spending money that candidates and political parties cannot raise and spend legally.

Some interest groups participate in elections through **527 committees,** which are organizations created by individuals and groups to influence the outcomes of elections by raising and spending money that candidates and political parties cannot raise and spend legally. Federal law limits the amount of money individuals and groups can legally give to candidates and parties, but it does not apply to 527 committees. Groups can contribute as much money as they like to a 527 committee, which can then use the money for voter mobilization and "issue advocacy." Although the law prevents 527 committees from running advertisements either for or against particular candidates, it allows issue advertisements that are typically designed to influence voter opinion on the candidates without explicitly telling people how to cast their vote.

Super PACs are the latest innovation in interest group politics. Super PACs can raise unlimited sums of money from corporations, unions, and individuals. Although they cannot donate directly to candidates, they can spend as much money as they like independently to advocate the election or defeat of candidates for office. Super PACs emerged in 2010 in response to Supreme Court rulings that found many campaign spending and contribution limits unconstitutional.[18] The biggest Super PAC in 2010 was American Crossroads, a conservative Super PAC organized by Republican strategist Karl Rove. American Crossroads spent $21.6 million on campaign advertising, mostly on attack ads targeting Democrats.[19]

Lobbying The communication of information by a representative of an interest group to a government official for the purpose of influencing a policy decision.

Lobbying

Interest groups attempt to influence policymaking by **lobbying,** which is the communication of information by a representative of an interest group to a government official for the purpose of influencing a policy decision. Groups lobby both the legislative and executive branches of government, attempting to influence every stage of the policy process. The number of Washington, DC, lobbyists, including support staffs, is estimated at more than 250,000.[20] Some interest groups have full-time lobbyists on their professional staffs, whereas other groups hire Washington law firms or consulting agencies to lobby on their behalf. More than 150 former members of Congress are lobbyists.[21] Former senator and presidential candidate Bob Dole, for example, became a lobbyist with the firm of Alston & Bird after his unsuccessful run for the White House in 1996, earning far more money as a lobbyist than he would have made had he been elected president. Other lobbyists are former congressional staff members, former employees of the executive branch, and even relatives of current members of Congress.

Lobbying is expensive whether interest groups employ full-time lobbyists or contract with established Washington lobbyists. In 2009, interest groups reported spending more than $2.5 billion for lobbying expenses. The U.S. Chamber of Commerce, for example, spent $527 million on its lobby activities. The AMA spent $213 million.[22]

Information is the key to lobbying. Successful lobbyists provide members of Congress with accurate facts and figures. Although lobbyists offer their own interpretation of data and voice arguments to support their group's particular policy preferences, they are honest because they know that their effectiveness depends on their credibility. In fact, lobbyists are an important information source for government officials.[23]

The most successful lobbying efforts of Congress are those that are supported by campaign contributions and buttressed by pressure from people living in a representative's district or a senator's home state. Interest groups lay the groundwork for effective lobbying by giving money to political campaigns. Lobbyists sometimes serve as campaign treasurers for members seeking reelection. Major trade associations have purchased Capitol Hill townhouses for fundraisers so that members of Congress can quickly go back to the Capitol to cast votes and then return to the event.[24] Although campaign contributions do not necessarily buy votes, they do generally guarantee lobbyists receive access to decision-makers. Once Congress is in session, well-organized groups attempt to support their lobbyists in Washington by encouraging group members in the home districts of key legislators to contact their representatives.

Interest groups use different approaches to influence policy. Most labor unions and business groups employ what might be called an insider's approach to achieving influence. These groups have a long-range interest in several policy areas. They give PAC contributions to gain access to officeholders for lobbyists who then work to get to know the public officials on a personal basis. Whatever pressure these groups bring to bear on public officials is subtle and unspoken. They believe threats are counterproductive and harmful to the construction of a long-term relationship between the interest group and the officeholder. In fact, interest groups give highest priority to lobbying their allies on the committees that formulate legislation. Lobbyists give friendly legislators facts, figures, and talking points in order to counter arguments raised by legislative opponents. Groups taking an insider's approach are usually able to take the outcome of elections in stride because they cultivate relationships with members of both political parties.

Lobbyists using the insider's approach do not expect to affect the way members of Congress vote on final passage of high-visibility legislation. Instead, their goal is to influence the details of legislation to include loopholes that benefit the interest group they represent. For example, a recent tax bill contained a provision limited to a single company, identified as a "corporation incorporated on June 13, 1917, which has its principal place of business in Bartlesville, Oklahoma." The only company fitting that description is Phillips Petroleum. Recent legislation increasing the minimum wage included a provision that "clarifies that foreign trade income of an FSC and export trade income of an ETC do not constitute passive income for purposes of the PFIC definition." That particular phrase was worth $22 million in tax savings for Hercules, Inc., a chemical manufacturer.[25]

In contrast, other groups, whose policy goals are more narrowly focused, follow an outsider's approach to influencing policy. The NRA, National Right to Life Committee, and some other cause groups focus on a relatively small set of high-profile issues. Members of Congress either support them on their pet issues or they are against them. Groups using an outsider's strategy are more heavy-handed in dealing with public officials than are interest groups with a broader range of policy concerns. Groups taking an outside approach are less willing to compromise on policy issues than are insider groups, and more likely to threaten (and attempt to carry out) political reprisals against officeholders who oppose them.

Creating Public Pressure

Some interest groups attempt to achieve their goals by generating public support for their policy positions and focusing it on government officials. Groups launch public relations campaigns to convince the general public that their particular point of view embodies the public interest. The NRA, for example, purchased a series of magazine advertisements designed to improve the group's public image. The advertisements featured hunters, police officers, and business people with the caption, "I am the NRA." Some tobacco companies have conducted high-profile media campaigns against underage smoking to counter criticism that tobacco advertisers have targeted youngsters.

Sometimes interest groups with negative public images will support other, less controversial groups that share their issue concerns. For example, Americans for Prosperity is a cause group that favors lower taxes and less government regulation. It opposes healthcare reform and tobacco regulations, and tries to cast doubt on global warming. Although Americans for Prosperity declares that it is a grassroots organization, the group was founded and heavily funded by the Koch Family Foundation, which is headed by two brothers who control Koch Industries, an oil-and-gas company.[26]

Some interest groups with large memberships have developed sophisticated procedures for mobilizing their members to pressure government officials. The National Federation of Independent Business (NFIB), which has more than 600,000 members, uses its membership to influence the legislative process. NFIB lobbyists first identify which senators and representatives are the swing votes in Congress on issues important to the group. The professional staff of the NFIB then sends direct mail or e-mail messages to NFIB members who live in the states and districts of the targeted lawmakers, asking them to contact their senator or representative in support of the group's goals.[27]

Protest Demonstrations

Tea Party movement A loose network of conservative activists organized to protest high taxes, excessive government spending, and big government in general.

Groups use protest demonstrations to show policymakers that a number of people have strong feelings—usually negative feelings—regarding a particular policy or program. Protests organized by the **Tea Party movement,** which is a loose network of conservative activists organized to protest high taxes, excessive government spending, and big government in general, were designed to draw attention to opposition to healthcare reform, government bailouts, and high taxes. Other contemporary protest movements focus on gay marriage, immigration reform, and the wars in Iraq and Afghanistan. In general, protest demonstrations are a tactic used by groups unable to achieve their goals through other means. Sometimes the protest catches the attention of the general public, which brings pressure to bear on behalf of the protesting group. Tea Party activists hope that their movement will change the direction of American politics. In many cases, however, protests have only a marginal impact on public policy.

Litigation

A number of interest groups specialize in the use of litigation (i.e., lawsuits) to achieve their goals. The ACLU provides legal assistance to individuals and groups involved in controversies involving individual rights and liberties, including disputes over freedom of religion, free speech, and the death penalty. The American Center for Law and Justice and the Liberty Counsel are organizations that litigate in support of conservative Christian goals, such as opposition to abortion rights and gay marriage. Other interest groups use litigation as one of several approaches to

Is animal research unethical?

achieving their policy goals. Both business organizations and environmental groups file suit against government agencies, charging that the executive branch is either going too far or not going far enough to implement the nation's environmental laws. Although courts generally defer to federal agencies in the implementation of policy, they will overrule an agency decision if it appears that the agency acted on the basis of politics rather than the law.

Political Violence

Some groups employ unconventional methods to achieve their goals. The Animal Liberation Front, Stop Animal Exploitation Now, and some other animal rights groups take aggressive action to oppose animal research. Although most animal rights demonstrations are peaceful and legal, some opponents of animal research resort to violence. Protestors have broken into university laboratories, releasing lab animals and destroying property. Some researchers have been threatened with physical assault and death, and had their homes vandalized.[28]

WHAT IS YOUR OPINION?

If you were a scientist, would animal rights protestors prevent you from using animals in laboratory research?

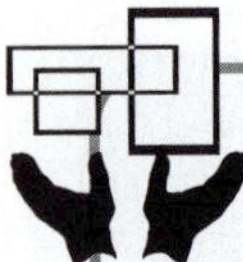

GETTING INVOLVED

Politics at the Movies

Some filmmakers aim not just to entertain but also to convey political messages. View a film with political themes and answer the following questions:

1. What is the title of the film and when was it released?
2. What is the film about? Summarize the storyline of the movie in your own words.
3. What political issue or issues does the film address?
4. What point of view does the film express?
5. Do you agree or disagree with the political views presented in the film? Why or why not?

Select one of the following films with political themes:

Absence of Malice, All the King's Men, American History X, An Inconvenient Truth, Apocalypse Now, Avatar, Boys Don't Cry, Capitalism: A Love Story, Charlie Wilson's War, Citizen Kane, District 9, Do the Right Thing, Dr. Strangelove, Fahrenheit 451, Fahrenheit 9/11, Frost/Nixon, Goodnight and Good Luck, Inherit the Wind, JFK, Man of the Year, Milk, Mississippi Burning, Mr. Smith Goes to Washington, The Manchurian Candidate, Network, No End in Sight, Nothing but the Truth, Once Were Warriors, Philadelphia, Platoon, Primary Colors, Recount, Sicko, Syriana, Thank You for Smoking, W., or *Wag the Dog.*

The Strength of Interest Groups

The policymaking influence of interest groups depends on several factors.

Alliances with Political Parties

In American politics, some interest groups have loose, informal alliances with political parties. Labor unions, African American rights groups, women's organizations, environmentalists, gun-control groups, abortion-rights organizations, and gay and lesbian rights groups are generally aligned with the Democratic Party. Business groups, the NRA, the National Right to Life Committee, anti-tax organizations, and conservative Christian organizations are tied to the Republican Party. Interest groups have more policymaking influence when the party with which they are allied is successful than when it is out of office. After the Republicans took control of the U.S. House in the 2010 election, labor unions, consumer groups, environmental organizations, minority rights groups, and other interest groups typically allied with the Democratic Party saw their influence fall, whereas business groups and trade associations gained influence.

Alliances with Members of Congress and Executive Branch Officials

The policymaking influence of interest groups depends on their ability to cultivate relationships with key officials in the legislative and executive branches of government, regardless of which party controls Congress or the White House. Business groups compensate for Democratic control of Congress by establishing ties with committee and subcommittee chairs through campaign contributions and effective lobbying. Frequently, business lobbyists succeeded in softening the impact of regulatory legislation on their particular industry.

Public Opinion

Public opinion affects the ability of interest groups to achieve their policy goals. The chief goal for the president and most members of Congress is reelection. Therefore, they will not support policy proposals that the public strongly opposes or adopt programs that they believe will prove unpopular with their constituents, regardless of PAC contributions, lobbying, or other interest group activities. Groups are most successful when their policy goals enjoy strong public support.

Unity Among Groups Representing the Same Cause

Interest groups have more influence when organizations representing the same or similar interests or points of view share goals and speak with one voice. For example, at least 11 major environmental organizations participate in national politics. Many more environmental groups operate at the state and local levels. Although environmental groups agree on the broadly defined goal of protecting the environment, they emphasize different aspects of the cause and disagree on tactics and strategy, sometimes quite vocally.[29] On those issues on which environmental groups agree, members of Congress who are already predisposed to be friendly to the environmental cause have clear direction for their efforts. When environmental groups disagree about policy, however, members of Congress who usually support their cause are less likely to proceed with enthusiasm. Furthermore, opponents of the environmentalist position will use the division among environmental groups to undermine their initiative.

Opposition from Other Groups

The policy influence of groups depends on the extent of opposition from other groups. Interest groups are most successful on issues over which there is no conflict among groups.[30] Conflict among groups is least likely on specific provisions of detailed legislation, such as an amendment to the tax code to grant a narrow tax break to a particular industry. Conflict is most likely on major policy issues that are high profile. Doctors' groups and lawyers' associations, for example, butt heads over the issue of medical malpractice insurance reform. Environmental and business groups often oppose one another on environmental issues. On many issues, public officials can choose which interests to court, playing one group against another.

Resources

Finally, groups with resources, especially money, organization, and volunteers, are more influential than groups without resources. The most effective interest group tactics—electioneering, lobbying, and creating public pressure—all require financial resources. Groups with a substantial number of committed members can generate pressure on Congress on behalf of group goals. Well-organized groups can provide campaign assistance to favored candidates through communications to members and perhaps volunteer support.

WHAT WE HAVE LEARNED

1. **Why do people join interest groups in spite of the free-rider barrier to group membership?**

   The free-rider barrier to group membership is the concept that individuals will have little incentive to join a group and contribute resources to it if the group's benefits go to members and nonmembers alike. Professor Mancur Olson says that groups attempt to compensate for the free-rider barrier by offering selective benefits that go only to group members, including material, purposive, and solidary incentives.

2. **What types of interest groups are active in American politics and what are their goals?**

   An interest group is an organization of people who join together voluntarily on the basis of some interest they share for the purpose of influencing policy. Business groups are concerned with government actions that affect their profits, costs, and operations, such as tax laws, environmental regulations, labor laws, and government contracts. Organized labor favors government policies aimed at making it easier for unions to organize and backs programs and policies designed to improve the quality of life for working people and their families. Professional associations are concerned with public policies that affect their members. Agricultural groups want government loan guarantees, crop subsidies, and the promotion of farm exports. Racial and ethnic minority groups share the goals of equality before the law, representation in elective and appointive office, freedom from discrimination, and economic advancement. Interest groups that are part of the religious right are concerned with such causes as abortion, same-sex marriage, and prayer in school, whereas groups associated with the religious left focus on the wars in Iraq and Afghanistan, immigration reform, environmental protection, and poverty relief. Citizen groups are organizations created to support government policies that they believe will benefit the public at large. Advocacy groups are organizations created to seek benefits on behalf of groups of persons who are in some way incapacitated or otherwise unable to represent their own interests. Cause groups are organizations whose members care intensely about a single issue or small group of related issues.

3. **What strategies and tactics do interest groups use to achieve their goals?**

   Interest groups employ a variety of tactics in an effort to achieve their goals, including electioneering, lobbying, creating public pressure, protest demonstrations, litigation, and political violence. Interest groups endorse candidates for office and form political action committees (PACs) to support them financially. They employ professional lobbyists to communicate the group's viewpoint to government officials. They may launch public relations campaigns to promote policies they favor. Some groups file lawsuits to achieve their goals, whereas others organize protest demonstrations or engage in political violence.

4. **What factors determine the relative strength of interest groups?**

   A number of factors affect the relative strength of interest groups, including alliances with political parties, alliances with members of Congress and executive branch officials, public opinion, unity among groups representing the same cause, opposition from other groups, and resources.

KEY TERMS

527 committee
AARP
access
advocacy groups
affirmative action programs
American Bar Association (ABA)
American Civil Liberties Union (ACLU)
American Federation of Labor-Congress of Industrial Organizations (AFL-CIO)
American Indian Movement (AIM)
American Medical Association (AMA)
anti-clericalism
bundling
card check
cause groups
Chamber of Commerce
citizen groups
Club for Growth
Common Cause
EMILY's List
free-rider barrier to group membership
friendly incumbent rule
Frostbelt
Human Rights Campaign (HRC)
interest group
League of United Latin American Citizens (LULAC)
lobbying
Medicare
minimum wage
Mothers Against Drunk Driving (MADD)
NARAL Pro-Choice America
National Association for the Advancement of Colored People (NAACP)
National Organization for Women (NOW)
National Rifle Association (NRA)
National Right to Life Committee

political action committee (PAC)
religious left
religious right
right-to-work laws
Sierra Club
Social Security
Sunbelt
Tea Party movement
trade associations
Voting Rights Act (VRA)

NOTES

1. Jeffrey M. Jones, "Public Believes Americans Have Right to Own Guns," March 27, 2008, available at www.gallup.com.
2. Gallup, available at www.gallup.com.
3. Mancur Olson, *The Logic of Collective Action* (Cambridge, MA: Harvard University Press, 1971).
4. Kelly D. Patterson and Matthew M. Singer, "Targeting Success: The Enduring Power of the NRA," in Allan J. Ciglar and Burdett A. Loomis, eds., *Interest Group Politics* (Washington, DC: CQ Press, 2007), pp. 41–42.
5. U.S. Chamber of Commerce, available at www.uschamber.com.
6. Center for Responsive Politics, available at www.opensecrets .org.
7. U.S. Census Bureau, "Union Members by Sector," *2011 Statistical Abstract of the United States*, available at www.census.gov.
8. Peter L. Francia, "Protecting America's Workers in Hostile Territory: Unions and the Republican Congress," in Paul S. Herrnson, Ronald G. Shaiko, and Clyde Wilcox, eds., *The Interest Group Connection: Electioneering, Lobbying, and Policymaking in Washington*, 2nd ed. (Washington, DC: CQ Press, 2005), p. 214.
9. American Federation of Labor-Congress of Industrial Organizations, available at www.aflcio.org.
10. Caryle Murphy and Alan Cooperman, "Seeking to Reclaim the Moral High Ground," *Washington Post National Weekly Edition*, May 29–June 4, 2006, p. 12.
11. John C. Green and Nathan S. Bigelow, "The Christian Right Goes to Washington: Social Movement Resources and the Legislative Process," in Herrnson, Shaiko, and Wilcox, eds., *The Interest Group Connection*, pp. 191–206.
12. John C. Green, Mark J. Rozell, and Clyde Wilcox, eds., *The Values Campaign? The Christian Right and the 2004 Election* (Washington, DC: Georgetown University Press, 2006), p. 4.
13. Center for Responsive Politics, available at www.opensecrets .org.
14. Federal Election Commission, "Summary of PAC Financial Activity, 2007–2008," available at www.fec.gov.
15. Federal Election Commission, "Top 50 PAC Disbursements," available at www.fec.gov.
16. Michael M. Franz, *Choices and Changes: Interest Groups in the Electoral Process* (Philadelphia, PA: Temple University Press, 2008), p. 174.
17. Center for Responsive Politics, available at www.opensecrets .org.
18. Dan Eggen and T. W. Farnam, "New 'Super Pacs' Bringing Millions into Campaigns," *Washington Post*, September 28, 2010, available at www.washingtonpost.com.
19. Center for Responsive Politics, available at www .opensecrets.org.
20. Professor James A. Thurber, quoted in Jeffrey H. Birnbaum, "Mickey Goes to Washington," *Washington Post National Weekly Edition*, February 25–March 2, 2008, p. 6.
21. Ronald G. Shaiko, "Making the Connection: Organized Interests, Political Representation, and the Changing Rules of the Game in Washington Politics," in Herrnson, Shaiko, and Wilcox, eds., *The Interest Group Connection*, p. 32.
22. Center for Responsive Politics, available at www.opensecrets .org.
23. Rogan Kersh, "The Well-Informed Lobbyist: Information and Interest Group Lobbying," in Ciglar and Loomis, ed., *Interest Group Politics*, pp. 390–406.
24. Thomas B. Edsall, "A Chill but Not the Cold Shoulder," *Washington Post National Weekly Edition*, January 16–22, 2006, p. 15.
25. Dan Clawson, Alan Neustadtl, and Mark Weller, *Dollars and Votes: How Business Campaign Contributions Subvert Democracy* (Philadelphia, PA: Temple University Press, 1998), pp. 67–69.
26. Dan Eggen and Philip Rucker, "Loose Network of Activists Drives Reform Opposition," *Washington Post*, August 16, 2009, available at www.washingtonpost.com.
27. Steven E. Schier, *By Invitation Only: The Rise of Exclusive Politics in the United States* (Pittsburgh, PA: University of Pittsburgh Press, 2000), pp. 179–181.
28. Richard Monastersky, "Protesters Fail to Slow Animal Research," *Chronicle of Higher Education*, April 18, 2008, pp. A1, A26–A28.
29. Tom Arrandale, "The Mid-Life Crisis of the Environmental Lobby," *Governing*, April 1992, pp. 32–36.
30. Diana Evans, "Before the Roll Call: Interest Group Lobbying and Public Policy Outcomes in House Committees," *Political Research Quarterly* 49 (June 1996): 287–304.

Chapter 8

Political Parties

CHAPTER OUTLINE

The Party System

Party Organization

Political Cycles and Party Realignment

Party Strength

Voting Patterns
- Income
- Race and Ethnicity
- Education
- Gender
- Age
- Family and Lifestyle Status
- Region
- Political Ideology
- Religion
- Place of Residence

Issues

Government, Opposition, and Divided Government

What We Have Learned

WHAT WE WILL LEARN

After studying Chapter 8, students should be able to answer the following questions:

1. Why does the United States have a two-party system?
2. What services do the national political party organizations provide to party candidates?
3. What factors explain the alternation in power between political parties in the American political system?
4. What is the party balance in party identification and offices held?
5. What groups of people typically vote Democratic and what groups typically vote Republican?
6. How do the Democratic and Republican Parties compare in terms of issue orientation?
7. What is the relationship between political parties, government, and democracy?

Republican Party leaders are divided on how best to return their party to power after devastating losses in the 2006 and 2008 national elections. Republicans lost their majorities in both the U.S. House and U.S. Senate in 2006. Two years later, they lost more seats in Congress and lost the White House as well, giving the Democratic Party complete control of the legislative and executive branches of American national government. Moderate Republican leaders believe that the party should soften its position on social issues and the environment in order to broaden the party's appeal to political independents, young people, and minorities, all of whom voted heavily Democratic in 2006 and 2008. In contrast, conservative leaders counter that the Republican Party lost power because it compromised its core principles during the George W. Bush administration by increasing government spending, expanding the size of government, and running up the national debt. They argue that the way forward for the Republican Party is to return to solidly conservative policy positions of tax cuts, spending reductions, and reduced government regulation.

The battle over the future direction of the Republican Party played itself out in a number of 2010 primary elections, including the contest for a seat in the U.S. Senate between Florida Governor Charlie Crist and Marco Rubio, the former speaker of the Florida House of Representatives. Governor Crist began the race as the heavy favorite because the polls showed that he was personally popular and, as the sitting governor, he could raise a good deal of money for the campaign. Nonetheless, many conservative activists considered Crist a **Republican in name only (RINO),** which is an accusation that a Republican candidate or elected official is insufficiently conservative to merit the support of party activists. In the eyes of the conservatives, Crist's greatest sin was accepting Florida's share of the $787 billion federal economic stimulus package while literally embracing President Barack Obama when he visited Florida. Crist defended the action, declaring that the federal money helped the state balance its budget and avoid the layoff of 20,000 teachers. Meanwhile, Florida conservatives, led by the **Tea Party movement,** a loose network of conservative activists organized to protest high taxes, excessive government spending, and big government in general, lined up behind Rubio, who promised not to compromise his principles.[1] Rather than risk defeat in the Republican primary, Crist changed parties and ran for the Senate as an independent. Unfortunately for Crist, the move failed to pay off. Rubio won easily with Crist finishing a distant second.

Republican in name only (RINO) An accusation that a Republican candidate or elected official is insufficiently conservative to merit the support of party activists.

Tea Party movement A loose network of conservative activists organized to protest high taxes, excessive government spending, and big government in general.

The 2010 election was a triumph for the Republican Party and vindication for Tea Party activists and other conservatives who believe that the Republican Party will return to political power by championing conservative principles. Republicans captured a majority of seats in the U.S. House in 2010, reduced the size of the Democratic majority in the U.S. Senate, and did very well in races for state executive and legislative offices. Moreover, many of the successful Republican candidates were staunch conservatives who, similar to Marco Rubio, won with Tea Party backing.

The primary election contest between Crist and Rubio introduces this chapter on political parties in America and their role in the policymaking process. The chapter describes the party system and discusses how parties are organized. It examines the concepts of political cycles and party realignment. It compares and contrasts the Democratic and Republican Parties in terms of their party identifiers, support

Florida Republican Governor Charlie Crist alienated conservative activists in his own party when he accepted Florida's share of the $787 billion federal economic stimulus package while literally embracing President Barack Obama when he visited Florida.

groups, and issue positions. Finally, the chapter explores the phenomenon of divided government with one political party controlling Congress and the other holding the White House.

The Party System

Political party An organization that seeks political power.

A **political party** is an organization that seeks political power. A party differs from an interest group in its effort to win control of the machinery of government. Both parties and interest groups participate in election campaigns, but only parties actually run candidates for office. Candidates for Congress run as Democrats or Republicans, not representatives of the NRA or Walmart.

The major political parties in the United States also have a broader base of support than interest groups and take positions on a wider range of policy issues than do most interest groups. The United Auto Workers (UAW), for example, is a labor union representing automobile workers. Its political concerns are limited to matters relevant to auto workers and their families, such as tax policy, Social Security, Medicare, laws affecting the ability of unions to organize workers, and the enforcement of workplace safety regulations. The National Rifle Association (NRA), meanwhile, focuses narrowly on gun issues. In contrast to the UAW, NRA, and other interest groups, the Democratic and Republican Parties have broad bases of support and take positions on the full spectrum of political issues. In fact, political scientists sometimes use the terms *umbrella party* or *big tent* to refer to the two major political parties in the United States because each party encompasses a broad set of social, political, and economic interests.

Two-party system The division of voter loyalties between two major political parties, resulting in the near exclusion of minor parties from seriously competing for a share of political power.

Third party A minor party in a two-party system.

Plurality election system A method for choosing public officials that awards office to the candidate with the most votes.

Electoral College The system established in the Constitution for indirect election of the president and vice president.

Multiparty system The division of voter loyalties among three or more major political parties.

Proportional representation (PR) An election system that awards legislative seats to each party approximately equal to its popular voting strength.

The number of political parties varies from country to country. The United States has a **two-party system,** which is the division of voter loyalties between two major political parties, resulting in the near exclusion of minor parties from seriously competing for a share of political power. After the 2010 election, 98 of the 100 U.S. senators were elected as either Democrats or Republicans. Bernie Sanders of Vermont and Joe Lieberman of Connecticut won office as independents, although they caucus with the Democrats and are counted as Democrats for the purpose of committee assignments. The two major parties held all 435 seats in the U.S. House and 49 of 50 offices of state governor. The exception is independent Lincoln Chafee, governor of Rhode Island.

A **third party** is a minor party in a two-party system. Third-party candidates and independents may compete for office in a two-party system, but usually with a notable lack of success. The roster of third parties in the United States includes Green, Reform, Libertarian, Natural Law, Official Constitution, Workers World, Socialist, and Socialist Equality Parties. The Green and the Libertarian Parties are the most successful, since they have won a handful of local races.

WHAT IS YOUR OPINION?

Would you ever seriously consider voting for a third-party candidate for president? Why or why not?

Why does the United States have a two-party system as opposed to a system with three or more major political parties, as occurs in most other democracies? Political scientists offer two sets of explanations—the electoral system and the absence of deep-seated political divisions in American society. Maurice Duverger, a French political scientist, wrote in the 1950s that a **plurality election system,** which is a method for choosing public officials that awards office to the candidate with the most votes, favors a two-party system.[2] Candidates for executive and legislative office in the United States run from geographic areas and the candidate with the most votes wins the office. Candidates who finish second or third win nothing, no matter how close the race. The **Electoral College,** which is the system established in the Constitution for indirect election of the president and vice president, is especially inhospitable to third-party candidates because it awards electoral votes, the only votes that really count, to candidates that win the most popular votes in a state. In 1992, for example, Reform Party candidate Ross Perot won no electoral votes despite taking 19 percent of the popular vote because he carried no states. The dilemma for minor parties in the United States is that if they do not quickly develop enough popular support to win elections, the voters do not take them seriously. If voters believe that a party and its candidates are unlikely to win, they often decide to choose between the major party candidates because they do not want to throw away their votes.[3]

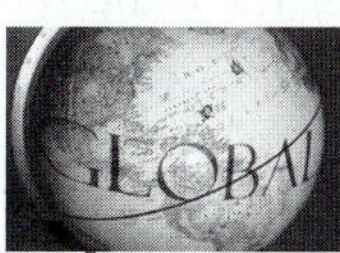

Around the World

The Israeli Party System

Israel has a **multiparty system,** which is the division of voter loyalties among three or more major political parties. The Knesset, the lower house of the Israeli national legislature, included 12 parties after the 2009 elections. Kadima, the largest party in the Knesset, held 28 of 120 seats. The Likud Party was the second largest party in the Knesset with 27 seats. Yisrael Beitenu had 15 seats. Labor had 13 seats and Shas had 11. No other party had more than five seats.* Several parties had to form a coalition in order to achieve a majority in the Knesset.

Israel has **proportional representation (PR),** which is an election system that awards legislative seats to each party approximately equal to its popular voting strength. As long as a party receives at least 2 percent of the total vote, the minimum threshold for gaining representation, the party wins seats in the Knesset in proportion to its share of the vote. In 2009, for example, Kadima won 23 percent of the seats in the Knesset based on 22 percent of the popular vote. Proportional representation is related to multiparty systems because voters know that their votes will count. Unless a party has almost no popular support, each vote it receives will enable it to increase its representation in the Knesset.

Voters in Israel cast their ballots for the party rather than individual candidates by choosing a letter symbol. Before the election, each party prepares a list of candidates for the Knesset and ranks them in order, placing party leaders at the top. If the party wins five seats, the first five candidates on the list become members of the Knesset. If it wins 10 seats, the first 10 candidates are elected. Candidates are chosen to represent their party in the Knesset rather than individual geographic districts as in the United States.†

Democracies with multiparty systems are countries with intense social and political divisions. People who disagree fundamentally about the nature of society and the role of government are less likely to form broad-based coalition parties such as those that exist in the United States. Instead, they create smaller, more narrowly based parties. Societies that are deeply divided are likely to have several political parties. The multiplicity of political parties in Israel reflects a nation deeply divided over the peace process, the creation of a Palestinian state, the economy, and the role of religion in society.

Many political scientists believe that electoral laws and a nation's social structure interact. Nations with deep social and political divisions create electoral systems based on proportional representation in order to allow the democratic expression of those divisions at the ballot box. In contrast, countries with fewer divisions establish election procedures that favor a two-party system.‡

Questions

1. If the United States were to adopt proportional representation, do you think that a multiparty system would soon develop? Why or why not?
2. If Israel were to adopt a plurality election system, do you think a two-party system would eventually emerge in that country? Why or why not?
3. What are the advantages and disadvantages of each type of party system?

*Knesset website, "Current Parliamentary Groups in the Knesset," available at www.knesset.gov.

†Asher Arian, *Politics in Israel: The Second Republic*, 2nd ed. (Washington, DC: CQ Press, 2005), p. 203.

‡Octavio Amorim Neto and Gary W. Cox, "Electoral Institutions, Cleavage Structures, and the Number of Parties," *American Journal of Political Science* 41 (January 1997): 149–174.

Scholars also believe that a party system reflects the nation's fundamental social and political divisions. The more intense the divisions, the more likely the nation will have a multiparty system. The United States has a two-party system, they say, because Americans are relatively united. Americans may disagree about the role of government in society, but they generally share the basic values of capitalism and democracy. People with opposing views on some issues can unite under the same party banner because they agree on other issues.

Party Organization

The organization of political parties in the United States reflects the federal system, with organizations at both the state and national levels of government. At the state level, the Democratic and Republican Party organizations are led by executive party committees, which are elected by party activists who participate in local party meetings, district conventions, and state party conventions. The executive committee usually elects the state party chair. In Texas, for example, the Texas Republican Executive Committee selects the chair of the Texas Republican Party, whereas the Democratic Executive Committee chooses the chair of the Texas Democratic Party.

A national committee and a national chair lead the national party organizations. The national committee consists of a committeeman and committeewoman chosen by the party organizations of each state and the District of Columbia. The national committee elects the national committee chair. When the party controls the White House, the president usually handpicks the national chairperson.

The Democratic National Committee (DNC) and Republican National Committee (RNC) work to increase the number of party officeholders. Each party tries to recruit a strong list of candidates for the next election. Although the national party organizations do not control nominations, they can encourage potential candidates to run. They also provide candidates with technical assistance and campaign advice. The DNC and RNC support their candidates with polling data, issue research, media assistance, and advice on campaign strategy. Both national parties offer campaign seminars, teaching inexperienced candidates how to do everything from raising money to dealing with the media. The most important service the national party organizations provide for their candidates, however, is money.

Figure 8.1 tracks Democratic and Republican Party fundraising from 2000 through the 2010 election. The Republicans have historically enjoyed a significant fundraising advantage over the Democrats because of the socioeconomic status of their support base and because of their fundraising expertise. People who identify with the Republican Party have more money than do people who consider themselves Democrats. The Republicans have also benefited from a more efficient fundraising operation, especially direct mail. As the figure shows, however, the Democrats erased the fundraising gap in 2008, primarily because they took better advantage of the Internet than their Republican opponents. The Democratic Party and

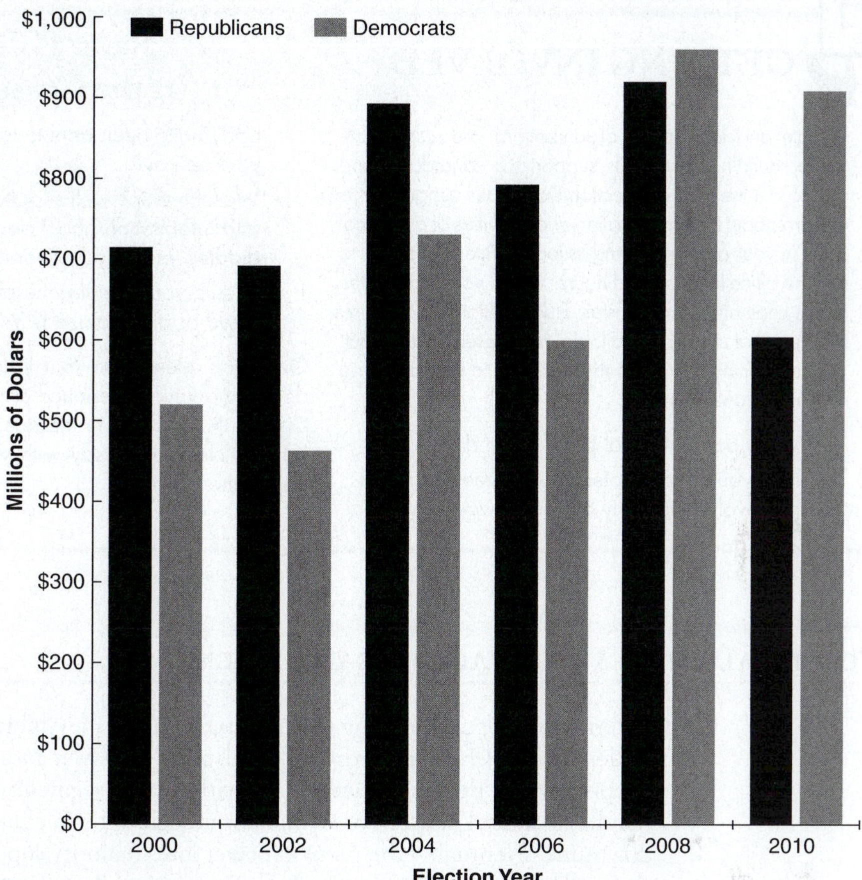

FIGURE 8.1 Party Fundraising, 2000–2010.
Source: Federal Election Commission.

its candidates now raise substantially more money online than the Republican Party and its candidates.[4] Although the Democratic Party raised considerably more money than the Republican Party in 2010, the Republicans narrowed the gap because they benefitted more than did the Democrats from spending by outside groups.[5]

Access The opportunity to communicate directly with legislators and other government officials in hopes of influencing the details of policy.

Political parties take a different approach to campaign finance than interest groups. Most interest groups contribute primarily to incumbent officeholders because they want to develop positive relationships with influential members of Congress. Their goal is **access,** which is the opportunity to communicate directly with legislators and other government officials in hopes of influencing the details of policy. In contrast, the goal of political parties is to control the government. Consequently, they contribute most of their money to candidates in competitive races, whether they are incumbents or challengers.[6]

GETTING INVOLVED — Party Politics at the Grassroots

State and local party organizations are responsible for building grassroots support for candidates and getting out the vote on Election Day. Your assignment is to learn about the organization and activities of a political party in your area by visiting its local office. Go online to find the office location and hours. When you arrive at the office, chat with the office staff, ask questions, collect any literature that might be available, and observe the layout.

Do your best to learn the answers to the following research questions:

- What does the local party office do?
- Had you been a potential volunteer, ready to get involved in party activities, would the local party have been able to take advantage of your energy?
- Was the office well supplied with literature and information about party officeholders, candidates, and issue positions?
- Would you describe the office as well organized or disorganized? Why?

Once you return from your visit, write a short essay describing your experience at the local party office. Discuss the answers to the questions in the previous list. Conclude the essay with your personal evaluation of the activity.

Political Cycles and Party Realignment

Alternation in power among political parties is an inevitable and essential element of democracy. Over time, the political party in power loses popularity because it adopts policies that prove unpopular with a large segment of the population, mishandles a natural disaster, or is unlucky enough to be in charge during an economic downturn. Eventually, the party in power loses majority support and the opposition party takes power. The success of the Democratic Party in the 2006 and 2008 elections, for example, reflected popular displeasure with the performance of the Republican Congress (before the 2006 election) and the George W. Bush administration. In early 2008, less than one in three Americans approved of President Bush's performance as president, seriously damaging the prospects of Republican Party candidates in that year's election.[7] Similarly, voters punished the Democratic Party in the 2010 midterm election, giving the Republicans control of the U.S. House and reducing the size of the Democratic majority in the U.S. Senate, primarily because of a sluggish economy with a high unemployment rate. Alternation in power is a critical component of democracy because it is the mechanism for holding the government accountable to the voters. The president and members of Congress have an incentive to do their best to provide an effective government because they know that they will eventually be held accountable at the ballot box.

Political scientists Samuel Merrill, III, Bernard Grofman, and Thomas L. Brunell offer a theory to explain partisan cycles in American politics. They note that the average American voter is moderate—less liberal on most policy issues than the Democratic Party and less conservative than the Republicans. When the Republicans are in power, the public mood grows more liberal because the Republicans adopt policies

Both Senator John McCain and Senator Barack Obama conducted campaigns designed to appeal to independent voters.

that are more conservative than the policy preferences of the average voter. Over a period of time, generally 12 to 15 years, the public grows dissatisfied and votes for change, putting a Democrat in the White House and electing a Democratic majority in Congress. The opposite happens when the Democrats are in power.[8]

Party era A period of time characterized by a degree of uniformity in the nature of political party competition.

Party realignment A change in the underlying party loyalties of voters that ends one party era and begins another.

Other political sciences use the concepts of party era and political party realignment to explain changes in the party balance. A **party era** is a period of time characterized by a degree of uniformity in the nature of political party competition. A **party realignment** is a change in the underlying party loyalties of voters that ends one party era and begins another. A party realignment has five basic characteristics: (1) changes in the regional bases of party support; (2) changes in the social bases of party support; (3) mobilization of new groups into the electorate; (4) emergence of divisive issues; and (5) changes not just in voting patterns but in how voters think about parties.[9] The 1932 election in which Democrat Franklin Roosevelt swept into office in the midst of the Great Depression is the classic example of a realigning election. The voters blamed the Republican Party for the Depression and turned control of the government over to the Democrats, who held onto their majority status for nearly 50 years. Although the nature of party competition has changed considerably since the New Deal realignment, no single election since 1932 has matched the criteria for a realigning election.

Party Strength

After the 2010 election, the Democratic and Republican Parties shared control of government. The Democrats held the White House and enjoyed a 53–47 majority in the Senate. The Republican Party was the majority party in the House, holding 242 seats compared with 193 Democratic seats. At the state level, Republican governors outnumbered Democratic governors, 29 to 20, with one independent. The Republican Party also enjoyed a sizable advantage over the Democratic Party in the number of state legislative seats held.

The Democratic Party enjoyed a narrow advantage in party identification. Political scientists measure party identification by asking survey respondents if they consider themselves Democrats, Republicans, or independents. In 2010, Democrats outnumbered Republicans by a margin of 31 percent to 29 percent, with another 38 percent declaring that they were independents. When asked whether they leaned more to the Democratic Party or the Republican Party, most of the Independents expressed a preference for one party or the other. Adding together party identifiers and leaning independents, the Democratic advantage shrank from 45 percent to 44 percent for the **Grand Old Party (GOP),** which is a nickname for the Republican Party.[10]

Grand Old Party (GOP) Nickname for the Republican Party.

WHAT IS YOUR OPINION?

Is it better to identify with a political party or to be an independent?

Voting Patterns

Voting patterns reflect differences in income, race and ethnicity, education, gender, age, family and lifestyle status, region, ideology, religion, and place of residence.

Income

Economic status is one of the most enduring bases for voting divisions in America. Since the 1930s, Republican candidates have typically done better among upper-income voters, whereas Democrats have scored their highest vote percentages among lower-income groups. In 2008, **exit polls,** surveys based on random samples of voters leaving the polling place, found that Obama outpolled McCain among voters with family incomes less than $50,000 a year by 60 percent to 38 percent. The two candidates evenly split the votes of people in families with annual incomes greater than $50,000.[11]

Exit polls Surveys based on random samples of voters leaving the polling place.

Race and Ethnicity

Voting patterns reflect the nation's racial divisions. White voters lean Republican. In 2008, 55 percent of whites backed McCain, whereas 45 percent backed Obama. In contrast, minority voters support the Democrats. In 2008, African Americans supported Obama over McCain by a lopsided 95 percent to 4 percent. Asian Americans

White voters lean Republican; minority voters tend to support the Democrats.

gave Obama 61 percent of their votes compared with 35 percent who supported McCain. Democratic candidates also enjoy support from most Latinos. In 2008, Obama won 66 percent of the Latino vote, compared with 32 percent for McCain.[12] Latino voters were especially important for Obama because they apparently provided his margin of victory in Colorado, Florida, Nevada, and New Mexico, four hotly contested states that George W. Bush won in 2004.[13] However, not all groups of Latinos share the same perspective on party affiliation. Whereas Mexican Americans and Puerto Ricans typically vote Democratic, most Cuban Americans support the GOP because of the Republican Party's strong anti-Castro position.[14]

Education

The Democratic Party is strongest with voters at either end of the education ladder. In 2008, Obama led McCain by 63 percent to 35 percent among voters who had not graduated from high school. Obama also won the votes of high school graduates, although by a more modest 52 percent to 46 percent, over his Republican opponent. The two parties evenly split the votes of college graduates. Among voters with postgraduate degrees, however, Obama led his Republican opponent by 58 percent to 40 percent.[15] For the most part, the relationship between education and party support reflects differences in income. As people move up the education ladder, they also move up the income ladder. Individuals in higher income brackets are more likely to vote Republican than are lower income voters. The pattern holds through college but not into graduate and professional school. People who have postgraduate college degrees tend to vote Democratic because many of them hold liberal positions on social issues such as abortion rights, environmental protection, and gay and lesbian rights.

Gender

Gender gap Differences in party identification and political attitudes between men and women.

For more than 40 years, American voters have divided along gender lines, producing a **gender gap,** the differences in party identification and political attitudes between men and women. The gender gap has emerged in American politics because men have moved away from the Democratic Party. In 1952, a majority of both men and women identified with the Democratic Party. Since then, the percentage of women identifying with the Democrats has risen while the proportion of men declaring themselves Democrats has declined. The gender gap was greatest in the 1996 presidential election at 14 percentage points. Subsequently, the gap has somewhat narrowed. In 2008, Democrat Barack Obama won the support of half of the male voters, but he carried 56 percent of the women's vote, a 6 percentage point gender gap.[16]

Age

Polling data reveal that younger voters have been moving toward the Democratic Party and away from the GOP. In fact, Obama won the presidency in 2008 because of his support from younger voters. He outpolled McCain among voters under the age of 30 by 66 percent to 32 percent. Obama won the 30–44 age bracket as well, but by a closer margin of 52 percent to 46 percent. The two candidates split the votes of people ages 45 to 64. McCain won a majority of voters over the age of 65, taking 53 percent compared with 45 percent for Obama.[17]

Family and Lifestyle Status

People who are members of traditional families tend to vote Republican, whereas unmarried adults and people who are gay, lesbian, or bisexual generally back the Democrats. In 2008, married voters supported McCain by 51 percent to 47 percent for Obama. In contrast, Obama led his Republican opponent among single people by 65 percent to 33 percent. Voters who identified as gay, lesbian, or bisexual supported Obama by 70 percent, compared with 27 percent for McCain.[18]

Region

Regional voting patterns have changed. The South was once the strongest region for the Democratic Party, whereas the Midwest was a stronghold for the GOP. Today, Democrats run best in the Northeast and on the West Coast. The GOP is strongest in the South, the Great Plains, and the Rocky Mountain West. The Midwest has become a battleground region between the two parties. In 2008, Obama was strongest in the Northeast, winning 59 percent of the vote and carrying every state in the region. McCain ran best in the South, outpolling Obama 53 percent to 46 percent, and winning every southern state except Florida, North Carolina, and Virginia.[19]

Political Ideology

The Democratic and Republican Parties are ideologically polarized. Conservatives are aligned with the GOP; liberals vote Democratic.[20] In 2008, liberals supported Obama over McCain by a substantial 88 percent to 10 percent. In contrast, conservatives backed McCain by an impressive 78 percent to 20 percent. Moderates tend to be swing voters. Obama won the White House because he captured 60 percent of the votes of moderates, compared with 39 percent for McCain.[21]

The political parties were once more ideologically diverse than they are today. Many conservatives identified with the Democratic Party, especially in the South, whereas the Republican Party had a liberal wing based principally in the Northeast. Important legislation frequently passed Congress with the support of bipartisan coalitions. For example, the Civil Rights Act of 1964 passed Congress because moderate and liberal Republicans joined with liberal Democrats to overcome the intense opposition of conservative southern Democrats.

The political parties are more ideologically distinct today because their coalitions of supporters have changed. The move of southern white conservatives from the Democratic Party to the GOP has made the Democrats more liberal and the Republicans more conservative. The Democratic Party has adopted liberal positions on a range of social issues in order to appeal to middle-class voters concerned with abortion rights, the environment, and gay and lesbian rights. The Republican Party, meanwhile, has taken conservative positions on social issues to bolster its support among conservative Christians.[22] In addition, the Tea Party movement is making the GOP more conservative on economic issues.

Religion

Religion and party support are closely related. During the last party era, voting patterns reflected religious affiliation. Protestants generally supported the Republican Party, Catholics leaned to the Democratic Party, and Jews were strongly Democratic. Today, party divisions based on religion have grown more complex. Although most Jews still vote for Democrats, Catholics have become a swing group. Conservative white evangelical Protestants (including Southern Baptists, Pentacostals, and members of the Assemblies of God) are firmly Republican as are members of the Church of Jesus Christ of Latter-day Saints (the Mormons). Latinos as a whole typically support the Democrats, but the GOP is stronger among Latino evangelicals than among Latino Catholics, who remain firmly Democratic.[23] White members of mainline Protestant denominations (including Methodists, Episcopalians, and Presbyterians) lean Republican as well, but less so than do evangelicals. Most African Americans are Democrats, regardless of their religious preferences.[24] In 2008, Jews supported Obama over McCain by 78 percent to 21 percent. Catholics backed Obama as well, but the margin was more narrow, 54 percent to 45 percent. Protestants voted for McCain over Obama by 54 percent to 45 percent.[25]

Today, voting patterns are also based on frequency of attendance at religious services. White Protestants and Catholics who attend worship services regularly are more likely to vote Republican than are people who attend services less frequently.[26] In 2008, McCain led among voters who said that they attended religious services more than once a week, taking 55 percent of the vote compared with 43 percent for Obama. In contrast, voters who declared that they seldom attended religious services voted for Obama by 59 percent to 40 percent. People who never attended services backed the Democrat by 67 percent to 30 percent.[27]

Place of Residence

Voting patterns reflect place of residence. Democrats win urban areas, Republicans carry rural areas, and the suburbs are a battleground between the two parties. In 2008, Obama outpolled McCain in large urban areas by 63 percent to 35 percent, whereas the Republican candidate won rural areas by 53 percent to 45 percent. The vote in the suburbs was 50 percent for Obama to 48 percent for McCain.[28]

Issues

Since the 1970s, the parties have grown further apart philosophically, with the Democrats generally taking liberal positions and the Republicans expressing conservative views. Voters who think that the government is too big and taxes are too high, who long for a return to traditional standards of morality and behavior, who support the war in Afghanistan, and who favor an aggressive foreign policy back the Republican Party. In contrast, citizens who favor the adoption of more social programs to address economic and racial inequality, who want the government to protect abortion rights and guarantee equal treatment for gay men and lesbians, who demand an end to the war, and who prefer a cautious foreign policy conducted in concert with allies vote for the Democrats.[29]

Party platform A statement of party principles and issue positions.

A **party platform** is a statement of party principles and issue positions. The 2008 Democratic and Republican Party platforms, which are excerpted in Table 8.1, show clear philosophical differences between the parties on many issues. The parties disagreed on tax policy, labor laws, abortion, gay and lesbian rights, and affirmative action. By no means, however, do the parties take opposite sides on all issues. Some differences are nuanced. Consider gun control. Both parties endorse a right of gun ownership, but they disagree on the efficacy of gun regulation. The Democrats endorse "reasonable regulation," while the Republicans declare that gun control penalizes law-abiding citizens without having an impact on crime. Finally, the two parties take similar positions on some issues. Both the Democratic and the Republican platforms declare support for Israel, even using the same phrase to pledge that the United States would ensure that Israel would always have better weapons ("a qualitative edge") than its adversaries.

TABLE 8.1 Selected 2008 Democratic and Republican Party Platform Positions

Issue	Democratic Position	Republican Position
Healthcare	Declares that every American should be guaranteed affordable, comprehensive healthcare and that healthcare should be a shared responsibility between employers, workers, insurers, providers, and government. Endorses government support for embryonic stem cell research.	Supports health savings accounts that provide tax breaks to individuals who save money to pay for their own health insurance coverage. Says employer-provided health insurance should no longer be tax exempt. Calls for expansion of research using adult stem cells but opposes embryonic stem cell research.
Education	Supports innovative ways to increase teacher pay that are negotiated between schools and teachers rather than imposed on teachers. Endorses $4,000 higher education tax credit; in exchange, students will perform community service. Supports age-appropriate sex education.	Supports school choice programs with vouchers for private schools, including religious schools. Advocates merit pay for teachers. Endorses abstinence-only sex education.
Environmental policy	Endorses a cap-and-trade system to reduce carbon emissions that cause global warming.	Favors market-based solutions for decreasing emissions, reducing greenhouse gasses, and mitigating the impact of climate change.
Social Security	Opposes Social Security privatization and increasing the retirement age. Promises to raise revenue to support the program by applying the Social Security payroll tax on income over $250,000 a year.	Promises that anyone now receiving Social Security benefits or close to receiving them will not have their benefits cut or their taxes increased. Calls for partial privatization through the creation of personal investment accounts.
Iran	Declares that the United States and its allies should use diplomacy, sanctions, and incentives to ensure that Iran will not be allowed to develop nuclear weapons.	Declares that the United States, in solidarity with the international community, should not allow Iran to develop nuclear weapons.
Iraq and Afghanistan	Promises to bring the war in Iraq to a responsible end. Declares that the war in Afghanistan and the fight against the Taliban should be the nation's top military priority.	Calls for increasing troop strength in Afghanistan.
Israel	Declares that the United States must ensure that Israel enjoys a qualitative edge for its national security and its right to self-defense.	Declares support for Israel and pledges that the United States will ensure that Israel enjoy a qualitative edge in defense technologies over any potential adversaries.
Energy	Declares the United States must reduce oil consumption by 35 percent by 2030. Says that the government should provide incentives to increase domestic production of clean and renewable energy. Calls for more fuel-efficient automobiles.	Calls for increasing energy development in the United States in an environmentally responsible way, including drilling in the Arctic National Wildlife Refuge (ANWR), on federal lands in the western United States, and offshore. Supports the construction of new nuclear power plants as well as alternative sources of energy, such as wind, solar, and geothermal.

(Continued)

TABLE 8.1 *(Continued)*

Issue	Democratic Position	Republican Position
Trade	Calls for the inclusion of international labor and environmental standards in trade agreements.	Supports free trade and open markets because free trade means more American jobs, higher wages, and a better standard of living.
Tax policy	Promises to eliminate income taxes on retirees making less than $50,000 a year. Says that families earning more than $250,000 a year will have to give back some of the tax cuts granted to them during the Bush administration.	Favors making the tax cuts enacted during the early years of the Bush administration permanent. Proposes a major reduction in the corporate income tax rate. Calls for giving tax-payers the option of filing under the current tax code or under a two-rate flat-tax alternative.
Budget policy	Supports a pay-as-you-go budget process in which Congress would have to balance any spending increases or tax reductions with equal spending reductions or tax increases.	Calls for the adoption of a Balanced Budget constitutional amendment. Says that additional spending should be offset by reductions in another program.
Immigration reform	Calls for securing the nation's borders. Endorses immigration reform that requires undocumented immigrants who are in good standing to pay a fine, pay taxes, learn English, and then have the opportunity to become citizens.	Declares that border security is essential to national security. Opposes amnesty. Supports English as the official language of the nation. Opposes drivers' licenses and in-state college tuition for illegal aliens.
Gun control	Promises to preserve the right to own and use firearms, while recognizing the need for reasonable regulation.	Strongly supports the individual right to own and bear arms. Declares that gun control penalizes only law-abiding citizens and is ineffective at preventing crime.
Affirmative action	Supports affirmative action to redress discrimination and achieve diversity in federal contracting and higher education.	Opposes discrimination while rejecting all preferences, quotas, and set-asides based on skin color, ethnicity, or gender.
Abortion	Strongly supports a woman's right to choose a safe and legal abortion, regardless of ability to pay.	Favors a constitutional amendment to prohibit abortion.
Gay and lesbian rights	Endorses federal legislation to prohibit job discrimination based on sexual orientation. Supports "equal responsibility, benefits, and protections" for same-sex couples, but does not mention gay marriage.	Endorses a constitutional amendment to define marriage as between one man and one woman. Opposes legal recognition of same-sex relationships or granting benefits to same-sex couples.

Government, Opposition, and Divided Government

Political parties are essential for democracy. The political party or party coalition holding the reins of government in a democracy is the **governing party.** After the 2008 election, the Democratic Party, with majorities in the U.S. House and U.S. Senate and control of the executive branch, was the governing power of American national government. It was in position to formulate, adopt, and implement government

Governing party The political party or party coalition holding the reins of government in a democracy.

Opposition party The political party out of power in a democracy.

Divided government The phenomenon of one political party controlling the legislative branch of government while the other holds the executive branch.

policies. Although the nature of America's political system typically prevents the governing party from enacting all (or sometimes even most) of its policy agenda, it is able to take the policy lead on most issues. The political party out of power in a democracy is the **opposition party.** The opposition party criticizes the policies of the governing party and offers alternatives. The opposition party ensures that citizens receive more information about government policies and programs than the official statements of government leaders. The opposition party has an incentive to highlight failures and seek out inefficiency and corruption, as doing so may help them become the governing party. Opposition parties help make democracy work by providing information to citizens and offering voters alternative policies and alternative sets of leaders to those put forward by the governing party.

American elections sometimes result in **divided government,** which is the phenomenon of one political party controlling the legislative branch of government while the other holds the executive branch. When different parties share control of Congress and the White House, no party is the governing party in the sense that it has complete control of the reins of political power, and no party is the opposition party in the sense that it is shut out of political power. Divided government can produce policy gridlock or cooperation. If party leaders in Congress and the president are unable to reach agreement on major policy issues, Congress may reject presidential initiatives while the president may veto measures passed by Congress, leaving the country in a policy gridlock. Alternatively, Congressional leaders and the White House may cooperate to adopt compromise policies. Some observers expect that the 2010 midterm election will ensure two years of conflict between the White House and Congress because many of the newly elected Republican members of Congress, especially members who won with the backing of the Tea Party movement, promised no compromise with the Democrats in Congress and the Obama administration.

WHAT IS YOUR OPINION?

Do you prefer divided government or would you rather have both the legislative and executive branches controlled by the same party?

Table 8.2 documents instances of divided and unified government since 1969. Although there have been periods when one party controlled both the legislative and executive branches of government, divided government has been more common than unified control of government. Historical research shows that divided government is not unique to the current era, although it has become more frequent. The first instances of divided government occurred before the Civil War. In the nineteenth century, 16 of 50 elections resulted in divided government, with different parties controlling the White House and at least one chamber of Congress.[30] Between 1900 and 1952, 22 elections produced unified government; four resulted in divided government. Divided government has now become commonplace. Between 1952 and 2010, 11 elections resulted in unified government whereas 18 elections produced divided government.[31] Divided government is common at the state level as well.

TABLE 8.2 Party Control of Executive and Legislative Branches of American National Government Since 1969

Year	Divided or Unified Control	Party Controlling Executive and Legislative Branches
1969–1977 (eight years)	Divided	Republican president, Democratic Congress
1977–1981 (four years)	Unified	Democratic president, Democratic Congress
1981–1987 (six years)	Divided	Republican president, Democratic House, Republican Senate
1987–1993 (six years)	Divided	Republican president, Democratic Congress
1993–1995 (two years)	Unified	Democratic president, Democratic Congress
1995–2001 (six years)	Divided	Democratic president, Republican Congress
2001–2003 (two years)	Divided	Republican president, Republican House, Democratic Senate*
2003–2007 (four years)	Unified	Republican president, Republican Congress
2007–2009 (two years)	Divided	Republican president, Democratic Congress
2009–2011 (two years)	Unified	Democratic president, Democratic Congress
Since 2011	Divided	Democratic president, Democratic Senate, Republican House

*After the 2000 election, the Senate was evenly divided between the two parties and the vote of Republican Vice President Richard Cheney enabled the GOP to claim majority status. In 2001, Republican Senator James Jeffords of Vermont switched his party allegiance from Republican to independent to allow the Democrats to claim the majority, which they held until 2003.

Separation of powers The division of political power among executive, legislative, and judicial branches of government.

The Constitution sets the stage for divided government. In a parliamentary system, the national legislature chooses the chief executive (often called a prime minister) by majority vote. Consequently, the party or coalition of parties that controls the legislature also controls the executive. In contrast, the United States has **separation of powers,** which is the division of political power among the executive, legislative, and judicial branches of government. Members of Congress and the president are elected independently from one another. They have different constituencies, serve terms of different length, and stand for election at different times. In particular, midterm elections are more likely to produce divided government than presidential election years. With relatively few exceptions, the president's party loses seats in the House in a midterm election. On 10 occasions since 1894, midterm elections have produced divided government or added a second chamber to opposition control.

The 2010 midterm election is an example of voters holding the governing party accountable. This time the Democrats were in charge and suffered big losses. The Republican Party won control of the U.S. House, added seats in the Senate, and made substantial gains at the state level as well. The outcome of the 2010 election reflected the sour mood of the nation. Polls taken just before the election found that Americans believed that the country was on the wrong track by a 64 percent to 31 percent margin. President Obama's job approval rating was 45 percent while the job approval rating for Congress was only 20 percent.[32] Exit polls taken the day of the election found that three-fourths of those people who voted indicated that they were dissatisfied or even angry with the way the federal government was working. Why were the voters so unhappy? It was primarily the economy. According to exit polls, 89 percent of voters said that the nation's economy was in bad shape, almost as many as in 2008. More than 40 percent said that their personal financial situations had grown worse off in the last two years and 87 percent were worried or very worried about the direction of the economy.[33]

Elections for president, Congress, and the Senate usually feature different issues. Whereas candidates for president stress national issues involving foreign policy, defense, and the strength of the nation's economy, candidates for the House of Representatives focus on local issues, such as cleaning up an area waterway or the proposed closure of a regional military base. Local voters may choose the presidential candidate that they believe will work the hardest to cut taxes while voting for the candidate for Congress who promises to support increased federal spending in the region.[34]

At any given time, Party A may have an advantage on national issues while Party B is perceived by voters as being stronger on local issues. During the 1980s, presidential elections focused on defense, tax rates, and cultural values—issues that favored the Republicans. In contrast, races for Congress focused on more specific policy concerns, such as protecting Social Security, helping farmers or unemployed workers, and promoting local economic development. These were issues that advantaged Democrats. Divided government reflected the divided issue preferences of Americans. Voters want low inflation, a less obtrusive government, and low taxes—positions associated with the GOP. Voters also want the government to ensure a safe

Polling data show that younger voters have been moving toward the Democratic Party and away from the GOP.

environment, promote education, and protect the integrity of the Social Security and Medicare programs—issues that favor the Democratic Party.

Political scientists disagree as to whether divided government is the result of conscious voter choice. Some research indicates that even though the proportion of voters who split their ticket in order to balance the House with a president of the other party is small, the number is large enough to affect election outcomes.[35] Other research, however, finds that voters who split their tickets in hopes of producing divided control of government are more than offset by people who cast straight tickets in order to minimize gridlock. In other words, strategic voting makes divided government less common, not more common.[36]

WHAT WE HAVE LEARNED

1. **Why does the United States have a two-party system?**

   The United States has a two-party system, which is the division of voter loyalties between two major political parties, resulting in the near exclusion of minor parties from seriously competing for a share of political power. Political scientists attribute America's two-party system to the nature of the country's election system, especially plurality elections and the Electoral College, as well as the absence of fundamental social and political divisions.

2. **What services do the national political party organizations provide for party candidates?**

   The national political party organizations recruit candidates, provide them with technical assistance and advice, and spend money on their behalf. Historically, the Republicans have enjoyed a fundraising advantage over the Democrats, but that advantage disappeared in 2008.

3. **What factors explain the alternation in power between political parties in the American political system?**

   Over time, the political party in power loses popularity and voters turn to the other party. This is the concept of alternation in power. Political scientists note that the average American voter is moderate. When the Republicans are in power, the public mood grows more liberal because the Republicans adopt policies that are more conservative than the policy preferences of the average voter and vice versa. Eventually, they vote for a change. Other political scientists use the concepts of party era and party realignment to explain changes in the party balance.

4. **What is the party balance in party identification and offices held?**

   The strength of a political party depends on its level of support among the electorate and the offices it holds. Although the two parties were at near parity in terms of party identification in 2010, the Democrats shared power with the GOP after the 2010 midterm. Republicans controlled the U.S. House whereas Democrats enjoyed a majority of seats in the U.S. Senate and held the White House.

5. **What groups of people typically vote Democratic and what groups typically vote Republican?**

   Democrats do better among middle- and low-income people, minority voters, high-school dropouts, people with graduate degrees, women, younger people, single persons, gay/lesbian/bisexual individuals, people living in the Northeast and the West Coast, liberals, Jews, people who seldom if ever attend religious services, and people living in urban areas. In contrast, Republicans are stronger with middle- and upper-income groups, white voters, people with bachelor's degrees, men, older people, married people, southerners, conservatives, white evangelical Protestants, people who attend religious services regularly, and people living in rural areas.

6. **How do the Democratic and Republican Parties compare in terms of issue orientation?**
   Since 1960, the parties have grown further apart philosophically, with the Democrats generally taking liberal positions and the Republicans expressing conservative views. Democrats believe that a strong government is needed to provide essential services and remedy social inequalities. They favor healthcare reform, government action to respond to climate change, and comprehensive immigration reform. They support abortion rights and affirmative action, and oppose discrimination against gay men and lesbians. Republicans believe that a strong government interferes with business and threatens individual freedom. They favor privatization of Social Security through investment accounts and advocate making the tax cuts adopted during the George W. Bush administration permanent. They oppose abortion, gay marriage, and affirmative action.

7. **What is the relationship between political parties, government, and democracy?**
   The political party or party coalition holding the reins of government in a democracy is the governing party. The political party out of power is the opposition party. The phenomenon of one political party controlling the legislative branch of government while the other holds the executive branch is known as divided government. The 2010 election ushered in another period of divided government with the GOP capturing the House and the Democrats holding the Senate and presidency.

KEY TERMS

access
divided government
Electoral College
exit polls
gender gap
governing party
Grand Old Party (GOP)
multiparty system
opposition party
party era
party platform
party realignment
plurality election system
political party
proportional representation (PR)
Republican in name only (RINO)
separation of powers
Tea Party movement
third party
two-party system

NOTES

1. Mark Leibovich, "The First Senator from the Tea Party?" *New York Times*, January 10, 2010, available at www.nytimes.com.
2. Maurice Duverger, *Political Parties* (New York: Wiley, 1954), p. 217.
3. A. James Reichley, "The Future of the American Two-Party System at the Beginning of a New Century," in John C. Green and Rick Farmer, eds., *The State of the Parties: The Changing Role of Contemporary American Parties*, 4th ed. (Lanham, MD: Rowman & Littlefield, 2003), pp. 20–21.
4. Michael Toner, "The Impact of the New Campaign Finance Law on the 2004 Presidential Election," in Larry Sabato, ed., *Divided States of America: The Slash and Burn Politics of the 2004 Presidential Election* (New York: Pearson Longman, 2006), p. 197.
5. Center for Responsive Politics, available at www.opensecrets.org.
6. Timothy P. Nokken, "Ideological Congruence versus Electoral Success: Distribution of Party Organization Contributions in

Senate Elections, 1990–2000," *American Politics Research* 31 (January 2003): 3–26.

7. "Bush Approval Static, Congress' Sinks Further," March 14, 2008, available at www.gallup.com.
8. Samuel Merrill, III, Bernard Grofman, and Thomas L. Brunell, "Cycles in American National Electoral Politics, 1854–2006: Statistical Evidence and an Explanatory Model," *American Political Science Review* 102 (February 2008): 1–17.
9. Paul R. Abramson, John H. Aldrich, and David W. Rohde, *Change and Continuity in the 2008 Election* (Washington, DC: CQ Press, 2010), p. 6.
10. Jeffrey M. Jones, "Democratic Party ID Drops in 2010, Tying 22-Year Low," January 5, 2011, available at www.gallup.com.
11. Exit poll data, available at www.cnn.com.
12. Ibid.
13. Juan Castillo, "Latinos Deliver on Potential, Turn Out Big for Obama," *Austin American-Statesman*, November 6, 2008, available at www.statesman.com.
14. David L. Leal, Stephan A. Nuño, Jongho Lee, and Rodolpho O. de la Garza, "Latinos, Immigration, and the 2006 Midterm Election," *PS: Political Science & Politics*, April 2008, p. 312.
15. Exit poll data.
16. Ibid.
17. Ibid.
18. Ibid.
19. Ibid.
20. Donald C. Baumer and Howard J. Gold, *Parties, Polarization, and Democracy in the United States* (Boulder, CO: Paradigm Publishers, 2010), p. 78.
21. Ibid.
22. Morris P. Fiorina, *Culture War? The Myth of a Polarized America*, 2nd ed. (New York: Pearson Education, 2006), pp. 61–70.
23. Jongho Lee and Harry P. Pachon, "Leading the Way: An Analysis of the Effect of Religion on the Latino Vote," *American Politics Research* 35 (March 2007): 252–272.
24. John C. Green, Lyman A. Kellstedt, Corwin E. Smidt, and James L. Guth, "How the Faithful Voted: Religious Communities and the Presidential Vote," in David E. Campbell, ed., *A Matter of Faith: Religion in the 2004 Presidential Election* (Washington, DC: Brookings Institution Press, 2007), pp. 1–28.
25. Exit poll data.
26. Frank Newport, "Church Attendance and Party Identification," May 18, 2005, available at www.gallup.com.
27. Exit poll data.
28. Ibid.
29. Mark D. Brewer and Jeffrey M. Stonecash, *Dynamics of American Political Parties* (New York: Cambridge University Press, 2009), p. 209.
30. Joel H. Silbey, "Divided Government in Historical Perspective, 1789–1996," in Peter F. Golderisi, ed., *Divided Government: Change, Uncertainty, and the Constitutional Order* (Lanham, MD: Rowman & Littlefield, 1996), pp. 9–34.
31. Morris Fiorina, *Divided Government*, 2nd ed. (Cambridge, MA: Harvard University Press, 1996), p. 7.
32. "RCP Poll Averages," available at www.realclearpolitics.com.
33. Gary Langer, "2010 Elections Exit Poll Analysis: The Political Price of Economic Pain," ABC News, November 3, 2010, available at www.abcnews.go.com.
34. John R. Petrocik and Joseph Doherty, "The Road to Divided Government: Paved Without Intention," in Golderisi, ed., *Divided Government: Change, Uncertainty, and the Constitutional Order*, p. 105.
35. Walter R. Mebane, Jr., "Combination, Moderation, and Institutional Balancing in American Presidential Elections," *American Political Science Review* 94 (March 2000): 37–57.
36. Michael Peress, "Strategic Voting in Multi-Office Elections," *Legislative Studies Quarterly* 33 (November 2008): 619–640.

Chapter 9

Elections

CHAPTER OUTLINE

WHAT WE WILL LEARN

After studying Chapter 9, students should be able to answer the following questions:

1. What types of elections are held in the United States?
2. What factors affect the redistricting process?
3. What are the goals of an election campaign, and how does money affect the ability of candidates to achieve their goals?
4. What are the similarities and differences in elections for the U.S. House and U.S. Senate?
5. What are the main steps in the nominating stage of the presidential election process?
6. What are the most important steps in the general election stage of the presidential election process?
7. How does each of the following factors affect voter choice: party identification, issues, personal qualities and image, campaigns, and retrospective and prospective voting?

The Republican Party won the 2010 midterm election. Republicans won a clear majority in the U.S. House, increasing the size of their representation by 63 seats. When Congress convened in 2011, Republicans outnumbered Democrats in the House 242 to 193. Although Republicans fell short of the goal of taking control of the U.S. Senate, they gained six seats in the chamber, reducing the Democratic majority to 53 Democratic senators compared with 47 Republicans. The Republican Party made sizable gains at the state level as well. It increased the number of Republican governors to 29 compared with 20 Democratic governors and 1 independent. In addition, the GOP picked up hundreds of seats in state legislatures.

The Republican Party won because of a heavy turnout by conservative Republican voters and strong support from independent voters. Polls conducted before the election found that Republicans, motivated at least in part by the Tea Party movement, were substantially more enthusiastic about going to the polls than were the Democrats.[1] The GOP also did well with independent voters. Whereas independents backed Obama in 2008 by 8 percentage points, they supported Republican congressional candidates in 2010 by a 55 percent to 39 percent margin.[2]

The 2010 off-year election outcome introduces this chapter on elections in America. This chapter focuses on elections, considering types of elections, election districts and redistricting, political campaigns, congressional elections, presidential elections, the factors that influence voter choice, and the relationship between elections and public policy.

Types of Elections

General election An election to fill state and national offices held in November of even-numbered years.

Straight ticket ballot Voters selecting the entire slate of candidates of one party only.

Split ticket ballot Voters casting their ballots for the candidates of two or more political parties.

Americans have the opportunity to cast ballots in several types of elections. A **general election** is held in November of even-numbered years to fill state and national offices. Voters choose among Democratic and Republican candidates, as well as occasional third-party candidates and independent candidates not affiliated with any political party. Some states allow voters to cast a **straight ticket ballot,** which refers to voters selecting the entire slate of candidates of one party only. In contrast, a **split ticket ballot** occurs when voters cast their ballots for the candidates of two or more political parties during a single election.

Most general elections are plurality elections. In every state but Georgia, the candidate with the most votes wins the general election, regardless of whether the candidate has a majority of ballots cast. Georgia requires a **runoff,** which is an election between the two candidates receiving the most votes when no candidate wins a majority in an initial election.

In most states, major parties choose their general election candidates in primary elections scheduled a month or more before the November general election. A **primary election** is held to determine a party's nominees for the general election ballot. Democrats compete against other Democrats; Republicans compete against Republicans. In a number of states, a candidate must achieve a certain threshold level of support at a state party convention in order to qualify for the primary ballot. The candidate with

Runoff An election between the two candidates receiving the most votes when no candidate got a majority in an initial election.

Primary election An intra-party election held to select party candidates for the general-election ballot.

Closed primary An election system that limits primary election participation to registered party members.

Open primary An election system that allows voters to pick the party primary of their choice without regard to their party affiliation.

Blanket primary A primary election system that allows voters to select candidates without regard for party affiliation.

Republican Bobby Jindal became governor of Louisiana in 2007, taking 54 percent of the blanket primary vote to win a four-way race without a runoff.

the most votes wins the primary election in most states, regardless of whether the candidate has a majority. Some states, including most southern states, require a runoff between the top two candidates if no one receives a majority in the first vote.

Some states conduct closed primaries, whereas other states hold open primaries. A **closed primary** is an election system that limits primary election participation to registered party members. Only registered Republicans can vote in the GOP primary; participants in the Democratic primary must be registered Democrats. In contrast, an **open primary** is an election system that allows voters to pick the party primary of their choice without regard to their party affiliation. California has adopted a **blanket primary,** which is a primary election system that allows voters to select candidates without regard for party affiliation. If no candidate receives a majority in the primary, the two leading candidates face each other in the general election regardless of party affiliation.

Election Districts and Redistricting

American voters select public officials in a combination of at-large and district elections. An **at-large election** is a method for choosing public officials in which the citizens of an entire political subdivision, such as a state, vote to select officeholders. U.S. senators, state governors, and other state executive-branch officials are elected at-large in statewide elections. States that are so sparsely populated that they have

At-large election A method for choosing public officials in which the citizens of an entire political subdivision, such as a state, vote to select officeholders.

District election A method for choosing public officials that divides a political subdivision, such as a state, into geographic areas called districts; each district elects one official.

Apportionment The allocation of legislative seats among the states.

Redistricting The process through which the boundaries of legislative districts are redrawn to reflect population movement.

Reapportionment The reallocation of legislative seats.

One person, one vote The judicial ruling that the Equal Protection Clause of the Fourteenth Amendment to the U.S. Constitution requires legislative districts to be apportioned on the basis of population.

only one representative in the U.S. House of Representatives, such as Alaska, Delaware, and Wyoming, choose their member of Congress in statewide at-large elections as well.

A **district election** is a method for choosing public officials that divides a political subdivision, such as a state, into geographic areas called districts. Voters in each district then elect one official. States with more than one U.S. representative choose their members of Congress from districts. Missouri, for example, with nine members of the U.S. House, has nine U.S. congressional districts, each of which elects one representative. The members of state legislatures are also chosen in district elections.

Reapportionment

Legislative district boundaries must be redrawn every 10 years after the national census is taken. Census data are used for apportioning the 435 seats of the U.S. House of Representatives among the states. **Apportionment** is the allocation of legislative seats among the states. States that grew rapidly since the last census gain seats in the House, whereas slowly growing states lose representation. After the 2010 Census, 10 states lost one or more seats in the House, whereas eight states gained one or more seats. New York, which lost two House seats, had to shuffle district boundaries to reduce the number of congressional districts in the state from 29 to 27. In contrast, Texas, which gained four seats, increased the number of its House districts from 32 to 36.

Legislative districts must also be redrawn if census data show population movement within a state. **Redistricting** is the process through which the boundaries of legislative districts are redrawn to reflect population movement. During the first half of the twentieth century, a number of states failed to redistrict despite dramatic population movement from rural to urban areas because rural state legislators did not want to relinquish control. As a result, the population size of some legislative districts varied dramatically. In Illinois, one U.S. congressional district in Chicago had a population of 914,053 by the early 1960s, whereas another district in rural Southern Illinois contained only 112,116 people.[3]

The U.S. Supreme Court dealt with the issue of legislative reapportionment in a series of cases, the most important of which were *Baker v. Carr* (1962) and *Wesberry v. Sanders* (1964).[4] **Reapportionment** is the reallocation of legislative seats. In these and other cases, the Supreme Court established the doctrine of **one person, one vote,** which is the judicial ruling holding that the Equal Protection Clause of the Fourteenth Amendment to the U.S. Constitution requires legislative districts to be apportioned on the basis of population. The Supreme Court has also stipulated that legislative district boundaries must be drawn to ensure nearly equal population size. Although the Court allows as much as 10 percent variation in the size of state legislative districts and local districts, it requires that U.S. congressional districts contain almost exactly the same number of people.[5] In 2002, for example, a federal court overturned Pennsylvania's redistricting plan because two U.S. House districts varied in size by 19 people—646,361 compared with 646,380.[6]

The Court's one-person, one-vote decisions have affected legislative representation and policy. When the rulings were first implemented in the 1960s, rural areas lost representation, whereas the nation's big cities gained seats. As a result, urban problems, such as housing, education, unemployment, transportation, and race relations took center stage on legislative agendas.[7] The distribution of public funds changed as well. Counties that were overrepresented before redistricting in the 1960s received relatively more government funds per person than they deserved on the basis of their population, whereas areas that were underrepresented received fewer government dollars per capita than their population size would dictate. After redistricting, the distribution of government funds changed to conform closely to relative population size. Nationwide, the effect of redistricting was to shift $7 billion of public funds annually from rural to urban areas.[8]

Recent census figures have shown that America's population has shifted away from generally liberal inner cities to more conservative suburbs and surrounding metropolitan areas. This time redistricting changes have led to fewer representatives from constituencies demanding big government and more representatives from areas where people are wary of government. Congress and many state legislatures have grown more conservative.[9]

Voting Rights Act (VRA)

Voting Rights Act (VRA) A federal law designed to protect the voting rights of racial and ethnic minorities.

The **Voting Rights Act (VRA)** is a federal law designed to protect the voting rights of racial and ethnic minorities. The VRA makes it illegal for state and local governments to enact and enforce election rules and procedures that diminish the voting power of racial, ethnic, and language minority groups. Furthermore, the VRA requires state and local governments in areas with a history of voting discrimination to submit redistricting plans to the U.S. Department of Justice for approval *before* they can go into effect, a procedure known as pre-clearance. Congress and the president included the pre-clearance provision in the VRA in order to stay one step ahead of local officials who adopted new discriminatory electoral practices as soon as the federal courts threw out an old procedure. The pre-clearance provision of the VRA only applies to states and parts of states that have substantial racial and language minority populations with relatively low rates of voter participation, including all or part of Alaska, Alabama, Arizona, California, Florida, Georgia, Louisiana, Michigan, Mississippi, New Hampshire, New York, North Carolina, South Carolina, South Dakota, Texas, and Virginia.

In the late 1980s and early 1990s, the Department of Justice in the first Bush administration interpreted amendments to the VRA adopted in 1982 to require that state legislatures create legislative districts designed to maximize minority representation. In short, the Justice Department declared that if a district *could* be drawn that would likely elect an African American or Latino candidate then it *must* be drawn. State legislatures would have to create the maximum possible number of **majority-minority districts,** which are legislative districts with populations that are more than 50 percent minority.[10]

Majority-minority districts Legislative districts whose population was more than 50 percent African American and Latino.

Why would a Republican administration choose to implement the VRA to increase African American and Latino representation in Congress and state legislatures? After all, most minority lawmakers are Democrats. The reason was simple: The policy also helped the Republican Party to gain seats.[11] In order to construct majority African American and Latino districts, state legislatures redrew district lines to shift minority voters away from adjacent districts into new majority-minority districts. Because most African American and Latino voters are Democrats, the redistricting reduced Democratic voting strength in surrounding districts, threatening the political survival of some white Democratic members of Congress. The Georgia congressional delegation, for example, went from one African American Democrat, eight white Democrats, and one white Republican before redistricting in 1991 to three African American Democrats and eight white Republicans after the 1994 election. Nationwide, the creation of majority-minority districts after the 1990 census helped white Republicans pick up about nine seats in Congress, defeating white Democrats who were stripped of some of their minority voter support.[12]

In the mid-1990s, the U.S. Supreme Court overruled the Justice Department's interpretation of the VRA. The Court responded to legal challenges filed against majority-minority districts created in Louisiana, Georgia, and other southern states by ruling that state governments cannot use race as the predominant factor in drawing district lines unless they have a compelling reason. The Court declared that the goal of maximizing the number of majority-minority districts is not a sufficient reason for race-based redistricting because Congress did not enact the VRA with the intent of forcing states to maximize the number of districts that would elect African American and Latino candidates. The purpose of the VRA was to prevent discrimination.[13] The Court has held that states are free to redistrict as long as the districts they draw do not diminish the political influence of minorities, but the VRA does not require states to create additional majority-minority districts in order to increase minority representation.[14] Furthermore, the Court ruled in 2003 that states have the leeway to create "coalitional districts" in which minority voters do not form a numerical majority, but are numerous enough so that black and white coalitional voting will give an African American candidate a realistic opportunity to be elected.[15]

In sum, the judicial climate for redistricting under the VRA has changed. After the 1990 U.S. Census, states acted under the assumption that they had to maximize the number of legislative districts that would elect African American and Latino candidates. State redistricting after the 2000 U.S. Census worked under the guidance of Supreme Court decisions interpreting the VRA to prohibit discrimination but not to require state legislatures to create majority-minority districts. In fact, the Supreme Court had held that a legislature could not consider race in creating districts unless it had a compelling reason. Finally, after the 2010 U.S. Census, states had the freedom to create coalitional districts instead of majority-minority districts if they desired.[16]

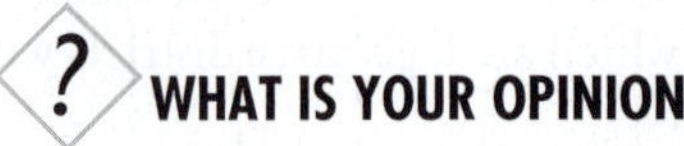

WHAT IS YOUR OPINION?

Are people who voted against (or for) Barack Obama because he is African American racist?

Gerrymandering

Gerrymandering The drawing of legislative district lines for political advantage.

Redistricting can be used to advance the interests of a political party or a particular individual. In fact, the practice is so common that there is a word for it, **gerrymandering,** which is the drawing of legislative district lines for political advantage. The term dates from early nineteenth-century Massachusetts when Governor Elbridge Gerry was behind the creation of a district that observers said resembled a salamander, hence the term Gerry-*mander*.

The Republican Party was positioned to control redistricting in a majority of states after the 2010 election because it held a majority of governorships and most state legislatures as well. If one political party holds a majority of seats in the state legislature and controls the governor's office as well, it will be in good position to draw congressional districts designed to protect its incumbents from serious challenges from the other party while shifting some of the seats held by the other party into its column. When Democrats and Republicans share control—say, the Republicans control the legislature but the governor is a Democrat—they typically compromise on redistricting by agreeing to protect the incumbents of both parties.

The federal courts have been more tolerant of political gerrymandering than they have been of efforts to draw districts to increase minority representation in Congress. The U.S. Supreme Court has held that partisan gerrymandering is unconstitutional if it can be demonstrated that the "electoral system is arranged in such a manner that will consistently degrade a . . . group of voters' influence on the political process as a whole."[17] In practice, however, this standard is so high that it has never been satisfied. The U.S. Supreme Court has yet to find a political gerrymander unconstitutional.[18]

Election Campaigns

Election campaign An attempt to get information to voters that will persuade them to elect a candidate or not elect a candidate's opponent.

An **election campaign** is an attempt to get information to voters that will persuade them to elect a certain candidate or not elect that candidate's opponent. Although many local election contests are modest affairs, presidential campaigns, statewide races, local elections in big cities, and many elections for Congress and state legislatures feature professional campaign consultants, sophisticated organizations, and big money.

The Role of Money

Money is the most controversial feature of American electoral politics.

The Cost of Campaigns Election campaigns cost money. In 2008, Obama and McCain raised and spent more than $1 billion in their race for the White House, with Obama raising almost twice as much as his Republican opponent. Races for Congress are expensive as well. In 2010, the average House incumbent raised $1.5 million compared with less than $300,000 for the average challenger. The cost of Senate races varied, depending on the size of the state. Running for office is far more expensive in a large urban state with multiple media markets than it is in a small rural state without a major media market. In 2010, the average Senate incumbent raised $11.2 million compared with less than a million dollars for the average challenger.[19]

Critics charge that campaigns are too expensive. Many potential candidates for office choose not to run because they do not think they can raise the necessary funds. Incumbents, meanwhile, must devote an inordinate amount of time to fundraising. The critics of the current campaign funding system worry that public officials will make policy decisions with an eye to pleasing contributors rather than serving the policy interests of ordinary constituents.

In contrast, some analysts believe that election campaigns are not especially expensive, at least not compared with commercial advertising campaigns. Proctor and Gamble, Ford Motor Company, Allstate Insurance, and other retail advertisers spend more money to promote their products than candidates spend informing voters. Citizens need more information to make intelligent choices at the ballot box, they say, not less. The problem with campaign spending is not the total amount of money spent but the disparity in resources among candidates. These analysts favor reforming the campaign finance system to make it easier for candidates and parties to raise and spend money. Then, voters will have more information on which to base their choices. An analysis of the campaigns for the U.S. House suggests that campaign spending enhances the quality of democracy by increasing voter knowledge, improving the ability of the public to accurately identify the issue positions of the candidates, and increasing voter interest in the campaign.[20]

Many observers believe that the media and the general public exaggerate the importance of money in the policy process. Money alone does not determine election results nor does it dictate policy outcomes. Political parties, the media, experts, elected and appointed officials, public opinion, individual policy entrepreneurs, and interest groups, both well-funded and poorly funded, all play a role. To be sure, money matters, but it would be a mistake, they say, to believe that it dominates everything. Furthermore, the number of individuals and groups who contribute to campaigns is so large that the influence of individual contributors is diluted.

The Campaign Budget The largest item in most campaign budgets is advertising, particularly on television. The cost of advertising time varies greatly, depending on the market and the medium. Television, especially network television during primetime, is the most expensive. Cable television, radio, and newspapers are less costly. Advertising in larger markets, such as New York City or Los Angeles, California, is substantially more expensive than advertising in smaller markets, such as Baton Rouge, Louisiana, or Albuquerque, New Mexico. Running a serious political campaign in a populous state with several major media markets is many times more costly than running a campaign in a less populous state without a major media market. Political campaigns also have expenses other than advertising. Campaigns have offices with telephone banks, computers, fax machines, furniture, supplies, and utility costs. Campaigns hire consultants and employ professionals for fundraising, event coordination, media relations, Internet connection, and volunteer coordination. Candidates for president or statewide office also spend a good deal of money for travel.[21]

Sources of Campaign Money Wealthy individuals sometimes finance their own election campaigns. In 2010, Linda McMahon ($50 million) of Connecticut, Jeff Greene of Florida ($24 million), and Ron Johnson ($9 million) of Wisconsin headed a list of 14 candidates for the U.S. House or U.S. Senate that invested at least $2 million of their personal funds in an attempt to win elective office. Johnson and two of the other big-spending candidates won, but the other 11 all lost.[22] Self-financing is usually a sign of weakness because candidates with enough support to win office can raise money for their campaigns.

Candidates who are not wealthy enough to bankroll their own campaigns (or who choose to hold onto their money) must rely on others to finance their election efforts. Individual campaign contributors are the most important overall source of campaign cash, accounting for 60 percent of total receipts for U.S. House and Senate candidates and more than 90 percent of the money raised by the two major-party presidential candidates in 2008, not counting federal funds.[23] Candidates raise money from individuals through direct solicitations, usually on the telephone or at fundraising dinners or receptions, by means of direct mail, and over the Internet. Candidates spend hours on the phone calling wealthy supporters asking for the maximum contribution under federal law, which in 2008 was $2,300 per individual contributor.

George W. Bush developed a bundling system for raising money from individuals that netted millions of dollars for his two presidential campaigns. In 2000, more than 500 Bush supporters called Pioneers (mostly wealthy energy company officials, lobbyists, and corporate executives) raised $100,000 each in individual contributions up to $1,000, which was then the maximum amount an individual could give.[24] Each of the Pioneers tapped at least 100 people for contributions and earmarked their contribution checks with a special identification code in order to get credit. The Bush campaign rewarded Pioneers with special receptions and individual meetings with the candidate. Subsequently, President Bush appointed at least 19 of the Pioneers as ambassadors to other countries.[25] In 2004, with the contribution limit raised to $2,000 a person, the Bush campaign created a second category of fundraisers called Rangers who agreed to raise at least $200,000 each for the president's reelection.

Direct mail is another important fundraising tool. Typically, Candidate A sends a long, detailed letter to supporters warning of dire consequences if the opposing candidate wins the election. The only way to prevent the calamity and save the country, the letter declares, is to contribute money to Candidate A by writing a check today and inserting it in the return envelope included in the mailing. Direct mail is an expensive fundraising tool because it takes time and money to develop an address list of people who are likely to respond positively to appeals for campaign money. Mailing expenses are costly as well. Nonetheless, direct mail can be effective. For years, the Republican Party held a fundraising advantage over the Democrats because it had a more sophisticated direct mail operation.

The Internet is the latest innovation in campaign fundraising. Campaigns create a sharp-looking website designed to attract the attention of supporters who can donate online with a credit card and a few mouse clicks or by sending a text message. The advantage of online fundraising is that it is relatively inexpensive, especially compared with direct mail. Campaigns can send e-mail or text messages again and again to supporters, giving them campaign updates and asking for funds at virtually no expense.[26] Most of the money raised in this fashion comes in relatively small contributions, but they can add up to big money. In 2008, the Obama campaign raised more than $200 million in donations in amounts of $200 or less, mostly in online contributions and through cell phone text messaging.[27]

Political action committee (PAC) An organization created to raise and distribute money in election campaigns.

Interest groups give money directly to candidates through **political action committees (PACs),** which are organizations created to raise and distribute money in election campaigns. PACs are an important source of funds in races for the U.S. House, accounting for more than a third of the total money raised by House candidates. In contrast, PACs give relatively little money directly to Senate or presidential candidates.[28] Federal law limits the amount of money a PAC can give a candidate for federal office to $5,000 for each election.

Bipartisan Campaign Reform Act (BCRA) A campaign finance reform law designed to limit the political influence of big money campaign contributors.

Soft money The name given to funds that are raised by political parties which are not subject to federal campaign finance regulations.

Hard money Funds that are raised subject to federal campaign contribution and expenditure limitations.

The role of political parties in campaign fundraising has changed because of the adoption of the **Bipartisan Campaign Reform Act (BCRA)** of 2002, which is a campaign finance reform law designed to limit the political influence of big money campaign contributors. The BCRA, which is also known as McCain-Feingold after its two Senate sponsors (Senator John McCain and Senator Russ Feingold), prohibited political parties from raising **soft money,** which is the name given to funds that are raised by political parties which are not subject to federal campaign finance regulations. Before the adoption of the BCRA, parties raised hundreds of millions of dollars in unregulated large contributions from individuals, corporations, and unions. The BCRA prohibited parties from raising soft money beginning with the 2004 election, forcing them to rely on **hard money,** which are funds that are raised subject to federal campaign contribution and expenditure limitations.[29]

Independent expenditures Money spent in support of a candidate but not coordinated with the candidate's campaign.

Political parties support their candidates primarily with **independent expenditures,** which is money spent in support of a candidate but not coordinated with the candidate's campaign. Although parties can contribute a limited amount of money directly to candidates, they can make unlimited independent expenditures. Parties also back candidates by providing them with polling data and conducting get-out-the-vote efforts.

527 Committee Organization created to influence the outcomes of elections by raising and spending money that candidates and political parties cannot raise and spend legally.

Individuals and groups can spend unlimited amounts of money on behalf of candidates they support or against candidates they oppose by creating 527 committees. A **527 committee** is an organization created to influence the outcomes of elections by raising and spending money that candidates and political parties cannot raise and spend legally. As long as 527 committees operate independently of political campaigns and stop short of explicitly calling for a candidate's election or defeat, they can raise and spend unlimited amounts of unregulated soft money. In the 2008 presidential campaign, 527 committees raised and spent millions of dollars to support one side or the other. America Votes, Fund for America, and Patriot Majority were 527 committees that helped the Democrats by registering voters, organizing activists, and purchasing political advertisements. In the meantime, American Solutions for Winning the Future, Club for Growth, and RightChange.com were 527 committees that worked to support Republicans. Because the 527 committees did not explicitly coordinate their work with either political party or presidential campaign, they claim that the BCRA did not apply to them.[30]

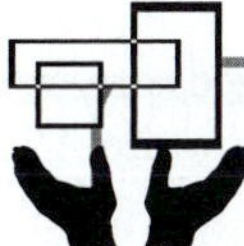

GETTING INVOLVED

Campaign Volunteers

Volunteers play an important role in election campaigns. They mail campaign literature to registered voters, telephone supporters to encourage them to vote, and drive citizens to the polls on Election Day. They are often the backbone of campaigns for local office. Your assignment is to research campaign activity by volunteering for the candidate of your choice. Contact the local political party organizations to identify local campaigns that are seeking volunteers. To verify your volunteer work, bring your instructor a signed note from the campaign office manager indicating the time you spent on the campaign. Also, prepare a written report discussing your work and your impressions of the campaign, covering the following points:

- Identify the candidate and the office the candidate seeks, noting whether the candidate is the incumbent.
- Describe the campaign office, including the location, physical layout, and level of organization.
- Describe the other people working in the campaign as to age, gender, race, and ethnicity.
- List the tasks you completed for the campaign.
- Describe your impression of the experience, discussing whether you had a good time, whether you believe your work was important to the campaign's success, and if you ever plan to volunteer to work for a campaign again.

The 2010 midterm election saw the emergence of super PACs. In contrast to traditional PACs, super PACs can raise unlimited amounts of money directly from corporations as well as from individuals. Although super PACs cannot contribute directly to candidates, they can spend money independently to help elect candidates they favor or defeat candidates they oppose. In future elections, they may replace 527 committees as the preferred means for legally circumventing campaign finance limits. [31]

Federal funds are a source of campaign money for presidential candidates who qualify and choose to accept the money. Although some reformers favor government funding for congressional elections, money is currently available only for presidential races. We discuss presidential campaign funding in more detail later in the chapter.

Campaign Organization and Strategy

Big-time campaigns are long, drawn-out affairs. Challengers begin planning and organizing their campaigns years before the election. Incumbents, meanwhile, never really quit campaigning. Many observers believe that American politics now features constant election campaigns because newly elected officeholders start work on their reelection the day they take the oath of office.

Campaigns start early because much has to be done. Candidates spend the early months of the race raising money, building an organization, seeking endorsements, and planning strategy. One of the first tasks of a campaign is to prepare the candidate. This often means outfitting the candidate with a new wardrobe, a new hairstyle, and a slimmer waistline. Some critics of George W. Bush believe that he purchased his ranch in Crawford, Texas, in 1999 because it would provide an attractive backdrop for television reports on the candidate during the 2000 presidential election campaign. It would also help him project an image as a regular guy rather than the privileged son of a famous family who graduated from Harvard and Yale. Candidates also memorize a basic speech and rehearse answers to questions reporters might ask.

Social media have become the latest campaign battleground. Candidates create Facebook fan pages, open Twitter accounts, and upload campaign videos on YouTube. Social media enable candidates to communicate regularly and personally with supporters, increasing name identification and building enthusiasm. Campaigns can use online tools such as Meetup to organize supporters or enable supporters to organize themselves.[32] The social media are especially important for younger supporters, many of whom use social media as their main source of news.[33]

Many factors shape the course of a campaign and influence strategy, including the type of office at stake, the nature of the constituency, the personalities and images of the candidates, the issues that concern the electorate, and whether one of the candidates is an incumbent seeking reelection. Incumbents generally use a different campaign strategy than do challengers seeking to unseat incumbents. Presidents

Movie actor Arnold Schwarzenegger enjoyed near universal name recognition before he decided to run for governor of California.

Rose garden strategy A campaign approach in which an incumbent president attempts to appear presidential rather than political.

running for reelection often employ a **rose garden strategy,** which is a campaign approach in which an incumbent president attempts to appear presidential rather than political. The president holds press conferences, meets foreign heads of state, makes "nonpolitical" trips to dedicate public-works projects, and announces the awarding of federal grants for projects in closely fought cities and states.

An important goal for many campaigns is to improve the candidate's name recognition, especially if the candidate is not an incumbent. Citizens generally will not vote for someone with whom they are unfamiliar. Races for less visible offices may never move beyond the name-recognition stage. It helps if voters are already familiar with the candidate. As an example, Tom Osborne easily won a seat in Congress from Nebraska after retiring from a long and successful career as the head football coach at the University of Nebraska.

Besides building name recognition, campaigns attempt to create a favorable image of the candidate. Candidates air campaign advertisements that stress their qualifications for the office and associate the candidate with popular themes and images. In 2008, for example, Senator McCain used his personal history as a prisoner of war in Vietnam as evidence that he was strong enough to be an effective commander-in-chief. Obama's image as an energetic relatively young man helped reinforce his message of change and reform.

As they build a positive view of a candidate, campaigns simultaneously try to create an unfavorable impression of the opponent. Negative campaigning is nothing new in American politics. Thomas Jefferson's enemies denounced him as the antichrist. Opponents accused President Grover Cleveland of beating his wife and fathering an illegitimate child. Critics attacked Theodore Roosevelt as a drunkard and a drug addict. In 1950, George Smathers defeated Senator Claude Pepper in Florida by calling Pepper "a shameless EXTROVERT" who has "a sister who was once a THESPIAN."[34] (If your dictionary is not handy, an extrovert is someone who is outgoing and a thespian is an actor or actress.)

Research is mixed on the effectiveness of negative campaigning. Sometimes it works, but sometimes it backfires. In general, negative campaigning is a more effective strategy for challengers than it is for incumbents, who are generally more successful with a positive campaign. Nonetheless, incumbents are often able to effectively counter a challenger's attacks. Political scientists find no evidence that personal attacks or attacks that distort the record are effective.[35] Political scientists also disagree as to whether negative campaign advertisements affect voter turnout. Some political scientists believe that negative campaign advertising diminishes the turnout of independents and people with weak ties to political parties. Negative advertisements make the public disenchanted with both candidates, they say, causing supporters of both sides to stay home.[36] In contrast, other scholars think that negative campaign accusations may actually engage voters in a campaign and increase turnout.[37] Some analysts even believe that negative campaigns are good for democracy because they inform the public about important issues and concerns.[38]

Early in a campaign, candidates work to build name identification and establish their credibility by producing a message that is primarily positive. As the election approaches, candidates who trail in the polls often decide that positive advertising alone will not close the gap with their opponents, so they go on the attack in hopes of undermining their opponent's support.[39] Incumbents sometimes launch attack ad campaigns against their challengers early in the election season in hopes of giving voters a negative image of the challenger before the challenger has a chance to establish a positive identification. Candidates who suffer attack are likely to respond in kind because they know that voters presume that an unanswered attack is true.[40]

Campaign advertising increases citizen knowledge of issues and candidates, affects voter evaluations of candidates, and increases a candidate's share of the vote.[41] Campaign advertising broadcast close to the election has a greater impact than advertising early in the contest. Research shows that advertising has its greatest influence on people who are moderately aware of the campaign. The least politically alert do not get the message, whereas the best informed citizens have already made up their minds.[42]

Issue ownership The concept that the public considers one political party more competent at addressing a particular issue than the other political party.

Campaigns also try to focus voter attention to the issues on which their political party has an advantage.[43] **Issue ownership** is the concept that the public considers one political party more competent at addressing a particular issue than the other political party. The Democratic Party has an advantage on the environment, education, Social Security, healthcare, and jobs; the Republicans are favored on taxes, law and order, and foreign policy.[44] During the 2008 presidential election, the Obama campaign stressed healthcare and the economy, especially unemployment and jobs, whereas the McCain campaign tried to shift the focus to taxes and foreign policy issues, particularly the war on terror.

Most candidates do their best to meet as many voters as possible. They shake hands in front of factory gates, discuss issues at town hall meetings, and wade into the crowd at campaign rallies. Voters like and know more about candidates that they meet in person, although people who seek out a particular candidate are disposed to like that candidate already. The effect of the meeting is primarily to reinforce an already established preference.[45]

Ground war Campaign activities featuring direct contact between campaign workers and citizens, such as door-to-door canvassing and personal telephone contacts.

Battleground states Swing states in which the relative strength of the two major party presidential candidates is close enough so that either candidate could conceivably carry the state.

Air war Campaign activities that involve the media, including television, radio, and the Internet.

Election campaigns for major offices are fought on the ground and in the air. Campaign professionals use the term **ground war** to refer to campaign activities featuring direct contact between campaign workers and citizens, such as door-to-door canvassing and personal telephone contacts. In 2008, the Obama and McCain campaigns deployed small armies of volunteers and paid campaign workers to register voters and get out the vote. The Democrats targeted inner-city minority residents, whereas the Republican campaign focused on increasing the turnout of conservative Christian voters. Both parties concentrated their efforts on the **battleground states,** which are swing states in which the relative strength of the two major party presidential candidates is close enough so that either candidate could conceivably carry the state. The **air war** refers to campaign activities that involve the media, including television, radio, and the Internet. In 2008, campaign professionals focused their television advertising on network shows and cable channels that data analyses showed were popular with people most likely to support the candidates of their party. If a campaign wants to target women, it advertises on Lifetime because its audience is mostly women. The ESPN audience is primarily male. The BET audience is African American; Latinos watch Univision. Independent voters ages 25–54 disproportionately watch E, HGTV, Lifetime, and Oxygen.[46]

Congressional Elections

In America's representative democracy, citizens elect the Congress. Voters choose members of the House from districts to serve two-year terms, except in states that have only one representative, who runs statewide. Senators run statewide for six-year terms. Because Senate terms are staggered, voters elect one-third of the Senate every two years.

House Elections

The most striking feature of elections for the U.S. House of Representatives is that most incumbents are reelected. Between 1954 and 2008, 93 percent of House incumbents seeking reelection won.[47] Even in 2010, a remarkably bad year for incumbents, 87 percent of incumbents won reelection.[48]

Political scientists identify a number of reasons for the high reelection rate of sitting members of Congress:

- **Incumbency has certain built-in advantages.** Incumbents are almost always better known than challengers. They have the money to staff one or more district offices, allowances to pay for trips home during congressional sessions, and free postage to mail newsletters to constituents. Incumbents send out press releases and give speeches throughout the district. They can also build goodwill among constituents by bringing spending projects to the district, voicing the concerns of the district residents, and helping constituents navigate the bureaucracy.[49]
- **Incumbents are almost always better funded than challengers.** To become known, and hence competitive, challengers need to spend hundreds of thousands of dollars on their campaigns. Most serious candidates for Congress will not run unless they believe they have a realistic chance of winning, and that means raising more than $500,000.[50] Potential challengers who doubt they can raise enough money to be competitive usually decide to wait for another opportunity. Furthermore, incumbent members of Congress try to scare off challengers by raising as much money as they can as early as they can. Most serious challengers are reluctant to run against an incumbent who already has nearly a million dollars in the bank.
- **Most incumbents are strong candidates.** They know how to run effective campaigns because they have run and won before. In contrast, many challengers are inexperienced campaigners. Furthermore, incumbents in danger of losing may retire rather than face a tough reelection battle.[51]
- **Many congressional districts are safe for one party or the other.** Even in 2010, a bad year for incumbents, fewer than 20 percent of House races were decided by 10 percentage points or less. Although some scholars blame the prevalence of safe districts on the redistricting process, other scholars attribute safe districts to the phenomenon of communities growing more like-minded over time.[52]

Historically, the political party holding the White House loses seats in the House of Representatives in midterm elections. Since 1920 and 1980, the president's party has lost ground in the House in all but three midterm elections, dropping an average of 33 seats. In 2010, the Democrats lost 63 seats in the House, the largest loss of seats by the incumbent president's party since 1938 when Democrat Franklin Roosevelt was president and his party lost 72 seats in the House.

Political scientists have developed two sets of theories to explain the phenomenon of a president's party losing seats in the midterm. One set of theories focuses on the withdrawal of coattails. The **coattail effect** is a political phenomenon in which a strong candidate for one office gives a boost to fellow party members on the same ballot seeking other offices. Coattails are particularly important in election contests in which voters have relatively little information about either candidate, such as open-seat races for the U.S. House. In presidential election years, some of the people who turn out to cast their ballots for a popular presidential candidate either vote a straight ticket or support candidates from the same party as their presidential choice even though they have no real candidate preference. Two years later, without a presidential race on the ballot, many of the congressional candidates who benefited from the coattail effect lose without it.

Coattail effect The political phenomenon in which a strong candidate for one office gives a boost to fellow party members on the same ballot seeking other offices.

A second set of theories attempts to explain the tendency of the president's party to lose House seats in the midterm on the basis of ideological balancing. Moderate voters support the opposition party in order to restrain the president from pushing policies that they perceive to be ideologically extreme. Some voters may also use their vote at midterm to punish the president's party for poor performance, especially in terms of the economy.[53]

The 2010 midterm election was a perfect storm for the Democrats for several reasons. First, the Democrats found themselves defending most of the swing seats, having won the 2006 and 2008 elections. Consequently, they had more seats at risk than did the Republicans. Second, the Republican base, energized by the Tea Party movement, turned out in large numbers. In contrast, many Democrats who voted in 2008 failed to cast ballots in 2010. Finally, the economy was weak and many voters blamed the Democrats for failing to take effective action to reduce unemployment.

Proportional representation (PR) An election system that awards legislative seats to each party approximately equal to its popular voting strength.

Senate Elections

Senate races are more competitive than House elections. Incumbency is a factor in Senate contests, but it is not the overwhelming advantage that it is in House races. Furthermore, Senate races are typically closer than House contests, even when the incumbent wins. In 2008, 8 of 37 Senate races were decided by less than 10 percent of the vote.

Pork barrel spending Expenditures to fund local projects that are not critically important from a national perspective.

Political scientists identify a number of differences between Senate and House races that account for the relatively greater vulnerability of Senate incumbents. First, Senate constituencies are more diverse than most House constituencies and hence more competitive. Many U.S. House districts are safe for one party or the other. In contrast, senators must run at-large statewide, and both parties are capable of winning statewide races in most states.

Around the World

Legislative Elections in Brazil

Brazil elects the members of its national legislature using a system in which each state is an at-large, multimember district. The size of a state's legislative delegation varies from 8 to 70 members, depending on its population. Political parties can nominate as many candidates as there are seats at stake, but only the names of the parties appear on the ballot. Voters can cast their ballots either for a party or for a particular candidate by writing in the candidate's name or number. The total number of votes a party receives is the sum of its party votes and the votes cast for its individual candidates.

The number of seats a party wins is based on **proportional representation (PR),** which is an election system that awards legislative seats to each party approximately equal to its popular voting strength. If the combined votes for a party and its candidates total 25 percent of the votes cast in the state, then the party wins 25 percent of the seats at stake. The candidates on the party slate with the most individual votes actually claim the seats. If a party has enough combined party and candidate votes to win five seats, for example, the five individual candidates on its party list who received the most votes are the individuals chosen to serve in the national legislature.*

The Brazilian electoral system provides for competition not just among political parties but also among candidates in the same party. In practice, legislative candidates focus on building their personal vote totals, often by campaigning in a geographical stronghold or targeting a particular group of voters, such as industrial workers, ethnic minorities, or members of Protestant Christian churches (who are a minority in Catholic Brazil). The electoral system affects policymaking because legislators worried about winning reelection focus their energy on **pork barrel spending,** which are expenditures to fund local projects that are not critically important from a national perspective. Political scientists also believe that the system increases the power of Brazil's president who trades support on local projects for legislative votes on national issues.†

Questions

1. How does the Brazilian legislative electoral system differ from the American system?
2. Is the Brazilian system democratic? Why or why not?
3. Do you think Brazilian legislators focus more on pork barrel spending than do the members of the U.S. Congress? Why or why not?

* David J. Samuels, "Incentives to Cultivate a Party Vote in Candidate-Centric Electoral Systems: Evidence from Brazil," *Comparative Political Studies* 32 (June 1999): 487–518.

† Barry Ames, "Electoral Rules, Constituency Pressures, and Pork Barrel: Bases of Voting in the Brazilian Congress," *Journal of Politics* 57 (May 1995): 324–343.

Second, incumbent senators generally face stronger challengers than House incumbents. A seat in the Senate is an important enough prize to attract the candidacies of governors, big-city mayors, members of the House, and well-known figures such as astronauts, war heroes, sports stars, and show business celebrities. As a result, Senate challengers can usually attract enough media attention and raise sufficient money to run at least a minimal campaign.

Finally, research has found that voters tend to perceive Senate races as national election contests. As a result, national issues often play a prominent role in Senate campaigns and national trends frequently affect Senate election outcomes. A study of the impact of presidential coattails on Senate contests found that a 10 percent gain in a party's presidential vote in a state adds about two percentage points to the vote of its Senate candidate.[54] Presidential popularity affects Senate races in off-year elections as well.

Presidential Elections: The Nomination Phase

The presidential election process consists of two distinct phases with different rules, requiring candidates to wage two separate campaigns. In the first phase of the presidential election process, candidates compete for their political party's nomination. In the summer of a presidential election year, the two major parties hold national conventions to which the party organizations in each state, the District of Columbia, and the various territories send delegates. The Democratic Party traditionally invites more delegates to its convention than does the GOP. In 2008, 4,049 delegates attended the Democratic National Convention in Denver, whereas 2,380 delegates attended the Republican National Convention in Minneapolis.

The size of each state's convention delegation varies, depending on a formula set by the party that includes both the state's population and the success of the

The 2008 Democratic National Convention was designed to present the nation with an image of a party united after a bruising nomination fight between Hillary Clinton and Barack Obama.

party in the state. In 2008, for example, California, the nation's largest state, sent 363 delegates to the Democratic convention and 161 delegates to the Republican convention. Arkansas, a relatively small state, sent 35 delegates to the Democratic convention, 31 to the GOP meeting.

The convention selects the presidential and vice presidential nominees to run on the party's ticket in the November general election by majority vote of the convention delegates. Until the conventions have done their work, the real contest is not between Democrats and Republicans, but among Democrats for the Democratic presidential nomination and among Republicans for their party's nomination. Because the convention delegates make the actual selection, candidates focus on the delegate-selection process in each state, hoping to get their supporters selected as delegates to the national convention. In 2008, New York Senator Hillary Clinton, Illinois Senator Barack Obama, and former North Carolina Senator John Edwards were the leading candidates for the Democratic nomination. Arizona Senator John McCain, former Massachusetts Governor Mitt Romney, former Arkansas Governor Mike Huckabee, and former New York City Mayor Rudy Giuliani contended for the GOP nomination.

The Delegate-Selection Process

Presidential preference primary An election in which party voters cast ballots for the presidential candidate they favor and in so doing help determine the number of national convention delegates that candidate will receive.

The process of selecting delegates to the national party conventions varies from state to state. Most delegates are chosen in presidential preference primaries. A **presidential preference primary** is an election in which party voters cast ballots for the presidential candidate they favor and in so doing help determine the number of national convention delegates that candidate will receive. Democratic voters select among Democratic candidates; Republican voters choose among GOP presidential contenders.

Presidential primary election campaigns are similar to other election campaigns except that the candidates must appeal to a different voter pool. Primary elections typically attract fewer voters than the general election. In 2008, 530,000 voters participated in the New Hampshire presidential preference primary compared with 700,000 who turned out for the November general election in that state.[55] Primary election voters differ from general election voters in that most people who participate in primaries identify strongly with the party in whose primary they vote. In contrast, the electorate for the general election includes a larger proportion of independents and people who identify weakly with a party.

The nature of the primary electorate affects the approaches candidates must take to win the nomination. People who identify strongly with the GOP are more conservative than voters as a group, whereas people who identify strongly with the Democratic Party are more liberal.[56] Consequently, Republican presidential contenders usually stress conservative themes during the nomination phase, whereas Democratic candidates emphasize liberal positions. Primary voters do not just consider policy preferences in choosing among candidates; they also evaluate each candidate's chances of winning the November general election.[57] The most liberal Democratic candidate and the most conservative Republican candidate may not win the nomination if large numbers of their party's primary voters believe they would not be strong candidates in the general election.

Caucus method of delegate selection A procedure for choosing national party convention delegates that involves party voters participating in a series of precinct and district or county political meetings.

States that do not conduct presidential preference primaries use the caucus method to choose national convention delegates. The **caucus method of delegate selection** is a procedure for choosing national party convention delegates that involves party voters participating in a series of precinct and district or county political meetings. The process begins with party members attending local precinct meetings or caucuses that elect delegates to district or county meetings. The district/county meetings in turn select delegates for the state party convention. Finally, the state convention chooses national-convention delegates.

Candidates who do well in presidential preference primaries and caucuses win delegates pledged to support their nomination at the national convention. The Democratic Party awards delegates in rough proportion to a candidate's level of support as long as the candidate surpasses a 15 percent threshold. In contrast, Republican Party rules typically award delegates on a winner-take-all basis.

Candidates use a different strategy for competing in caucus states than they employ in states with primary elections. Because caucus meetings require more time and effort than simply voting in a primary, the number of people who participate in them is generally fewer than primary participants and far fewer than the number of people who turn out for general elections. In 2008, for example, 350,000 people took part in the Iowa caucus compared with 1.5 million who voted in the general election.[58] Furthermore, most caucus participants are party activists who tend to be more liberal (in the Democratic Party) or more conservative (in the Republican Party) than party voters or the electorate as a whole. Consequently, in each party, ideologically extreme candidates (i.e., strong conservatives in the GOP, strong liberals in the Democratic Party) typically do better in caucus states than primary states.[59]

Super delegates Democratic Party officials and officeholders selected to attend the national party convention on the basis of the offices they hold.

In addition to delegates selected through presidential preference primaries and caucuses, the national Democratic Party convention includes several hundred Democratic officeholders and party officials who are called **super delegates.** The 2008 Democratic National Convention included 796 superdelegates, 19 percent of the total. The superdelegates are chosen on the basis of the offices they hold rather than their support for a particular candidate. In contrast to delegates selected through presidential preference primary elections and caucuses, superdelegates are officially uncommitted, pledged to support no candidate. The superdelegate system ensures that Democratic officeholders and party leaders can attend the convention as delegates, regardless of their candidate preferences. The system also bolsters the position of insider candidates who enjoy the support of party leaders. In 2008, superdelegates found themselves in a position to name a presidential nominee because the closeness of the Obama-Clinton race prevented either candidate from winning a majority of pledged delegates. Most superdelegates chose to go with Obama because he was the candidate who won the most pledged delegates.

WHAT IS YOUR OPINION?

Should superdelegates play a role in choosing a party's presidential nominee?

Reforming the Delegate-Selection Process

The delegate-selection process has changed a great deal in recent years. For more than a century, the Democratic and Republican Parties nominated their presidential candidates at national conventions that were dominated by elected officials and local party leaders. The main concern of the party leaders was the selection of a candidate whose popularity would boost the election chances of their party's candidates at the state and local level. They also hoped that their party's nominee would cooperate with state party leaders once elected. Fewer than 20 states held primaries, and serious candidates would focus on only one or two primaries in order to demonstrate their voter appeal to the party leadership. Many delegates arrived at the national party conventions uncommitted to any of the announced presidential candidates, allowing state governors, big-city mayors, and other party leaders leverage to negotiate the outcome of the nomination process.[60] Critics of this system charged that it was undemocratic because the process allowed for relatively little input from ordinary party members and voters. In 1952, for example, Senator Estes Kefauver of Tennessee won 12 of the 13 Democratic primaries he entered, but he did not get the nomination because party leaders did not like him.[61]

The 1968 Democratic National Convention was the catalyst for reforming the delegate-selection process. Although party leaders' control over the presidential selection process had already begun to slip because of the long-term decay of party organization in the United States, the process of change accelerated in 1968. Party reformers were outraged that Vice President Hubert Humphrey was able to win the Democratic presidential nomination without entering a single primary. The reformers charged that too much power was in the hands of party bosses such as Mayor Richard J. Daley of Chicago. Because Humphrey and the party leadership needed the support of the reformers to win the general election against Republican Richard Nixon (they lost anyway), they granted them a major concession: the formation of a reform commission chaired by Senator George McGovern of South Dakota.

The McGovern Commission revised the Democratic Party delegate-selection process in a fashion consistent with the goals of the reformers. First, the commission opened the process to greater participation for rank-and-file party members and activists, giving no special advantage to party insiders. Second, the commission mandated representation in the process by groups favored by the reformers—African Americans, women, and young people. Later, the party added Latinos, Native Americans, and gay men and lesbians to the list. Finally, the commission pushed for a system that would award convention delegates to candidates in rough proportion to their voting strength in a state rather than a winner-take-all system.

By the end of the 1970s, a number of Democrats thought that the reforms had gone too far. The attempt to reduce the power of party leaders had worked so well that many Democratic members of Congress and Democratic governors did not attend the 1972 and 1976 conventions. The power of the leaders over delegates had been largely lost to candidates and interest-group representatives. Furthermore, many Democrats feared that the new process produced weak nominees outside the mainstream of the party, such as McGovern in 1972 and Jimmy Carter in 1976. After

Former Arkansas Governor Mike Huckabee won the 2008 Iowa Caucus, disappointing these supporters of former Massachusetts Governor Mitt Romney who had been favored to win the caucus.

Carter's defeat for reelection in 1980, Democratic Party regulars pushed through rule changes that would reserve delegate seats for party officials and elected officeholders—superdelegates. Nonetheless, few observers believed that party leaders had regained their lost power over presidential selection.

While the Democrats struggled over reforming delegate-selection procedures, the national Republican Party was content to leave most delegate-selection decisions to state parties, acting only to ensure more participation by poorly represented groups, especially women. Nonetheless, the Republican nomination process did not go unchanged. As political parties grew weaker, GOP leaders, similar to their Democratic counterparts, were hard pressed to maintain control over the presidential nomination process. Furthermore, many state legislatures responded to the Democratic Party reforms by changing delegate-selection procedures in their states.

The effect of the changes in the presidential nomination process in both parties has been to weaken the authority of party leaders in the presidential nomination process while increasing the power of party voters and activists. The nomination process has been opened to millions of ordinary Americans voting in primaries and participating in caucuses. In 2008, for example, 55 million people participated in the presidential nomination process.[62]

Today, a new generation of reformers wants to spread out the nominating process to reduce the importance of early contests. In 1976, only 10 percent of convention delegates had been chosen by March 2 compared with 70 percent in 2008 as more states move their nomination contests to January, February, and early March.[63] The frontloading of the process benefits candidates who are already well known and/or can raise a substantial amount of money. Today's reformers want to eliminate frontloading by pacing primaries and caucuses throughout the winter and spring months of an election year. Spreading out the delegate-selection process will increase the importance of voters in states holding primary elections later and reward candidates who can appeal to voters throughout the nation and not just in a few early contests.[64]

The Road to the Nomination

In 2008, the presidential nomination process had six stages:

Invisible primary The period between the time when candidates announce their intention to run for the presidency and the actual delegate selection begins.

The Invisible Primary The **invisible primary** is the period between the time when candidates announce their intention to run for the presidency and the actual delegate-selection process begins. The men and women who want to be president begin the process of seeking their party's nomination more than a year before any votes are cast by assembling campaign teams, collecting endorsements, establishing campaign organizations in key primary and caucus states, building name recognition among party voters and activists, and raising money. The latter is particularly important. Because the nomination process is frontloaded, candidates need to have millions of dollars on hand in order to conduct campaigns in dozens of states in the space of just a couple of months. Furthermore, media attention mirrors fundraising success.

Federal campaign finance laws allow for partial federal funding of presidential campaigns during the nomination stage. In order to qualify for federal matching funds, candidates must prove they are serious contenders by raising at least $5,000 in each of 20 states in individual contributions of $250 or less. Once a candidate qualifies for federal funding, the government will match individual contributions dollar for dollar up to $250. Candidates who accept the money must agree to an overall pre-convention spending ceiling and state-by-state limits that vary based on the population of a state. Candidates who reject federal funding are free to raise and spend as much money as they can.

Most serious presidential candidates no longer participate in the federal funding system because they are unwilling to accept the spending and fundraising limits. In 2008, candidates who took federal matching funds were limited to $54 million during the nomination period, including federal funds. Among the major contenders, only John Edwards accepted the federal money.[65] In contrast, Obama and Clinton, both of whom rejected federal funds, collected well over $250 million in campaign contributions for the nomination fight.[66]

Party insiders, including elected officials, key interest groups, donors, and activists, are more influential during the invisible primary than at any time in the nomination process. If one candidate emerges from the invisible primary as the clear choice of party insiders, that person usually wins the nomination. In 2000, Republican insiders favored George W. Bush whereas Democratic insiders backed Al Gore. Both won their parties' nominations. In contrast, the 2008 invisible primary failed to produce clear frontrunners in either party. Hillary Clinton had more support among Democratic

Party insiders than Obama, but the difference between the two in endorsements and fundraising was close enough to indicate that the race would be tight. Meanwhile, no candidate emerged as the clear favorite of party insiders among the Republicans.[67]

The Early Contests By tradition, the Iowa Caucus and the New Hampshire primary, which follows soon after, are the first delegate-selection events of the presidential election season. The two early contests help define the candidate field by establishing some candidates as frontrunners and eliminating others as serious contenders. The Iowa Caucus and New Hampshire Primary receive enormous media attention simply because they are first. Each of the two contests receives 10 percent to 20 percent of the total media coverage devoted to the nomination campaign compared with no more than 2 percent that other individual states receive.[68] Consequently, candidates who do well in Iowa and New Hampshire gain name recognition and momentum that can be used to raise money and win votes in later contests, whereas candidates who do poorly are doomed to failure, with neither media attention nor an ability to raise campaign money.[69] The eventual nominee almost always finishes in the top three in Iowa and the top two in New Hampshire.

Success or failure in Iowa and New Hampshire depends on media and voter perceptions of whether a candidate exceeds expectations. Candidates build momentum by exceeding expectations; they lose momentum by falling short of expectations.[70] In 1972, for example, Senator Edmund Muskie, the early frontrunner for the Democratic nomination, was expected to do especially well in New Hampshire because he was from the neighboring state of Maine. Although Muskie won the New Hampshire primary, the media discounted his victory because his margin over runner-up George McGovern was less than anticipated. Muskie's campaign never recovered and McGovern went on to win the nomination.

In 2008, Iowa and New Hampshire produced upset winners and upset losers. On the Republican side, Romney spent heavily in Iowa and New Hampshire in hopes of locking up the nomination early, but he was upset in both races, by Huckabee in Iowa and McCain in New Hampshire. Whereas Romney failed to meet expectations, both Huckabee and McCain exceeded expectations. Meanwhile, on the Democratic side, Iowa and New Hampshire narrowed the Democratic field to two main contestants—Clinton and Obama. The strategy of the Obama campaign was to finish ahead of Clinton in Iowa and Obama succeeded by winning the caucus while Clinton finished third behind John Edwards. Obama hoped to become the clear frontrunner for the nomination by winning the New Hampshire primary, held in early January just a few days after the Iowa caucus. Riding a wave of favorable publicity generated by his Iowa caucus win, Obama moved up in the polls in New Hampshire and seemed poised to deliver another blow to the Clinton campaign.[71] Nonetheless, Clinton won a narrow victory in New Hampshire.

The contests in the weeks following Iowa and New Hampshire further define the field. In 2008, the Nevada Caucus and the South Carolina Primary clearly established Clinton and Obama as the co-frontrunners for the Democrats, with Clinton winning Nevada and Obama taking South Carolina. As for the Republicans, Romney breathed life back into his candidacy by winning in Nevada while McCain built on his victory in New Hampshire and established himself as the leading contender for the nomination by capturing the South Carolina primary.

WHAT IS YOUR OPINION?

Do Iowa and New Hampshire play too great a role in the presidential nomination process?

Super Tuesday Over the years, state legislatures around the country have moved their nomination contests to early in the year in hopes that their states will have more influence in the nomination process. In 2008, 24 states scheduled primaries or caucuses on February 5, including the big states of California, New York, Illinois, and New Jersey. Candidates with money, organization, and name recognition benefit from the frontloaded nomination process because they have the resources to compete in dozens of states within a matter of a few days. Both Obama and Clinton were able to compete in 2008 because they had well-funded campaign organizations in place in all of the Super Tuesday states.

Super Tuesday often settles the nomination contest, at least for the Republicans. With so many delegates at stake, one candidate usually wins enough delegates to claim the nomination or at least build an insurmountable delegate lead. The GOP contest is likely to wrap up first because of the party's winner-take-all delegate rule. Senator McCain became the inevitable Republican nominee because he won the most votes and, consequently, all of the delegates at stake in California, New York, New Jersey, and Illinois. The other major contenders soon dropped from the race.

The Democratic nomination often takes longer to settle because the Democratic Party awards delegates on a proportional basis. In 2008, Clinton and Obama split the Super Tuesday contests. Even though Clinton won New York, California, and New Jersey, she earned only a few more delegates than her opponent in each state because the vote was relatively close and the party's proportional rule ensured a near equal division of delegates between the two candidates. The two candidates emerged from the Super Tuesday voting nearly even in delegates won.

Post–Super Tuesday Contests After Super Tuesday, Obama was better positioned to win the nomination than Clinton. The Clinton campaign assumed that she would effectively capture the nomination on Super Tuesday, whereas the Obama organization prepared for the nomination fight to continue well beyond the Super Tuesday voting. The Obama campaign created an organization in each of the states holding caucuses and primaries in the days and weeks immediately following Super Tuesday, but Clinton did not.[72] Obama also took the fundraising lead. At the end of April 2008, more than halfway through the nomination process, Obama had raised $272 million compared with Clinton's $222 million.[73] Between February 5 and March 5, Obama won 11 consecutive contests, building a delegate lead of more than 150. Clinton recovered to win primaries in Texas, Ohio, Pennsylvania, and other states, but Obama won contests as well and she failed to close the gap. When the last primaries were held in early June, Obama had a clear delegate lead and enough superdelegates announced their support to give him the nomination.

The Transition The period from the end of the nomination contest until the national party conventions in mid-summer is a time of transition. Once the frontrunner has enough delegates to ensure nomination, party leaders begin urging the remaining candidates still in the race to drop out in the name of party unity. In the meantime, the campaign of the eventual nominee begins to change focus. The candidate's speeches start to emphasize themes geared toward general election voters rather than the hardcore party voters who participate in primaries and caucuses. Campaign spokespersons redirect their attacks from their nomination opponents to the candidate of the other party. In 2008, the transition began for McCain shortly after Super Tuesday, whereas Obama had to wait until early June to begin the transition phase.

Party platform A statement of party principles and issue positions.

The National Party Conventions The national party conventions are the last step in the nomination process. The official role of a convention is to adopt a party platform and nominate a presidential and a vice presidential candidate. A **party platform** is a statement of party principles and issue positions. Traditional wisdom holds that platforms are meaningless documents, forgotten by Labor Day. To be sure, platforms often include general language because they represent compromise among different factions within the party. Nonetheless, research shows that American political parties keep about two-thirds of their platform promises.[74]

The most important business of a convention is the official selection of the presidential nominee, ratifying the choice made during the primary season. Traditionally, the nomination takes place during primetime on the third evening of the convention. Festivities begin as speakers place the names of prospective nominees before the convention and their supporters respond with exuberant (and planned) demonstrations. Eventually, the time comes to call the roll of the states and the delegates vote. A majority of the delegates must agree on a nominee. At every convention for more than 60 years, the delegates have selected a winner on the first ballot. Unless the nomination process changes dramatically, that pattern is likely to continue.

The final official business of the convention is to pick a vice presidential candidate. Although the selection process is formally identical to the method for choosing a presidential nominee, the presidential candidate usually makes the choice weeks before the convention meets and the delegates ratify it. Above all else, presidential nominees look for running mates that will help them win in November. Historically, presidential candidates have tried to **balance the ticket,** which is an attempt to select a vice presidential candidate who will appeal to different groups of voters than the presidential nominee. Presidential candidates consider different types of balances in selecting a vice presidential running mate:

Balance the ticket An attempt to select a candidate for vice president who will appeal to different groups of voters than the presidential nominee.

- Racial, ethnic, religious, and gender diversity;
- Regional balance;
- Ideological balance;
- Experience;
- Factional balance (in hopes of healing divisions produced by a bruising primary battle); and
- Personal characteristics, such as age, style, and personal appeal.[75]

Also, it is helpful if the vice presidential candidate comes from a populous state, such as California, Texas, New York, or Florida. (Ironically, research finds that voter evaluations of vice presidential candidates have no impact on voter choice for president.[76]) In recent years, most presidential candidates have chosen established political figures as their running mates with less regard for regional balance and state size. A well-known vice presidential nominee has already been vetted by the press and is less likely to make mistakes during the campaign than a less experienced candidate.[77]

Both Obama and McCain used their vice presidential selections to shore up perceived weaknesses by adding balance to their tickets. Obama chose Senator Joe Biden of Delaware, a 35-year veteran of the U.S. Senate and chair of the Senate Foreign Relations Committee. Obama wanted Biden to balance his own relative lack of experience, especially in foreign and defense policymaking. Obama may have also hoped that Biden, a Roman Catholic who was born in Pennsylvania, would attract white working-class voters in the Midwest and Catholic voters nationwide. McCain, meanwhile, surprised almost everyone by choosing Alaska's 44-year-old governor, Sarah Palin, as his running mate. McCain hoped to energize the conservative base of his party by choosing Palin because she is an outspoken opponent of abortion and

In 2008, Barack Obama chose Senator Joe Biden of Delaware to be his running mate. Was Biden a good choice?

gay marriage. He may have also hoped to attract the support of some women who were disappointed that Hillary Clinton did not win the Democratic nomination.

Exit polls Surveys based on random samples of voters leaving the polling place.

Biden probably did more to help Obama than Palin did to assist McCain. Except for occasional verbal missteps, Biden avoided controversy while campaigning vigorously for the ticket. **Exit polls,** which are surveys based on random samples of voters leaving the polling place, found that two-thirds of the electorate believed that Biden would be qualified to be president should it become necessary. Palin excited the conservative base of the Republican Party, attracting huge crowds at campaign events and mobilizing volunteers to work for the ticket, but her lack of experience and shaky interview performances left many observers questioning her fitness for the job. According to the exit polls, 60 percent of the electorate said she was not qualified to be president.[78]

The national party conventions are political rituals. The presidential candidates, vice presidential choices, and platform positions are all known well in advance of the convention and approved without significant opposition. For roughly a week, each party presents itself and its candidates in the best possible light while trashing the opposition. Nonetheless, conventions are important to the election process because many citizens decide how to vote at the time of the conventions.[79] On average, the party convention is worth from 5 to 7 percentage points in the polls for the party's ticket.[80]

Presidential Elections: The General Election Phase

After the party conventions, the presidential election process enters its second and decisive phase. The field of presidential candidates has narrowed to one Democrat, one Republican, and several other candidates running on third-party tickets or as independents. The rules of the political game have changed as well as each campaign considers what it must do to win an Electoral College majority.

The Electoral College

True or false: The candidate with the most votes is elected president. Answer: Not necessarily. Ask Al Gore. In 2000, Gore won 51 million votes nationwide compared with 50.5 million votes for George W. Bush, a difference of more than 500,000 votes. Nonetheless, Bush captured the White House because he won a majority of the votes in the Electoral College, 271 for Bush to 267 for Gore.

Electoral College The system established in the Constitution for indirect election of the president and vice president.

The **Electoral College** is the system established in the Constitution for the indirect election of the president and vice president. The framers of the Constitution disagreed on a procedure for selecting a president. Some delegates at the Constitutional Convention of 1787 favored letting Congress choose the president, but a majority rejected the idea because they worried that congressional selection would make the chief executive subservient to Congress. Another group of delegates favored direct popular election, but they faced opposition as well. Delegates from less populous states were afraid that popular election would afford their states little influence. A number of delegates also believed that voters scattered across the nation would be unaware of the merits of all of the candidates for president. Citizens would vote for local favorites from their region of the country, perhaps overlooking better-qualified candidates from other states. The Electoral College was a compromise between a system of congressional selection of the president and direct popular election.[81] The Electoral College also reflected the **federal system,** which is the division of power between a central government, with authority over the whole nation, and a series of state governments. By basing electoral votes in the states, the Electoral College ensured that presidents would respond to the interests of the states.[82]

Federal system A political system that divides power between a central government, with authority over the whole nation, and a series of state governments.

Under the Electoral College system, each state is entitled to as many electoral votes as the sum of its representatives in the U.S. House and Senate. Florida, for example, with 27 representatives and 2 senators, has 29 electoral votes; California, with 53 representatives and 2 senators, has 55. Altogether, the number of electoral votes is 538, based on 435 members of the House, 100 senators, and three electors for the District of Columbia. It takes a majority, 270 electoral votes, to elect a president.

Electors Individuals selected in each state officially to cast that state's electoral votes.

Electors are individuals selected in each state officially to cast the state's electoral votes. Each state selects as many electors as it has electoral votes. The framers of the Constitution anticipated that the members of the Electoral College would be experienced state leaders who would exercise good judgment in the selection of a president and vice president. In practice, however, the electors have been people chosen by party leaders to cast the state's electoral ballots for their party's nominees for president and vice president if their party's ticket carries the state. Electors are usually long-time party activists selected as a reward for their service to the party. (The U.S. Constitution prohibits members of Congress from serving as electors.) Instead of exercising their own judgment to choose candidates for president and vice president, electors almost always cast their votes for their party's candidates.

The Constitution empowers the states to determine the manner for selecting electors. Every state but Maine and Nebraska uses a winner-take-all election system. The entire slate of electors backing the presidential candidate winning the most popular votes in the state earns the right to serve as the official set of electors, regardless of the margin of victory or whether the candidate won a majority of the state's vote. Bush won the presidency in 2000 because he was finally declared the winner of Florida's electoral votes after weeks of recounts, lawsuits over recounts, and allegations of election irregularities. Bush claimed all of Florida's electoral votes even though his official margin of victory was less than 600 votes of almost 6 million ballots cast and he won only 49 percent of the state's vote.

The states of Maine and Nebraska award electors based on the total statewide vote *and* the vote in each congressional district. In 2008, Obama and McCain split Nebraska's five electoral votes four to one. Obama earned one electoral vote because he had the most votes in the state's Second Congressional District. McCain took Nebraska's other four electoral votes by winning the First and Third Congressional Districts and having the most votes statewide.

When voters choose among candidates in November, they are literally casting their ballots for electors pledged to support particular presidential and vice presidential candidates. In 32 states, the names of the electors do not even appear on the ballot. A California voter casting a ballot for Obama in 2008 was really voting for a slate of 55 electors pledged to vote for the Obama-Biden ticket for president and vice president. A McCain voter in California cast a ballot for a different set of 55 electors, a slate pledged to back the McCain-Palin ticket.

In December, the electors selected on Election Day in November gather in their state's capital city to officially mark their ballots for president and vice president. The electors chosen by the voters of Georgia, for example, meet in Atlanta, the state's capital city. New York's electors gather in Albany, that state's capital. In January, Congress convenes in joint session (both chambers meeting together), opens the ballots, counts the vote, and announces the official outcome.

If no candidate receives a majority of electoral votes, Congress picks the president and vice president. The Constitution states that the House chooses the president from among the three presidential candidates with the most electoral votes. Each state delegation has one vote, and a majority (26 states) is needed for election. In the meantime, the Senate names the vice president from the top two vice-presidential candidates. Each senator has one vote and a majority is required for election.

The Fall Campaign

The goal of the general election campaign is to win 270 electoral votes. Each campaign targets states based on their electoral votes and the perception of the closeness of the race in the state and allocates campaign resources accordingly.[83] Wyoming, Alaska, Montana, Delaware, and other states with few electoral votes receive little attention from the candidates, whereas California, Texas, New York, Florida, and other large states are preeminently important. If polls in a state show that one candidate leads the other by a substantial margin, then neither side is likely to devote many campaign resources to that state, focusing instead on places where the race is closer. In recent presidential elections, Texas, California, and New York have seen relatively little campaign activity because they have not been politically competitive. The Republicans have dominated presidential races in Texas, whereas the Democrats have had a lock on California and New York. In contrast, Florida, Ohio, Pennsylvania, and Michigan have been battleground states.

The campaign funding rules are different for the general election period than they are during the primary season. Once the major party nominees are chosen, they are eligible for complete funding for the general-election campaign, in the amount of $84 million in 2008. Candidates who accept the money may neither raise nor spend additional funds. In 2008, McCain accepted public financing, but Obama refused it because he thought he would be able to raise and spend more money than federal funding would have provided; he was right. Obama raised several hundred million dollars for the general election campaign, giving him a substantial financial advantage over McCain. The Obama campaign put its funding advantage to good use, opening more campaign offices in key states than the McCain campaign and spending more money on advertising. More than one in four voters reported being contacted by the Obama campaign compared with fewer than one in five contacted by the McCain campaign.[84]

Third-party and independent candidates may also benefit from federal funding. Third-party and independent candidates receive federal money *if* they win 5 percent or more of the popular vote in November. The catch is that the amount of money they receive depends on the size of their vote, and they must wait until after the election to collect, at least in their initial year. If a third party does well enough to qualify for federal funds, it receives a proportional amount of money at the beginning of the next general election period. Third-party and independent candidates who apply for federal funds must abide by contribution and spending limits, including the requirement that they spend no more than $50,000 of personal funds.

The presidential and vice presidential debates are often the most publicized events of the fall campaign. They are watched closely by the public and reported about extensively by the media. Debates affect peoples' views of the candidates both because of the presentations made by the candidates themselves and because of media analyses.[85] Nonetheless, research shows that debates typically have little impact on election outcomes. The debate between John Kennedy and Richard Nixon is widely regarded as the turning point of the 1960 presidential race but only because of the closeness of that contest. Most people who watched or heard the debate thought that the candidate they already favored had won. Most debates have little lasting effect on either voter preferences or knowledge about candidates and issues.[86]

Most campaign events, not just debates, have relatively little impact on the election outcomes because relatively few voters are open to persuasion. In 2008, 60 percent of the electorate decided how to vote before the national party conventions.

Although presidential debates are highly publicized affairs, they usually have little impact on the outcome of the election.

Only 10 percent of the 2008 electorate made their voting choice within a week of Election Day.[87]

Base voters Rock solid Republicans or hardcore Democrats who are firmly committed to voting for their party's nominee.

Swing voters Citizens who could vote for either the Democratic or the Republican nominee.

The electorate includes both base voters and swing voters. **Base voters** are rock solid Republicans or hardcore Democrats, firmly committed to voting for their party's nominee. In contrast, **swing voters** are citizens who could vote for either the Democratic or the Republican nominee. Base voters typically outnumber swing voters by a large margin. Bush won the 2004 election because his party had the larger base that year and the Republicans did a better job than the Democrats at turning out their base. Swing voters make a difference only when the base vote for each party is nearly equal in size and one candidate or the other attracts a substantial majority of the swing vote.[88] In 2008, voters identifying with the Democratic Party outnumbered Republican Party identifiers 39 percent to 32 percent, giving Obama a distinct advantage. Obama also captured 52 percent of independents, which represented 29 percent of the electorate.[89]

In the last few days of the campaign, the candidates frantically crisscross the country, making as many appearances as possible in large states that are expected to be close. Research shows that candidate appearances increase turnout, especially late in the campaign season, but have relatively little impact on voter choice.[90] Consequently, the candidates focus on party strongholds. Republicans hold rallies in the suburbs; Democrats campaign in inner-city neighborhoods.

Blue States and Red States

Red states Republican states.

Blue states Democratic states.

Some political observers believe that the United States is deeply and closely divided along regional lines into Republican **red states** and Democratic **blue states,** so named because of the colors used on the Electoral College map to show states that went Republican (red) or Democratic (blue). In this view, red states are pro-gun, pro-life, anti-gay Christian conservative strongholds opposed to government regulation and high taxes, whereas blue states are secular liberal bastions that favor gun control, abortion rights, gay rights, and well-funded government programs aimed at alleviating societal problems.

The 2004 Electoral College map, which is shown in Figure 9.1, graphically illustrates the blue state/red state divide. President Bush won reelection by carrying every state in the South, every state in the Great Plains, and every state in the Rocky Mountains. Kerry won the Northeast and every state on the West Coast except Alaska. The two candidates split the Midwest. The 2004 electoral vote division closely resembled the 2000 election. The only states that flipped from one party to the other were New Mexico and Iowa, which went for Gore in 2000 but Bush in 2004, and New Hampshire, which switched from Bush in 2000 to Kerry in 2004.

In 2008, Obama broke out of the blue state-red state stalemate by winning a series of formerly red states. In addition to holding onto every state that Kerry took in 2004, Obama expanded his base in the Northeast by winning New Hampshire. He shored up his position in the Midwest, taking Ohio, Indiana, and Iowa. Obama made inroads in the South, the most Republican region in the nation, winning Virginia, North Carolina, and Florida. Finally, he carved out a section of the Southwest, taking Colorado, New Mexico, and Nevada (Figure 9.2).

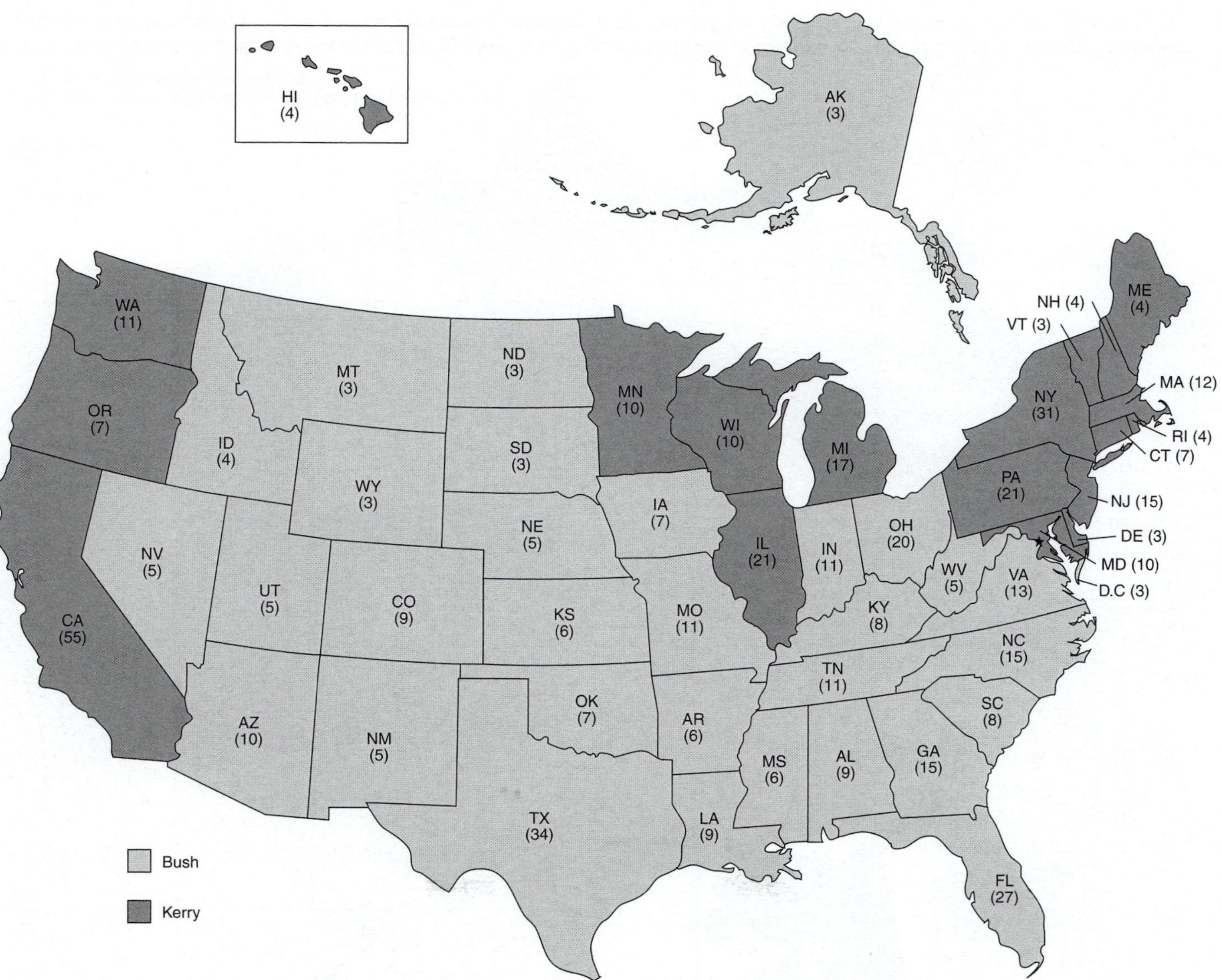

FIGURE 9.1 President Bush won reelection in 2004 by capturing 31 states with 286 electoral votes, sweeping the South, the Great Plains, and the Rocky Mountain States.

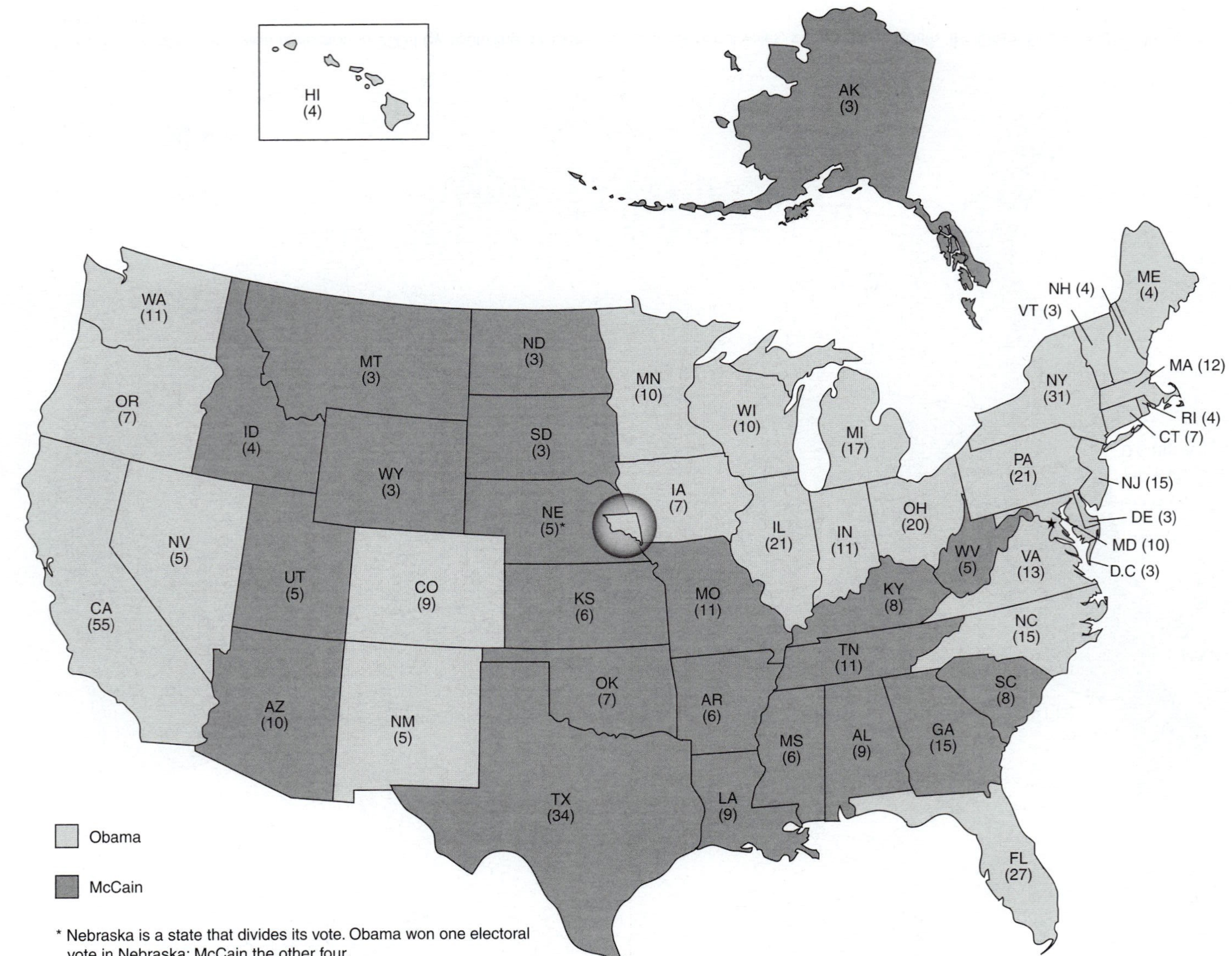

* Nebraska is a state that divides its vote. Obama won one electoral vote in Nebraska; McCain the other four.

FIGURE 9.2 Barack Obama won the White House in 2008 by carrying 28 states and the District of Columbia for a total of 365 electoral votes. Obama won every state taken by Kerry and added several formerly red states, including the large states of Ohio, Florida, North Carolina, Virginia, and Indiana.

Political scientist Morris P. Fiorina believes that the red state-blue state division is overblown. He points out that most of the red states have major enclaves of blue voters and vice versa. Even though Texas is a red state on the Electoral College map, many of its cities voted for Kerry as did the region along the border with Mexico. Meanwhile, a majority of the counties in California, a blue state, voted for Bush.[91]

Electoral College Reform

The 2000 presidential election made the Electoral College the center of controversy. Gore won the popular vote because he piled up huge margins of victory in California and New York, whereas Bush won other states by smaller margins. Gore carried California and New York, the two largest states he won, by a combined victory margin of 2.9 million votes. In contrast, Bush won Texas and Florida, the two states with the most electoral votes in his column, by a combined margin of only 1.4 million votes. Bush also benefited from the federalism bonus that awards every state three electoral votes (because of its two senators and one representative) regardless of size. Because Bush carried 11 of 18 smaller states, he won more electoral votes than he would have received on the basis of population alone.[92]

Bush is not the only person to be elected president despite losing the national popular vote. In 1876, Samuel Tilden lost to Rutherford B. Hayes even though he received more popular votes than did his opponent. Similarly, Grover Cleveland won the popular vote in 1888 but lost the Electoral College—and the presidency—to Benjamin Harrison. The chances of a "wrong winner" electoral vote outcome are about one in three when the popular vote margin is 500,000 votes or fewer.[93] Nonetheless, election outcomes that close are rare. Only two presidential races in the twentieth century had popular vote margins of fewer than 500,000 votes—the Kennedy–Nixon election in 1960 and the Nixon–Humphrey contest in 1968.

The critics of the Electoral College warn that the electors may vote for persons other than their party's presidential and vice presidential candidates. Fewer than half the states legally require the electors to cast their ballots for their party's nominees. In 2004, for example, one Democratic elector from Minnesota cast an official presidential ballot for vice presidential candidate John Edwards instead of John Kerry, apparently by accident because none of the state's 10 electors owned up to the action. The 2000 election was so close that two Bush electors could have changed the outcome had they switched their votes from Bush to Gore. Nonetheless, academic observers downplay the seriousness of this problem because most electoral vote margins are large enough that dozens of electors would have to change their votes to affect an election's outcome. Also, electors rarely prove unfaithful. Since 1789, only 10 out of nearly 22,000 electors have voted "against instructions."[94] None affected the outcome of an election.

Another criticism of the Electoral College is that Congress picks the president and vice president if no candidate receives a majority of the electoral vote. Although this procedure is part of the Constitution, many Americans would likely be disturbed by the prospect of a chief executive chosen through behind-the-scenes maneuvering. It might also weaken the office of the presidency by making the incumbent dependent on congressional selection.[95] In 1824, the last time Congress named the president, the selection of John Quincy Adams over Andrew Jackson was marred by dark rumors of a backroom deal. In recent years, the closest the nation has come to seeing an election go to Congress was in 1968, when independent candidate George Wallace won 46 electoral votes. Despite winning 19 percent of the popular vote in 1992 and 8.5 percent in 1996, Ross Perot won no electoral votes because he failed to carry any states.

Political legitimacy The popular acceptance of a government and its officials as rightful authorities in the exercise of power.

The strength of the Electoral College is that it conveys political legitimacy to the winner in closely fought presidential elections. **Political legitimacy** is the popular acceptance of a government and its officials as rightful authorities in the exercise of power. If citizens and other public officials believe that a president lacks political legitimacy, the president will have difficulty exercising authority. The proponents of the Electoral College argue that it enhances the president's legitimacy by ensuring that even fairly close presidential elections produce a clear winner. Even though Bill Clinton took only 43 percent of the popular vote in 1992, he won 69 percent of the electoral vote. The Electoral College turned a badly divided popular vote, split 43 percent for Clinton to 38 percent for Bush to 19 percent for Perot, into a one-sided Electoral College victory. The morning after the election some newspapers even used the word *landslide* to describe Clinton's victory. Figure 9.3 compares the popular vote with the electoral vote percentage for the winning presidential candidate from 1940 through 2008. In every election, the winning candidate's electoral vote

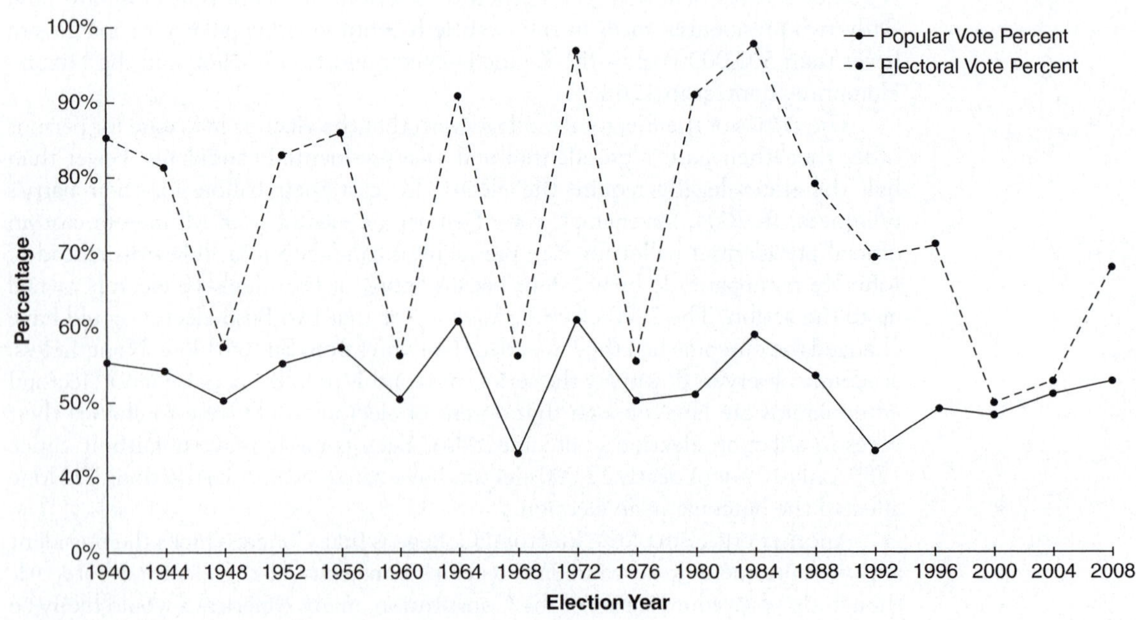

FIGURE 9.3 Popular Vote and Electoral Vote Percent.

percentage was greater than the popular vote percentage, even in the 2000 election when the Electoral College turned a popular vote loser into an Electoral College winner. The defenders of the Electoral College believe that it is beneficial because it gives the winning presidential candidate the appearance of the majority support necessary to be an effective president.

Nonetheless, the 2000 election showed that the Electoral College sometimes undermines the political legitimacy of a president. The outcome of the national Electoral College vote depended on the result of the popular vote in Florida, which was too close to call. For more than a month, county canvassing boards, state officials, the Florida legislature, Florida judges, the Florida Supreme Court, and the U.S. Supreme Court struggled over ballot counting issues. The outcome of the Florida vote ultimately hinged on the decision whether and how to count more than 40,000 ballots which voting machines had failed to count. Many observers believed that a hand count of 40,000 additional ballots would give the election to Gore because most of the ballots were from counties that voted heavily for the vice president. After a district court judge in Florida ruled against a hand count, the Florida Supreme Court, all of whose members were Democrats, voted four to three to order a hand count. Within less than a day, the U.S. Supreme Court voted five to four to halt the count. The five justices in the majority were all appointees of President Reagan or President George H. W. Bush, the father of the presidential candidate who benefited from the decision. Many observers believed that the involvement of the courts in the election outcome would undermine the legitimacy of the new president, regardless of the outcome of the dispute. Had Gore won because the Florida Supreme Court ordered a hand recount, Republicans would have charged that his victory was tainted by the intervention of a partisan court. As it were, many Democrats argued that Bush's election was illegitimate because of the intervention of a narrow partisan majority on the U.S. Supreme Court.

In the aftermath of the 2000 election, some members of Congress proposed constitutional amendments to abolish the Electoral College and replace it with direct popular election. The advocates of direct election point out that their system is simpler than the Electoral College and more democratic because it ensures that the candidate with the most votes nationwide wins. They also think direct election would increase turnout because every vote would count equally regardless of the state in which it was cast.[96]

Nonetheless, direct election of the president has its detractors. Some critics complain that candidates would make fewer public appearances, concentrating even more on television than they do now. Other opponents fear that a proliferation of independent and minor-party candidates would undermine the legitimacy of the eventual winner. Once again, consider the 1992 presidential election. Had Clinton won the presidency based on 43 percent of the popular vote instead of 69 percent of the electoral vote, would his administration have enjoyed the same level of political legitimacy as it did with his solid Electoral College victory?

Most political scientists think that it is unlikely that Congress and the states will adopt a constitutional amendment to abolish the Electoral College, despite the 2000 election. Constitutional amendments must be proposed by a two-thirds vote of the House and Senate and then ratified by three-fourths of the states, margins that are not easily achieved. Will small states agree to an amendment that would reduce their influence in the presidential election process? Furthermore, interest groups that are disproportionately powerful in states with large numbers of electoral votes will oppose eliminating the Electoral College because it would reduce their influence. African Americans, Latinos, Jews, gay men and lesbians, and organized labor all enjoy considerable influence in large states rich in electoral votes. No candidate who hopes to win in California, for example, can afford to ignore the interests of Latino voters. Similarly, Jewish voters are disproportionately important in the large states of New York and Florida. Cuban American voters enjoy considerable influence in American politics because of their concentration in Florida.

The most recent effort to reform the Electoral College involves a proposed agreement among states to cast their electoral votes for the national popular vote winner regardless of each state's vote. The U.S. Constitution allows states with congressional approval to enter into agreements or compacts with other states. If states with electoral votes totaling 270 agreed to the compact, the candidate with the most votes would be guaranteed of winning the election. The advantage of this effort is that it effectively repeals the Electoral College without having to propose and ratify a constitutional amendment. To date, however, only a few states have signed on to the approach.[97]

WHAT IS YOUR OPINION?

Do you think the Electoral College should be replaced with direct popular election of the president?

The Voters Decide

Political scientists identify a number of factors influencing voter choice.

Party Identification

Voter choice is closely related to political party identification. Democrats vote for Democratic candidates; Republicans back Republicans. In 2008, 89 percent of Republicans voted for McCain whereas 89 percent of Democrats backed Obama.[98] Keep in mind, however, that party identification is a complex phenomenon. People identify with one party or the other because they agree with its issue positions, have confidence in its leaders, or feel comfortable with groups associated with the party. When citizens decide to vote for Candidate A because Candidate A is a Democrat (or Republican), their choice is more than blind allegiance to a party label; it is also a response to the perceived issue positions and image of the party.

Issues

The role of issues varies, depending on the strength of a voter's party attachment and knowledge of the candidates' issue positions. Informed voters consider issues in selecting candidates although they tend to be biased in favor in candidates who share their party identification. Well-informed independents base their voting decisions strictly on how closely the candidates' issue positions match their own.[99] Less well-informed voters fall back on party identification. Poorly informed voters and people who are ambivalent on parties and issues base their voting decisions on other factors, such as their judgment about the state of the economy.[100]

Personal Qualities and Image

Political science research shows that perceptions of a candidate's personal qualities influence voter choice. One study finds that voters evaluate presidential candidates on the basis on their mental image of what a president should be. Citizens want a president who is competent, honest, and reliable, and they pick the candidate they believe best matches those qualities.[101] Another study concludes that voters respond to candidates on the basis of their emotional evaluation of a candidate's moral leadership and competence.[102]

Campaigns

Campaigns educate voters about candidates and issues.[103] Candidates who choose not to conduct a campaign or who lack the necessary funding to get their message across almost never win. Challengers for congressional seats who have less than a quarter million dollars to spend have less than a 1 percent chance of winning.[104]

Research shows that campaign tactics vary in their effectiveness. Campaign advertising affects voters in concert with their party identification, making Democrats more likely to vote Democratic and Republicans more likely to support GOP candidates. The issues that work best for the Democrats are education, childcare, and healthcare. In contrast, Republicans benefit when they can shift the issue focus to taxes, morality, economic growth, and foreign policy.[105]

Although campaigns affect election outcomes, they are not as important as the state of the economy and the political context in which the race is run. Presidential campaigns after Labor Day affect the national vote by an average of four percentage points, enough to make a difference in the outcome of only about one in five elections.[106] The results of most election contests are determined by the following underlying factors: (1) the incumbent president's approval rating in the months before the election; (2) the growth rate of the economy in the quarter prior to the election; and (3) the length of time the president's party has held the White House.[107] All three of the factors worked against McCain in the 2008 presidential campaign. He was a Republican trying to keep his party's hold on the White House for the third election in a row despite incumbent President Bush's low approval rating and a serious economic downturn. In 2008, 71 percent of the voters told pollsters that they disapproved of the way Bush was handling his job, and two-thirds of them cast their ballots for Obama. Half the electorate described the economy as "poor" or "not so good"; 54 percent of them voted for Obama compared with 44 percent for McCain.[108]

Retrospective and Prospective Voting

Retrospective voting The concept that voters choose candidates based on their perception of an incumbent candidate's past performance in office or the performance of the incumbent party.

Prospective voting The concept that voters evaluate the incumbent officeholder and the incumbent's party based on their expectations of future developments.

Citizens make voting decisions based on their evaluations of the past and expectations for the future. **Retrospective voting** is the concept that voters choose candidates based on their perception of an incumbent candidate's past performance in office or the performance of the incumbent party. If voters perceive that things are going well, incumbent officeholders and their party usually get the credit. They get the blame, though, if voters think the situation is poor. The economy is the most important factor affecting retrospective voters, but war and peace matter as well.[109] In 2008, 75 percent of the electorate told survey researchers that the country was "seriously off on the wrong track"; 62 percent of them voted for Obama.[110]

Voter evaluations of candidates have a prospective component as well. **Prospective voting** is the concept that voters evaluate the incumbent officeholder and the incumbent's party based on their expectations of future developments. Voters compare candidate promises and make assessments about the ability of candidates and parties to fulfill their promises.[111]

WHAT IS YOUR OPINION?

What are the most important qualities a candidate for president should have in order to get your vote?

WHAT WE HAVE LEARNED

1. **What types of elections are held in the United States?**

   Americans have the opportunity to cast ballots in several types of elections. A general election is an election held in November of even-numbered years to fill state and national offices. General election voters can cast a straight ticket or a split ticket ballot. In most states, major parties choose their general election candidates in primary elections scheduled a month or more before the November general election. Some states have closed primaries; other states have open primaries.

2. **What factors affect the redistricting process?**

   American voters select public officials in a combination of at-large and district elections. An at-large election is a method for choosing public officials in which the citizens of an entire political subdivision, such as a state, vote to select officeholders. A district election is a method for choosing public officials that divides a political subdivision, such as a state, into geographic areas called districts with each district electing one official. Legislative district boundaries must be redrawn every 10 years after the national census is taken. States that grow relatively rapidly gain seats in the U.S. House; states that grow slowly or not at all lose seats. Legislative districts must also be redrawn because of population movement within a state. According to the one person, one vote rulings of the U.S. Supreme Court, legislative districts must be nearly equal in population.

The Voting Rights Act (VRA), meanwhile, makes it illegal for state and local governments to enact and enforce election rules and procedures that diminish the voting power of racial, ethnic, and language minority groups. Nonetheless, redistricting is highly political and can be used to advance the interests of a political party or a particular individual. Gerrymandering is the drawing of legislative district lines for political advantage.

3. **What are the goals of an election campaign, and how does money affect the ability of candidates to achieve their goals?**

   An election campaign is an attempt to get information to voters that will persuade them to elect a candidate or not elect a candidate's opponent. Advertising, particularly television, is the largest item in most campaign budgets. Wealthy candidates can fund their own campaigns, but most raise money from individual contributors (either through direct mail or online) and PACs. Political parties, 527 committees, and super PACs may also spend money to support or defeat candidates. Candidates spend the early months of the race raising money, building an organization, seeking group endorsements, and planning strategy. An important goal for many campaigns is to improve the candidate's name recognition, especially if the candidate is not an incumbent. Campaigns try to create a positive image of their candidates and a negative image of their opponent. Campaign advertising increases citizen knowledge of issues and candidates, affects voter evaluations of candidates, and increases a candidate's share of the vote.

4. **What are the similarities and differences in elections for the U.S. House and U.S. Senate?**

   The most striking feature of elections for the U.S. House of Representatives is that most incumbents are reelected. Incumbents are usually better known and better funded than their opponents. Voters typically like their representative even if they disapprove of the performance of Congress as a whole. Many House districts are safe for one or the other political party. Historically, the political party holding the White House loses seats in the House of Representatives in midterm elections. Senate races are more competitive than House elections. Incumbency is not as important in Senate races as it is in House races. Senate constituencies are usually more diverse than House constituencies. Incumbent senators typically face stronger challengers than incumbent House members.

5. **What are the main steps in the nominating stage of the presidential election process?**

   The presidential election process consists of two distinct phases with different rules, requiring candidates to wage two separate campaigns. The first phase is the contest for the nomination. Republicans compete against other Republicans, Democrats against other Democrats in a series of primaries and caucuses designed to select delegates to each party's national nominating convention. Each candidate's goal is for his or her supporters to be chosen as convention delegates because the delegates, by majority vote, select the party's presidential nominee. In 2008, the presidential nomination process had six stages: (1) the invisible primary; (2) the early contests; (3) Super Tuesday; (4) post-Super Tuesday contests; (5) transition; and (6) the national party conventions.

6. **What are the most important steps in the general election stage of the presidential election process?**

   The general election phase is a contest between the two major party tickets and, perhaps, a serious independent or third-party candidate. Because the Electoral College determines the winner of the general election, the general election phase is actually 51 elections, a contest in every state and the District of Columbia. The winner is the candidate who can win a set of states whose combined electoral votes total at least 270, the majority of electoral votes at stake. With the exception of Maine and Nebraska, the candidate with the most votes in each state receives all of the state's electoral votes. In the general election phase, each campaign targets states with large numbers of electoral votes that are perceived to be close, known as battleground states. The electorate includes both base voters and swing voters. Most elections are decided by the relative size of each party's base vote and how effective the party is at turning out its base.

The 2000 presidential election made the Electoral College the center of controversy because the winner of the popular vote, Al Gore, lost the election. George W. Bush captured a majority of Electoral College votes because he won a number of states by relatively small margins and because he carried more small states, each of which has three electoral votes regardless of its population. Critics of the Electoral College also worry about electors casting their ballots contrary to the will of the voters in their states and the prospect that Congress will pick a president and vice president if no candidate receives a majority of electoral votes. Reformers offer a number of alternatives to the Electoral College, including direct popular election, but no proposal has come close to winning the level of support needed to propose and ratify a constitutional amendment. The latest reform effort is a proposal for states to enter into an interstate compact to award their electoral votes to the national popular vote winner regardless of the outcomes in individual states.

7. **How does each of the following factors affect voter choice: party identification, issues, personal qualities and image, campaigns, and retrospective and prospective voting?**

Voter choice is closely related to political party identification. As for issues, informed voters base their voting decisions on ideology and the issue positions of the candidates; uninformed voters base their voting decisions on other factors, such as their judgment about the state of the economy. Perceptions of a candidate's personal qualities and image influence voter choice. Campaigns educate voters about candidates and issues. Campaigns influence election outcomes, but they are typically not decisive. The three most important underlying factors affecting the outcome of a presidential race are the following: (1) the incumbent president's approval rating in the months before the election; (2) the growth rate of the economy in the quarter prior to the election; and (3) the length of time the president's party has held the White House. Finally, citizens make voting decisions based on their evaluations of the past (retrospective voting) and expectations for the future (prospective voting).

KEY TERMS

527 committee
air war
apportionment
at-large election
balance the ticket
base voters
battleground states
Bipartisan Campaign Reform Act (BCRA)
blanket primary
blue states
caucus method of delegate selection
closed primary
coattail effect
district election
election campaign
Electoral College
electors
exit polls
federal system
general election
gerrymandering
ground war
hard money
independent expenditures
invisible primary

issue ownership
majority-minority districts
one person, one vote
open primary
party platform
political action committee (PAC)
political legitimacy
pork barrel spending
presidential preference primary
primary election
proportional representation (PR)
prospective voting
reapportionment
red states
redistricting
retrospective voting
rose garden strategy
runoff
soft money
split ticket ballot
straight ticket ballot
superdelegates
swing voters
Voting Rights Act (VRA)

NOTES

1. Jeffrey M. Jones, "Record Midterm Enthusiasm as Voters Head to Polls," November 2, 2010, available at www.gallup.com.
2. Gary Langer, "2010 Elections Exit Poll Analysis: The Political Price of Economic Pain," November 3, 2010, available at www.abcnews.go.com.
3. Robert E. Cushman and Robert F. Cushman, *Cases in Constitutional Law*, 3rd ed. (New York: Appleton-Century-Crofts, 1968), p. 42.
4. *Baker v. Carr*, 369 U.S. 186 (1962) and *Wesberry v. Sanders*, 376 U.S. 1 (1964).
5. David Lublin, "Race and Redistricting in the United States: An Overview," in Lisa Handley and Bernie Grofman, eds., *Redistricting in Comparative Perspective* (New York: Oxford University Press, 2008), p. 142.
6. *Vieth v. Commonwealth of Pennsylvania*, 195 F. Supp. 2d 672 (M.D. Pa. 2002).
7. Thomas Brunell and Bernard Grofman, "The Partisan Consequences of *Baker v. Carr* and the One Person, One Vote Revolution," in Handley and Grofman, eds., *Redistricting in Comparative Perspective*, pp. 225–236.
8. Stephen Ansolabehere, Alan Gerber, and James Snyder, "Equal Money: Court-Ordered Redistricting and Public Expenditures in the American States," *American Political Science Review* 96 (December 2002): 767–777.
9. Harold Wolman and Lisa Marckini, "The Effect of Place on Legislative Roll-Call Voting: The Case of Central-City Representatives in the U.S. House," *Political Science Quarterly* 81 (September 2000): 763–781.
10. Mark Monmonier, *Bushmanders and Bullwinkles: How Politicians Manipulate Electronic Maps and Census Data to Win Elections* (Chicago, IL: University of Chicago Press, 2001), p. 62.
11. David Lublin and D. Stephen Voss, "Racial Redistricting and Realignment in Southern State Legislatures," *American Journal of Political Science* 44 (October 2000): 792–810.
12. Lublin, "Race and Redistricting in the United States: An Overview," p. 148.
13. *Shaw v. Reno*, 509 U.S. 630 (1993) and *Miller v. Johnson*, 515 U.S. 900 (1995).
14. *Reno v. Bossier Parish School Board*, 528 U.S. 320 (2000).
15. *Georgia v. Ashcroft*, 539 U.S. 461 (2003).
16. Richard H. Pildes, "Political Competition and the Modern VRA," in David L. Epstein, Richard H. Pildes, Rodolfo O. de la Garza, and Sharyn O'Halloran, eds., *The Future of the Voting Rights Act* (New York: Russell Sage Foundation, 2006), p. 7.
17. *Davis v. Bandemer*, 478 U.S. 109 (1986).
18. Richard L. Engstrom, "The Post-2000 Round of Redistricting: An Entangled Thicket Within the Federal System," *Publius: The Journal of Federalism* 32 (Fall 2002): 60–64.
19. Center for Responsive Politics, available at www.opensecrets.org.
20. John J. Coleman and Paul F. Manna, "Congressional Campaign Spending and the Quality of Democracy," *Journal of Politics* 62 (August 2000): 757–789.
21. Paul S. Herrnson, *Congressional Elections: Campaigning at Home and in Washington*, 5th ed. (Washington, DC: CQ Press, 2008), p. 83.
22. Center for Responsive Politics.
23. Federal Election Commission, available at www.fec.gov.
24. Richard A. Oppel, Jr., "Campaign Documents Show Depth of Bush Fund-Raising," *New York Times*, May 5, 2003, available at www.nytimes.com.
25. Wayne Slater, "Elite Donors Lifted Bush," *Dallas Morning News*, May 5, 2003, available at www.dallasnews.com.
26. Kirsten A. Foot and Steven M. Schneider, *Web Campaigning* (Cambridge, MA: MIT Press, 2006), pp. 197–198.
27. Jack Citrin and David Karol, ed., *Nominating the President: Evolution and Revolution in 2008 and Beyond* (Lanham, MD: Rowman & Littlefield, 2009), pp. 27–36.
28. Center for Responsive Politics.
29. Michael J. Malbin, *The Election After Reform: Money, Politics, and the Bipartisan Campaign Reform Act* (Lanham, MD: Rowman & Littlefield, 2006), pp. 3–4.

30. Glen Justice and Jim Rutenberg, "Advocacy Groups Step Up Costly Battle of Political Ads," *New York Times*, September 25, 2004, available at www.nytimes.com.
31. Dan Eggen and T. W. Farnam, "New 'Super Pacs' Bringing Millions into Campaigns," *Washington Post*, September 28, 2010, available at www.washingtonpost.com.
32. Matthew R. Kerbel, *Netroots: Online Progressives and the Transformation of American Politics* (Boulder, CO: Paradigm Publishers, 2009), pp. 135–139.
33. Doug Beizer, "Social Media Swings Tight Mass. Senate Race," *Federal Computer Week*, January 20, 2010, available at http://fcw.com.
34. Kerwin C. Swint, *Mudslingers: The Top 25 Negative Political Campaigns of All Time* (Westport, CT: Praeger, 2006), p. 47.
35. Richard R. Lau and Gerald M. Pomper, "Effectiveness of Negative Campaigning in U.S. Senate Elections," *American Journal of Political Science* 46 (January 2002): 47–66.
36. Stephen Ansolabehere and Shanto Iyengar, *Going Negative: How Attack Ads Shrink and Polarize the Electorate* (New York: Free Press, 1995), pp. 89–113.
37. Ken Goldstein and Paul Freedman, "Campaign Advertising and Voter Turnout: New Evidence for a Stimulation Effect," *Journal of Politics* 64 (August 2002): 721–740.
38. John G. Geer, *In Defense of Negativity: Attack Ads in Presidential Campaigns* (Chicago, IL: University of Chicago Press, 2006), pp. 153–164.
39. David E. Damore, "Candidate Strategy and the Decision to Go Negative," *Political Research Quarterly* 55 (September 2002): 669–685.
40. Steven Ansolabehere and Shanto Iyengar, "Winning Through Advertising: It's All in the Context," in James A. Thurber and Candice J. Nelson, eds., *Campaigns and Elections American Style* (Boulder, CO: Westview, 1995), p. 109.
41. Lynda Lee Kaid, "Political Advertising," in Stephen C. Craig, ed., *The Electoral Challenge: Theory Meets Practice* (Washington, DC: CQ Press, 2006), p. 82.
42. Gregory A. Huber and Kevin Arceneaux, "Identifying the Persuasive Effects of Presidential Advertising," *American Journal of Political Science* 51 (October 2007): 957–977.
43. John R. Petrocik, William L. Benoit, and Glenn J. Hansen, "Issue Ownership and Presidential Campaigning," *Political Science Quarterly* 118 (Winter 2004–2005): 599–626.
44. Jeremy C. Pope and Jonathan Woon, "Measuring Changes in American Party Reputation, 1939–2004," *Political Research Quarterly* 62 (December 2009): 653–661.
45. Lynn Vavreck, Constantine J. Spiliotes, and Linda L. Fowler, "The Effects of Retail Politics in the New Hampshire Primary," *American Journal of Political Science* 46 (July 2002): 595–610.
46. Kate Kenski, Bruce W. Hardy, and Kathleen Hall Jamieson, *The Obama Victory: How Media and Message Shaped the 2008 Election* (New York: Oxford University Press, 2010), pp. 279–280.
47. Paul R. Abramson, John H. Aldrich, and David W. Rohde, *Change and Continuity in the 2008 Election* (Washington, DC: CQ Press, 2010), p. 229.
48. Alexander C. Hart, "Election by Numbers," *Washington Post*, November 5, 2010, available at www.washingtonpost.com.
49. David C. W. Parker and Craig Goodman, "Making a Good Impression: Resource Allocation, Home Styles, and Washington Work," *Legislative Studies Quarterly* 34 (November 2009): 493–524.
50. Michael E. Toner and Melissa L. Laurenza, "Emerging Campaign Finance Trends and Their Impact on the 2006 Midterm Election," in Larry J. Sabato, ed., *The Sixth Year Itch: The Rise and Fall of the George W. Bush Presidency* (New York: Pearson, 2008), p. 132.
51. Robert S. Erickson and Gerald C. Wright, "Voters, Candidates, and Issues in Congressional Elections," in Lawrence C. Dodd and Bruce I. Oppenheimer, eds., *Congress Reconsidered*, 9th ed. (Washington, DC: CQ Press, 2009), pp. 79–82.
52. Bill Bishop and Robert Cushing, "The Big Sort: Migration, Community, and Politics in the United States of 'These People,'" in Texiera, ed., *Red, Blue, and Purple America*, p. 69.
53. Robert S. Erikson and Gerald C. Wright, "Voters, Candidates, and Issues in Congressional Elections," in Lawrence C. Dodd and Bruce I. Oppenheimer, eds., *Congress Reconsidered*, 7th ed. (Washington, DC: CQ Press, 2001), p. 72.
54. James E. Campbell and Joe A. Sumners, "Presidential Coattails in Senate Elections," *American Political Science Review* 84 (June 1990): 513–524.
55. Secretary of State of New Hampshire, available at www.sos.nh.gov.
56. John S. Jackson, Nathan S. Bigelow, and John C. Green, "The State of Party Elites: National Convention Delegates, 1992–2000," in John C. Green and Rick Farmer, eds., *The State of the Parties: The Changing Role of Contemporary American Parties* (Lanham, MD: Rowman & Littlefield, 2003), pp. 54–78.
57. Paul R. Abramson, John H. Aldrich, Phil Paolino, and David W. Rohde, "'Sophisticated' Voting in the 1988 Presidential Primaries," *American Political Science Review* 86 (March 1992): 55–69.
58. "State-by-state Election Results," available at www.govote.com.
59. Barbara Norrander, "Nomination Choices: Caucus and Primary Outcomes, 1976–88," *American Journal of Political Science* 37 (May 1993): 343–364.
60. Elaine C. Kamarck, *Primary Politics: How Presidential Candidates Have Shaped the Modern Nominating System* (Washington, DC: Brookings Institution Press, 2009), pp. 18–23.
61. William G. Mayer, "Voting in Presidential Primaries: What Can We Learn from Three Decades of Exit Polling?" in Mayer, ed., *The Making of the Presidential Candidates 2008* (Lanham, MD: Rowman & Littlefield, 2008), p. 169.

62. Available at www.realclearpolitics.com.
63. Caroline Tolbert and Peverill Squire, "Reforming the Presidential Nomination Process," *PS: Political Science & Politics*, January 2009, p. 27.
64. Lonna Rae Atkeson and Cherie D. Maestas, "Meaningful Participation and the Evolution of the Reformed Presidential Nominating System," *PS: Political Science & Politics*, January 2009, pp. 59–64.
65. Anthony Corrado and Molly Corbett, "Rewriting the Playbook on Presidential Campaign Financing," in Dennis W. Johnson, ed., *Campaigning for President 2008: Strategy and Tactics, New Voices and New Techniques* (New York: Routledge, 2009), p. 126.
66. Federal Election Commission.
67. Marty Cohen, David Karol, Hans Noel, and John Zalla, *The Party Decides: Presidential Nominations Before and After Reform* (Chicago, IL: University of Chicago Press, 2008), pp. 187–235, 339–348.
68. Paul-Henri Gurian and Audrey A. Haynes, "Presidential Nomination Campaigns: Toward 2004," *PS: Political Science & Politics*, April 2003, p. 177.
69. Christopher C. Hull, *Grassroots Rules: How the Iowa Caucus Helps Elect American Presidents* (Stanford, CA: Stanford University Press, 2008), p. 49.
70. Todd Donovan and Rob Hunsaker, "Beyond Expectation: Effects of Early Elections in U.S. Presidential Nomination Contests," *PS: Political Science & Politics*, January 2009, pp. 45–52.
71. Jackie Calmes, "Clinton Braces for Second Loss; Union, Senators May Back Obama," *Wall Street Journal*, January 8, 2008, available at www.wsj.com.
72. Tad Devine, "Obama Wins the Nomination: How He Did It," in Johnson, ed., *Campaigning for President 2008*, pp. 31–43.
73. Federal Election Commission.
74. François Pétry and Benoît Colleteet, "Measuring How Political Parties Keep Their Promises: A Positive Perspective from Political Science," in Louis M. Imbeau, *Do They Walk Like They Talk? Speech and Action in Policy Processes* (New York: Springer, 2009), pp. 65–80.
75. Jody C. Baumgartner, *The American Vice Presidency Reconsidered* (Westport, CT: Praeger, 2006), p. 78.
76. David W. Romero, "Requiem for a Lightweight: Vice Presidential Candidate Evaluation and the Presidential Vote," *Presidential Studies Quarterly* 31 (September 2001): 454–463.
77. Mark Hiller and Douglas Kriner, "Institutional Change and the Dynamics of Vice Presidential Selection," *Presidential Studies Quarterly* 38 (September 2008): 401–421.
78. Exit polls, available at www.cnn.com.
79. Gerald M. Pomper, "The New Role of the Conventions as Political Rituals," in Costas Panagopoulos, ed., *Rewiring Politics: Presidential Nominating Conventions in the Media Age* (Baton Rouge, LA: LSU Press, 2007), pp. 189–197.
80. James E. Campbell, Lynn L. Cherry, and Kenneth A. Wink, "The Convention Bump," *American Politics Quarterly* 20 (July 1992): 287–307.
81. Lawrence D. Longley and Neal R. Peirce, *The Electoral College Primer* (New Haven, CT: Yale University Press, 1996), pp. 17–19.
82. Randall E. Adkins and Kent A. Kirwan, "What Role Does the 'Federalism Bonus' Play in Presidential Selection?" *Publius: The Journal of Federalism* 32 (Fall 2002): 71–90.
83. Daron R. Shaw, *The Race to 270: The Electoral College and the Campaign Strategies of 2000 and 2004* (Chicago, IL: University of Chicago Press, 2006), p. 143.
84. James Thurber, "Understanding the Dynamics and the Transformation of American Campaigns," in James Thurber and Candice J. Nelson, eds., *Campaigns and Elections American Style*, 3rd ed. (Boulder, CO: Westview Press, 2010), pp. 12–16.
85. Kim J. Fridkin, Patrick J. Kenney, Sarah Allen Gershon, Karen Shafer, and Gina Serignese Woodall, "Capturing the Power of a Campaign Event: The 2004 Presidential Debate in Tempe," *Journal of Politics* 69 (August 2007): 770–785.
86. David J. Lanoue, "The 'Turning Point': Viewers' Reactions to the Second 1988 Presidential Debate," *American Politics Quarterly* 19 (January 1991): 80–95.
87. Exit Poll, available at www.cnn.com.
88. James E. Campbell, "Do Swing Voters Swing Elections?" in William G. Mayer, ed., *The Swing Voter in American Politics* (Washington, DC: Brookings Institution, 2008), pp. 118–132.
89. Exit poll.
90. Jeffrey M. Jones, "Does Bringing Out the Candidate Bring Out the Vote?" *American Politics Quarterly* 26 (October 1998): 395–419.
91. Morris P. Fiorina, *Culture War? The Myth of a Polarized America*, 2nd ed. (New York: Pearson Education, 2006), pp. 57–60.
92. Ibid.
93. David W. Abbott and James P. Levine, *Wrong Winner: The Coming Debacle in the Electoral College* (New York: Praeger, 1991), p. 32.
94. Lawrence D. Longley and Neal R. Peirce, *The Electoral College Primer 2000* (New Haven, CT: Yale University Press, 1999), p. 24.
95. George C. Edwards III, *Why the Electoral College Is Bad for America* (New Haven, CT: Yale University Press, 2004), p. 150.
96. Ann N. Crigler, Marion R. Just, and Edward J. McCaffery, *Rethinking the Vote: The Politics and Prospects of American Electoral Reform* (New York: Oxford University Press, 2004).
97. Brian J. Gaines, "Compact Risk: Some Downsides to Establishing National Plurality Presidential Election by Contingent Legislation," in Gary Bugh, ed., *Electoral*

College Reform: Challenges and Possibilities (Burlington, VT: Ashgate Publishing Co., 2010), pp. 113–126.

98. Exit poll.
99. Stephen A. Jessee, "Partisan Bias, Political Information and Spatial Voting in the 2008 Presidential Election," *Journal of Politics* 72 (April 2010): 327–340.
100. Scott J. Basinger and Howard Lavine, "Ambivalence, Information, and Electoral Choice," *American Political Science Review* 99 (May 2005): 169–184.
101. Arthur H. Miller, Martin P. Wattenberg, and Oksana Malachuk, "Schematic Assessments of Presidential Candidates," *American Political Science Review* 80 (June 1986): 521–540.
102. George E. Marcus, "The Structure of Emotional Response: 1984 Presidential Candidates," *American Political Science Review* 82 (September 1988): 737–761.
103. Thomas M. Holbrook, "Do Campaigns Matter?" in Craig, ed., *The Electoral Challenge: Theory Meets Practice*, pp. 12–13.
104. Edward Roeder, "Not Only Does Money Talk, It Often Calls the Winners," *Washington Post National Weekly Edition*, September 26–October 2, 1994, p. 23.
105. Brian F. Schaffner, "Priming Gender: Campaigning on Women's Issues in U.S. Senate Elections," *American Journal of Political Science* 49 (October 2005): 803–817.
106. James E. Campbell, *The American Campaign: U.S. Presidential Campaigns and the National Vote*, 2nd ed. (College Station, TX: Texas A&M University Press, 2008), p. 191.
107. Alan I. Abramowitz, "Can McCain Overcome the Triple Whammy?" May 29, 2008, Larry J. Sabato's Crystal Ball 2008, available at www.centerforpolitics.org.
108. Exit polls.
109. David Karol and Edward Miguel, "The Electoral Cost of War: Iraq Casualties and the 2004 U.S. Presidential Election," *Journal of Politics* 69 (August 2007): 633–648.
110. Exit polls.
111. Brad Lockerbie, *Do Voters Look to the Future? Economics and Elections* (Albany, NY: State University of New York Press, 2008), pp. 110–126.

Chapter 10

Congress

CHAPTER OUTLINE

WHAT WE WILL LEARN

After studying Chapter 10, students should be able to answer the following questions:

1. How do the U.S. House and U.S. Senate compare and contrast in terms of structures, responsibilities, and characteristics?
2. What is the profile of the membership of Congress, considering qualifications, background, compensation, personal styles, relationship with their districts, and turnover?
3. How is Congress organized both on the floor and in its committee structure?
4. What are the steps of the legislative process, considering not just the traditional model but also how Congress has modified that model to increase the chances of passing major legislation?

In early 2010, President Barack Obama and the Democratic Party leadership in Congress made history with the enactment of comprehensive healthcare reform. The legislation had two primary goals: first, to provide insurance coverage to most of the 32 million Americans without health insurance, and second, to slow the rapidly increasing cost of healthcare. The measure included a number of important provisions:

- Insurance companies will no longer be able to refuse coverage based on pre-existing conditions or to drop coverage of people who become ill.
- Businesses with 50 or more workers must provide health insurance coverage for their employees or pay a fine to the government.
- People who are not already covered must purchase a health insurance policy or pay an annual fine of $695. Families earning less than four times the federal poverty level, which was $88,200 a year in 2010, qualify for federal financial assistance to help them cover the cost.
- The measure expands **Medicaid,** which is a federal health insurance program for low-income persons, people with disabilities, and elderly people who are impoverished.
- State governments will set up health insurance exchanges, which are marketplaces where businesses and individuals will be able to shop for insurance policies.
- Funding for the program comes from increasing tax rates on families making $250,000 a year ($200,000 for individuals) as well as a 10 percent tax on indoor tanning services.[1]

Medicaid A federal health insurance program for low-income persons, people with disabilities, and elderly people who are impoverished.

Healthcare reform was quite controversial. Whereas President Obama and most Democrats in Congress declared that the new law was a balanced solution to the nation's most pressing domestic policy priority, Republicans in Congress unanimously opposed the bill's passage, calling it an expensive government takeover of the healthcare industry. They said that it would expand government regulation of healthcare, increase healthcare costs for consumers, limit consumer choice of healthcare providers, and increase taxes. Republican leaders made healthcare reform an election issue, promising to repeal and replace the program if voters put them in power.

The enactment of healthcare reform provides a backdrop for studying the processes and politics of the U.S. Congress. This chapter highlights the differences in the two chambers of Congress. It profiles the membership of Congress and explains how Congress is organized. Finally, the chapter traces the steps of the legislative process using the adoption of healthcare reform to illustrate the dynamics of the process.

Bicameralism

Bicameral legislature Legislature with two chambers.

Article I of the U.S. Constitution declares that the legislative power of the United States is vested in a **bicameral legislature,** which is a legislature with two chambers. The legislative branch of American national government is the Congress. Its two chambers are the Senate and the House of Representatives.

States enjoy equal representation in the U.S. Senate. California and Wyoming each have two senators, even though the population of California exceeds 36 million

President Obama signs the Patient Protection and Affordable Care Act into law. It will eventually provide health insurance coverage to millions of Americans who are not currently insured.

people and Wyoming has a population of just over half a million. The original Constitution stipulated that each state would be represented by two senators chosen by its state legislature. The Seventeenth Amendment, ratified in 1913, provided for the direct popular election of senators. Today, the 50 states elect 100 senators, running statewide to serve six-year staggered terms, with one-third of the Senate standing for reelection each election year (2010, 2012, 2016, etc.). Because senators run for election statewide, they have more diverse constituencies than do members of the House, most of whom run from relatively small districts.

The size of a state's delegation in the U.S. House depends on the state's population, with the requirement that each state, no matter how small, must have at least one representative. California has 53 representatives in the House; Wyoming has one. In 1911, Congress capped the size of the House at 435 representatives. Today, the House membership also includes nonvoting delegates from the District of Columbia, American Samoa, the Virgin Islands, and Guam, as well as a resident commissioner from Puerto Rico. Representatives run for election from districts to serve two-year terms with the entire House standing for reelection every other year.

The Constitution assigns certain responsibilities exclusively to the Senate. The Senate ratifies treaties by a two-thirds vote. It confirms presidential appointments of federal judges, ambassadors, and executive branch officials, all by majority vote. The only major appointment also requiring House approval is for the office of vice president. The Twenty-fifth Amendment provides that both the House and Senate confirm the president's nomination for vice president if the office becomes vacant.

The Senate and House share other duties. Both chambers must vote by a two-thirds margin to propose constitutional amendments and both houses must agree by majority vote to declare war. The government can neither raise nor spend money without majority approval of both chambers although bills that raise revenue must originate in the House. The Constitution specifies that the House of Representatives can **impeach** (formally accuse) an executive or judicial branch officeholder by majority vote. The accused official can be removed from office by a two-thirds vote of the Senate. Legislation does not pass Congress unless it passes both the House and the Senate in identical form.

Impeach To formally accuse.

Because of their different constitutional structures and responsibilities, the Senate and the House have developed into distinct legislative bodies. The Senate is often likened to a great debating society, where senators discuss the grand design of national policy. It is individualistic and dependent on informally devised decision-making practices. Many of the decisions made in the Senate require the approval of a **supermajority,** which is a voting majority that is greater than a simple majority. Because the Senate conducts much of its business under agreements requiring the unanimous consent of its members, individual senators enjoy considerable power over the legislative process.[2] Furthermore, the rules of debate in the Senate allow a minority of 41 senators to extend debate endlessly, preventing a measure from ever coming to a vote.

Supermajority A voting margin which is greater than a simple majority.

Members of the House have a reputation for devotion to technical expertise, personalized constituency service, and responsiveness to local political interests. Because of its size, the House is a relatively impersonal institution that depends on formal rules to structure the decision-making process. In contrast to the Senate, the House makes decisions by majority vote. As long as a measure enjoys the support of more than half of the members of the House, its opponents are powerless to stop it. The House is also considered a less prestigious body than the Senate. Members of the House frequently give up their seats to run for the Senate, but senators never leave their positions to run for the House.

Membership

The U.S. Constitution requires that members of the House be no less than 25 years of age, American citizens for at least seven years, and residents of the state in which their district is located. Senators must be at least 30 years old, citizens for nine years, and residents of the state they represent. If disputes arise about qualifications or election results, each chamber of Congress determines the eligibility of its own members. The House and Senate can also expel a member for misconduct.

Profile of the Membership

Because of the impact of the Voting Rights Act (VRA) and changing social and cultural values, Congress is more diverse now than at any time in its history.[3] As recently as 1965, the year the VRA became law, only six African Americans and four Latinos served in Congress. In contrast, the 112th Congress, which took office in 2011, was relatively diverse. Seventeen women, two Asian Americans, and two Latinos served in the Senate. The House of Representatives included 72 women, 42 African Americans, 24 Latinos, nine Asian Americans, one Native American, three openly gay men, and one lesbian. Despite the influx of women and minority members over the last few decades, more than three-fourths of the members of the 112th Congress were white males of European ancestry.

Most members of Congress are older, affluent, established members of society. Almost every member of Congress is a college graduate and nearly two-thirds of the members hold advanced college degrees. Law and public service are the most popular professions, followed by business and education. Many members of the House and Senate are personally wealthy. The most commonly cited religious affiliations are Roman Catholic, Episcopalian, Methodist, Baptist, and Presbyterian. Most members of Congress held elective offices before winning election to Congress. In the 112th Congress, the average age in the House was 57; it was 63 in the Senate.[4]

Compensation

Congress determines the compensation of its members. In 2011, rank-and-file members of the House and Senate received $174,000 a year, with members of the leadership earning higher salaries. Under a federal law enacted in 1989, lawmakers get an annual cost of living raise unless both the House and Senate vote to block it.

Congressional compensation is controversial. Many observers (including most members of Congress) believe that high pay is needed to attract good people. Although congressional salaries are more than adequate by most standards, the advocates of higher pay point out that senators and representatives earn less money than corporate executives and probably less than they could make working in private business, practicing law, or lobbying. Also, most members of Congress must maintain two residences—one in Washington, DC, and another residence in their district or state. In contrast, the opponents of increasing congressional pay argue that high salaries are elitist. How can Congress be a representative institution, they ask, if its members earn several times more money than the average American makes? Furthermore, many critics believe that high salaries are unjustified considering the inability of Congress to solve some of the nation's most pressing problems.

In addition to their salaries, members of Congress have provided themselves with a number of perks. Senators and representatives have an allowance sufficient to cover regular trips home. They can also travel abroad for free on official business. Members enjoy free parking on Capitol Hill and at Washington, DC, airports, long-distance telephone use, and postage for official correspondence—a perk known as the **franking privilege.** Members of Congress also benefit from a generous pension system.

Franking privilege Free postage provided to members of Congress.

Personal Styles

Traditionally, members of Congress got things done and advanced their careers by building relationships with colleagues, deferring to senior members, and bargaining. New members of Congress, especially in the House, were expected to learn the ropes from more experienced members before speaking out on policy matters. They earned

Logrolling An arrangement in which two or more members of Congress agree in advance to support each other's favored legislation.

respect from their colleagues by specializing in a particular policy area rather than trying to have an impact on a broad range of issues. Members of Congress were expected to cooperate with one another, exchanging favors and engaging in **logrolling,** which is an arrangement in which two or more members of Congress agree in advance to support each other's favored legislation. The ideal lawmaker was someone who regarded the House or Senate as a career rather than a stepping-stone to higher office.[5]

In today's Congress, individual members have greater latitude than did their predecessors. Some members are skilled media entrepreneurs, using policy issues to gain media coverage so they can establish themselves as national political figures. They are less interested in passing legislation than in advancing their own political careers. Other members use the media to promote their legislative agendas. Through news conferences, press releases, televised speeches on C-Span, and other staged media events, they influence the legislative agenda, define policy alternatives, and shape public opinion about proposed legislation.[6] Consider the career of Minnesota Republican Congresswoman Michelle Bachmann. Bachmann is an outspoken social conservative who has become the darling of her party's activist base. In a speech that was seen by two million YouTube viewers, she wondered if healthcare reform would allow a 13-year-old girl to use a school sex clinic to get an abortion and "go home on the school bus that night." She speculated in another speech that the reforms would deny healthcare to the ill: "So watch out if you are disabled." Bachmann has made herself into a political celebrity, able to raise substantially more money in campaign contributions than the average member of Congress. In 2010, Bachmann raised $4.5 million.[7] Bachmann has also become a political lightning rod, attracting well-funded opponents.

Congresswoman Michelle Bachmann is an outspoken social conservative who has become the darling of her party's activist base.

Home Styles

Most members of Congress believe that they have a responsibility to "vote their district," that is, to take policy positions in accordance with the views of the majority of their constituents. Senators and representatives from agricultural states, for example, back farm support legislation whereas members of Congress from oil-producing states support measures favored by the oil industry. Senators and representatives know that if they stray too far and too frequently from the policy preferences of the majority of their constituents, they may pay the price at the ballot box. Future election opponents will accuse them of losing touch with the folks back home and charge them with voting against the interests of the state or district.[8] Consequently, members of Congress go home often, stress their local ties, and spend considerable time in their districts.[9]

Political scientist Richard F. Fenno points out that members of Congress perceive more than one constituency whose support they cultivate. The Geographic Constituency includes everyone who lives within the boundaries of a state (for a senator) or congressional district (for a representative). In sheer numbers, the Geographic Constituency is the largest, but least important, constituency to the member of Congress because it includes many people who do not vote or who consistently support candidates of the other party.

The Reelection Constituency is those voters who support the senator or representative at the polls in general elections. It consists of loyal party voters and swing voters, including independents and people who identify with the other party but are willing to vote for candidates of the opposing party under certain circumstances. Incumbent members of Congress focus on this constituency, especially in districts that are competitive between the two major political parties. Representatives and senators who potentially face strong general election opposition often take moderate policy positions to win the support of swing voters, who are usually less conservative/less liberal than core party voters. Most of the Democrats in Congress who voted against healthcare reform represented competitive districts and they worried that a vote for healthcare reform would be used against them in the upcoming general election.

The Primary Constituency includes the people who would back the incumbent against a serious challenger in a party primary.[10] Although any senator or member of Congress could face a primary election challenge, members of Congress who represent districts that are solidly Democratic or Republican are unlikely to have serious opposition in any election other than the primary. Consequently, GOP members of Congress from safe districts often take more conservative policy positions than Republicans from competitive districts because they want to cultivate the support of Republican primary voters who tend to be more conservative than the electorate as a whole. For similar reasons, Democrats from safe districts are frequently more liberal than Democrats representing swing districts. Congressional partisanship is more intense today than it was 20 or 30 years ago because most members of Congress win election from districts that are safe for candidates from their political party.[11]

Constituency pressure was a key factor in the battle over healthcare reform. Although polls showed that most Democratic voters favored healthcare reform, the measure was highly unpopular with Republicans, especially party activists who were stirred up by conservative talk show hosts and cable TV commentators.[12] Members of Congress are quite reluctant to vote against the strong preferences of party activists on a high profile issue such as healthcare reform because they worry about giving potential primary election opponents an issue that can be used against them. Moreover, interest groups such as EMILY's List (for Democrats) and Club for Growth (for Republicans) are willing to recruit and fund primary challengers to incumbent members of Congress who do not support the party line on key issues.[13] Ultimately, not a single Republican member of either the House or the Senate voted in favor of healthcare reform on final passage.

Constituency service The actions of members of Congress and their staffs while attending to the individual, particular needs of constituents.

Members of Congress work to shore up support through **constituency service,** which is the action of members of Congress and their staffs attending to the individual, particular needs of constituents. Citizens sometimes ask senators or representatives to resolve problems with federal agencies, such as the Social Security Administration (SSA) or the U.S. Citizenship and Immigration Services (USCIS). Constituents may ask members and their staffs to supply information about federal laws or regulations. Also, local civic clubs and other organizations frequently invite members of Congress to make public appearances at functions in their districts or states and meet with various groups of constituents about problems of local concern.

Membership Turnover

Members of Congress seeking reelection are usually successful, especially members of the House. Members of Congress win reelection despite the general unpopularity of Congress because the voters make a distinction between the performance of their representative and the performance of Congress as an institution. Polls consistently show that the voters like their own member of Congress even when they disapprove of the actions of Congress as a whole.[14]

GETTING INVOLVED — Contacting Your Representative

Members of the U.S. House recognize that if they fail to represent the wishes of their constituents satisfactorily, then they may risk reelection defeat. Your assignment is to participate in America's representative democracy by sending an e-mail message about a current policy issue to your representative in the U.S. House. You can find the name and e-mail address of your U.S. representative online at www.house.gov. The following guidelines will help you write an effective letter:

- Know what you are writing about. If you do not understand an issue, your message will have little impact. Choose an issue discussed in the textbook or in the news, and research it sufficiently to speak about it intelligently.
- Use correct grammar. E-mail messages filled with grammatical errors and misspelled words will not have a positive impact.
- Make your point clearly and succinctly. Present your opinion and give the reasons behind your position in no more than a few paragraphs. Long, rambling messages are ineffective.

Submit a copy of your letter or e-mail message to your instructor. He or she will not grade you on your point of view, but will evaluate your work on the criteria stated above.

Despite relatively high reelection rates, Congress experiences significant turnover. In the 111th Congress, the average tenure for members of the House was 11 years; it was 13 years for members of the Senate.[15] Turnover is greater than statistics on incumbent reelection success rates suggest because many members decide not to seek reelection. Some members retire, some quit to run for higher office, and some leave Congress to pursue other opportunities, including work as lobbyists. For example, Representative Billy Tauzin of Louisiana, the former chair of the House Ways and Means Committee and the principal author of the **Medicare** prescription drug benefit, retired from Congress to become president of the Pharmaceutical Research and Manufacturers of America (PhRMA), the chief lobby group for brand-name drug companies. In 2009, Tauzin represented the pharmaceutical industry in negotiations with congressional leaders over the details of healthcare reform, a measure that PhRMA ultimately supported.[16] (Tauzin retired in 2010.)

Medicare A federal health insurance program for people 65 and older.

Term limitation The movement to restrict the number of terms public officials may serve.

Many critics of Congress favor **term limitation,** which is the movement to restrict the number of terms public officials may serve. The supporters of term limitation want to restrict the number of terms incumbents serve in order to open public service to new people with fresh ideas. Term limitation advocates also believe that career politicians grow cautious in office, constantly worrying about reelection. In contrast, officials who are prevented from holding office for more than a few years are free to adopt creative new ideas that may entail some political risk. The proponents of term limitation think that term limits will weaken the influence of special interest groups because officeholders will have less need to solicit money from interest groups to fund expensive reelection campaigns.

The longest-serving member of Congress is Representative John D. Dingell of Michigan. Dingell, who was born in 1924, first took office in 1955.

The opponents of term limitation argue that it is a gimmick that will cause harm rather than good. Term limits are undemocratic, they say, because they deny voters the chance to elect the candidates of their choice. If a majority of voters want to reelect an officeholder for a third, fourth, or even fifth term, they ask, should that not be their right? Furthermore, the opponents of term limitation worry that inexperienced officeholders will lack the knowledge and expertise to formulate effective public policy. Lacking personal knowledge of the workings of government, officials may have to rely on the advice of lobbyists and bureaucrats. Finally, the critics of term limitation warn that short-term officeholders may focus on securing future employment, and some future employers may be interest groups seeking special favors from government.[17]

Organization

The organization of the House and Senate is based on political party.

Organization of the Floor

Floor The full House or full Senate taking official action.

The "floor of the House" and "floor of the Senate" are the large rooms in which the members of each chamber assemble to do business. As a practical matter, the **floor** refers to the full House or the full Senate taking official action. The organization of the floor refers to the structures that organize the flow of business that is conducted by the House or Senate as a whole.

The organization of the floor is based on party strength in each chamber. In the 111th Congress, which served from January 2009 through December 2010, the Democratic Party controlled both the House and the Senate. Democrats outnumbered Republicans in the House, 257 to 178. The party balance in the Senate was 57 Democrats, 41 Republicans, and two independents, both of whom voted with the Democrats to organize the chamber, effectively giving the Democrats a 59–41 advantage. After Republican Senator Arlen Specter of Pennsylvania switched parties in early 2009, the party balance in the Senate became 60 Democrats and 40 Republicans.

The sizable Democratic Party majorities in both the House and Senate during the 111th Congress were indispensable to the passage of healthcare reform because they allowed the Democrats to organize the floor of the House and Senate and dominate every congressional committee. Considering the determined opposition of almost every Republican to healthcare reform, the measure would almost certainly have failed had the Republican Party controlled either chamber of Congress or even if the margin between the two parties was closer, especially in the Senate.

The 2010 election changed the party balance in Congress. The Republican Party became the majority party in the House by adding more than 60 seats formerly held by Democrats. Although the Democrats continued to hold a majority of seats in the Senate, their margin fell to 53–47. House Republicans promised to do their best to repeal healthcare reform, and repeal legislation passed the House in early 2011. However, without control of either the Senate or the presidency they were unlikely to achieve their goal.

Although the Constitution designates the vice president as the "President of the Senate," the legislative role of the vice president is relatively unimportant. The vice president may not address the Senate without permission of the chamber and only votes in case of a tie, which is rare. During eight years as vice president, Dick Cheney cast only eight tie-breaking votes in the Senate. More often than not, the vice president attends to other tasks, leaving the chore of presiding in the Senate to others.

Senate president pro tempore The official presiding officer in the Senate in the vice president's absence.

The Constitution designates the **Senate president pro tempore** as the presiding officer in the Senate in the vice president's absence. The Senate as a whole selects the president pro tempore, customarily electing the senator from the majority party with the greatest length of service, or **seniority,** in the chamber. In practice, the post of Senate president pro tempore is more honorary than substantive, and the rather tedious chore of presiding in the Senate is usually left to junior members of the majority party.

Seniority Length of service.

Real power on the floor of the Senate (and the House) is in the hands of the political party organizations. At the beginning of each session of Congress, the Republican and Democratic members of each chamber elect party leaders. In the Senate, the head of the majority party is called the **Senate Majority Leader.** The Majority Leader's first assistant is the Majority Whip. A Minority Leader and a Minority Whip lead the minority party. **Whips** are assistant floor leaders in Congress. Both the Majority Whip and the Minority Whip coordinate the work of a number of assistant whips. Each party also selects a policy committee to consider party positions on legislation, a committee to appoint party members to standing committees, and a campaign committee to prepare for the next election.

Senate Majority Leader The head of the majority party in the Senate and that chamber's most important figure.

Whips Assistant floor leaders in Congress.

The **Speaker of the House** is the presiding officer in the House of Representatives and the leader of the majority party in that chamber. The entire House membership selects the Speaker, but because almost all members vote for their party's candidate, the Speaker is invariably the leader of the majority party. As in the Senate, the Democratic and Republican members of the House meet at the beginning of each session to choose leaders. The person chosen to lead the majority party will become the Speaker, whereas the second ranking figure in the majority party becomes the **House Majority Leader.** The third ranking leader of the majority party is the Majority Whip. In the meantime, the minority party elects a Minority Leader and a Minority Whip. As in the Senate, the House whips head extensive networks of assistant whips, numbering dozens of members in the House.

Speaker of the House The presiding officer in the House of Representatives and the leader of the majority party in that chamber.

House Majority Leader The second ranking figure in the majority party in the House.

The Senate Majority Leader and the Speaker of the House are the most important legislators in their respective chambers. Speaker Nancy Pelosi and Senate Majority Leader Harry Reid played a critical role in the adoption of healthcare reform in 2010 by managing the measure through the legislative process to its eventual passage. The Senate Majority Leader and the Speaker appoint members to special committees and influence assignments to standing committees. They refer legislation to committee and control the flow of business to the floor. These latter two powers are especially important for the Speaker who can use them to control the timing of legislation and determine the policy options available to House members voting on the floor. Although the Speaker cannot force passage of unpopular legislation, the Speaker can usually prevent consideration of a measure that he or she opposes, even when the measure enjoys enough support to pass the full House if it were to come to a vote.

In 2007, Nancy Pelosi became Speaker of the House, the first woman ever to hold the position.

The Senate Majority Leader and the Speaker hold positions of high visibility and great prestige, both in Congress and the nation. As party leaders, they work with fellow party members in Congress to set policy goals and assemble winning coalitions. They consult widely with various party factions, working to compromise differences among party members and maintain party unity. As national political leaders, the Senate Majority Leader and Speaker publicize the achievements of Congress, promote their party's positions in the media, and react to presidential initiatives. When the same political party controls the White House and Congress, as it did in 2011, the Speaker and Majority Leader work with the president on legislative strategy.[18]

Because party leadership posts are elective, the Senate Majority Leader and the Speaker maintain their power by helping members achieve their goals: reelection, influence in national politics, policy enactment, and election to higher office. Party leaders create political action committees (PACs) to raise and distribute campaign money to fellow party members running for reelection. By playing the campaign money game, party leaders can support their parties in Congress while building personal loyalty among party members.[19] In the 2010 election, Speaker Pelosi's PAC to the Future contributed nearly $700,000 to Democratic congressional candidates. Meanwhile, Republican Leader John Boehner's PAC, Freedom Project, gave nearly $900,000 to Republican candidates.[20]

Leadership in Congress is both collegial and collective. It is collegial in the sense that the Senate Majority Leader and the Speaker of the House base their power on tact and persuasion rather than threats or criticism of other members. The two leaders generally do their best to satisfy the needs of rank-and-file party members, gathering IOU's that can be cashed in later. Leadership is collective in that top party leaders consult regularly with a broad range of party members, attempting to involve every party faction in setting party policy in the chamber. The whip networks transmit information between party leaders and members. Furthermore, on particular pieces of legislation, the Speaker of the House often appoints a group of rank-and-file party members to serve on party task forces to plan strategy for the passage of the party's program.

The Speaker and Majority Leader are political party leaders, working to advance their party's policy interests and maintain their majority. Democrats favor liberal policies; Republicans prefer conservative policies. When the Democratic Party controls Congress, the leadership promotes liberal policy alternatives while preventing the consideration of conservative bills (and vice versa when Republicans control). Although a Democratic majority in Congress cannot ensure the enactment of liberal legislation, it can usually prevent the passage of conservative measures.[21]

Members of Congress have a strong incentive to cooperate with their party leadership because their success is tied to the success of their political party, especially in the House. Members of the majority party chair all committees and subcommittees, and have a greater opportunity for input on the details of legislation, at least in the House where the majority party tightly controls deliberations in committee and on the floor. Furthermore, the election prospects of senators and members of the House elected from districts that are competitive between the two parties depend at least in part on the standing of their political party in the eyes of the voters.[22] Democratic members of the House and Senate voted overwhelmingly in favor of healthcare reform not just because they favored the measure personally but also because its defeat would be perceived as a defeat for their party and their party's president, weakening the position of the party in the 2010 midterm election. Republican members of Congress, even those who had previously supported similar healthcare proposals, voted unanimously against healthcare reform on final passage because they wanted to tarnish the image of President Obama by defeating him on his signature issue.[23]

The role of the minority party leadership in the House and Senate is similar to that of the majority party leadership with some important exceptions. The Minority Leader and the Minority Whip work to define a party program in their chamber, plan strategy, and unite party members behind party positions. As with the Senate Majority Leader and the Speaker, the Senate and House Minority Leaders may become media spokespersons for their party. In practice, minority party leaders spend a good deal of time working to help their party become the majority party by recruiting candidates, raising money, and planning strategy. Fundraising ability has even become an important criterion in each congressional party's leadership selection process.[24] House Minority Leader John Boehner and Senate Minority Leader Mitch McConnell led the opposition to healthcare reform, uniting their party in Congress against the bill. After the measure passed, the Republican leaders called on the voters to elect a Republican majority in the House and Senate so the bill could be repealed.

Because of their party's minority status, the leadership of the minority party lacks the influence that their majority party counterparts enjoy, especially in the House. Although the Majority Leader in the Senate and the Speaker of the House may consult with the minority-party leadership on bill scheduling, the authority to control the flow of business to the floor lies with the majority party leadership. Furthermore, the ability of the minority leadership in the House and Senate to influence legislative policy is limited by their party's minority status, especially in the House of Representatives, where the rules enable a simple majority to conduct business. As long as the majority party in the House is united or nearly united, depending on the size of its majority, it can pass legislation without having to compromise with the minority party. Because the rules of the Senate allow a minority of senators—or sometimes even a single senator—to delay or defeat legislation, the minority party leadership plays a more substantive legislative role in the Senate than in the House.

The style of party leadership in Congress depends to a large degree on the occupant of the White House. When the opposition party controls the White House, congressional leaders act independently from and frequently in opposition to the White House. They scrutinize presidential appointments, aggressively investigate policy missteps, and critically evaluate presidential initiatives. In contrast, congressional leaders usually have a positive relationship when the same party controls both the legislative and executive branches of government. Congressional leaders worked closely with President Obama to enact his policy proposals during his first two years in office when Democrats controlled the House and Senate with large majorities. After the 2010 election, Republican leaders in the House promised to undermine implementation of healthcare reform even if they lacked the power to repeal it outright.

Committee and Subcommittee Organization

The detailed work of Congress takes place in committees. The advantage of the committee system is that it allows Congress to divide legislative work among a number of subgroups while giving individual members the opportunity to specialize, developing

Around the World — Healthcare in Canada

Canada provides its citizens with universal healthcare offered on the basis of need rather than ability to pay. Canada administers its healthcare program through the nation's ten provinces, which are the Canadian equivalent of states, and its three territories. Because the provinces have some leeway to design their own plans, healthcare funding and delivery varies somewhat from one part of the nation to another. Some provinces assess their citizens a monthly premium or charge a fee for each visit to a physician, whereas others fund the program entirely from tax money. Coverage varies somewhat from province to province and waits for services are longer in some areas than others.*

Although Canadian healthcare is publicly funded, it is privately provided. Citizens seeking medical services go to private physicians or visit hospitals and clinics that are either for-profit businesses or nonprofits governed by boards of trustees. Many Canadians also have supplemental insurance coverage, often provided through their employers, to pay for services not covered or only partially covered by the national health system, including dental, optical, and prescription drug service.

Is the Canadian healthcare system better than its counterpart in the United States? Proponents of the Canadian system note that life expectancy is greater in Canada than it is in the United States and that infant mortality rates are lower. Furthermore, Canada devotes a smaller share of its GDP to healthcare than does the United States. In contrast, critics of the Canadian healthcare system complain that wait times for non-emergency services are sometimes long. Canadian medicine may also be relatively slow to adopt new treatments and technologies.†

QUESTIONS

1. Would you prefer the Canadian healthcare system to that in the United States?
2. What individuals and groups in the United States would support moving to a system similar to the Canadian system? Which would oppose?
3. Does the healthcare reform plan adopted by Congress and signed into law by President Obama move the United States closer to the Canadian system? Why or why not?

* Health Canada, available at www.hc-sc.gc.ca.

† Gerard W. Boychuk, *National Health Insurance in the United States and Canada* (Washington, DC: Georgetown University Press, 2008), pp. 3–21.

expertise in particular policy areas. The disadvantage of the committee system is that the division of broad issues into smaller sub-issues may impede the development of comprehensive and coordinated national policy. Because Congress deals with policy problems on a piecemeal basis, it tends to offer piecemeal solutions.

Standing committee A permanent legislative committee with authority to draft legislation in a particular policy area or areas.

A **standing committee** is a permanent legislative committee with authority to draft legislation in a particular policy area or areas. The House Agriculture Committee, for example, deals with subjects related to agriculture, including rural economic conditions, crop insurance, agricultural trade, commodity futures trading, agricultural research and promotion, conservation, farm credit, welfare and food nutrition programs, and food safety inspection. The jurisdiction of the Senate Foreign Relations Committee includes matters relating to American national security policy, foreign policy, and international economic policy.

Special or **select committee** A committee established for a limited time only.

Joint committee A committee that includes members from both houses of Congress.

In addition to standing committees, Congress has special or select committees and joint committees. A **special** or **select committee** is a committee established for a limited time only. A **joint committee** is a committee that includes members from both houses of Congress. In contrast to standing committees, joint committees and special or select committees do not usually have the legislative authority to draft legislation. They can only study, investigate, and make recommendations.

Committees are often divided into subcommittees. Not all committees have subcommittees, and not all bills are referred to subcommittee. However, in the House in particular, subcommittees have become the center of legislative work. For example, the House Ways and Means Committee, which deals with tax issues, trade, and Social Security, has six subcommittees, each of which addresses a different aspect of the committee's responsibilities.

Senators typically have more committee assignments than do members of the House because the Senate has fewer members. Senator Dianne Feinstein of California, for example, serves on four standing committees and one select committee: the Appropriations Committee, Energy and Natural Resources Committee, Judiciary Committee, Rules and Administration Committee, and the Select Committee on Intelligence. Feinstein is also a member of a number of subcommittees. Because senators are stretched thin, they pick and choose when to get involved in committee processes. Consequently, committee decisions in the Senate usually reflect the work of less than half the committee membership except on especially high-profile matters such as immigration reform or a major tax bill.[25] Most members of the House serve on no more than two committees and four subcommittees. Representative Lincoln Diaz-Balart of Florida, for example, serves on one committee, the Rules Committee, and one subcommittee. Because members of the House have fewer committee assignments than their Senate counterparts, they have more time to devote to committee work and are more likely to develop policy expertise in the issues dealt with by the committees on which they serve. As a result, committees play a more important role in the legislative process in the House than they do in the Senate.

When senators and representatives are first elected, they request assignment to standing committees that they believe will help them win reelection, gain influence in national politics, and/or affect policy. Committees dealing with money qualify on all three counts and are in great demand. The money committees in the Senate are Appropriations, Budget, and Finance. In the House, the committees dealing with money are Appropriations, Budget, and Ways and Means. The other Senate committees that are considered prestigious assignments are Foreign Relations, Armed Services, and Judiciary.[26] In the House, members want to serve on the Energy and Commerce Committee because it deals with a broad range of important legislation. The Transportation and Infrastructure Committee is popular as well because members see it as a way to procure projects for their districts. Senators and representatives frequently request assignments on committees that deal with policy issues that are particularly relevant to their states and districts. Members of Congress from financial centers are attracted to the banking committees; members from agricultural areas favor membership on the agricultural committees. Finally, some members of Congress request particular committee assignments for personal reasons. For example, members of the House with prior military service may seek membership on the Armed Services Committee.[27]

Party committees in each chamber make committee assignments for members of their party. Party leaders control these committees; in theory, they could use them to reward friends and punish enemies. In practice, however, the party committees try to accommodate the preferences of members, usually giving them either their first or second choices of committee assignments. If members are unhappy with a committee assignment, they may request a transfer when openings occur on committees they prefer. Committee switching is not especially common, particularly among senior members, because members who change committees must start over on the seniority ladder of the new committee. Nonetheless, it is not unusual for members to request transfer to one of the really choice committees.

The nature of the committee assignment process has an impact on the composition of committees. Membership on the major committees mirrors the membership of Congress as a whole because senators and representatives seek to serve on the major committees without regard for ideology or constituency.[28] Consequently, legislation emerging from major committees is likely to be acceptable to a majority of members of Congress. In contrast, members of committees that deal with particular policy areas, such as agriculture and armed services, are generally composed of members whose constituencies are directly impacted by the committee's work.[29] Legislation emerging from these committees tends to reflect the concerns of particularized interests, such as defense contractors and farmers, rather than broader policy perspectives.[30]

Members choose subcommittees based on seniority. When committee members change committees, die, retire, or suffer defeat at the polls, other committee members volunteer for their subcommittee assignments in order of seniority. The most senior members get their choice; the least senior members get the leftovers.

The majority party controls each committee and subcommittee. Before the 2010 election, the Democratic Party was the majority party in the House and Senate. Democrats accounted for a majority of the membership of each committee and subcommittee and chaired every committee and subcommittee in both chambers. In 2010, the Republicans won a majority in the House while Democrats maintained their majority in the Senate. Beginning in 2011, Republicans were a majority in every House committee and subcommittee and Republicans chaired every committee and subcommittee.

Ranking member The leader of the minority party on a committee.

Party caucus All of the party members of a chamber meeting as a group.

Each party has its own procedures for selecting committee leaders. The committee chair is the leader of the majority party on the committee, whereas the **ranking member** is the leader of the minority party on the committee. Republican Party rules stipulate that the party committee that makes initial committee assignments nominates chairs or ranking members with confirmation by the **party caucus,** which is all of the party members of a chamber meeting as a group. The Republicans select chairs or ranking members based on party loyalty and ability to raise campaign money for party candidates, rather than using seniority as the basis for selection.[31] Each Republican member of the House is expected to contribute money to the party's campaign fund, ranging from $70,000 to $600,000, depending on the member's position. Party members who fail to meet their financial obligations will be passed over for leadership positions.[32] Democrats, meanwhile, provide for the selection of committee chairs and ranking members by a secret-ballot vote of the party caucus. The Democrat with the most seniority on a particular committee usually wins the vote except on those rare occasions when a senior member has alienated his or her colleagues. Both parties limit chairs and subcommittee chairs to six-year terms.

The Legislative Process

Conference committee A special congressional committee created to negotiate differences on similar pieces of legislation passed by the House and Senate.

Omnibus bills Complex, highly detailed legislative proposals covering one or more subjects or programs.

The traditional image of the legislative process is that a member introduces a bill, it is referred to committee, it goes from committee to the floor, from the floor to a **conference committee,** and, if it passes every step, to the president. In today's Congress, the legislative process no longer conforms to the traditional "bill-becomes-a-law" formula, especially for major pieces of legislation. Congress has adopted modifications in the traditional legislative process to increase the likelihood that it can pass major legislation. The key differences between the traditional model and the new model of legislative policymaking are the following:

- Major legislation is often written in the form of **omnibus bills,** which are complex, highly detailed legislative proposals covering one or more subjects or programs. The healthcare reform measure, for example, included provisions dealing with Medicaid, insurance regulation, healthcare delivery, and a set of tax increases to pay for the package. Congressional leaders assemble omnibus bills in order to attract as much support as possible.
- Pieces of major legislation are frequently referred to more than one standing committee. Involving several committees in the legislative process provides a measure's supporters with an opportunity to draft legislation that enjoys a broader base of support than a bill considered by one committee. Furthermore, the strategy avoids the danger of a hostile committee chair bottling up the bill in committee, which sometimes happens to measures referred to only one committee.
- The legislative leadership, especially in the House, coordinates the work of the standing committees. The leadership sets timetables to move legislation through the committee stage.
- The legislative leadership, especially in the House, fashions the details of the legislation and develops a strategy for winning passage of the measure on the floor. Even after a bill clears committee, the leadership may change its provisions to broaden its base of support and increase its chances of success.
- A conference committee including dozens, maybe even hundreds, of members works out the final compromise language of the bill. Once again, the goal is to build a broad enough coalition of support for the measure to ensure its passage.[33]

Figure 10.1 (pages 252–253) outlines the basic steps of the legislative process.

Origin and Introduction

Bill A proposed law.

Resolution A legislative statement of opinion on a certain matter.

In the 111th Congress, members introduced 13,675 bills and resolutions—8,789 in the House and 4,886 in the Senate.[34] A **bill** is a proposed law. Except for revenue-raising bills, which must begin in the House, any bill may be introduced in either chamber. A **resolution** is a legislative statement of opinion on a certain matter. Resolutions may be introduced in either chamber. A member who introduces a measure is known as its sponsor. Bills and resolutions may have multiple sponsors, which are known as cosponsors. For example, Rep. John D. Dingell of Michigan sponsored healthcare reform in the House. The measure had six cosponsors. Over the years, legislative measures have grown longer and more complex. Since the 1940s, the length of the average bill has increased from 2.5 pages to more than 19 pages.[35] Omnibus bills are far longer. The healthcare reform act, for example, was 906 pages long.[36]

Although the formal introduction of legislation is a privilege limited to actual members of Congress, the ideas and initiative for legislation are varied. Interest groups, the president, executive branch agencies, journalists, constituents, individual members of Congress, and other political actors may advance policy proposals that are embodied in formal legislation. Executive branch agencies and major interest groups may even draft the text of a bill, turning a policy proposal into formal legislation. Many of the ideas contained in the healthcare reform bill had been discussed for years and some key aspects of the plan, including the individual mandate, were modeled on the Massachusetts healthcare reform plan.

There is less legislative activity today than there was 30 years ago. In the 1960s, senators and representatives introduced on average more than 50 bills and resolutions apiece during a two-year session of Congress. In contrast, the average member of Congress introduced only 26 measures in the 111th Congress.[37] The decline in legislative activity reflects a political climate that has grown skeptical of government solutions to the nation's problems. Many members of Congress, especially Republicans, won office by campaigning against government programs. Their goal is to reduce the scope of government activity rather than passing legislation to create new programs.

Committee and Subcommittee Action

Once a bill or resolution is introduced, it is assigned a number and referred to committee. A measure introduced in the House has the initials H.R. for House of Representatives, whereas Senate measures begin with the letter S. for Senate. The healthcare reform measure passed by Congress was H.R. 3590. (The number signifies the order in which a measure was introduced.) The sponsors of a bill also give it a popular title designed to put the measure in a favorable light. For example, Democrats in Congress called their bill the Patient Protection and Affordable Care Act. The chamber parliamentarian, working under the oversight of the Speaker of the House or the Senate Majority Leader, refers the measure to committee based on the subject covered by the bill or resolution.

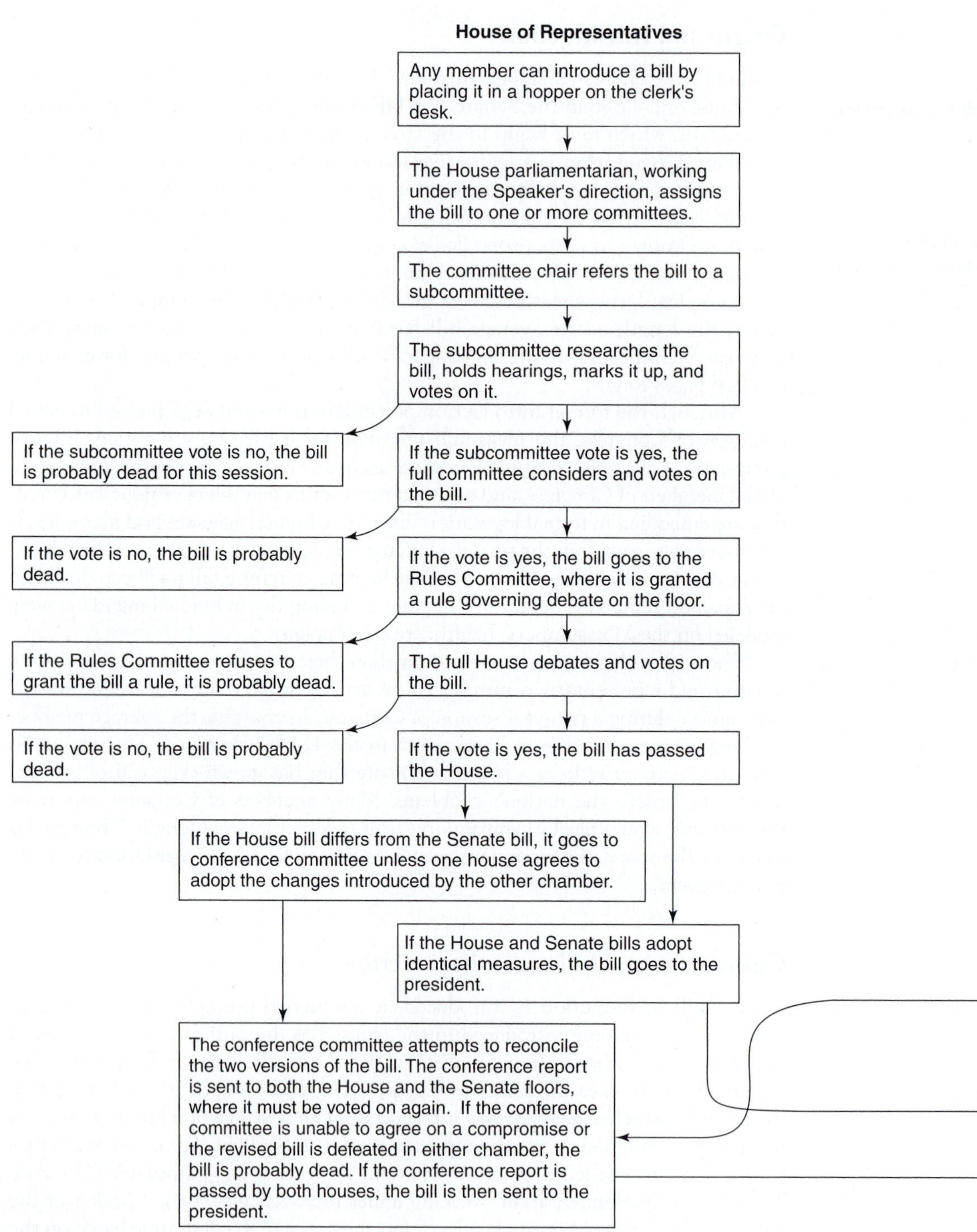

FIGURE 10.1 The Legislative Process.

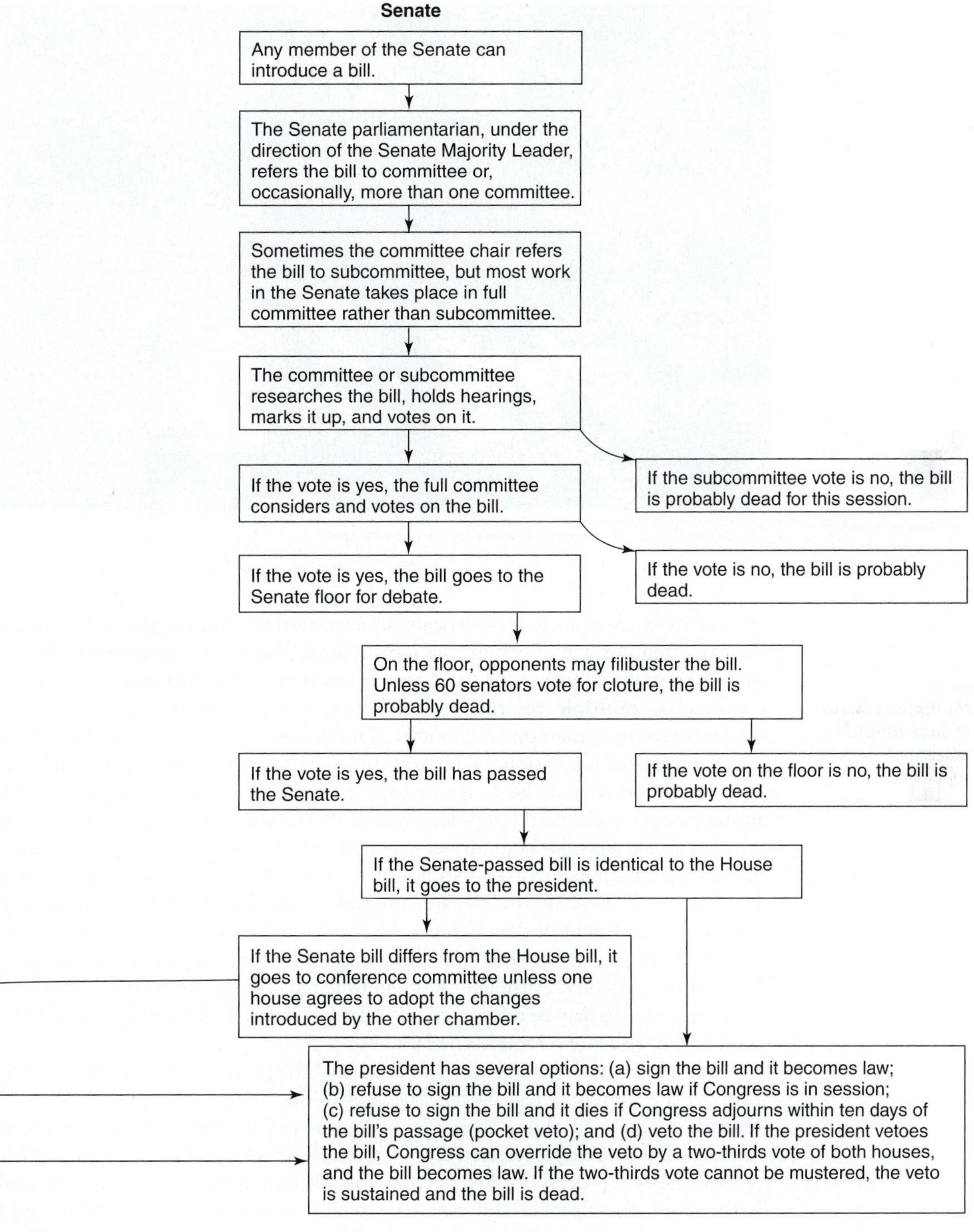

FIGURE 10.1 *(Continued)*

The detailed work of Congress takes place in committees.

Multiple referral of legislation The practice of assigning legislation to more than one committee.

Complex issues such as healthcare, immigration reform, energy, and homeland security often cut across committee jurisdictions. Sometimes committees develop arrangements to cooperate or defer to one another.[38] At other times, the leadership employs **multiple referral of legislation,** which is the practice of assigning legislation to more than one committee. The Senate permits joint, sequential, and partial referrals of legislation. House rules allow only sequential and partial referrals, and one committee may be designated the committee of primary jurisdiction. The Speaker makes multiple referral decisions in the House. The Speaker may also appoint an *ad hoc* (special) committee, which may be called a task force, to consider a measure whose subject matter does not fit neatly within the jurisdiction of a single standing committee. In the Senate, multiple referral of legislation requires the unanimous agreement of the chamber. Multiple referral of legislation is more common in the House than the Senate and more likely to be used for major legislation than routine measures. Although most multiple referrals go to only two committees, complex measures may be referred to several committees. Eight standing committees dealt with healthcare reform in the House.

Multiple referral of legislation has enhanced the power of the legislative leadership over the content of legislation, especially in the House. The Speaker can devise referral arrangements that enhance policy goals and set timetables for committee consideration of multiple referred bills. A multiple referred measure cannot continue in the legislative process until each committee dealing with it has finished its work. Furthermore, the Speaker can negotiate policy compromises among the various committees considering a multiple referred measure. In practice, multiple referral of legislation is also a means for moving legislation through the process because it enables the Speaker to intervene to prevent one committee from stalling a measure.[39]

Committees are gatekeepers in the lawmaking process, killing most of the bills and resolutions referred to them. In the 111th Congress, committees reported 1,249 measures to the floor of 13,675 bills and resolutions introduced, for a report rate of 9 percent.[40] The following measures are most likely to receive detailed committee and subcommittee consideration:

- Measures that committee and subcommittee chairs personally favor.
- Measures that have the support of the legislative leadership.
- Measures that enjoy broad support in Congress as a whole.
- Measures that benefit from the backing of important interest groups.
- Measures that deal with issues that many members of Congress and a large segment of the general public consider important.
- Measures that are pushed by the White House.

In contrast, measures that lack support or are opposed by the committee or party leadership seldom emerge from committee.

Committees and subcommittees do the detailed work of Congress. Once a measure is sent to committee or subcommittee, the chair and the ranking minority member ask their staffs to prepare separate reports on its merits. For major legislation, the committee or subcommittee chair schedules hearings to allow the measure's supporters and opponents a chance to make their case. Full committees generally conduct Senate hearings, whereas subcommittees hold most hearings in the House.

Legislative markup The process in which legislators go over a measure line-by-line, revising, amending, or rewriting it.

The next step is **legislative markup.** In this process, legislators go over a measure line-by-line, revising, amending, or rewriting it. In the House, markup usually takes place in subcommittee. Markup in the Senate, in contrast, generally occurs in full committee.

The primary avenue for policymaking in committee is not formal markup itself, but informal negotiations that take place before and during markup. The most important participants in these negotiations are the committee and subcommittee chairs and the ranking minority members on the committee and subcommittee. On major legislation, the party leadership, the president, and major interest groups will probably be involved as well.[41]

Table Postpone consideration of a legislative measure.

Once markup is complete, the subcommittee and then the full committee vote on whether to recommend passage. If the measure is voted down at either stage or members vote to **table** it (that is, postpone consideration), it is probably dead, at least for the session. If the measure is approved in subcommittee and committee, the next step is the floor of the full House or Senate.

Discharge petition A procedure whereby a majority of the members of the House of Representatives can force a committee to report a bill to the floor of the House.

The rules of the House provide a mechanism for members to bring a bill to the floor that has been tabled or defeated in committee, but the procedure is seldom used and almost never successful. A bill's supporters can compel a committee to report a measure to the floor by means of a **discharge petition,** which is a procedure whereby a majority of the members of the House of Representatives can force a committee to report a bill to the floor of the House. Since 1910, only three measures forced from committee through the use of a discharge petition eventually became law.[42] Most members of Congress are reluctant to sign a discharge petition because they do not want to undermine committee authority. Furthermore, the threat of a discharge petition is sometimes enough to stimulate a committee to act on stalled legislation.

Floor Action

In the House, the process for moving measures from committee to the floor varies, depending on the type of measure involved. The House considers noncontroversial measures of relatively minor importance through a shortcut procedure on designated special days set aside for that purpose. Budget resolutions and appropriation bills may go directly from committee to the House floor. (An **appropriation bill** is a legislative authorization to spend money for particular purposes.)

Appropriation bill A legislative authorization to spend money for particular purposes.

The leadership brings some major pieces of legislation to the floor either without committee consideration or with only cursory committee examination. If a measure was carefully studied in committee in the previous session of Congress, the leadership may determine that no additional committee consideration is necessary. Sometimes, the leadership wants to move quickly for political reasons. In 2005, the House leadership put legislation to provide aid for people impacted by Hurricane Katrina on a fast track, moving it directly to the floor without committee consideration.[43] In 2011, the Republican leadership of the House brought repeal of healthcare reform without committee consideration in order to score political points by fulfilling an election promise.

House Rules Committee A standing committee that determines the rules under which a specific bill can be debated, amended, and considered on the House floor.

Most measures that clear standing committee are assigned to the Rules Committee before they go to the floor. The **House Rules Committee** is a standing committee that determines the rules under which a specific bill can be debated, amended, and considered on the House floor. Because more measures clear committee than the full House has time to consider, the Rules Committee determines which bills go forward. Measures that are not assigned rules are not considered on the House floor and therefore have no chance of passage unless supporters can succeed in forcing the legislation out of the Rules Committee by means of a discharge petition.

Open rule A rule that opens a measure to amendment on the House floor without restriction.

Closed rule A rule that prohibits floor consideration of amendments on the House floor.

Structured rules Rules that specify which amendments are allowed and under what conditions, the time available for debate, and/or the method of voting on amendments.

When the Rules Committee refers a bill to the floor, it sets a time limit for debate and determines the ground rules for amendments. Debate in the House is defined by the rule under which a measure is considered. A rule that opens a measure to amendment on the House floor without restriction is an **open rule.** In contrast, a **closed rule** is a rule that prohibits floor consideration of amendments on the House floor. The measure must be voted up or down without amendment. In practice, most rules, especially rules for major legislation, are **structured rules,** which are rules that specify which amendments are allowed and under what conditions, the time available for debate, and/or the method of voting on amendments.[44] The Rules Committee limited debate on the healthcare reform bill to four hours, divided equally between proponents and opponents. The Rules Committee allowed consideration of two amendments to healthcare reform—a Republican alternative bill, which failed, and an amendment to prohibit the expenditure of federal funds for healthcare coverage that included abortion services, which passed. The anti-abortion amendment was added to win the votes on final passage of a number of anti-abortion Democrats.

In 2011, the healthcare reform repeal measure came to the floor with a closed rule—no amendments.

Rules are a means for structuring debate on the House floor. Rules that force members to choose between comprehensive alternative pieces of legislation focus debate on big choices rather than the details of legislation. Rules can also prevent a measure's opponents from forcing votes on the most unpopular provisions of a bill or offering amendments that the leadership opposes.[45] The Rules Committee is an important element of the Speaker's power. In contrast to other House committees, the Speaker personally appoints the majority party members of the Rules Committee subject to approval by the party caucus, thereby ensuring control. The Speaker uses the Rules Committee not only to determine which measures reach the floor, but also to structure the policy choices available to members on the floor.

The role of the House Rules Committee in the legislative process is controversial. Its defenders contend that it enables the House to conduct business efficiently, especially in comparison with the plodding Senate, by allowing the chamber's majority to work its will. In contrast, critics charge that the majority party in the House, regardless of which party has been in charge of the chamber, uses the rules process to shut the minority party out of the legislative process entirely, bypassing intraparty discussion, debate, negotiation, and compromise necessary for the formulation of good legislation.[46]

Unanimous consent agreement (UCA) A formal understanding on procedures for conducting business in the Senate that requires the acceptance of every member of the chamber.

Filibuster An attempt to defeat a measure in the Senate through prolonged debate.

Nongermane amendments Amendments which are unrelated to the subject matter of the original measure.

Killer amendment An amendment designed to make a measure so unattractive that it will lack enough support to pass.

Majority rules on the floor of the House. If all 435 members are present and voting, 218 votes are necessary for final passage of legislation, a simple majority. Healthcare reform passed the House 220–215. Democrats favored the measure 219–39. Every Republican except for Congressman Joseph Cao of New Orleans, Louisiana, voted against the bill.

In the Senate, a measure typically reaches the floor through the mechanism of a **unanimous consent agreement (UCA),** which is a formal understanding on procedures for conducting business in the Senate that requires the acceptance of every member of the chamber. UCAs limit debate and determine the amendments that can be offered, similar to the rules granted by the Rules Committee in the House. Except for measures that are noncontroversial, UCAs reflect negotiation between the Senate leadership and the membership that considers the needs of every member, because a single senator can prevent the adoption of an agreement. A member who objects to a UCA is said to have placed a hold. The Majority Leader may choose to bring the measure to the floor despite the hold, but the motion to proceed may face a **filibuster,** which is an attempt to defeat the measure through prolonged debate. If that is overcome, then the bill itself may be filibustered.

Nonetheless, senators can usually get their legislation to the floor. A senator can often obtain unanimous consent by accepting policy compromises or threatening to place holds on the legislation favored by the measure's opponents. A senator can also bring a measure to the floor by offering it as an amendment to another bill because Senate rules allow consideration of **nongermane amendments,** which are unrelated to the subject matter of the original measure. Nongermane amendments are not allowed in the House.

Senators can offer amendments strategically to weaken legislation or to raise other, unrelated issues. A **killer amendment** is an amendment designed to make a measure so unattractive that it will lack enough support to pass. Opponents of term limitation legislation, which Congress considered in 1995, offered an amendment to the measure that would count time already served in the calculation. Were it adopted, many members of Congress voting for term limits would effectively be voting themselves out of office.[47] Killer amendments that succeed are rare.[48]

Congress has a reputation as one of the great debating bodies of the world, but it is unusual for debates to sway many votes. Floor debates are often poorly attended and many of the members who are present may be inattentive. The real work of Congress does not take place on the floor, but in committee and subcommittee, congressional offices, the cloakroom, and elsewhere around the capital. Debates allow members to read into the record the case for and against a measure and to justify their own position to their constituents. Debates serve to inform the world outside of Congress rather than sway opinion within. They also have symbolic value, demonstrating to the world that Congress respects majority and minority opinion and that it makes decisions democratically.

Floor proceedings are relatively less structured in the Senate than the House. Although disgruntled House members can sometimes delay action through parliamentary maneuvers, the Rules Committee system generally ensures that House proceedings move forward in a predictable fashion. In contrast, the rules of the Senate

The 1964 Civil Rights Bill became law after Senate supporters were able to invoke cloture, ending a 57-day filibuster.

are designed to maximize the rights of expression of individual senators. One senator or a group of senators is often able to produce chaos on the Senate floor if desired.

Indeed, senators sometimes take advantage of the rules to defeat legislation they oppose. Because Senate rules do not limit the amount of time a senator or the chamber as a whole can spend discussing a measure, a bill's opponents may filibuster. Under Senate rules, each senator who wishes to speak must be recognized and cannot be interrupted without consent. The Senate cannot vote on a piece of legislation until every senator has finished speaking.[49]

Cloture The procedure for ending a filibuster.

The procedure for ending a filibuster is known as **cloture.** Senators wanting to halt a filibuster must announce their intentions and gather the signatures of a sixth of the Senate, 16 senators, to force a vote on cloture, which, in turn, requires a three-fifths vote of the Senate membership (60 votes) to succeed. Although Senate rules limit post-cloture debate to 30 hours, a measure's opponents often delay action even longer through parliamentary maneuvering.

Filibusters have grown more common. In the 1950s, the Senate had more the atmosphere of an exclusive social club than it does today and senators reserved the filibuster for issues of great import and emotion. The Senate averaged one filibuster per Congress in the 1950s, five per Congress in the 1960s, 11 in the 1970s, and, most recently, 52 per Congress.[50] In the 111th Congress, the Republican Party in the Senate used the filibuster as a partisan weapon and not just against healthcare reform. In 2009, Republicans filibustered 80 percent of major legislation.[51] Healthcare reform legislation was able to move forward to a final vote only after the chamber's 60 Democratic senators voted to invoke cloture, overcoming the unanimous opposition of the Senate's Republican members.

The nature of the filibuster has changed. In the 1950s and 1960s, senators conducting a filibuster engaged in longwinded debate while Senate leaders kept the chamber in an overnight marathon session in order to break the filibuster and move on with a vote. Today, classic filibusters are a thing of the past. Senators simply announce their intention to filibuster and the Senate goes on with other business while the leadership works to gather sufficient support to invoke cloture. Sometimes, Senate leaders file a cloture petition to end debate even before a filibuster materializes.

The filibuster is controversial, probably more controversial than the role of the Rules Committee in the House. Whereas the rules process in the House promotes majority rule, the filibuster undermines it. The proponents of the filibuster argue that it improves the policymaking process by forcing the majority to debate with, listen to, and negotiate with the minority. A bill that can win the support of 60 senators rather than just 51 is probably a better bill and one that will be more likely to win popular support in the country than legislation rammed through the Senate with a bare majority.[52] In contrast, critics of the filibuster warn that the current use of the filibuster as a partisan weapon is undermining Congress's institutional role as a legislative body. If the minority party in the Senate filibusters every issue except the most routine, then the Senate will be unable to act unless the majority party has 60 senators and that is rare. Congress will consequently be unable to respond legislatively to major national problems, such as immigration and energy. The role of the executive branch will expand as the president and executive branch agencies act through executive orders and the rulemaking process, actions that do not require congressional approval.[53]

The Senate, similar to the House, decides the fate of legislation on final passage by majority vote. Although the proponents of a measure may need the support of 60 senators to bring a measure to a vote because of the filibuster, once a final vote is taken, only a simple majority is necessary for final passage. Healthcare reform passed the Senate by a vote of 60–39, with every Democrat voting yes and every Republican voting no. (One Republican senator was absent when the vote was taken.)

WHAT IS YOUR OPINION?

If you were a member of the Senate, would you use the filibuster to defeat legislation you opposed?

Conference Committee Action

A measure does not pass Congress until it clears both the House and Senate in identical form. If the House and Senate pass similar but not identical bills, the chamber that initially passed the measure can agree to the changes made by the other chamber or the two houses can resolve their differences by adopting a series of reconciling amendments. When the differences between the two houses are too great for easy resolution, the two chambers appoint a conference committee, which is a special congressional committee created to negotiate differences on similar pieces of legislation passed by the House and Senate. Although Congress resorts to the conference committee process for only about 10 percent of the measures that ultimately become law, conference committees are typical for major legislation.[54]

Conferees The members of a conference committee.

The Speaker and the Senate Majority Leader appoint the members of a conference committee (called **conferees**) from lists given to them by committee leaders. Although the Speaker and Majority Leader can appoint any member of Congress to serve on a conference committee, they almost always select members of the standing committee or committees that considered the bill, including the committee chair(s) and ranking member(s). If the Speaker and Majority Leader are concerned that the conferees may not uphold the position of the majority party, they may also appoint members who are sympathetic to the party's position.[55] Because of the increased use of multiple referrals and the increasing tendency of Congress to write omnibus bills, the size of conference committees has grown, sometimes including dozens or even hundreds of members.

A conference committee is sometimes called the third house of Congress because it writes the final version of legislation. The conferees are not bound to stick with the version of the measures passed by either the House or the Senate. The conference committee can delete provisions passed by both houses and include provisions passed by neither. In practice, the final version of major legislation produced by a conference committee reflects not just a compromise between the House and Senate, but a compromise among the party leadership in each chamber, the president, and key interest groups with a stake in the legislation.

Conference report A revised bill produced by a conference committee.

Once a majority of each chamber's conferees, voting separately, agree on a compromise, the revised measure, called the **conference report,** goes back to the floor of the House and Senate. The first chamber to vote on the conference report has three options: to accept, reject, or return to conference for more negotiations. If the first chamber accepts the measure, the second chamber has two options: to adopt or reject. If both chambers accept the conference report, the measure has passed Congress and goes to the president.

The healthcare reform bills passed by the House and Senate were similar but not identical. Democratic leaders planned to create a conference committee where party leaders would negotiate a compromise final bill with significant input from the White House. Their plan was undone, however, by the results of a special election in Massachusetts. During the debate over healthcare reform in 2009, Democratic Senator Ted Kennedy of Massachusetts died. The state's Democratic governor appointed Democrat Paul Kirk to fill the seat until a special election could be held. Kirk voted with the other Democrats in the chamber to end the Republican filibuster and pass healthcare reform in late 2009. Much to the dismay of President Obama and Democrats in Congress, Scott Brown, a Republican, won the special election to fill Kennedy's old seat in early 2010. Brown promised to vote against cloture, preventing Senate Democrats from having the 60 votes necessary to end a Republican filibuster of the conference report.

Democratic congressional leaders and the president developed an alternative strategy for passing healthcare reform. First, the House voted to accept the version of healthcare reform passed by the Senate. The vote was 220–215 with every Republican voting no, including Congressman Cao of New Orleans. All but 39 Democrats in the House voted yes. With this action, healthcare reform passed Congress because the measure had already passed the Senate. The bill went to the White House for President Obama's signature. Second, the House passed a budget reconciliation measure dealing with funding matters in the bill. The rules of Congress prohibit filibustering budget reconciliation bills. Although the budget reconciliation process was created to keep spending in line with overall budget goals, Republicans and Democrats in Congress have often used the process to enact policy measures, including the tax cut and Medicare reform legislation adopted during the George W. Bush administration. The Democrats used the reconciliation process to change some of the provisions in the Senate bill that House Democrats opposed. Without having to overcome a filibuster, Senate Democrats had more than enough votes to pass the reconciliation bill, which also went to the president for signature. Finally, President Obama signed an executive order making it clear that tax money could not be used to purchase insurance policies as part of healthcare reform that covered abortion services. Obama took the action to win over the support of a number of anti-abortion Democrats in the House that threatened to vote against the Senate version of healthcare reform because they did not believe that its anti-abortion language was strong enough.

Presidential Action

The Constitution gives the president several options for dealing with legislation passed by Congress. If the president signs a measure, it becomes law. If the president does not sign the measure, it becomes law anyway after 10 days unless Congress is

Republican Scott Brown won a special election to fill Ted Kennedy's vacant Senate seat in Massachusetts, promising to support a Republican filibuster to defeat healthcare reform. The election of Brown was full of ironies. Not only was Kennedy a lifelong proponent of healthcare reform, but the bill that Brown promised to derail was remarkably similar to the Massachusetts healthcare program, which Brown had supported when he served in the state legislature.

Pocket veto The action of a president allowing a measure to die without signature after Congress has adjourned.

Veto An action by the chief executive refusing to approve a measure passed by the legislature.

Rider A provision, unlikely to become law on its own merits, which is attached to an important measure so that it will ride through the legislative process.

adjourned, in which case it dies. The action of a president allowing a measure to die without signature after Congress has adjourned is known as a **pocket veto.** In practice, modern presidents rarely use the latter two options. Because Congress now stays in session nearly year-round, presidents have few opportunities for pocket vetoes. Furthermore, image-conscious presidents believe it appears more decisive either to sign a measure or veto it outright.

If the president opposes a measure passed by Congress, the president can issue a **veto,** an action by which the chief executive refuses to approve a measure passed by the legislature. A president vetoes a bill by returning it to Congress with a statement of objections. If Congress overrides the veto by a two-thirds vote of each house, the measure becomes law anyway. Should either house fall short of two-thirds, the veto is sustained and the measure fails. Since the administration of Franklin Roosevelt, presidents have vetoed 1,349 measures, with Congress overriding 60 vetoes for an override rate of 4.4 percent.[56]

The president must accept or reject a measure in its entirety. Congress takes advantage of this situation by passing omnibus bills hundreds or even thousands of pages long that combine provisions the president wants with measures the president would veto if they were standing alone. A **rider** is a provision, unlikely to become law on its own merits, which is attached to an important measure so that it will ride through the legislative process. Appropriation bills are favorite vehicles for riders because they are must-pass legislation that presidents are reluctant to veto.

For example, Congress enacted a prohibition against smoking on commercial airline flights as a rider attached to an appropriation measure.[57]

Statistics on presidential vetoes indicate that presidents are more likely to veto measures and have their vetoes overridden when the opposition party controls Congress. Since 1960, the presidents who issued the most vetoes were, in order of veto frequency, Ronald Reagan, Gerald Ford, George H. W. Bush, and Richard Nixon, all Republican presidents operating with Congresses that were controlled, in part or in whole, by Democrats. Ford, Reagan, and Nixon suffered the largest number of veto overrides.[58]

The modifications in the legislative process adopted to increase the likelihood that major legislation will become law have been effective. Although the overall success rate for bills is poor, a majority of the major pieces of legislation considered by Congress become law. In the 111th Congress, only 328 bills of 13,675 measures introduced in the House and Senate became law for a success rate of 2 percent.[59] In contrast, major pieces of legislation fare much better. Over the last decade, 59 percent of major bills have become law.[60]

WHAT WE HAVE LEARNED

1. **How do the U.S. House and U.S. Senate compare and contrast in terms of structures, responsibilities, and characteristics?**

   The United States has a bicameral legislature with a House and a Senate. Whereas states are equally represented in the Senate, representation in the House depends on a state's population. Senators run for election statewide to serve six-year terms; House members run from districts to serve two-year terms. Although the Constitution assigns certain responsibilities to the Senate, the two chambers share other tasks, including enacting legislation. The Senate is individualistic, with many important decisions requiring supermajority approval, either because of the Constitution (in the case of treaty ratification) or Senate rules (in the case of the filibuster). Members of the House have a reputation for devotion to technical expertise, personalized constituency service, and responsiveness to local political interests.

2. **What is the profile of the membership of Congress, considering qualifications, background, compensation, personal styles, relationship with their districts, and turnover?**

   The U.S. Constitution requires that members of the House be no less than 25 years of age, American citizens for at least seven years, and residents of the state in which their district is located. Senators must be at least 30 years old, citizens for at least nine years, and residents of the state they represent. Although Congress is more diverse than at any time in its history, white males of European ancestry are still overrepresented. In 2011, members of Congress earned $174,000 in salary. Traditionally, members of Congress got things done and advanced their careers by building relationships with colleagues, deferring to senior members, and bargaining. In today's Congress, some members have become skilled media entrepreneurs, using policy issues to gain media coverage so they can establish themselves as national political figures. Members of Congress go home often to cultivate ties with their districts, which are important for their reelection. In particular, members of Congress work to shore up constituent support through constituency service. Despite the absence of term limits, congressional turnover is substantial because members often choose not to seek reelection.

3. **How is Congress organized both on the floor and in its committee structure?**
The organization of the House and Senate is based on political party. The Senate Majority Leader and the Speaker of the House are the most important legislators in their respective chambers. They appoint members to special committees, such as conference committees, and influence the membership of standing committees. They refer legislation to committee and control the flow of business to the floor, which is especially important in the House. The Speaker and Majority Leader are political party leaders, working to advance their party's policy interests and maintain their majority. Members of Congress have a strong incentive to cooperate with their party leadership because their success is tied to the success of their political party, especially in the House.
The detailed work of Congress takes place in committee and subcommittee. Senators typically serve on more committees because the Senate has fewer members. House members, with fewer committee assignments, are better able to specialize than are senators. When individuals are first elected to the House or Senate, they request committee assignments from party committees in each chamber that make assignment decisions. Committees dealing with money are in great demand. The majority party enjoys a majority on and chairs every committee and subcommittee. Each party has its own procedures for selecting committee chairs (for the majority party) and ranking members (for the minority party).

4. **What are the steps of the legislative process, considering not just the traditional model but also how Congress has modified that model to increase the chances of passing major legislation?**
In today's Congress, the legislative process no longer conforms to the traditional "bill-becomes-a-law" formula, especially for major pieces of legislation. Congress has adopted modifications in the traditional legislative process to increase the likelihood that it can pass major legislation. Although the privilege of introducing bills and resolutions is limited to members of Congress, the ideas and initiative for legislation are varied. Once a bill or resolution is introduced, it is assigned a number and referred to committee, where the detailed work of Congress takes place. Major legislation is often referred to more than one committee, especially in the House. Committees and subcommittees hold hearings, debate the details of legislation, and revise, amend, and rewrite a measure, a process known as legislative markup. In the House, most measures that clear the standing committees go to the Rules Committee, which sets a time limit for debate and the ground rules for amendments. In the Senate, a measure typically reaches the floor through the mechanism of a unanimous consent agreement (UCA). A senator who objects to a UCA is said to place a hold on the measure. The Majority Leader may choose to bring the measure to the floor despite the hold, but the motion to proceed may face a filibuster; if that is overcome, the bill itself may face a filibuster. Cloture, the procedure for shutting off a filibuster, requires 60 votes. A measure must pass the House and Senate in identical form before it has passed Congress. If the two chambers pass similar but not identical bills, one chamber can accept the version of the legislation passed by the other chamber or the two chambers can pass a series of reconciling amendments. When differences between the two houses are too great for easy reconciliation, they create a conference committee to negotiate a single measure, which must then be voted on again and passed by the House and Senate. After a bill passes Congress, it goes to the president who can sign, veto, or permit it to become law without signature. If Congress has adjourned, the president can take no action and the bill dies—this is called a pocket veto.

KEY TERMS

appropriation bill
bicameral legislature
bill
closed rule
cloture
conferees
conference committee
conference report
constituency service
discharge petition
filibuster
floor
franking privilege
House Majority Leader
House Rules Committee
impeach
joint committee
killer amendment
legislative markup
logrolling
Medicaid
Medicare
multiple referral of legislation
nongermane amendments
omnibus bills
open rule
party caucus
pocket veto
ranking member
resolution
rider
Senate Majority Leader
Senate president pro tempore
seniority
Speaker of the House
special or select committee
standing committee
structured rules
supermajority
table
term limitation
unanimous consent agreement (UCA)
veto
whips

NOTES

1. Karen Tumulty and Kate Pickert with Alice Park, "America, The Doctor Will See You Now," *Time*, April 5, 2010, pp. 24–32.
2. Charles B. Cushman, Jr., *An Introduction to the U.S. Congress* (Armonk, NY: M.E. Sharpe, 2006), p. 5.
3. Robert V. Remini, *The House: The History of the House of Representatives* (New York: HarperCollins, 2006), p. 496.
4. "Membership in the 112th Congress: A Profile," Congressional Research Service, available at http://assets.opencrs.com.
5. Donald R. Matthews, *U.S. Senators and Their World* (New York: Vintage Books, 1960), pp. 116–117.
6. Burdett Loomis, *The New American Politician: Ambition, Entrepreneurship, and the Changing Face of Political Life* (New York: Basic Books, 1988), pp. 233–244.
7. Center for Responsive Politics, available at www.opensecrets.org.
8. Brandice Canes-Wrone, David W. Brady, and John F. Cogan, "Out of Step, Out of Office: Electoral Accountability and House Members' Voting," *American Political Science Review* 96 (March 2002): 127–140.
9. Sally Friedman, *Dilemmas of Representation: Local Politics, National Factors, and the Home Styles of Modern U.S. Congress Members* (Albany, NY: State University of New York Press, 2007), pp. 223–225.
10. Richard F. Fenno, *Home Style* (Boston, MA: Little, Brown, 1978), p. 18.
11. Richard G. Forgette, *Congress, Parties, and Puzzles: Politics as a Team Sport* (New York: Peter Lang, 2004), p. 174.
12. Lydia Saad, "By Slim Margin, Americans Support Healthcare Bill's Passage," Gallup, March 23, 2010, available at www.gallup.com.
13. Michael H. Murekami, "Divisive Primaries: Party Organizations, Ideological Groups, and the Battle Over Party Unity," *PS: Political Science & Politics*, October 2008, pp. 918–923.
14. Michael L. Mezey, *Representative Democracy: Legislators and Their Constituents* (Lanham, MD: Rowman & Littlefield, 2008), pp. 170–172.
15. "Membership of the 111th Congress: A Profile."
16. Dan Eggen, "Billy Tauzin, Key Player in Health-Care Push, Leaving PhRMA," *Washington Post*, February 13, 2010, available at www.washingtonpost.com.
17. Rebekah Herrick and Samuel H. Fisher III, *Representing America: The Citizen and the Professional Legislator in the House of Representatives* (Lanham, MD: Lexington Books, 2007), pp. 93–96.
18. Matthew N. Green, *The Speaker of the House: A Study of Leadership* (New Haven, CT: Yale University Press, 2010), p. 12; Andrea C. Hatcher, *Majority Leadership in the U.S. Senate* (Amherst, NY: Cambria Press, 2010), pp. 154–157.

19. Kristin Kanthak, "Crystal Elephants and Committee Chairs: Campaign Contributions and Leadership Races in the U.S. House of Representatives," *American Politics Research* 35 (May 2007): 389–406.
20. Center for Responsive Politics.
21. Sean M. Theriault, *Party Polarization in Congress* (New York: Cambridge University Press, 2008), pp. 4–9.
22. Gary W. Cox and Mathew D. McCubbins, *Legislative Leviathan: Party Government in the House*, 2nd ed. (New York: Cambridge University Press, 2007), pp. 256–257.
23. Frances E. Lee, *Beyond Ideology: Politics, Principles, and Partisanship in the U.S. Senate* (Chicago, IL: University of Chicago Press, 2009), pp. 8–10.
24. Eric S. Heberlig and Bruce A. Larson, "Party Fundraising, Descriptive Representation, and the Battle for Majority Control: Shifting Leadership Appointment Strategies in the U.S. House of Representatives, 1990–2002," *Social Science Quarterly* 88 (June 2007): 404–421.
25. Barbara Sinclair, "The New World of U.S. Senators," in Lawrence C. Dodd and Bruce I. Oppenheimer, eds., *Congress Reconsidered*, 9th ed. (Washington, DC: CQ Press, 2009), pp. 1–22.
26. Laura W. Arnold, "The Distribution of Senate Committee Positions: Change or More of the Same?" *Legislative Studies Quarterly* 26 (May 2001): 227–248.
27. Scott A. Frisch and Sean Q. Kelly, *Committee Assignment Politics in the U.S. House of Representatives* (Norman, OK: University of Oklahoma Press, 2006), pp. 328–330.
28. D. Roderick Kiewiet and Mathew D. McCubbins, *The Logic of Delegation: Congressional Parties and the Appropriations Process* (Chicago: University of Chicago Press, 1991), pp. 232–233.
29. Barry Rundquist, Jungho Rhee, Jeong-Hwa Lee, and Sharon E. Fox, "Modeling State Representation on Defense Committees in Congress, 1959–1989," *American Politics Quarterly* 25 (January 1997): 35–55.
30. Richard L. Hall and Bernard Grofman, "The Committee Assignment Process and the Conditional Nature of Committee Bias," *American Political Science Review* 84 (December 1990): 1149–1166.
31. Paul R. Brewer and Christopher J. Deering, "Musical Chairs: Interest Groups, Campaign Fund-Raising, and Selection of House Committee Chairs," in Paul S. Herrnson, Ronald G. Shaiko, and Clyde Wilcox, eds., *The Interest Group Connection: Electioneering, Lobbying, and Policymaking in Washington*, 2nd ed. (Washington, DC: CQ Press, 2005), pp. 141–146.
32. Jeff Zeleny, "Of Party Dues and Deadbeats on Capitol Hill," *New York Times*, October 1, 2006, available at www.nytimes.com.
33. Barbara Sinclair, *Unorthodox Lawmaking: New Legislative Processes in the U.S. Congress*, 3rd ed. (Washington, DC: Congressional Quarterly Press, 2007), pp. 5–8.
34. Congressional Record, Daily Digest, "Résumé of Congressional Activity, 111th Congress," available at www.senate.gov/reference/resources/pdf/110_1.pdf.
35. Roger H. Davidson and Walter J. Oleszek, *Congress and Its Members*, 7th ed. (Washington, DC: CQ Press, 2000), p. 31.
36. Steven Brill, "On Sale: Your Government. Why Lobbying Is Washington's Best Bargain," *Time*, July 12, 2010, p. 32.
37. "Résumé of Congressional Activity, 111th Congress."
38. John Baughman, *Common Ground: Committee Politics in the U.S. House of Representatives* (Stanford, CA: Stanford University Press, 2006), pp. 175–179.
39. Sinclair, *Unorthodox Lawmaking*, p. 12.
40. "Résumé of Congressional Activity, 111th Congress."
41. C. Lawrence Evans, "Participation and Policy Making in Senate Committees," *Political Science Quarterly* 106 (Fall 1991): 490.
42. Davidson and Oleszek, *Congress and Its Members*, 7th ed. p. 242.
43. Sinclair, *Unorthodox Lawmaking*, p. 19.
44. Matthew Green and Daniel Burns, "What Might Bring Regular Order Back to the House?" *PS: Political Science & Politics*, April 2010, pp. 223–226.
45. Ibid., p. 32.
46. Thomas E. Mann and Norman J. Ornstein, *The Broken Branch: How Congress Is Failing America and How to Get It Back on Track* (New York: Oxford University Press, 2006), p. 170.
47. John D. Wilerson, "'Killer' Amendments in Congress," *American Political Science Review* 93 (September 1999): 535–552.
48. Charles J. Finocchiaro and Jeffery A. Jenkins, "In Search of Killer Amendments in the Modern U.S. House," *Legislative Studies Quarterly* 33 (May 2008): 263–294.
49. Gregory J. Wawro and Eric Schickler, *Filibuster: Obstruction and Lawmaking in the U.S. Senate* (Princeton, NJ: Princeton University Press, 2006), pp. 13–14.
50. Sinclair, "The New World of U.S. Senators," in *Congress Reconsidered*, p. 7.
51. Peter Beinart, "Why Washington's Tied Up in Knots," *Time*, March 1, 2010, p. 23.
52. Ruth Marcus, "Why the Filibuster Is Frustrating but Necessary," *Washington Post*, January 27, 2010, available at www.washingtonpost.com.
53. Francis E. Lee, "Senate Deliberation and the Future of Congressional Power," *PS: Political Science & Politics*, April 2010, pp. 227–230.
54. Sinclair, *Unorthodox Lawmaking*, p. 76.
55. Jeffrey Lazarus and Nathan W. Monroe, "The Speaker's Discretion: Conference Committee Appointments in the 97th through 106th Congresses," *Political Research Quarterly* 60 (December 2007): 593–606.
56. Based on the data included in John Woolley and Gerhard Peters, "The American Presidency Project," available at www.presidency.ucsb.edu.
57. Dan Morgan, "Along for the Rider," *Washington Post National Weekly Edition*, August 19–25, 2002, p. 15.
58. Based on the data included in John Woolley and Gerhard Peters, "The American Presidency Project."
59. "Résumé of Congressional Activity, 111th Congress."
60. Sinclair, *Unorthodox Lawmaking*, p. 272.

Chapter 11

The Presidency

CHAPTER OUTLINE

The Constitutional Presidency
- Qualifications and Backgrounds
- Term of Office
- Impeachment and Removal
- Presidential Succession and Disability
- The Vice Presidency

Presidential Powers
- Diplomatic Powers
- Military Powers
- Inherent Powers
- Judicial Powers
- Executive Powers
- Legislative Powers

The Development of the Modern Presidency

The Organization of the Presidency
- White House Staff
- Executive Office of the President
- Presidential Bureaucracy and Presidential Influence

Theories of Presidential Leadership
- Presidential Character
- Leadership Style
- The Power to Persuade
- Going Public
- Unilateral Tools of Presidential Power

Presidential Popularity

The Presidency in Context

What We Have Learned

WHAT WE WILL LEARN

After studying Chapter 11, students should be able to answer the following questions:

1. How does the Constitution define the office of the presidency?
2. What are the diplomatic, military, inherent, judicial, executive, and legislative powers of the presidency?
3. What factors contributed to the development of the modern presidency?
4. How is the office of the presidency organized to assist the chief executive in carrying out the duties of the office?
5. How do various political scientists approach the concept of presidential power?
6. What factors affect presidential popularity?
7. How does the political context affect the ability of a president to influence the policymaking process?

The United States has been at war in Afghanistan since 2001 when American forces entered the country to overthrow the Taliban government for harboring the al Qaeda terror network responsible for the 9/11 attacks. After quickly defeating Taliban and al Qaeda forces, the United States and its allies installed a democratic government in Afghanistan with Hamid Karzai at its head. Karzai was subsequently elected the country's president. Meanwhile, the Taliban and al Qaeda regrouped in the mountainous region along the Afghan-Pakistani border and began an insurgency against the Afghan government and American forces stationed in the country.

When Barack Obama became president in January 2009, the situation in Afghanistan was grim. The Karzai government was widely regarded as corrupt and ineffective. Taliban forces controlled much of the Afghan countryside and were capable of launching deadly strikes throughout the country, including the capital city of Kabul. American casualties were steadily rising and General Stanley McChrystal, the American military commander in the region, warned that the war was in danger of being lost.

Few decisions are more difficult for a president than deciding when to fight a war and when to end it. While General McChrystal was requesting additional troops, some liberal Democrats were urging the president to begin a withdrawal. Committing more troops to the region would inevitably lead to an increase in American casualties and cost billions of dollars a year in military spending. Furthermore, Obama was certainly aware of the effect of an unpopular war on presidential popularity. President Harry Truman in 1948 and President Lyndon Johnson in 1968 chose not to seek reelection because unpopular wars in Korea (for Truman) and Vietnam (for Johnson) undermined their standing in opinion polls. Similarly, an unpopular war in Iraq contributed to the record low approval rating for President George W. Bush when he ended his second term in 2009. If the United States withdrew its forces too soon, however, the Taliban could regain power and al Qaeda might once again have a safe haven from which to launch attacks against the United States and its allies.

Obama chose a middle course. He ordered 30,000 more troops to Afghanistan by the summer of 2010, bringing the total American force commitment to nearly 100,000. He also promised to begin a withdrawal in 2011. Obama's strategy was to halt the Taliban advance, step up the air war against al Qaeda leaders inside the Pakistani border, and train the Afghan army. If the strategy works, the Taliban and al Qaeda will be on the defensive and Afghan forces will be capable of replacing American forces as they leave the country. If the strategy does not work, however, the failure will be apparent just in time for the 2012 presidential election.

President Obama's strategy for fighting the war in Afghanistan introduces this chapter on the presidency by drawing attention on the factors that affect the president's ability to accomplish policy goals. The chapter begins with the constitutional profile of the office. It examines the powers and responsibilities of the office, traces the development of the modern presidency, and describes the organization of the executive branch. The chapter continues by exploring various theories of presidential leadership. It discusses presidential popularity and concludes by examining the presidency in the context of American politics.

The Constitutional Presidency

The Constitution describes the office of the presidency in Article II.

Qualifications and Backgrounds

The Constitution declares that the president must be at least 35 years of age, a natural-born American citizen (as opposed to a naturalized citizen), and a resident of the United States for at least 14 years. Before the 2008 election, all the nation's presidents had been white males of Western European ancestry. Two sets of presidents were father and son (John and John Quincy Adams and George and George W. Bush); two were grandfather and grandson (William Henry and Benjamin Harrison); and two were cousins (Theodore and Franklin D. Roosevelt). All were Protestant Christians except for John Kennedy, who was Roman Catholic. Most presidents have been fairly wealthy; the majority of them have been experienced politicians. Most presidents have come from states outside the South. In recent years, however, social barriers have begun to fall as the nation has elected a Roman Catholic (Kennedy), three Southerners (Jimmy Carter, Bill Clinton, and George W. Bush), and a divorced person (Ronald Reagan) to the White House. The election of Barack Obama, the son of a white woman from Kansas and a black immigrant from Kenya, shattered the barriers of race and ethnicity.

Source: © Fischer/www.CartoonStock.com.

Furthermore, Hillary Clinton's strong showing in the race for the Democratic presidential nomination in 2008 suggested that gender was no longer a major barrier to the White House. The myth that anyone born in the United States can grow up to become president has come closer to reality than ever before in the nation's history.

Term of Office

Lame duck An official whose influence is diminished because the official either cannot or will not seek reelection.

The president's constitutional term of office is four years. The framers of the Constitution placed no limit on the number of terms presidents could serve, believing that the desire to remain in office would compel presidents to do their best. George Washington, the nation's first chief executive, established a custom of seeking no more than two terms, which every president honored until Franklin D. Roosevelt broke tradition in the early 1940s. After Roosevelt, a Democrat, won election to a third and then a fourth term, unhappy Republicans launched a drive to amend the Constitution to limit the president to two terms. They succeeded with the ratification of the Twenty-second Amendment in 1951. The proponents of the two-term limit argued that it prevented a president from becoming too powerful. In contrast, critics believed that the two-term limit unnecessarily weakened the office of the presidency by making a second-term president a **lame duck,** which is an official whose influence is diminished because the official either cannot or will not seek reelection. The opponents of the Twenty-second Amendment also complained that it was undemocratic because it denied voters the right to reelect a president they admired.

WHAT IS YOUR OPINION?

Should presidents be permitted to run for more than two terms?

Impeachment and Removal

Impeachment The process in which an executive or judicial official is formally accused of an offense that could warrant removal from office.

Impeachment is a process in which an executive or judicial official is formally accused of an offense that could warrant removal from office. The Constitution states that the president may be impeached for "treason, bribery, or other high crimes and misdemeanors." The Founders foresaw two broad, general grounds on which a president could be impeached and removed from office. First, impeachment could be used against a president who abused the powers of office, thereby threatening to become a tyrant. Second, it could be employed against a president who failed to carry out the duties of the office. In practice, however, impeachment has been understood primarily as a legal process, with Congress basing impeachment on violations of law rather than political misdeeds.[1]

Articles of impeachment A document listing the impeachable offenses that the House believes the president committed.

The actual process of impeachment and removal involves both houses of Congress. The House drafts **articles of impeachment,** which is a document listing the impeachable offenses that the House believes the president committed. Technically, *impeach* means to accuse; therefore, when the House impeaches the president by majority vote, it is accusing the president of committing offenses that may warrant removal from office. The Senate then tries the president, with the chief justice presiding. The Senate must vote by a two-thirds margin to remove the president from office.

The election of Barack Obama shattered the barriers of race and ethnicity that had limited the presidency to white males of Western European descent.

Andrew Johnson's Impeachment In 1868, Andrew Johnson became the first president to be impeached. Johnson was a former Democratic senator from Tennessee who was chosen by the Republican Party to be President Abraham Lincoln's running mate in the 1864 election. The Republicans hoped that adding Johnson to the ticket would broaden its appeal to Democrats who supported the Union during the Civil War. When Johnson became president after Lincoln's assassination, he quarreled with the Republican Congress over which branch of government would control **Reconstruction,** which was the process whereby the states that had seceded during the Civil War were reorganized and reestablished in the Union. Congress overrode Johnson's veto to pass several laws aimed at limiting the president's power. One of these measures, the Tenure of Office Act, stipulated that any official appointed by the president and confirmed by the Senate could not be removed from office until the Senate had confirmed a replacement. Johnson challenged the law by removing Secretary of War Edwin M. Stanton and appointing General Ulysses S. Grant as his interim successor. The House of Representatives responded to Johnson's challenge by voting to impeach him 126 to 47. The Senate voted 35 to 19 for conviction, just one vote short of the two-thirds vote necessary to remove President Johnson from office.

Reconstruction The process whereby the states that had seceded during the Civil War were reorganized and reestablished in the Union.

Richard Nixon's Resignation More than a century after Andrew Johnson survived impeachment, President Nixon resigned in the face of impeachment proceedings stemming from the Watergate scandal. The Watergate affair began in June 1972 when five men were arrested for breaking into the Democratic National Committee headquarters in the Watergate office complex in Washington, DC. The burglars, employed by the Committee to Reelect the President, were hired to plant electronic eavesdropping devices in the opposition's headquarters. Their mission was part of a conspiracy formed by aides of President Nixon to manipulate the Democratic Party's presidential nomination process to assist the weakest Democratic candidate possible and defeat any potential nominee strong enough to beat Nixon. It was many months, however, before these facts were generally known.

Once the burglars were arrested, Nixon and his aides attempted to conceal the nature of the initial conspiracy. They paid more than $300,000 in hush money to the burglars and their supervisors to keep them quiet. In the meantime, the White House played down the significance of the break-in, calling the event a third-rate burglary.

The cover-up did not begin to unravel until early 1973 when the burglars stood trial. Although they remained silent, Judge John Sirica voiced the opinion that the truth had not come out. In the meantime, two investigative reporters for the *Washington Post* newspaper, Carl Bernstein and Bob Woodward, began to uncover facts and ask questions about the affair.

By early summer 1973, the investigation was proceeding on several fronts. In the Senate, a special committee, chaired by Senator Sam Ervin, conducted televised hearings at which presidential aides told startling tales of political dirty tricks and cover-ups in the White House. "What did the president know and when did he know it?" asked Senator Howard Baker. While the hearings continued, Special Counsel Archibald Cox conducted an investigation on behalf of the Justice Department. In October, Nixon decided that Cox's probe was coming too close to the truth and he fired Cox in what came to be known as the Saturday Night Massacre. For the first time, congressional leaders publicly considered impeachment.

Nixon clung to his presidency for another nine and a half months. He called on the nation "to put Watergate behind us," but each week brought new accusations and revelations. In 1974, the House Judiciary Committee held hearings on proposed articles of impeachment against the president, eventually recommending impeachment to the full House. Meanwhile, a new special counsel, Leon Jaworski, pursued the investigation, aided immeasurably by tape recordings the president had made secretly of conversations with his aides.

Watergate came to a climax in midsummer 1974 when the U.S. Supreme Court ordered Nixon to hand over a key group of tapes to the special prosecutor. One tape, containing a conversation between the president and Chief of Staff H. R. Haldeman, proved to be the smoking gun that linked Nixon directly to the cover-up. What support Nixon still had in Congress and the Republican Party crumbled. In August, he resigned the presidency.

The Impeachment of Bill Clinton In 1998, President Clinton became the second president to be impeached. An investigation by Special Counsel Kenneth Starr provided the basis for the case against Clinton. Starr was initially appointed to look into allegations of the president's involvement in a failed Arkansas land development called Whitewater when Clinton was governor of Arkansas. The scope of Starr's investigation subsequently expanded to include allegations that Clinton had lied under oath about an alleged sexual liaison with White House intern Monica

Lewinsky and that Clinton encouraged Lewinsky to lie as well. Starr's focus on Lewinsky stemmed from a sexual harassment lawsuit filed against Clinton by Paula Corbin Jones over an incident that allegedly occurred while Clinton was governor of Arkansas. In her lawsuit, Jones charged that then Governor Clinton engaged in illegal sexual harassment by asking her for sexual favors. Her attorneys subpoenaed both Lewinsky and Clinton in hopes of establishing a pattern of sexual misconduct by Clinton. Starr investigated the matter to ascertain whether President Clinton had lied under oath while giving a deposition in the case and whether he had illegally encouraged Lewinsky to lie under oath as well.

Starr's report to Congress included 11 specific allegations of impeachable offenses. Starr charged that Clinton committed perjury by lying under oath about having an affair during the Jones deposition and while testifying to a grand jury convened by the special counsel. He accused the president of obstructing justice by helping Lewinsky find a job after she left the White House and making false statements to his staff about his relationship with her. Finally, Starr charged Clinton with abusing his constitutional authority by lying to the public and Congress about the affair. Starr supported his allegations by filling his report with page after page of explicit details of the sexual encounters between the president and Lewinsky.

Clinton responded to the crisis by admitting to an "inappropriate relationship" with Lewinsky. Clinton said that he had made a mistake and began a series of apologies to his wife, staff, members of Congress, cabinet, and the American people. All the while, Clinton and his lawyers declared that technically he had not perjured himself by lying under oath and that he had not committed an impeachable offense. The investigation should end, they said, so the president and Congress could get on with the nation's business.

But the investigation did not end, at least not before the impeachment process played itself out. The House Judiciary Committee held hearings on the charges and recommended four articles of impeachment on a strict party-line vote, with every Republican on the committee voting for at least one of the articles and every Democrat voting against all of them. In late 1998, the House impeached Clinton by voting in favor of Article I, which accused the president of lying under oath, and Article III, which charged Clinton with the obstruction of justice in the investigation of his testimony in the Jones case. The vote in the House was close, with all but five Republicans voting for at least one article of impeachment and all but five Democrats voting against all the articles. In February 1999, the Senate failed to convict the president and remove him from office. The vote was 45 to 55 in favor of Article I and 50 to 50 on Article III. All 45 Senate Democrats voted against both articles, whereas 10 Republican Senators voted against Article I and five Republicans opposed Article III.

WHAT IS YOUR OPINION?

If you were a member of the Senate, would you have voted to remove Clinton from office? Why or why not?

Presidential Succession and Disability

The vice president succeeds a president who is removed, resigns, or dies in office. After the vice president, the line of succession passes to the Speaker of the House, president pro tempore of the Senate, secretary of state, and through the cabinet. In American history, nine vice presidents have succeeded to the presidency, but no Speakers or Senate presidents pro tempore. Furthermore, because of the Twenty-fifth Amendment, the order of succession probably will never extend beyond the office of vice president.

The Twenty-fifth Amendment was ratified in 1967, after President Dwight Eisenhower's heart attack and President Kennedy's assassination focused attention on the issue of presidential succession and disability. The amendment authorizes the president to fill a vacancy in the office of vice president subject to majority confirmation by both houses of Congress. This procedure was first used in 1973, when President Nixon nominated Gerald Ford to replace Vice President Spiro Agnew, who resigned under accusation of criminal wrongdoing. When Nixon himself resigned in 1974, Ford moved up to the presidency and appointed former governor of New York Nelson Rockefeller to be the new vice president.

Franklin D. Roosevelt was elected to four terms. Because of the Twenty-second Amendment, the president is now limited to two terms.

Other provisions of the Twenty-fifth Amendment establish procedures for the vice president to become acting president should the president become disabled and incapable of performing the duties of the office. The president may declare disability by written notice to the Senate president pro tempore and the Speaker of the House. The vice president then becomes acting president until the president declares in writing the ability to resume the responsibilities of office. If the president is unable or unwilling to declare disability, the vice president can declare the president disabled in conjunction with a majority of the cabinet. Should the vice president/cabinet and president disagree on the question of the president's disability, Congress may declare the president disabled by two-thirds vote of each house.

The Vice Presidency

The Constitution gives the vice president two duties. The vice president is president of the Senate and votes in case of a tie. The vice president also becomes president of the United States if the office becomes vacant. For most of American history, however, the vice president was the forgotten person of Washington. In 1848, Daniel Webster, a prominent political figure of the time, rejected the vice presidential nomination of his party by saying "I do not propose to be buried until I am dead."[2] John Nance Garner, one of Franklin Roosevelt's vice presidents, once declared the job was not worth a "bucket of warm piss." Before the last half of the twentieth century, the vice president had no staff and few responsibilities. The vice president represented the nation at selected ceremonial occasions, such as the funeral of a foreign leader, but had no policy responsibilities.

Today, the vice presidency has become a more visible and important office. The death in office of President Franklin Roosevelt, Eisenhower's heart attack, Kennedy's assassination, Nixon's resignation, and the assassination attempt against Reagan all called attention to the possibility that the vice president could become president at any time. A contemporary president who kept the vice president uninformed and uninvolved in policy issues would be generally regarded as an irresponsible chief executive. Furthermore, the vice presidency has become the most common path to the office of the presidency, either through succession or election. Since 1950, five presidents (Harry Truman, Lyndon Johnson, Nixon, Ford, and the elder Bush) held office as vice president prior to becoming president. Men and women of stature are now willing to serve as vice president.

Walter Mondale, who served under President Carter, is regarded as the first modern vice president. Carter used Vice President Mondale as an advisor, troubleshooter, and emissary to interest groups and Congress. Since Mondale, every vice president has had an office in the White House, a sizable staff, and an open invitation to attend any meeting on the president's schedule.[3] Presidents have used their vice presidents to chair commissions, take on political opponents, serve as an emissary to Congress, and advise them on policy matters. Vice President Dick Cheney was such a powerful figure in the George W. Bush administration that some critics accused him of being co-president.[4] Bush saw himself as chairman of the board with Cheney as chief operating officer. Cheney developed great influence because he was detail-oriented and willing to assert himself. Many observers believe that Cheney was the architect of every significant policy initiative in the Bush administration, including the response to the terrorist attacks of 9/11, energy policy, the war in Iraq, judicial nominations, the budget, and tax policy.[5] Vice President Joe Biden has become an important advisor for President Obama, especially on foreign and defense policy issues, such as the war in Afghanistan. Biden also serves as the president's emissary to Congress, negotiating with both Republicans and Democrats, and as a messenger to foreign governments.[6]

Presidential Powers

The powers of the presidency have developed through the give-and-take of the political process. Although the Constitution outlines the powers to the office in Article II, many of the provisions are not clearly defined.[7] The ambiguity of Article II has enabled presidents to expand the limits of presidential power beyond the initial understanding of the authority granted to the office.[8]

Diplomatic Powers

Chief of state The official head of government.

The Constitution gives the president, as **chief of state** (the official head of government), broad diplomatic authority to conduct foreign relations. The president has the power to officially recognize the governments of other nations and to receive and appoint ambassadors. For example, the United States broke off diplomatic relations with China after the communist takeover in 1940. President Nixon later began the process of normalizing relations with the People's Republic of China as the legitimate government of mainland China. President Carter completed the process and the two nations exchanged ambassadors. The only constitutional limitation on the president's power of diplomatic recognition is that ambassadorial appointments must be approved by majority vote of the Senate.

The Constitution empowers the president to negotiate treaties with other nations, subject to a two-thirds vote of ratification by the Senate. Since 1789, the Senate has rejected only 21 of more than 1,500 treaties submitted to it, but that figure underestimates the Senate's role in the ratification process. Most treaties that lack sufficient support to pass the Senate are either withdrawn from consideration by the president or bottled up in committee. For example, the Law of the Sea Treaty, which is an international agreement governing the oceans, has languished in the Senate Foreign Relations Committee since 1982, even though it has been ratified by more than a hundred other nations. At least 85 treaties have been withdrawn because the Senate failed to act on them. The Senate may make its approval of a treaty conditional, depending on the acceptance of amendments, interpretations, understandings, or other reservations. The president and the other countries involved must then decide whether to accept the conditions, renegotiate the provisions, or abandon the treaty altogether.[9]

Executive agreement An international understanding between the president and foreign nations that does not require Senate ratification.

Presidents use executive agreements to expand their diplomatic authority beyond the treaty power. An **executive agreement** is an international understanding between the president and foreign nations that does not require Senate ratification. Although the Constitution says nothing about executive agreements, the Supreme Court has upheld their use based on the president's diplomatic and military powers. Executive agreements are more numerous than treaties. The United States is currently a party to nearly 900 treaties and more than 5,000 executive agreements.[10] Many executive agreements involve relatively routine matters, such as the exchange of postal service between nations. Congress has passed legislation authorizing the executive branch to make executive agreements with other countries in certain fields, such as agriculture, trade, and foreign aid. Some executive agreements also require congressional participation because they involve changes in American law.

Military Powers

The Constitution names the president commander-in-chief of the armed forces. As commander-in-chief, the president makes military policy, including decisions involving the use of force, operational strategy, and personnel. President Franklin Roosevelt, for example, chose the time and place of the Normandy invasion in World War II. Truman decided to drop the atomic bomb on Japan during World War II and fired General Douglas MacArthur for publicly disagreeing with the administration's war policy during the Korean conflict. Reagan ordered the marines to invade the Caribbean nation of Grenada and directed air strikes against Libya. The first President Bush sent American forces to the Persian Gulf to roll back the Iraqi invasion of Kuwait. Clinton dispatched American forces on peacekeeping missions to Somalia and Bosnia, ordered air strikes against Iraq, and directed the U.S. Air Force to conduct an air war to protect ethnic Albanian civilians from attack by Serbian forces in the Yugoslavian province of Kosovo. President George W. Bush ordered American forces to take military action against the Taliban government in Afghanistan and the al Qaeda terrorists that it sheltered. He also ordered the American military to overthrow the government of Saddam Hussein in Iraq. President Obama demanded the resignation of General McChrystal, the commander of U.S. forces in Afghanistan, after his remarks critical of Vice President Biden and other administration officials were quoted in *Rolling Stone* magazine.

Civilian supremacy of the armed forces The concept that the armed forces should be under the direct control of civilian authorities.

The president's role as commander-in-chief embodies the doctrine of **civilian supremacy of the armed forces,** which is the concept that the armed forces should be under the direct control of civilian authorities. The doctrine of civilian supremacy is based on the belief that military decisions should be weighed in light of political considerations. The concept of civilian supremacy also reflects the view that the preservation of representative democracy depends on keeping the military out of politics. In many nations, the armed forces are a powerful political force and military men sometimes seize the reigns of government from civilian authorities. The government of Burma (also known as Myanmar), for example, is a military government, headed by generals whose power depends on the support of the armed forces rather than the votes of the nation's people. In the United States, the president, a civilian, stands at the apex of the command structure of the armed forces. The government controls the military rather than the military controlling the government.

Presidents sometimes use their power as commander-in-chief as the basis for exercising authority beyond the scope of direct military action. After Japan bombed Pearl Harbor in 1941 and the United States entered World War II, President Franklin Roosevelt issued an executive order authorizing the military to relocate all persons of Japanese ancestry from the West Coast to inland war relocation centers. More than 120,000 persons were interned, including 70,000 native-born American citizens, and the U.S. Supreme Court upheld the constitutionality of the action.[11] After the terrorist attacks of September 11, 2001, President Bush exercised his authority as commander-in-chief to order the arrest and detention of persons suspected of involvement in terrorist activity.

Congress and the president have frequently quarreled over the relative authority of the legislative and executive branches to make military policy. Although the president is commander-in-chief, the Constitution grants Congress sole authority to declare war. The last war in which the United States participated that was declared, however, was World War II. The president has initiated all subsequent American military actions, including the Korean War and the War in Vietnam, without benefit of a congressional declaration of war. Although Congress authorized the use of force in Iraq before the U.S. invasion, it did not issue a declaration of war.

In 1973 during the War in Vietnam, Congress responded to what it considered an infringement of its constitutional power to declare war by enacting

President Bush ordered that enemy combatants in the war on terror be held at Guantánamo Bay, Cuba.

War Powers Act A law limiting the president's ability to commit American armed forces to combat abroad without consultation with Congress and congressional approval.

the **War Powers Act,** which is a law limiting the president's ability to commit American armed forces to combat abroad without consultation with Congress and congressional approval.[12] The measure includes a number of important provisions:

- The president should consult with Congress "in every possible instance" before introducing American forces into situations where hostilities would be likely.
- The president must make detailed, periodic reports on the necessity and scope of the operation.
- American forces must be withdrawn after 60 days of the first reports of fighting (with a 30-day grace period to ensure safe withdrawal) unless Congress declares war or votes to authorize the presence of the American forces.
- Congress can order the withdrawal of American forces by majority vote of both houses at any time, even before the 60-day period has expired. This last provision was apparently invalidated by a 1983 Supreme Court decision that found similar measures unconstitutional.[13]

The War Powers Act has been a source of conflict between the president and Congress. The two branches of government have often disagreed about the measure's consultation requirement. Whereas some members of Congress believe that the law requires that the president discuss the use of force with Congress and seek advice, presidents have generally only informed congressional leaders in advance of pending military actions. Chief executives have also tried to avoid the application of the War Powers Act by denying that the military actions they ordered fell under the scope of the law.

In practice, the War Powers Act is probably a less effective check on the president's military power than is public opinion. If a president's actions enjoy broad public support, as was the case with the first war in the Persian Gulf, Congress is unlikely to order a withdrawal of American forces. In contrast, the risk of adverse public reaction may deter some military initiatives or cut short others. In 1983, for example, Reagan ordered American forces withdrawn from Beirut, Lebanon, well in advance of a War Powers Act cut-off date after several hundred marines were killed in a terrorist bombing. Perhaps more significantly, the ordered withdrawal came well in advance of the 1984 presidential election.

Professor Robert Kennedy believes that Congress has failed to provide a check and balance on the military power of the modern presidency. Even though the Constitution gives Congress broad authority, including the power to declare war, raise forces, and provide the funds for military operations, the legislative branch of government has largely abdicated its responsibility to check the war-making power with the chief executive. When presidents have chosen to act militarily, Congress has either endorsed the endeavor or acquiesced in the president's action. For example, Congress failed to assess the quality of intelligence supporting the Bush administration's erroneous claim that Iraq was developing weapons of mass destruction (WMD) before giving the president enormous discretionary power to go to war.[14]

WHAT IS YOUR OPINION?

Is the president's authority as commander-in-chief too broad?

Inherent Powers

Inherent powers Those powers vested in the national government, particularly in the area of foreign and defense policy, which do not depend on any specific grant of authority by the Constitution, but rather exist because the United States is a sovereign nation.

Louisiana Purchase The acquisition from France of a vast expanse of land stretching from New Orleans north to the Dakotas.

Inherent powers are those powers vested in the national government, particularly in the area of foreign and defense policy, which do not depend on any specific grant of authority by the Constitution, but rather exist because the United States is a sovereign nation. Consider the **Louisiana Purchase,** which was the acquisition from France of a vast expanse of land stretching from New Orleans north to the Dakotas. President Thomas Jefferson justified his decision to acquire the territory on the basis of inherent powers because the Constitution says nothing about purchasing land from another country. Similarly, Lincoln claimed extraordinary powers to defend the Union during the Civil War on the basis of inherent powers. President George W. Bush used the doctrine of inherent powers to justify the use of military tribunals to try enemy combatants captured in the war on terror, designate U.S. citizens as enemy combatants, send terror suspects to countries that practice torture, and authorize eavesdropping on American citizens by the National Security Agency (NSA).[15]

Presidential assertions of inherent powers are almost invariably controversial because they involve an expansion of government authority and presidential power not authorized by the Constitution. Critics of the Louisiana Purchase, for example, called Jefferson a hypocrite because he had long argued that the authority of the national government was limited to powers clearly delegated by the Constitution. Critics accused President George W. Bush of not just exceeding his power but violating the Constitution. They challenged his actions in Congress and the courts.

Judicial Powers

The president plays a role in judicial policymaking. The president nominates all federal judges pending majority-vote confirmation by the Senate. The Senate usually approves nominees, but not without scrutiny, especially for Supreme Court selections. The Senate rejected two consecutive Supreme Court appointments by President Nixon before confirming his third choice. Similarly, the Senate rejected Reagan's nomination of Robert Bork to the Supreme Court.

The power of appointment gives a president the opportunity to shape the policy direction of the judicial branch of American government, especially a president who serves two terms. During his eight years in office, President Clinton appointed 374 federal judges; George W. Bush named more than 300 judges during his presidency. Clinton and Bush each appointed two Supreme Court justices.[16] During his first two years in office, President Obama made two Supreme Court appointments, Sonia Sotomayor and Elena Kagan.

Pardon An executive action that frees an accused or convicted person from all penalties for an offense.

The Constitution empowers the president to grant pardons and reprieves. A **pardon** is an executive action that frees an accused or convicted person from all

Reprieve An executive action that delays punishment for a crime.

penalties for an offense. A **reprieve** is an executive action that delays punishment for a crime. With some exceptions, such as President Ford's pardon of former President Nixon, most presidential pardons and reprieves are not controversial.

Executive Powers

Chief executive The head of the executive branch of government.

Executive order A directive issued by the president to an administrative agency or executive department.

The president is the nation's **chief executive,** that is, the head of the executive branch of government. The Constitution grants the president authority to require written reports of department heads and enjoins the president to "take care that laws be faithfully executed." As head of the executive branch of government, presidents can issue executive orders to manage the federal bureaucracy. An **executive order** is a directive issued by the president to an administrative agency or executive department. Although the Constitution says nothing about executive orders, the courts have upheld their use based on law, custom, and the president's authority as head of the executive branch.

Presidents have used executive orders to enact important (and sometimes controversial) policies. President Lincoln, for example, used an executive order to issue the Emancipation Proclamation. President Eisenhower issued an executive order to send federal troops into Little Rock, Arkansas, in 1957 to protect African American youngsters attempting to attend a whites-only public high school. President Obama

In 1957, President Dwight Eisenhower issued an executive order to send the National Guard into Little Rock, Arkansas, to protect African American youngsters attempting to attend a whites-only public high school.

issued executive orders to prohibit the use of torture in the interrogation of prisoners held in the war on terror and order the closure of the detention camp at Guantánamo Bay, Cuba.

The president's power to issue executive orders is not unlimited. Presidents may only issue executive orders that fall within the scope of their constitutional powers and legal authority.[17] In 1952, for example, during the Korean War, the U.S. Supreme Court overturned an executive order by President Truman to seize the nation's steel mills and head off a strike that would have disrupted steel production and hurt the war effort. The Court declared that the president lacked the legal authority to seize private property and that the president's power as commander-in-chief did not extend to labor disputes.[18] Congress can also overturn an executive order legislatively. Because the president would likely veto a measure reversing an executive order, Congress would need to vote not only to repeal the order but then to vote again by a two-thirds margin to override the veto.

Legislative Powers

Finally, the Constitution grants the president certain tools for shaping the legislative agenda. From time to time, it says, the president shall "give to Congress information of the state of the Union, and recommend to their consideration such measures as he shall judge necessary and expedient." Traditionally, the president makes a State of the Union address each January before a joint session of Congress and a national television audience. The speech gives the president the opportunity to raise issues and frame the terms of their discussion. Although the State of the Union address allows the president the opportunity to present himself or herself as the nation's chief legislator, it may also create unrealistic public expectations. In practice, Congress approves only 43 percent of the policy initiatives included in the average State of the Union speech, either in whole or in part.[19]

The president can use veto power to shape the content of legislation. The Constitution empowers the president to return measures to Congress along with objections. A vetoed measure can become law only if both the House and Senate vote to override by a two-thirds margin. The veto is a powerful weapon. Since 1789, Congress has overridden only 7 percent of presidential vetoes.[20] Political scientists consider the actual use of the veto a sign of weakness rather than strength because influential presidents can usually prevent passage of measures they oppose by threatening a veto.[21]

Presidential signing statement A pronouncement issued by the president at the time a bill passed by Congress is signed into law.

A **presidential signing statement** is a pronouncement issued by the president at the time a bill passed by Congress is signed into law. Presidents historically have used signing statements to comment on the bill they are signing, score political points, identify areas of disagreement with the measure, and discuss its implementation. President George W. Bush went further than any of his predecessors in using signing statements to expand the powers of his office. Bush signing statements identified more than 800 provisions in 500 measures that he signed into law that he considered unconstitutional limitations on his authority as president, and asserted his intention to ignore the provisions or treat them as advisory. Bush declared, for example, that legislative provisions that establish qualifications for executive branch officials were advisory rather than mandatory because he believed that they unconstitutionally restricted the presidential power of appointment. He asserted his intention to withhold information from Congress and rejected legislative provisions that he believed would limit his power as commander-in-chief. Much to the unhappiness of congressional leaders, especially Democrats, President Obama has continued the use of signing statements to challenge the constitutionality of certain legislative provisions and to declare his intention not to enforce them.[22]

Presidential signing statements are controversial. Political scientist Phillip J. Cooper believes that signing statements are a vehicle for revising legislation without issuing a veto, which is subject to congressional override, and that violates the letter and spirit of the Constitution.[23] The American Bar Association (ABA) declares that the recent use of signing statements is "contrary to the rule of law and our constitutional system of separation of powers" because the Constitution requires that the president sign legislation or veto it in its entirety.[24] In contrast, law professors Curtis A. Bradley and Eric A. Posner argue that signing statements are legal and useful because they provide a way for the president to disclose his or her views about the meaning and constitutionality of legislation.[25]

The Development of the Modern Presidency

In the nineteenth century, the presidency was an institution on the periphery of national politics. Early presidents generally confined their initiatives to foreign affairs, leaving domestic policymaking to Congress. The nation's first chief executives did not negotiate with Congress over policy and rarely used the veto.[26] Three of the first six presidents vetoed no legislation at all. In contrast, President Reagan cast 78 vetoes in eight years; the first President Bush issued 46 vetoes in four years.[27]

Jefferson, Andrew Jackson, and Lincoln expanded the powers of the presidency. Jefferson, as we previously noted, negotiated the Louisiana Purchase in 1803. Jackson, who served as president from 1829 to 1837, vetoed legislation on policy grounds, issuing more vetoes than the first six presidents combined. He asserted his legislative leadership by asking the voters to elect different people to Congress who would be more supportive of his policy priorities. President Lincoln, who held office during the Civil War from 1861 to 1865, used his authority as commander-in-chief to justify taking actions without congressional authorization. He declared martial law, ordered the blockade of southern ports, freed slaves in the rebelling territories, stationed troops in the South, and spent money not appropriated by Congress.

In the twentieth century, the president's role grew as the role of the national government grew. Early twentieth-century presidents were more active than their nineteenth-century counterparts, especially Theodore Roosevelt and Woodrow Wilson. In foreign affairs, Roosevelt, who held office from 1901 to 1909, sent the navy halfway around the globe and schemed to acquire the Panama Canal. Domestically, Roosevelt attacked monopolies, crusaded for conservation, and lobbied legislation through Congress. Wilson, who served from 1913 through 1921, was the first president to recommend a comprehensive legislative program to Congress. He was also the first president to conduct face-to-face diplomacy with foreign leaders, negotiating the League of Nations Treaty. In addition, he made direct policy appeals to the public, campaigning across the nation in support of the ratification of the League of Nations Treaty.[28]

Franklin D. Roosevelt, who served from 1933 to 1945, is widely regarded as the first modern president. FDR, as President Franklin Roosevelt was known, was first elected during the Great Depression and held office through most of World War II. Both of these events served to increase the scope of federal government activities and centralize policymaking in the executive branch. The Depression generated public pressure for the national government to act to revive the nation's economy, help those Americans hardest hit by the collapse, and regulate business and industry in an effort to prevent recurrence of the disaster. FDR responded with the **New Deal,** the legislative package of reform measures proposed by President Franklin Roosevelt for dealing with the Great Depression that involved the federal government more deeply in the nation's economy than ever before.

New Deal The legislative package of reform measures proposed by President Franklin Roosevelt for dealing with the Great Depression.

World War II also increased presidential power. Presidential power grows during wartime and other periods of international tension because the president has the opportunity to exercise authority as commander-in-chief. The general public and Congress tend to defer to presidential leadership in the face of international threats. Also, Congress delegates extraordinary powers to the chief executive to expedite the war effort. During World War II, Congress ceded so many powers to the presidency that scholars often refer to FDR during the war years as a constitutional dictator.

The modern president is a chief executive who is active and visible. The modern president often takes the lead in legislative policymaking. Roosevelt offered the New Deal, Truman presented a set of policy initiatives labeled the Fair Deal, Kennedy put forward the New Frontier, and Lyndon Johnson proposed the Great Society. President Reagan called for major tax and spending cuts. Although the chief executive was not the original author of most of these legislative proposals, the president focused attention on them and lobbied successfully for their enactment. The modern president uses executive orders to act without congressional approval. Truman issued executive orders to racially integrate the armed forces and commit troops to combat in Korea. Reagan used an executive order to direct agencies in the executive branch of government to balance the costs and benefits of proposed regulations before putting them into effect. The modern president has the support of an expanded presidential bureaucracy. The White House staff is now both larger and more involved in the policymaking process than it was before the Franklin Roosevelt administration. The modern presidency has become personalized. The media, especially television, have made the president the central figure of American government. No other political actor in the nation is better positioned to influence the policymaking process.[29]

Political scientists Matthew Crenson and Benjamin Ginsberg identify a number of factors contributing to the president's emergence as the chief actor in the political system. First, the United States has become a world power, thrusting foreign policy and national security issues to the top of the policy agenda. These are areas where the president's constitutional powers are stronger than they are in domestic policy. Second, the modern presidential selection process favors the election of assertive individuals with big ideas rather than individuals chosen primarily for their loyalty to their political parties. Finally, the executive branch of the national government has grown, giving the president the means to expand influence.[30]

The Organization of the Presidency

The development of the modern presidency has been accompanied by a significant growth in the size and power of the presidential bureaucracy, that is, the White House staff and the Executive Office of the President. Early chief executives wrote their own speeches and even answered their own mail. They had only a few aides, whom they paid from their own funds. Jefferson, for example, had one messenger and one secretary. Eventually, Congress appropriated money for the president to hire aides and advisors and the presidential bureaucracy grew. The administration of George W. Bush employed 1,703 executive staff members, including 403 White House staffers, 477 employees working for the Office of Management and Budget, 62 National Security Council employees, and 25 staffers working for the Council of Economic Advisers.[31]

White House Staff

The White House is the administrative center of the executive branch of American national government. It contains 135 offices, including a chief of staff, press secretary, speechwriter, appointments secretary, national security advisor, legislative liaison, counselor to the president, and various special assistants. The White House staff gives the president advice on policy issues and politics, screens key appointments, manages press relations, organizes the president's workday, and ensures that the president's wishes are carried out.[32]

The president selects the White House staff without Senate confirmation. As with most presidential appointees (the exceptions are federal judges and regulatory commissioners), White House staff members serve at the president's pleasure, which means that the president can remove them at will. Political and personal loyalty is usually the foremost criterion the president uses in selecting a staff. When George W. Bush became president, he recruited his staff primarily from his father's administration, his own administration as governor of Texas, and his presidential campaign. Andrew H. Card, Jr., the White House chief of staff during Bush's first term, was Secretary of Transportation in the administration of George H. W. Bush. Similarly, President Obama selected Rahm Emanuel, a member of Congress from Chicago, Illinois, Obama's political home base, to serve as his chief of staff. When Emanuel resigned to run for mayor of Chicago, Obama replaced him with former Secretary of Commerce Bill Daley, another Chicago politician.

Although every presidential candidate promises to keep politics out of the White House, the White House staff focuses on politics as if the last presidential campaign had never ended or the next one had already begun. Bush appointed Karl Rove, his campaign manager in the 2000 presidential election, to coordinate policy development in the White House in order to integrate policy with political strategy.[33]

Similarly, Obama named David Axelrod, the chief political strategist of his 2008 election campaign, as a senior advisor in the White House. When healthcare reform appeared stalled in Congress, Obama turned to David Plouffe, his former campaign manager, to work as a political advisor to the White House.

Professor Stephen J. Farnsworth worries that the intense focus on marketing the president undermines sound policy development. Instead of educating the public about the issues of the day and discussing the tradeoffs that come with making policy choices, presidents concentrate on winning the 24-hour news cycle. By playing to the camera, presidents focus on short-term payoffs that can sometimes cause long-term problems for the country. They oversimplify problems, downplay the cost of solutions, and make promises they often cannot keep.[34]

Executive Office of the President

Executive Office of the President The group of White House offices and agencies that develop and implement the president's policies and programs.

The **Executive Office of the President** is the group of White House offices and agencies that develop and implement the president's policies and programs. Congress established the Executive Office in 1939 after a special investigative commission concluded that the responsibilities of the presidency were too great for any one individual. "The president needs help," the commission said. The legislation creating the Executive Office allowed the president to create and disband components without further congressional authorization. Consequently, the size and composition of the Executive Office changes somewhat from administration to administration. The Executive Office had 11 units during the Obama administration.[35]

National Security Council (NSC) The agency in the Executive Office of the President that advises the chief executive on matters involving national security.

The major agencies of the Executive Office are the National Security Council (NSC), Office of Management and Budget (OMB), Council of Economic Advisers (CEA), Council on Environmental Quality, Office of Science and Technology Policy, Office of the United States Trade Representative, and Domestic Policy Council. The first two are the most prominent. The **National Security Council (NSC)** is an agency in the Executive Office of the President that advises the chief executive on matters involving national security. It includes the president, vice president, secretaries of state and defense, and other officials the president may choose to include, such as the national security advisor, the head of the Joint Chiefs of Staff, and the director of the Central Intelligence Agency (CIA). Although the NSC was created primarily as an advisory body, in some administrations it has participated in policy formulation and implementation.

Office of Management and Budget (OMB) An agency that assists the president in preparing the budget.

The **Office of Management and Budget (OMB)** is an agency that assists the president in preparing the budget. The OMB is an important instrument of presidential control of the executive branch. It assists the president in preparing the annual budget to be submitted to Congress, screens bills drawn up by executive branch departments and agencies to ensure that they do not conflict with the president's policy goals, monitors expenditures by executive branch departments, and evaluates regulations proposed by executive agencies. As with other federal agencies, most OMB personnel below the level of executive management are career employees chosen through a merit hiring system. The president appoints the director of the OMB and other top-level agency officials pending Senate confirmation.

Around the World — The Russian Presidency

Russia elects a president by popular vote to serve a four-year term. If no candidate receives a majority in the first election, the two candidates with the most votes face each other in a runoff election a month later. Russia has no vice president. If the office of president becomes vacant, the prime minister becomes acting president for 90 days and a special election is held.

The Russian Constitution makes the president the most powerful office in the government. The president appoints the prime minister to head the cabinet and administer the government. The Duma, the lower chamber of the Russian parliament, must approve the president's choice for prime minister. If the Duma rejects the president's nominee three times, the president must either select a different prime minister or call for new parliamentary elections. The Duma can also vote "no confidence" in the prime minister. Upon a second vote of no confidence, the president must either replace the prime minister or call for new parliamentary elections. In practice, the Duma is unlikely to reject a prime minister or vote no confidence because its members would have to face reelection, whereas the president would not.

The Russian president plays a role in the legislative process somewhat similar to the role played by the American president in the legislative process. Measures passed by the parliament go to the president who may sign or reject them. If the president rejects a bill, the parliament may vote to override the rejection by a two-thirds vote of both chambers. If parliament cannot override the rejection, it creates a conciliation commission along with representatives of the president in an attempt to reach compromise. The president also has the power to make laws by decree. The Russian Constitution declares that presidential decrees may not contradict existing laws. Furthermore, the parliament can rescind a presidential decree by majority vote.

The presidency was the dominant institution of Russian politics during the administration of Vladimir Putin, who served from 2000 through 2008. Putin crushed his opponents and consolidated power. President Putin won reelection in 2004 with 72 percent of the vote against several unknown opponents because the government disqualified, on the basis of technicalities, every candidate with enough support to seriously challenge Putin. The government also took control of the news media to ensure that Putin received flattering coverage while political opponents were either ignored or attacked. News editors who dared to exercise their independence were beaten or prosecuted for criticizing the government.*

The importance of the presidency in Russian government is now in decline, ironically, because of Putin. The Russian Constitution limits the president to two four-year terms. Rather than attempting to change the Constitution to remain as president, Putin promoted the candidacy of a handpicked successor, Dmitry Medvedev, a relatively unknown bureaucrat who won easily over token opposition. Putin then became prime minister. Many observers believed that the Russian system will evolve to resemble most parliamentary systems in which the real power is in the hands of the prime minister, whereas the president is the ceremonial head of state without significant decision-making influence.†

QUESTIONS

1. Is there a difference between the Russian president ruling by decree and the American president issuing executive orders?
2. Could a future American political leader execute a maneuver similar to that accomplished by Putin to stay in power despite the end of a second term in the White House?
3. What keeps the American president from taking actions similar to those taken by Putin?

* M. Steven Fish, *Democracy Derailed in Russia: The Failure of Open Politics* (New York: Cambridge University Press, 2005), pp. 30–80.

† Clifford J. Levy, "With Tight Grip on Ballot, Putin Is Forcing Foes Out," *New York Times*, October 14, 2007, available at www.nytimes.com.

Presidential Bureaucracy and Presidential Influence

The presidential bureaucracy is essential to the effective operation of the modern presidency. An efficient, knowledgeable White House staff is an important element of presidential power. Members of the staff not only advise the president on policy issues and political strategy, but they often act on behalf of the president in dealing with Congress, members of the executive branch bureaucracy, and the media. An efficient, professional staff can further the president's policy goals and create an image of presidential competence. A White House staff that is accessible to members of Congress and maintains open lines of communication will help promote the president's policies while keeping the president well enough informed to prevent surprises.[36] In contrast, an inefficient staff makes the president appear incompetent. During the first two years of the Clinton administration, a disorganized White House staff contributed to the president's penchant for putting off decisions and failing to stick to decisions once they were made. As a result, Clinton developed a reputation for indecision and inconsistency, a reputation that contributed to substantial Democratic losses in the 1994 congressional elections. Leon Panetta, whom Clinton named chief of staff in 1994, brought discipline to the White House, enabling the president to rehabilitate his image and win reelection in 1996.[37]

The tendency of newly elected presidents to select old friends and campaign aides who are unfamiliar with Washington politics to serve in the White House often undermines the president's effectiveness. The problem is made worse if the president is also inexperienced in national politics. Healthcare reform was the foremost goal of Clinton's first term in office. The president appointed a task force chaired by Hillary Clinton to hold hearings and develop a plan to be presented to Congress. Because the task force lacked broad-based representation and conducted much of its work in secret, it failed to develop a plan with enough support to pass Congress and the effort became an embarrassing failure.

The challenge for a president is to develop a leadership style that neither delegates too little or too much. Because a president's time, energy, and abilities are limited, the president must delegate some tasks. To be effective, a president must know which tasks can be delegated and which cannot. The president must also have a strong enough grasp of policy issues to recognize when the proposals of subordinates make sense and when they do not.[38]

Weapons of mass destruction (WMD) Nuclear, chemical, and biological weapons that are designed to inflict widespread military and civilian casualties.

President George W. Bush's decision to go to war against Iraq was based on a flawed decision-making process within the administration. Bush ordered the overthrow of Saddam Hussein because he believed that Iraq possessed **weapons of mass destruction (WMD),** which are nuclear, chemical, and biological weapons that are designed to inflict widespread military and civilian casualties. The United States had to act, the president declared, before Iraq gave WMD to terrorist groups that could then use them against the United States or its allies. The conclusion that Iraq possessed WMD, however, was wrong. The administration not only misinterpreted some of the intelligence it received but also attempted to influence the nature of that intelligence to support its position. It sought evidence to prove that Iraq possessed WMD while ignoring information to the contrary. Furthermore, Bush decided to go

President George W. Bush's decision to go to war against Iraq was based on a flawed decision-making process within the administration.

to war without deliberating with his advisors as to whether war was necessary. The White House shut out Secretary of State Colin Powell from the decision-making process and ignored warnings from the military.[39]

Theories of Presidential Leadership

Political scientists take different approaches to describing and explaining presidential leadership.

Presidential Character

Political scientist James David Barber believes that a president's performance in office depends on personality traits formed primarily during childhood, adolescence, and early adulthood. Barber classifies personality along two dimensions. The first dimension involves the amount of energy an individual brings to the office. Active presidents throw themselves into their work, immersing themselves in the details of the office, whereas passive presidents devote relatively little energy and effort to the job. The second dimension to Barber's personality classification scheme involves the president's attitude toward the job. Positive presidents enjoy their work. They have an optimistic, positive attitude. Negative presidents feel burdened by the weight of the office. They tend to be pessimists.

Barber uses these two dimensions to create four general types of presidential personalities: active-positive, active-negative, passive-positive, and passive-negative. According to Barber, the best type of personality for a president is active-positive. This president is self-confident, optimistic, flexible, and enjoys the job. Active-positive presidents use their office as an "engine of power." Franklin Roosevelt, for example, was a supremely self-confident man who set out to master the intricacies of his office. He was a flexible, skillful politician who truly enjoyed being president. Barber also classifies Truman, Kennedy, Ford, Carter, George H. W. Bush, and Clinton as active-positive presidents.

Barber believes that the most dangerous chief executive is the active-negative president. This type of president puts great energy into work, but derives little pleasure from it. Barber says that active-negative presidents suffer from low self-esteem and tend to view political disputes in terms of personal success or failure. They are pessimistic, driven, and compulsive. Active-negative presidents tend to overreact to crises and continue failed policies long after it is clear they do not work because to admit error would be to lose control. Barber classifies Richard Nixon as active-negative because he was personally insecure, combative, tough, and vindictive. He was a loner who saw himself as a righteous leader besieged by enemies. Barber says that Herbert Hoover and Lyndon Johnson were active-negative presidents as well.

Barber lists two other categories of presidential personalities: passive-positive and passive-negative. Barber identifies Eisenhower as a passive-negative president, that is, one who is involved in politics out of a sense of duty. The passive-negative president avoids conflict and uncertainty and just plain dislikes politics. Finally, the passive-positive president is indecisive and superficially optimistic. This president tends to react rather than initiate. Barber classifies Reagan as passive-positive.[40]

Scholars identify a number of weaknesses with Barber's classification scheme. It is not always clear in which category a president should be placed. President Reagan can be labeled *passive* because of his inattentiveness and willingness to allow aides to carry a good deal of his workload. Nonetheless, the Reagan administration had a substantial impact on public policy, taking important initiatives in a wide range of policy areas. Is that the record of a passive president? Some critics complain that Barber's categories are so broad that they are of little help in differentiating among presidents. Barber puts Presidents Franklin Roosevelt, Carter, and the first President Bush in the same category—active-positive. How helpful is Barber's classification scheme if such different presidents fit in the same category? Historians typically rank Franklin Roosevelt among the best of the nation's presidents, whereas Carter and George H. W. Bush are considered only average. Finally, Barber's scheme ignores the political climate in which a president serves. The success or failure of a chief executive depends on a number of factors in addition to the president's personality traits.[41]

Leadership Style

Some scholars believe that the president's ability to effectively use the powers of the office depends on leadership style. Political scientist Fred I. Greenstein takes this approach by identifying six qualities associated with effective presidential leadership.

- **Communication skills.** Greenstein identifies Franklin Roosevelt, Kennedy, Reagan, Clinton, and Obama as effective public communicators. In contrast, he says that both George H. W. Bush and George W. Bush were relatively ineffective communicators because they were prone to misstatements.
- **Organizational capacity.** According to Greenstein, Truman, Eisenhower, Kennedy, Ford, and the elder Bush had strong organizational skills, but Lyndon Johnson, Carter, and Clinton did not. Greenstein says that George W. Bush failed to create an organizational structure that would facilitate an effective decision-making process.
- **Political skills.** Greenstein says that Johnson was a skilled, determined political operator; in contrast, Carter had a poor reputation among fellow policymakers. Greenstein gives both George W. Bush and Obama high marks for being politically skilled.
- **Vision.** Eisenhower, Kennedy, Nixon, Reagan, and George W. Bush all had a capacity to inspire support for achieving a set of overarching goals. In the meantime, Greenstein believes that George H. W. Bush was weak in this area.
- **Cognitive skill.** Both Carter and Nixon were skilled at understanding complex issues by reducing them to their component parts. Truman and Reagan were less skilled. Greenstein faults George W. Bush for a management style that relied too heavily on his staff to provide the backup for his policy actions. That approach may have led him to error when evaluating the question of WMD in Iraq. Obama's cognitive style is marked by "intelligence, analytic detachment, and a capacity for complex thinking."[42]
- **Emotional intelligence.** Greenstein says that Eisenhower, Ford, and both George H. W. and George W. Bush were emotionally mature individuals who were able to focus on their responsibilities without distraction. In contrast, he labels Johnson, Nixon, Carter, and Clinton as "emotionally handicapped." Greenstein says that Obama is cool under pressure, but has difficulty conveying sympathy or compassion.[43]

The Power to Persuade

Political scientist Richard Neustadt believes that presidents succeed or fail based on their skills as political bargainers and coalition builders. Although the presidency is regarded as a powerful office, Neustadt points out that presidents lack authority to command public officials other than the members of the White House staff, some executive branch appointees, and the members of the armed forces. Under America's constitutional system, the members of Congress, federal judges, and state officials do not take orders from the president. Because presidents cannot command, they must convince other political actors to cooperate with them voluntarily. The power of the president, Neustadt says, is the power to persuade.

Persuasion is often difficult for the president, Neustadt notes, because the interests of other political actors do not always coincide with the concerns of the chief executive. Whereas presidents worry about their reelection by voters nationwide, members of Congress focus on winning reelection from their districts or states, whose voters are often more concerned about local problems than national issues. Former Republican Congressman Tom DeLay once gave this explanation for opposing Republican President George H. W. Bush on a particular issue: "I represent the Twenty-second District [of Texas], not George Bush."[44]

The president cannot necessarily even count on the cooperation of the federal bureaucracy. Except for the White House staff, the heads of Executive Office agencies, and members of the cabinet, all of whom serve at the pleasure of the president, the loyalty of federal employees lies with their jobs in their own niches in the bureaucracy, not with the president's program. A chief executive who wants to reorganize the bureaucracy or cut federal programs invariably meets resistance from within the executive branch.

Consequently, Neustadt says, presidents must bargain with other political actors and groups to try to win their cooperation. Presidents are brokers and consensus builders. In this task, presidents have several assets: they have a number of appointments to make; they prepare the budget; they can help supporters raise money for reelection; and they can appeal to others on the basis of the national interest or party

President Obama outlines his strategy for fighting the war in Afghanistan in a speech to the cadets at West Point.

loyalty. To use these assets to their fullest, presidents must understand the dynamics of political power.[45]

Neustadt's approach can be used to explain the presidencies of Lyndon Johnson and Jimmy Carter. President Johnson learned as Majority Leader in the Senate how to build a political coalition to get legislation passed. In the White House, he put those skills to work and won passage for his legislative program, which was known as the **Great Society.** In contrast, President Carter never mastered the mechanics of political power. He ran for president as an outsider, someone who was not tainted by Washington politics. Once in office, Carter appeared standoffish. He had won the Democratic nomination and been elected president without having to bargain with the Washington establishment, and he thought he could govern without bargaining. He was wrong. Politics involves negotiation, give-and-take, and compromise. Carter never understood that and consequently failed to accomplish many of his goals.

Great Society The legislative program of President Lyndon Johnson.

Going Public

Political scientist Samuel Kernell updates the Neustadt approach. Kernell believes that contemporary presidents often must adopt a media-oriented strategy, which he calls "going public," if they are to achieve their goals in today's political environment. In 1981, for example, President Reagan went on television to ask citizens to contact their representatives in Congress to support his economic program. The public responded and Congress approved the president's budget proposals.

Media-oriented approaches are not new—Franklin Roosevelt was famous for his fireside chats on the radio—but the strategy has become more common. Modern communications and transportation technologies make going public relatively easy. Furthermore, today's presidential selection process tends to favor people who are better at public appeals than political bargaining.[46] Contemporary presidents advance their policy agendas through speeches, public appearances, political travel, and targeted outreach aimed at particular groups of voters.[47]

The George W. Bush administration illustrates both the strengths and limitations of the going public strategy. Bush effectively used the going public strategy to bring the threat of Iraq to the top of the public agenda and put pressure on Congress to approve his war policy. Public concern over Iraq made Democrats in Congress wary about opposing the president on Iraq because Saddam Hussein was a highly unpopular figure. Many Democrats believed that Saddam actually did have WMD and was a threat to national security. Opposing Bush on Iraq could open them to the charge that they were soft on national defense. Nearly 40 percent of House Democrats and 57 percent of Senate Democrats joined nearly every Republican member of Congress in voting in favor of the resolution to authorize the use of military force in Iraq.[48] In contrast, President Bush's effort to reform **Social Security** by allowing workers to invest some of their payroll tax payments in private accounts was a failure. Although President Bush succeeded in elevating the issue to the top of the policy agenda, he failed to convince a majority of the public that private retirement accounts were a good idea. As a result, it was easy for Democrats in Congress

Social Security A federal pension and disability insurance program funded through a payroll tax on workers and their employers.

to oppose the president on the issue and difficult for Republicans to support him. Going public is an ineffective strategy if the president's proposed initiative lacks public support.[49]

Unilateral Tools of Presidential Power

A number of political scientists believe that presidents have tools they can use to influence the policymaking process that do not depend on political bargaining or persuasion. These "power tools," as Professor Christopher S. Kelley calls them, allow the president to take unilateral action without direct congressional authorization or approval.[50] They include the following:

- **Executive orders.** They enable the president to adopt a number of important policies without legislative approval.
- **Executive agreements.** They give the president an important tool for conducting foreign relations that does not require Senate ratification.[51]
- **Presidential signing statements.** They enable the president to define the scope and limitations of legislation passed by Congress.
- **Recess appointments.** By filling vacancies during a period of time when Congress is in recess, the president can make temporary appointments without the advice and consent of the Senate.[52]

Presidential Popularity

Presidential popularity influences presidential power. A president's personal popularity affects the president's position as a political broker and the president's ability to appeal to the public for policy support. A president who is politically popular can offer more benefits and inducements to other political actors for their cooperation than can an unpopular chief executive. Campaign help from a popular president is more valuable and support for legislative proposals is more effective. Similarly, a popular president can claim to speak for the national interest with greater credibility.

A popular president enjoys more success with Congress than an unpopular chief executive. After September 11, 2001, President Bush's approval rating soared. Republican members of Congress eagerly associated themselves with the president, whereas Democrats were reluctant to oppose him. Congress passed legislation embodying the president's policy proposals dealing with taxes, the budget, government reorganization, Iraq, and the war on terror. By 2006, however, Bush's approval rating had fallen below 40 percent and members of Congress from both parties found it easy to oppose the president's legislative agenda. Democrats attacked Bush at every opportunity while Republican members of Congress boasted of their independence from the White House.

Honeymoon effect The tendency of a president to enjoy a high level of public support during the early stages of an administration.

New presidents are popular, at least for a few months. The tendency of a president to enjoy a high level of public support during the early stages of an administration is known as the **honeymoon effect.** In the first few months of a new administration, opposition political leaders and the press usually reserve judgment, waiting for the president to act before offering comment. Most voters, regardless of party affiliation, tell polltakers that they approve of the president's performance in office because they have heard few complaints on which to base disapproval. President Obama enjoyed an initial approval rating of 68 percent; he averaged 63 percent during his first three months in office. Those figures were about average for recent presidents—higher than comparable numbers for Clinton, Reagan, and both Bushes, but lower than the ratings for Kennedy, Nixon, and Carter. Once an administration begins making controversial policy decisions, however, opposition leaders and the media begin to criticize the president's performance. As the criticism mounts, the president's popularity invariably falls, especially among people who identify with the opposition political party. Obama's honeymoon lasted about seven months, which is average for recent presidents. After beginning his presidency with approval ratings in the 60 percent range, Obama's popularity fell below 55 percent by late summer 2009. Obama's honeymoon was longer than that enjoyed by George W. Bush and Clinton, but shorter than the honeymoons of Richard Nixon and George H. W. Bush.[53]

Presidential approval responds to events. In domestic policy matters, presidential popularity rises with good news and falls with bad news, especially news concerning the economy. Although President Reagan was called the "Teflon President"—regardless of what went wrong, no blame stuck to him—he was an unpopular president during the recession of 1982. Only when the economy began to recover did Reagan's popular standing again exceed the 50 percent approval mark. President Clinton got off to such a slow start that the Democratic Party lost control of both houses of Congress in the 1994 midterm elections. Subsequently, a strong economy helped the president recover in the polls and win reelection in 1996 by a comfortable margin.

Rally effect The tendency of the general public to express support for the incumbent president during a time of international threat.

Presidential popularity rises dramatically during times of international crisis because of the **rally effect,** which is the tendency of the general public to express support for the incumbent president during a time of international threat. Political scientist John Mueller defines the rally effect as "being associated with an event which (1) is international and (2) involves the United States and particularly the president directly." Mueller says that the event must be "specific, dramatic, and sharply focused."[54] Mueller found that the "public seems to react to both 'good' and 'bad' international events in about the same way"—with a burst of heightened presidential approval.[55] For example, President George W. Bush's standing in the polls soared after September 11, 2001. The percentage of Americans who told survey researchers that they approved of Bush's performance in office leaped from 51 percent in early September to 90 percent later in the month.[56] Bush's popularity level also jumped when the United States invaded Iraq and then again when Saddam Hussein was captured.

The appearance and size of a rally effect depends on how the crisis is presented to the public in terms of media coverage, comments from opposition political leaders, and statements from the White House.[57] When the nation appears threatened from abroad, the political criticism that generally accompanies presidential action is muted. The White House is able to get its interpretation of events before the public because opposition political leaders do not want to be accused of undermining the president during an international crisis. The public tends to support the president because the only messages it hears about the president's handling of the crisis are positive messages, usually conveyed by the White House itself or the president's allies in Congress.[58] Even though September 11, 2001, was a national disaster, President Bush's approval rating soared because no one publicly raised questions about the administration's failure to foresee or prevent the terrorist attack, at least not initially. Instead, the media were filled with images of the president comforting the families of the victims and declaring that the United States would punish the people responsible for the attack.[59]

The public responds differently to a domestic crisis than it does to an international crisis. Whereas opposition political leaders and the press typically withhold judgment in an international crisis, they are quick to criticize if something goes wrong domestically. Consider the reaction to Hurricane Katrina and its impact on President Bush's standing in the polls. Within days of the hurricane's coming ashore, opposition political leaders and the news media were blasting the Bush administration for inadequately responding to the disaster. Between late August and October 2005, the president's popularity rating fell by 5 percentage points.[60]

A rally effect usually has only a short-term impact on presidential popularity. According to a study conducted by the Gallup organization, a president's approval rating reverts to previous levels within seven months of an international crisis unless other factors intervene, such as changing economic conditions.[61] At the beginning of an international crisis, the president enjoys near unanimous support from members of the president's political party and strong support from independents and members of the other party. As the political climate returns to normal, the press and opposition party leaders begin voicing criticism, initially about domestic policy matters and eventually about foreign affairs as well. Although members of the president's party usually continue to support the incumbent, members of the other party and independents begin to register their displeasure with the president's performance and the president's overall standing in the polls falls.[62]

Most presidents leave office less popular than they were when they first took office. New presidents are popular because of the honeymoon effect. Over time, presidents lose support because negative events and controversial decisions generate criticism that undermines their support, especially among independents and people who identify with the opposition party. Even though presidents enjoy successes as well as suffer failures, presidential approval ratings trend downward over time because negative news has a greater psychological impact than positive news. Economic downturns hurt a president's standing in the polls more than economic upswings help the president's approval ratings.[63]

The Presidency in Context

Many political scientists attempt to explain the role of the presidency in the policymaking process by focusing on contextual factors, such as the international environment, the state of the nation's economy, and the party balance in Congress.[64]

Some international developments can expand presidential power while other international developments can weaken the president. An international crisis, such as the terrorist attacks of September 11, 2001, can enhance the president's opportunity to exert policymaking influence as members of Congress of both parties turn to the president for leadership and the president's popularity soars. Presidential power grows during wartime as well because a military conflict provides the president with the opportunity to exercise authority as commander-in-chief. The other branches of government generally defer to executive leadership for fear of impeding the war effort or being accused of failing to support the troops. If a war drags on, however, and grows unpopular, it can undermine a president's political standing.

The party balance in Congress has a major impact on the ability of presidents to achieve their goals. Presidents are more effective when their party controls Congress because congressional leaders work with the White House to enact the president's priorities into law and to derail legislation the president opposes. For example, President Obama benefited from lopsided Democratic majorities in both the U.S. House and Senate during his first two years in office. Congress passed and Obama signed healthcare reform, financial regulatory reform, and a major economic stimulus package. In contrast, presidents are far more likely to issue veto threats and to veto legislation when the opposition controls Congress.[65] Congress is also more likely to

GETTING INVOLVED

Why Do They Run?

Have you ever wondered why people seek political office? Do they want personal power? Do they hope to accomplish policy objectives? Are they motivated by a desire to serve the community?

Investigate the answers to these questions by interviewing an elected official in your area. Keep in mind that most public officials are busy, so local judges, school board members, community college trustees, and city council members may prove more accessible. Call or e-mail the official's office to introduce yourself and request 15 minutes or so for an interview, either on the phone or in person. Before you conduct the interview, learn as much as you can about the office and the official so you can make the most of the opportunity. Study the questions you want to ask so you will be able to speak in a conversational tone of voice. Begin the interview by thanking the official for his or her time. Explain that you will report to your class on what you learn. The following questions can serve as a guideline for your interview.

- Is this the first elected office you have held? (If not, ask what other posts the official has held.)
- Why did you decide to seek this office?
- About how many hours a week do you spend on the job?
- What do you like most about your position in local government?
- What do you like least about your position?
- Are you glad you sought this office and won? Why or why not?

Once you have completed the interview, thank the official again for his or her time. You will also want to write the official a thank-you letter for taking time to chat with you. Prepare a short oral report for your class on the interview, including your impressions of the official and whether you are interested in running for office yourself.

investigate the executive branch during periods of divided government than times when the same party controls the executive and legislative branches.[66]

The economy is the most important single factor affecting presidential success. Presidential popularity is closely tied to economic performance. The public blames the president for hard times and rewards the president for good times. Whereas a weak economy led to the defeat of President George H. W. Bush in 1992, a strong economy helped President Clinton win reelection in 1996. A president also benefits from a strong economy because economic growth generates tax revenue that can be used to finance government programs or fund tax cuts. In contrast, a weak economy forces the president and Congress to cut spending, increase taxes, or borrow to balance the budget.

WHAT WE HAVE LEARNED

1. **How does the Constitution define the office of the presidency?**

   The Constitution declares that the president must be at least 35 years of age, a natural-born American citizen, and a resident of the United States for at least 14 years. The Constitution declares that no president can be elected to more than two four-year terms. The House has the authority to impeach a president by majority vote, with the Senate deciding by a two-thirds vote whether to remove the president from office. The vice president succeeds a president who is removed, resigns, or dies in office. After the vice president, the line of succession passes to the Speaker of the House, president pro tempore of the Senate, secretary of state, and through the cabinet. The vice president presides in the Senate and votes in case of a tie. In recent administrations, the vice president has been given an important role as a presidential advisor.

2. **What are the diplomatic, military, inherent, judicial, executive, and legislative powers of the presidency?**

   The president, as chief of state, has broad diplomatic authority to conduct foreign relations. Presidents have the power of diplomatic recognition and they negotiate treaties and executive agreements with other nations. The former are subject to Senate confirmation by a two-thirds vote; the latter are not. The president is commander-in-chief of the armed forces. During the Vietnam War, Congress responded to what it considered an infringement of its constitutional power to declare war by enacting the War Powers Act. The act has generally been an ineffective check on presidential war-making powers. The president is able to take some actions, such as making the Louisiana Purchase, because of inherent powers. These powers are vested in the national government, particularly in the area of foreign and defense policy, and do not depend on any specific grant of authority by the Constitution, but rather exist because the United States is a sovereign nation. The president nominates all federal judges pending majority-vote confirmation by the Senate and has the authority to grant pardons and reprieves. The president is the chief executive, that is, the head of the executive branch of government. As chief executive, the president is empowered to issue executive orders. Presidents have used executive orders to enact important policies, such as Lincoln using an executive order to issue the Emancipation Proclamation. The Constitution gives the president some tools for influencing the legislative process including the veto. Presidents also issue signing statements to comment on the bills they are signing, score political points, identify areas of disagreement with the measure, and discuss its implementation. Recent presidents have used signing statements to identify provisions that they considered unconstitutional limitations on their authority as president that they intend to ignore or treat as advisory.

3. **What factors contributed to the development of the modern presidency?**

   Since the nineteenth century, the presidency has moved from the periphery of national politics to its center. Presidential power grows during times of crises, such as wars and economic depressions, because they increase public pressure for the government to act. The Great Depression served to increase the scope of federal government activities and centralize policymaking in the executive branch. Presidential power also grows during wartime and other periods of international tension because the president has the opportunity to exercise authority as commander-in-chief. Political scientists identify three factors responsible for the modern presidency: (1) the United States has emerged as a world power, (2) the presidential selection process favors individuals with big ideas, and (3) the executive branch of government has grown.

4. **How is the office of the presidency organized to assist the chief executive in carrying out the duties of the office?**

   The development of the modern presidency has been accompanied by a significant growth in the size and power of the presidential bureaucracy. The White House staff, which is chosen without need of Senate confirmation, gives the president advice on policy issues and politics, screens key appointments, manages press relations, organizes the president's workday, and ensures that the president's wishes are carried out. The Executive Office of the President is the group of White House offices and agencies that develop and implement the president's policies and programs. It includes the OMB, NSC, and CEA. An efficient, professional staff can further the president's policy goals and create an image of presidential competence. An inefficient staff makes the president appear incompetent.

5. **How do various political scientists approach the concept of presidential power?**

   Political scientists take different approaches to describing and explaining presidential leadership. Barber believes that a president's performance in office depends on personality traits formed primarily during childhood, adolescence, and early adulthood. Barber classifies personality along two dimensions—the amount of energy an individual brings to the office and the president's attitude toward the job. Greenstein identifies six qualities associated with effective presidential leadership: communication skills, organizational skills, political skills, vision, cognitive skill, and emotional intelligence. Neustadt believes that presidents succeed or fail based on their skills as political bargainers and coalition builders. The power of the president, he says, is the power to persuade. Kernell contends that contemporary presidents often must adopt a media-oriented strategy, which he calls "going public," if they are to achieve their goals in today's political environment. A number of political scientists point out that presidents have tools they can use to influence the policymaking process that do not depend on political bargaining or persuasion. These unilateral tools of presidential power include executive orders, executive agreements, presidential signing statements, and recess appointments.

6. **What factors affect presidential popularity?**

   Popular presidents are more influential than unpopular presidents. The tendency of a president to enjoy a high level of public support during the early stages of an administration is known as the honeymoon effect. Once a new president begins making policy decisions, opposition leaders and the media begin to criticize the performance and the president's popularity falls. In domestic policy matters, presidential popularity rises with good news and falls with bad news, especially news concerning the economy. Presidential popularity rises dramatically during times of international crisis because of the rally effect.

7. **How does the political context affect the ability of a president to influence the policymaking process?**
   Many political scientists attempt to explain the role of the presidency in the policymaking process by focusing on contextual factors, such as the international environment, the state of the nation's economy, and the party balance in Congress. Presidential power grows during wartime and when the economy is strong. Presidents are also in a stronger position when their party controls Congress than when the opposition party controls Congress.

KEY TERMS

articles of impeachment
chief executive
chief of state
civilian supremacy of the armed forces
executive agreement
Executive Office of the President
executive order
Great Society
honeymoon effect
impeachment
inherent powers
lame duck
Louisiana Purchase
National Security Council (NSC)
New Deal
Office of Management and Budget (OMB)
pardon
presidential signing statement
rally effect
Reconstruction
reprieve
Social Security
War Powers Act
weapons of mass destruction (WMD)

NOTES

1. Jeffrey K. Tulis, "Impeachment in the Constitutional Order," in Joseph M. Bessette and Jeffrey K. Tulis, eds., *The Constitutional Presidency* (Baltimore, MD: Johns Hopkins Press, 2009), p. 235.
2. Quoted in Michael Nelson, "Choosing the Vice President," *PS: Political Science and Politics*, Fall 1988, p. 859.
3. Jack Lecholt, *The Vice Presidency in Foreign Policy: From Mondale to Cheney* (El Paso, TX: LFB Scholarly Publishing, 2009), pp. 277–278.
4. Jody C. Baumgartner, *The American Vice Presidency Reconsidered* (Westport, CT: Praeger, 2006), p. 133.
5. Joel K. Goldstein, "The Rising Power of the Modern Vice Presidency," *Presidential Studies Quarterly* 38 (September 2008): 374–389.
6. Helene Cooper, "As the Ground Shifts, Biden Plays a Bigger Role," *New York Times*, December 11, 2010, available at www.nytimes.com.
7. Harold J. Krent, *Presidential Powers* (New York: New York University Press, 2005), pp. 215–216.
8. Ryan J. Barilleaux, "Venture Constitutionalism and the Enlargement of the Presidency," in Christopher S. Kelley, *Executing the Constitution: Putting the President Back into the Constitution* (Albany, NY: State University of New York, 2006), pp. 40–42.
9. "Learning About the Senate: Treaties," available at www.senate.gov.
10. Ibid.
11. *Korematsu v. United States*, 323 U.S. 214 (1944).
12. Public Law 93-148 (1973).
13. *Immigration and Naturalization Service (INS) v. Chadha*, 462 U.S. 919 (1983).
14. Robert Kennedy, *The Road to War: Congress' Historic Abdication of Responsibility* (New York: Praeger, 2010), pp. 132–134.

15. Louis Fisher, "The Scope of Inherent Powers," in George C. Edwards and Desmond King, *The Polarized Presidency of George W. Bush* (New York: Oxford University Press, 2007), p. 53.
16. Administrative Office of the U.S. Courts, "Federal Judicial Vacancies," available at www.uscourts.gov.
17. Kenneth R. Mayer, "Executive Orders," in Bessette and Tulis, eds., *The Constitutional Presidency*, p. 155.
18. *Youngstown Sheet and Tube Co. v. Sawyer*, 343 U.S. 579 (1952).
19. Donna R. Hoffman and Alison D. Howard, *Addressing the State of the Union: The Evolution and Impact of the President's Big Speech* (Boulder, CO: Lynne Rienner, 2006), p. 194.
20. Harold W. Stanley and Richard G. Niemi, *Vital Statistics on American Politics 2007–2008* (Washington, DC: CQ Press, 2008), p. 268.
21. Rebecca A. Deen and Laura W. Arnold, "Veto Threats as a Policy Tool: When to Threaten?" *Presidential Studies Quarterly* 32 (March 2002): 30–45.
22. Charlie Savage, "Obama's Embrace of a Bush Tactic Riles Congress," *New York Times*, August 8, 2009, available at www.nytimes.com.
23. Phillip J. Cooper, "George W. Bush, Edgar Allan Poe, and the Use and Abuse of Presidential Signing Statements," *Presidential Studies Quarterly* 35 (September 2005): 515–532.
24. Robert Pear, "Legal Group Faults Bush for Ignoring Parts of Bills," *New York Times*, July 24, 2006, available at www.nytimes.com.
25. Curtis A. Bradley and Eric A. Posner, "Presidential Signing Statements and Executive Power," *Constitutional Commentary* 23 (Winter 2006): 307–364.
26. Nolan McCarty, "Presidential Vetoes in the Early Republic: Changing Constitutional Norms or Electoral Reform?" *Journal of Politics* 71 (April 2009): 369–384.
27. Michael A. Sollenberger, *Presidential Vetoes, 1789–Present: A Summary Overview*, Congressional Research Service, available at www.house.gov.
28. Kevan M. Yenerall, "Executing the Rhetorical Presidency: William Jefferson Clinton, George W. Bush, and the Contemporary Face of Presidential Power," in Kelly, *Executing the Constitution*, pp. 132–133.
29. Joseph A. Piker and John Anthony Maltese, *The Politics of the Presidency*, 7th ed. (Washington, DC: CQ Press, 2008), pp. 3–4.
30. Matthew Crenson and Benjamin Ginsberg, *Presidential Power: Unchecked and Unbalanced* (New York: W.W. Norton, 2007), pp. 11–13.
31. Lynn Ragsdale, *Vital Statistics on the Presidency: George Washington to George W. Bush*, 3rd ed. (Washington, DC: CQ Press, 2009), p. 327.
32. Bradley H. Patterson, *To Serve the President: Continuity and Innovation in the White House Staff* (Washington, DC: Brookings Institution Press, 2008), p. 103.
33. Matthew J. Dickinson, "The Executive Office of the President: The Paradox of Politicization," in Aberbach and Peterson, eds., *The Executive Branch*, p. 154.
34. Stephen J. Farnsworth, *Spinner in Chief: How Presidents Sell Their Policies and Themselves* (Boulder, CO: Paradigm Publishers, 2009), pp. 6–8, 130–144.
35. The Executive Office of the President, available at http://first.gov/Agencies/Federal/Executive/EOP.shtml.
36. Dickinson and Lebo, "Reexamining the Growth of the Institutional Presidency, 1940–2000," pp. 206–219.
37. Paul J. Quirk, "Presidential Competence," in Nelson, *The Presidency and the Political System*, 8th ed., pp. 156–158.
38. Ibid., pp. 179–189.
39. James P. Pfiffner, "Intelligence and Decision Making Before the War with Iraq," in Edwards and King, *The Polarized Presidency of George W. Bush*, p. 235.
40. James David Barber, *The Presidential Character*, 4th ed. (Englewood Cliffs, NJ: Prentice-Hall, 1992); "Carter and Reagan: Clues to Their Character," *U.S. News & World Report*, October 27, 1980, pp. 30–33.
41. Michael Nelson, "The Psychological Presidency," in Nelson, ed., *The Presidency and the Political System*, 8th ed., pp. 170–194.
42. Fred I. Greenstein, "The Leadership Style of Barack Obama: An Early Assessment," *The Forum* 7 (2009): Article 6.
43. Fred I. Greenstein, *The Presidential Difference: Leadership Style from FDR to Barack Obama*, 3rd ed. (Princeton, NJ: Princeton University Press, 2009).
44. Quoted in Kathy Lewis, "Republicans Join Sharp Opposition to New Tax Plans," *Houston Post*, October 20, 1990, p. A-1.
45. Richard E. Neustadt, *Presidential Power: The Politics of Leadership* (New York: Wiley, 1980).
46. Samuel Kernell, *Going Public: New Strategies of Presidential Leadership*, 3rd ed. (Washington, DC: Congressional Quarterly Press, 1997).
47. Joseph A. Pike and John Anthony Maltese, *The Politics of the Presidency*, 6th ed. (Washington, DC: CQ Press, 2004), p. 118.
48. Scott B. Blinder, "Going Public, Going to Baghdad: Presidential Agenda-Setting and the Electoral Connection in Congress," in Edwards and King, eds., *The Polarized Presidency of George W. Bush*, pp. 336–344.
49. Brandice Canes-Wrone, *Who Leads Whom? Presidents, Policy, and the Public* (Chicago, IL: University of Chicago Press, 2006), p. 185.
50. Kelly, *Executing the Constitution*, pp. 4–5.
51. Steven A. Shull, *Policy by Other Means: Alternative Adoption by Presidents* (College Station, TX: Texas A&M University Press, 2006), pp. 30–35.
52. Ryan C. Black, Anthony J. Madonna, Ryan J. Owens, and Michael S. Lynch, "Adding Recess Appointments to the President's 'Tool Chest' of Unilateral Powers," *Political Research Quarterly* 60 (December 2007): 645–654.

53. Jeffrey M. Jones, "Obama Honeymoon Continues; 7 Months Is Recent Average," July 3, 2009, available at www.gallup.com.
54. John E. Mueller, *War, Presidents, and Public Opinion* (New York: Wiley, 1973), p. 208.
55. Ibid., p. 212.
56. Jeffrey M. Jones, "Bush's High Approval Ratings Among Most Sustained for Presidents," *Gallup Poll Monthly*, November 2001, p. 32.
57. William D. Baker and John R. O'Neal, "Patriotism or Opinion Leadership? The Nature and Origins of the 'Rally 'round the Flag' Effect," *Journal of Conflict Resolution* 45 (October 2001): 661–687.
58. Richard Brody, "International Crises: A Rallying Point for the President?" *Public Opinion*, December/January 1984, pp. 41–43, 60.
59. Marc J. Hetherington and Michael Nelson, "Anatomy of a Rally Effect: George W. Bush and the War on Terrorism," *PS: Political Science and Politics*, January 2003, pp. 37–42.
60. Gallup Poll, "Presidential Job Approval in Depth," available at www.gallup.com.
61. *Gallup Poll Monthly*, June 1991, p. 27.
62. Frank Newport, "Bush Job Approval Update," Gallup News Service, July 29, 2002, available at www.gallup.com.
63. Stuart N. Soroka, "Good News and Bad News: Asymmetric Response to Economic Information," *Journal of Politics* 68 (May 2006): 372–385.
64. George C. Edwards III, *The Strategic President: Persuasion and Opportunity in Presidential Leadership* (Princeton, NJ: Princeton University Press, 2009), pp. 189–190.
65. Barbara Sinclair, "Leading and Competing: The President and the Polarized Congress," in Edwards and Davies, *Challenges for the American Presidency*, p. 96.
66. Douglas Kriner and Liam Schwartz, "Divided Government and Congressional Investigations," *Legislative Studies Quarterly* 33 (May 2008): 295–321.

Chapter 12

The Federal Bureaucracy

CHAPTER OUTLINE

Organization of the Bureaucracy
- Cabinet Departments
- Independent Executive Agencies
- Government Corporations
- Foundations and Institutes
- Independent Regulatory Commissions
- Quasi-Governmental Companies

Personnel

Rulemaking

Politics and Administration
- The President
- Congress
- Interest Groups
- Bureaucrats

Subgovernments and Issue Networks

What We Have Learned

WHAT WE WILL LEARN

After studying Chapter 12, students should be able to answer the following questions:

1. What are the major administrative structures of the executive branch of American national government?
2. What is the history of federal employee personnel policies?
3. What are the steps in the rulemaking process?
4. What perspectives and political resources does each of the following political actors have in the administrative process: the president, Congress, interest groups, and bureaucrats?
5. What approaches do political scientists take in explaining the administrative process?

Global warming The gradual warming of Earth's atmosphere, reportedly caused by the burning of fossil fuels and industrial pollutants.

Addressing the problem of climate change caused by global warming is one of the foremost goals of the Obama administration. **Global warming** is the gradual warming of Earth's atmosphere reportedly caused by the burning of fossil fuels and industrial pollutants. Many environmental scientists believe that climate change caused by global warming will inflict catastrophic harm to the planet. Rising sea levels caused by melting polar ice will inundate coastal areas, displacing millions of people. Climate change will negatively affect water supplies in many areas, increase the frequency of extreme weather events, and cause the extinction of many plants and animals adapted to the current climate.

Cap and trade An approach to pollution control in which the government sets a limit on the amount of emissions allowed (the cap) and then permits companies to buy and sell emissions allowances (the trade).

In 2009, Democratic Congressman Henry Waxman from California introduced the American Clean Energy and Security (ACES) Act.[1] The measure, which enjoyed the support of President Barack Obama and many environmental groups, would create a cap and trade system designed to reduce greenhouse gas emissions. **Cap and trade** is an approach to pollution control in which the government sets a limit on the amount of emissions allowed (the cap) and then permits companies to buy and sell emissions allowances (the trade). The goal is to steadily reduce emissions in an economically efficient fashion. Each company responsible for substantial emissions of greenhouse gases would have a limit on the amount of emissions it could emit in a year. The government would provide polluting firms with an emissions permit for each ton of carbon dioxide and other greenhouse gases released into the atmosphere. Over time, the government would shrink the total number of permits available, thus reducing pollution. The ACES Act requires a 17 percent reduction in emissions by 2020 and an 80 percent reduction by 2050.[2] Companies that are able to reduce their emissions more rapidly than required can sell their excess pollution permits to firms that are unable to meet their goals. Consequently, utilities, manufacturers, and other greenhouse gas producers have an economic incentive to reduce their emissions as rapidly as possible.

The ACES Act passed the House in 2009 but bogged down in the Senate. Some Senate Republicans opposed the measure because they are either skeptical that global warming exists or do not believe that it is the result of human activity. Other Republicans and many business interests argued that cap and trade is effectively a tax on energy that will harm the nation's economy and force companies to lay off workers. Some Senate Democrats opposed the measure as well because they represent states that are dependent on coal for electricity or heavy manufacturing for jobs and would thus be more negatively affected by the legislation than other parts of the country. The 2010 midterm election in which Republicans took over the House and made gains in the Senate ensured that the ACES Act would not pass Congress anytime soon, at least not in its original form.

Environmental Protection Agency (EPA) The federal agency responsible for enforcing the nation's environmental laws.

With climate change legislation bogged down in Congress, the Obama administration turned to the regulatory process to achieve its policy goals. In late 2009, the **Environmental Protection Agency (EPA),** which is the federal agency responsible for enforcing the nation's environmental laws, formally declared that greenhouse gases jeopardize the public health, thus paving the way for the eventual adoption of regulations designed to limit carbon dioxide emissions from refineries, chemical facilities, and power plants. The EPA acted under authority granted to it by Congress in the Clean Air Act, which was originally enacted in 1963. The Clean

Air Act requires the EPA to develop and enforce regulations to protect the public from exposure to contaminants that are known to be hazardous to human health. By declaring that greenhouse gases jeopardize the public health, the EPA was serving notice that it was preparing to adopt regulations requiring major companies to reduce their emissions or face penalties.[3]

Addressing global warming through the regulatory process offered some advantages to the Obama administration. First, it allowed the president to move forward on achieving his policy goals without waiting for Congress to pass legislation. Second, the EPA's action might prod business interests to compromise on legislation pending in Congress, preferring the cap and trade approach to controlling greenhouse gas emissions to regulations adopted by the EPA.

The Obama administration's efforts to address climate change introduce this chapter on the federal bureaucracy. The chapter begins by describing the major administrative units that comprise the executive branch of American national government. It then examines federal personnel policies. The chapter explains the rulemaking process and discusses the politics of administrative policymaking from the perspectives of various important political actors, including the president, Congress, interest groups, and federal bureaucrats. Finally, the chapter compares and contrasts the concepts of subgovernments and issue networks.

Many environmental scientists believe that climate change caused by global warming will cause catastrophic harm to the planet.

Organization of the Bureaucracy

The organization of the executive branch of American national government seems haphazard. The Constitution is silent about the organization of the executive branch other than discussing the selection, powers, and responsibilities of the president and vice president. The agencies and departments that make up the rest of the executive branch have been created by Congress and the president through the legislative process over the last 220 years of American history.

Cabinet Departments

Cabinet departments The major administrative units of the federal government that have responsibility for the conduct of a wide range of government operations.

The **cabinet departments** are the major administrative units of the federal government that have responsibility for the conduct of a wide range of government operations. The 15 cabinet departments (in the order of their creation) are as follows: State, Defense, Treasury, Justice, Interior, Agriculture, Commerce, Labor, Housing and Urban Development (HUD), Transportation, Energy, Health and Human Services, Education, Veterans' Affairs, and Homeland Security. The largest departments in terms of personnel are Defense and Veterans' Affairs. In 2008, the Department of Defense had 682,000 civilian employees; the Department of Veterans' Affairs employed 265,000 workers. In contrast, 4,210 employees worked for the Department of Education, the smallest department.[4] Each cabinet department includes a number of smaller administrative units with a variety of titles, such as bureau, agency, commission, administration, center, service, and institute. For example, the Department of Homeland Security includes Customs and Border Protection, Transportation Security Administration, Immigration and Customs Enforcement, U.S. Coast Guard, U.S. Secret Service, and Citizenship and Immigration Service.

With the exception of the head of the Justice Department, who is the attorney general, the people who lead the cabinet departments are called secretaries. The secretary of defense, for example, heads the Department of Defense. The secretary of the interior leads the Department of the Interior. The president appoints the heads of the cabinet departments and their chief assistants, who are called undersecretaries, deputy undersecretaries, and assistant secretaries, pending Senate confirmation.

Although the Senate confirms most presidential appointments, the approval process has grown increasingly time-consuming. The average time between presidential nomination and Senate confirmation for executive branch appointees has increased steadily from 2.35 months for the nominees of President John Kennedy[5] to nine months for individuals nominated by President George W. Bush.[6] More than 170 nominees remained unconfirmed two years after President Obama took office.[7] Confirmation delays have steadily increased, regardless of party control of Congress and the White House, because of bureaucratic red tape and because individual senators have increased the use of a parliamentary procedure called a hold that allows an individual senator to privately delay a vote on a nomination. Holds are used as bargaining chips to extract concessions from the administration on unrelated matters or to retaliate over other issues.[8] In early 2010, for example, Republican Senator Richard Shelby of Alabama placed a blanket hold on more than 70 administration nominees because he was concerned about a pair of government spending projects in his home state. The holds had nothing to do with the qualifications of the nominees.[9] If a senator puts a hold on a nominee and refuses to remove it, the Senate can vote on confirmation only if the Senate as a whole invokes cloture, which is a time-consuming procedure that requires 60 votes.

Presidents can sometimes avoid the confirmation process by making recess appointments when the Senate is in recess. According to the Constitution, recess appointees serve until the end of the next session of the Senate. Senator Shelby dropped most of his holds after President Obama made it known that he intended to use the 2010 Presidents' Day holiday to fill vacant positions with recess appointments.[10]

Presidents employ a number of criteria in selecting department heads. They look for knowledge, administrative ability, experience, loyalty, and congeniality. Some cabinet posts may be given to reward campaign assistance. Modern presidents want a cabinet that includes both men and women, and that reflects the ethnic and racial diversity of the United States. Presidents also seek individuals that fit the style and image of their department and that will be acceptable to the interest groups with which their department works most closely. The secretary of the treasury, for example, is typically someone with a background in banking or finance. The secretary of agriculture is often a farmer, usually from the Midwest.

Finding qualified men and women who are willing to lead cabinet departments is often a challenge. Some potential cabinet officials will not accept an appointment because the position does not pay as well as executive positions in private industry and it lacks job security. Also, some potential cabinet secretaries turn down appointments because they and their families do not want to go through a long and often intrusive confirmation process.

President's cabinet A body that includes the executive department heads and other senior officials chosen by the president, such as the U.S. ambassador to the United Nations.

The heads of the cabinet departments are all part of the **president's cabinet,** which is a body that includes the executive department heads and other senior officials chosen by the president, such as the U.S. ambassador to the United Nations. The policymaking role of the cabinet varies from president to president. President Dwight Eisenhower delegated considerable responsibilities to cabinet members. He met with his cabinet two or three times a month. In contrast, contemporary presidents seldom convene their cabinets, relying instead on the White House staff, the Executive Office of the President, and individual department heads. The cabinet includes too many people working from too many different perspectives to be an effective policymaking body. Furthermore, the White House usually grows to distrust the cabinet. Eventually, members of the White House staff begin to suspect that department heads have grown too attached to the programs their departments administer and too friendly with the interest groups most closely associated with their departments. Most presidents pay lip service to the cabinet, but seldom consult with it and never defer to its judgment. Instead, they rely on cabinet members to run their departments in the president's interest.[11]

The traditional image of the cabinet is that its members are primarily responsible for advising the president on policy formulation and leading their departments in policy implementation. In practice, however, most executive department heads do not do much of either activity. Presidents usually turn to smaller groups of aides, advisors, and selected department heads for policy advice. When President Obama

Inner cabinet The four cabinet officials—the secretary of state, secretary of defense, secretary of the treasury, and the attorney general—that are considered the most important because of the critical nature of the issues that their departments address.

Independent executive agencies Executive branch agencies that are not part of any of the 15 cabinet-level departments.

Peace Corps The agency that administers an American foreign aid program under which volunteers travel to developing nations to teach skills and help improve living standards.

National Aeronautics and Space Administration (NASA) The federal agency in charge of the space program.

Central Intelligence Agency (CIA) The federal agency that gathers and evaluates foreign intelligence information in the interest of national security.

considered his options for managing the war in Afghanistan, he assembled a diverse group of policy advisors, including political advisor David Axelrod, Secretary of State Hillary Clinton, Secretary of Defense Robert Gates, National Security Advisor General James Jones, White House Chief of Staff Rahm Emanuel, Central Intelligence Agency (CIA) Director Leon Panetta, and Vice President Joe Biden.[12] Four cabinet officials—the secretary of state, secretary of defense, secretary of the treasury, and the attorney general—are known as the **inner cabinet,** because of the importance of the policy issues their departments address.[13] Full cabinet meetings tend to become forums for presidential pep talks or show-and-tell sessions for cabinet members to discuss the latest developments in their departments. As for leading their departments, many secretaries soon learn that their departments are not easily led. Also, most department heads do not have the time to concentrate on the details of administration. They are too busy dealing with Congress, doing public relations work with their department's constituents, selling the president's program, and campaigning for the president's reelection.

Independent Executive Agencies

Congress and the president have created a number of executive branch agencies that are not part of any of the 15 cabinet-level departments, hence the designation **independent executive agencies.** The EPA is an independent executive agency headed by an individual administrator, as are the Peace Corps, National Aeronautics and Space Administration (NASA), Central Intelligence Agency (CIA), Social Security Administration (SSA), and the Small Business Administration (SBA). The Federal Election Commission (FEC) is an independent executive agency headed by a multimember commission. The president appoints both individual agency heads and board members, pending confirmation by the Senate. The heads of independent executive agencies report directly to the president and serve at the president's pleasure.

Independent executive agencies perform a range of administrative and regulatory activities. The **Peace Corps,** for example, is an agency that administers an American foreign aid program under which volunteers travel to developing nations to teach skills and help improve living standards. The **National Aeronautics and Space Administration (NASA)** is the federal agency in charge of the space program. The **Central Intelligence Agency (CIA)** is the federal agency that gathers and evaluates foreign intelligence information in the interest of national security. The **Social Security Administration (SSA)** is a federal agency that operates the Social Security system. The **Small Business Administration (SBA)** is a federal agency established to make loans to small businesses and assist them in obtaining government contracts. The **Federal Election Commission (FEC)** is the agency that enforces federal campaign finance laws.

Government Corporations

Government corporations are organizationally similar to private corporations except that the government owns them rather than stockholders. Their organizational rationale is that an agency that makes a product or provides a service should

Social Security Administration (SSA) The federal agency that operates the Social Security system.

Small Business Administration (SBA) The federal agency established to make loans to small businesses and assist them in obtaining government contracts.

Federal Election Commission (FEC) The agency that enforces federal campaign finance laws.

U.S. Postal Service (USPS) A government corporation responsible for mail service.

National Railroad Passenger Service Corporation (AMTRAK) A federal agency that operates inter-city passenger railway traffic.

Federal Deposit Insurance Corporation (FDIC) A federal agency established to insure depositors' accounts in banks and thrift institutions.

be run by methods similar to those used in the private sector. For example, the **U.S. Postal Service (USPS)** is a government corporation responsible for mail service. An 11-member board of governors appointed by the president to serve nine-year, overlapping terms leads the agency. The board names a postmaster general to manage the day-to-day operation of the service. In addition to the Postal Service, the list of government corporations includes the National Railroad Passenger Corporation (AMTRAK), Federal Deposit Insurance Corporation (FDIC), and the Tennessee Valley Authority (TVA). The **National Railroad Passenger Service Corporation (AMTRAK)** is a federal agency that operates intercity passenger railway traffic. The **Federal Deposit Insurance Corporation (FDIC)** is a federal agency established to insure depositors' accounts in banks and thrift institutions. The **Tennessee Valley Authority (TVA)** is a federal agency established to promote the development of the Tennessee River and its tributaries.

An important principle behind government corporations is that they should be self-financing, at least to a significant degree. Users cover the cost of operating the U.S. Postal Service (USPS) by purchasing stamps and paying service charges, at least in theory. The USPS is currently facing a funding crisis because people are using the Internet to send messages and pay bills rather than buying stamps to mail letters. In the meantime, the cost of operating the Postal Service continues to rise because of increasing personnel costs and the rising price of gasoline. The USPS is considering a number of options for balancing revenues and expenditures, including increasing the price of stamps, reducing its workforce, slowing mail delivery, and eliminating Saturday mail service.

AMTRAK is another government corporation that is not financially self-sufficient. AMTRAK requires a subsidy from Congress to keep its trains rolling. AMTRAK's critics argue that the agency should be forced to pay its own way or go out of business. If the demand for passenger rail is not sufficient to support AMTRAK's operation, then the service should end. In contrast, the defenders of AMTRAK believe that the agency provides an important service that should be continued. Furthermore, they point out that the government also subsidizes automobile transportation by building highways and air transportation by constructing airports.

WHAT IS YOUR OPINION?

If you were a member of Congress, would you vote in favor of government subsidies for AMTRAK?

Foundations and Institutes

Foundations and institutes administer grant programs to local governments, universities, nonprofit institutions, and individuals for research in the natural and social sciences or to promote the arts. These agencies include the National Science Foundation (NSF) and the National Endowment for the Arts (NEA). The **National Science Foundation (NSF)** is a federal agency established to encourage scientific advances and improvements in science education. The **National Endowment for**

Tennessee Valley Authority (TVA) A federal agency established to promote the development of the Tennessee River and its tributaries.

National Science Foundation (NSF) A federal agency established to encourage scientific advances and improvements in science education.

National Endowment for the Arts (NEA) A federal agency created to nurture cultural expression and promote appreciation of the arts.

Independent regulatory commission An agency outside the major executive departments that is charged with the regulation of important aspects of the economy.

Federal Trade Commission (FTC) An agency that regulates business competition, including enforcement of laws against monopolies and the protection of consumers from deceptive trade practices.

the Arts (NEA) is a federal agency created to nurture cultural expression and promote appreciation of the arts. Foundations and institutes are governed by multimember boards appointed by the president with Senate concurrence from lists of nominees submitted by various scientific and educational institutions.

Independent Regulatory Commissions

An **independent regulatory commission** is an agency outside the major executive departments that is charged with the regulation of important aspects of the economy. The **Federal Trade Commission (FTC),** for example, is an agency that regulates business competition, including enforcement of laws against monopolies and the protection of consumers from deceptive trade practices. The **Federal Communications Commission (FCC)** is an agency that regulates interstate and international radio, television, telephone, telegraph, and satellite communications, as well as licensing radio and television stations. The **Securities and Exchange Commission (SEC)** is an agency that regulates the sale of stocks and bonds as well as investment and holding companies. The **Equal Employment Opportunity Commission (EEOC)** is an agency that investigates and rules on charges of employment discrimination.

Congress has attempted to insulate independent regulatory commissions from direct political pressure, especially from the White House. These agencies are headed by boards of three to seven members who are appointed by the president with Senate approval. In contrast to cabinet members and the heads of other executive departments, the president cannot remove regulatory commissioners. Instead, they serve fixed, staggered terms ranging from 3 to 14 years. As a result, a new president must usually wait several years before having much impact on the composition of the boards. Furthermore, the law generally requires that no more than a bare majority of board members be from the same political party.

Congress has designed independent regulatory commissions to provide closer, more flexible regulation than Congress itself can offer through **statutory law,** which is law that is written by the legislature. Congress has delegated authority to these agencies to control various business practices using broad, general language. Congress has authorized the FTC, for example, to regulate advertising in the "public convenience, interest, or necessity." It has empowered the EEOC "to prevent any person from engaging in any unlawful employment practice."

Quasi-Governmental Companies

A **quasi-governmental company** is a private, profit-seeking corporation created by Congress to serve a public purpose. For example, Congress created the Federal National Mortgage Association (Fannie Mae) and Federal Home Loan Mortgage Corporation (Freddie Mac) to increase the availability of credit to home buyers. Fannie Mae and Freddie Mac are profit-making corporations run by 18-member boards of governors appointed by the president with Senate confirmation. They are exempt from state and federal taxation and enjoy a line of credit at the U.S.

Federal Communication Commission (FCC) An agency that regulates interstate and international radio, television, telephone, telegraph, and satellite communications, as well as licensing radio and television stations.

Securities and Exchange Commission (SEC) An agency that regulates the sale of stocks and bonds as well as investment and holding companies.

Equal Employment Opportunity Commission (EEOC) An agency that investigates and rules on charges of employment discrimination.

Statutory law Law that is written by a legislature, rather than constitutional law.

Quasi-governmental company A private, profit-seeking corporation created by Congress to serve a public purpose.

Treasury. Because of the perception that Congress would bail them out if they got in financial trouble, Fannie Mae and Freddie Mac pay lower interest rates than they would if they were strictly private enterprises. Lower rates benefit home buyers, some of whom would not be able to purchase a home at all without lower interest rates. The Export-Import Bank and the Government National Mortgage Association (Ginnie Mae) are other examples of quasi-governmental companies. The Export-Import Bank provides loan guarantees to foreign purchasers to enable them to acquire American goods. Ginnie Mae, meanwhile, purchases mortgages, pools them, and then issues mortgage-backed securities to investors.[14]

In 2008, Congress passed, and President George W. Bush signed, legislation to commit federal funds to Fannie Mae and Freddie Mac to ensure that they would not collapse under the weight of losses incurred in the housing foreclosure crisis. The federal government eventually took over the operation of Fannie Mae and Freddie Mac, at least temporarily, to prevent their financial collapse, which would have been catastrophic for the home mortgage industry. The action kept Fannie and Freddie in business, but potentially put taxpayers on the hook for billions of dollars in bad loans.

In 2008, Congress passed, and the president signed, legislation to commit federal funds to Fannie Mae and Freddie Mac to ensure that they would not collapse under the weight of losses incurred in the housing foreclosure crisis.

Personnel

The size of the federal civilian bureaucracy has grown dramatically since the early days of the nation. In 1800, only about 3,000 persons worked for the U.S. government. That figure grew to 95,000 by 1881 and half a million in 1925. Today, the federal bureaucracy is the largest civilian workforce in the western world, with 2.7 million civilian employees stationed in every state and city in the country and almost every nation in the world.[15]

As Figure 12.1 indicates, the number of federal civilian employees fell during the 1990s. Between 1991 and 2001, the federal payroll decreased from 3.1 million to 2.7 million, a decline of nearly 13 percent. After September 11, 2001, the number of federal employees inched up. Congress passed, and the president signed, legislation to make airport baggage screeners federal employees, adding thousands of people to the federal payroll. Employment in other federal agencies that deal with security issues, including the Border Patrol, increased as well. The post-9/11 surge in federal employment peaked in 2003. Thereafter, the size of the federal workforce declined before increasing once again in 2008.

Although the official size of the federal workforce is less than it was in the early 1990s, the actual number of people employed directly and indirectly by the federal

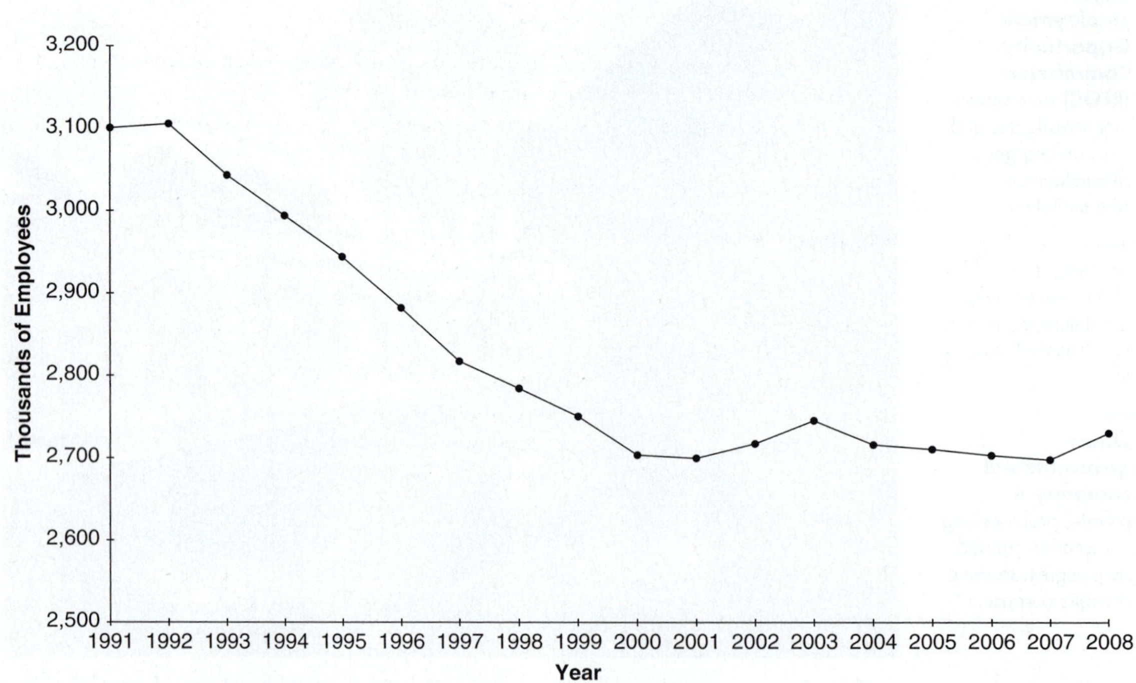

FIGURE 12.1 Federal Civilian Employment, 1991–2008.
Source: Office of Personnel Management.

GETTING INVOLVED

Working for Uncle Sam

More than 2.7 million people work for the federal government in every state and city in the country and in almost every nation in the world. Even small towns are home to federal employees working for the U.S. Postal Service and other agencies. Find a friend, relative, or neighbor who works for the federal government. Chat with him or her about federal employment, and take notes so you can discuss the conversation in class. Use the following questions to guide your discussion:

- For which department or agency do you work, and how long have you been a federal employee?
- What are the advantages and disadvantages of working for the federal government as opposed to a private employer?
- Have you enjoyed your job with the government? Why or why not?
- Do you believe that federal employee compensation should be based on job performance?
- Would you recommend a career in the federal workforce to a college student?

government has risen sharply over the same period of time. Political scientist Paul C. Light estimates that the true size of the federal civilian workforce is 14.6 million employees instead of the 2.7 million on the official payroll.[16] In addition to civilian employees working directly for the federal government, Light's figure includes millions of contract workers, state and local government employees working on federally funded programs, and federal grant beneficiaries at colleges and universities. The federal government pays their salaries, but their names do not appear on federal personnel rosters. Contract workers collect taxes, prepare budget documents, take notes at meetings, and perform hundreds of other governmental functions. The Department of Defense even hires private security guards to protect military bases in the United States.[17] Furthermore, Congress and the president rely on millions of state and local bureaucrats to administer federal programs, including Medicaid and the Supplemental Nutrition Assistance Program.

Employment practices in the early days of the nation emphasized character, professional qualifications, and political compatibility with the administration in office. Under President Andrew Jackson (1829–1837), political considerations became paramount. A new president would fire many of the employees of the previous administration and replace them with friends and supporters. To the victor belonged the spoils (that is, the prizes of victory), they said, and federal jobs were the spoils. The method of hiring government employees from among the friends, relatives, and supporters of elected officeholders was known as the **spoils system.**

Spoils system The method of hiring government employees from among the friends, relatives, and supporters of elected officeholders.

When a disgruntled office seeker assassinated President James Garfield in 1881, Congress passed, and the president signed, legislation to reform the federal hiring process. The measure, which was called the Pendleton Act, created a Civil Service Commission to establish a hiring system based on competitive examinations and protect federal workers from dismissal for political reasons. Initially, the civil service system covered only about 10 percent of federal jobs, but Congress gradually expanded coverage to include more than 90 percent of federal workers.[18] In 1939, Congress enacted another reform, the **Hatch Act,** which was a measure designed to restrict the political activities of federal employees to voting and the private expression of views. The rationale behind the law was to protect government workers from being forced by their superiors to work for particular candidates.

Hatch Act A measure designed to restrict the political activities of federal employees to voting and the private expression of views.

Although civil service ended the spoils system, it too became the target of criticism. Many observers charged that the civil service system was too inflexible to reward merit, punish poor performance, or transfer civil servants from one agency to another without having to scale a mountain of red tape. In 1978, Congress and the president responded to complaints against the civil service system by enacting a package of reforms. The legislation established a Senior Executive Service (SES) composed of approximately 8,000 top civil servants who would be eligible for substantial merit bonuses but who could be transferred, demoted, or fired more easily than other federal employees. The reform measure replaced the old Civil Service Commission with two new agencies: an Office of Personnel Management to manage the federal workforce and a Merit Systems Protection Board to hear employee grievances. The reforms also provided greater protection for **whistleblowers**—that is, workers who report wrongdoing or mismanagement—and streamlined procedures for dismissing incompetent employees.[19]

Whistleblowers Workers who report wrongdoing or mismanagement.

Congress and the president have given federal employees limited rights to organize. Federal workers won the right to form unions in 1912. Fifty years later, President John Kennedy signed an executive order giving federal workers the right to bargain collectively over a limited set of issues but not pay and benefits. **Collective bargaining** is a negotiation between an employer and a union representing employees over the terms and conditions of employment. The civil service reform legislation adopted in 1978 guaranteed federal employees the right to bargain collectively over issues other than pay and benefits, but it prohibited federal workers from striking. When the Professional Air Traffic Controllers Association (PATCO) called a strike in 1981, President Reagan fired every controller who failed to return to work. More than 11,000 air traffic controllers lost their jobs.

Collective bargaining A negotiation between an employer and a union representing employees over the terms and conditions of employment.

Democratic presidents typically have a more positive relationship with federal employee organizations than do Republican presidents. Labor unions in general, and public employee unions in particular, are allied with the Democratic Party, whereas the GOP has stronger ties to management. Democratic President Bill Clinton issued an executive order directing federal agencies to develop partnerships with the employee unions. Clinton justified the approach as a means to reform government by making it more efficient. In contrast, Republican President George W. Bush took an adversarial approach toward employee unions. He dissolved the partnership councils created during the Clinton administration and asked Congress to change personnel policies in light of the war on terror.[20]

When Congress created the Department of Homeland Security (DHS), it gave President George W. Bush authority to relax civil service rules to make it easier for the administration to hire, transfer, promote, cross-train, discipline, and fire employees in the new department without having to worry about union rules and civil service procedures. The president argued that the administration needed more flexibility over personnel than the old civil service system provided in order to create a modern workforce capable of responding to the threat of international terrorism. In particular, the administration wanted to base annual salary increases on performance tied to job evaluations rather than giving every employee an annual raise based on longevity. The Bush administration set out to create a pay-for-performance system, not just for the DHS, but for the whole federal government, that would replace the old general schedule system with its 15 GS levels and 10 steps within each level. The new system will make it easier for managers to reward good work and punish poor performance while making it more difficult for unions to intervene on behalf of their members.[21] Soon after taking office, however, President Obama signed an executive order ending the performance-based system for DHS, and Congress, then under Democratic control, passed legislation to return DHS employees to the previous pay system.[22]

WHAT IS YOUR OPINION?

Does a performance-based pay system improve employee performance or is it just a way for managers to reward their friends?

Rulemaking

Rule A legally binding regulation.

Rulemaking A regulatory process used by government agencies to enact legally binding regulations.

Regulatory negotiation A structured process by which representatives of the interests that would be substantially impacted by a rule work with government officials to negotiate agreement on the terms of the rule.

Independent regulatory commissions and many agencies in the executive branch have regulatory authority. When Congress passes regulatory legislation, it frequently delegates authority to the bureaucracy to make rules to implement the legislation. A **rule** is a legally binding regulation. **Rulemaking** is the regulatory process used by government agencies to enact legally binding regulations. The Clean Air Act requires that the EPA adopt rules to protect the public from exposure to contaminants that are known to be hazardous to human health. The Patient Protection and Affordable Care Act of 2010, the new healthcare reform law, requires various government agencies to adopt hundreds of rules to implement its provision. On average, federal agencies produce between four and five thousand rules a year.[23]

The rulemaking process begins with an agency giving advance notice that it is considering issuing a rule in a particular policy area. The agency publishes the text of the proposed rule in the *Federal Register* and allows a period of time at least 30 days long in which the public can comment on the proposed rule. Concerned parties, usually interest groups affected by the proposed rule, submit written comments or offer testimony at public hearings. When an agency officially adopts a rule, it is published in the *Code of Federal Regulations*.

Rules are sometimes the product of formal negotiations among government agencies and affected interest groups. **Regulatory negotiation** is a structured process by which representatives of the interests that would be substantially impacted by a rule work with government officials to negotiate agreement on the terms of the rule. The federal agency considering the adoption of a rule employs a neutral third party to identify interests that would be affected by the rule. The agency interviews representatives of the interest groups, determines what issues should be considered, assesses the willingness of interest groups to participate in a negotiation, and evaluates the likelihood that an agreement can be reached among the parties. The goal of a regulatory negotiation is to produce an agreement to which all parties will sign. The signed agreement stipulates that the parties participating in the negotiation will neither attempt to prevent the rule's adoption nor challenge the rule in court once it is adopted.[24]

The Office of Management and Budget (OMB) is a regular participant in the rulemaking process. In 1981, President Ronald Reagan issued an executive order requiring that any executive branch agency issuing a new rule with an economic impact of $100 million or more must prepare a cost-benefit analysis and submit it to the OMB for approval. A **cost-benefit analysis** is an evaluation of a proposed policy or regulation based on a comparison of its expected benefits and anticipated costs. Reagan's order applied to executive branch agencies such as the EPA, but not to independent regulatory commissions such as the FCC because they are not technically part of the executive branch. Although subsequent presidents have kept Reagan's requirement for a cost-benefit analysis of regulations, they have approached the issue from different perspectives. In Republican administrations, the OMB functions as an appeals court for business and trade groups worried about the impact of regulation on their activities. In contrast, environmentalists, consumer groups, and organized labor have more influence in the OMB review process during Democratic administrations.[25]

Cost-benefit analysis An evaluation of a proposed policy or regulation based on a comparison of its expected benefits and anticipated costs.

Congress exercises oversight of agency rules. Agencies must submit all proposed new rules to Congress, which has 60 days to overturn them through the legislative process, subject to a presidential veto and a possible override attempt. If Congress does not act within 60 days, the rule goes into effect.

Federal courts also play a role in the rulemaking process. Individuals and groups unhappy with agency decisions sometimes turn to the federal courts for relief. Courts hear challenges not just from business groups who believe that federal regulations have gone too far, but also from consumer and environmental groups who argue that regulations are not strict enough. In general, the courts have ruled that agency decisions must be supported by evidence and reasoned explanations and that the agencies must follow statutory requirements to give notice, hold hearings, and consult with parties outside the affected industries.[26]

Politics and Administration

Bureaucratic policymaking is a complex process involving the president, Congress, interest groups, and the bureaucracy itself. Each of the participants has a perspective and a set of political resources for achieving its goals.

The President

Presidents have several tools for influencing the bureaucracy. The president has the authority to name most of the top administrators in the bureaucracy, including department secretaries and undersecretaries, agency heads, and regulatory

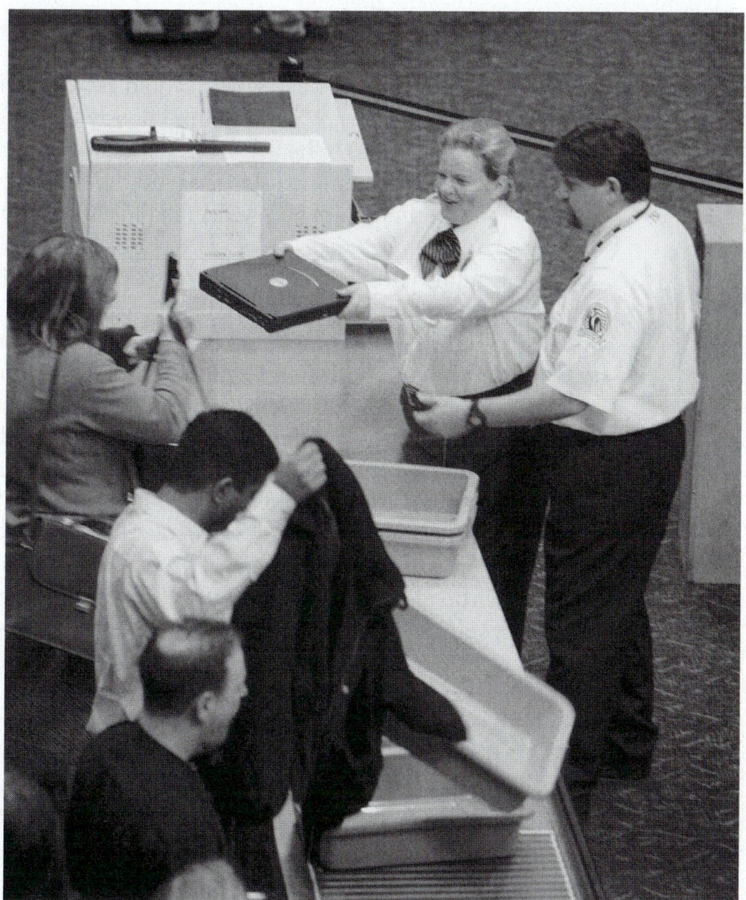

After September 11, 2001, Congress passed, and the president signed, legislation to make airport baggage screeners federal employees, adding thousands of people to the federal payroll.

commissioners. President George W. Bush ordered each executive branch agency to create a regulatory policy office run by a presidential appointee to ensure that rules and other actions taken by the agency conformed to the president's policy priorities.[27] Except for members of the independent regulatory commissions, presidents also have the power to dismiss their appointees. The president can use the OMB to evaluate agency performance and screen rules proposed by executive branch agencies. Furthermore, the president can ask Congress to reorganize the bureaucracy and propose agency budgets to Congress.

Consider the Reagan administration's efforts to reduce the regulatory activities of such agencies as the EPA, EEOC, Occupational Safety and Health Administration (OSHA), and the Office of Surface Mining. President Reagan believed that many government regulations were excessive, particularly in the areas of environmental protection, consumer rights, and workplace safety. The Reagan White House carefully screened the presidential appointees to head these agencies to ensure they were business-oriented conservatives who would be loyal to the president. For example, Reagan chose an attorney who had previously defended corporations against antidiscrimination lawsuits to head the EEOC. Reagan selected an anti-environmentalist to run the EPA. Furthermore, Reagan used the SES to transfer or demote career civil servants whom the White House deemed insufficiently supportive of the president's policy goals.[28]

Reagan also attempted to limit regulatory activities by asking Congress to cut agency budgets and reduce their personnel. At the president's urging, Congress reduced total EPA funding by 24 percent in 1982 alone. Between 1980 and 1983, expenditures for air pollution regulation and monitoring fell by 42 percent and the number of personnel authorized for clean air activities declined by 31 percent.[29]

Finally, the Reagan administration used the OMB to prevent the adoption of rules by executive branch agencies that the White House considered burdensome to industry. In 1984, for example, the OMB forced the EPA to ease proposed pollution regulations for diesel vehicles.[30] Between 1981 and 1985, the OMB forced agencies to modify or withdraw 19 percent of proposed rules. Furthermore, that figure underestimated the real impact of the OMB because agencies often revised rules to make them acceptable to the White House before submitting them for OMB review.[31]

Reagan's efforts to reduce regulatory activities enjoyed mixed success. In the short run, regulatory enforcement levels in the agencies Reagan targeted declined. The EPA's air quality monitoring fell by 41 percent in 1982 while its pollution abatement activities declined by 69 percent.[32] Food and Drug Administration (FDA) seizures of improperly manufactured food and drugs fell by 54 percent under Reagan.[33] Similarly, FTC reduced its enforcement activities by about 50 percent.[34]

In at least two agencies, however—the EEOC and the EPA—Reagan's impact on regulatory enforcement proved short-lived, evaporating even before the end of Reagan's first term in office. The Reagan appointees heading the agencies were highly controversial and were eventually forced to resign amid allegations of improper or even illegal conduct. Their replacements were experienced bureaucrats who were sympathetic with the mission of the regulatory agencies they were appointed to head. Furthermore, Congress responded to the public controversy surrounding the EEOC and the EPA by conducting investigations and restoring budget cuts.[35]

The experience of the Reagan administration demonstrates that a determined president has sufficient power to have an impact on bureaucratic policymaking. Through the use of his appointive powers, the OMB, and his authority to propose budgets to Congress, Reagan succeeded in reducing the regulatory activities of a number of targeted agencies. To a considerable degree, however, the president's success at influencing the bureaucracy depends on the role of other political actors, including Congress, interest groups, and agency administrators. Reagan failed to achieve all of his regulatory goals because he faced a hostile environment in that the Democratic Party controlled the House of Representatives. Labor unions, environmental organizations, and consumer groups were able to delay and eventually defeat many of Reagan's regulatory reforms because they enjoyed the support of Democratic allies in the House. In contrast, President George W. Bush, whose regulatory policy goals were similar to those of President Reagan, succeeded at modifying the impact of federal regulation on business interests because his political party controlled both the House and Senate during most of his first six years in office. The EPA, OSHA, and other regulatory agencies sharply reduced their enforcement activities between 2001 and 2006. The EPA, for example, cut criminal prosecutions of polluters by 36 percent.[36] OSHA, meanwhile, changed its approach from issuing regulations to a voluntary compliance strategy aimed at reaching agreements with industry associations and companies to police themselves.[37]

Congress

Congress has strong legal authority to oversee the actions of the federal bureaucracy. Congress can abolish an agency, reorganize its structure, change its jurisdiction, cut its budget, audit its expenditures, investigate its performance, and overrule its decisions. In short, Congress has effective means for getting an agency's attention. The Smithsonian Institution is a national museum and educational institution chartered by Congress. When the Smithsonian's governing board failed to provide Congress with a satisfactory justification for an exclusive deal with Showtime Network to use materials in the Smithsonian collection to make films, the House Appropriations Committee cut $15 million from the agency's budget and sought a cap on salaries for agency administrators.[38]

Some political scientists believe that congressional oversight is generally ineffective. Congress is unable to provide clear, consistent policy oversight for the bureaucracy, they say, because Congress itself lacks consensus on administrative policy goals. Whereas some members of Congress will think an agency has gone too far, others will believe that it has not gone far enough. Furthermore, members of Congress depend on executive branch agencies for help in providing services to constituents. Members of Congress who have built mutually beneficial relationships with the bureaucracy are not going to undermine those relationships through aggressive oversight.

Fire-alarm oversight An indirect system of congressional surveillance of bureaucratic administration characterized by rules, procedures, and informal practices that enable individual citizens and organized interest groups to examine administrative decisions, charge agencies with violating legislative goals, and seek remedies from agencies, courts, and the Congress itself.

Some political scientists believe that Congress has developed an effective method of administrative oversight through a process that some observers call **fire-alarm oversight.** It is an indirect system of congressional surveillance of bureaucratic administration characterized by rules, procedures, and informal practices that enable individual citizens and organized interest groups to examine administrative decisions, charge agencies with violating legislative goals, and seek remedies from agencies, courts, and Congress itself. In other words, Congress exercises oversight when media reports, interest group demands, lawsuits, or citizen complaints call attention to a problem.

Interest Groups

Every agency has several to perhaps dozens of interest groups vitally concerned with the programs it administers. Broadcasters are concerned with the FCC. The airline industry, aircraft manufacturers, airline employee associations, and consumer groups have an interest in the Federal Aviation Administration (FAA). Western land interests and environmentalists monitor the activities of the Interior Department. Postal workers unions, direct-mail advertisers, publishers, and consumer groups focus on the work of the U.S. Postal Service.

Interest groups have a number of tools for influencing the bureaucracy. Groups lobby bureaucratic agencies. They also lobby Congress to pressure the bureaucracy on their behalf. Sometimes groups file lawsuits to block or reverse an agency's decisions.

Captured agencies Agencies that work to benefit the economic interests they regulate rather than serving the public interest.

Critics charge that federal agencies often become **captured agencies,** that is, agencies that work to benefit the economic interests they regulate rather than serving the public interest. The Federal Maritime Commission, for example, historically has worked closely with shippers. The Federal Power Commission has been accused of acting on behalf of the electric-utility industry. Proponents of the captured-agencies thesis point to what they describe as a revolving door between industry and the bureaucracy as evidence of the comfortable relationship between the regulatory commissions and industry. Presidents appoint corporate lawyers and industry executives to serve as commissioners. When the commissioners eventually leave government, they often take jobs in the industries they once regulated.

Many political scientists believe that the captured-agencies thesis is too simplistic. Studies have found that capture is not the norm, and when it does occur, it does not always last.[39] Instead, a range of factors, including presidential appointments, congressional committees and subcommittees, judicial actions, economic conditions, and agency staffs, affect agency decisions. Professor Steven P. Croley notes that government agencies do not always take the side of special interests against the

Postal worker unions, direct-mail advertisers, publishers, and consumer groups focus on the work of the U.S. Postal Service.

public interest. The FTC, for example, adopted the National Do Not Call Registry despite the opposition of the telemarketing industry.[40] The captured-agencies thesis assumes that the political environment for each government agency consists of a single set of interest groups with a similar perspective, but that is not usually the case. The debate over the adoption of the National Do Not Call Registry involved not just an industry group, but also consumer organizations and the AARP.

Bureaucrats

Each agency has two sets of administrators—a small group of presidential appointees, typically called political appointees, and a larger group of career civil servants. Nineteen presidential appointees and 284 SES managers lead the Department of Health and Human Services. Five presidential appointees and 20 SES managers head the EEOC.[41] In contrast to presidential employees who serve no more than four or eight years, depending on the number of terms of the president who appoints them, SES managers are career bureaucrats who stay with a single agency for most of their careers. SES managers have interests of their own that may differ from those of the president and political administrators appointed to run their agencies. Career SES managers typically want to preserve and enhance their positions, their programs, and their budgets. Furthermore, agencies often attract employees who are personally committed to the mission of their department. Environmentalists work for the EPA, whereas people with agricultural backgrounds seek employment with the Department of Agriculture.

Career bureaucrats have resources for defending their turf. Sometimes career employees resort to subtle, behind-the-scenes resistance to policy changes they oppose, sort of a bureaucratic guerrilla warfare. In an organization as large as the federal bureaucracy, presidential initiatives can be opposed in a number of quiet ways. Changes can be delayed. In addition, bureaucrats may follow the letter but not the spirit of directives. Officials may "forget" to pass along orders to subordinates, and news of mistakes or internal bickering can be leaked to the press.[42]

Bureaucracy finds power in alliances with important members of Congress and interest groups. Executive branch agencies are some of the most vigorous and effective lobbyists. By assisting key members of Congress with problems involving constituent complaints, agencies build friendships. Furthermore, most agencies have interest group constituencies that are willing to use their political resources on behalf of the agency. Teacher groups lobby for the Department of Education; defense contractors fight for the defense budget. Medical professionals support the Public Health Service.

Executive branch officials know that they are more likely to achieve their goals if they can find a way to connect their policy preferences with the self-interest of members of Congress. Consider NASA's successful strategy for winning congressional support for continued funding of the International Space Station (ISS). NASA distributed work on the ISS to 68 prime contractors and 35 major subcontractors in 22 states, including California, Texas, Florida, New York, Illinois, Ohio, and Pennsylvania—all states with large, politically influential congressional delegations.[43]

Around the World — Egypt and Swine Flu

The Egyptian government responded to international concerns about the H1N1 virus, better known as the swine flu, by ordering the slaughter of every pig in the country. The government acted even though Egypt had no reported cases of the H1N1 virus when it took the action.* When international health officials explained that the transmission of infection from swine to humans is rare to nonexistent, Egyptian bureaucrats justified their action as a general public health measure taken because the pigs lived in too close proximity to humans and domestic animals.†

The government's action directly affected relatively few Egyptians. The overwhelming majority of Egyptians are Muslims whose religion forbids them to raise swine or eat pork. The slaughtered pigs were the property of members of the nation's Christian minority who made their living collecting garbage door-to-door on the streets of Cairo, Egypt's largest city. The Christian garbage collectors separated their garbage into items that could be recycled and sold, and organic material that could be fed to their swine.

The Egyptian government's decision to slaughter the nation's pigs not only failed to prevent a swine flu outbreak, but it created a public health crisis on the streets of Cairo. As of February 2010, the Egyptian health ministry reported 16,000 cases of H1N1 virus with more than 250 deaths from the illness.‡ Meanwhile, the streets of Cairo filled with garbage. The Christian garbage collectors, infuriated by the slaughter of their livestock, stopped collecting the organic garbage. The government hired multinational corporations to collect garbage and they placed bins around the city, but the people, accustomed to the door-to-door service provided by the Christian garbage collectors, generally did not use them, preferring instead to pile their trash on the streets.§

Questions

1. Why is it that bureaucracies sometimes make decisions that make no sense?
2. Would the Egyptian government have slaughtered the pigs had they been owned by a more prominent segment of the community?
3. If you were a government official in Egypt, what would you propose to improve the situation for the residents of Cairo?

*"Swine Flu: Egypt Slaughters All Pigs to Prevent Outbreak," April 29, 2009, available at www.huffingtonpost.com.

†Catharine Paddock, "Egypt's Pig Cull Not a Swine Flu Measure, Says Government," May 1, 2009, available at www.medicalnewstoday.com.

‡"Egypt Says Swine Flu Cases on the Decline," February 10, 2010, available at http://bikyamasr.com.

§ Michael Slackman, "Belatedly, Egypt Spots Flaws in Wiping Out Pigs," *New York Times,* September 20, 2009, available at www.nytimes.com.

Subgovernments and Issue Networks

Subgovernment or **iron triangle** A cozy, three-sided relationship among government agencies, interest groups, and key members of Congress in which all parties benefit.

Political scientists use different concepts to explain administrative policymaking. One approach to understanding the administrative process is the concept of subgovernments or iron triangles. A **subgovernment** or **iron triangle** is a cozy, three-sided relationship among government agencies, interest groups, and key members of Congress in which all parties benefit.

- On one point of the subgovernment triangle, the bureaucracy and interest groups benefit from a special relationship. Agencies enhance the economic status of the interest group through favorable regulation or the awarding of government contracts. Interest groups return the favor by lobbying Congress on behalf of the agency.

- On the second point of the triangle, interest groups and members of Congress enjoy a mutually beneficial relationship. Interest groups assist senators and members of the House by contributing to their reelection campaigns. In return, members of Congress vote to appropriate money for programs the interest groups support.
- The third point of the triangle focuses on the interaction between agencies and members of Congress. Politically wise bureaucrats know that it is important to keep key members of Congress happy by providing all the information they request, solving problems members of Congress bring to their attention, and paying special notice to the needs of the home states and districts of key senators and representatives.

Consider the highway subgovernment. On one point of the highway triangle are interest groups that benefit from highway construction: auto manufacturers, the United Auto Workers Union (UAW), tire companies, asphalt and cement dealers, road contractors, long-haul trucking firms, the Teamsters Union, and oil companies. The second point is the Federal Highway Administration, which, of course, is interested in the preservation of the programs it administers. On the third point of the triangle are the congressional committees that consider highway-construction bills—the Environment and Public Works Committee in the Senate and the Committee on Transportation and Infrastructure in the House. Senators and representatives from states with extensive interstate highway systems, such as Texas, California, and Oklahoma, are also involved.

Each part of the subgovernment serves and is served by the other two. The members of Congress involved work to maintain federal support for highway construction and maintenance. The interest groups lobby Congress on behalf of highway programs, and their political action committees (PACs) contribute campaign money to members of Congress on key committees. The agency, meanwhile, makes sure that the districts and states of the members of Congress involved get their share of new highways and bridges. Also, if some town in the district wants a special favor, local officials call their representative or senator, who passes the request along to the agency. The agency is eager to please and happy to give the member of Congress the credit.

The political scientists who study subgovernments believe that a great deal of public policy is made through behind-the-scenes understandings among interest groups, key members of Congress, and the federal bureaucracy. When issues arise, the participants in the subgovernment settle the matter, with little input from political actors outside the triangle, including the president. The result is that public policy is tailored to the wishes of those groups most closely associated with the policy itself. Energy policy, they say, reflects the interests of the oil and gas industry. Highway programs are geared to match the concerns of the highway lobby.

In recent years, however, many political scientists have concluded that although subgovernments exist in American politics, their influence is less than it was during the 1940s and 1950s. Subgovernments prospered in a time when public policy was the work of a relatively small number of fairly autonomous participants: a handful of powerful committee chairs, a small number of interest groups, and a few agency administrators. Furthermore, most policy decisions were made outside public view.

Today's policy environment has changed. Power in Congress is centralized in the party leadership. Committee chairs are less influential. Interest groups are more numerous. Furthermore, new issues have arisen for which it is all but impossible to identify clearly the dominant actors, including energy, consumer protection, illegal immigration, and the environment.[44]

Issue network A group of political actors that is concerned with some aspect of public policy.

Political scientist Hugh Heclo believes that the concept of issue networks more accurately describes administrative policymaking today than the concept of subgovernments. An **issue network** is a group of political actors that is concerned with some aspect of public policy. Issue networks are fluid, with participants moving in and out. They can include technical specialists, members of Congress, journalists, the president, interest groups, bureaucrats, academic experts, and individual political activists. Powerful interest groups may be involved, but they do not control the process. Instead, policy in a particular area results from conflict among a broad range of political actors both in and out of government.[45]

Consider the fate of the Highway Trust Fund. A subgovernment once dominated federal highway policy, but that is no longer the case. During the 1970s, the number of interest groups concerned with highway construction grew. Environmentalists worried about the effect of highway construction on the environment. Minority rights groups became alarmed about the impact of freeway construction on minority neighborhoods. Groups advocating energy conservation argued that government should divert money from highways to mass transit. In the meantime, congressional committees and subcommittees with jurisdiction over highway programs began to include members of Congress allied to groups opposed to highway spending. As a result, federal highway policy is now made in a more contentious, uncertain environment than before.[46] In 1991, Congress passed, and the president signed, the Intermodal Surface Transportation Efficiency Act (ISTEA), granting states considerable leeway in deciding whether to spend federal transportation money for highways or mass transit. The legislation also required that states use a certain amount of money to fund "enhancement programs," which were local transportation-related projects designed to aid a community's quality of life, such as hike and bike trails. The passage of ISTEA reflected the participation of a broad range of interests concerned with transportation policy, not just the traditional set of interest groups involved with highway funding.[47]

WHAT WE HAVE LEARNED

1. **What are the major administrative structures of the executive branch of American national government?**

   Congress and the president have created the agencies and departments that comprise the executive branch over the last 220 years. The cabinet departments, including the Department of State and the Department of Defense, are the major administrative units of the federal government that have responsibility for the conduct of a wide range of government operations. Congress and the president have created a number of independent executive agencies that are not part of any of the 15 cabinet-level departments, including the Peace Corps, National Aeronautics and Space Administration (NASA), Central Intelligence Agency (CIA), Environmental Protection Agency (EPA), Social Security Administration (SSA), and the Small Business Administration (SBA). Government corporations, such as the U.S. Postal Service, AMTRAK, and the FDIC, are organizationally similar to private corporations except that the government owns them rather than stockholders. Foundations and institutes administer grant programs to local governments, universities, nonprofit institutions, and individuals for research in the natural and social sciences or to promote the arts. Independent regulatory commissions, such as the FCC, FTC, and SEC, are agencies outside the major executive departments that are charged with the regulation of important aspects of the economy. Quasi-governmental companies, such as Fannie Mae and Freddie Mac, are private, profit-seeking corporations created by Congress to serve a public purpose, such as increasing the availability of credit to home buyers.

2. **What is the history of federal employee personnel policies?**

   The size of the federal civilian bureaucracy has grown dramatically since the early days of the nation, peaking in the early 1990s at more than three million employees. Today, 2.7 million people work for the federal government, although that number is misleading because millions of other people work indirectly for the federal government as private contractors, or as state employees and university faculty paid by federal grant money. When Andrew Jackson was president, federal employees were hired primarily on the basis of their political connections. It was a spoils system. After Garfield's assassination by a disappointed office seeker, Congress reformed the hiring process to emphasize merit. Congress subsequently established a Senior Executive Service (SES) of upper-level civil servants who would be eligible for big bonuses but could be more easily transferred, reassigned, and so on. Federal workers have a limited right to organize. They can bargain collectively over matters other than pay and benefits; they may not strike.

3. **What are the steps in the rulemaking process?**

   When Congress passes regulatory legislation, it frequently delegates authority to the bureaucracy to make legally binding rules to implement the legislation. The rulemaking process begins with an agency giving advance notice that it is considering issuing a rule in a particular policy area. Rules are sometimes the product of formal negotiations among government agencies and affected interest groups called regulatory negotiation. The OMB reviews rules before they go into effect. Congress can overturn rules through the legislative process subject to presidential veto and possible override.

4. **What perspectives and political resources does each of the following political actors have in the administrative process: the president, Congress, interest groups, and bureaucrats?**

   Bureaucratic policymaking is a complex process involving the president, Congress, interest groups, and the bureaucracy itself. Presidents have an important stake in the faithful and efficient implementation of federal programs, but they must work to influence the administrative process and their success is not assured. A determined president has sufficient power to have an impact on bureaucratic policymaking through appointive powers, the OMB, and his authority to propose budgets to Congress. Congress can abolish an agency, reorganize its structure, change its jurisdiction, cut its budget, audit its expenditures, investigate its performance, and overrule its decisions. Although some political scientists believe that congressional oversight is generally ineffective, others believe that Congress has developed an effective method of oversight through a process that some observers call fire-alarm oversight. Every agency has several to perhaps dozens of interest groups vitally concerned with the programs it administers. Groups lobby agencies, lobby Congress, and sometimes file suits to influence administrative actions. Career bureaucrats have interests of their own that may not necessarily coincide with those of the president, and they have resources to defend their interests. Bureaucrats find power in alliances with interest groups and key members of Congress.

5. **What approaches do political scientists take in explaining the administrative process?**
Some political scientists believe that administrative policymaking reflects the activity of subgovernments or iron triangles, which are cozy, three-sided relationships among government agencies, interest groups, and key members of Congress in which all parties benefit. In recent years, however, many political scientists have concluded that although subgovernments exist in American politics, their influence is less than it was during the 1940s and 1950s. They believe that the concept of issue networks best describes administrative policymaking. Issue networks are groups of political actors that are concerned with some aspect of public policy.

KEY TERMS

cabinet departments
cap and trade
captured agencies
Central Intelligence Agency (CIA)
collective bargaining
cost-benefit analysis
Environmental Protection Agency (EPA)
Equal Employment Opportunity Commission (EEOC)
Federal Communications Commission (FCC)
Federal Deposit Insurance Corporation (FDIC)
Federal Election Commission (FEC)
Federal Trade Commission (FTC)
fire-alarm oversight
global warming
Hatch Act
independent executive agencies
independent regulatory commission
inner cabinet
issue network
National Aeronautics and Space Administration (NASA)
National Endowment for the Arts (NEA)
National Railroad Passenger Service Corporation (AMTRAK)
National Science Foundation (NSF)
Peace Corps
president's cabinet
quasi-governmental company
regulatory negotiation
rule
rulemaking
Securities and Exchange Commission (SEC)
Small Business Administration (SBA)
Social Security Administration (SSA)
spoils system
statutory law
subgovernment or iron triangle
Tennessee Valley Authority (TVA)
U.S. Postal Service (USPS)
whistleblowers

NOTES

1. John M. Broder, "House Passes Cap and Trade Legislation," *New York Times*, June 27, 2009, available at www.nytimes.com.
2. HR 2454, 2009.
3. Jennifer A. Diouhy, "EPA Declares Greenhouse Gases Pose Health Risk," *San Francisco Chronicle*, December 8, 2009, available at www.sfgate.com.
4. "Federal Civilian Employment by Branch and Agency: 1970 to 2008," *Statistical Abstract of the United States, 2010*, available at www.census.gov.
5. G. Calvin MacKenzie, "The Real Invisible Hand: Presidential Appointees in the Administration of George W. Bush," *PS: Political Science & Politics*, March 2002, p. 28.
6. Paul C. Light, "Late for Their Appointments," *New York Times*, November 16, 2004, available at www.nytimes.com.
7. Congressional Record, Daily Digest, "Résumé of Congressional Activity, 111th Congress," available at www.senate.gov/reference/resources/pdf/110_1.pdf.
8. Nolan McCarty and Rose Razaghian, "Advice and Consent: Senate Responses to Executive Branch Nominations, 1885–1996," *American Journal of Political Science* 43 (October 1999): 1122–1143.
9. Scott Wilson and Ed O'Keefe, "Administration Faults GOP Tactic of Blocking Presidential Appointments," *Washington Post*, February 5, 2010, available at www.washingtonpost.com.
10. Manu Raju, "Reid Ready to Play at Recess," February 7, 2010, available at www.politico.com.
11. Andrew Rudalevige, "The President and the Cabinet," in Michael Nelson, ed., *The Presidency and the Political System*, 8th ed. (Washington, DC: CQ Press, 2006), p. 533.
12. Peter Baker, "How Obama Came to Plan for 'Surge' in Afghanistan," *New York Times*, December 6, 2009, available at www.nytimes.com.
13. Joseph A. Pika and John Anthony Maltese, *The Politics of the Presidency*, 6th ed. (Washington, DC: CQ Press, 2004), p. 230.
14. Jonathan G. S. Koppel, *The Politics of Quasi-Government* (New York: Cambridge University Press, 2003), pp. 187–195.
15. "Federal Civilian Employment, by Branch and Agency: 1970 to 2008," *Statistical Abstract of the United States 2010*.
16. Paul C. Light, "The New True Size of Government," Robert F. Wagner Graduate School, New York University, available at http://wagner.nyu.edu.
17. Scott Shane and Ron Nixon, "In Washington, Contractors Take on Biggest Role Ever," *New York Times*, February 4, 2007, available at www.nytimes.com.
18. O. Glenn Stahl, *Public Personnel Administration*, 8th ed. (New York: Harper & Row, 1983), p. 42.
19. Stewart Liff, *The Complete Guide to Hiring and Firing Government Employees* (New York: American Management Association, 2010), pp. 6–8.
20. James R. Thompson, "Federal Labor-Management Relations Under George W. Bush: Enlightened Management or Political Retribution?" in James S. Bowman and Jonathan P. West, eds., *American Public Service: Radical Reform and the Merit System* (Boca Raton, FL: RC Press, 2007), p. 240.
21. Ann Gerhart, "Homeland Insecurity," *Washington Post National Weekly Edition*, April 4-10, 2005, pp. 6–7.
22. 2010 Defense Authorization Act, Public Law 111-84.
23. Cornelius M. Kerwin, *Rulemaking: How Government Agencies Write Law and Make Policy*, 3rd ed. (Washington, DC: CQ Press, 2003), p. 21.
24. Alana S. Knaster and Philip J. Harter, "The Clean Fuels Regulatory Negotiation," *Intergovernmental Perspective*, Summer 1992, pp. 20–22.
25. Terry M. Moe, "The Presidency and the Bureaucracy: The Presidential Advantage," in Michael Nelson, ed., *The Presidency and the Political System*, 6th ed. (Washington, DC: CQ Press, 2000), pp. 465–468.
26. Alan B. Morrison, "Close Reins on the Bureaucracy: Overseeing the Administrative Agencies," in Herman Schwartz, ed., *The Burger Years* (New York: Viking, 1987), pp. 191–205.
27. Robert Pear, "Bush Directive Increases Sway on Regulation," *New York Times*, January 30, 2007, available at www.nytimes.com.
28. Marissa Martino Golden, *What Motivates Bureaucrats? Politics and Administration During the Reagan Years* (New York: Columbia University Press, 2000), pp. 152–159.
29. B. Dan Wood, "Principals, Bureaucrats, and Responsiveness in Clean Air Enforcement," *American Political Science Review* 82 (March 1988): 218.
30. Kay Lehrman Schlozman and John T. Tierney, *Organized Interests and American Democracy* (New York: Harper & Row, 1986), p. 353.
31. Joseph Cooper and William F. West, "Presidential Power and Republican Government: The Theory and Practice of OMB Review of Agency Rules," *Journal of Politics* 50 (November 1988): 864–895.
32. Wood, "Principals, Bureaucrats, and Responsiveness in Clean Air Enforcements," pp. 222–226.
33. B. Dan Wood and Richard W. Waterman, "The Dynamics of Political Control of the Bureaucracy," *American Political Science Review* 85 (September 1991): 813.
34. Ibid., p. 811.

35. Ibid., pp. 806–807, 818–821.
36. John Solomon and Julier Eilperin, "Dwindling Pursuit of Polluters," *Washington Post National Weekly Edition*, October 8–14, 2007, p. 34.
37. Stephen Labaton, "OSHA Leaves Worker Safety in Hands of Industry," *New York Times*, April 25, 2007, available at www.nytimes.com.
38. Edward Wyatt, "House Panel Challenges Smithsonian," *New York Times*, May 11, 2006, available at www.nytimes.com.
39. Schlozman and Tierney, *Organized Interests and American Democracy*, pp. 341–346.
40. Steven P. Croley, *Regulation and Public Interests: The Possibility of Good Regulatory Government* (Princeton, NJ: Princeton University Press, 2008), pp. 214–230.
41. Colin Campbell, "The Complex Organization of the Executive Branch: The Legacies of Competing Approaches to Administration," in Joel D. Aberbach and Mark A. Peterson, eds., *The Executive Branch* (New York: Oxford University Press, 2005), p. 254.
42. Dennis D. Riley and Bryan E. Brophy-Baermann, *Bureaucracy and the Policy Process* (Lanham, MD: Rowman & Littlefield Publishers, 2006), p. 98.
43. Jeffrey Kluger, "Space Pork," *Time*, July 24, 2000, pp. 24–26.
44. Jeffrey M. Berry, "Subgovernments, Issue Networks, and Political Conflict," in Richard A. Harris and Sidney M. Milkis, *Remaking American Politics* (Boulder, CO: Westview Press, 1989), pp. 239–260.
45. Hugh Heclo, "Issue Networks and the Executive Establishment," in Anthony King, ed., *The New American Political System* (Washington, DC: American Enterprise Institute, 1978), pp. 87–124.
46. John R. Provan, "The Highway Trust Fund: Its Birth, Growth, and Survival," in Theodore W. Taylor, ed., *Federal Public Policy* (Mt. Airy, MD: Lomond Publications, 1984), pp. 221–258.
47. Jonathan Walters, "Revenge of the Highwaymen," *Governing*, September 1997, p. 13.

Chapter 13

The Federal Courts

CHAPTER OUTLINE

WHAT WE WILL LEARN

After studying Chapter 13, students should be able to answer the following questions:

1. What role do courts and judges play in the policy process?
2. What is the policymaking history of the U.S. Supreme Court?
3. How is the federal court system organized?
4. How are U.S. district court judges selected and what sorts of cases do district courts hear?
5. What role do the U.S. Courts of Appeals play in the judicial system?
6. How is the Supreme Court structured and what role does it play in the policy process?
7. How closely do court decisions reflect public opinion?

Associate Justice Anthony Kennedy may be the key member of the U.S. Supreme Court. When the Court's nine justices divide 5–4, Kennedy is in the majority more than any other justice. Since the 2006–2007 term, Kennedy has voted with the majority in 53 of 74 cases decided 5–4.[1]

Kennedy is the swing vote on a Court that is closely divided philosophically. In 2009–2010, Associate Justices John Paul Stevens, Ruth Bader Ginsburg, Stephen Breyer, and Sonia Sotomayor formed a liberal bloc while four other justices—Chief Justice John Roberts and Associate Justices Antonin Scalia, Clarence Thomas, and Samuel Alito—voted together as the conservative wing of the Court. Justice Stevens retired after the term, but his replacement, Elena Kagan, was expected to join the liberals.[2]

Although Kennedy is conservative, he is not consistently conservative. More often than not, Kennedy sides with the conservative wing of the Court. During the 2008–2009 session, he joined with Roberts, Scalia, Thomas, and Alito to rule that the Second Amendment guarantees an individual the right to own a firearm rather than just the right of states to maintain an armed militia.[3] In the following year, Kennedy voted with the conservatives to overturn campaign finance laws that limited the amount of money unions and corporations could spend on election advertising.[4] On some issues, however, Kennedy votes with the Court's liberal wing to form a 5–4 majority. During the Court's 2009–2010 session, for example, he sided with Stevens, Ginsburg, Breyer, and Sotomayor to hold that a sentence of life in prison without the possibility of parole for juvenile offenders violates the Eighth Amendment's prohibition against "cruel and unusual punishments."[5]

This chapter considers the place of the courts in American government. It begins by examining the role of judges and courts in the policy process. The chapter traces the political history of the Supreme Court. It describes the federal court system, distinguishing between trial courts and appellate courts. The chapter examines district courts and then appellate courts, considering judicial selection and court jurisdiction. The chapter then turns to the U.S. Supreme Court, discussing judicial selection, judicial processes, and the impact of Court decisions. Finally, the chapter discusses the position of the courts in the political system.

Judicial Policymaking

Judicial review The power of courts to declare unconstitutional the actions of the other branches and units of government.

Courts make policy by interpreting the law and the Constitution.[6] When courts interpret the law, they modify policies adopted by the executive and legislative branches by aggressively expanding or narrowly restricting the provisions of a law. When courts interpret the Constitution, they exercise **judicial review,** which is the power of courts to declare unconstitutional the actions of the other branches and units of government. Altogether, the Supreme Court has overturned at least one provision in more than 160 federal laws and nearly 1,300 state laws and local ordinances.[7]

In 2009, Sonia Sotomayor made history when she became the first Latino member of the U.S. Supreme Court.

Strict construction The doctrine of constitutional interpretation holding that the document should be interpreted narrowly.

Loose construction A doctrine of constitutional interpretation holding that the document should be interpreted broadly.

Judicial activism The charge that judges are going beyond their authority by making the law and not just interpreting it.

Judicial restraint The concept that judges should defer to the policymaking judgment of the legislative and executive branches of government unless their actions clearly violate the law or the Constitution.

Controversy rages over the leeway courts should exercise in interpreting the Constitution. **Strict construction** is a doctrine of constitutional interpretation holding that the document should be interpreted narrowly. Advocates of strict construction believe that judges should stick close to the literal meaning of the words in the Constitution and place themselves in harmony with the purpose of the framers. In contrast, **loose construction** is a doctrine of constitutional interpretation holding that the document should be interpreted broadly. Loose constructionists argue that strict construction is neither possible nor desirable. They point out that it is often difficult to ascertain original intent because no complete and accurate records exist to indicate what the authors of the Constitution had in mind. Furthermore, those records that are available show that the nation's founders often disagreed with one another about the Constitution's basic meaning.

A similar and related debate involves the role of judges. Conservative opponents of the Supreme Court sometimes accuse it of **judicial activism,** which is the charge that judges are going beyond their authority by making the law and not just interpreting it. For example, critics of *Roe v. Wade*, the Supreme Court's landmark abortion decision, call it an activist ruling because the U.S. Constitution does not specifically address the issue of abortion. Republican presidential candidates typically promise to nominate men and women to the Supreme Court that will practice **judicial restraint,** which is the concept that judges should defer to the policymaking judgment of the legislative and executive branches of government unless their actions clearly violate the law or the Constitution.

Many political scientists believe that the debate between judicial activism and judicial restraint is more about politics than judicial behavior. Professors Kermit Roosevelt III and Thomas M. Keck contend that the accusation of judicial activism is a convenient line of attack for people who disagree with a court ruling for whatever reason.[8] The real dispute is not between the advocates of judicial activism and judicial restraint, but between liberal and conservative activism. All judges regard the Constitution as a charter of fundamental principles that courts are pledged to uphold. The real controversy is that conservative and liberal judges disagree as to what those principles are.[9]

WHAT IS YOUR OPINION?

If you were a member of the Supreme Court, how would you approach the job?

Political History of the Supreme Court

Throughout most of its history, the U.S. Supreme Court has been an active participant in some of the nation's most significant public policy debates. In its first decade, however, the Court was relatively unimportant. It decided only 50 cases from 1789 to 1800. Some of its members even resigned to take other, more prestigious jobs.[10]

After John Marshall was named Chief Justice, the Supreme Court's role in the policy process began to take shape. Under his leadership from 1801 to 1835, the Court claimed the power of judicial review in *Marbury v. Madison* (1803)[11] and assumed the authority to review the decisions of state courts on questions of federal law in *Martin v. Hunter's Lessee* (1816).[12] The Marshall Court also decided a number of landmark cases dealing with commercial law and the nature of the federal system. In the *Dartmouth College Case* (1819), the Court held that the Constitution protected private contracts from infringement by state legislatures.[13] This decision played an important role in the nation's economic development because it assured private investors that the courts would enforce the terms of contractual agreements.

The Marshall Court ruled in favor of a strong national government in controversies concerning the relative power of the national government and the states. In *McCulloch v. Maryland* (1819), the Court struck down a Maryland tax on the national bank and gave broad scope to federal authority under the Constitution.[14] In *Gibbons v. Ogden* (1824), the Court ruled that a New York law that established a monopoly for a steamboat company was a state infringement of the constitutional power of the federal government to regulate interstate commerce.[15]

States' rights An interpretation of the Constitution that favors limiting the authority of the federal government while expanding the powers of the states.

Under Chief Justice Roger Taney (1836–1864), Marshall's successor, the Supreme Court's involvement in the slavery controversy led the Court away from support for a strong national government toward a states' rights position. The doctrine of **states' rights** is an interpretation of the Constitution that favors limiting the

New Deal The legislative package of reform measures proposed by President Franklin Roosevelt for dealing with the Great Depression.

Jim Crow laws Legal provisions requiring the social segregation of African Americans in separate and generally unequal facilities.

Civil liberties The protection of the individual from the unrestricted power of government.

Civil rights The protection of the individual from arbitrary or discriminatory acts by government or by other individuals based on an individual's group status, such as race or gender.

Exclusionary rule The judicial doctrine stating that when the police violate an individual's constitutional rights, the evidence obtained as a result of police misconduct or error cannot be used against the defendant in a criminal prosecution.

authority of the national government while expanding the powers of the states. In the infamous *Dred Scott* decision (1857), the Supreme Court declared the Missouri Compromise unconstitutional and held that the federal government had no power to prohibit slavery in the territories.[16]

After the Civil War, the Supreme Court turned its attention to the protection of property rights, reviewing government efforts to regulate business activity. Initially, the Court was ambivalent, allowing some regulations while disallowing others. By the 1920s and early 1930s, however, the Court had grown hostile to government regulation of business. It scrutinized state and federal taxation and regulatory policies and found many of them unconstitutional under the Due Process Clauses of the Fifth and Fourteenth Amendments, which declare that neither the national government nor state governments may deprive persons of property without due process of law. The Court struck down state laws prohibiting child labor and invalidated a number of federal laws passed during the early days of the **New Deal,** which was the legislative package of reform measures proposed by President Franklin Roosevelt for dealing with the Great Depression.

While the Supreme Court protected the property rights of business corporations, it ignored the civil rights of African Americans. Around the turn of the century, a number of states, primarily in the South, enacted **Jim Crow laws,** which were legal provisions requiring the social segregation of African Americans in separate and generally unequal facilities. In the meantime, many states, again mostly in the South, adopted fiendishly clever devices to prevent African Americans from voting. The Supreme Court responded to this situation by legitimizing racial segregation in *Plessy v. Ferguson* (1896)[17] and essentially overlooking voting rights violations.

In 1937, the Supreme Court changed course. In a remarkable turn of events, the Court began to uphold the constitutionality of New Deal legislation. No longer would the Court protect business against government regulation. Although the Supreme Court generally required that government agencies follow proper procedures in their regulatory activities, it broadly and consistently endorsed the right of government to regulate business and the nation's economy.

After 1937, the agenda of the U.S. Supreme Court focused primarily on civil liberties and civil rights. **Civil liberties** refer to the protection of the individual from the unrestricted power of government. **Civil rights** concern the protection of the individual from arbitrary or discriminatory acts by government or by individuals based on that person's group status, such as race and gender.

Under the leadership of Chief Justice Earl Warren (1953–1969), the Supreme Court adopted liberal policy positions on a number of civil liberties and civil rights issues. The Court strengthened the First Amendment guarantees of freedom of expression and religion, broadened the procedural rights of persons accused of crimes, and ruled decisively in favor of civil rights for African Americans and other minorities. In *Brown v. Board of Education of Topeka* (1954), the Court struck down laws requiring school segregation, overturning the *Plessy Decision*.[18] In *Mapp v. Ohio* (1961), the Court extended the exclusionary rule to the states.[19] The **exclusionary rule** is the judicial doctrine stating that when the police violate an individual's constitutional rights, the evidence obtained as a result of police misconduct or error cannot be used against the defendant. In *Miranda v. Arizona*, the Court held that persons arrested for crimes must be informed of their constitutional rights before being interrogated by police officers.[20]

During Warren Burger's tenure as Chief Justice (1969–1986), the Supreme Court continued to focus primarily on civil liberties and civil rights, but its policy preferences were neither consistently liberal nor consistently conservative. In some issue areas, such as abortion rights, **capital punishment,** education for the children of illegal aliens, affirmative action, school busing, and gender discrimination, the Burger Court broke new ground. In *Roe v. Wade*, the Court held that states could not prohibit abortion in the first two trimesters of pregnancy.[21] In other policy areas, however, particularly on issues involving the rights of persons charged with crimes, the Burger Court limited or qualified Warren Court positions without directly reversing any of the major precedents set during the Warren years.

Capital punishment The death penalty.

The Supreme Court continued to defy labels during the tenure of Chief Justice Rehnquist (1986–2005). On some policy issues, the Rehnquist Court adopted conservative positions. The Court declared that government programs designed to remedy the effects of discrimination in government contracting were unconstitutional unless the government could demonstrate a compelling interest to justify their creation.[22] The Rehnquist Court also pleased conservatives by upholding a school voucher program that allowed students to use public funds to attend religious schools. The Court ruled that the program did not violate the First Amendment's prohibition against an establishment of religion.[23] On other issues, however, the Rehnquist Court adopted liberal positions. The Court consistently blocked government efforts to include spoken prayer in school activities, ruling against clergy-led invocations and benedictions at graduation[24] as well as student-led prayers before high school football games.[25] The Rehnquist Court broke new ground on the issue of gay and lesbian rights by overturning the Texas sodomy law that prohibited sexual relations between adults of the same gender even in the privacy of the home.[26]

The Rehnquist Court addressed a number of policy controversies by taking moderate, compromise positions. The Court allowed state governments to restrict abortion rights without overturning *Roe*. Similarly, the Rehnquist Court upheld the constitutionality of the death penalty while ruling against the execution of mentally retarded murderers.[27] It struck down college admissions procedures that gave a numerical advantage to minority applicants,[28] but allowed college officials to consider race and ethnicity in order to achieve a diverse student body as long as they did not grant minority applicants a numerical advantage.[29]

The Rehnquist Court was more willing than any Supreme Court since the 1930s to limit federal regulatory power, especially over state governments. The Supreme Court overturned the Gun-Free School Zone Act of 1990, which was a federal law banning firearms within 1,000 feet of a school. The Court said that Congress could regulate only those economic activities that substantially affect interstate commerce and that the possession of a firearm in the vicinity of a school does not meet that criterion.[30] The Supreme Court also ruled that Congress lacks the constitutional authority to enact laws that override the **sovereign immunity** of a state government,

Sovereign immunity The legal concept that individuals cannot sue the government without the government's permission.

which is the legal concept that individuals cannot sue the government without the government's permission.[31]

Ironically, the Rehnquist Court may be best remembered for a case that ended the 2000 presidential election by overturning the decision of a state supreme court. *Bush v. Gore* involved an appeal by the George W. Bush campaign of the Florida Supreme Court's decision to order a manual recount of thousands of punch-card ballots that had not been counted by machine. Vice President Al Gore wanted a hand count because he hoped that it would give him enough additional votes to carry the state of Florida and thus win the presidency. The Gore campaign argued that a hand count was the only way to determine the true outcome of the race because it would ensure that every legal vote was counted. In contrast, the Bush campaign charged that a hand recount would introduce subjectivity into the vote count. When the Florida Supreme Court ordered a manual recount of uncounted ballots in every county in the state, the Bush campaign appealed to the U.S. Supreme Court, charging that the Florida court had violated both federal law and the U.S. Constitution.

Equal Protection Clause A provision found in the Fourteenth Amendment of the U.S. Constitution that declares that "No State shall . . . deny to any person within its jurisdiction the equal protection of the laws."

The U.S. Supreme Court halted the recount, ensuring that Bush would be the next president. The Court ruled that the recount violated the **Equal Protection Clause,** which is a provision of the Fourteenth Amendment of the U.S. Constitution that declares that "No State shall . . . deny to any person within its jurisdiction the equal protection of the laws." Because the Florida Supreme Court had not established a uniform statewide standard for determining a legal vote, different counties could treat votes differently, thereby giving more weight to some voters than others. Although the state of Florida could fix the problem by setting a statewide standard, the U.S. Supreme Court ruled by a five-to-four margin that it was too late for them to try because the Florida Legislature had set December 12, 2000, as the last date for naming presidential electors. The Court issued its ruling at 10 p.m. on December 11, two hours before the deadline.[32]

The Supreme Court's decision in *Bush v. Gore* was controversial. Many Democrats accused the Court of conservative judicial activism. They charged that the Court's conservative five-judge majority, all of whom had been appointed either by President Reagan or the first President Bush, had abandoned their principles to overturn a state court so they could hand the presidency to George W. Bush.[33] In contrast, the Court's defenders argued that the Court had merely applied established judicial principles to resolve a difficult dispute, thus sparing the nation weeks of political turmoil and a possible constitutional crisis.[34]

The Supreme Court under Chief Justice Roberts has been difficult to characterize because it is closely divided philosophically. Some rulings have satisfied conservatives; others have gratified liberals. On one hand, the Court pleased conservatives by striking down a District of Columbia ordinance banning handgun possession. For the first time in the history of the Court, it ruled that the Constitution guarantees an individual the right of gun ownership. The vote on the Court was 5–4 with Justice Kennedy joining the four conservative-leaning justices to overturn the ordinance.[35] On the other hand, the Court satisfied liberals with its decision holding unconstitutional a Louisiana law that provided for the death penalty for a defendant convicted of sexually assaulting a child who did not die as a result of the assault. In this case, Kennedy joined the Court's four liberal-leaning justices to provide a 5–4 majority limiting the death penalty to murder and treason.[36]

The U.S. Supreme Court halted the Florida recount in 2000, ensuring that George W. Bush would win the state and be elected president.

The Federal Court System

The Constitution says relatively little about the organization of the federal court system. "The judicial Power of the United States," it declares, "shall be vested in one supreme Court, and in such inferior Courts as the Congress may from time to time ordain and establish." Over the years, Congress and the president have created the federal court system through the legislative process.

Trial The formal examination of a judicial dispute in accordance with law before a single judge.

Figure 13.1 diagrams the federal court system. Trial courts make up the lowest tier of federal courts. A **trial** is the formal examination of a judicial dispute in accordance with law before a single judge. Trials involve attorneys, witnesses, testimony, evidence, judges, and, occasionally, juries. The U.S. District Courts are the most important federal trial courts, hearing nearly all federal cases. The U.S. Court of Federal Claims and the U.S. Court of International Trade are specialized trial courts, created to deal with some of the more complex areas of federal law. The U.S. Court of Federal Claims hears disputes over federal contracts and cases involving claims for monetary damages against the U.S. government; the U.S. Court of International Trade hears cases involving international trade and customs issues.

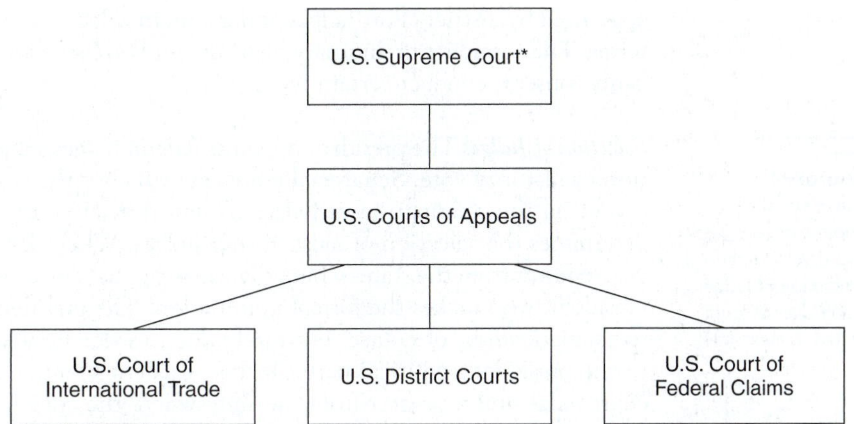

FIGURE 13.1 The U.S. Federal Courts.
*The U.S. Supreme Court also hears appeals from the state court systems.

Appeal The taking of a case from a lower court to a higher court by the losing party in a lower court decision.

An **appeal** is the taking of a case from a lower court to a higher court by the losing party in a lower court decision. The procedures of appeals courts differ notably from those of trial courts. In general, trial courts are concerned with questions of fact and the law as it applies to those facts. In contrast, appeals are based on issues of law and procedure. Appellate courts do not retry cases appealed to them. Instead, appellate court justices (juries do not participate in appellate proceedings) make decisions based on the law and the Constitution, the written and oral arguments presented by attorneys for the litigants in the lawsuit, and the written record of the lower-court proceedings. Also, appellate court justices usually make decisions collectively in panels of three or more judges rather than singly, as do trial court judges.

The U.S. Courts of Appeals and the U.S. Supreme Court are primarily appellate courts. The courts of appeals hear appeals from the federal trial courts and administrative agencies. The U.S. Supreme Court stands at the apex of the American court system. Although it has authority to try a limited range of cases, it is in practice an appellate court, hearing appeals from both the federal and state court systems.

U.S. District Courts

Congress has created 94 district courts, with at least one court in every state and one each in the District of Columbia, Guam, Northern Mariana Islands, Puerto Rico, and the Virgin Islands. Although only one judge presides in each courtroom, most districts have enough business to warrant more than one courtroom, each with its own judge. The number of judges per district ranges from 1 to 28. Congress has authorized the appointment of 678 district court judges who, along with more than a hundred semi-retired senior judges, staff the district courts. In addition, each district court has a clerk, a U.S. marshal, and one or more bankruptcy judges, probation officers, court reporters, and magistrates attached to it. The magistrates are attorneys appointed by district court judges under a merit selection system to serve eight-year terms. They conduct preliminary hearings, set bail, issue arrest warrants, and, if litigants consent, conduct certain types of trials.[37]

Senatorial courtesy The custom that senators have a veto on the nomination of judges to staff district courts located in their states.

Selection of Judges The president appoints federal judges subject to Senate confirmation by majority vote. **Senatorial courtesy,** which is the custom that senators have a veto on the nomination of judges to staff district courts located in their states, determines the selection of most district judges. When district court vacancies occur, senators from the states where the vacancies have occurred submit names to the president, who makes the formal nomination. The president can reject a senator's recommendation, of course, but rarely does, especially when the senator belongs to the president's political party. If the president nominates a prospective district court judge and a senator from the state where the court is located objects to the nomination, the Senate Judiciary Committee will honor the objection by refusing to consider the nomination, forcing the president to submit another name.

The Senate Judiciary Committee evaluates district court nominees. After the committee staff conducts a background check, the committee chair schedules a hearing to allow the nominee and interested parties an opportunity to be heard. The confirmation of district court judges is usually a quiet affair, with few nominees rejected. Confirmation is not necessarily speedy, however, especially when the Senate and White House are in the hands of different political parties. Toward the end of a presidential term, the chair of the Senate Judiciary Committee and the Senate Majority Leader will sometimes delay the confirmation process in hopes that the White House changes parties and the new president can then fill pending vacancies. Even early in a term, the confirmation process takes anywhere from four months to two years or even more.[38]

Presidents typically nominate judges whose party affiliation and political philosophy are compatible with their own. Democratic presidents appoint Democratic judges; Republican presidents select Republicans. Some presidents also seek judges with particular political philosophies. In general, Republican presidents choose judges with conservative political philosophies, whereas Democratic presidents select liberal judges. Conservative judges tend to favor government interests over criminal defendants, interpret narrowly the constitutional guarantees of equal rights for women and minorities, support corporate interests against the claims of individual workers or consumers, and rule against federal government involvement in local policy issues. In contrast, liberal judges are more inclined than their conservative counterparts to favor judicial underdogs, such as consumers, workers, criminal defendants, and members of minority groups. They tend to support the federal government in federalism disputes over the relative power of the states and the national government.[39]

Federal judges hold lifetime appointments, with "good behavior," as the Constitution puts it. They may not be retired involuntarily or removed for political reasons, but they are subject to impeachment by the House and removal by the Senate. Although members of Congress occasionally threaten to impeach judges with whom they have policy disagreements, impeachment is rare and only directed against judges who are accused of misconduct. In American history, only eight federal judges have been impeached and removed from office. Most judges who get in trouble resign rather than face the humiliation of impeachment.[40]

WHAT IS YOUR OPINION?

Do you think federal judges should be appointed for life? Why or why not?

Jurisdiction The authority of a court to hear a case.

Civil case A legal dispute concerning a private conflict between two parties—individuals, corporations, or government agencies.

Criminal case A legal dispute dealing with an alleged violation of a penal law.

Writ of *habeas corpus* A court order requiring that government authorities either release a person held in custody or demonstrate that the person is detained in accordance with law.

Jurisdiction The term ***jurisdiction*** refers to the authority of a court to hear and decide a case. The jurisdiction of district courts includes both civil and criminal matters. A **civil case** is a legal dispute concerning a private conflict between two parties—individuals, corporations, or government agencies. A **criminal case** is a legal dispute dealing with an alleged violation of a penal law. More than 80 percent of district court cases are civil disputes.[41] In sheer volume, the main chores of the district courts are naturalizing new citizens and granting passport applications. District courts also have jurisdiction over bankruptcy cases filed under federal law, civil cases involving more than $75,000 in which the U.S. government is a party, and if either litigant requests it, lawsuits in which the parties live in different states and in which more than $75,000 is at stake. In these latter types of cases, federal judges apply the laws of the applicable state rather than federal law.

As for criminal matters, district courts try all cases involving violations of federal law as well as criminal offenses occurring on federal territory, federal reservations, or the high seas. District judges must also rule on *habeas corpus* petitions filed by inmates in both state and federal prisons. A **writ of *habeas corpus*** is a court order requiring government authorities either to release a person held in custody or demonstrate that the person is detained in accordance with law. *Habeas corpus* petitions allege that a prisoner is held contrary to law and ask a court to inquire into the matter. An inmate's attorney may charge, for example, that a state trial court erred in admitting certain evidence, thereby violating the Fourth and Fourteenth Amendments to the U.S. Constitution. If the judge sees merit in the petitioner's complaint, the judge can direct the jailer to reply and a suit will be joined. Death row inmates often use *habeas corpus* petitions to avoid or at least delay their execution. Litigants who lose their district court cases may appeal to a U.S. Court of Appeal. In practice, however, less than 20 percent of district court decisions are appealed.[42]

U.S. Courts of Appeals

The U.S. Courts of Appeals (also known as circuit courts of appeals) are the primary intermediate appellate courts in the federal system, hearing appeals from the federal trial courts. There are 13 courts of appeals, one for each of the 12 judicial circuits (or regions), and a thirteenth circuit called the U.S. Court of Appeals for the Federal Circuit. The latter court hears appeals in specialized cases, such as patent law, and cases appealed from the Court of International Trade and the Court of Federal Claims. The number of justices for each of the circuits ranges from 3 to 24. Altogether, 179 justices staff the courts of appeals along with another 40 senior justices.

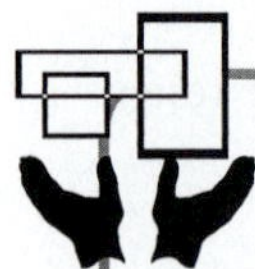

GETTING INVOLVED

A Day in Court

Learn about the judicial branch of government by visiting a courtroom in your community.

Large cities will be home to federal courts and state courts, whereas small towns may have only municipal courts or justice of the peace courts. Go online to locate a court in your area and find out when it is in session. Visit the court for at least an hour. Then, write an essay in which you address the following questions:

- Which court did you visit (give its official title) and when did you go?
- Who was the presiding judge, by name and title?
- How many cases did you witness? Were the cases civil or criminal? How do you know? What issue(s) did the case(s) address?
- How many people were in the courtroom and who were they (defendants, lawyers, jurors, law officers, etc.)?
- Did the court run smoothly? Do you think the court ran fairly? Why do you say so?
- If you could make one change in the manner in which the court was run, what would it be?
- Did you have a good time? Discuss.

Selection of Justices The White House generally takes more care with nominations to the courts of appeals than it does with district court selections. Because the judicial circuits usually include several states, senatorial courtesy does not dictate the selection of justices on the courts of appeals.[43] Consequently, presidents are able to seek out men and women who not only share their political party affiliation but also their policy preferences.[44] When a vacancy occurs, a deputy attorney general gathers names of potential nominees, asking party leaders, senators, and members of the House for suggestions. Eventually, the deputy attorney general suggests a name or perhaps a short list of names for the president's consideration and the president makes a choice.

The Senate examines appellate court nominees more closely than it considers district court selections, especially when the opposition party controls the Senate. Furthermore, as with district court nominees, delays are not unusual. The length of confirmation delays depends on the size of the president's opposition in the Senate, the proximity of the next presidential election, and whether the nominee is a woman or minority. Appellate court nominees who are women or minority take twice as long to confirm as white males.[45] The Senate is more likely to reject nominees when the opposition party controls the Senate and in the last year of a president's term. In 2008, the U.S. Senate, under Democratic control, approved only 10 of 24 Bush nominees to the federal courts of appeals in hopes that a Democratic president would be in place to choose replacement nominees in 2009. The odds of confirmation in any event decline by 25 percent in a presidential election year. Since 1992, less than 60 percent of appeals court nominees have been confirmed compared with 80 percent in earlier years.[46] Most of the unsuccessful nominees failed not because the Senate voted down their confirmations but because the Senate failed to act and their nominations were withdrawn.

The nomination process for courts of appeals judges has become an arena for conflict between the two political parties. After Republicans won control of the Senate in 1994, Democrats accused the Judiciary Committee of blocking many Clinton judicial nominees by failing to hold hearings on them. When George W. Bush won the White House in 2000, he was able to appoint judges to fill the vacancies left at the end of Clinton's term. During Bush's first term, Democrats filibustered 10 of 52 appellate court nominees, declaring that the judicial philosophies of the 10 were so conservative that they were outside the judicial mainstream. Republicans responded to the Democrats' tactic by threatening a procedure they labeled the "constitutional option." Democrats called it the "nuclear option." The strategy involved Republican senators asking the presiding officer of the Senate, probably Vice President Dick Cheney, to rule that it was unconstitutional to filibuster judicial nominees. Because a simple majority would be sufficient to uphold the vice president's ruling, Senate Republicans, who outnumbered Democrats 55 to 45, would be able to end the Democratic filibuster and force a vote on Bush's nominations whose appointments had been blocked. Democrats responded to the Republican strategy by threatening to use various parliamentary maneuvers to shut down or at least seriously delay Senate business.[47] Eventually, a group of 14 senators, seven Democrats and seven Republicans, brokered a compromise to allow the confirmation of some of the filibustered judicial nominees. The compromise defused the crisis temporarily but did not resolve the issue.

The confirmation process for courts of appeals judges has become an arena for conflict between the two political parties because of the importance and finality of the decisions of the appeals courts. Appellate courts decide thousands of cases per year, compared with fewer than a hundred decided by the U.S. Supreme Court, which agrees to hear relatively few appeals.[48] In addition, political parties in Congress are more ideologically polarized now than they were in the past. Republican members of Congress are almost all conservative, whereas their Democratic counterparts are almost all liberal. Most important votes in Congress break down along party lines, so it should be no surprise for judicial confirmation votes to become a partisan battleground as well. Finally, the stakes are high because of the close partisan balance on the courts, in which individual judges can tip the balance in a case.

Jurisdiction The courts of appeals are exclusively appellate courts, usually hearing cases in panels of three justices each. They accept appeals from the U.S. District Courts, the Court of International Trade, and the Court of Federal Claims. The courts of appeals also hear appeals on the decisions of the regulatory commissions, with the rulings of the National Labor Relations Board (NLRB) producing the most appeals. The courts of appeals are generally not required to hold hearings in every case. After reading the legal briefs in a case (a **legal brief** is a written legal argument) and reviewing the trial court record, the appeals court may uphold the lower court decision without hearing formal arguments.

Legal brief Written legal argument.

When an appeals court decides to accept an appeal, the court usually schedules a hearing at which the attorneys for the two sides in the dispute present oral arguments and answer any questions posed by the justices. Appeals courts do not retry cases. Instead, they review the trial court record and consider legal arguments. After hearing oral arguments and studying legal briefs, appeals court justices discuss the case and eventually vote on a decision, with a majority vote of the justices required to decide a case. The court may **affirm** (uphold) the lower court decision, reverse it, modify it, or affirm part of the lower court ruling while reversing or modifying the rest. Frequently, an appeals court may **remand** (return) a case to the trial court for reconsideration in light of the appeals court decision. The courts of appeals have the final word on more than 95 percent of the cases they hear because the Supreme Court rarely intervenes on appeal.[49]

Affirm Uphold the decision of a lower court.

Remand Return a case to a lower court.

Supreme Court of the United States

The Supreme Court of the United States is the highest court in the land. Its rulings take precedence over the decisions of other federal courts. On matters involving federal law and the U.S. Constitution, the decisions of the U.S. Supreme Court take precedence over state court rulings as well.

The Constitution says nothing about the size of the Supreme Court, letting Congress and the president determine its membership legislatively. Through the years, the size of the Court has varied from 5 to 10 justices. The present membership of nine justices has been in effect for more than a century. In the 1930s, President Franklin Roosevelt attempted to enlarge the Court in order to appoint new justices friendly to the New Deal, but his effort was popularly attacked as a court-packing plan and defeated by Congress. Since then, no serious efforts have been made to change the Court's size.

Today's Court includes a chief justice and eight associate justices. The justices are equal and independent, similar to nine separate law firms, but the chief justice is first among them. The chief presides over the Court's public sessions and private conferences. The chief justice can call special sessions of the Court and helps administer the federal court system. The chief justice also assigns justices the responsibility of writing the Court's majority opinion in cases when the chief votes with the majority.

The chief justice is a political leader who, to be successful, must deal effectively with political pressures both inside and outside the Court. Internally, the chief attempts to influence the other members of the Court. Externally, the chief justice lobbies Congress, responding and/or reacting to attacks against the Court. Regular sessions of the Supreme Court run from the first Monday in October until the end of June or early July. The summer months are a time for vacation and individual study by the Court's members, although the chief justice can call a special session to consider particularly pressing matters.

Jurisdiction Technically, the Supreme Court can be both a trial court and an appellate court. The Constitution gives the Court a limited **original jurisdiction,** which is the set of cases a court may hear as a trial court. The Supreme Court may try "cases affecting ambassadors, other public ministers and consuls, and those in which a state shall be a party," except for cases initiated against a state by the citizens of another

Original jurisdiction The set of cases a court may hear as a trial court.

state or nation. In practice, however, the Court does not conduct trials. The Court shares jurisdiction with the U.S. District Courts on the matters included in its original jurisdiction and leaves most of those cases for the district courts to decide. Even for the few cases of original jurisdiction that the justices consider worthwhile, the Supreme Court does not hold a trial. Instead, the Court appoints a special master to conduct a hearing to determine the facts before it decides the legal issues.

The Court's appellate jurisdiction is set by law, and through the years, Congress has made the Supreme Court of the United States the nation's highest appellate court for both the federal and the state judicial systems. In the federal system, the courts of appeals generate the largest number of appeals by far. Cases may arise from the court of military appeals and special three-judge courts, which Congress has authorized to hear redistricting cases and some civil rights cases. Cases can also be appealed to the Supreme Court from the highest court in each state, usually the state supreme court.

Congress can reduce the jurisdiction of the Supreme Court if it chooses. After the Civil War, Congress removed the Court's authority to review the constitutionality of Reconstruction legislation. Since then, Congress has been reluctant to tamper with the jurisdiction of the federal courts on grounds that it would interfere with the independence of the judicial branch. In recent years, most attempts to limit the jurisdiction of federal courts in cases involving such controversial issues as abortion, school prayer, busing, and the rights of criminal defendants have all failed.[50]

Selection of Justices Nominating individuals to the Supreme Court is one of the president's most important responsibilities. Certainly it is an opportunity that may not come often. President Richard Nixon was able to appoint four justices in less than six years in office, but President Carter was unable to make any appointments during his four-year term. Furthermore, each appointment has the potential to affect public policy for years to come, particularly if the Court is closely divided or the president has the chance to name a new chief justice. Members of the Court often time their retirements to maintain the ideological balance on the Court. Whereas conservative jurists want a Republican president to name their successor, liberal justices wait for a Democratic president before they retire.[51]

The formal procedures of appointment and confirmation of Supreme Court justices are similar to those for appellate court justices except they are generally performed more carefully and receive considerably more publicity. The attorney general begins the task by compiling a list of possible nominees. The president narrows the list to a few names and the FBI conducts background checks on each.

In selecting individuals to serve on the Supreme Court, presidents look for nominees who share their political philosophy: Conservative presidents prefer conservative justices, whereas liberal presidents want liberal justices. When President Franklin Roosevelt finally had the chance to make appointments to the Supreme Court, he was careful to select nominees sympathetic to the New Deal. In contrast, President Reagan screened nominees to ensure their political conservatism.

The Senate scrutinizes Supreme Court nominations more closely than lower-court appointments. The Judiciary Committee staff and the staffs of individual

Thurgood Marshall, appointed by President Lyndon Johnson, was the first African American to serve on the Supreme Court.

senators carefully examine the nominee's background and past statements on policy issues. The committee conducts hearings at which the nominee, interest group spokespersons, and other concerned parties testify. The Senate as a whole then debates the nomination on the floor before voting to confirm or reject.

The confirmation process is highly political with the White House and interest groups conducting public relations campaigns in hopes of putting pressure on wavering senators to confirm or reject the president's choice.[52] For example, the nomination of Clarence Thomas by President George H. W. Bush became a political tug-of-war between women's groups and the White House over Thomas's fitness to serve after Anita Hill, a former employee of Thomas at the Equal Employment Opportunity Commission (EEOC), accused him of sexual harassment. Thomas eventually won confirmation by a narrow margin.

The Senate confirms most Supreme Court nominees. Since 1789, the Senate has approved 124 of 153 nominations.[53] Senators routinely vote to confirm nominees who are perceived as well qualified and whose political views are close to those of their constituents. When nominees are less well qualified or hold controversial views, the outcome of the confirmation vote depends to a large degree on the political environment.[54] Opponents of a nomination attempt to identify negative information about a nominee to justify rejection. They hope to expand the conflict over the nomination to the general public through committee hearings and the media. Consider the fate of Harriet Miers, President George W. Bush's first choice to replace the retiring Sandra Day O'Connor on the Supreme Court. She asked the president to withdraw her nomination even before the Senate Judiciary Committee held hearings in the face of withering criticism from conservative commentators that she was both poorly qualified and insufficiently conservative for the job.

The Senate is most likely to reject Supreme Court nominees when the opposition party controls the Senate and/or when a nomination is made in the last year of a president's term.[55] When both these conditions apply, the failure rate for Supreme Court nominees is 71 percent. It is 19 percent when one condition applies and only 10 percent when neither condition exists.[56] The confirmation process has become so contentious that presidents have begun to seek out nominees who have written little so as to minimize the opportunity for opponents to build a case for rejection.

The backgrounds of individuals selected to serve on the Supreme Court are less diverse than in the past. Historically, members of the Supreme Court came to the bench from a variety of backgrounds. Chief Justice Warren had been governor of California. Justice O'Connor was a member of the Arizona legislature. Justice Marshall was chief counsel for the National Association for the Advancement of Colored People (NAACP). In contrast, most justices chosen in the last 40 years have been federal judges, serving on the courts of appeal. Justice Kagan, a former solicitor general (the lawyer who represents the federal government before the Supreme Court) and Harvard Law School dean, is the only current member of the Court without prior judicial experience.

Similar to other federal judges, members of the Supreme Court enjoy the ultimate in job security. With "good behavior," they can serve for life, and many have continued on the bench well past traditional retirement age. Associate Justice Hugo Black, for example, served until age 85; William O. Douglas stayed on the Court until he was 77, despite suffering a debilitating stroke. Justices can be impeached and removed from office, but Congress is unlikely to act without clear evidence of misconduct. Politics or old age and ill health are probably not reason enough for Congress to initiate impeachment proceedings. Furthermore, because of advances in medicine, life tenure means more today than it did when the Constitution was written. Between 1789 and 1970, the average justice served fewer than 15 years, with vacancies occurring on average every two years. Since 1970, the average justice serves more than 26 years and a vacancy occurs every three years.[57] Because modern justices are serving longer, some Court observers advocate the adoption of term limits for Supreme Court justices in hopes of reducing the partisan intensity of the confirmation process and ensuring that each president has the opportunity to make one or two appointments.[58]

WHAT IS YOUR OPINION?

Do you think that federal judges should be periodically subject to reappointment or should serve limited terms? Why or why not?

Deciding to Decide Supreme Court justices set their own agenda. Each year, litigants appeal 7,000 to 10,000 cases to the Supreme Court, far more cases than the Court can reasonably handle. As a result, the justices screen the cases brought to them to decide which ones merit their attention.

Cases are the raw material from which the Supreme Court makes policy. An important judicial ground rule is that the Court must wait for a case to be appealed to it before it can rule. The Supreme Court does not issue advisory opinions. Although the members of the Court decide themselves what cases they will hear, their choices are limited to those cases that come to them on appeal. During the Civil War, for example, Chief Justice Taney and perhaps a majority of the members of the Supreme Court believed that the draft law was unconstitutional. They never had the opportunity to rule on the issue, however, because no case challenging the law ever reached the Court. Today, questions have been raised about the constitutionality of the limitations of the War Powers Act on the president's prerogatives as commander-in-chief, but the issue remains undecided because a case has yet to arise under the law.

Test case A lawsuit initiated to assess the constitutionality of a legislative or executive act.

In forma pauperis The process whereby an indigent litigant can file an appeal of a case to the Supreme Court without paying the usual fees.

Conference A closed meeting of the justices of the Supreme Court.

Rule of Four Decision process used by the Supreme Court to determine which cases to consider on appeal, holding that the Court will hear a case if four of the nine justices agree to the review.

Certiorari or ***Cert*** The technical term for the Supreme Court's decision to hear arguments and make a ruling in a case.

The legal requirement that the Supreme Court can only rule when presented a case gives interest groups an incentive to promote and finance **test cases,** which are lawsuits initiated to challenge the constitutionality of a legislative or executive act. *Brown v. Board of Education of Topeka*, for example, was a test case initiated by the NAACP. Linda Brown was a public-school student who was denied admission to a whites-only school near her home. The NAACP recruited several families, including the Brown family, to file suit and provided the legal and financial resources necessary for carrying the case through the long and expensive process of trial and appeals.

Lawyers for losing parties in lower court proceedings begin the process of appeal to the Supreme Court by filing petitions and submitting briefs explaining why their clients' cases merit review. Appellants must pay a filing fee and submit multiple copies of the paperwork, but the Court will waive these requirements when a litigant is too poor to hire an attorney and cover the expenses of an appeal. The Court allows indigent appellants to file ***in forma pauperis,*** which is the process whereby an indigent litigant can file an appeal of a case to the Supreme Court without paying the usual fees. Frequently, pauper petitions come from prison inmates who study law books and prepare their own appeals. In 2008, 79 percent of the cases appealed to the Supreme Court were *in forma pauperis*.[59] The Court rejects most of these petitions, but a few make the Court's docket for full examination. When the Court decides to accept a case from the *in forma pauperis* docket, it appoints an attorney to prepare and argue the case for the indigent petitioner.

The actual selection process takes place in **conference,** a closed meeting of the justices of the Supreme Court. The justices decide which cases to hear based on the **Rule of Four,** a decision process used by the Supreme Court to determine which cases to consider on appeal, holding that the Court will hear a case if four of the nine justices agree to the review. In practice, the Supreme Court grants ***certiorari*** or ***cert,*** for short, which is the technical term for the Supreme Court's decision to hear arguments and make a ruling in a case, to only about 1 percent of all the cases appealed to it. In its 2008 term, the Court heard arguments on only 83 of 7,738 cases appealed to it.[60]

What kinds of cases does the Supreme Court accept? The justices choose cases with legal issues of national significance that the Court has not already decided, cases involving conflicts among courts of appeals or between a lower court and the Supreme Court, and cases in which the constitutionality of a state or federal law is under attack. The Court rejects cases it considers trivial or local in scope, and cases that raise issues already decided by earlier rulings. The Court will not accept appeals from state courts unless the appellant can demonstrate that a substantial national constitutional question is involved.

In practice, the justices of the Supreme Court set their own rules for deciding which cases to accept, and follow or violate the rules as they see fit. For years, the Court refused to consider whether legislative districts that varied considerably in population size violated the Constitution. It was a political question, the justices said, declaring that the legislative and executive branches of government should address the issue rather than the judicial branch. In 1962, however, in *Baker v. Carr*, the Court chose to overlook its political questions doctrine and rule on the dispute.[61]

Political scientists search for clues as to which cases the Court will agree to decide. In general, studies have found that the justices are more likely to accept a case when the U.S. government is the appellant, civil liberties or race-related issues are involved, a number of interest groups file supporting briefs in a case, and lower courts disagree with one another. The members of the Supreme Court also choose cases that enable them to express their policy preferences with maximum impact. During the 1950s and 1960s, the Warren Court accepted cases to extend the guarantees of the Bill of Rights to the poor and other underdog litigants in both federal and state courts. In contrast, the more conservative Burger and Rehnquist Courts often selected cases in order to adopt conservative policy positions. "Upperdogs," such as the government and business corporations, were more successful in having their appeals heard.

***Per curiam* opinion** An unsigned written opinion issued by the Supreme Court.

***Amicus curiae* or friend of the court briefs** Written legal arguments presented by parties not directly involved in the case.

Deciding the Case The Supreme Court usually deals with the cases it chooses to hear in one of two ways. It decides some cases without oral arguments, issuing a ruling accompanied by an unsigned written opinion called a ***per curiam* opinion** that briefly explains the Court's decision. The justices may use this approach, for example, to reverse a lower court ruling that is contrary to an earlier decision of the Court.

The Court more extensively reviews the remainder of the cases it accepts. The attorneys for the litigants submit briefs arguing the merits of the case and the Court schedules oral arguments. The Court may also receive ***amicus curiae*** or **friend of the court briefs,** which are written legal arguments presented by parties not directly involved in the case, including interest groups and units of government. *Amicus* briefs offer the justices more input than they would otherwise receive and provide interest groups and other units of government an opportunity to lobby the Court. The justices sometimes use information contained in *amicus* briefs to justify their rulings.

Attorneys for the litigants present oral arguments publicly to the nine justices in the courtroom of the Supreme Court building. The Court usually allows each side half an hour to make its case and answer any questions the justices may ask. The members of the Court use the oral arguments to gather information about the case and identify their policy options.[62] A few days after oral arguments, the justices meet in closed conference to discuss the case and take a tentative vote. If the chief

Around the World

Islamic Law in Nigeria

Nigeria is an ethnically and religiously diverse country. Its population includes several major ethnic groups (the Hausa-Fulani, Yoruba, and Igbo) as well as hundreds of smaller groups. The most important religions are Islam, Christianity, Orisha (the traditional Yoruba religion), and Animism, which is the belief that souls inhabit most bodies, including people, animals, plants, and even inanimate objects, such as stones.

After military rule ended in Nigeria in 1999 and the country established a federal system, 12 of the northern states adopted Sharia, which is Islamic law based on the Koran. Sharia addresses issues of sexual morality and alcohol consumption in addition to other crimes. Punishments under Sharia can be harsh. Adulterers may be stoned to death or flogged. Thieves may suffer the amputation of a hand. Public intoxication is punishable by flogging.

The adoption of Sharia in the northern states of Nigeria has been controversial. Even though Sharia applies only to Muslims, some aspects of it, including banning alcohol and prostitution, apply generally. Critics declare that the use of Sharia violates the principle of separation of state and religion. Furthermore, they charge that the status of women under Sharia and its imposition of harsh punishments cast the nation in an unfavorable light. They point to the 2002 case that provoked international outrage in which a divorced Muslim woman was sentenced to death after having a child out of wedlock. Islamic courts eventually overturned the sentence on the basis of a technicality. Sharia courts have subsequently avoided high-profile controversial cases.*

QUESTIONS

1. In a country as diverse as Nigeria, is it better for different regions to follow their own legal traditions or would it be preferable for the entire nation to have a uniform system?
2. Should a nation's laws be based on its religious traditions?
3. To what extent, if any, is American law grounded in Judeo-Christian legal traditions?

*John N. Paden, *Muslim Civic Cultures and Conflict Resolution: The Challenge of Democratic Federalism in Nigeria* (Washington, DC: Brookings Institution Press, 2005), pp. 139–174.

Majority opinion The official written statement of the Supreme Court that explains and justifies its ruling and serves as a guideline for lower courts when similar legal issues arise in the future.

Concurring opinion A judicial statement that agrees with the Court's ruling but disagrees with the reasoning of the majority opinion.

justice sides with the Court's majority on the initial vote, the chief either writes the majority opinion or assigns another justice the task. If the chief justice does not vote with the majority, the most senior justice in the majority is responsible for opinion assigning. The **majority opinion** is the official written statement of the Supreme Court that explains and justifies its ruling and serves as a guideline for lower courts when similar legal issues arise in the future. The majority opinion is more important than the actual decision of the Court because the majority opinion establishes policy.

When the initial opinion assignment is made, everything is still tentative. Over the next several months, some justices may switch sides and others may threaten to change if the majority opinion is not written to their liking. The justice drafting the majority opinion searches for language to satisfy a majority of the Court's members. Inevitably, the opinion will be a negotiated document, reflecting compromise among the justices. While the majority opinion is being drafted, other justices may be preparing and circulating concurring or dissenting opinions. A **concurring opinion** is a

Sandra Day O'Connor, appointed by President Ronald Reagan, was the first woman to serve on the Supreme Court.

judicial statement that agrees with the Court's ruling but disagrees with the reasoning of the majority opinion. A justice may write a concurring opinion to point out what the Court did not do in the majority opinion and identify the issues that remain open for further litigation.[63] A **dissenting opinion** is a judicial statement that disagrees with the decision of the court's majority. Justices write dissenting opinions in order to note disagreement with the Court's ruling, emphasize the limits of the majority opinion, and express the conscience of the individual justice. Only the majority opinion of the Court has legal force.

Dissenting opinion A judicial statement that disagrees with the decision of the court's majority.

The Decision Eventually, the positions of the justices harden or coalesce and the Supreme Court announces its ruling. The announcement takes place in open court and the final versions of the majority, concurring, and dissenting opinions are published in the *United States Reports*. The Court decides cases by majority vote—9–0, 5–4, or anything in between, assuming, of course, that the Court is fully staffed and every justice participates.

Many observers believe that the strength of a Supreme Court decision depends on the level of agreement among the justices. *Brown v. Board of Education* was decided unanimously; the death or resignation of one or two justices was not going to reverse the majority on the issue should a similar case come before the Court in the near future. Furthermore, the Court issued only one opinion, the majority opinion written by Chief Justice Warren. The decision offered no comfort to anyone looking for a weakness of will on the Court. In contrast, the Court's decision in *Furman v. Georgia* (1972) was muddled. In *Furman*, the Court ruled that the death penalty as then practiced was discriminatory and hence unconstitutional. The Court did not say, however, that the death penalty as such was unconstitutional. The ruling's weakness, perhaps fragility, came from the closeness of the vote, 5–4, and the number of opinions—four concurring and four dissenting opinions besides the majority opinion. The justices could not agree on which facts were important in the case or what goals the Court should pursue.[64]

Implementation Political scientists Charles Johnson and Bradley Canon divide the judicial policymaking process into three stages. First, higher courts, especially the U.S. Supreme Court, develop policies. Although major policy cases make headlines, the Supreme Court frequently clarifies and elaborates on an initial decision with subsequent rulings on related issues. Second, lower courts interpret the higher court rulings. In theory, lower federal courts apply policies formulated by the U.S. Supreme Court without modification. In practice, however, Supreme Court rulings are often general, leaving room for lower courts to adapt them to the circumstances of specific cases. The third stage of Johnson and Canon's model of judicial policymaking is the implementation by relevant government agencies and private parties.[65] State legislatures had to rewrite death penalty statutes to comply with the *Furman* ruling, for example. Local school boards had the task of developing integration plans to comply with the *Brown* decision.

Although the implementation of Supreme Court rulings is not automatic, direct disobedience is rare because Court actions enjoy considerable symbolic legitimacy. When the Supreme Court ordered President Nixon to turn over key Watergate tapes to the special prosecutor, for example, Nixon complied. Had the president made a bonfire of them, as some observers suggested, he probably would have been impeached. Instead of defiance, unpopular Supreme Court decisions are often met with delay and subtle evasion.

Impact Supreme Court decisions have their greatest impact when the Court issues a clear decision in a high profile case and its position enjoys strong support from other branches and units of government, interest groups, and public opinion. Figure 13.2 traces the impact of the Court's rulings on abortion. In 1973, when *Roe v. Wade* was decided, the abortion ratio, which is the number of abortions out of every hundred pregnancies resulting in an abortion or live birth, was 19.3. (Abortion was already legal in many states.) Four years later, the abortion ratio had risen to 28.6 and continued climbing until 1983. During the same period, the number of adoptions was falling, apparently because legalized abortion was reducing the number of unwanted infants. In 1970, before *Roe v. Wade*, the total number of adoptions in the nation was 175,000. In 1975, after the decision, the number of adoptions had declined to 129,000.[66]

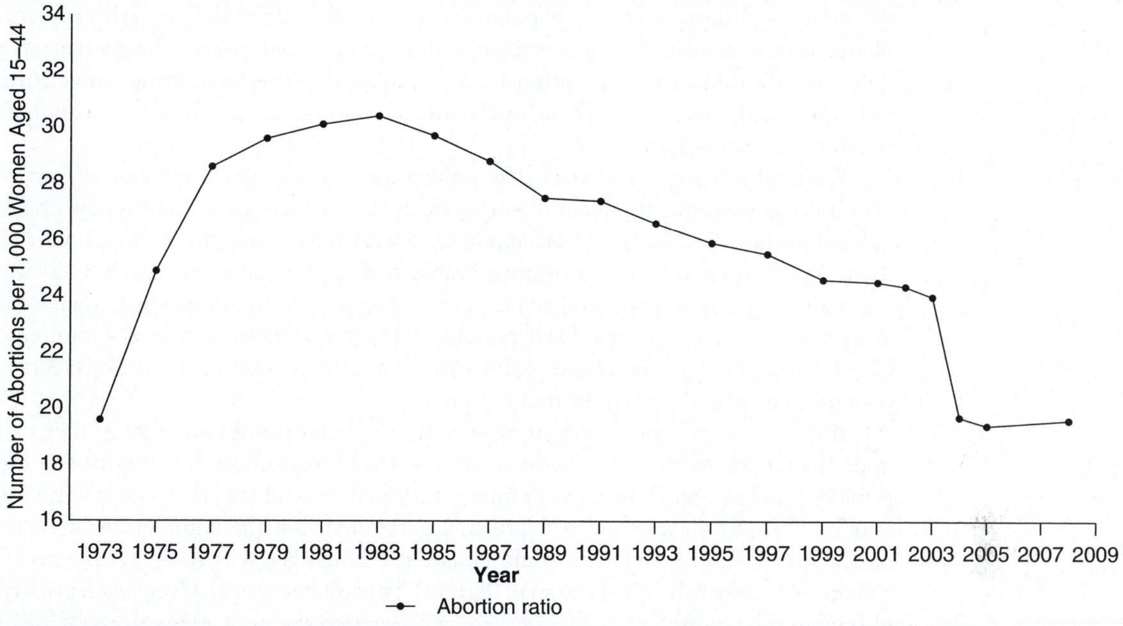

FIGURE 13.2 Abortion Ratio, 1973–2008.
Source: Alan Guttmacher Institute.

As the opponents to abortion have grown more aggressive and the Supreme Court has modified its policy position, the impact of *Roe v. Wade* has lessened. Compared with the middle 1970s, fewer physicians are performing abortions and the number of hospitals and clinics offering abortion services has declined. Some aggressive anti-abortion groups have not only picketed abortion clinics but also the homes of doctors who perform abortions. Some abortion clinics have been bombed and abortion providers threatened with violence. Several doctors who perform abortions have been shot and killed by abortion opponents. Furthermore, the Supreme Court has somewhat backed away from the *Roe* decision, allowing states more leeway to restrict access to abortion. Declining abortion rates may be due to other factors as well, including better access to contraceptives and pregnancy counseling, and changing attitudes about family size.[67]

Power, Politics, and the Courts

How much influence do federal courts have in the policymaking process? How responsive are they to public concerns? On different occasions in American history, various groups and individuals have attacked the federal courts as both too powerful and undemocratic. In the early 1930s, liberals said that the members of the Supreme Court were "nine unelected old men" who abused their power to unravel the New Deal despite strong popular support for President Roosevelt's program. In the 1960s and 1970s, conservatives complained about court rulings that gave rights to accused criminals, atheists, and political protesters, while preventing state and local governments from outlawing abortion or controlling the racial balance of local schools.

Political scientists who study the judicial branch identify a number of restrictions on the power of the federal courts. Both the Constitution and the law check judicial authority. The president appoints federal judges and the Senate confirms their appointments. In the long run, Franklin Roosevelt won his battle with the Supreme Court by waiting for justices to die or retire and then replacing them with individuals friendly to New Deal policies. Voters who believe that the Supreme Court is too liberal or too conservative can eventually reverse the Court by electing conservative/liberal presidents and senators.

If Congress and the president believe that judicial rulings are wrong, they can undo the Court's work by changing the law or the Constitution. If Congress and the president disagree with the Court's interpretation of federal law, they can rewrite the law. In 1978, for example, the Supreme Court ruled that the completion of a dam on the Little Tennessee River would violate the Endangered Species Act because it threatened a tiny fish called the snail darter.[68] The following year, Congress legislated to reverse the Court.

Statutory law Law that is written by a legislature, rather than constitutional law.

Constitutional law Law that involves the interpretation and application of the Constitution.

Congress and the president cannot overrule Supreme Court decisions that are based on interpretations of the Constitution by simply passing legislation. **Statutory law,** which is law that is written by the legislature, does not supersede **constitutional law,** which is law that involves the interpretation and application of the Constitution. Amending the Constitution to overturn court rulings is a more difficult procedure than changing statutory law, of course, but it has been done. The Twenty-sixth Amendment, giving 18-year-olds the right to vote, was passed and ratified after the Supreme Court held that Congress could not legislatively lower the voting age because of constitutional restrictions.[69] Congress and the states have overturned four Supreme Court decisions by enacting constitutional amendments.[70]

The power of the federal courts is also limited by the practical nature of the judicial process. Courts are reactive institutions. They respond to policies adopted in other branches and at other levels of government, and then only when presented with a case to decide. For example, the Supreme Court cannot rule on the constitutionality of the War Powers Act until given a case dealing with the issue.

Because the courts cannot enforce their own rulings, they must depend on the cooperation and compliance of other units of government and private parties to implement their decisions. Consider, for example, the difficulty in enforcing the Supreme Court's school prayer rulings. Despite the Supreme Court's longstanding decision against government-prescribed official prayers in public school classrooms, they continue to take place in a substantial number of schools, especially in the South, in rural and less educated communities, and in areas with relatively high concentrations of conservative Christians.[71]

Political scientist Robert Dahl believes that the courts are not out of step with Congress and the executive branch for long. Dahl conducted a study in which he traced the fate of 23 "important" laws that had been struck down by the Supreme Court. Three-fourths of the time, Dahl found that the original policy position adopted by Congress and the president ultimately prevailed. In most instances, Congress simply passed legislation similar to the measure that had been initially invalidated. The second time around, however, the Court ruled the legislation constitutional. The role of the courts, Dahl said, is to legitimize the policy decisions made by the elected branches of government rather than to make policy on their own.[72]

In contrast, other political scientists believe that Dahl underestimated the policy influence of the courts. They note that whereas Dahl examined issues that he considered important, many so-called unimportant decisions are not unimportant at all, particularly to the groups most directly affected. Even on important matters, Dahl admits that court rulings affect the timing, effectiveness, and details of policy.[73]

The federal courts are important participants in America's policy process, but their influence depends on the political environment, the issue, and the political skills and values of the judges. One study concludes that the power of the federal courts, particularly the Supreme Court, hinges on their capacity to forge alliances with other political forces, including interest groups and the executive branch. In the 1960s, for example, the Supreme Court joined forces with civil rights groups and the White House under Presidents Kennedy and Johnson to promote the cause of African American civil rights.[74] Another study finds that federal judges are more likely to rule against presidential policy when the chief executive has lost popularity than when the president enjoys strong public support.[75]

The role of the courts varies from issue to issue. In today's policy process, the courts are most likely to defer to the other branches of government on issues involving foreign and defense policy, as well as economic policy. The courts are least likely to follow the lead of other branches and units of government on matters dealing with civil rights and civil liberties.

Legal scholar Jeffrey Rosen believes that the courts reflect the views of a majority of Americans on most issues. Judges can nudge the country in one policy direction or another, but they are sensitive to public opinion through pressure by Congress and the president. They recognize that their policy decisions will not be accepted by the country unless those decisions are perceived as being rooted in constitutional principles rather than the personal preferences of judges. On those occasions when courts stray too far away from mainstream public opinion, they get slapped down.[76]

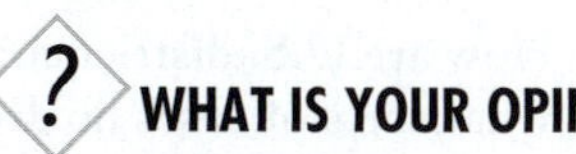

WHAT IS YOUR OPINION?

If you were a member of the Supreme Court, when, if ever, would you consider public opinion in making decisions?

WHAT WE HAVE LEARNED

1. **What role do courts and judges play in the policy process?**

   Courts make policy by interpreting the law and the Constitution. When courts interpret the Constitution, they exercise judicial review. Some justices believe in strict construction, which is the doctrine of constitutional interpretation holding that the document should be interpreted narrowly. Other justices favor loose construction, which is a doctrine of constitutional interpretation holding that the document should be interpreted broadly. Justices also disagree about their role. Judicial activism is the charge that judges are going beyond their authority by making the law and not just interpreting it. Judicial restraint is the concept that judges should defer to the policymaking judgment of the legislative and executive branches of government unless their actions clearly violate the law or the Constitution. Many political scientists believe that all judges regard the Constitution as a charter of fundamental principles that must be upheld, but liberal and conservative judges disagree as to what those principles are.

2. **What is the policymaking history of the U.S. Supreme Court?**

   After a decade of relative unimportance, the Supreme Court asserted its authority to declare acts of Congress unconstitutional in 1803 in *Marbury v. Madison*. The Marshall Court subsequently decided a number of cases important for the nation's political and economic development, including *Martin v. Hunter's Lessee*, the *Dartmouth College Case*, *McCulloch v. Maryland*, and *Gibbons v. Ogden*. The Taney Court moved the Court away from support of a strong national government to advocacy of states' rights, especially in the infamous *Dred Scott* decision. After the Civil War, the Supreme Court focused on protecting property rights from regulation while largely ignoring individual rights and civil rights. In *Plessy v. Ferguson*, for example, the Court upheld state Jim Crow laws. Beginning in 1937, the Court changed course. It upheld the constitutionality of New Deal measures and other government efforts to regulate the economy while adopting the role of protector of individual rights and liberties. The Warren Court in particular strengthened the First Amendment guarantees of freedom of expression and religion, broadened the procedural rights of persons accused of crimes, and ruled decisively in favor of civil rights for African Americans and other minorities. *Brown v. Board of Education*, for example, overturned the *Plessy* decision. In subsequent years, the Supreme Court was neither consistently conservative nor consistently liberal. It issued a number of liberal rulings, including *Roe v. Wade*, but it also made conservative decisions, especially in cases involving the rights of persons accused of crimes and the constitutionality of government efforts to remedy the effects of past racial discrimination. The most controversial recent decision of the Supreme Court was *Bush v. Gore*, which decided the 2000 presidential election.

3. **How is the federal court system organized?**

   The federal court system has three layers. The U.S. District Courts are trial courts, conducting all federal criminal and civil trials except those heard by the U.S. Court of Federal Claims and the U.S. Court of International Trade, which are specialized trial courts. The U.S. Courts of Appeals hear appeals from the federal trial courts and administrative agencies. The U.S. Supreme Court, the highest court in the land, has the authority to try a limited range of cases but in practice is almost exclusively an appellate court.

4. **How are U.S. district court judges selected and what sorts of cases do district courts hear?**

   The president appoints district court judges with Senate confirmation, following the custom of senatorial courtesy. The overwhelming majority of district court nominees are approved, although the confirmation process is sometimes time consuming. Presidents typically nominate judges whose party affiliation and political philosophy are compatible with their own. All federal judges serve for life "with good behavior." District courts hear bankruptcy cases, civil cases in which the U.S. government is a party, and some lawsuits of at least $75,000 in which the litigants live in different states. They hear all federal criminal cases and rule on *habeas corpus* petitions filed by inmates in both state and federal prisons.

5. **What role do the U.S. Courts of Appeals play in the judicial system?**

   The U.S. Courts of Appeals are the intermediate appellate courts in the federal system, hearing appeals from the federal trial courts and from federal regulatory commissions. Both the White House and the Senate take more care with courts of appeals nominees than with district court nominees. Since 1992, less than 60 percent of appeals court nominees have been confirmed, with the Senate failing to act on the unsuccessful nominees rather than voting them down. The courts of appeals hear cases in panels of three justices each. After hearing oral arguments and reviewing briefs, the justices may affirm, reverse, or modify a lower court ruling. The courts of appeals have the final say on most cases because the U.S. Supreme Court seldom accepts appeals of their rulings.

6. **How is the Supreme Court structured and what role does it play in the policy process?**

   The Supreme Court is the highest court in the land. The Constitution is silent about the size of the Court. Congress has set its size at nine—a chief justice, who presides, and eight associate justices. Although the Supreme Court can be both a trial court and an appellate court, in practice it is exclusively an appeals court, hearing cases brought to it from the courts of appeals and the highest court in each state, usually a state supreme court. The president fills vacancies on the Supreme Court by appointment pending Senate confirmation. Presidents are careful to select nominees whose policy preferences mirror their own and the Senate closely scrutinizes nominees. The confirmation process is often highly political. Similar to other federal judges, Supreme Court justices serve for life "with good behavior." The justices select which cases to hear among the thousands that are appealed to it, using the Rule of Four decision-making process. Whereas the Court settles some cases quickly with *per curiam* opinions, most cases involve the justices reading briefs, including *amicus* briefs, and hearing oral arguments. After an initial vote, the chief, if in the majority, or the most senior justice in the majority, either begins writing the majority opinion or assigns it to another justice. Justices may also write concurring and dissenting opinions. Although the Supreme Court decides cases by majority vote, many observers believe that the strength of a ruling depends on the level of agreement among the justices. After the Supreme Court sets policy, lower courts adapt the policies to particular circumstances. Government agencies and private parties implement the policies. Direct disobedience of Supreme Court decisions is rare, but delay and evasion of rulings is not uncommon. Supreme Court decisions have their greatest impact when the Court issues a clear decision in a high profile case and its position enjoys strong support from other branches and units of government, interest groups, and public opinion.

7. **How closely do court decisions reflect public opinion?**

   Political scientists who study the judicial branch identify a number of restraints on the power of the federal courts. Courts will eventually reflect the will of the voters because judges are appointed and confirmed by elected officials. Judicial decisions can be reversed by changing the law or the Constitution. Furthermore, courts are reactive institutions in that they must wait for a case before they can rule and they cannot enforce their own decisions. Political scientist Robert Dahl believes that the courts are not out of step with Congress and the executive branch for long. The role of the courts, Dahl said, is to legitimize the policy decisions made by the elected branches of government rather than to make policy on their own. Political scientist Jeffrey Rosen believes that the courts reflect the views of a majority of Americans on most issues.

KEY TERMS

affirm
amicus curiae or friend of the court brief
appeal
capital punishment
certiorari or *cert*
civil case
civil liberties
civil rights
concurring opinion
conference
constitutional law
criminal case
dissenting opinion
Equal Protection Clause
exclusionary rule
in forma pauperis
Jim Crow laws
judicial activism
judicial restraint
judicial review
jurisdiction
legal brief
loose construction
majority opinion
New Deal
original jurisdiction
per curiam opinion
remand
Rule of Four
senatorial courtesy
sovereign immunity
states' rights
statutory law
strict construction
test case
trial
writ of *habeas corpus*

NOTES

1. Linda Greenhouse, "Is the 'Kennedy Court' Over?" *New York Times*, July 15, 2010, available at www.nytimes.com.
2. Richard Brust, "The 'Super Median': On an Ideological Court, It's All About Keeping Justice Kennedy," *ABA Journal*, July 2010, pp. 20–21, 43.
3. *District of Columbia v. Heller*, 554 U.S. 290 (2008).
4. *Citizens United v. Federal Election Commission*, No. 08-205 (2010).
5. *Graham v. Florida*, No. 08-7412 (2010).
6. Richard L. Pacelle, Jr., *The Role of the Supreme Court in American Politics: The Least Dangerous Branch* (Boulder, CO: Westview, 2002), p. 35.
7. Harold W. Stanley and Richard G. Niemi, *Vital Statistics on American Politics 2007–2008* (Washington, DC: Congressional Quarterly Press, 2008), p. 301.
8. Kermit Roosevelt III, *The Myth of Judicial Activism: Making Sense of Supreme Court Decisions* (New Haven, CT: Yale University Press, 2006), p. 3.
9. Thomas M. Keck, *The Most Activist Supreme Court in History: The Road to Modern Judicial Conservatism* (Chicago, IL: University of Chicago Press, 2004), pp. 286–289.
10. Robert A. Carp, Ronald Stidham, and Kenneth L. Manning, *Judicial Process in America*, 6th ed. (Washington, DC: Congressional Quarterly Press, 2004), p. 28.
11. *Marbury v. Madison*, 1 Cranch 137 (1803).
12. *Martin v. Hunter's Lessee*, 1 Wheaton 304 (1816).
13. *Dartmouth College v. Woodward*, 4 Wheaton 518 (1819).
14. *McCulloch v. Maryland*, 4 Wheaton 316 (1819).
15. *Gibbons v. Ogden*, 9 Wheaton 1 (1824).
16. *Dred Scott v. Sandford*, 19 Howard 393 (1857).

17. *Plessy v. Ferguson*, 163 U.S. 537 (1896).
18. *Brown v. Board of Education of Topeka*, 347 U.S. 483 (1954).
19. *Mapp v. Ohio*, 367 U.S. 643 (1961).
20. *Miranda v. Arizona*, 377 U.S. 201 (1966).
21. *Roe v. Wade*, 410 U.S. 113 (1973).
22. *City of Richmond v. J. A. Croson Co.*, 488 U.S. 469 (1989).
23. *Zelman v. Simmons-Harris*, 536 U.S. 639 (2002).
24. *Lee v. Weisman*, 505 U.S. 577 (1992).
25. *Santa Fe School District v. Doe*, 530 U.S. 290 (2000).
26. *Lawrence v. Texas*, 539 U.S. 558 (2003).
27. *Atkins v. Virginia*, 492 U.S. 302 (2002).
28. *Gratz v. Bollinger*, 539 U.S. 244 (2003).
29. *Grutter v. Bollinger*, 539 U.S. 306 (2003).
30. *United States v. Lopez*, 514 U.S. 549 (1995).
31. *Florida Prepaid Postsecondary Ed. Expense Bd. v. College Savings Bank*, 527 U.S. 666 (1999) and *Alden et al. v. Maine*, 527 U.S. 706 (1999); *Kimel v. Florida Board of Regents*, 528 U.S. 62 (2000).
32. *Bush v. Gore*, 531 U.S. 98 (2000).
33. Jeffrey Rosen, *The Most Democratic Branch: How the Courts Serve America* (New York: Oxford University Press, 2006), p. 148.
34. Elizabeth Garrett, "The Impact of *Bush v. Gore* on Future Democratic Politics," in Gerald M. Pomper and Marc D. Weiner, eds., *The Future of American Democratic Politics: Principles and Practices* (New Brunswick, NJ: Rutgers University Press, 2003), pp. 141–142.
35. *District of Columbia v. Heller*, 554 U.S. 290 (2008).
36. *Kennedy v. Louisiana*, 554 U.S. (2008).
37. Carp, Stidham, and Manning, *Judicial Process in America*, pp. 43–44.
38. Karl Derouen, Jr., Jeffrey S. Peake, and Kenneth Ward, "Presidential Mandates and the Dynamics of Senate Advice and Consent, 1885–1996," *American Politics Research* 33 (January 2005): 106–131.
39. Cass R. Sunstein, David Schkade, Lisa M. Ellman, and Andres Sawicki, *Are Judges Political? An Empirical Analysis of the Federal Judiciary* (Washington, DC: Brookings Institution, 2006), pp. 147–149.
40. Ibid., p. 141.
41. Ibid., p. 52.
42. Ibid., p. 53.
43. Ashlyn Kuersten and Donald Songer, "Presidential Success Through Appointments to the United States Courts of Appeals," *American Politics Research* 31 (March 2003): 119.
44. Michael W. Giles, Virginia A. Hettinger, and Todd Peppers, "Picking Federal Judges: A Note on Policy and Partisan Selection Agendas," *Political Research Quarterly* 54 (September 2001): 623–641.
45. David C. Nixon and David L. Gross, "Confirmation Delay for Vacancies on the Circuit Courts of Appeals," *American Politics Research* 29 (May 2001): 246–274.
46. Sarah A. Binder and Forrest Maltzman, "The Politics of Advice and Consent: Putting Judges on the Federal Bench," in Lawrence C. Dodd and Bruce I. Oppenheimer, eds., *Congress Reconsidered*, 9th ed. (Washington, DC: CQ Press, 2009), pp. 244–245.
47. Helen Dewar and Mike Allen, "GOP May Target Use of Filibuster," *Washington Post*, December 13, 2004, p. A01.
48. R. Jeffrey Smith, "Back-Bench Politics," *Washington Post National Weekly Edition*, December 15–21, 2008, p. 7.
49. Joan Biskupic, "Barely a Dent on the Bench," *Washington Post National Weekly Edition*, October 24–30, 1994, p. 31.
50. Charles Gardner Geyh, *When Courts and Congress Collide: The Struggle for Control of America's Judicial System* (Ann Arbor, MI: University of Michigan Press, 2006), p. 19.
51. Kjersten R. Nelson and Eve M. Ringsmuth, "Departures from the Court: The Political Landscape and Institutional Constraints," *American Politics Research* 37 (May 2009): 486–507.
52. Timothy R. Johnson and Jason M. Roberts, "Presidential Capital and the Supreme Court Confirmation Process," *Journal of Politics* 66 (August 2004): 663–683.
53. Updated data, based on Lawrence Baum, *The Supreme Court* (Washington, DC: CQ Press, 1981), p. 25.
54. Charles M. Cameron, Albert D. Cover, and Jeffrey A. Segal, "Senate Voting on Supreme Court Nominees: A Neoinstitutional Model," *American Political Science Review* 84 (June 1990): 525–534.
55. Keith E. Whittington, "Presidents, Senates, and Failed Supreme Court Nominations," *2006 The Supreme Court Review* (Chicago, IL: University of Chicago Press, 2006), pp. 412–422.
56. John Massaro, *Supremely Political: The Role of Ideology and Presidential Management in Unsuccessful Supreme Court Nominations* (Albany, NY: State University of New York Press, 1990), p. 136.
57. Linda Greenhouse, "New Focus on the Effects of Life Tenure," *New York Times*, September 10, 2007, available at www.nytimes.com.
58. Linda Myers, "Law Professors Propose Term Limits for Supreme Court Justices," January 27, 2005, available at www.cornell.edu.
59. U.S. Supreme Court, "2009 Year-End Report on the Federal Judiciary," available at www.supremecourtus.gov.
60. Ibid.
61. *Baker v. Carr*, 369 U.S. 186 (1962).
62. Timothy R. Johnson, "Information, Oral Arguments, and Supreme Court Decision Making," *American Politics Research* 29 (July 2001): 331–351.
63. David O. Stewart, "A Chorus of Voices," *ABA Journal* (April 1991), p. 50.
64. *Furman v. Georgia*, 408 U.S. 238 (1972).
65. Charles A. Johnson and Bradley C. Canon, *Judicial Policies: Implementation and Impact* (Washington, DC: Congressional Quarterly Press, 1984), Ch. 1.

66. *Statistical Abstract of the United States, 1991*, 111th ed. (Washington, DC: U.S. Department of Commerce, 1991), p. 71.
67. Naseem Sowti, "Fewer Abortions," *Washington Post National Weekly Edition*, July 25–31, 2006, p. 29.
68. *Tennessee Valley Authority v. Hill*, 437 U.S. 153 (1978).
69. *Oregon v. Mitchell*, 400 U.S. 112 (1970).
70. Carp, Stidham, and Manning, *Judicial Process in America*, p. 371.
71. Kevin T. McGuire, "Public Schools, Religious Establishments, and the U.S. Supreme Court: An Examination of Policy Compliance," *American Politics Research* 37 (January 2009): 50–74.
72. Robert Dahl, "Decision-Making in a Democracy: The Supreme Court as a National Policy-Maker," *Journal of Public Law* 6 (Fall 1957): 279–295.
73. Johnson and Canon, *Judicial Policies*, pp. 231–232.
74. Mark Silverstein and Benjamin Ginsberg, "The Supreme Court and the New Politics of Judicial Power," *Political Science Quarterly* 102 (Fall 1987): 371–388.
75. Craig R. Ducat and Robert L. Dudley, "Federal District Judges and Presidential Power During the Postwar Era," *Journal of Politics* 51 (February 1989): 98–118.
76. Rosen, *The Most Democratic Branch*, pp. 7–8.

Chapter 14

Economic Policymaking

CHAPTER OUTLINE

WHAT WE WILL LEARN

After studying Chapter 14, students should be able to answer the following questions:

1. What are the primary goals of American economic policy?
2. What are the most important revenue sources of the federal government?
3. What are the most important issues facing the nation's tax system and what reforms have been proposed for addressing them?
4. What is the history of federal budget deficits and surpluses since the 1940s, and what impact do budget deficits have on the nation's economy?

5. What are the most important spending priorities of the federal government?
6. What is the process through which Congress and the president make fiscal policy?
7. What is the policymaking role of the Federal Reserve System?
8. How is American economic policy made?

Budget deficit The amount by which annual budget expenditures exceed annual budget revenues.

The federal government is spending more money than it collects in taxes, much more. In 2010, federal expenditures exceeded revenues by $1.3 trillion. It was the largest federal **budget deficit,** which is the amount by which expenditures exceed revenues, since the end of World War II when the government borrowed huge sums of money to fund the war effort.[1] Furthermore, the Congressional Budget Office (CBO) projects that the cumulative deficit between 2010 and 2020 will be nearly $10 trillion.[2] Although most economists agree that running a budget deficit is sometimes an appropriate economic policy, they warn that large annual deficits incurred over a long period of time threaten the nation's economic health.

Policymakers disagree about economic policy. President Barack Obama and his Democratic allies in Congress believe that the country needs to adopt a long-term plan for reducing the deficit, including both tax increases and spending reductions. In the short run, however, they contend that the government should increase spending in order to stimulate the economy and reduce the unemployment rate, which exceeded 9 percent in early 2011. In contrast, Republicans counter that government spending and the deficit are the real threat to the economy. They say that the best way to attack the deficit and help the economy is by cutting government spending.

The debate over government spending and the budget deficit introduces this chapter on economic policymaking. The chapter begins by discussing the goals of economic policy. It identifies the most significant revenue sources of the federal government. The chapter examines some of the key issues facing the nation's tax system and the reforms that have been proposed for addressing those issues. It discusses budget deficits and the national debt, and their potential effect on the economy's health. The chapter then examines the major spending priorities of the federal government. It discusses how the government makes fiscal policy as well as the policymaking role of the Federal Reserve System. Finally, the chapter details the economic policymaking process.

The Goals of Economic Policy

Policymakers adopt economic policies in order to achieve the goals of funding government services, encouraging/discouraging private sector activity, redistributing income, and promoting economic growth with stable prices.

Fund Government Services

Americans disagree over spending priorities and the appropriate level of funding for federal government activity. In fiscal year 2010, which ran from October 1, 2009, through September 30, 2010, the federal government spent $3.5 trillion funding

Critics of the NEA are offended by some of the art that the agency supports, such as *Piss Christ*, a 1987 photograph of a small plastic crucifix submerged in a glass of urine.

government programs, including healthcare, Social Security, and national defense.[3] In general, liberals believe that government can play a positive role in addressing the needs of society. They favor programs to improve the nation's health, education, and welfare. In contrast, conservatives believe that the role of government should be limited to the provision of basic services. They support spending for national defense and to promote economic development, but they are wary about spending for social programs, especially by the federal government, because they think that high taxes and big government suppress economic growth.

Consider the controversy over the National Endowment for the Arts (NEA), which is a government agency created to nurture cultural expression and promote appreciation of the arts. The NEA helps fund art exhibitions, drama productions, and musical performances all over the United States. Many conservative members of Congress want to end funding for the NEA. They are angry because some NEA money has gone to support controversial artistic works that they consider sacrilegious or that they believe promote homosexuality. Conservative members of Congress also question whether the federal government has a role in funding art. Why should taxpayers support art, they ask, especially art that may offend them? In contrast, liberal members of Congress defend the NEA. Government should support the arts, they declare, because it enriches the cultural life of the nation. Theatrical productions, musical performances, and art exhibits enhance local economic development by promoting tourism. Sometimes art will be controversial, but the government should not dictate to artists what their art should embody.

WHAT IS YOUR OPINION?

Do you think that tax money should support the National Endowment for the Arts (NEA)? Why or why not?

Welfare state A government that takes responsibility for the welfare of its citizens through programs in public health, public housing, old-age pensions, unemployment compensation, and the like.

Americans also disagree about the future of the **welfare state,** which is a government that takes responsibility for the welfare of its citizens through programs in public health, old-age pensions, public housing, unemployment compensation, and the like. The most important welfare programs in the United States are health insurance coverage and pensions for older Americans, unemployment insurance for workers, agricultural support for farmers, and various assistance programs for the poor. Most of these programs were enacted during the administrations of two Democratic presidents, Franklin Roosevelt in the 1930s and Lyndon Johnson in the 1960s. The adoption of healthcare reform in 2010 was the latest expansion of the welfare state. Liberals supported healthcare reform and favor updating other programs to assist two-wage earner families in balancing the demands of work and family. In contrast, conservatives opposed healthcare reform and favor cutting back the welfare state to reduce the size and cost of government.[4]

Encourage/Discourage Private Sector Activity

The Patel and Martinez families live next door to one another in a middle-class suburb of Los Angeles, California. The two families are the same size, have the same family income, and live in homes of equal value. Nonetheless, the Patel family pays more money in income tax than the Martinez family pays. The only difference between the two families is that the Patel family rents, whereas the Martinez family owns its home. Money paid for real estate taxes and home mortgage interest is tax deductible, but rent payments are not.

Congress and the president use economic policy to encourage some private sector activities while discouraging others. By making home mortgage interest and real estate taxes deductible, the federal government promotes housing construction and home ownership. Similarly, the government uses tax breaks to encourage people to give money to charity, save for retirement, and invest in state and local government bonds. Congress and the president also use tax policy to discourage certain activities.

Increasing cigarette taxes, for example, reduces the smoking rate for teenagers. Raising gasoline taxes saves energy and decreases pollution by discouraging driving.

Subsidy A financial incentive given by government to an individual or a business interest to accomplish a public objective.

A **subsidy** is a financial incentive given by government to an individual or a business interest to accomplish a public objective. The federal government encourages people to go to college by providing students with low-interest loans. It keeps the U.S. Merchant Marine in business by requiring that goods shipped between American ports travel on American-flag vessels with American crews rather than less expensive foreign-registered ships. Government subsidizes farm production, cattle grazing on western lands, offshore oil production, and the marketing of American products and goods overseas.

The government operates a number of agricultural subsidy programs. It gives some farmers price-support loans. Farmers borrow money from the government, using their crops as collateral. The value of the crops, and hence the amount of money the farmer can borrow, is determined by a target commodity price set by the U.S. Department of Agriculture (USDA). If the market price rises above the target price, the farmer sells the crop, repays the loan, and makes a profit. Should the market price stay below the target price, the farmer is allowed to forfeit the crop to the government as full repayment for the loan. In addition, some farmers receive direct subsidies from the government. If the market price falls below the target price, the government pays farmers the difference between the two prices, either in cash or in certificates for government-stored commodities. The government also subsidizes farmers by intervening to limit commodity production, thus driving up market prices. No one can grow peanuts, for example, without a federal license. Because the number of licenses is limited, the number of peanut growers is limited as well. New farmers cannot get into the business unless they buy or rent a license from someone who already owns one. In practice, the expense of renting a license is usually the single largest cost of doing business for peanut farmers.

WHAT IS YOUR OPINION?

Do you think the government should subsidize farm production? Why or why not?

Tax incentives and subsidies are controversial. Their defenders argue that tax incentives and subsidies enable the government to accomplish worthwhile goals, such as promoting home ownership and the export of American-made goods. Farm subsidies are necessary, they say, to preserve the family farm and support the rural economy. Just because everyone may not agree with every tax break or subsidy, they say, is not a good reason to discredit the approach. In contrast, the critics of tax incentives and subsidies charge that they are based more on politics than the desire to achieve worthwhile policy goals. Tax breaks and subsidies drive up taxes and product costs for ordinary Americans and consumers. Congress and the president persist in reauthorizing and funding farm programs because of the political power of agricultural interest groups. Even though consumers and taxpayers are much more numerous than farmers, they are typically indifferent to farm subsidies because the cost to the average American is only a few dollars a year. In contrast, agricultural interests have a strong incentive to fight to defend and even expand their subsidies because they receive thousands of dollars in annual benefits.[5]

Redistribute Income

Income redistribution The government taking items of value, especially money, from some groups of people and then giving items of value, either in cash or services, to other groups of people.

Income redistribution involves the government taking items of value, especially money, from some groups of people and then giving items of value, either in cash or services, to other groups of people. Those people who favor income redistribution believe that government has an obligation to reduce the income gap between the poorest and wealthiest income groups in the nation. They advocate the adoption of programs that provide benefits based on need and a tax structure whose burden falls most heavily on businesses and the wealthy. Furthermore, many scholars believe that extreme levels of income inequality are incompatible with democracy. They note that the world's democracies tend to be countries with a large middle class, whereas countries that are divided between a small group of very rich families and a huge group of the very poor typically do not have democratic governments. In contrast, the opponents of income redistribution believe that government should adopt tax systems and spending programs designed to foster economic development because in the long run economic development will benefit all segments of society, including low-income groups, more than programs designed to redistribute wealth. In practice, they warn, programs designed to redistribute wealth hinder economic development, hurting everyone. They believe that government has a role to ensure a level playing field in which everyone can compete fairly to get ahead, but that government should not intervene to dictate economic winners and losers.

Social Security A federal pension and disability insurance program funded through a payroll tax on workers and their employers.

Many government programs redistribute income. Healthcare reform transfers wealth from upper-income earners to low- and middle-income people. Whereas the program primarily benefits low- and middle-income people who lack health insurance and cannot afford to purchase policies on their own, most of the money to pay for healthcare reform comes from taxes on people earning more than $200,000 a year for individuals and $250,000 for families.[6] Not all redistributive programs transfer money from upper-income groups to lower-income earners, however. For example, **Social Security** is a federal pension and disability insurance program funded through a payroll tax on workers and their employers. It transfers money from current wage earners and their employers to retirees and people with disabilities.

Depression A severe and prolonged economic slump characterized by decreased business activity and high unemployment.

Recession An economic slowdown characterized by declining economic output and rising unemployment.

Inflation A decline in a currency's purchasing power.

Promote Economic Growth with Stable Prices

A final goal of economic policy is to promote economic growth by avoiding depression, minimizing the severity of recession, and controlling inflation.[7] A **depression** is a severe and prolonged economic slump characterized by decreased business activity and high unemployment. It is more severe than a **recession,** which is an economic slowdown characterized by declining economic output and rising unemployment. **Inflation** is a decline in the purchasing power of the currency. Consider the government's response to the severe recession of 2008–2009. Early in 2008, Congress passed, and President George W. Bush signed, legislation to give most taxpayers a $600 tax rebate in hopes that they would spend the money and thus boost the economy. The rebates, which cost the government $170 billion, helped stimulate economic growth but only temporarily. Later in the year, with economic conditions worsening, the Bush administration loaned billions of dollars to companies to keep them from failing, including GM and Chrysler. Meanwhile, Congress authorized the U.S. Department of the Treasury to spend $700 billion to bail out the financial industry in hopes that banks and mortgage companies would begin making loans again, freeing the credit market. The Federal Reserve reduced interest rates to near zero and loaned money to financial institutions as well. In early 2009, Congress passed, and President Barack Obama signed, a $787 billion stimulus package of tax cuts and spending programs designed to get the economy moving again. Congress passed, and the president signed, a measure in 2010 to give $26 billion more to states to minimize the number of teachers who would otherwise lose their jobs and to help states cover the cost of providing healthcare to low-income people. Finally, in late 2010, Congress passed, and the president signed, legislation to extend tax cuts adopted during the Bush administration for two years and continue unemployment benefits for millions of unemployed workers.

Government efforts to manage the economy are controversial. Liberal economists believe that the government can play a positive role in promoting economic growth with stable prices. They credit the actions of the Bush and Obama administrations with saving the nation from another Great Depression. Although the recession was severe, so severe that it is often called the Great Recession, it could have been much worse.[8] In contrast, conservatives argue that government interventions in the economy are counterproductive. Government bailouts and stimulus spending drive up the deficit, they say, without making the economy more efficient. In their view, the best government policies for promoting economic growth are low taxes, low spending, and minimal regulation.

Revenues—How Government Raises Money

In 2010, the U.S. government raised $2.2 trillion in revenue. As the pie chart in Figure 14.1 shows, the individual income tax and payroll taxes together generated nearly 85 percent of federal government revenue. The corporate income tax, along with a variety of other sources, accounted for the remainder.

Individual Income Tax

Fiscal year
Budget year.

The individual income tax is the largest single source of revenue for the national government, producing 43.2 percent of the nation's total tax revenue in **fiscal year** (budget year) 2010. The income tax system divides taxable income into brackets and applies a different tax rate to the portion of income falling into each bracket, with higher incomes taxed at higher rates than lower incomes. Table 14.1 shows the taxable income ranges for each bracket for couples and singles in 2010. Because the income tax brackets are adjusted annually for inflation, the cutoff points between

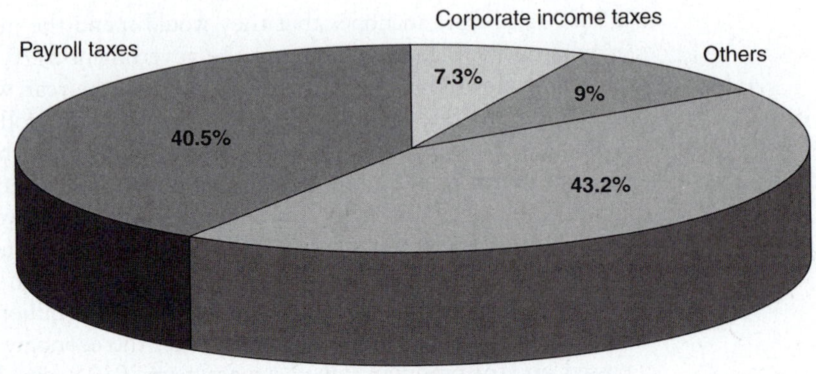

FIGURE 14.1 Sources of Tax Revenue, 2010.
Source: Office of Management and Budget, available at www.omb.gov.

TABLE 14.1 Federal Income Tax Brackets, 2010

Tax Rate	Married Couple Filing Jointly	Singles
10%	Not over $16,750	Not over $8,375
15%	$16,751–$68,000	$8,375–$34,000
25%	$68,001–$137,300	$34,001– $82,400
28%	$137,301–$209,250	$82,401–$171,850
33%	$209,251–$373,650	$171,851–$373,650
35%	Over $373,650	Over $373,650

Source: Internal Revenue Service, available at www.irs.gov.

brackets change somewhat from year to year. A married couple filing jointly that had $150,000 of taxable income in 2010 paid a 10 percent tax on the first $16,750 of taxable income, 15 percent on money earned from $16,751 to $68,000, 25 percent on taxable income from $68,001 through $137,300, and 28 percent on the remainder of their income. Their tax bill would have been calculated as follows:

10% × $16,750	=	$ 1,675
15% × $51,250 ($68,000 – $16,750)	=	$ 7,688
25% × $69,300 ($137,300 – $68,000)	=	$17,325
28% × $12,700 ($150,000 – $137,300)	=	$ 3,556
Total tax owed		$30,244

Because of the bracket system, the couple's income tax bill amounted to 20 percent of their *taxable* income.

Income tax rates are a source of political conflict. When President Bill Clinton left office in 2001, the tax tables included five brackets with tax rates of 15, 28, 31, 36, and 39.6 percent. Shortly after taking office, President George W. Bush

Estate tax A tax levied on the value of an inheritance.

proposed, and Congress passed, a major income tax cut that increased the number of brackets to six and reduced the rates to 10, 15, 25, 28, 33, and 35 percent. They also agreed gradually to repeal the **estate tax,** which is a tax levied on the value of an inheritance. Congress and the president subsequently reduced taxes on dividend income, and exempted or deferred taxes on interest income from savings. In order to avoid a Senate filibuster, Republican leaders phased the tax cuts in over the following decade and then allowed them all to expire in 2011. President Obama has proposed making the Bush tax cuts permanent for everyone but families earning more than $250,000 a year and individuals making more than $200,000 annually. He would then use the extra revenue to reduce the deficit. Republicans, meanwhile, want to make all the Bush tax cuts permanent, arguing that increasing taxes, even if limited to the top brackets, would hurt the economy. In late 2010, President Obama and Republican leaders in Congress agreed to extend the Bush tax cuts for two years while extending unemployment benefits for the long-term unemployed.

Tax preference A tax deduction or exclusion that allows individuals to pay less tax than they would otherwise.

Tax exemption The exclusion of some types of income from taxation.

Because of tax preferences, not all income is taxable. A **tax preference** is a tax deduction or exclusion that allows individuals to pay less tax than they would otherwise. Tax preferences include tax exemptions, deductions, and credits. A **tax exemption** is the exclusion of some types of income from taxation. Veterans' benefits, pension contributions and earnings, and interest earned on state and local government bonds are exempt from the income tax. Social Security benefits are exempt for retired couples with a taxable annual income less than $32,000 a year and retired individuals who have a taxable annual income that is less than $25,000. Retirees earning more than those amounts pay income taxes on 85 percent of the Social Security benefits they receive. Taxpayers are also allowed to claim personal exemptions for themselves and their dependents. In 2010, the personal exemption was $3,650 for every taxpayer and each dependent.

Tax deduction An expenditure that can be subtracted from a taxpayer's gross income before figuring the tax owed.

A **tax deduction** is an expenditure that can be subtracted from a taxpayer's gross income before figuring the tax owed. Taxpayers can itemize deductions for such expenditures as home-mortgage interest payments, charitable contributions, and state and local real estate taxes. For example, a family that contributes $5,000 to charity reduces its taxable income by $5,000.

Tax credit An expenditure that reduces an individual's tax liability by the amount of the credit.

A **tax credit** is an expenditure that reduces an individual's tax liability by the amount of the credit. A tax credit of $500 reduces the amount of tax owed by $500. The Hope Scholarship, for example, grants first- and second-year college students tax credits up to $1,500 to cover the cost of college tuition and fees. Likewise, a family tax credit of $5,000 to purchase health insurance reduces the family's income tax burden by $5,000.

Tax preferences have both critics and defenders. Their opponents say that tax preferences erode taxpayer confidence in the income tax. The U.S. Tax Code is more than 70,000 pages long and the Internal Revenue Service (IRS) has published thousands of pages of regulations to explain it.[9] Tax preparation has become a major industry. Tax preferences also reduce tax receipts. In 2010, tax preferences reduced individual and corporate income tax collections by nearly $1 trillion.[10] Nonetheless, every tax preference has its defenders. One person's loophole is another's sacred right. Homeowners, wage earners, the elderly, churches, schools, businesses, and

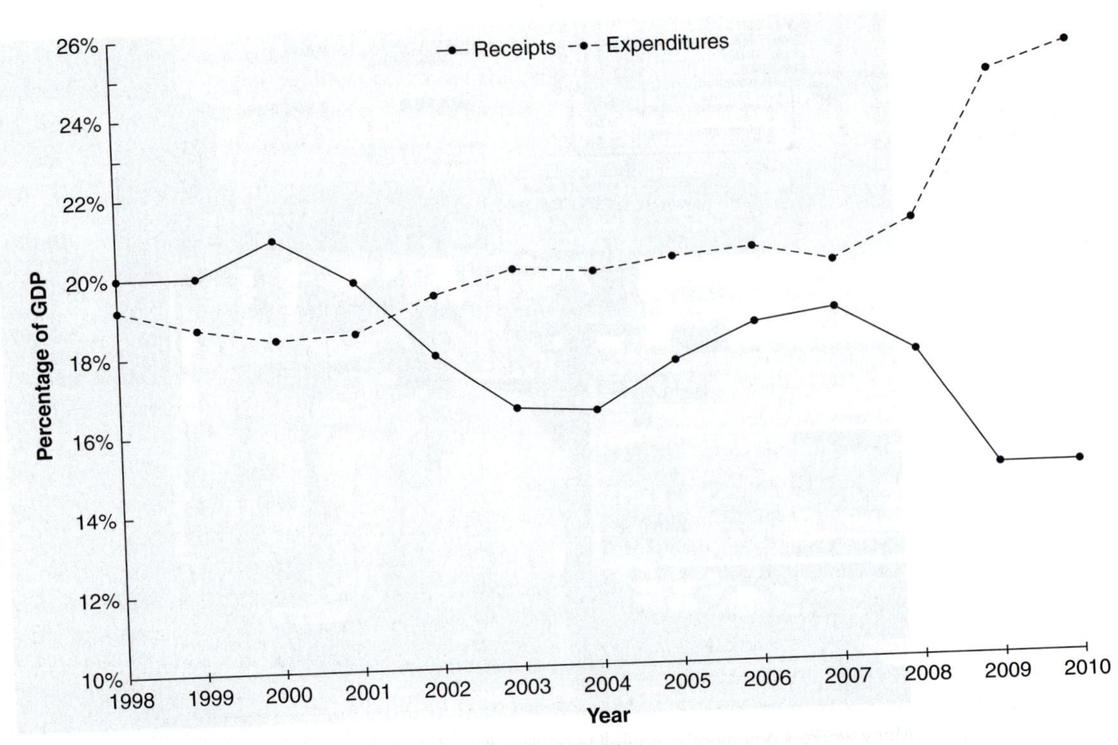

FIGURE 14.2 Receipts and Expenditures as Pct. of GDP, 1998–2010.
Source: Office of Management and Budget.

Japan (35 percent), and the United Kingdom (41.9 percent) all allocate more of their national income to government than does the United States.[12] In contrast, other scholars contend that Americans are overtaxed and they warn that high tax rates depress economic growth. In general, Republicans believe that high taxes undermine economic prosperity, whereas Democrats resist tax cuts because they want to ensure that the government has sufficient revenue to fund essential government services.

Progressive tax A levy that taxes people earning higher incomes at a higher rate than it does individuals making less money.

Proportional tax A levy that taxes all persons at the same percentage rate, regardless of income.

Regressive tax A levy whose burden falls more heavily on lower-income groups than on wealthy taxpayers.

Tax Fairness

Social scientists classify taxes as progressive, proportional, or regressive based on how a particular tax affects different income groups. A **progressive tax** is a levy that taxes people earning higher incomes at a higher rate than it does individuals making less money. The federal income tax is a progressive tax because people earning higher incomes pay a higher tax rate than persons making less money. A **proportional tax** is a levy that taxes all persons at the same percentage rate, regardless of income, whereas a **regressive tax** is a levy whose burden falls more heavily on lower-income groups than on wealthy taxpayers. Economists generally classify sales and excise taxes as regressive taxes because lower-income persons spend a greater proportion of their earnings on items subject to taxation than do upper-income persons.

Ability to pay theory of taxation An approach to government finance that holds that taxes should be based on an individual's ability to pay.

Observers disagree about the fairest tax system. The advocates of progressive taxation often defend the concept on the basis of the **ability to pay theory of taxation,** which is the approach to government finance that holds that taxes should be based on an individual's ability to pay. Well-to-do persons can better afford taxes than lower-income individuals, so they should pay more.[13] Furthermore, the advocates of income redistribution point out that a progressive tax helps to narrow the income differential between the poor and the affluent.

Other experts on public finance believe that the best tax system is one that encourages economic growth. They favor sales and excise taxes because those levies discourage people from spending their money on consumer goods. They want people to save and invest their incomes. They also believe that progressive taxes such as the income tax are harmful to the economy because they reduce the amount of money middle- and upper-income individuals have available to invest in economic development.

Economists conclude that the current federal tax system is either slightly progressive or slightly regressive, depending on the set of assumptions one accepts. The personal income tax is progressive, but payroll taxes and excise taxes are regressive. Most economists believe that the corporate income tax is progressive as well because the burden of the tax falls primarily on stockholders who as a group are more affluent than the average American.[14] Although the payroll tax *appears* proportional, it is actually regressive because, until the adoption of healthcare reform, it was assessed only on wages and not on other types of income, such as dividends and interest earned on savings. Extending the Medicare tax to the dividend and interest income of upper-income taxpayers makes the payroll tax less regressive.

? WHAT IS YOUR OPINION?

Do you think people who make more money should pay a greater proportion of their earnings in taxes than people with lower incomes?

Tax Reform

Critics of the nation's tax system offer a number of prescriptions for reform. The advocates of progressive tax systems favor increasing income tax rates on corporations and upper-income taxpayers while cutting taxes for people at the lower end of the income ladder. They also support reducing or eliminating deductions that allow upper-income persons and corporations to avoid paying taxes. In contrast, the opponents of progressive income tax systems charge that raising taxes on upper-income families and corporations would hurt the economy by discouraging savings and investment.

Flat tax An income tax that assesses the same percentage tax rate on all income levels above a personal exemption while allowing few, if any, deductions.

Instead of making the income tax more progressive, some reformers favor making it proportional. They want the United States to replace the current income tax system with a **flat tax,** which is an income tax that assesses the same percentage tax rate on all income levels above a personal exemption while allowing few if any deductions. The advocates of the flat tax prefer it to the current income tax system because it is simpler and because it would close loopholes that allow wealthy individuals to escape taxation. Moreover, people who work harder and earn more money would no longer be penalized by having a greater proportion of their earnings taken by the government in taxes.

Not everyone thinks the flat tax is a good idea. Critics charge that it would increase the tax bite on middle-income Americans while cutting taxes for the wealthy. The current income tax system is graduated in that it assesses a higher tax rate on higher incomes than on lower incomes. A flat tax that was designed to generate the same amount of revenue as the current income tax system would lower taxes on wealthy families while increasing taxes for lower- and middle-income families. Another criticism of the flat tax is that it would eliminate popular tax deductions. If homeowners cannot deduct mortgage interest and real estate taxes, the cost of owning a home would rise significantly. Charities, religious organizations, colleges, and universities would suffer because gifts to them would no longer be tax deductible. Businesses that lose tax breaks would probably pass along their additional costs to consumers.

WHAT IS YOUR OPINION?

Would you be better off with the current income tax or with a flat tax?

Sales tax A levy on the retail sale of taxable items.

Value added tax (VAT) A tax on the estimated market value added to a product or material at each stage of its manufacture or distribution, which is ultimately passed on to the consumer.

European Union (EU) An economic and political union of 27 member states, mostly in Europe.

International Monetary Fund (IMF) An international organization created to promote economic stability worldwide.

Some reformers want to replace the income tax with a national **sales tax,** which is a levy assessed on the retail sale of taxable items. Because the national sales tax could be collected through the systems that the states now use to collect state and local sales taxes, the IRS could be eliminated and taxpayers would no longer have to spend time and money keeping tax records. Furthermore, a national sales tax would provide a powerful incentive for savings and investment because investment income would not be taxed. Nonetheless, the proposal for a national sales tax has its share of critics. Opponents point out that a national sales tax rate would have to be set at 18 to 20 percent on top of existing state and local sales taxes in order to raise as much money as the current personal income tax. Also, the burden of the sales tax would fall most heavily on low- and middle-income wage earners because they spend a greater proportion of their earnings on retail purchases, which are taxed. In contrast, upper-income families who devote a greater share of their earnings to real estate purchases and investments in stocks and bonds, transactions that are not typically subject to sales taxes, would pay less than they do now.

Some members of Congress have begun discussing the possible adoption of a **value added tax (VAT),** which is a tax on the estimated market value added to a product or material at each stage of its manufacture or distribution, ultimately passed on to the consumer. Assume that a manufacturer buys raw material for $1,000 and uses it to create a consumer product worth $1,500. The value added is $500 and that amount is subject to the tax. The VAT is similar to a sales tax, but more difficult to evade because manufacturers pay the tax rather than consumers. The VAT, which is used extensively around the world, can raise a great deal of money. It is also

Around the World

Debt Crisis in Greece

Governments borrow money by selling various types of securities to investors. These securities are essentially promissory notes that the government will repay the debt with interest on a certain date. The interest rate that government pays depends on the confidence investors have in the government's ability to repay its debt. As notes mature, the government pays them off with tax revenues if the budget is in surplus. If the budget is in deficit, the government must borrow not just to fund its current deficit but also to refinance old debt that has come due.

In 2010, the Greek government faced a debt crisis when it found itself unable to refinance its debt. Investors were wary of loaning more money to Greece because the Greek national debt was larger than its GDP and growing rapidly.* To make matters worse, investors were not certain they could trust Greece to honor its financial commitments because the Greek government admitted that the previous government had lied about the size of its deficit in order to win admittance to the **European Union (EU),** which is an economic and political union of 27 member states, mostly in Europe.†

The Greek debt crisis threatened not just Greece but the world economy. If Greece defaulted on its debt because it could not borrow the funds needed to refinance it, the investors who had initially loaned Greece money would lose their money. Those investors included banks in Europe and the United States. A Greek default would likely make future investors wary about loaning money to governments in general, driving up interest rates worldwide. Furthermore, a default would put pressure on Portugal, Italy, and Spain, countries which, along with Greece, are known as the PIGS, after their initials, because of their high level of debt.‡

Other members of the EU and the **International Monetary Fund (IMF),** which is an international organization created to promote economic stability worldwide, eventually agreed to help Greece finance its debt. Wealthier EU members, particularly Germany and France, and the IMF put together a financial plan of more than $100 billion to guarantee loans to Greece. The guarantee was the international financial equivalent of co-signing on a loan. Investors would now be willing to lend to Greece because their investments were guaranteed by the IMF and EU countries with better credit. In exchange for the guarantee, the Greek government agreed to raise taxes, crack down on tax evasion, and cut spending.

The Greek bailout was widely unpopular. Greece was rocked by violent protests against pay cuts and layoffs of government workers, an increase in the retirement age, and a series of tax increases.§ Meanwhile, people in other EU countries, especially Germany, resented having their tax dollars put at risk to support what they regarded as irresponsible budget policies in Greece. Why should Germany, with a retirement age of 67, bail out Greece, where the retirement age is 61?**

Questions

1. How closely does the debt situation in the United States resemble that of Greece?
2. Would you be willing to pay higher taxes and receive fewer services in order to reduce the federal budget deficit?
3. Do you think candidates in the United States (or anywhere, for that matter) would be successful if they ran for office promising to cut spending and increase taxes? Why or why not?

*"Greece's Financial Crisis Explained," CNN, March 26, 2010, available at www.cnn.com.

†Sheldon Filger, "Greek Debt Crisis Gets Steadily Worse Amid a Sea of Fiscal Deception," *Huffington Post*, April 22, 2010, available at www.huffingtonpost.com.

‡David McHugh, "Q & A on the Greek Debt Crisis," *Bloomberg Businessweek*, March 4, 2010, available at www.businessweek.com.

§"Greece's Austerity Measures," BBC, May 5, 2010, available at www.bbc.co.uk.

**Kate Connolly, "Greek Debt Crisis: The View from Germany," *Guardian*, February 11, 2010, available at www.guardian.co.uk.

relatively invisible to consumers (and voters) because it is included in the final cost of an item rather than added on at the point of purchase similar to a sales tax. Critics charge that the VAT is regressive for the same reason sales taxes are regressive—low-income people spend more of their incomes on items subject to the tax than do upper-income people.[15]

Deficits and the Debt

Budget surplus The sum by which annual budget revenues exceed annual budget expenditures.

Balanced budget Budget receipts that equal budget expenditures.

National debt The accumulated indebtedness of the federal government.

The terms *budget deficit*, *budget surplus*, and *balanced budget* all refer to the relationship between annual budget revenues and budget expenditures. In contrast to a budget deficit, which is the amount of money by which annual budget *expenditures* exceed annual budget *receipts*, a **budget surplus** is the sum by which annual budget *receipts* exceed annual budget *expenditures*. If budget receipts equal budget expenditures, the government has a **balanced budget.** Finally, the **national debt** is the accumulated indebtedness of the federal government. An annual budget deficit increases the debt by the amount of the deficit, whereas a surplus decreases the debt. In 2010, for example, federal receipts were $2.2 trillion compared with outlays of $3.5 trillion, for a budget deficit of $1.3 trillion.[16] As a result, the national debt grew by $1.3 trillion during 2010.

By graphing both budget receipts and budget outlays as a percentage of GDP, Figure 14.2 also graphs the relative size of budget deficits and surpluses between 1998 and 2010. The government began the period with a surplus and some economists actually predicted that it was on course to pay off the national debt. The surplus turned into a deficit in 2002, and the deficit grew wider until 2006 when rising tax revenues began to close the gap. In 2008, 2009, and 2010, the deficit gap expanded dramatically as expenditures rose while revenues fell.

Changes in budget deficits and surpluses reflect fluctuations in the health of the nation's economy and the policy decisions of Congress and the president. The widening budget gap of the late 2000s and 2010 was a direct result of the Great Recession. During a recession, tax revenues fall because personal income and corporate profits are down. In the meantime, expenditures increase as welfare payments and unemployment compensation claims rise. For opposite reasons, economic booms increase government revenues while decreasing expenditures. The mounting surpluses of the late 1990s and 2000 were largely the result of an economic boom that produced rapidly growing tax collections.

Deficits and surpluses also reflect policy decisions. The record budget surpluses of 2000 and 2001 turned into record deficits because of tax cuts and increased government spending. Shortly after taking office, President George W. Bush proposed, and Congress passed, a series of tax cuts that reduced government revenues by $5 trillion over the next decade. Meanwhile, government spending soared. Some of the increased expenditures were earmarked to conduct the war on terror, fight wars in Afghanistan and Iraq, and provide for homeland security. The president and Congress added hundreds of billions of dollars more to the budget imbalance by increasing spending for education, transportation, healthcare, and farm subsidies.[17]

When the federal budget is in deficit, the Department of the Treasury borrows money to close the gap between revenues and expenditures. Much of the money needed to cover the deficit is borrowed from surplus funds in other federal accounts, such as the Social Security Old Age and Survivors Insurance (OASI) Trust Fund, which by law must be invested in U.S. Treasury securities. The government borrows the rest of the money from public sources, such as savings and loan institutions, corporations, insurance companies, commercial banks, state and local governments, foreign investors, foreign governments, and individual Americans. The U.S. government increasingly relies on foreign lenders to finance the debt.[18] The most important foreign investors in American securities in 2009 were China ($768 billion) and Japan ($687 billion).[19] In early 2011, the national debt stood at $14 trillion, including $9.4 trillion publicly held and $4.6 trillion held in U.S. government accounts.[20]

The national government pays interest on debt that is owed to the public. In 2010, the government paid $188 billion in interest on the debt, 5 percent of expenditures. As the size of the debt grows and as the record low interest rates of 2009–2010 inevitably increase, interest payments will go up. The Office of Management and Budget (OMB) estimates that interest on the debt will be $571 billion in 2015, a figure representing 13 percent of government expenditures.[21] Even if the federal budget is balanced in 2015, a development no one currently predicts, American taxpayers will be paying billions not for current government services but to finance earlier spending.

The relationship of the deficit and the national debt to economic growth is complex. Economists generally agree that deficit spending is an appropriate government response to a recession. People thrown out of work during a recession reduce their spending and that causes others to lose their jobs as the economy spirals downward. Business reduces its spending as well because of the slowing economy. The government can help reverse the cycle by running a deficit.[22] Congress and the president followed this strategy in 2008 through 2010 when they adopted economic stimulus packages designed to pump money into the economy with spending programs and tax cuts. Many economists also believe that deficits can be justified if the money is spent on projects that enhance long-term economic growth, such as improving transportation and education. In theory, at least, these sorts of programs pay for themselves by generating future tax revenues.

The deficit becomes an economic crisis if and when investors decide that the U.S. government is no longer a safe place to invest their money. U.S. government securities have long been considered the safest investment in the world. In 2010, investors purchased one- and two-year treasury notes that paid less than 1 percent annual interest. Ten-year securities sold for less than 4 percent annual interest.[23] These rates were low by historic standards. In the late 1990s, for example, when the federal budget was in surplus, 10-year treasury securities sold for 5.7 percent.[24] Low interest rates are an indication that investors are confident that the U.S. government will repay their loans with interest. Nonetheless, many economists worry that investors will not always be so optimistic about the U.S. government's ability to repay its debts, especially as the government borrows trillions of additional dollars in the years ahead. At some point, investors may demand substantially higher interest rates before they loan the U.S. government their money, dramatically increasing the cost of the debt to U.S. taxpayers. In the worst possible scenario, Chinese, Japanese, and other foreign investors will tell U.S. officials that they will no longer loan the U.S. government money unless it dramatically increases taxes and cuts spending in order to reduce its deficit. Those steps would likely harm the U.S. economy.[25]

Congress and the president could take steps to close the budget gap before the nation faces a debt crisis, but the policy options—increased taxes and/or reduced spending—are politically unpopular. Most Republican members of Congress are adamantly opposed to increasing taxes.[26] In fact, many Republican leaders favor tax

Millions of elderly Americans rely on Social Security and Medicare benefits.

cuts. Although Republicans support reducing government spending to cut the deficit, most Republican members of Congress are reluctant to specify which programs should be cut and by how much. Democrats, meanwhile, stand firmly opposed to any cuts in Social Security, Medicare, or the other major components of the welfare state. Although most Democrats voted in favor of increasing taxes on upper-income families and individuals in 2010, they used the money to fund healthcare reform rather than reduce the deficit.

Expenditures—How Government Spends Money

As the pie chart in Figure 14.3 shows, federal government expenditures in 2010 were closely divided among five budget categories—healthcare (22.3 percent), Social Security (19.4 percent), national defense (19.3 percent), income security (18.4 percent), and everything else (20.1 percent). The "everything else" category included transportation, agriculture, energy, housing, education, and other government programs. (The percentages do not sum to 100 because of rounding.)

Healthcare

Although health expenditures include money for medical research and disease control, by far the largest federal health programs are Medicare and Medicaid. More than 45 million people participate in the Medicare program at a cost of $457 billion, including premiums and deductibles paid by program participants, and general revenue expenditures.[27] Part A of Medicare is compulsory hospitalization insurance that covers the cost of inpatient care after beneficiaries pay a deductible. It is financed from premiums deducted from the Social Security checks of retirees and by a 2.9 percent payroll tax, divided evenly between workers and their employers. Medicare Part B is

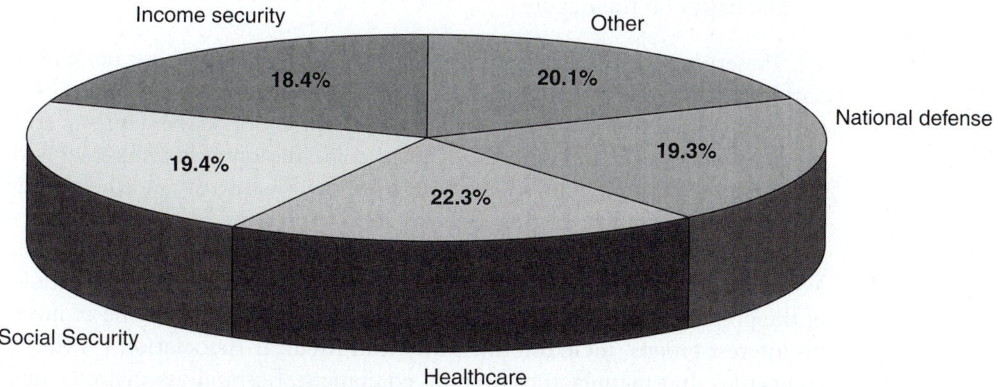

FIGURE 14.3 Federal Government Expenditures, 2010.
Source: Office of Management and Budget.

a voluntary medical insurance plan that covers certain physician fees and nonhospital services after beneficiaries pay a deductible. It is funded by premiums deducted from the Social Security checks of retired persons who choose to participate. In 2010, the premium was $96.40 a month for most recipients. Medicare recipients earning more than $85,000 in adjusted annual income had to pay a surcharge equal to 1.4, 2.6, or 3.2 times the standard premium, depending on their income level.[28] Medicare Part D is a prescription drug benefit offered and managed by private insurers under contract with the government. Medicare recipients who choose to participate pay a monthly premium, which averaged just under $40 in 2010, along with various deductibles and co-pays.[29]

Baby-boom generation The exceptionally large number of Americans born after the end of World War II.

The aging of the **baby-boom generation,** which is the exceptionally large number of Americans born after the end of World War II, is a demographic time bomb for the Medicare program. Between 2010 and 2030, the number of people on Medicare will more than double, adding huge costs to the system.[30] Furthermore, inflation in the healthcare industry is driving up the cost of medical care faster than wages are rising to provide tax revenues to cover the cost. The addition of the prescription drug benefit to Medicare makes the program's financial crisis more severe because the cost of prescription drugs is rising more rapidly than healthcare costs in general. The Medicare Board of Trustees estimates that program expenditures will exceed assets by 2012.[31]

In order to preserve the financial integrity of the Medicare system, Congress and the president will have to adopt reforms involving benefit reductions, tax increases, and greater charges to recipients. The most commonly offered reform proposals are the following:

- Slow the growth of healthcare expenditures by reducing government payments to hospitals and doctors, and encouraging recipients to participate in managed care programs.
- Increase the 2.9 percent payroll tax.
- Push back the age at which beneficiaries can qualify for benefits from 65 to 67.
- Increase premiums and service charges to recipients, especially to retirees who are better off financially.

Preserving the Medicare program is a political necessity, but none of the alternatives will be politically easy to adopt. The Medicare Board of Trustees estimates it would take a reduction of program expenditures of 53 percent, an increase in program revenues of 134 percent, or some combination of tax increases and benefit cuts to ensure the program's long-term solvency.[32] Congress and the president may have no choice but to take the necessary steps to preserve Medicare because it enjoys strong public support, not just among the elderly but also among their children who would otherwise have to help cover their parents' medical bills. Nonetheless, each of the policy options for fixing Medicare faces opposition from one or more powerful interest groups, including the American Medical Association (AMA), AARP, companies that manufacture hospital equipment, hospital associations, and groups philosophically opposed to tax increases. If Congress and the president do nothing, the Medicare shortfall will just be added to the budget deficit.

Medicaid A federal health insurance program for low-income persons, people with disabilities, and elderly people who are impoverished.

Medicaid is another large and rapidly growing federal healthcare program. In 2010, Medicaid served 58 million clients at a cost to the federal government of $277 billion. The poor—particularly pregnant women, mothers, and their young children—are the largest group of recipients, accounting for three-fourths of Medicaid beneficiaries. Nearly two-thirds of Medicaid spending, however, goes to the other 25 percent of recipients—the blind, disabled, and impoverished elderly—because their medical needs are greater and therefore more expensive to meet. All told, Medicaid covers the cost of healthcare for one in every three children. It pays for 40 percent of births and funds two-thirds of the nursing home care in the country.[33]

The Congressional Budget Office (CBO) estimates that Medicaid costs will double over the next decade. The CBO projects that Medicaid enrollment of elderly persons will increase by an average of 2.5 percent a year over the next ten years because of the aging of the baby-boom generation. Rising Medicaid costs also reflect inflation in the healthcare industry, which has been greater than in the economy as a whole, particularly with the introduction of expensive new technologies and prescription drugs.[34]

The healthcare reform legislation passed by Congress and signed into law by President Obama in 2010 will significantly affect almost all elements of American healthcare. The most important features of the new legislation are as follows:

- **Insurance reform.** Insurance companies will no longer be able to refuse coverage based on pre-existing conditions or drop coverage of people who become ill. Insurers will not be able to set annual or lifetime coverage limits. Young people will be able to remain on their parents' insurance plans until they reach age 26.
- **Employer mandate.** Businesses with 50 or more workers must provide health insurance coverage for their employees or pay a fine to the government. Small businesses can receive tax credits to help cover the cost of insuring their employees.
- **Medicaid expansion.** The measure expands Medicaid to cover individuals earning at least 133 percent of the federal poverty level ($14,484 in 2011), adding 10 million to 14 million people to Medicaid rolls. Although the federal government will initially pay the entire cost of the additional enrollees, state governments will be required to pick up 5 percent of the extra cost in 2017, 7 percent by 2019, and then 10 percent from 2020 going forward.[35]
- **Individual mandate.** Most people who are not already covered will be required to purchase a health insurance policy or pay an additional tax of $695. Families earning less than four times the federal poverty level, which was $88,200 a year in 2010, qualify for federal financial assistance to help them cover the cost.
- **Insurance exchanges.** State governments will set up health insurance exchanges, which are marketplaces where businesses and individuals will be able to shop for insurance policies. The exchanges will allow insurance companies to compete for customers by providing quality products at affordable prices. Illegal immigrants will not be able to purchase from the exchanges even if they pay entirely with their own money.

- **Medicare reform.** In 2010, the Medicare prescription drug benefit covered annual drug costs up to $2,700. Patients then lost coverage until they reached $6,154 in drug costs, at which point the government again picked up the tab. The healthcare reform legislation progressively eliminates this doughnut hole in coverage.
- **Cost control mechanisms.** Insurance companies will pay a 40 percent tax on policies worth more than $27,500 for families and $10,000 for individuals, not counting the cost of dental and vision plans. These expensive plans are known as Cadillac plans because they require very low co-payments. With little or no out-of-pocket expense, beneficiaries have no incentive to control costs. The bill also includes a number of experimental approaches to cost-cutting designed to identify approaches that work.
- **Funding.** The estimated cost of healthcare reform is $940 billion over the next decade, which will be covered by increasing tax rates on families making $250,000 a year ($200,000 for individuals). The measure raises additional revenue by taxing the so-called Cadillac insurance plans and from a 10 percent tax on indoor tanning services.[36]

Social Security

Are you counting on Social Security for your retirement? Six in ten of all Americans who are not now retired and three-fourths of adults below the age of 35 believe that Social Security will be unable to pay them a benefit when they retire.[37] Is their pessimism about the future of Social Security warranted?

Congress created the program in 1935 to provide limited coverage to workers upon their retirement at age 65. Through the years, Congress has extended the program's scope and increased its benefits. Even before the first benefit checks were mailed, Congress expanded coverage to include the aged spouse and children of a retired worker as well as the young children and spouse of a covered worker upon the worker's death. Congress subsequently added disability insurance to the package and provided for early retirement.

Consumer price index (CPI) A measure of inflation that is based on the changing cost of goods and services.

Cost-of-living adjustment (COLA) An increase in the size of a payment to compensate for the effects of inflation.

Congress and the president have also increased Social Security benefits. They raised benefits 15 percent in 1970, 10 percent in 1971, and 20 percent in 1972. Beginning in 1975, Congress and the president indexed benefits to the **consumer price index (CPI),** a measure of inflation that is based on the changing cost of goods and services. As a result, Social Security beneficiaries receive an annual **cost-of-living adjustment (COLA),** which is an increase in the size of a payment to compensate for the effects of inflation. Social Security recipients enjoyed a 6.2 percent cost-of-living adjustment (COLA) in their benefit checks because the CPI rose 6.2 percent in 2008. However, Social Security beneficiaries received no increase in 2010 because inflation was negligible the year before. The average retired worker received a monthly Social Security check of $1,067.[38]

The Social Security program can most accurately be described as a tax on workers to provide benefits to elderly retirees and disabled persons. Contrary to popular belief, Congress did not create Social Security as a pension/savings plan in which the government would simply refund the money retirees contributed over the years.

Instead, current payroll taxes pay the benefits for current recipients. Because the initial tax rate was relatively low, current retirees draw substantially more money in Social Security benefits than they paid in payroll taxes. The average person who is retired today got back all the money he or she paid into Social Security with interest in about seven years. Because tax rates are higher today, workers who are now in their thirties will likely pay more money in taxes during their lifetimes than they will collect in benefits after they retire.

Even though payroll taxes were initially low, the Social Security trust funds maintained healthy surpluses into the early 1970s. With the baby-boom generation coming of age and more women entering the workforce than ever before, the pool of workers paying taxes into the system grew more rapidly than did the number of retirees collecting benefits. Furthermore, the system benefited from a healthy economy and rising wages.

Eventually, demographic and economic changes combined with political decisions to drive the Social Security system into near bankruptcy. Early retirement, increased longevity, and falling birthrates served to swell the ranks of Social Security beneficiaries while slowing the increase in the number of employees paying taxes. When Social Security was created, the average worker retired at age 69 and lived another eight years. Today, the average worker retires at 64 and draws retirement benefits for 19 years.[39] In the meantime, Congress and the president increased benefits and pegged future increases in Social Security payments to the inflation rate. When the economy slumped and inflation soared in the late 1970s, the Social Security system faced a financial crisis.

In 1983, Congress and the president responded to the situation by adopting a Social Security bailout plan that increased payroll taxes significantly while somewhat limiting future benefit payments. The plan provided for an increase in the retirement age by small annual increments after the year 2000 until the retirement age reaches 67. Also, the bailout legislation provided that half the benefits of upper-income recipients would be counted as taxable income for income tax purposes. In 1993, Congress increased the share of taxable Social Security for middle- and upper-income recipients from 50 percent to 85 percent.

The goal of the Social Security bailout plan was not only to keep the program solvent for the short term but also to ensure its long-term stability despite unfavorable demographic trends. In 1950, 16 workers paid taxes for every person drawing benefits. In 2000, the ratio was down to three to one. By the year 2030, when the baby-boom generation will have retired, the ratio of workers to retirees will be only two to one.[40] The architects of the bailout plan hoped that the payroll tax increases would be sufficient to allow the Social Security trust funds to build up sizable surpluses that could be used to pay benefits well into the twenty-first century. At the end of 2009, the Social Security trust funds held assets worth $2.5 trillion.[41]

Although the bailout plan has put Social Security in the black for now, the retirement of the baby-boom generation threatens the system's long-term financial viability. Benefit payments will regularly begin to exceed payroll tax revenue in 2016 and the trust funds will be exhausted by 2037. At that point, payroll tax collections will cover only 76 percent of the cost of the program.[42] Once the annual cost of Social

Security benefits exceeds payroll tax revenues, benefits will have to be reduced unless Congress and the president make up the shortfall from general revenues.

A number of reformers want to go beyond tinkering with benefits and funding mechanisms to change the basic structure of Social Security. Some reformers want to make Social Security a **means-tested program,** which is a government program that provides benefits to recipients based on their financial need. Under the current system, recipients qualify for benefits based on their age and contributions, regardless of personal wealth or other income. If Social Security were a means-tested program, benefit levels would be based on the financial need of the recipients. The advantage of this approach is that it would reduce benefits without hurting low-income retirees. The disadvantage is that middle- and upper-income taxpayers might be unwilling to continue supporting the program if their benefits were decreased.

Means-tested program A government program that provides benefits to recipients based on their financial need.

Privatization A process that involves the government contracting with private business to implement government programs.

Many conservatives favor reforming Social Security through **privatization,** which is a process that involves the government contracting with private business to implement government programs. President George W. Bush proposed supplementing Social Security with a pension plan system in which workers would invest some of the money they would have contributed to Social Security in private savings accounts. Bush and other proponents of privatization believe that employees would have a better return on an investment in stocks and bonds than they could count on from the Social Security system. The returns on the private accounts would cushion the impact of future reductions in Social Security benefits. In contrast, the critics of privatization warn that private investments carry risk. Falling stock prices could endanger retirement income. Furthermore, even if privatization succeeds in the long run, the government would have to put additional funds into the Social Security system to make up for the money diverted into private accounts.

WHAT IS YOUR OPINION?

If you were a member of Congress, what actions would you favor to ensure the long-term solvency of the Social Security program?

National Defense

National defense is the third largest category of federal government expenditures. This budget category includes funding for the Department of Defense as well as nuclear weapons-related activities of the Department of Energy and defense-related expenditures by several other agencies, such as the Coast Guard and the Federal Bureau of Investigation (FBI). Chapter 17 examines defense spending in detail.

Income Security

The income security category of federal government spending encompasses a variety of domestic spending programs, including unemployment insurance, federal retirement, and, with the major exception of Medicaid, most welfare programs. Federal Civilian Retirement and Federal Military Retirement collectively represent almost

Welfare programs Government programs that provide benefits to individuals based on their economic status.

Earned Income Tax Credit (EITC) A federal program designed to give cash assistance to low-income working families by refunding some or all of the taxes they pay and, if their wages are low, giving them an additional refund.

Supplemental Nutrition Assistance Program (SNAP) A federal program (once called the Food Stamp program) that provides vouchers to low-income families and individuals that can be used to purchase food from grocery stores.

Supplemental Security Income (SSI) A federal program that provides money to low-income people who are elderly, blind, or disabled who do not qualify for Social Security benefits.

half the expenditures in the category. **Welfare programs,** means-tested government programs that provide benefits to individuals based on their economic status, account for most of the rest.

The most important welfare programs are the Earned Income Tax Credit (EITC), Supplemental Nutrition Assistance, Supplemental Security Income (SSI), Temporary Assistance to Needy Families (TANF), and Medicaid, which was discussed earlier in the chapter. The **Earned Income Tax Credit (EITC)** is a federal program designed to give cash assistance to low-income working families by refunding some or all of the taxes they pay and, if their wages are low, giving them an additional refund. The **Supplemental Nutrition Assistance Program (SNAP)** is a federal program (once called the Food Stamp program) that provides vouchers to low-income families and individuals that can be used to purchase food from grocery stores. **Supplemental Security Income (SSI)** is a federal program that provides money to low-income people who are elderly, blind, or disabled and do not qualify for Social Security benefits. **Temporary Assistance to Needy Families (TANF)** is a federal program that provides temporary financial assistance and work opportunities to needy families.

Federal welfare policy changed in the mid-1990s with the adoption of welfare reform. Before 1996, the unofficial goal of the nation's welfare system was to provide welfare recipients with a minimum standard of living.[43] In 1996, Congress passed, and President Bill Clinton signed, sweeping welfare reform legislation that explicitly changed the underlying philosophy of American welfare policy. Instead of attempting to supply low-income individuals and families with cash and benefits sufficient to meet basic human needs, the goal of welfare reform was to move recipients from the welfare rolls to the workforce. The legislation limited the amount of time able-bodied adult recipients could draw benefits by placing a lifetime cap of five years on welfare assistance. Furthermore, childless adults between the ages of 18 and 50 could receive SNAP (Food Stamp) benefits for no more than three months in any three-year period. Welfare reform instituted work requirements for welfare recipients. The heads of families on welfare would have to find work within two years or the family would lose benefits. It reduced the amount of federal money available for public assistance programs. Welfare reform also included a number of provisions aimed at changing the behavior of welfare recipients. In order to collect benefits, unmarried teenage mothers would have to live at home and stay in school. States were given the option to deny assistance to children born to welfare recipients in order to discourage welfare mothers from having additional children. The measure even offered a cash prize to the states that were most successful in reducing the number of children born outside of marriage.

WHAT IS YOUR OPINION?

Should states cut off welfare benefits to women who have children while on welfare?

Welfare reform has shifted the focus of government assistance to the poor from cash benefits to services designed to help poor people get and keep jobs. Cash

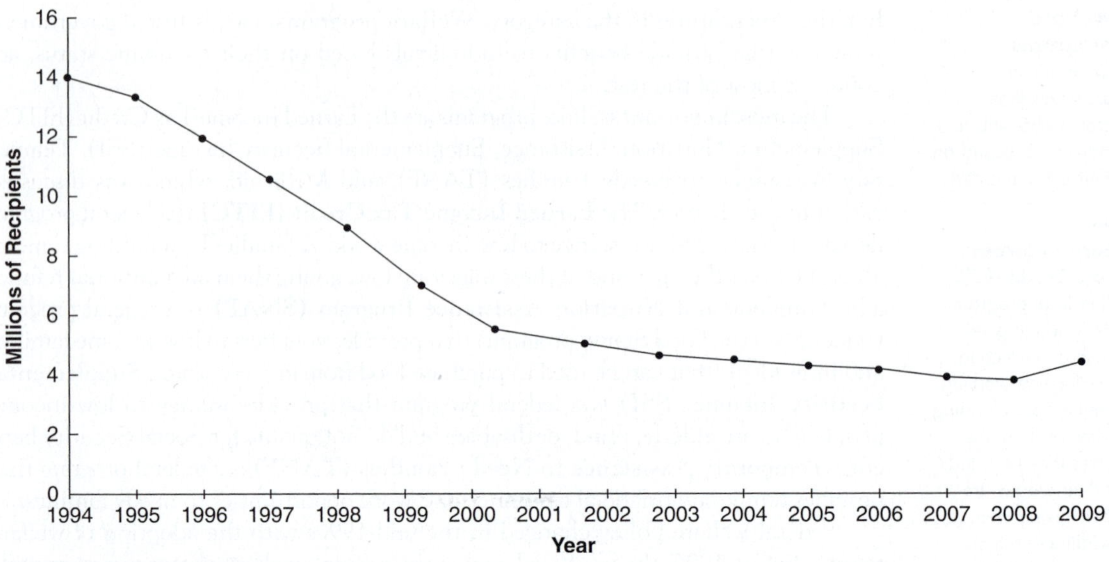

FIGURE 14.4 TANF Recipients, 1994–2009.
Source: Administration for Children and Families.

Temporary Assistance to Needy Families (TANF) A federal program that provides temporary financial assistance and work opportunities to needy families.

assistance now counts for less than half of all spending under TANF. Instead, states are using their welfare dollars to help meet the transportation needs of welfare recipients to get to work, address drug abuse and mental health problems, and provide childcare for single parents.[44]

Welfare reform has helped reduce the welfare rolls, but it has not eliminated poverty. As Figure 14.4 shows, the number of TANF recipients fell dramatically from 14.2 million in 1994 to 3.8 million in 2008 before increasing to 4.4 million in 2009 in the midst of the Great Recession. Government data show that most people leaving welfare find work and earn enough money so that they are better off than they were before.[45] Nonetheless, most of the people who have left welfare still rely heavily on public assistance, especially EITC, which is now larger than TANF, SNAP (Food Stamp) benefits, or SSI.[46] Most of the people that have made their way off welfare lack the skills necessary to get jobs that pay much more than $7 or $8 an hour. As a result, they remain dependent on government assistance. The impact of welfare reform has been to change from a system that subsidized families unconditionally to one that subsidizes families in work. Although people who have left welfare are no longer totally dependent on the government for their livelihood, most of them still rely on government assistance.[47] Furthermore, critics of welfare reform are alarmed by the slow rise in the number of TANF recipients in 2009–2010 despite rising unemployment rates. They worry that states are making it difficult for people to enroll in TANF because the amount of federal money provided to the states does not increase as the number of recipients increases.[48]

Fiscal Policymaking

Fiscal policy The use of government spending and taxation for the purpose of achieving economic goals.

Fiscal policy is the use of government spending and taxation for the purpose of achieving economic goals. Congress and the president make fiscal policy when they adopt the annual budget and enact tax laws.

Ground Rules for Budgeting

Congress and the president work under certain ground rules as they formulate and adopt an annual budget.

Entitlement program A government program providing benefits to all persons qualified to receive them under law.

Entitlements An **entitlement program** is a government program providing benefits to all persons qualified to receive them under law. Social Security, Medicare, Medicaid, unemployment compensation, federal retirement programs, and most agriculture programs are entitlements. Spending for entitlement programs depends on the number of recipients collecting benefits. Anyone who qualifies for Medicaid, for example, is entitled to receive benefits. Entitlement programs consume more than half of the federal budget.

Contractual Commitments The budgetary discretion of Congress and the president is limited by contractual commitments made in previous years. Congress and the president often stretch weapons purchases over several years, contracting with the manufacturer to supply a certain number of ships or planes each year for several years. Money for the purchase must be included in each year's budget. Similarly, the federal government is legally committed to pay interest on the national debt.

Budget Agreements Between 1990 and 2002, Congress and the president—first President George H. W. Bush and then President Clinton—prepared the annual budget on the basis of negotiated budget agreements that established spending limits for that part of the budget which is not predetermined because of entitlements or prior contractual agreements. The negotiated budget agreements set bottom-line budget limits but did not mandate spending amounts for individual budget items. The budget agreement negotiated between the president and Congress covering the period from 1990 through 2002 set strict spending caps for three spending areas—domestic, defense, and international expenditures—and prohibited shifting money among the categories.[49] As a result, the annual budget debate revolved around the distribution of a predetermined amount of money among items within the three categories. Instead of debating spending priorities between domestic and defense spending, for example, Congress and the president considered how to allocate budget resources among budget items within each category. The budget agreements also included a **PAYGO** provision, which is a pay-as-you-go budget rule that requires any tax cut or spending increase to be offset by tax increases or spending cuts elsewhere in the budget. In 2002, however, Congress and the president allowed the budget agreement to expire so they could enact tax cuts and increase spending without adopting corresponding tax increases and budget reductions. Without the discipline of a budget agreement, federal spending increased dramatically, from 18.5 percent of GDP in 2001 to 25.4 percent in 2010.[50] Spending associated with homeland security, the war on terror, and wars in Iraq and Afghanistan drove up the cost of government, of course, but the absence of a budget agreement made it easier for Congress and the president to also increase spending for education, agriculture, transportation, healthcare, and other programs. Although Congress reinstated PAYGO rules in 2010, it provided for several large exceptions to the rule, including any expenditure that Congress decided to declare an emergency.[51] When Republicans took control

PAYGO A pay-as-you-go budget rule that requires that any tax cut or spending increase be offset by tax increases or spending cuts elsewhere in the budget.

The cost of wars in Iraq and Afghanistan has helped drive up the cost of government.

of the House after the 2010 election, they further weakened PAYGO by exempting tax cuts. Whereas spending increases require offsetting spending cuts, tax cuts do not require offsetting tax increases.

The Budget Process

The White House begins the process of formulating a budget in March, a year and a half before the start of the fiscal year, when the president sets economic goals and establishes overall revenue and expenditure levels. The president may map plans for spending initiatives in some areas, retrenchments in others.

Mandatory spending Budgetary expenditures that are mandated by law, including entitlements and contractual commitments made in previous years.

Discretionary spending Budgetary expenditures that are not mandated by law or contract.

Appropriations process The procedure through which Congress legislatively provides money for a particular purpose.

Authorization process The procedure through which Congress legislatively establishes a program, defines its general purpose, devises procedures for its operation, specifies an agency to implement the program, and indicates an approximate level of funding for the program (but does *not* actually provide money).

Once the president has set administration priorities, the OMB sends spending guidelines to the various departments of the executive branch and directs them to prepare detailed budgets. Several months later, the agencies send the OMB their budget proposals, which are often over the original ceiling. The OMB questions the size of some of the spending requests and the agencies respond by justifying their proposals. The head of the agency, the director of the OMB, and a member of the White House staff, and, perhaps, even the president negotiate a final budget request for inclusion in a detailed budget proposal, which the president submits to Congress in January or February. The budget document, which is the size of a telephone book for a large city, includes specific spending recommendations to fund every agency of the federal government and for all federal activities.

Budget expenditures are classified as mandatory or discretionary. **Mandatory spending** refers to budgetary expenditures that are mandated by law, including entitlements and contractual commitments made in previous years. Interest on the debt is also mandatory spending because the government has no choice but to pay interest on money it has borrowed. **Discretionary spending** includes budgetary expenditures that are not mandated by law or contract, including annual funding for education, the Coast Guard, space exploration, highway construction, defense, foreign aid, and the Federal Bureau of Investigation (FBI). More than 60 percent of total government expenditures are mandatory.

Discretionary expenditures must be approved through the **appropriations process,** which is the procedure through which Congress legislatively provides money for a particular purpose. Appropriation bills begin in the appropriations committees in each house although, by tradition, the House Appropriations Committee takes the lead in the process. Congress appropriates money annually. The House Appropriations Committee divides the discretionary part of the budget into 13 separate categories for assignment to its 13 subcommittees. Congress never reunites the budget into a single document; instead, it passes 13 separate appropriation bills. Spending for entitlement programs is included in the budget but does not go through the appropriations process.

Spending programs must be authorized, regardless of whether they are entitlements or programs funded by discretionary spending. The **authorization process** is the procedure through which Congress legislatively establishes a program, defines its general purpose, devises procedures for its operation, specifies an agency to implement the program, and indicates an approximate level of funding for the program

GETTING INVOLVED

Tax Breaks for College Students

The Hope Credit and Lifetime Learning Credit are tax breaks for college students. Your assignment is to research the tax rules to determine whether you or your parents can benefit from these credits. You can find information about these credits online at the IRS website, www.irs.gov.

Research these tax breaks for college students, review your family's tax situation, and answer the following questions:

- How do the Hope Credit and Lifetime Learning Credit programs differ?
- Who qualifies? Do you have to be a full-time student? Are the credits available for both public and private school students?
- If parents have two children in college at the same time, can they claim a tax credit for each of them?
- Can you claim the cost of this textbook as an educational expense? Why or why not?
- Do you or your parents qualify for either the Hope Credit or the Lifetime Learning Credit? Why or why not?
- If you qualify for either, how will the credit affect your tax liability?
- Did you or your parents claim a credit last year? Will you claim it next year?

(but does *not* actually provide money). The standing legislative committees in each chamber, such as Agriculture and Armed Services, consider authorization bills. Congress may authorize a program for one year only or for several years. The budget timetable calls for Congress and the president to complete work on the budget by October 1, the beginning of the fiscal year. If Congress and the president have not agreed on appropriation legislation by then, Congress typically votes to continue government operations at their current funding rate. If Congress fails to act, the government must shut down nonessential services, but that is rare. Congress allowed some parts of government to cease operations for lack of funds in late 1995 and early 1996 in a standoff between the Republicans who controlled the House and Senate and Democratic President Clinton. Congress backed down and voted to restore the money, however, when polls showed that public opinion sided with the president.

Congress and the president adopt tax measures through the legislative process with the constitutional stipulation that revenue-raising bills must originate in the House. Consequently, tax legislation must pass the House before it passes the Senate. The Ways and Means Committee has jurisdiction over tax measures in the House. In the Senate, the Finance Committee considers tax bills.

Monetary Policymaking and the Role of the Fed

Most Americans are concerned with interest rates. Consumers pay interest on credit card debt and when they borrow money to purchase vehicles or homes. Investors earn interest on the money they save. Interest rates also affect the economy. Low interest rates encourage companies to borrow money to expand their operations. Likewise, low interest rates for automobile loans and home mortgage interest promote consumer purchases. In contrast, high interest rates promote savings and discourage borrowing by business and consumers alike.

Many economists believe that the government can influence the performance of the nation's economy by adjusting interest rates. Increasing interest rates can cool inflation by slowing down economic activity, whereas cutting interest rates can stimulate economic growth. The government affects interest rates through its control of the money supply. **Monetary policy** is the control of the money supply for the purpose of achieving economic goals.

Monetary policy The control of the money supply for the purpose of achieving economic goals.

The **Federal Reserve System (Fed)** is the central banking system of the United States with authority to establish banking policies and influence the amount of credit available in the economy. It consists of 12 Federal Reserve banks, each located in one of the nation's 12 Federal Reserve districts. A seven-member board of governors, which is appointed by the president with Senate confirmation to serve fixed, overlapping terms of 14 years, heads the Fed, as the agency is often called. The president designates one member of the board as the chair to serve a four-year term, pending Senate confirmation. President George W. Bush appointed economist Ben Bernanke to chair the Fed in 2006. Obama named Bernanke to serve a second term as chair in 2009.

Federal Reserve System (Fed) The central banking system of the United States with authority to establish banking policies and influence the amount of credit available in the economy.

Congress has ordered the Fed to make policy with the aim of achieving two goals: full employment and price stability. The **Federal Open Market Committee (FOMC)** is a committee of the Federal Reserve that meets eight times a year to review the economy and adjust monetary policy to achieve its goals. The FOMC is a 12-member group that includes the seven members of the Federal Reserve board, the president of the Federal Reserve Bank of New York, and 4 of the 11 other Federal Reserve Bank presidents who serve on a rotating basis. If the FOMC determines that the demand for goods and services is growing faster than businesses can supply them, it tightens monetary supply to fight inflation. It does this by reducing the funds available to banks for loans and by raising interest rates to make businesses and individuals less eager to borrow money. In contrast, if the FOMC believes that businesses are not selling as many goods and services as they can produce and fewer people have jobs than want them, it eases monetary policy to prevent recession. It lowers interest rates by increasing the funds that banks can lend, hoping to encourage businesses and consumers to borrow to make purchases.

Federal Open Market Committee (FOMC) A committee of the Federal Reserve that meets eight times a year to review the economy and adjust monetary policy to achieve its goals.

The Fed moved aggressively in 2008–2009 to shore up the economy and stave off financial crisis. As economic activity slowed throughout 2008, the Fed lowered interest rates. By late 2008, the federal funds rate, which is the rate banks charge each other for loans, was effectively zero percent. Nonetheless, the economy continued to falter in the face of a serious financial crisis. According to Fed Chair Bernanke, virtually every large financial institution in the world was in danger of going bankrupt and that likely would have led to another Great Depression. The Fed acted to prop up banks and other financial institutions by loaning them money with the goal of keeping the financial markets functioning smoothly. The Fed financed the private acquisition of Bear Stearns, a global investment bank. It assisted with the government takeover of Fannie Mae and Freddie Mac, the giant mortgage lenders.

President George W. Bush appointed Ben Bernanke to head the Fed in 2006 after Alan Greenspan retired.

It brokered the sale of investment firm Merrill Lynch to Bank of America and bailed out American International Group (AIG), a giant insurance and financial services corporation. Altogether, the Fed loaned $1.6 trillion.[52]

The Fed's actions were controversial. Bernanke and many economists believe that the Fed helped save the nation from another Great Depression. The ensuing recession with 10 percent unemployment was painful but nothing in comparison with the 25 percent unemployment of the Great Depression of the 1930s. Moreover, most of the money the Fed loaned to banks and other financial institutions was paid back with interest.[53] In contrast, critics blame the Fed for failing to anticipate the nature and severity of the financial crisis. They also complain that the Fed put taxpayer dollars at risk bailing out the institutions whose risky lending practices were responsible for the financial crisis.[54]

Making Economic Policy

The most important elements of the environment for economic policymaking are public opinion, the strength of the economy, and party control of the executive and legislative branches of government. Conventional wisdom holds that people "vote their pocketbooks," that is, they reelect incumbent officeholders if the economy is strong, but turn them out of office if the economy is weak. In this case, political science research supports the conventional wisdom. Economic conditions have an important impact on voter choices.[55] Furthermore, many Americans pay careful attention to specific economic policy issues that affect them directly, such as Social Security, Medicare, tax reform, and agriculture policy.

The strength of the economy expands or limits the policy options available to economic policymakers. A growing economy generates revenue that can be used to fund new spending programs or provide tax cuts. Strong economic growth in the mid- and late-1990s did at least as much to eliminate the budget deficit as the policy choices of elected officials. In contrast, a weak economy reduces the options available to policymakers. Although the president and Congress may want to respond to a recession by cutting taxes or increasing government programs to help the unemployed, they will not have the money to fund tax cuts or new programs unless they borrow it.

It matters which party controls Congress. Democrats generally back policies designed to assist their traditional support groups: organized labor, inner-city voters, and lower- and middle-income families. Republicans, meanwhile, steer economic policy to benefit their support groups: businesspeople and professionals, suburban voters, and middle- and upper-income families. When Congress and the presidency are in the hands of different parties, economic policy typically reflects compromise between the parties.

Agenda Setting

A number of political actors participate in elevating economic issues to the official policy agenda. Candidates often highlight economic issues during election campaigns. Independent presidential candidate Ross Perot made deficit reduction a major talking point when he ran for president as an independent in 1992 and 1996. Clinton stressed welfare reform when he first ran for president, promising to "end welfare as we know it." George W. Bush promised to cut taxes during his presidential campaign in 2000. Barack Obama pushed healthcare reform. Interest groups frequently emphasize economic issues. The **AARP,** an interest group representing the interests of older Americans, stresses the need to preserve Social Security and Medicare. Business groups are concerned with tax issues. Farm groups, such as the American Farm Bureau, lobby for farm support programs. The media play a role by emphasizing economic developments, such as the unemployment rate or the size of the deficit. Finally, economic developments set the agenda as well. High unemployment rates focus the attention of policymakers on creating jobs. Policymakers discuss energy when the price of a gallon of gasoline goes up.

AARP An interest group representing the concerns of older Americans.

Policy Formulation, Adoption, and Legitimation

Economic policy formulation takes place in congressional committees, executive branch agencies, and the White House. It involves officials from all levels of government as well as a wide range of interest group participants. The president and the president's staff, department heads, and the OMB prepare detailed budget proposals for submission to Congress. The appropriations committees in each house draft budget legislation; standing committees work on authorization measures. The Ways and Means Committee in the House and the Finance Committee in the Senate deal with tax measures. Conference committees iron out the final details for most appropriation bills, tax measures, and authorization bills. The Fed formulates monetary policy.

Individual members of Congress focus on issues important to their states and districts. Farm-belt senators and representatives pay special attention to legislation affecting agriculture. Members with defense bases or defense industries in their districts are concerned with the defense appropriation bill. Senators and representatives are also interested in special projects that benefit their states and districts, including **earmarks,** which are provisions directing that funds be spent for particular purposes. In 2010, Congress earmarked almost $11 billion for special projects, including money for water resource development, local transportation projects, tourist attractions, and special projects for colleges and universities.[56] The opponents of earmarks charge that they are nothing more than **pork barrel spending,** which are expenditures to fund local projects that are not critically important from a national perspective. Although congressional leaders have pledged to eliminate earmarks, many members of Congress defend them as a tool the legislative branch has over the executive branch. They note that earmarks account for much less than 1 percent of government spending and that they have funded many worthwhile projects, including most federal breast cancer research and the Boys & Girls Clubs of America. Colleges and universities are major recipients of earmarks.[57] Moreover, the congressional leadership uses earmarks as bargaining chips to win support for appropriation bills that might not otherwise pass.[58]

Earmarks Provisions that direct funds to be spent for particular purposes.

Pork barrel spending Expenditures to fund local projects that are not critically important from a national perspective.

Interest groups also take part in policy formulation. Corporations lobby Congress to affect the impact of tax policies on their firms. Weapons manufacturers attempt to influence decisions on defense spending. The AARP participates in negotiations over reform of the Medicare program and changes in Social Security.

The executive and legislative branches of American national government are primarily responsible for the adoption of fiscal policy. The judiciary plays relatively little role. Congress and the president create government programs and appropriate money to fund them. They raise funds through taxation and borrowing. In the meantime, the Fed adopts monetary policies.

Political battles over economic policymaking do not always end with policy adoption but continue into the policy legitimation stage of the policy process. Consider the fight over healthcare reform. No sooner had President Obama signed the bill into law than he began a speaking tour designed to explain the measure and sell it to the nation. Democratic members of Congress who supported the bill held events in their districts as well, discussing the benefits of healthcare reform to their communities. In contrast, Republican leaders in Congress reiterated their opposition and called for the bill's repeal. Meanwhile, a number of state officials opposed to healthcare reform filed lawsuits that challenged the measure's constitutionality.

Policy Implementation, Evaluation, and Change

The implementation of economic policy involves nearly the whole of government in America. The Treasury Department, especially the IRS, is responsible for tax collection and borrowing. The Federal Reserve System and its member banks implement monetary policy. Money is spent by the agencies of the executive branch and, through federal programs, by an array of state and local governments as well. State governments, for example, are responsible for implementing federal transportation policies, Medicaid, and most welfare programs.

Congress and the president often leave considerable discretion to officials who implement economic policies. Welfare reform initially allowed states considerable flexibility to design their welfare programs. For example, states could grant hardship exemptions to individual recipients who had exhausted their benefits or were unable to find work. In general, the legislation set goals and allowed state governments to develop their own strategies for achieving the goals. States who met the goals would receive financial rewards; states falling short of goals would suffer penalties. When Congress reauthorized welfare reform in 2006, however, it tightened the definitions of work and work-related activities, reducing state flexibility.[59]

Both the executive and legislative branches of American government have mechanisms for evaluating economic policy. The OMB assesses the operation of programs within the executive branch for the president, whereas the Government Accountability Office (GAO) performs a similar role for Congress, investigating agency activities and auditing expenditures. Outside of the GAO, however, efforts at oversight are haphazard and unsystematic. Furthermore, when they do occur, they tend to focus on nickel-and-dime matters, such as expense accounts and limousine use, or on well-publicized abuses, such as cost overruns on weapons systems purchased by the Department of Defense.

Economic policies change because of changes in party control of Congress and the presidency, and because of changes in the state of the economy. Healthcare reform legislation would not have passed in 2010 without a Democratic president and sizable Democratic majorities in both the House and Senate. Certainly, the measure would not have been funded by increasing taxes on upper-income individuals and families had Democrats not been in charge. Economic policies change with variations in the state of the economy. When the economy slowed in 2008, Congress and the president adopted a stimulus plan and the Fed cut interest rates.

WHAT WE HAVE LEARNED

1. **What are the primary goals of American economic policy?**

   The first goal of economic policy is to fund government services. Americans disagree over spending priorities and the appropriate level of funding for federal government activity, with liberals preferring a more active government than conservatives. A second goal of economic policy is to encourage/discourage private sector activity. The government taxes behavior it wishes to discourage, such as smoking, and subsidizes activities it wants to promote, such as home ownership. A third goal of economic policy is to redistribute income. Healthcare reform, for example, transfers wealth from upper-income taxpayers to low- and middle-income people who currently lack health insurance. A final goal of economic policy is to promote economic growth by avoiding depression, minimizing the severity of recession, and controlling inflation. In 2008 and 2009, for example, policymakers took action to avert another Great Depression.

2. **What are the most important revenue sources of the federal government?**

The individual income tax, which is the largest source of revenue for the national government, divides taxable income into brackets and applies a different tax rate to the portion of income falling into each bracket, with higher incomes taxed at higher rates than lower incomes. Because of tax preferences, not all income is subject to the income tax. Payroll taxes, which are levied primarily on wages and salaries, represent the second most important tax source. They fund both Medicare and Social Security, and help fund healthcare reform. Other sources of federal revenue include the corporate income tax and excise taxes levied on such items as gasoline, alcohol, tobacco, tires, and airplane tickets. The government also raises revenue through customs duties, fines, penalties, and inheritance taxes.

3. **What are the most important issues facing the nation's tax system and what reforms have been proposed for addressing them?**

Are taxes too high or not high enough? Compared with other nations, the tax burden in the United States is relatively light. In general, Republicans believe that high taxes undermine economic prosperity, whereas Democrats resist tax cuts because they want to ensure that the government has sufficient revenue to fund essential government services. Social scientists identify three general types of taxes: progressive, proportional, and regressive. The federal income tax is progressive; sales and excise taxes are considered regressive. The advocates of progressive taxation justify it on the basis of the ability to pay theory of taxation. In contrast, other experts on public finance believe that the best tax system is one that focuses on consumption taxes because they encourage economic growth.

Critics of the nation's tax system offer a number of prescriptions for reform. The advocates of progressive tax systems favor increasing income tax rates on corporations and upper-income taxpayers while cutting taxes for people at the lower end of the income ladder. Some reformers favor a flat tax, which is a proportional tax with few if any deductions. Still other reformers prefer a national sales tax. Some members of Congress have begun discussing the adoption of a value added tax (VAT) to help reduce the deficit. Critics of the flat tax, a national sales tax, and the VAT contend that they would shift the tax burden from middle- and upper-income earners to lower- and middle-income families.

4. **What is the history of federal budget deficits and surpluses since the 1940s, and what impact do budget deficits have on the nation's economy?**

The U.S. government began the twenty-first century in surplus, but it soon dissolved into record-high deficits. Changes in budget deficits and surpluses reflect fluctuations in the health of the nation's economy and the policy decisions of Congress and the president. The government must pay interest on publicly held debt, which in 2010 amounted to 5 percent of expenditures. Economists generally agree that deficit spending is an appropriate government response to a recession and deficit spending that finances economic growth may be acceptable as well. A debt crisis would take place if and when investors decide that the U.S. government is no longer a safe place to invest their money. Congress and the president could take steps now to head off a possible debt crisis, but they are reluctant to act because the options—increased taxes and/or spending cuts—are politically unpopular. They may also retard economic growth.

5. **What are the most important spending priorities of the federal government?**

The most important spending priorities in 2010 were healthcare, Social Security, national defense, and income security. Medicare and Medicaid are by far the largest federal healthcare programs. Healthcare reform legislation adopted in 2010 will impact virtually all elements of American healthcare, including Medicare and Medicaid. The Social Security program can most accurately be described as a tax on workers to provide benefits to elderly retirees and disabled persons. The retirement of the baby-boom generation threatens the long-term solvency of Medicare, Medicaid, and Social Security. National defense, the third largest budget category, includes funding for the Department of Defense as well as nuclear weapons-related activities of the Department of Energy and defense-related expenditures by several other agencies. The income security category of federal government spending encompasses a variety of domestic spending programs, including unemployment insurance, federal retirement, and, with the major exception of Medicaid, most welfare programs. Since the adoption of welfare reform in the late 1990s, the goal of welfare has changed from ensuring that poor people have basic necessities to moving the poor from welfare to work.

6. **What is the process through which Congress and the president make fiscal policy?**

Fiscal policy is the use of government spending and taxation for the purpose of achieving economic goals. The ground rules that Congress and the president must follow in formulating fiscal policy include the following: (1) entitlement spending must be included automatically because people qualified for entitlement programs are guaranteed those benefits regardless of budgetary considerations; (2) contractual agreements made in previous years must be honored; and (3) budget agreements, such as PAYGO, must be followed. The OMB assists the president in preparing a budget, which is submitted to Congress at the beginning of the year. Budget expenditures are classified as mandatory or discretionary. Only the latter must be approved through the appropriations process. Spending programs must be authorized, regardless of whether they are entitlements or programs funded by discretionary spending. Congress and the president adopt tax bills through the legislative process.

7. **What is the policymaking role of the Federal Reserve System?**

The Federal Reserve System (Fed) is the central banking system of the United States with authority to establish banking policies and influence the amount of credit available in the economy. Congress has ordered the Fed to make monetary policy with the aim of achieving two goals: full employment and price stability. The Fed moved aggressively in 2008–2009 to shore up the economy and stave off a financial crisis by lowering interest rates and by loaning money to banks and other financial institutions.

8. **How is American economic policy made?**

The most important elements of the environment for economic policymaking are public opinion, the strength of the economy, and party control of the executive and legislative branches of government. A number of political actors participate in setting the agenda for economic policymaking, including candidates for office, interest groups, and the media. Events, such as recessions and bouts with inflation, set the agenda as well. Economic policy formulation takes place in congressional committees, executive branch agencies, and the White House. It involves government officials and interest group representatives. Whereas the executive and legislative branches of American national government are primarily responsible for the adoption of fiscal policy, the Fed adopts monetary policy. Political battles over economic policymaking do not always end with policy adoption but continue into the policy legitimation stage of the policy process. The implementation of economic policy involves nearly the whole of government in America, including the Federal Reserve System, executive branch agencies, and state and local governments. Both the executive and legislative branches of American government have mechanisms for evaluating economic policy. Economic policies change because of changes in party control of Congress and the presidency, and because of changes in the state of the economy.

KEY TERMS

AARP
ability to pay theory of taxation
appropriations process
authorization process
baby-boom generation
balanced budget
budget deficit
budget surplus
consumer price index (CPI)
cost-of-living adjustment (COLA)
depression
discretionary spending
earmarks
Earned Income Tax Credit (EITC)
entitlement program
estate tax
European Union (EU)
excise taxes
Federal Open Market Committee (FOMC)
Federal Reserve System (Fed)
fiscal policy
fiscal year
flat tax
gross domestic product (GDP)
income redistribution
inflation
International Monetary Fund (IMF)
mandatory spending
means-tested program
Medicaid
Medicare
monetary policy
national debt
PAYGO
pork barrel spending
privatization
progressive tax
proportional tax
recession
regressive tax
sales tax
Social Security
subsidy
Supplemental Nutrition Assistance Program (SNAP)
Supplemental Security Income (SSI)
tax credit
tax deduction
tax exemption
tax preference
Temporary Assistance for Needy Families (TANF)
value added tax (VAT)
welfare programs
welfare state

NOTES

1. Office of Management and Budget, *President's Budget: Historical Tables*, available at www.omb.gov.
2. Congressional Budget Office, "Budget Projections," March 24, 2010, available at www.cbo.gov.
3. Office of Management and Budget, *Fiscal Year 2009, Mid-Session Review*, available at www.omb.gov.
4. Jacob S. Hacker, "Privatizing Risk Without Privatizing the Welfare State: The Hidden Politics of Social Policy Retrenchment in the United States," *American Political Science Review* 98 (May 2004): pp. 251–256.
5. Randal R. Rucker and E. C. Pasour, Jr., "The Growth of U.S. Farm Programs," in Price V. Fishback, et al., *Government &*

the American Economy: A New History (Chicago, IL: University of Chicago Press, 2007), p. 483.

6. David Leonhardt, "In Health Care Bill, Obama Attacks Wealth Inequality," *New York Times*, March 23, 2010, available at www.nytimes.com.
7. Chris J. Dolan, John Frendreis, and Raymond Tatalovich, *The Presidency and Economic Policy* (Lanham, MD: Rowman & Littlefield, 2008), p. 3.
8. Paul Krugman, "Averting the Worst," *New York Times*, August 10, 2009, available at www.nytimes.com.
9. "Federal Tax Law Keeps Piling Up," available at http://voices.washingtonpost.com.
10. Office of Management and Budget, *Budget of the United States Government, Analytical Perspectives, Fiscal Year, 2011*, available at www.omb.gov.
11. Office of Management and Budget, *The Budget for Fiscal Year 2010, Historical Tables*, available at www.omb.gov.
12. U.S. Census Bureau, "Gross Public Debt, Expenditures, and Receipts by Country: 1990–2008," *The 2011 Statistical Abstract*, available at www.census.gov.
13. Anthony J. Cataldo II and Arline A. Savage, *U.S. Individual Federal Income Taxation: Historical, Contemporary, and Prospective Policy Issues* (Oxford, UK: Elsevier Science, 2001), pp. 39–40.
14. Office of Management and Budget, *Fiscal Year 2009, Mid-Session Review.*
15. Shawn Tully, "VAT Trap: The Inevitable Fix for the Deficit," *Fortune*, February 10, 2010, available at www.cnnmoney.com.
16. Congressional Budget Office, available at www.cbo.gov.
17. David Leonhardt, "For U.S., a Sea of Perilous Red Ink, Years in the Making," *New York Times*, June 10, 2009, available at www.nytimes.com.
18. James J. Gosling, *Economics, Politics, and American Public Policy* (Armonk, NY: M.E. Sharpe, 2008), pp. 90–91.
19. U.S. Department of the Treasury, "Major Foreign Holders of U.S. Securities," available at www.ustreas.gov.
20. Bureau of the Public Debt, available at www.treasurydirect.gov.
21. Office of Management and Budget, *President's Budget: Historical Tables*.
22. Robert H. Frank, "When 'Deficit' Isn't a Dirty Word," *New York Times*, March 22, 2009, available at www.nytimes.com.
23. U.S. Treasury, "Daily Treasury Yield Curve Rates," June 2010, available at www.ustreas.gov.
24. Graham Bowley and Jack Healy, "Worries Rise on the Size of the U.S. Debt," *New York Times*, May 4, 2009, available at www.nytimes.com.
25. Robert J. Samuelson, "With Health Bill, Obama Has Sown the Seeds of a Budget Crisis," *Washington Post*, March 29, 2010, available at www.washingtonpost.com.
26. Catherine E. Rudder, "Transforming American Politics Through Tax Policy," in Lawrence C. Dodd and Bruce I. Oppenheimer, *Congress Reconsidered*, 9th ed. (Washington, DC: CQ Press, 2009), p. 269.
27. Congressional Budget Office, "CBO's March 2008 Baseline: Medicare," available at www.cbo.gov.
28. Medicare.gov, available at www.medicare.gov.
29. Centers for Medicare and Medicaid Services, available at www.cms.hhs.gov.
30. Congressional Budget Office, "Budget Options," available at www.cbo.gov.
31. *Social Security and Medicare Boards of Trustees 2009 Annual Reports*, available at www.ssa.gov.
32. Ibid.
33. Congressional Budget Office, "Spending and Enrollment Detail for CBO's March 2010 Baseline: Medicaid," available at www.cbo.gov.
34. Donald B. Marron, "Medicaid Spending Growth and Options for Controlling Costs," Testimony Before the Senate Select Committee on Aging, available at www.cbo.gov.
35. John Buntin, "Dueling Diagnosis," *Governing*, February 2010, p. 24.
36. Karen Tumulty and Kate Pickert with Alice Park, "America, The Doctor Will See You Now," *Time*, April 5, 2010, pp. 24–32.
37. Frank Newport, "Six in 10 Workers Hold No Hope of Receiving Social Security," Gallup Poll, July 20, 2010, available at www.gallup.com.
38. Social Security Administration, available at www.ssa.gov.
39. Jesse J. Holland, "Raise Retirement Age to Save Social Security?" *Business Week*, August 1, 2008, available at www.businessweek.com.
40. *Social Security and Medicare Boards of Trustees 2009 Annual Reports.*
41. Social Security Administration, Trust Fund Data, available at www.ssa.gov.
42. *Social Security and Medicare Boards of Trustees 2009 Annual Reports.*
43. William A. Kelso, *Poverty and the Underclass: Challenging Perceptions of the Poor in America* (New York: New York University Press, 1994), p. 4.
44. Robert Pear, "Welfare Spending Shows Huge Shift from Checks to Services," *New York Times*, October 13, 2003, available at www.nytimes.com.
45. U.S. Department of Health and Human Services, Office of Family Assistance, Temporary Assistance for Needy Families, *Sixth Annual Report to Congress*, November 2004, available at www.acf.hhs.gov.
46. Congressional Budget Office, "The Budget and Economic Outlook: An Update."
47. Jonathan Walters, "Is Welfare Working?" *Governing*, February 2008, pp. 28–33.
48. Jason Deparle, "Welfare Aid Not Growing as Economy Drops Off," *New York Times*, February 2, 2009, available at www.nytimes.com.

49. Roger H. Davidson and Walter J. Oleszek, *Congress and Its Members*, 7th ed. (Washington, DC: CQ Press, 2000), p. 372.
50. Office of Management and Budget, *Budget of the United States Government, Fiscal Year 2011*.
51. Lori Montgomery, "House Votes to Revive Pay-as-You-Go Budget Rules," *Washington Post*, February 5, 2010, available at www.washingtonpost.com.
52. Interview with Ben Bernanke, *Time*, December 28, 2009–January 4, 2010, pp. 76–78.
53. Michael Grunwald, "Ben Bernanke," *Time*, December 28, 2009–January 4, 2010, pp. 47–62.
54. Sewell Chan, "Is Ben Bernanke Having Fun Yet?" *New York Times*, May 14, 2010, available at www.nytimes.com.
55. Alan I. Abramowitz, "Can McCain Overcome the Triple Whammy?" May 29, 2008, Larry J. Sabato's Crystal Ball 2008, available at www.centerforpolitics.org.
56. Walter Alarkon, "$11 Billion in Disclosed Earmarks Expected in Fiscal Year 2010," *The Hill*, December 12, 2009, available at www.thehill.com.
57. Kevin Kiley, "Earmark Ban Would Cost Colleges Dearly," *Chronicle of Higher Education*, December 17, 2010, pp. A1, A15.
58. Jonathan Weisman, "Bush Puts the Kibosh on Lawmakers' Pet Projects—Later," *Washington Post National Weekly Edition*, February 4–10, 2008, p. 7.
59. Sheri Steisel and Jack Tweedle, "TANF Rules Tough on States," *State Legislatures*, March 2006, p. 23.

Chapter 15

Civil Liberties

CHAPTER OUTLINE

The Constitution and Civil Liberties
- U.S. Constitution
- State Constitutions

Government and Religion
- Establishment of Religion
- Free Exercise of Religion

Freedom of Expression
- Anti-Government Speech
- Expression that Threatens the Public Order
- Symbolic Expression
- Expression Versus Action
- Hate Crimes Legislation
- Commercial Speech

Freedom of the Press
- Obscenity
- Defamation
- Prior Restraint and National Security

The Right to Bear Arms

Privacy Rights

Due Process of Law and the Rights of the Accused
- Searches and Seizures
- The Exclusionary Rule
- The Miranda Warning
- Double Jeopardy
- Fair Trial
- Cruel and Unusual Punishments

Civil Liberties and the War on Terror

Making Civil Liberties Policy
- Agenda Setting
- Policy Formulation, Adoption, and Legitimation
- Policy Implementation, Evaluation, and Change

What We Have Learned

WHAT WE WILL LEARN

After studying Chapter 15, students should be able to answer the following questions:

1. What is the constitutional basis for civil liberties in America, including both the U.S. Constitution and state constitutions?
2. What is the legal/constitutional relationship between government and religion?
3. What is the current status of constitutional law concerning freedom of expression, including statements of anti-government

views, symbolic expression, expression that might lead to a disruption of the public order, expression versus action, hate crimes, and commercial speech?

4. How does the constitutional guarantee of freedom of the press affect the issues of obscenity, defamation, and prior restraint?
5. Do individuals enjoy a constitutional right to own a gun?
6. What is the basis for a constitutional right to privacy and to what sorts of controversies has the right to privacy been applied?
7. What is the current status of constitutional law concerning the rights of people accused of crimes involving searches and seizures, the exclusionary rule, the Miranda warning, double jeopardy, fair trial, and cruel and unusual punishments?
8. What civil liberties issues are raised by the conduct of the war on terror?
9. How is civil liberties policy made?

Terrance Graham was sentenced to life in prison in the state of Florida without the possibility of parole for the offenses of armed burglary and a subsequent probation violation. In 2009–2010, Graham became the focus of a constitutional controversy because of his age at the time of his offense. Graham was 16 when he committed the burglary and 17 when he violated probation.[1]

The Eighth Amendment of the U.S. Constitution prohibits "cruel and unusual punishments." Is sentencing a juvenile offender to life in prison without the possibility of parole cruel and unusual? The practice is unusual at least from an international perspective because most of the world's nations prohibit life sentences for juveniles.[2] Furthermore, the American Psychological Association (APA) notes that research indicates that juveniles, compared with adults, have less capacity for mature judgment, are more vulnerable to negative external influences, and are more likely to reform their behavior. Because juveniles are different from adults, the APA contends, they should be treated differently from adults.[3]

In contrast, the state of Florida and several conservative legal foundations defend the practice of sentencing juveniles to life without parole. They note that life without parole for juvenile offenders is not unusual in the United States because most states allow the sentence for some juvenile offenders. More than 2,000 people are currently serving life sentences in the United States for crimes committed when they were under the age of 18. As for international comparisons, they contend that the United States assesses tougher sentences to juveniles because juveniles in the United States commit more serious violent crimes than juveniles in most other countries. Juveniles who commit adult crimes should receive adult sentences. The best approach to the issue, they argue, is to allow the states to deal with each juvenile offender on a case-by-case basis.[4]

Civil liberties The protection of the individual from the unrestricted power of government.

The legal controversy over juvenile sentencing practices introduces this chapter on **civil liberties,** which is the protection of the individual from the unrestricted power of government. The chapter begins by examining the constitutional basis of civil liberties in the United States, and then discusses a number of important civil liberties issues.

The Constitution and Civil Liberties

Both the U.S. Constitution and state constitutions affect civil liberties policymaking.

U.S. Constitution

Bill of Rights A constitutional document guaranteeing individual rights and liberties. The first ten amendments to the U.S. Constitution constitute the U.S. Bill of Rights.

Selective incorporation of the Bill of Rights against the states The process through which the U.S. Supreme Court interpreted the Due Process Clause of the Fourteenth Amendment of the U.S. Constitution to apply most of the provisions of the national Bill of Rights to the states.

Fundamental right A constitutional right that is so important that government cannot restrict it unless it can demonstrate a compelling or overriding public interest for so doing.

The Bill of Rights and the Fourteenth Amendment are the most important constitutional provisions affecting civil liberties policymaking. The **Bill of Rights,** which is contained in the first ten amendments to the Constitution, is a constitutional document guaranteeing individual rights and liberties. Initially, the Bill of Rights restricted the national government but not the states. It prohibited Congress from passing laws abridging the freedom of speech, for example, but it did not affect the actions of state and local governments.

The Due Process Clause of the Fourteenth Amendment provided the mechanism by which the U.S. Supreme Court eventually applied most of the provisions of the Bill of Rights to the states. Section 1 of the Fourteenth Amendment reads as follows: "No State shall . . . deprive any person of life, liberty, or property, without due process of law." The Supreme Court has interpreted the word *liberty* in the Due Process Clause to include most of the individual rights and liberties protected by the Bill of Rights. As a result, most of the provisions of the Bill of Rights now apply not just to the national government but to state and local governments as well. The process through which the U.S. Supreme Court interpreted the Due Process Clause of the Fourteenth Amendment of the U.S. Constitution to apply most of the provisions of the national Bill of Rights to the states is known as the **selective incorporation of the Bill of Rights against the states.** If Congress passed a law abridging freedom of speech, it would violate the First Amendment. If a state legislature enacted a similar law, it would violate both the Fourteenth and the First Amendments because the Due Process Clause of the Fourteenth Amendment applies the provisions of the First Amendment to the states.

The Supreme Court has held that the guarantees of the Bill of Rights are not absolute. Note the wording of the Due Process Clause: "No State shall . . . deprive any person of life, liberty, or property, *without due process of law*" (emphasis added). The Supreme Court has interpreted the Constitution to allow government restrictions on individual rights and liberties when government can demonstrate sufficient reason.

Furthermore, the Bill of Rights only applies to the actions of government, not those of individuals or private employers. Consider the controversy surrounding Don Imus, the former radio talk show host of *Imus in the Morning*. CBS cancelled the show after Imus referred to the members of the Rutgers University women's basketball team as "nappy-headed hos." Because of the First Amendment's guarantee of freedom of expression, the government could not fine Imus or put him in jail because of his views. The Constitution did not protect him, however, from losing his job because of his statements.

The Supreme Court has determined that some rights are more important than other rights. A **fundamental right** is a constitutional right that is so important that government cannot restrict it unless it can demonstrate a compelling or overriding public interest for doing so. Freedom of expression, freedom of religion, the right to vote, and the right to be free from cruel and unusual punishments are examples of fundamental rights. To restrict rights that are not fundamental, government need only show that it is acting in pursuit of a legitimate public purpose. Suppose a city government prohibited both holding political rallies and drinking alcoholic beverages in a public park. Because the U.S. Supreme Court has recognized freedom of expression as a fundamental right, the city would have to show a compelling or overriding public interest in prohibiting political rallies for that policy to survive legal challenge. In contrast, because the Supreme Court has not held that drinking alcoholic beverages is a fundamental right, the city government would only need to demonstrate a legitimate public purpose to justify its policy on alcohol consumption.

State Constitutions

State constitutions affect civil liberties policymaking as well. In America's federal system of government, states must grant their residents all the rights guaranteed by the U.S. Constitution (as interpreted by the Supreme Court). If state governments so choose, they may offer their residents *more* rights than afforded in the U.S. Constitution.[5] All state constitutions include bills of rights, many of which are longer and use more expansive language than the national document. Since 1970, state supreme courts around the nation have issued hundreds of rulings in which they have granted broader rights protection under state constitutions than the U.S. Supreme Court has allowed under the U.S. Constitution. In several states, for example, courts have ruled that their state constitution gives same-sex couples the same right to marry as traditional couples enjoy. The policy areas that state supreme courts have addressed include freedom of speech, freedom of religion, criminal procedure, privacy, and due process of law.[6]

WHAT IS YOUR OPINION?

Do you believe that juvenile offenders should be subject to life in prison without possibility of parole?

Government and Religion

The First Amendment addresses the relationship between church and state with these well-known words: "Congress shall make no law respecting an establishment of religion, or prohibiting the free exercise thereof." The provision has two separate and distinct elements. On one hand, the First Amendment prohibits the establishment of religion. It concerns the degree to which the government may constitutionally support religion or promote religious belief. On the other hand, the First Amendment prohibits the government from interfering with the free exercise of religion. It addresses the extent to which government actions may constitutionally interfere with individual religious practice.

Around the World

Population Policy in China

With a population of more than 1.3 billion people, China is the most populous country in the world. Because of medical advances and nutritional improvements, life expectancy in China has increased dramatically and the population has more than doubled since 1949. Chinese families have traditionally been large because Chinese couples want children to care for them when they are old. Male children are especially prized because sons traditionally live near their parents, whereas daughters marry and leave home. Chinese couples want to bear sons because their daughters-in-law will care for them in their old age, whereas their own daughters will be caring for someone else.*

The Chinese government believes that population control is a prerequisite for economic development. Rapid population growth strains the nation's agricultural resources and contributes to the shortage of adequate housing. Substantial economic growth is necessary just to provide jobs for the growing population.

Since the 1980s, the government has implemented a one-child policy. Couples are to bear no more than one child unless they receive permission from the government based on special circumstances. Some local officials have taken drastic steps to enforce the policy, including forced abortions, sterilization for women who have too many children, and destroying the assets of families that are too large. Because of the cultural preference for male children, some families abort female children. According to Chinese demographic figures, the ratio of male to female children under the age of five in China is 117 to 100. According to the International Planned Parenthood Federation, China aborts seven million fetuses a year and about 70 percent are female. Chinese families apparently abandon millions of other girls to state-run orphanages.†

The population policy has worked more effectively in urban centers than in rural areas. In urban areas, women average only one child, whereas rural women have two or more children.‡ Urban couples more readily comply with the policy because they are more subject to government sanctions than are people living in the countryside. Traditional cultural practices are also stronger in rural China than they are in urban centers.

QUESTIONS

1. How does China's population policy compare and contrast with America's abortion policy?
2. Would you expect a democracy to adopt a population policy similar to China's policy?
3. Do you believe that the need for economic development is sufficient to justify China's population policy?

*Alan Hunter and John Sexton, *Contemporary China* (London: MacMillan Press, 1999), pp. 59–60.

† Beth Nonte Russell, "The Mystery of the Chinese Baby Shortage," *New York Times*, January 23, 2007, available at www.nytimes.com.

‡ Cecilia Nathansen Milwertz, *Accepting Population Control: Urban Chinese Women and the One-Child Family Policy* (Richmond Surrey, UK: Curzon Press, 1997), p. 11.

Establishment of Religion

The First Amendment prohibits government from making laws "respecting an establishment of religion." Historians agree that the authors of this provision intended to prohibit the naming of an official state church, but they disagree as to what other forms of church/state involvement constitute establishment. Some experts believe that the framers intended to build a wall of separation between church and state. The affairs of government and the affairs of religion should never intermix. In contrast, other scholars argue that the founders never envisioned so extreme an interpretation of the Establishment Clause. They believe that the authors of the Constitution favored a society in which government would accommodate the interests of religion, especially Christian religion.[7]

WHAT IS YOUR OPINION?

Do you believe in the strict separation of government and religion or should the government accommodate the interests of religion?

The Supreme Court has adopted a middle ground on the issue of establishment of religion, attempting to balance the concerns of groups favoring a strict separation of church and state and the values of groups calling for accommodation between government and religion.[8] Consider the controversy over state aid to religious schools. Parents who send their children to private, church-supported schools frequently complain that they pay twice for education, once when they pay school taxes and a second time when they pay private school tuition. Religious school systems save taxpayers millions of dollars. Besides, many church-related schools desperately need financial aid. On the opposite side of the issue are those individuals and groups who contend that tax money should not be used to support religious education.

The battle over public assistance to religious schools generally begins in state legislatures and school boards but winds up in the federal courts. In 1941, the New Jersey legislature authorized school districts to subsidize the transportation of students to and from school and, if districts chose, to extend the aid to parochial school students as well. When Ewing Township did just that, a taxpayer named Arch Everson sued, challenging the constitutionality of the action. The Supreme Court's decision in *Everson v. Board of Ewing Township* set an important precedent on the meaning of the Establishment Clause. The Court ruled that New Jersey's transportation plan was constitutional because it had a "secular legislative purpose"—safe transportation for school children—and "neither advance[d] nor inhibit[ed] religion." Thus, the Court created a standard for determining the constitutionality of state aid to religious schools: Aid that serves a public purpose is constitutional; aid that serves a religious purpose is not.[9]

Parental choice An educational reform aimed at improving the quality of schools by allowing parents to select the school their children will attend.

The controversy over parental choice and school vouchers is a recent manifestation of the battle over public funding for church-related schools. **Parental choice** is an educational reform aimed at improving the quality of schools by allowing parents to select the school their children will attend. The theory behind the concept is that public schools will have to improve in order to hang onto students and funding. Under a parental choice program, the state gives parents a voucher that provides a type of scholarship to be paid to the school that the parents choose for their child to attend. Some parental choice programs allow parents to select not only among public schools but also among private schools, including parochial schools. For example, the state of Ohio created a parental choice program for low-income families attending the Cleveland City School District. Students who qualified could attend the private school of their parents' choice or a public school in an adjacent district and receive tuition assistance grants from the state. Although the overwhelming majority of private schools chosen by parents for student transfer were religiously affiliated, the U.S. Supreme Court ruled the program constitutional. The Court upheld the program because it had a valid secular purpose (providing educational assistance to poor children in a weak school system), it was neutral toward religion (parents could choose any private school or even another public school), and it provided assistance to families rather than to the schools.[10]

School prayer is perhaps the most controversial Establishment Clause issue. In *Engel v. Vitale* (1962), the Supreme Court ruled that the daily classroom recitation of a prayer written by New York's state board of regents violated the First Amendment. "[I]t is no part of the business of government to compose official prayers for any group of the American people to recite as part of a religious program carried on by the government," declared the Court. Furthermore, it was irrelevant that the prayer was voluntary and students were not forced to recite it. "When the power, prestige, and financial support of government [are] placed behind a particular religious belief," the Court said, "the indirect coercive pressure upon religious minorities to conform to the prevailing officially approved religion is plain."[11]

WHAT IS YOUR OPINION?

Do you agree with the Supreme Court's decision in Engel v. Vitale*? Why or why not?*

Consider the school prayer controversy in Santa Fe, Texas. The school district allowed students at Santa Fe High School to vote on whether to have an invocation before home football games and then held a second election to select a student to deliver the prayer. The district stipulated that the invocation had to be nonsectarian and that the student could not attempt to convert other students to her religion. Two families—one Mormon and the other Catholic—sued the school district and the case reached the Supreme Court in 2000. The Court's majority ruled that the invocation was an unconstitutional infringement on the Establishment Clause, rejecting the school district's argument that the student delivering the invocation was exercising her free speech rights. Students and other spectators have a constitutional right to pray at a school football game if they are acting on their own, but that was not the situation at Santa Fe High School. The girl voicing the prayer was acting under the supervision of school faculty, pursuant to a school policy that encouraged public prayer. Consequently, her prayer was not private speech but a statement sanctioned by the school, an arm of the government.[12]

The constitutionality of public displays of religious symbols depends on the history and purpose of their display. In 2005, the Court ruled that a six-foot-tall monument of the Ten Commandments on the grounds of the Texas Capital was constitutional while holding that the display of framed copies of the Commandments on the walls of two courthouses in Kentucky was unconstitutional. The vote in each case was 5–4. The Fraternal Order of Eagles gave the Ten Commandments monument to the state of Texas more than 40 years ago with the hope of reducing

The U.S. Supreme Court declared that the student-led invocations before football games in Santa Fe, Texas, violated the Establishment Clause of the Constitution.

juvenile delinquency. The Court held that its display was constitutional because it was erected to achieve a valid secular purpose—reducing juvenile delinquency—rather than advancing religion.[13] In contrast, the Court ruled against the Kentucky display because it determined that the county governments in Kentucky that posted the Ten Commandments did so in order to advance a religious agenda in violation of the Establishment Clause.[14]

Free Exercise of Religion

The First Amendment prohibits the adoption of laws interfering with the free exercise of religion. In practice, disputes concerning free exercise fall under two general categories. The first category involves the deliberate effort of government to restrict the activities of small, controversial religious groups. For example, some localities have enacted local laws aimed at preventing Jehovah's Witnesses and other religious groups from distributing religious literature door to door. The Supreme Court has upheld these sorts of restrictions on religious practice only when the government has been able to justify its action on the basis of a compelling or overriding government interest that could not be achieved in a less restrictive fashion. Because the compelling interest test is a high standard, the Supreme Court more often than not has struck down laws and regulations aimed against particular religions or religious

The First Amendment protects the right of Jehovah's Witnesses, Mormons, and other religious believers to go door-to-door to spread word of their faith.

practices. The Court has ruled, for example, that Jehovah's Witnesses may distribute religious literature door to door and in public places without the permission of local authorities.[15]

The second category of disputes concerns the impact on religious practice of general laws and government procedures that are otherwise neutral with respect to religion. Prison inmates who are Muslim or Jewish, for example, demand that they be provided meals that do not violate the dietary restrictions imposed by their religious faiths. Christian Scientists often object to state and local regulations requiring that their children be immunized against disease. Amish parents protest school attendance laws. For years, the Supreme Court subjected these sorts of incidental restrictions on religious practice to the compelling government interest test. Since *Employment Division v. Smith* (1990), however, the Supreme Court has held that states can enact laws that have an incidental impact on religious freedom so long as they serve a valid state purpose and are not aimed at inhibiting any particular religion. The *Smith* case involved a decision by the state of Oregon to deny unemployment benefits to state employees who were fired because a drug test showed that they had used peyote, which is an illegal hallucinogenic drug that is used in Native American religious practices. The Court upheld the firing and denial of unemployment benefits because the law under which they were dismissed served a valid state purpose, was not aimed at any particular religion, and had only an incidental impact on religious belief. [16]

Freedom of Expression

The First Amendment guarantees freedom of expression. "Congress shall make no law . . . abridging the freedom of speech, or of the press; or the right of the people peaceably to assemble to petition the government for a redress of grievances." People have a constitutional right to criticize the government and its officials, even if the criticism is outrageous, intemperate, and unfair.[17]

Anti-Government Speech

The courts have held that the government cannot restrict political expression because of its content unless it has a compelling interest that cannot be achieved by less restrictive means. Although the courts have ruled that federal laws that make it a crime to threaten the president or vice president are constitutional, most governmental efforts to restrict criticism of the government are unconstitutional.[18] Consider the 1960s case of Clarence Brandenburg, a Ku Klux Klan leader from Ohio. Standing before a group of hooded men preparing to burn a cross, Brandenburg made a series of negative remarks about African Americans and Jews and then added the following statement: "We're not a revengent [sic] organization, but if our President, our Congress, our Supreme Court, continues [sic] to suppress the white, Caucasian race, it's possible that there might have to be some revengeance [sic] taken." After footage of the speech was broadcast on a Cincinnati television station, Brandenburg was arrested, tried, convicted, and sentenced to prison under an Ohio law that made it a crime to "advocate crime, sabotage, violence, or unlawful methods of terrorism as a means of accomplishing industrial or political reform." The U.S. Supreme Court ruled the Ohio law unconstitutional and overturned Brandenburg's conviction because, it said, the law was punishing "mere advocacy." Although the government can take action against individuals plotting to commit a crime, Brandenburg was speaking in the abstract rather than directing the men to take specific action. The Court ruled that the state does not have a compelling interest in outlawing "mere abstract teaching." Instead, the state must prove that the "advocacy is directed to inciting or producing imminent lawless action and is likely to incite or produce such action."[19]

Expression That Threatens the Public Order

Can the government punish expression that may lead to a disruption of public order? Consider the controversy generated by Paul Cohen and his jacket. In 1968, during the Vietnam War, Cohen wore a jacket into the Los Angeles County Courthouse upon which the words "F___ the Draft" were clearly visible. Cohen was arrested and subsequently convicted by a local court for disturbing the peace. The judge reasoned that the jacket might provoke others to commit acts of violence and sentenced Cohen to 30 days in jail. Cohen appealed and the case eventually reached the Supreme Court, which overturned the conviction. The Court held that government cannot forbid shocking language that is not legally obscene and that is not directed at an individual listener (or reader) in such a way as to provoke violence. Otherwise, government risks the unconstitutional suppression of ideas.[20]

Symbolic Expression

Symbolic expression, such as flying the flag or burning a cross, enjoys the same constitutional protection as speech or written communication. Congress and the states can restrict symbolic expression only when they can demonstrate a compelling government interest that cannot be achieved in a less restrictive fashion. Consider the issue of flag burning. In 1989, the Supreme Court overturned a Texas flag desecration law under which Gregory Lee Johnson was convicted for burning an American

"It is a fair summary of history to say that the safeguards of liberty have been forged in controversies involving not very nice people." Justice Felix Frankfurter.

flag at the 1984 Republican convention in Dallas, ruling that Johnson's action was a form of symbolic speech. "If there is any bedrock principle underlying the First Amendment," wrote Justice William Brennan in the majority opinion, "it is that the government may not prohibit the expression of an idea simply because society finds the idea itself offensive or disagreeable."[21] Congress responded to the uproar over the Court's decision by passing a federal anti-flag burning statute, which, a year later, the Court also declared unconstitutional.[22]

WHAT IS YOUR OPINION?

Do you think that the Constitution should protect people who burn the American flag from prosecution? Why or why not?

Expression versus Action

The Supreme Court distinguishes between expression and action. Protestors do not have a constitutional right to disrupt traffic, block sidewalks, or impede access to public places. The Supreme Court has upheld lower court orders preventing anti-abortion protesters from blocking access to abortion clinics because the government has an interest in "ensuring public safety . . . promoting the free flow of traffic . . . protecting property rights, and protecting a woman's freedom to seek pregnancy related services."[23] The Court has ruled that these are all legitimate goals that justify governmental action. Nonetheless, the government may not burden expression more than is necessary to achieve its legitimate goals. Court orders creating fixed buffers around the entrances of abortion clinics and parking lot entrances are acceptable, whereas "floating buffers" around women walking in and out of clinics are not.[24]

Hate Crimes Legislation

Hate crimes law A legislative measure that increases penalties for persons convicted of offenses, motivated by prejudice based on race, religion, national origin, gender, or sexual orientation.

A **hate crimes law** is a legislative measure that increases penalties for persons convicted of offenses motivated by prejudice based on race, religion, national origin, gender, or sexual orientation. Suppose a group of young white men beat up an African American man who has just moved his family into a predominantly white neighborhood. During the assault, the white men use racial slurs and warn the man to move out of the area. The white men could be charged with the crime of assault. Because they acted out of racial animosity, they could also be charged with a hate crime. In recent years, many states have adopted hate crimes legislation, enhancing penalties for persons convicted of crimes motivated by bias.

Hate crimes legislation is controversial. Critics charge that hate crimes laws infringe on freedom of speech. They also believe that hate crimes provisions inhibit expression because they rely on speech as evidence of biased motive. In contrast, the proponents of hate crimes laws claim they are justified because crimes motivated by hate inflict not only physical harm but also psychological damage on their victims. Furthermore, they argue that violent crimes aimed at groups of persons are more threatening to society than crimes against particular individuals because they increase racial and social divisions.[25]

The Supreme Court has upheld hate crimes legislation, drawing a distinction between speech and action. Although biased speech is constitutionally protected, violent behavior motivated by bias is not. "A physical assault is not by any stretch of the imagination . . . protected by the First Amendment," said the Court. Because hate crimes are perceived as inflicting "greater individual and societal harm" than ordinary crimes, states are justified in providing greater penalties for their commission.[26]

WHAT IS YOUR OPINION?

Do people who commit crimes out of prejudice deserve more severe punishment than do other criminals? Why or why not?

Commercial Speech

Advertising and other forms of commercial speech are constitutionally protected forms of expression, but they do not enjoy the same level of constitutional protection as political expression. The Supreme Court has established a four-pronged test for protecting commercial speech:

1. Whether the speech concerns lawful conduct.
2. Whether the government interest in banning the speech is substantial.
3. Whether the regulation directly advances the government interest.
4. Whether the regulation is no more extensive than necessary to advance the government interest.[27]

In sum, the government can regulate advertising and other forms of commercial speech only if the regulation promotes a substantial government interest and is not more extensive than necessary to serve that interest. Commercial speech that is misleading or that promotes illegal activity does not enjoy constitutional protection.[28]

Freedom of the Press

Freedom of the press is a fundamental right, which means that government cannot restrict it unless it can demonstrate a compelling or overriding public interest for so doing. For example, the U.S. Supreme Court has ruled that the government has a compelling interest in prohibiting obscenity and protecting individuals from defamation of character.

Obscenity

The U.S. Supreme Court narrowly defines obscenity. In order for material to be legally obscene, it must meet all three elements of the following criteria:

1. It must depict or describe sexual conduct. Although depictions of graphic violence may offend many people, the legal definition of obscenity does not encompass violent images.

2. The material must be such that the "average person, applying contemporary . . . standards, would find that the work taken as a whole appeals to prurient interest." (The word *prurient* is defined as an excessive interest in sex.)
3. The work taken as a whole must lack serious literary, artistic, political, or scientific value.[29]

The definition of obscenity is so narrowly drawn as to exclude most material that ordinary citizens consider pornographic. With the exception of cases involving child pornography, obscenity prosecutions are rare and seldom successful.

Defamation

Libel False written statements that lower a person's reputation or expose a person to hatred, contempt, or ridicule.

Slander False spoken statements that lower a person's reputation or expose a person to hatred, contempt, or ridicule.

Defamation involves false written (**libel**) or spoken (**slander**) statements that lower a person's reputation or expose a person to hatred, contempt, or ridicule. Defamation lawsuits are fairly common and sometimes successful. In 2007, for example, the *National Enquirer* settled a defamation lawsuit filed by actress Cameron Diaz over an allegation that she had an affair with a married man.[30]

The U.S. Supreme Court has long held that the First Amendment does not protect defamatory expression. In recent decades, however, the Court has adopted a relatively strict standard for the defamation of public figures, which the Court defines as individuals who thrust themselves to the forefront of a particular public controversy in order to influence the resolution of the issues involved. Ordinary citizens can win defamation suits merely by proving that a statement is false and that it lowers their reputation or exposes them to hatred, contempt, or ridicule. In contrast, public figures must also show that the statement was made with malice or reckless disregard for the truth. The justification for this approach is that public figures, in contrast to private individuals, have access to channels of effective communication to combat allegations about their conduct. Furthermore, public figures have voluntarily subjected themselves to public scrutiny.[31] Consequently, elected officials and high-profile government appointees seldom file defamation suits against the media and are almost never successful.

Prior Restraint and National Security

In early 1979, *Progressive* magazine announced plans to publish an article on how to build an H-bomb. The magazine's editors explained that their purpose in printing the article was to inform the public about nuclear weapons. Because the information in the article was gleaned from unclassified sources, the article revealed no real secrets. Nonetheless, the federal government asked a judge to block publication of the article on national security grounds.

Prior restraint Government action to prevent the publication or broadcast of objectionable material.

This is an example of **prior restraint,** that is, government action to prevent the publication or broadcast of objectionable material. Expression involving defamation or obscenity can be held punishable *after* its utterance or publication. The issue of prior restraint considers whether government can block the expression of objectionable material *before* the fact. The Supreme Court has held that prior restraint is such an extreme limitation on freedom of the press that it can be used only in exceptional circumstances, such as time of war.[32]

The Supreme Court has had difficulty deciding prior restraint cases involving national security. In the *Pentagon Papers Case* (1971), the Court refused to block newspaper publication of government documents detailing the history of American involvement in Vietnam. Although the Nixon administration claimed the documents included military secrets, the newspaper charged that the government's only real concerns were political because no national security issues were at stake. The Court was deeply divided, however, and its opinion gave little guidance as to how similar disputes might be resolved in the future.[33] Nor did the *Progressive* controversy enable the Court to clarify the law in this area. After several newspapers published H-bomb articles, the government dropped its case against the magazine and the issue never reached the Supreme Court. The Court has yet to clarify the matter.

The Right to Bear Arms

The U.S. Constitution addresses the issue of gun ownership in the Second Amendment: "A well regulated Militia being necessary to the security of a free State, the right of the people to keep and bear Arms, shall not be infringed." Historically, the courts have interpreted the amendment to guarantee the right of states to maintain an armed militia rather than protecting an individual right to own a firearm. In 2008, however, the U.S. Supreme Court voted 5–4 to overturn a District of Columbia ban against handgun possession, declaring that the Second Amendment protects an individual right to possess a firearm in the home for purposes of self-defense. The Court made clear that the right to bear arms is not absolute and that the ruling against the ban on handgun ownership should not cast doubt on the constitutionality of "longstanding prohibitions on possession of firearms by felons and the mentally ill, or laws forbidding the carrying of firearms in sensitive places such as schools and government buildings, or laws imposing conditions and qualifications on the commercial sale of arms."[34] Two years later in another 5–4 decision, the Court ruled that the individual right to bear arms is a fundamental right that applies to state and local governments as well as the federal government.[35]

Privacy Rights

Do Americans enjoy a constitutional right of privacy? Although the Constitution does not specifically mention privacy, the Supreme Court has interpreted the Due Process Clause of the Fourteenth Amendment to include a right of privacy. In 1965, the Court struck down a seldom-enforced Connecticut law that prohibited the use of contraceptives and the dispensing of birth control information even to married couples on the grounds that its enforcement would involve government's invading "the privacy of the bedroom." The Court declared that various constitutional guarantees found in the Bill of Rights create "zones of privacy." The Third Amendment's prohibition against quartering soldiers in private homes and the Fourth Amendment's protection against unreasonable searches and seizures also imply a right of privacy.[36] In contrast, conservative legal scholars believe that the Supreme Court simply invented a right of privacy that does not exist in the Constitution because a majority of the justices disagreed with the Connecticut law and wanted to find an excuse to strike it down. Although few conservatives want to defend Connecticut's statute against contraception, which some label "an uncommonly silly law," they have been outraged that the Court has used the right of privacy as the basis for major decisions involving abortion and gay rights.

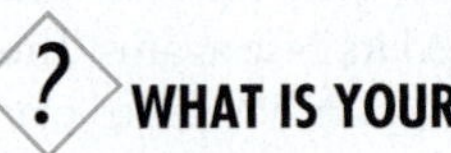

Should privacy be a constitutional right? Why or why not?

The Supreme Court based *Roe v. Wade*, its landmark abortion decision, on a right of privacy. The case dealt with a challenge by an anonymous Dallas woman, "Jane Roe," to a Texas law prohibiting abortion except to save the life of a woman. The Court found the Texas statute unconstitutional, declaring that a woman's right to personal privacy under the U.S. Constitution included her decision to terminate a pregnancy. The Court said, however, that a woman's right to privacy was not absolute and must be balanced against the state's interest in protecting health, medical standards, and prenatal life.

The Supreme Court balanced these competing interests by dividing a pregnancy into trimesters. During the first trimester, state governments could not interfere with a physician's decision, reached in consultation with a pregnant woman patient, to terminate a pregnancy. In the second trimester, the state could regulate abortion but only to protect the health of a woman. In the third trimester, after the fetus had achieved viability (the ability to survive outside the womb), the Court ruled that state governments could prohibit abortion except when it was necessary to preserve the life or health of a woman.[37]

In the years since *Roe* was decided, the Supreme Court has upheld its original decision while allowing states greater leeway to regulate abortion. In 1989, the Court upheld a Missouri law limiting access to abortion. The statute prohibited the use of public employees or facilities to perform or assist an abortion except to save a woman's life, and outlawed the use of public funds, employees, or facilities to encourage or counsel a woman to have an abortion not necessary to save her life. Citing recent medical advances, the Court abandoned the trimester system adopted in *Roe* by allowing Missouri to require physicians to perform medical tests to determine fetal viability beginning at 20 weeks.[38] The Court subsequently ruled that a state could regulate abortion throughout a pregnancy as long as the regulations did not place an "undue burden" on a woman's right to terminate a pregnancy before viability. The Court defined an undue burden as one that presented an "absolute obstacle or severe limitation" on the right to decide to have an abortion. State regulations that simply "inhibited" that right were permissible. After viability, the state could prohibit abortion except when necessary to protect the life of the woman.[39]

The Court upheld a number of restrictions on abortion, including the following:

- Women seeking abortions must be given information about fetal development and alternatives to ending their pregnancies.
- Women must wait at least 24 hours after receiving that information before having an abortion.
- Doctors must keep detailed records on each abortion performed.
- Abortion records must be subject to public disclosure.
- Unmarried girls under the age of 18 must get the permission of one of their parents or the certification of a state judge that they are mature enough to make the decision on their own.

The only provision in the law that the Court considered an undue burden was a requirement that married women notify their husbands of their plans to have an abortion.[40]

The Supreme Court's most recent application of the right of privacy involved a legal challenge to the Texas sodomy law, which criminalized private, consensual sexual conduct between two adults of the same gender. When police in Houston, Texas, arrived at the home of John Lawrence because of an unrelated call, they found Lawrence and another man, Tyron Garner, engaged in sexual intercourse. They arrested the men and charged them with violating the Texas homosexual conduct law for "engaging in deviate sexual intercourse with another person of the same sex." In *Lawrence v. Texas*, the Court ruled that the Texas law violated the Due Process Clause of the Fourteenth Amendment because it intruded into the personal and private lives of individuals without furthering a legitimate state interest.[41]

Due Process of Law and the Rights of the Accused

Several provisions of the Bill of Rights protect the rights of persons under investigation or accused of crimes, including the better part of the Fourth, Fifth, and Eighth Amendments. The key constitutional phrase is found in the Fifth Amendment and repeated in the Fourteenth Amendment: No person shall be deprived of "life, liberty, or property, without due process of law." **Due process of law** is the constitutional provision that declares that government must follow fair and regular procedures in actions that could lead to an individual's suffering loss of life, liberty, or property. Neither the national government nor the states may resort to stacked juries, coerced confessions, self-incrimination, denial of counsel, cruel and unusual punishments, or unreasonable searches and seizures.

Due process of law The constitutional principle holding that government must follow fair and regular procedures in actions that could lead to an individual's suffering loss of life, liberty, or property.

Searches and Seizures

The Fourth Amendment guarantees the "right of the people to be secure in their persons, houses, papers, and effects, against unreasonable searches and seizures . . . and no warrants shall issue, but upon probable cause . . . and particularly describing the place to be searched, and the persons or things to be seized." In general, this

Warrant An official authorization issued by a judicial officer.

Probable cause The reasonable suspicion based on evidence that a particular search will uncover contraband.

provision means that the police need a **warrant** (that is, an official authorization issued by a judicial officer) for most searches of persons or property. Judges or other magistrates issue warrants after the law-enforcement authorities have shown probable cause that certain items will be found. **Probable cause** is the reasonable suspicion based on evidence that a particular search will uncover contraband.

Through the years the Supreme Court has permitted a number of exceptions to the basic warrant requirement. The police do not need a warrant, for example, to search suspects who consent to be searched or to search suspects after valid arrests. If police officers have a reasonable suspicion of criminal activity, they may stop and search suspicious individuals. The Court has ruled, for example, that the police are justified in searching an individual in a high crime area who flees when the police appear.[42] The authorities can also search luggage in airports and may fingerprint suspects after arrests.

The Supreme Court has been more willing to authorize searches of automobiles without warrants than it has offices and homes. Consider the *Ross* case. An informant tipped off the District of Columbia police about a narcotics dealer known as Bandit who sold drugs from the trunk of his purplish maroon Chevrolet Malibu. When the police spotted a car fitting the description, they pulled it over and searched the trunk, even though they did not have a warrant. Sure enough, they found heroin and cash in the trunk. The car's driver, Albert Ross, Jr., was subsequently tried and convicted of possession of narcotics with intent to distribute. He appealed his case to the Supreme Court. Did the police search of Ross's car trunk without a warrant violate his constitutional rights? The Court said that it did not because the police had legitimately stopped the car and had probable cause to believe it contained contraband. As a result, the police could search the vehicle as thoroughly as if they had a warrant. The Court added, however, that a search "must be limited by its object," that is, the police cannot conduct a general search to see what might turn up. If authorities have probable cause to believe that illegal aliens are being transported in a van, for example, they may search the van, but they have no justification for searching the glove compartment or luggage where no illegal aliens could possibly be hiding.[43]

The Exclusionary Rule

Exclusionary rule The judicial doctrine stating that when the police violate an individual's constitutional rights, the evidence obtained as a result of police misconduct or error cannot be used against the defendant in a criminal prosecution.

The **exclusionary rule** is the judicial doctrine stating that when the police violate an individual's constitutional rights, the evidence obtained as a result of police misconduct or error cannot be used against the defendant in a criminal prosecution. In 1914, the Supreme Court established the exclusionary rule in federal prosecutions in the *Weeks case*. The police arrested Fremont Weeks at his place of business and then searched his home. Both of these actions were taken without a warrant. Papers and articles seized in the search were used in federal court against Weeks and he was convicted. He appealed his conviction, arguing that the judge should not have admitted into evidence illegally seized materials. The Supreme Court agreed.

> The tendency of those who execute the criminal laws of the country to obtain convictions by means of unlawful seizures and enforced confessions . . . should find no sanction in the judgment of the courts. . . . If letters and private documents can thus be seized and held and used in evidence against a citizen accused of an offense, the protection of the Fourth Amendment . . . might as well be stricken from the Constitution.[44]

In 1961, the Supreme Court extended the exclusionary rule to the states in the case of *Mapp v. Ohio*.[45]

The exclusionary rule is controversial. Its defenders say that is a necessary safeguard to ensure that police authorities do not intentionally violate individual rights. In contrast, critics point out that the United States is the only country to take the position that police misconduct must automatically result in the suppression of evidence. In other countries, the trial judge determines whether the misconduct is serious enough to warrant the exclusion of the evidence.[46]

In recent decades, the Supreme Court has weakened the exclusionary rule without repealing it by carving out major exceptions to its application. In 1984, the Court adopted a "good faith" exception to the exclusionary rule requirement, allowing the use of illegally seized evidence in criminal prosecutions as long as the police acted in good faith.[47] Subsequently, the Court added a "harmless error" exception, allowing a criminal conviction to stand despite the use of illegally obtained evidence when other evidence in the case was strong enough to convict the defendant anyway.[48] In 2009, the Court ruled that evidence obtained from an unlawful arrest based on careless record keeping rather than intentional police misconduct could be used in a prosecution.[49]

WHAT IS YOUR OPINION?

If the police obtain evidence in an unlawful search that conclusively proves a defendant guilty, should the evidence be used to prosecute the defendant? Why or why not?

The Miranda Warning

Ernesto Miranda was an Arizona man who was arrested for kidnapping and raping a young woman. Under questioning, Miranda confessed. On appeal, Miranda challenged the use of his confession as a violation of the Fifth Amendment's guarantee against self-incrimination because the police had not informed him of his constitutional rights to remain silent and consult an attorney.

The Supreme Court reversed Miranda's conviction. The Court's majority held that the prosecution could not use a statement against an accused person in a court of law unless the authorities observe adequate procedural safeguards to ensure that the statement was obtained "voluntarily, knowingly, and intelligently." The **Miranda warning** is the requirement that police inform suspects of their rights before questioning them. Before questioning, accused persons must be warned that (1) they have a right to remain silent, (2) that any statements they give may be used against them, and (3) that they are entitled to the presence of an attorney, either retained or appointed.[50]

Miranda warning
The requirement that police inform suspects of their rights before questioning them.

The Court's *Miranda* ruling has sparked an ongoing debate. Critics say that it makes law enforcement more difficult by preventing police from interrogating suspects quickly before they have a chance to concoct an alibi or reflect on the consequences of telling the truth.[51] In contrast, *Miranda*'s defenders call it the "poor

Are the Miranda warnings a necessary protection against police misconduct or just a device for releasing criminals on the basis of technicalities?

person's Fifth Amendment." Educated, middle-class defendants do not need the Miranda warning—they know their rights. Miranda protects poor, uneducated, first-time offenders from police coercion.

The Supreme Court has weakened the *Miranda* ruling without reversing it. The Court has held that in cross-examining defendants, prosecutors can use statements that do not meet the *Miranda* standard.[52] The Court has also ruled that police need not give the Miranda warning before questioning a suspect when the public safety is immediately and directly threatened.[53] The Court even upheld a conviction when the police refused to allow an attorney hired by a suspect's relatives to see him because the suspect had not asked to see a lawyer.[54]

Double Jeopardy

Double jeopardy The government trying a criminal defendant a second time for the same offense after an acquittal in an earlier prosecution.

The Fifth Amendment prohibits **double jeopardy,** which involves the government trying a criminal defendant a second time for the same offense after an acquittal in an earlier prosecution. No person shall be "twice put in jeopardy of life and limb" for the same criminal offense, the amendment declares. The goal of this provision is to protect individuals from the harassment of repeated prosecutions on the same charge after an acquittal. Because of the Double Jeopardy Clause, no one who has been acquitted of an offense can be retried for the same crime even if incontrovertible evidence of the person's guilt is discovered. A person acquitted of murder, for example, could walk out of the courtroom and declare, "I did it and I got away with it!" on national television and not have to worry about being retried for murder.

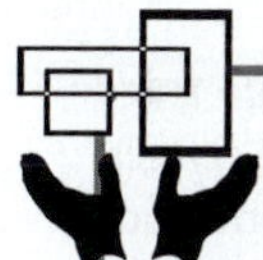

GETTING INVOLVED

Talking about Miranda

Is the Miranda warning a meaningful constitutional safeguard or a technical formality that has no impact on justice? The class project is to research the implementation of the Miranda warning by interviewing police officers or members of the campus police at your college. Before conducting the interviews, prepare a set of questions designed to focus on the following topics:

- **Police training.** How do police academies cover the topic of Miranda? Is it presented as a necessary evil or as an important element of civil liberties in a free society?
- **Police supervision.** How seriously does management take the Miranda warning? Do police supervisors frequently review implementation procedures or is that left to the discretion of individual officers?
- **Miranda implementation.** When, if ever, do officers recite the Miranda warning to suspects? Do they read the warning from a card, or do they have it memorized? What steps, if any, do officers take to ensure that suspects understand the meaning of the warning?
- **Miranda impact.** Do law enforcement officers believe that the Miranda warning has an impact on their work? Do they think the warning discourages guilty persons from confessing? Do they believe that Miranda plays a positive role in law enforcement by reminding innocent people of their constitutional rights? Or do they believe that the Miranda warning is meaningless, a waste of time to satisfy the courts that has no impact in the real world of law enforcement?

After the interviews are complete, students should organize their notes and prepare to participate in class discussion. In particular, the instructor will invite students to discuss their assessment of the Miranda warning. Is it harmful or beneficial, or is it just a meaningless technicality that neither police officers nor criminal suspects take seriously?

The prohibition against double jeopardy is not absolute. A defendant can be tried multiple times for multiple offenses committed in a single incident.[55] An individual charged with killing a gas station attendant during a holdup, for example, can be tried first for murder and then for robbery. Furthermore, separate prosecutions by different levels of government do not constitute double jeopardy, even for the same offense.[56] Timothy McVeigh and Terry Nichols, the men charged with the deadly bombing of the Oklahoma City federal building, were tried in federal court because the offense took place on federal property and a number of federal employees were killed. Nichols was also tried for murder in the state courts of Oklahoma because the crime took place in that state. Similarly, persons who have allegedly engaged in criminal activity that has transcended state lines can be tried in each state involved.[57]

The Supreme Court has held that the Double Jeopardy Clause does not protect persons convicted of child molestation from involuntary commitment to mental hospitals after they have served their prison sentences. Consider the case of *Kansas v. Hendricks*. Leroy Hendricks was a pedophile, an adult who sexually abuses children. He had five convictions for child molestation in the state of Kansas and admitted that he could not stop trying to have sex with children. In 1994, after Hendricks finished serving his most recent sentence for child molestation, the state of Kansas transferred him to a mental health facility, where he was confined indefinitely under provisions of the state's Sexually Violent Predator Act. A state judge ruled that Hendricks was "mentally abnormal" and likely to commit additional crimes. Hendricks and his attorneys filed suit against the state, charging that his continued confinement was a sort of double jeopardy in that he was tried and punished twice for the same crime. The case eventually reached the U.S. Supreme Court, which ruled against Hendricks. The Court declared that Hendricks could be confined against his will because he was being held in a mental institution rather than a prison. Technically, he was no longer being punished.[58] Although no one was sympathetic with Hendricks, a number of observers worried about the precedent set by the case. "Today we're dealing with sexual predators," said Steven Shapiro of the ACLU. "Who is it tomorrow that we're going to label as abnormal and potentially dangerous?"[59]

WHAT IS YOUR OPINION?

Should child molesters be kept in confinement even after they have served their criminal sentences? Why or why not?

Fair Trial

A number of provisions in the Sixth Amendment are aimed at guaranteeing that defendants receive a fair trial. For example, the amendment promises a speedy and public trial. Although the Supreme Court has been reluctant to set timetables for trials, the federal government and many states have adopted speedy trial laws to ensure that justice will not be long delayed. As for the public trial requirement, the Supreme Court has held that the public (and the press) may not be excluded from the courtroom except in rare circumstances.[60] Furthermore, the Court has said that states may permit the unobtrusive use of television in a courtroom if they wish.[61]

The Sixth Amendment guarantees trial by an impartial jury. Although juries are traditionally 12 persons, the Supreme Court has said that juries with as few as six people are acceptable.[62] The Court has also held that jury selection processes must ensure that the jury pool represents a cross-section of the community, holding, for example, that prosecutors may not systematically exclude racial minorities from jury service.[63]

The Sixth Amendment grants defendants the right to legal counsel. In *Gideon v. Wainwright*, the Supreme Court ruled that states must provide attorneys for indigent defendants charged with serious crimes.[64] The Court has also held that assigned counsel must meet a standard of reasonable competence.[65]

Cruel and Unusual Punishments

Should mentally retarded offenders be held fully accountable for their crimes? Daryl Renard Atkins is a murderer, convicted and sentenced to death by the state of Virginia for the robbery and slaying of a U.S. airman in 1996. Atkins is also severely retarded, at least according to his defense attorneys. Would executing Atkins violate the prohibition against cruel and unusual punishments contained in the Eighth

Amendment to the U.S. Constitution? In general, the Supreme Court has interpreted this provision to mean that the punishment must fit the crime. The Court, for example, has held that a life sentence without the possibility of parole for a series of nonviolent petty offenses is cruel and unusual.[66] The Court has also ruled that it is unconstitutional to impose the death penalty on a defendant who rapes a child but does not kill the victim.[67] Finally, in 2010, the Supreme Court resolved the issue discussed in the opener to this chapter by ruling that sentencing juveniles to life in prison without the possibility of parole violates the Eighth Amendment prohibition against cruel and unusual punishments.[68]

Capital punishment The death penalty.

No issue has generated more controversy under the Eighth Amendment than the death penalty (**capital punishment**). The supporters of capital punishment quote the Bible, "an eye for an eye, a tooth for a tooth," and declare that the death penalty is an effective deterrent to serious crime. In contrast, opponents call the death penalty barbaric and say that it is little less than legalized murder. In 1972, the opponents of capital punishment won a temporary victory in the case of *Furman v. Georgia*. By a 5–4 vote, the Supreme Court declared that the death penalty, *as then applied*, was unconstitutional because it allowed too much discretion, thereby opening the door to discriminatory practices. Getting the death penalty, the Court said, was similar to being struck by lightning.[69] Because of the *Furman* decision, death row inmates around the nation escaped execution, having their sentences commuted to life in prison. Many state legislatures responded to *Furman* by adopting new capital punishment laws designed to satisfy the Court's objections. As the states began to implement their new death penalty statutes, cases began to make their way through the court system. In 1976, the U.S. Supreme Court ruled that capital punishment was constitutional in the case of *Gregg v. Georgia*, which involved a constitutional challenge to Georgia's new death penalty statute.[70] Thirty-eight states and the federal government adopted capital punishment statutes and 32 states carried out executions, with Texas taking the lead, carrying out more than a third of the nation's executions.[71] The federal government carried out one execution, Timothy McVeigh, the convicted Oklahoma City bomber. As Figure 15.1 shows, the number of executions increased during the 1990s, peaking at 98 in 1999.

The increased rate of executions was accompanied by increased controversy. The opponents of the death penalty charged that the process of trials and appeals was so flawed that innocent people might face execution. A study published by Columbia University law professor James S. Liebman found that two-thirds of the death sentences given by American courts between 1973 and 1995 were overturned on appeal. When death penalty cases were retried, 7 percent of defendants were found not guilty.[72] Furthermore, the critics of the death penalty argued that it was inefficient because only 5 percent of death sentences were actually carried out and then only after years of evaluation.[73] In contrast, the proponents of capital punishment defended the process, saying that it was scrupulously fair. They pointed out that people given the death penalty were entitled to an appeals process that lasts for years. According to the Bureau of Justice Statistics, the average time on death row for the convicted murderers before their executions is nearly 12 years, long enough for their cases to be thoroughly examined for error.[74]

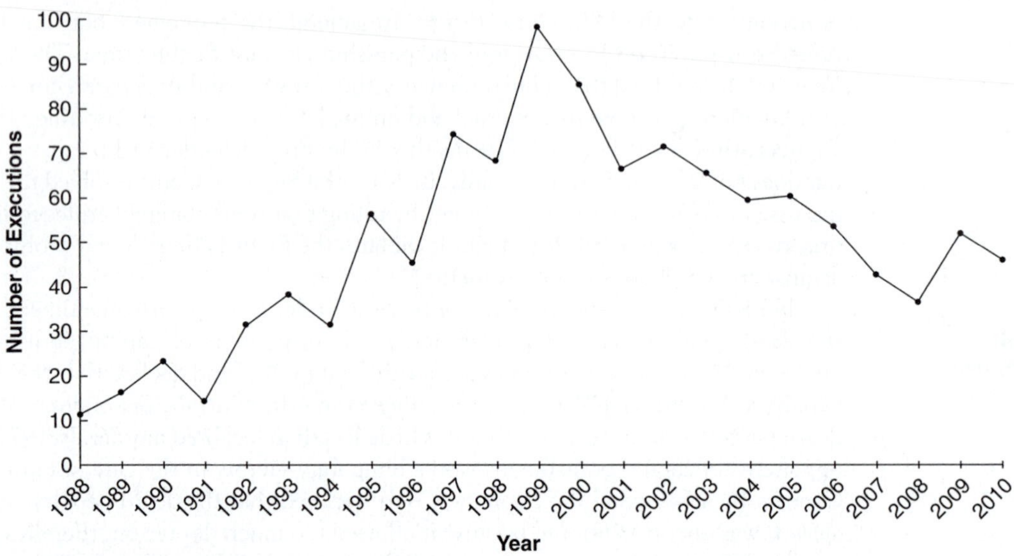

FIGURE 15.1 Executions in the United States, 1988–2010.
Source: Bureau of Justice Statistics.

The renewed debate over capital punishment has been accompanied by a decline in the implementation of the death penalty. As Figure 15.1 shows, the number of people executed in the United States peaked in 1999 at 98 and then began to fall. States carried out 46 executions in 2010, less than half the number of executions in 1999. New Jersey, New Mexico, and Illinois repealed their death penalty statutes and 18 states adopted laws to prohibit the execution of mentally retarded criminals.[75]

In this context, the U.S. Supreme Court declared that the execution of defendants who are mentally retarded is a violation of the Cruel and Unusual Punishment Clause of the Eighth Amendment. The Court reversed a position it had taken in 1989 when only two states excluded mentally retarded individuals from the death penalty, arguing that a national consensus had developed against executing the mentally retarded.[76] The Court returned the *Atkins* case (which we discussed at the beginning of this section) to a trial court in Virginia to determine whether the defendant was indeed mentally retarded. Ironically, a jury found Atkins mentally competent and a judge sentenced him to death. His case is once again on appeal.

Civil Liberties and the War on Terror

Executive authority grows during wartime, sometimes at the expense of civil liberties. In the midst of war, presidents exercise extraordinary powers and declare that their actions are necessary to defend the nation and win the war. Although civil libertarians often challenge the president's actions as infringements on personal liberty, other political actors and the general public either support the president's initiatives or mute their criticism for fear of being accused of failing to stand up to the enemy. Over time, public passions over the war recede and either a new administration or the other branches of government reverse the policies that compromised civil liberties.[77]

Consider the Japanese internment during World War II. In early 1942, shortly after the Japanese attack on Pearl Harbor, President Franklin Roosevelt issued an executive order to forcibly relocate nearly 120,000 people of Japanese ancestry living on the West Coast into internment camps until the end of the war. Most were American citizens. The president justified the order as necessary to prevent sabotage and espionage. When Fred Korematsu, an American citizen of Japanese descent, challenged his detention, the U.S. Supreme Court upheld the constitutionality of the executive order.[78] The U.S. government eventually began to regard the Japanese internment with regret. In 1988, Congress passed, and President Ronald Reagan signed, legislation officially apologizing for the internment and providing reparation payments of $20,000 each to the survivors or their heirs.

After the terrorist attacks of September 11, 2001, President George W. Bush took actions that critics charged threatened civil liberties. He approved wiretapping of overseas telephone calls without benefit of court order. He ordered terror suspects captured in the war on terror held at Guantánamo Bay, Cuba, without benefit of prisoner-of-war status or the rights of suspected criminals under the U.S. Constitution. The president authorized the use of aggressive interrogation techniques against terror suspects, and had some detainees transported to third countries where they were allegedly tortured. American citizens suspected of terrorism were held indefinitely without trial. Bush also declared his intent to try some enemy combatants in military tribunals without many of the civil liberties guarantees afforded by civilian courts.[79]

The U.S. Supreme Court and the Obama administration overturned or modified many of the Bush administration's actions. In a case involving Yaser Esam Hamdi, an American citizen who was taken into custody in Afghanistan, the Court held that the president could not deprive detainees of their right to due process.[80] The Court ruled against Bush's plan to put detainees on trial before military tribunals because Congress had not authorized the action.[81] In *Boumediene v. Bush*, the Supreme Court also declared that terror suspects held at Guantánamo have a constitutional right to seek their release in federal court.[82]

Similarly, President Obama reversed many Bush administration policies concerning the war on terror. In addition to banning the use of aggressive interrogation techniques, Obama ordered the closure of the Guantánamo prison within a year and made plans to try terror suspects in civilian courts within the United States. Obama soon discovered the difficulty of implementing his plans. The prison at Guantánamo Bay remained open because the U.S. government was unable to find countries willing to take all the inmates and American communities opposed efforts to transfer them to federal prisons in the United States. President Obama ran into a similar problem with his plan to try Khalid Sheik Mohammed, the alleged al Qaeda mastermind of the 9/11 attacks, in New York City when Mayor Michael Bloomberg rejected the proposal because of concerns over security and worry about the trial's effect on traffic congestion.

Making Civil Liberties Policy

Constitutional law is the most important contextual factor affecting civil liberties policymaking. Civil liberties questions are constitutional questions. Policy debates over prayer in public schools, pornography, and capital punishment invariably are also debates about constitutional law. Did the founders intend for the Establishment Clause to prohibit organized spoken prayer in public schools? Is it cruel and unusual punishment under the Eighth Amendment to sentence juvenile offenders to life without parole? The Constitution and its interpretation affect every stage of the civil liberties policy process.

Because of the constitutional nature of civil liberties policymaking, judges, especially the men and women who serve on the Supreme Court of the United States, are the most important civil liberties policymakers. Liberal judges are more likely than conservative judges to rule in favor of unpopular litigants, such as atheists, Jehovah's Witnesses, members of the Ku Klux Klan, criminal defendants, and prison inmates. During the 1960s, a liberal bloc of justices led by Chief Justice Earl Warren dominated the Supreme Court. Many of the decisions of that era, including *Engel v. Vitale* and *Miranda v. Arizona,* reflected their policy preferences. In contrast to liberal members of the judiciary, judges with conservative policy preferences tend to decide cases in favor of the police, criminal prosecutors, majority religious preferences, and traditional values. The Supreme Court today is closely divided on most civil liberties issues and many cases are decided by the narrowest margin.

Civil liberties policymaking is affected by the presence of interest groups and other organizations capable and willing to participate in the policy process. The American Civil Liberties Union (ACLU) is a frequent participant in civil liberties policymaking. Other interest groups involved with various civil liberties issues include the National Organization for Women (NOW), Planned Parenthood, National Abortion Rights Action League (NARAL), National Rifle Association (NRA), and National Right to Life Committee.

Public opinion affects the civil liberties policymaking process. Legislatures and executives respond to public demands by enacting death penalty statutes, school prayer requirements, and other measures related to civil liberties. At times, judges seem to respond to public opinion. Historically, the Supreme Court has been more willing to support presidential actions to limit civil liberties during wartime than after the war is over.

In the long run, the president's policy preferences affect civil liberties policymaking because the president appoints judges. Republican presidents tend to select conservative judges, whereas Democratic presidents appoint liberals. Because federal judges enjoy lifetime appointments, a president's influence on judicial policymaking will be slow to materialize but continues well after the president leaves office. In the early years of the twenty-first century, former Presidents Reagan, Bush, and Clinton continue to impact the judicial branch of government because their appointees still serve on the Court. The survival of the *Roe* precedent depends on future presidential and senatorial elections.

Agenda Setting

A number of political actors help set the agenda for civil liberties policymaking. Interest groups and other organizations are particularly important. Conservative groups call on the government to get tough on pornography and crime, and to limit access to abortion. Groups with unpopular views, such as Nazis and members of the Ku Klux Klan, stimulate debate on the First Amendment by attempting to march and demonstrate. Many of the civil liberties disputes reaching the Supreme Court are test cases initiated by groups such as the ACLU or the Jehovah's Witnesses. The latter have been responsible for more than 50 cases involving religious liberty, winning 90 percent of them. A **test case** is a lawsuit initiated to assess the constitutionality of a legislative or executive act. Furthermore, interest groups ranging from the Chamber of Commerce to B'nai B'rith, a Jewish organization, join other civil liberties cases by means of the *amicus* brief. An ***amicus curiae*** or **friend of the court brief** is a written legal argument presented by a party not directly involved in a case.

Test case A lawsuit initiated to assess the constitutionality of a legislative or executive act.

Amicus curiae or **friend of the court briefs** Written legal arguments presented by parties not directly involved in the case.

Individuals can raise civil liberties issues to the public agenda. Many criminal justice disputes arise from appeals filed by convicted felons, such as Ernesto Miranda. Other individuals raise civil liberties issues on the basis of principle. Madalyn Murray O'Hair, for example, was famous for initiating test cases to challenge what she regarded as unconstitutional government support of religion.

Policy Formulation, Adoption, and Legitimation

Many civil liberties policies are formulated and adopted in the executive and legislative branches of government, both at the national level and in the states. After the terrorist attacks of September 11, 2001, for example, Congress passed, and President George W. Bush signed, the USA Patriot Act. This Act makes it easier for federal officials to get wiretapping orders from judges to investigate terrorism, and authorizes nationwide search warrants for computer information in terrorism investigations.[83] State governments adopt policies dealing with the death penalty, state aid to parochial schools, abortion, and other civil liberties issues.

The courts become involved in civil liberties policymaking only when a civil liberties policy adopted by another unit of government is challenged on constitutional grounds. The U.S. Supreme Court has addressed the issues of school prayer and school choice because of legal challenges filed against state and local policies. Court rulings then serve as guidelines for other institutions of government. The Court's decision to uphold the school voucher program in Ohio did not require state legislatures to adopt similar programs for their states; the impact of the ruling was to inform state legislatures that school voucher programs similar to the one in Ohio were constitutional. The decision was permissive in that it allowed states to adopt voucher programs, but it did not require them to adopt a program.

If the Supreme Court overturns *Roe v. Wade*, the issue of abortion will return to the states. Before *Roe*, states set their own abortion policies. Some states allowed abortion, whereas other states prohibited it except when necessary to protect the life of the woman. In *Roe*, the Supreme Court ruled that women have a constitutional right to an abortion during the first trimester. States could regulate second trimester abortions; they could prohibit late-term abortions. If the Supreme Court overturns the *Roe* precedent, some states, such as South Dakota, will prohibit abortion except when the woman's life is in jeopardy, whereas others will allow most abortions. Other states will likely take a moderate approach, allowing abortion under certain circumstances but prohibiting abortions otherwise.

The debate over civil liberties policies frequently extends beyond policy adoption to the policy legitimation stage. Whereas President George W. Bush defended the USA Patriot Act as an appropriate action in light of the war on terror, civil libertarians attacked it as an infringement on the constitutional rights of Americans. *Roe v. Wade* hardly ended the debate over abortion policy; instead, it may have added to the controversy.

Policy Implementation, Evaluation, and Change

A broad range of government entities participates in the implementation of civil liberties policy. The Supreme Court's willingness to allow states to enact school voucher programs may not necessarily lead to the adoption of voucher programs, at least not in all states. Some state legislatures will adopt programs, but other legislatures will not. The Supreme Court's decision effectively moves the policymaking arena from the courthouse to the legislature, the governor's mansion, and the school district.

Scholars have completed a number of studies evaluating certain aspects of civil liberties policy. For example, research suggests that the primary impact of the *Miranda* decision has been psychological and that the ruling has had little appreciable effect on confessions and convictions.[84] Another observer concludes that *Miranda* has had no measurable impact on reducing police misconduct.[85] The Liebman study of capital punishment was designed to assess the effectiveness of the death penalty.

Civil liberties policy changes because of changes in public opinion and the makeup of the Supreme Court. Consider the approach of the U.S. Supreme Court toward criminal justice issues, especially the Fourth Amendment's prohibition against unreasonable searches and seizures and the Fifth Amendment's guarantee against self-incrimination. In the 1960s, the Warren Court extended the Exclusionary Rule to state prosecutions and added the Miranda warnings to police procedures to ensure lawful police conduct and proper prosecutorial procedures. Future Courts, responding to citizen concerns about crime, changed the focus of criminal justice rulings from protecting the innocent to convicting the guilty by undermining both the Exclusionary Rule and the Miranda warnings.[86]

WHAT WE HAVE LEARNED

1. **What is the constitutional basis for civil liberties in America, including both the U.S. Constitution and state constitutions?**

   Both the U.S. Constitution and state constitutions affect civil liberties policymaking. The Bill of Rights and the Fourteenth Amendment are the most important constitutional provisions affecting civil liberties policymaking. The Due Process Clause of the Fourteenth Amendment is the basis for the selective incorporation of the Bill of Rights to the states. The rights guaranteed by the Bill of Rights are not absolute. The government can restrict individual rights and liberties when it has sufficient reason. A fundamental right, such as freedom of expression or freedom of religion, is a constitutional right that is so important that government cannot restrict it unless it can demonstrate a compelling or overriding public interest for so doing. To restrict rights that are not fundamental, government need only show that it is acting in pursuit of a legitimate public purpose. State governments must grant their residents all the rights guaranteed by the U.S. Constitution (as interpreted by the Supreme Court). If state governments so choose, they may offer their residents *more* rights than afforded in the U.S. Constitution

2. **What is the legal/constitutional relationship between government and religion?**

   The First Amendment prohibits government from making laws "respecting an establishment of religion." The sorts of issues that arise under this constitutional provision include state aid to religious schools, parental choice and school vouchers, school prayer, and public displays of religious symbols. With the exception of government-sponsored school prayer, which the Supreme Court has always ruled unconstitutional, the Court has adopted a middle ground on the issue of establishment of religion, attempting to balance the concerns of groups favoring a strict separation of church and state and the values of groups calling for accommodation between government and religion.

   The First Amendment prohibits the adoption of laws interfering with the free exercise of religion. It is unconstitutional for the government to deliberately restrict the activities of religious groups unless the government can justify its action on the basis of a compelling government interest. In contrast, the Supreme Court has held that states can enact laws that have an incidental impact on religious freedom so long as they serve a valid state purpose and are not aimed at inhibiting any particular religion.

3. **What is the current status of constitutional law concerning freedom of expression, including statements of anti-government views, symbolic expression, expression that might lead to a disruption of the public order, expression versus action, hate crimes, and commercial speech?**

   The First Amendment protects freedom of expression. The Supreme Court has held that the government can restrict political expression only if it has a compelling interest that cannot be achieved by less restrictive means. Although the courts have ruled that federal laws that make it a crime to threaten the president or vice president are constitutional, most governmental efforts to restrict criticism of the government are unconstitutional. The government cannot forbid shocking language that is not legally obscene and that is not directed at an individual listener (or reader) in such a way as to provoke violence. Otherwise, government risks the unconstitutional suppression of ideas. The Court has ruled that symbolic expression, such as flying a flag or burning it, should be treated the same as other types of expression. The Supreme Court distinguishes between expression and action. Protestors do not have a constitutional right to disrupt traffic, block sidewalks, or impede access to public places. Moreover, the Court has upheld the constitutionality of hate crimes laws, holding that violent behavior motivated by bias is not constitutionally protected. Advertising and other forms of commercial speech are constitutionally protected forms of expression, but they do not enjoy the same level of constitutional protection as political expression.

4. **How does the constitutional guarantee of freedom of the press affect the issues of obscenity, defamation, and prior restraint?**

   Freedom of the press is a fundamental right, which means that government cannot restrict it unless it can demonstrate a compelling or overriding public interest for so doing. The U.S. Supreme Court has ruled that the government has a compelling interest in prohibiting obscenity and protecting individuals from defamation of character. Successful obscenity prosecutions are rare because the definition of obscenity is narrowly drawn. Defamation involves false written or spoken statements that lower a person's reputation or expose a person to hatred, contempt, or ridicule. Ordinary citizens are more likely to win defamation suits than are public figures. Prior restraint is government action to prevent the publication or broadcast of objectionable material. The Supreme Court has held that prior restraint is such an extreme limitation on freedom of the press that it can be used only in exceptional circumstances, such as time of war.

5. **Do individuals enjoy a constitutional right to own a gun?**

   Historically, the courts have interpreted the Second Amendment to guarantee the right of states to maintain an armed militia rather than protecting an individual right to own a firearm. In 2008, however, the U.S. Supreme Court declared that the Second Amendment protects an individual's right to possess a firearm in the home for purposes of self-defense.

6. **What is the basis for a constitutional right to privacy and to what sorts of controversies has the right to privacy been applied?**

   Although the Constitution does not specifically mention privacy, the Supreme Court has interpreted the Due Process Clause of the Fourteenth Amendment to include a right of privacy. After striking down a Connecticut law that prohibited the use of contraceptives, the Supreme Court based *Roe v. Wade*, the famous abortion decision, on a right to privacy. The Supreme Court also based its decision to overturn the Texas sodomy law on a constitutional right of privacy.

7. **What is the current status of constitutional law concerning the rights of people accused of crimes involving searches and seizures, the exclusionary rule, the Miranda warning, double jeopardy, fair trial, and cruel and unusual punishments?**

   Due process of law is the key constitutional provision protecting the rights of persons investigated for or accused of crimes. The Fourth Amendment protects against unreasonable searches and seizures. In general, police need a warrant, obtained on the basis of probable cause, to conduct a search of a person or property. The exclusionary rule is the judicial doctrine stating that when the police violate an individual's constitutional rights, the evidence obtained as a result of police misconduct or error cannot be used against the defendant in a criminal prosecution. In recent decades, the Supreme Court has weakened the exclusionary rule without repealing it by carving out major exceptions to its application. The Miranda warning is the requirement that police inform suspects of their rights before questioning them. As with the exclusionary rule, the Supreme Court in recent decades has weakened *Miranda* without overturning it. The Constitution prohibits double jeopardy, which is the government trying a criminal defendant a second time for the same offense after an acquittal in an earlier prosecution. The Constitution guarantees a fair trial, including trial by an impartial jury and the right to counsel. If defendants cannot afford to hire an attorney, the government will provide one for them. The death penalty is the most controversial issue arising under the prohibition against cruel and unusual punishments. A growing debate over the fairness and efficacy of capital punishment has been accompanied by a decline in the implementation of the death penalty.

8. **What civil liberties issues are raised by the conduct of the war on terror?**

   Executive authority grows during wartime, sometimes at the expense of civil liberties. In the midst of war, presidents exercise extraordinary powers and declare that their actions are necessary to defend the nation and win the war. Once the war has ended, civil libertarians are typically able to reverse actions taken during wartime. After 9/11, President George W. Bush took actions that some critics charged threatened civil liberties protections. Subsequently, the U.S. Supreme Court and the Obama administration overturned or modified many of the Bush administration's actions.

9. **How is civil liberties policy made?**

   Constitutional law is the most important contextual factor affecting civil liberties policymaking. Consequently, judges—especially the men and women who serve on the Supreme Court of the United States—are the most important civil liberties policymakers. Interest groups, public opinion, and the policy preferences of presidents and senators affect civil liberties policymaking as well. Interest groups, such as the ACLU, and individuals set the agenda for civil liberties policymaking. Many civil liberties policies are formulated and adopted in the executive and legislative branches of government, both at the national level and in the states. The courts become involved in civil liberties policymaking when a civil liberties policy adopted by another unit of government is challenged on constitutional grounds. The debate over civil liberties policies frequently extends beyond policy adoption to the policy legitimation stage. A broad range of government entities participates in the implementation of civil liberties policy. Scholars have completed a number of studies evaluating certain aspects of civil liberties policy. Civil liberties policy changes because of changes in public opinion and the makeup of the Supreme Court.

KEY TERMS

amicus curiae or friend of the court brief
Bill of Rights
capital punishment
civil liberties
double jeopardy
due process of law
exclusionary rule
fundamental right
hate crimes law
libel
Miranda warning
parental choice
prior restraint
probable cause
selective incorporation of the Bill of Rights against the states
slander
test case
warrant

NOTES

1. Adam Liptak, "Justices Consider the Role of Age in Life Sentences," *New York Times*, November 10, 2009, available at www.nytimes.com.
2. "A Shameful Record," February 6, 2010, *New York Times*, available at www.nytimes.com.
3. Friend of the Court brief filed by the American Psychological Association, *Sullivan v. Florida*, No. 08-7621 (2010) and *Graham v. Florida*, No. 08-7412 (2010).
4. Friend of the Court brief filed by the Heritage Foundation, *amicus* brief, *Sullivan v. Florida*, No. 08-7621 (2010) and *Graham v. Florida*, No. 08-7412 (2010).
5. *Pruneyard Shopping Center v. Robins*, 447 U.S. 74 (1980).
6. Jeffrey M. Shaman, *Equality and Liberty in the Golden Age of State Constitutional Law* (New York, NY: Oxford University Press, 2008), p. xviii.
7. John Witte, Jr., and Joel A. Nichols, *Religion and the American Constitutional Experiment*, 3rd ed. (Boulder, CO: Westview Press, 2011), p. 237.
8. Patrick M. Garry, *Wrestling with God: The Court's Tortuous Treatment of Religion* (Washington, DC: Catholic University of America Press, 2006), pp. 70–72.
9. *Everson v. Board of Ewing Township*, 330 U.S. 1 (1947).
10. *Zelman v. Simmons-Harris*, 536 U.S. 639 (2002).
11. *Engel v. Vitale*, 370 U.S. 421 (1962).
12. *Santa Fe School District v. Doe*, 530 U.S. 290 (2000).
13. *Van Orden v. Perry*, 545 U.S. 667 (2005).
14. *McCreary County v. American Civil Liberties Union*, 545 U.S. 844 (2005).
15. *Watchtower Bible & Tract Society v. Village of Stratton, NY* (536 U.S. 150) (2002).
16. *Employment Division, Oregon Department of Human Resources v. Smith*, 493 U.S. 378 (1990).
17. Suzanna Sherry, "The First Amendment and the Right to Differ," in Bodenhammer and Ely, eds., *The Bill of Rights in Modern America*, pp. 49–66.
18. *United States v. Barbour*, 70.F3d 580 (1995).
19. *Brandenburg v. Ohio*, 395 U.S. 444 (1969).
20. *Cohen v. California*, 403 U.S. 15 (1971).
21. *Texas v. Johnson*, 491 U.S. 397 (1989).
22. *United States v. Eichman*, 396 U.S. 310 (1990).
23. *Madsen v. Women's Health Center*, 512 U.S. 753 (1994).
24. *Schenck v. Pro Choice Network*, 519 U.S. 357 (1997).
25. "Hate Is Not Speech: A Constitutional Defense of Penalty Enhancement for Hate Crimes," *Harvard Law Review* 106 (April 1993): 1314–1331.
26. *Wisconsin v. Mitchell*, 508 U.S. 47 (1993).
27. *Central Hudson Gas & Electric Corp. v. Public Service Commission of New York*, 447 U.S. 557 (1980).
28. Richard H. Fallon, Jr., *The Dynamic Constitution: An Introduction to American Constitutional Law* (New York: Cambridge University Press, 2004), p. 49.
29. *Miller v. California*, 413 U.S. 15 (1973).
30. Richard Johnson, "A Win for Diaz," *New York Post*, February 17, 2007, available at www.nypost.com.
31. *New York Times v. Sullivan*, 376 U.S. 254 (1964).
32. *Near v. Minnesota*, 283 U.S. 697 (1931).
33. *New York Times v. United States*, 403 U.S. 713 (1971).
34. *District of Columbia v. Heller*, 554 U.S. 290 (2008).
35. *McDonald v. Chicago*, 08-1521 (2010).
36. *Griswold v. Connecticut*, 381 U.S. 479 (1965).
37. *Roe v. Wade*, 410 U.S. 113 (1973).
38. *Webster v. Reproductive Health Services*, 492 U.S. 490 (1989).
39. Ken T. Kersch, "The Right to Privacy," in Bodenhammer and Ely, eds., *The Bill of Rights in Modern America*, pp. 215–240.
40. *Planned Parenthood of Southeastern Pennsylvania v. Casey*, 505 U.S. 833 (1992).
41. *Lawrence v. Texas*, 539 U.S. 558 (2003).
42. *Illinois v. Wardlow*, 528 U.S. 119 (2000).

43. *United States v. Ross*, 456 U.S. 798 (1982).
44. *Weeks v. United States*, 232 U.S. 383 (1914).
45. *Mapp v. Ohio*, 367 U.S. 643 (1961).
46. Adam Liptak, "U.S. Alone in Rejecting All Evidence if Police Err," *New York Times*, July 19, 2008, available at www.nytimes.com.
47. *Massachusetts v. Shepherd*, 468 U.S. 981 (1984) and *United States v. Leon*, 468 U.S. 897 (1984).
48. *Arizona v. Fulminante*, 499 U.S. 270 (1991).
49. *Herring v. United States*, 07-513 (2008).
50. *Miranda v. Arizona*, 384 U.S. 436 (1966).
51. Gary L. Stuart, *Miranda: The Story of America's Right to Remain Silent* (Tucson, AR: University of Arizona Press, 2004), p. 100.
52. *Harris v. New York*, 401 U.S. 222 (1971).
53. *New York v. Quarles*, 467 U.S. 649 (1984).
54. *Moran v. Burdine*, 475 U.S. 412 (1986).
55. *Cucci v. Illinois*, 356 U.S. 571 (1958).
56. *United States v. Lanza*, 260 U.S. 377 (1922).
57. *Heath v. Alabama*, 474 U.S. 82 (1985).
58. *Kansas v. Hendricks*, 521 U.S. 346 (1997).
59. Quoted in *Time*, July 7, 1997, p. 29.
60. *Globe Newspaper Co. v. Superior Court*, 457 U.S. 596 (1982).
61. *Chancler v. Florida*, 449 U.S. 560 (1981).
62. *Williams v. Florida*, 399 U.S. 78 (1970).
63. *Snyder v. Louisiana*, No. 06-10119 (2008).
64. *Gideon v. Wainwright*, 372 U.S. 335 (1963).
65. *Tollett v. Henderson*, 411 U.S. 258 (1973).
66. *Solem v. Helm*, 463 U.S. 277 (1983).
67. *Kennedy v. Louisiana*, 554 U.S. (2008).
68. *Graham v. Florida*, No. 08-7412 (2010).
69. *Furman v. Georgia*, 408 U.S. 238 (1972).
70. *Gregg v. Georgia*, 428 U.S. 153 (1976).
71. Bureau of Justice Statistics, "Capital Punishment Statistics," available at www.ojp.usdoj.gov.
72. James S. Leibman, *A Broken System: Error Rates in Capital Cases, 1973–1995*, available at www.thejusticeproject.org.
73. Ibid.
74. Bureau of Justice Statistics, "Capital Punishment 2007—Statistical Tables," available at www.ojp.usdoj.gov.
75. "Supreme Court Bars Executing Mentally Retarded," June 20, 2002, available at www.cnn.com.
76. *Atkins v. Virginia*, 536 U.S. 304 (2002).
77. Otis H. Stephens, Jr., "Presidential Power, Judicial Deference, and the Status of Detainees in an Age of Terrorism," in David B. Cohen and John W. Wells, eds., *American National Security and Civil Liberties in an Era of Terrorism* (New York: Palgrave MacMillan, 2004), p. 82.
78. *Korematsu v. United States*, 323 U.S. 214 (1944).
79. Richard M. Pious, "Military Tribunals, Prerogative Power, and the War on Terrorism," in Joseph M. Bessette and Jeffrey K. Tulis, eds., *The Constitutional Presidency* (Baltimore, MD: Johns Hopkins University Press, 2009), pp. 123–148.
80. *Hamdi v. Rumsfeld*, 542 U.S. 507 (2004).
81. *Hamdan v. Rumsfeld*, 548 U.S. 557 (2006).
82. *Boumediene v. Bush*, 553 U.S. 723 (2008).
83. Ranata Lawson Mack and Michael J. Kelly, *Equal Justice in the Balance: America's Legal Responses to the Emerging Terrorist Threat* (Ann Arbor, MI: University of Michigan Press, 2004), p. 238.
84. Otis H. Stephens, Jr., *The Supreme Court and Confessions of Guilt* (Knoxville, TN: University of Tennessee Press, 1973).
85. Donald L. Horowitz, *The Courts and Social Policy* (Washington, DC: Brookings Institution, 1977), p. 223.
86. David J. Bodenhammer, "Reversing the Revolution: Rights of the Accused in a Conservative Age," in Bodenhammer and Ely, eds., *The Bill of Rights in Modern America*, p. 147.

Chapter 16

Civil Rights

CHAPTER OUTLINE

WHAT WE WILL LEARN

After studying Chapter 16, students should be able to answer the following questions:

1. What is the constitutional basis for civil rights in America, including both the U.S. Constitution and state constitutions?
2. How does the Equal Protection Clause affect African American civil rights, immigrant rights, women's rights, and gay and lesbian rights?
3. What is the history of voting rights in America, both for women and African Americans?
4. What steps has government taken to protect women and minorities from discrimination?
5. To what extent are colleges, universities, and employers legally able to use affirmative action to increase enrollment and employment of women and minorities?
6. How is civil rights policy made?

The battle over gay marriage has been fought state by state. Massachusetts became the first state to legalize same-sex marriage in 2004 when the Massachusetts Supreme Judicial Court (SJC) ruled that the state could not discriminate against same-sex couples when it issued marriage licenses. The SJC, which is the state's highest court, based its decision on the Massachusetts state constitution rather than the U.S. Constitution.[1] Gay marriage opponents proposed an amendment to the U.S. Constitution that would declare that marriage is limited to the union of a man and a woman. The Marriage Amendment, as its supporters labeled it, would have overturned any action taken at the state level, including the decision of the SJC, but it failed to win the necessary two-thirds vote in the U.S. House and Senate.

The defeat of the Marriage Amendment left the issue of same-sex marriage for each individual state to decide. Whereas 30 states have adopted state constitutional amendments limiting marriage to opposite-sex couples, five states have legalized gay marriage—Vermont, Connecticut, New Hampshire, Iowa, and Massachusetts. In Iowa and Vermont, same-sex marriage was the result of judicial rulings based on state constitutions similar to the decision of the SJC in Massachusetts. State legislatures also adopted laws legalizing same-sex marriage in New Hampshire and Connecticut.[2]

Referendum An election in which state voters can approve or reject a state law or constitutional amendment.

Two states, California and Maine, approved gay marriage and then repealed it by **referendum,** which is an election in which state voters can approve or reject a state law or constitutional amendment. After the California Supreme Court ruled in favor of gay marriage, opponents gathered signatures to put the issue to a vote. In 2008, California voters repealed same-sex marriage in the state by approving a ballot measure known as Proposition 8 by 52 percent to 48 percent. Proposition 8 amended the California Constitution to include the following words: "Only marriage between a man and a woman is valid or recognized in California." Similarly, Maine voters overturned a gay marriage statute adopted by the Maine legislature by a 53 percent to 47 percent margin.

In 2010, gay rights forces launched a legal battle aimed at establishing a national constitutional right to marry for gay couples. The lawsuit, which was filed on behalf of two same-sex couples in California, challenged the constitutionality of Proposition 8 under the U.S. Constitution. Court cases take years to work their way through the court system, but if the U.S. Supreme Court eventually agrees that state bans on same-sex marriage violate the U.S. Constitution, gay men and lesbians in every state will have the right to marry. Furthermore, the U.S. government will be required to recognize the validity of those marriages for Social Security survivor benefits, income tax filing status, and other legal matters.[3]

Civil rights The protection of the individual from arbitrary or discriminatory acts by government or by other individuals based on an individual's group status, such as race or gender.

The legal and constitutional battle over same-sex marriage introduces this chapter on **civil rights,** which is the protection of the individual from arbitrary or discriminatory acts by government or by other individuals based on an individual's group status, such as race or gender. Whereas civil liberties issues involve individual rights, civil rights issues concern group rights. Civil liberties policy issues revolve around the rights of individuals to be free from unwarranted government restrictions on expression, religious belief, and personal liberty. In contrast, civil rights policy issues concern the government's relationship to individuals based on their status as members of a group. The chapter examines the constitutional basis of civil rights and then considers a number of important civil rights issues, including equal rights, voting rights, freedom from discrimination, and affirmative action.

WHAT IS YOUR OPINION?

Do you support same-sex marriage? Why or why not?

The Constitution and Civil Rights

Equal Protection Clause A provision found in the Fourteenth Amendment of the U.S. Constitution that declares that "No State shall . . . deny to any person within its jurisdiction the equal protection of the laws."

Both the U.S. Constitution and state constitutions affect civil rights policymaking. The most important provisions in the U.S. Constitution dealing with civil rights are the Fourteenth and Fifteenth Amendments. The Fourteenth Amendment includes the **Equal Protection Clause:** "No State shall . . . deny to any person within its jurisdiction the equal protection of the laws." The Fifteenth Amendment declares that the right to vote "shall not be denied or abridged by the United States or by any State on account of race, color, or previous condition of servitude." Both

The current legal/constitutional status of gay marriage is that each state is free to define marriage as it wishes, either to limit marriage to opposite-sex couples or to extend marriage rights to same-sex couples.

the Fourteenth and Fifteenth Amendments contain sections granting Congress authority to pass legislation to enforce their provisions.

Most state constitutions include provisions prohibiting discrimination and/or guaranteeing equal protection of the laws. In recent years, a number of state supreme courts have interpreted their state constitutions to require equitable funding for public schools, guarantee equal rights for women, and offer marriage rights to same-sex couples. In each of these cases, state courts adopted policy positions embracing a more expansive interpretation of civil rights than were taken at the time either in the U.S. Constitution or federal law.[4]

Equal Rights

Although the Fourteenth Amendment guarantees individuals equal protection under the law, the U.S. Supreme Court has never required that laws deal with everyone and everything in precisely the same fashion. By their nature, laws distinguish among groups of people, types of property, and kinds of actions. The Court has recognized that most distinctions are necessary and desirable, and hence permissible under the Constitution. Only certain types of classifications that the Court considers arbitrary and discriminatory violate the Equal Protection Clause.

Suspect classifications Policy distinctions among persons based on their race, ethnicity, and citizenship status.

Strict judicial scrutiny The judicial decision rule holding that the Supreme Court will find a government policy unconstitutional unless the government can demonstrate a compelling interest justifying the action.

The Supreme Court has ruled that policy distinctions among persons based on their race, ethnicity, and citizenship status are **suspect classifications,** which are distinctions among persons that must be justified on the basis of a compelling government interest. The Supreme Court has declared that it will apply "strict judicial scrutiny" to any law that distinguishes among persons based on their race and ethnicity or citizenship. **Strict judicial scrutiny** is the judicial decision rule holding that the Supreme Court will find a government policy unconstitutional unless the government can demonstrate a compelling interest justifying the action. In other words, government cannot constitutionally adopt policies that treat people differently on the basis of race, ethnicity, or citizenship status unless it can demonstrate an overriding public interest in making that distinction. Furthermore, the government must prove that a policy that distinguishes among persons based on their race, ethnicity, or citizenship status is the least restrictive means for achieving the compelling policy objective.

The Supreme Court has chosen not to look so closely at laws that discriminate against persons on grounds other than race and ethnicity or citizenship status. It has held that government need only demonstrate some "reasonable basis" in order to justify public policies that distinguish among persons on the basis of such factors as relative wealth, physical ability, marital status, residency, or sexual orientation. As for gender, the Court has ruled that the government must offer an "exceedingly persuasive justification" that gender-based distinctions are necessary to achieve some "important governmental objective." Commentators see this standard as somewhere between "compelling government interest" and "reasonable basis."[5]

Racial Equality

Although the Equal Protection Clause of the Fourteenth Amendment was intended to protect the civil rights of freed slaves, it initially did little to shelter African Americans from discrimination. In the late nineteenth and early twentieth centuries, southern state legislatures enacted **Jim Crow laws,** which were legal provisions requiring the social segregation of African Americans in separate and generally unequal facilities. Jim Crow laws prohibited blacks from sharing schools, hospitals, hotels, restaurants, passenger railcars, and a wide range of other services and public facilities with whites.

Jim Crow laws Legal provisions requiring the social segregation of African Americans in separate and generally unequal facilities.

Did Jim Crow laws violate the Equal Protection Clause? The U.S. Supreme Court addressed the question in 1896 in the famous case of *Plessy v. Ferguson*. Homer Plessy purchased a first-class ticket on the East Louisiana Railway to travel from New Orleans to Covington, Louisiana. Plessy, who is described in court papers as a man "of mixed descent, in the proportion of seven-eighths Caucasian and one-eighth African blood," took a seat in the railcar reserved for whites. He was arrested and charged with violating a state law that prohibited most members of either race from occupying accommodations set aside for the other. Plessy initially insisted that he was white. When that argument failed, he contended that the Louisiana law violated his rights under the U.S. Constitution to equal protection. By an 8–1 vote, the U.S. Supreme Court ruled that the law was a reasonable exercise of the state's power, holding that states can constitutionally require separate facilities for whites and African Americans as long as the facilities are equal. Thus, the Court adopted the policy known as **separate-but-equal,** which is the judicial doctrine holding that separate facilities for whites and African Americans satisfy the equal protection requirement of the Fourteenth Amendment. Justice John Marshall Harlan, the Court's lone dissenter in *Plessy*, called the decision "a compound of bad logic, bad history, bad sociology, and bad constitutional law. . . . Our Constitution is color-blind," he said, "and neither knows nor tolerates classes among citizens."[6]

Separate-but-equal The judicial doctrine holding that separate facilities for whites and African Americans satisfy the equal protection requirement of the Fourteenth Amendment.

The Supreme Court allowed state and local governments to determine whether racially segregated facilities were actually equal. In 1899, for example, the Court held that a Georgia school district's decision to close the only African American high school in the county did not violate the Equal Protection Clause even though two white high schools remained open.[7] In another case, the Court permitted a Mississippi school district to force a youngster of Chinese descent to attend an African American school in a neighboring district rather than a nearby whites-only school. As far as the Supreme Court was concerned, state and local officials could determine school assignments without interference from federal courts.[8]

The Supreme Court began to reassess the constitutional status of racial segregation in the late 1930s. The Court started chipping away at the *Plessy* decision in 1938 in *Missouri ex rel Gaines v. Canada*, the beginning of a long line of test cases brought by the National Association for the Advancement of Colored People (NAACP). A **test case** is a lawsuit initiated to assess the constitutionality of a legislative or executive act. Gaines, who was an African American citizen of Missouri, applied to attend the University of Missouri Law School. The state denied him admission, but

Test case A lawsuit initiated to assess the constitutionality of a legislative or executive act.

offered to pay his tuition at a law school in a neighboring state where he could be accepted. Gaines sued, charging that the arrangement violated the Equal Protection Clause, and the Court agreed. Separate-but-equal had to be in the same state.[9]

The Supreme Court further undermined *Plessy* in two cases decided in 1950. In *Sweatt v. Painter*, it ruled that Texas's hasty creation of an African American law school did not satisfy the constitutional criterion of equal protection.[10] In *McLaurin v. Oklahoma State Regents*, the Court ruled against segregation within an institution. The University of Oklahoma admitted G. W. McLaurin, an African American man, to graduate school but forced him to sit in a particular seat, study in a particular carrel in the library, and eat at a particular table in the cafeteria. All of these facilities were labeled, "Reserved for Colored." The Supreme Court ordered that McLaurin be treated like other students.[11]

In 1954, the Court took the final step, unanimously overturning *Plessy* with the landmark decision known as *Brown v. Board of Education of Topeka*. The case involved a lawsuit brought by a group of African American families in Topeka, Kansas, whose youngsters had been denied admission to the "whites-only" public schools nearest their homes. The Court ruled that racial segregation mandated by law denied African American students an equal educational opportunity. "Segregation of white and colored children in public schools has a detrimental effect upon the colored children," wrote Chief Justice Earl Warren in the Court's majority opinion. "A sense of inferiority affects the motivation of the child to learn." In essence, the Court declared that separate-but-equal was a contradiction in terms. Once the law requires racial separation, it stamps the badge of inferiority on the minority race.[12] In the following year, the Supreme Court ordered the lower federal courts to oversee the transition to a nondiscriminatory system "with all deliberate speed."[13]

Implementation proved more deliberate than speedy. Although states in the Upper South made some progress toward desegregation, public officials in the Deep South responded to the *Brown* decision with delay, evasion, defiance, and massive resistance. Alabama Governor George Wallace spoke for many white Southerners: "I say segregation now, segregation tomorrow, segregation forever."[14]

For years, *Brown* was a hollow victory for civil rights forces. Congress did nothing, and President Dwight Eisenhower stood silent. The president finally took action in 1957, ordering federal troops into Little Rock, Arkansas, to enforce a school desegregation order against a stubborn governor and an angry mob. Nonetheless, a decade after the *Brown* decision, only 1 percent of African American students living in the South attended public schools that were not racially segregated.[15]

The civil rights movement of the 1960s succeeded in rallying support for the cause of African American civil rights. African American protest demonstrations, vividly displayed on the television evening news, moved public opinion to support the cause. Presidents John Kennedy and Lyndon Johnson called for action, and Congress responded with the Civil Rights Act of 1964, which authorized the Department of Health, Education, and Welfare (which has since been divided to form the Department of Health and Human Services and the Department of Education) to cut off federal money to school districts practicing segregation. The department set guidelines and some progress took place. Finally, the Supreme Court lost patience

School desegregation in Little Rock, Arkansas, in 1957.

with the slow pace of school desegregation, declaring an end to "all deliberate speed" and ordering immediate desegregation.[16] By the 1972–1973 school year, 91 percent of African American students living in the South attended integrated schools.[17]

Brown v. Board of Education prohibited racial discrimination in assigning children to public schools. State laws requiring segregated schools were clearly unconstitutional.[18] What was less clear after *Brown* was whether the Equal Protection Clause required the side-by-side instruction of students of different races in the same schools and classrooms. Many schools remained racially segregated after the *Brown* decision because of racially segregated housing patterns or because some white parents decided to withdraw their children from racially mixed public schools. Was the end of laws requiring racially segregated schools constitutionally sufficient or did the Equal Protection Clause require local officials to ensure that minority students and white youngsters attended the same schools?[19]

During the 1970s, the Supreme Court ordered school districts to take race into account in assigning students to schools in order to increase racial integration. In *Swann v. Charlotte-Mecklenburg Board of Education* (1971), the Court held that busing, racial quotas, school pairing or grouping, and gerrymandered attendance zones could all be used to eliminate the remnants of state-supported segregation.[20] Two years later, the Court ordered the integration of Denver schools, not because they were segregated by force of law, but because the local school board had manipulated attendance zones to create one-race schools.[21] Court-ordered efforts to increase racial integration in schools proved controversial, even with some African American parents who resented busing plans that forced their children to take long bus rides to schools outside their neighborhoods.

Since the 1980s, the Supreme Court has abandoned efforts to compel the racial integration of public schools in favor of a stance that requires local officials to ignore race in making school assignment decisions. In *Missouri v. Jenkins* (1995), the Supreme Court reversed a district court order forcing the state of Missouri to pay for a plan to upgrade predominantly African American schools in Kansas City, Missouri. The goal of the district court had been to improve the inner-city schools in hopes of enticing white parents who live in the suburbs to voluntarily send their children to the inner city. The Supreme Court held that local desegregation plans could not go beyond the purpose of eliminating racial discrimination. Once the lingering effects of legally enforced segregation were eradicated, it would be legal for the district to operate schools that happened to be all black or all white.[22] Finally, in *Parents Involved in Community Schools v. Seattle School District No. 1* (2007), a closely divided Supreme Court struck down a Seattle school assignment procedure that used race as a "tiebreaker" in making student assignments to high schools, even though the goal of the plan was to achieve racial integration rather than segregation.[23] Instead of using the *Brown* precedent to further efforts to achieve racial integration of public schools, the Court declared that *Brown* required school districts to follow color-blind school assignment policies.

WHAT IS YOUR OPINION?

How important is it for your children to attend schools that are racially diverse?

Today, racial segregation no longer has a legal basis. Few issues of constitutional law are more firmly established than the principle that any law or procedural requirement compelling the physical separation of people by race or ethnicity is unconstitutional. The old Jim Crow laws are gone, either repealed or rendered unenforceable by court rulings. Nonetheless, the end of legal segregation has not necessarily brought about meaningful racial integration in the public schools. Today, African American and Latino students have less contact with white students than their counterparts had in 1970. A third of African American and Latino children sit in classrooms that are 90 to 100 percent black and Latino.[24] Racial segregation in the schools is growing because of a major increase in enrollment by minority students, continued migration of white families from urban neighborhoods, housing patterns that isolate racial and ethnic groups, and the end of court-ordered racial integration.[25]

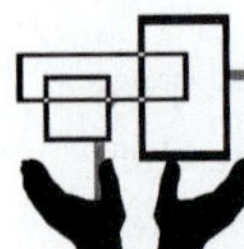

GETTING INVOLVED

Voices from the Past

The African American civil rights movement was one of the most important political developments of the twentieth century. Laws that once prevented African Americans from voting and attending public schools with white children were repealed or struck down by the courts. Today, more African Americans hold elective office and have joined the ranks of the middle class than ever before. Nonetheless, racism and its vestiges have not been eliminated. African Americans are disproportionately impacted by unemployment and poverty. They are underrepresented in corporate boardrooms and college campuses but overrepresented in prison.

Your class project is to interview older African American adults in your community to ascertain their perspective on the impact of the civil rights movement on their lives and on the United States. Identify African Americans 50 years of age and older who are friends, relatives, acquaintances, or coworkers who will agree to participate in short interviews with members of the class. Plan and conduct interviews that cover the following topics:

- What was it like for African Americans where you lived when you were growing up? What was good and what was bad? What events do you remember?
- What are the most important changes that have taken place? Which changes are most important? Have all the changes been positive?
- What still needs to be done? What do you see as the biggest remaining barrier to full equality for African Americans?
- How do you feel about Barack Obama's election?
- Are you optimistic or pessimistic about the future? Why?

After the interviews are complete, the instructor will lead the class in discussing what students have learned. Students will want to compare and contrast the recollections of different interview subjects who may have different perspectives, depending on their personal life experiences and points of view. The instructor will also ask students to relate the content of their interviews with the information contained in the textbook. Did some of the interview subjects mention historical events discussed in the textbook, such as the Supreme Court's decision in *Brown v. Board of Education*? To what extent do their current concerns about the status of African American civil rights mirror the controversies discussed in the text?

Other Equal Protection Issues

Not all equal protection claims involve African Americans or school desegregation. The Supreme Court has declared that citizenship status is a suspect classification similar to race, justifiable only by a compelling government interest. For example, the Court has struck down state laws that prohibited noncitizen permanent residents from becoming lawyers, engineers, or notary publics, and declared that states may not deny legal residents who are not citizens the opportunity to apply for financial aid for higher education.[26] In each case, the Court ruled that the government had failed to establish that it had a compelling interest in making the distinction. In contrast, the Court has held that states do indeed have a compelling interest in excluding noncitizens from playing a role in government, either by voting, running for office, or working as police officers.

After the terrorist attacks of September 11, 2001, Congress passed, and President George W. Bush signed, the Aviation and Transportation Security Act, which included a provision restricting employment as airport screeners to U.S. citizens.

Thousands of noncitizen legal residents who had been employed as airport screeners lost their jobs because of the measure and several of them filed suit, attacking the constitutionality of the new law. A federal district judge ruled that the provision excluding noncitizens from employment as security screeners was unconstitutional. The judge concluded that the government had a compelling interest in protecting aviation security, but held that the exclusion of noncitizens from screening jobs was not the least restrictive means for achieving that goal.[27]

Over the years, the Supreme Court has considered a number of equal protection issues raised on the basis of gender. For nearly a century after the adoption of the Fourteenth Amendment, the Court refused to apply the Equal Protection Clause to gender discrimination. Instead, the Court accepted discrimination against women as a necessary protection for the weaker sex. In 1873, for example, the Supreme Court upheld an Illinois law denying women the opportunity to practice law with the following explanation: "The natural and proper timidity and delicacy which belong to the female sex evidently unfit it for many of the occupations of civil life."[28]

Within the last 30 years, the Supreme Court has begun to look closely at claims of gender discrimination. Although the Court has not added gender to its list of suspect classifications, it has required that state governments prove that sex-based distinctions are necessary to achieve some important governmental objective. The Court has also declared that the government must offer an "exceedingly persuasive justification" for gender-based distinctions if they are to be held constitutional.[29] The Court ruled, for example, that Virginia Military Institute (VMI), a state-supported

States must demonstrate that laws that distinguish among individuals based on their gender have been enacted to fulfill an important government function, that they are a least restrictive method of achieving the function, and that they are not based on stereotypical notions about men and women.

Around the World

Women's Rights in Saudi Arabia

Women in Saudi Arabia have limited legal rights. Under Saudi law, which is based on a conservative interpretation of Islam, women are socially and legally dependent on their male guardians—their fathers at birth and their spouses upon marriage. Women cannot even have their own legal identity cards. Their names are added to their father's identity card when they are born and transferred to their husband's identity card when they marry. As a result, a woman cannot travel, purchase property, or enroll in college without the written permission of a male relative.*

The traditional role of women in Saudi Arabia is to be stay-at-home mothers. Women must cover themselves fully in public and wear the veil. They cannot attend classes or work with men. Women's education is aimed at making women better wives and mothers. Women cannot study law or become pilots. Instead, they are directed toward occupations deemed suitable for their gender, such as medicine, banking, and teaching in a girls' school. Women are not allowed to vote or drive a vehicle. Women who fail to conform to societal norms are subject to harassment by the religious police. They may be arrested, imprisoned, and even caned. Companies who hire women to work in nontraditional areas face social pressure. In 2010, for example, a major Saudi retailer reversed its decision to hire female cashiers after a conservative religious leader called for a boycott of the chain.†

Nonetheless, Saudi Arabia has a women's rights movement. Many Saudi women are aware of the status of women in other countries, including Muslim countries, because of the Internet, satellite TV, and travel abroad, and they are demanding better treatment. Young Saudi women in particular, who are better educated than most of the older women, are challenging their society's conservative interpretation of Islam. They are demanding access to education and employment opportunities.

The Saudi government has made some concessions to women's rights in part because it recognizes that the nation's economic progress depends on having a large skilled workforce and men alone are not numerous enough to meet the need for skilled workers. Women are now permitted to stay in a hotel alone without the presence of a male relative. Even though some leading universities only admit men, women now constitute a majority of university students.‡ The Saudi government is also reportedly considering lifting the ban against women driving.§

QUESTIONS

1. Is the treatment of women in Saudi Arabia a concern for people around the world or should it be an internal matter for the Saudis alone to address?
2. Should the United States pressure Saudi Arabia to improve the status of women?
3. Do you think most women in Saudi Arabia are comfortable with their legal and social status?

*Stephen Schwartz, "Shari'a in Saudi Arabia, Today and Tomorrow," in Paul Marshall, ed., *Radical Islam's Rules: The Worldwide Spread of Extreme Shari'a Law* (Lanham, MD: Rowman & Littlefield, 2005), pp. 33–34.

†"Saudi Retailer Fires Women Cashiers," *Times of India*, August 27, 2010, available at http://timesofindia.indiatimes.com.

‡Andrew Mills, "Saudi Universities Reach Toward Equality for Women," *Chronicle of Higher Education*, August 7, 2009, pp. A1, A21–A22.

§Damien McElroy, "Saudi Arabia to Lift Ban on Women Drivers," *Daily Telegraph*, January 21, 2008, available at www.telegraph.co.uk.

military university, could not constitutionally exclude women and that the state's offer to create a separate military college for women was unacceptable. The Court held that the state of Virginia had failed to show an exceedingly persuasive justification for maintaining a male-only university.[30] Nonetheless, the Court still upholds some gender-based laws, such as Congress's decision to exclude women from having to register for possible military service, on the basis of traditional attitudes about the respective roles of men and women in society.[31]

In 1996, the Supreme Court issued its first equal protection ruling favoring gay and lesbian rights in the case of *Romer v. Evans*. The legal dispute concerned a challenge to an amendment to the constitution of Colorado approved by state voters in 1992. Amendment Two, as it was known, not only repealed all local ordinances and statewide policies protecting gay men and lesbians from discrimination but also prohibited the future enactment of similar measures. The Supreme Court declared that the state of Colorado would have to demonstrate that the amendment bore a rational relationship to some legitimate end in order to meet the requirements of the Equal Protection Clause. The amendment was so broadly drawn, however, that the only logical explanation for its enactment was animosity toward gay men and lesbians. The real purpose of the measure was evidently "to make homosexuals unequal to everyone else," which, the Court said, is not a legitimate goal of state government. Consequently, Amendment Two violated the Equal Protection Clause of the Fourteenth Amendment.[32] The lawsuit challenging the constitutionality of California's Proposition 8 is based on the Equal Protection Clause. The groups bringing the lawsuit hope that the Supreme Court will conclude that the government lacks a reasonable basis for limiting marriage to opposite-sex couples.

Voting Rights and Representation

Suffrage The right to vote.

Disfranchisement The denial of voting rights.

White primary An electoral system used in the South to prevent the participation of African Americans in the Democratic primary.

Primary election An intra-party election held to select party candidates for the general-election ballot.

Although the right to vote is a fundamental civil right, universal adult **suffrage** (the right to vote) is a relatively recent development in the United States. The original Constitution (Article I, Section 2) allowed the states to establish voter qualifications, and initially most states limited the right to vote to adult white males who owned property. Popular pressure forced states to drop the property qualification in the early decades of the nineteenth century. Women won the right to vote with the ratification of the Nineteenth Amendment in 1920.

The struggle for voting rights for African Americans was particularly difficult despite the Fifteenth Amendment, which declared that the right to vote could not be abridged on account of race or color. In the late nineteenth and early twentieth centuries, southern white authorities adopted an array of devices designed to prevent African Americans from exercising meaningful voting rights. **Disfranchisement** is the term used to describe the denial of voting rights. Disfranchisement methods included tests of understanding, literacy tests, the white primary, grandfather clauses, and poll taxes.

The **white primary** was an electoral system used in the South to prevent African Americans from participating in the Democratic primary. (A **primary election** is an intra-party election held to select party candidates for the general-election ballot.) Because Democrats dominated southern politics from the 1870s through the 1950s, the Democratic Party primary was by far the most important election in most southern states. By excluding African Americans from the Democratic primary, southern

Women won the right to vote in 1920 with the ratification of the Nineteenth Amendment.

Test of understanding A legal requirement that citizens must accurately explain a passage in the United States or state constitution before they can register to vote.

Literacy test A legal requirement that citizens must demonstrate the ability to read and write before they can register to vote.

Poll tax A tax levied on the right to vote.

Grandfather clause A provision that exempted those persons whose grandfathers had been eligible to vote at some earlier date from tests of understanding, literacy tests, and other difficult-to-achieve voter qualification requirements.

officials effectively prevented them from participating meaningfully in state politics. The Supreme Court invalidated the white primary in 1944.[33]

Tests of understanding, literacy tests, and poll taxes were often used for disfranchisement in combination with a grandfather clause. A **test of understanding** was a legal requirement that citizens must accurately explain a passage in the United States or state constitution before they could register to vote. A **literacy test** was a legal requirement that citizens demonstrate an ability to read and write before they could register to vote. A **poll tax** was a tax levied on the right to vote. A **grandfather clause** was a provision that exempted those persons whose grandfathers had been eligible to vote at some earlier date from tests of understanding, literacy tests, and other difficult-to-achieve voter qualification requirements. The effect of the grandfather clause was to allow prospective white voters to escape voter requirements used to discourage or disqualify prospective African American voters.

Although the Supreme Court invalidated the grandfather clause in 1915,[34] tests of understanding, literacy tests, and poll taxes survived constitutional challenge for decades. The Court finally knocked down the use of tests of understanding in 1965, holding that they were often used to deny African Americans the right to vote.[35] In the same year, Congress passed, and the president signed, legislation that suspended the use of literacy tests throughout the South. Five years later, Congress extended the ban on literacy tests to the entire nation. The poll tax lasted until 1964 when the Twenty-fourth Amendment eliminated the use of poll taxes for elections to federal office. In 1966, the Supreme Court held that the poll tax was an unconstitutional requirement for voting in state and local elections as well.[36]

Voting Rights Act (VRA) A federal law designed to protect the voting rights of racial and ethnic minorities.

The **Voting Rights Act (VRA)** is a federal law designed to protect the voting rights of racial and ethnic minorities. The VRA makes it illegal for state and local governments to enact and enforce election rules and procedures that diminish African American and Latino voting power. Furthermore, the VRA requires state and local governments in areas with a history of voting discrimination to submit redistricting plans to the federal Department of Justice for approval *before* they can go into effect. This procedure is known as pre-clearance. Congress and the president included the pre-clearance provision in the VRA in order to stay one step ahead of local officials who would adopt new discriminatory electoral procedures as soon as the federal courts threw out an old procedure. The pre-clearance provision of the VRA only applies to states and parts of states that have substantial racial and language minority populations with relatively low rates of voter participation.

Majority-minority districts Legislative districts whose population was more than 50 percent African American and Latino.

The VRA was instrumental in the election of record numbers of African American and Latino candidates during the 1990s. Under pressure from the Justice Department, state legislatures across the nation, but especially in the South, created a number of **majority-minority districts.** These were legislative districts whose population was more than 50 percent African American and Latino. Most of these districts elected minority candidates.

The creation of majority-minority districts is controversial. Many supporters of minority rights believe that African American candidates, especially in the South, do not stand a realistic chance of winning office in majority white districts. In contrast, critics of majority-minority districts believe that creating election districts on the basis of race is wrong, regardless of whether the goal is electing minority or nonminority candidates. Furthermore, the practical impact of majority-minority districts is to limit the influence of minority voters to a relatively small number of districts. In order to draw majority-minority districts, legislatures must group minority voters in a few districts, removing them from surrounding districts.

WHAT IS YOUR OPINION?

Does the election of Barack Obama as president indicate that the Voting Rights Act (VRA) is no longer necessary because people are now open to electing someone of a different race? Why or why not?

The future of majority-minority districts is in doubt because of *Shaw v. Reno* (1993) and *Miller v. Johnson* (1995). These cases involved constitutional challenges to redistricting plans in North Carolina and Georgia. The Court ruled that a state could not create legislative districts based on the race of district residents unless it could demonstrate a compelling government interest. Satisfying the requirements of the VRA would not be a satisfactory reason, the Court said, because Congress and the president adopted the VRA to prohibit discrimination rather than to maximize the number of majority-minority districts. In sum, the Court ruled that districts drawn in order to favor racial and ethnic minorities are no more justifiable than districts created to discriminate against them.[37]

Has the VRA outlived its purpose, especially the pre-clearance provision, which applies to the South but not to most of the rest of the country? Critics charge that the VRA was created for a world that no longer exists, in large part because of the effectiveness of the VRA.[38] In contrast, the NAACP and other civil rights groups argue that the VRA remains vitally important because of the continued existence of racial discrimination, especially in the redistricting process. In 2009, the U.S. Supreme Court sidestepped a challenge to the constitutionality of the pre-clearance provision but hinted broadly that it was skeptical that the law, written more than 35 years ago, could still be justified in light of the changes that have taken place in the South in the last three decades.[39]

Freedom from Discrimination

Civil rights concerns the protection of the individual, not just against government action, but also against discrimination by *private* parties, such as hotels, restaurants, theaters, and business firms. Most individual rights claims against private discrimination are based on **statutory law,** which is law that is written by a legislature, rather than constitutional law.

Statutory law Law that is written by a legislature, rather than constitutional law.

After the Civil War, Congress enacted two important laws designed to protect the civil rights of former slaves. The Civil Rights Act of 1866 declared that citizens "of every race and color" were entitled "to make and enforce contracts, to sue . . . , give evidence, to inherit, purchase, lease, sell, hold, and convey real and personal property."[40] The Civil Rights Act of 1875 declared that "all persons within the jurisdiction of the United States shall be entitled to the full and equal enjoyment of the accommodations . . . of inns, public conveyances on land or water, theaters, and other places of public amusement."[41]

In the *Civil Rights Cases* (1883), however, the U.S. Supreme Court found the Civil Rights Act of 1875 unconstitutional. These cases involved disputes over theaters that would not seat African Americans, hotels and restaurants that would not serve African Americans, and a train that refused to seat an African American woman in the "ladies" car. The Court held that the Fourteenth Amendment protected individuals from discrimination by government but not by private parties.[42] The Court's decision in the *Civil Rights Cases* opened the door for private individuals, businesses, and organizations to discriminate in housing, employment, and a broad range of public accommodations.

It took civil rights forces more than 80 years to overcome the precedent set in the *Civil Rights Cases*. Consider the issue of housing discrimination. Although the Supreme Court ruled in 1917 that cities could not establish exclusive residential zones for whites and blacks,[43] housing developers often achieved the same result through **racially restrictive covenants,** which were private deed restrictions that prohibited property owners from selling or leasing property to African Americans or other minorities. The NAACP finally succeeded in undercutting restrictive covenants in *Shelley v. Kraemer* (1948). The Supreme Court held that private contracts calling for discrimination could be written, but state courts could not

Racially restrictive covenants Private deed restrictions that prohibited property owners from selling or leasing property to African Americans or other minorities.

constitutionally enforce them because enforcement would make the state a party to discrimination.[44]

The executive and legislative branches of government participated in the battle against housing discrimination as well. In 1962, President Kennedy issued an executive order banning discrimination in property owned, sold, or leased by the federal government. Subsequently, Title IV of the Civil Rights Act of 1964 extended nondiscrimination provisions to all public housing and urban renewal developments receiving federal assistance. The most important legislative move against housing discrimination was the Fair Housing Act of 1968, which prohibited discrimination in all transactions involving realtors.

A few weeks after the passage of the Fair Housing Act, the Supreme Court ruled that the Civil Rights Act of 1866 prohibited discrimination in all real estate transactions, including those among private individuals. The Court held that Congress in 1866 intended to ban all discrimination in the purchase or lease of property, including discrimination by private sellers. Furthermore, the Court ruled that Congress's action in prohibiting private housing discrimination was a constitutional exercise of authority granted by the Thirteenth Amendment, which prohibits slavery. "[W]hen racial discrimination herds men into ghettoes and makes their ability to buy property turn on the color of their skin, then it . . . is a relic of slavery."[45]

Civil rights forces used litigation and legislation to attack other forms of private discrimination. In the late 1950s and early 1960s, African American activists staged sit-ins at segregated dime store lunch counters and refused to leave until served. Local police would arrest the protesters, charging them with disturbing the peace or breaking a local Jim Crow ordinance. With NAACP legal assistance, the demonstrators would appeal their conviction to the federal courts, where it would be reversed and the local segregation ordinance overturned. This case-by-case approach desegregated many public facilities, but it was slow and expensive.

Interstate Commerce Clause The constitutional provision giving Congress authority to "regulate commerce . . . among the several states."

The Civil Rights Act of 1964 was a more efficient tool for fighting discrimination. Title II of the Act outlawed discrimination based on race, religion, color, sex, or national origin in hotels, restaurants, gas stations, and other public accommodations. Congress based Title II on the Interstate Commerce Clause in order to overcome the precedent set in the *Civil Rights Cases* that the Fourteenth Amendment prohibits discrimination by the government but not discrimination by private individuals and firms. The **Interstate Commerce Clause** is the constitutional provision giving Congress authority to "regulate commerce . . . among the several states." Because hotels, restaurants, gas stations, and the like serve individuals traveling from state to state, and because they purchase products that have been shipped in interstate commerce, Congress reasoned that they are part of interstate commerce and, consequently, subject to regulation by Congress. In *Heart of Atlanta Motel v. United States* and *Katzenbach v. McClung* (1964), the Supreme Court upheld the constitutionality of Congress's action.[46]

Americans with Disabilities Act (ADA) A federal law intended to end discrimination against persons with disabilities and to eliminate barriers preventing their full participation in American society through imposing a broad range of federal mandates.

Congress and the president have enacted legislation extending civil rights protection to groups based on criteria other than race, religion, color, gender, or national origin. The **Americans with Disabilities Act (ADA)** is a federal law intended to end discrimination against disabled persons and eliminate barriers to their full participation in American society. Other federal legislation prohibits age discrimination and protects families with children from housing discrimination. Title IX of the Education Amendments of 1972 is a federal law that prohibits gender discrimination in programs at educational institutions that receive federal funds. Because of Title IX, high schools, colleges, and universities have expanded athletic opportunities for women.

The Civil Rights Act of 1991 dealt with hiring practices that are not overtly discriminatory but which nonetheless limit employment opportunities for women and minorities. Suppose a city government requires prospective police officers to stand at least 5 feet 5 inches tall. That requirement would disproportionately reduce the number of women eligible to apply for jobs because women are typically shorter than men. The Civil Rights Act of 1991 declared that hiring practices that have a disproportionate impact on women and minorities must be "job-related for the position in question and consistent with business necessity." Therefore, the city's height requirement for police officers would be illegal unless the city could show that a height of at least 5 feet 5 inches was necessary to do the job. Furthermore, the Civil Rights Act of 1991 allowed women, minorities, and the disabled to sue for monetary damages in cases of intentional job discrimination and harassment.

In recent years, however, the Supreme Court has made it more difficult for women and minorities to win discrimination lawsuits. In 1989, for example, the Court reversed a 13-year-old precedent that interpreted the Civil Rights Act of 1866 to allow workers to sue employers for job discrimination. The Court ruled that the law only prohibited hiring discrimination but not racial harassment in the workplace or discrimination in promotions.[47] Furthermore, the Court ruled that workers who lose their jobs must specifically prove that their firing was motivated by unlawful bias. The case that prompted this ruling involved an African American man who claimed that he was demoted and then fired from his job at a prison in Missouri because of his race. The Court ruled that it was insufficient for the man to show that the reasons given by his employer for firing him were untrue. He had to prove that he was fired because of racial bias rather than personal dislike.[48]

State and local governments have also adopted policies protecting various groups from discrimination. Many state and local governments offer protection from discrimination based on race, ethnicity, gender, age, color, national origin, and disability, similar to those contained in federal law. Some state and local governments go beyond federal law, offering protection from discrimination based on sexual orientation and sexual identity (to protect transgendered persons from discrimination).

The U.S. Supreme Court has held, however, that state and local civil rights laws must be balanced against individual rights. Consider the case of *Boy Scouts of America v. Dale* (2000). James Dale had been a scout since he was 8, earning the rank of Eagle Scout at the age of 18. Dale became an adult member of the scouts and served as an assistant scoutmaster while he was a student at Rutgers University. After a story appeared in a local newspaper identifying Dale as the co-president of the Rutgers University Lesbian/Gay Alliance, the Boy Scouts sent him

In 2008, Congress passed, and President George W. Bush signed, the Genetic Information Nondiscrimination Act. It prohibited health insurance companies from using genetic information to deny benefits or raise premiums. It also prohibited employers from using genetic information to make employment decisions.

a letter revoking his membership, stating that the organization specifically forbids membership by homosexuals. Dale sued the Boy Scouts, charging that their action violated a New Jersey law prohibiting discrimination in public accommodations on the basis of sexual orientation. The U.S. Supreme Court ruled that applying the New Jersey law to the Boy Scouts would violate the organization's First Amendment right of "expressive association." The Boy Scouts claimed that opposition to homosexuality was an integral part of its organizational message. The Court decided that forcing the Scouts to include an openly gay member would unconstitutionally violate the organization's freedom of expression because it would make it difficult for the Scouts to convey their value system to members and the general public.[49]

The decision in the *Dale* case extended an earlier ruling that dealt with the exclusion of an Irish gay and lesbian organization from a privately organized St. Patrick's Day parade in Boston. The Supreme Court held that the state of Massachusetts could not enforce a law prohibiting discrimination in public accommodations on the basis of sexual orientation against the parade organizers. The Court said that a parade is a form of expression. By forcing the parade organizers to include a group whose message the organizers did not wish to convey, the government would be violating the free speech rights of the parade organizers. The Court held that Massachusetts could not limit free speech unless it could demonstrate a compelling government interest that could not be achieved in a less restrictive manner.[50]

WHAT IS YOUR OPINION?

Should gay men and lesbians enjoy the same legal protection from discrimination that women and the members of racial and ethnic minority groups have?

Affirmative Action

The University of Michigan Law School is one of the most prestigious law schools in the nation. Each year it receives more than 3,500 applications from which it selects a first-year class of 350 students. The law school looks for capable students with the promise of success in the classroom and in the future profession of law. It also strives to admit a mixture of students with varying backgrounds and experiences who will learn from each other. In particular, the law school attempts to ensure that its student body is racially and ethnically diverse by enrolling a critical mass of students from groups that have historically suffered discrimination—African Americans, Latinos, and Native Americans. In order to achieve its admissions goals, the law school rejects some academically strong applicants in favor of other applicants who add diversity to its student body. Barbara Grutter was one such student rejected by the law school. Grutter, a white woman, had a college grade point average of 3.8 and a high score on the Law School Admissions Test (LSAT). When the law school rejected her application, Grutter accused it of favoring minority applicants who were less qualified academically. She filed suit, charging that the school discriminated against her on the basis of race in violation of the Fourteenth Amendment and the Civil Rights Act of 1964.[51]

Affirmative action programs Programs designed to ensure equal opportunities in employment and college admissions for racial minorities and women.

The admissions procedure at the University of Michigan Law School was an example of an **affirmative action program,** which is a program designed to ensure equal opportunities in employment and college admissions exist for racial minorities and women. Affirmative action takes a number of forms. A corporation may target colleges and universities with substantial minority enrollments in hopes of increasing the number of African Americans, Latinos, and Asians in its applicant pool. A local government taking bids for the construction of a new sports stadium may stipulate that contractors make a good faith effort to ensure that at least 25 percent of subcontracts go to firms owned by women or minorities. A federal grant program designed to provide scholarships to college students studying to become teachers may be limited to students who are members of racial and ethnic minority groups. A law school may reserve 20 percent of the places in its first-year class for African Americans and Latinos. A city government may require that 30 percent of city contracts go to firms owned by women or minorities.

Few issues in American government are more controversial than affirmative action. The proponents of race- and gender-based preferences believe they are necessary to remedy the effects of past discrimination. Colleges and universities assert that they benefit from a diverse student body. Employers value a diverse workforce. In contrast, the opponents of racial and gender preferences argue that the only fair way to determine college admissions and employment decisions is merit. It is wrong, they say, to hire or promote someone because of race or gender.

Federal government efforts to remedy the effects of discrimination began in the early 1960s. Presidents Kennedy and Johnson ordered affirmative action in federal employment and hiring by government contractors, but their orders had little practical effect until the late 1960s when the Department of Labor began requiring government contractors to employ certain percentages of women and minorities. For the following decade, affirmative action took on a momentum all its own. For some, affirmative action meant nondiscrimination. For others, it required seeking out qualified women and minorities. For still others, affirmative action stood for hiring set percentages of women and minorities—a quota system. All the while, employers kept careful records of how many women and minority group members were part of their operations.

The election of Ronald Reagan as president in 1980 was a major setback for the proponents of affirmative action. During the Reagan administration, the Equal Employment Opportunity Commission (EEOC) under the leadership of Clarence Thomas dismantled affirmative action programs and anything that resembled a quota system for women and minorities. In Reagan's view, civil rights laws should offer relief not to whole groups of people, but only to specific individuals who could prove that they were victims of discrimination. Hiring goals, timetables, and racial quotas, the administration argued, were reverse discrimination against whites. Reagan's most lasting impact on affirmative action was in the judicial branch of government. Reagan appointees, later reinforced by justices appointed by President George H. W. Bush, created a Supreme Court majority who shared Reagan's conservative philosophy on affirmative action issues.

Minority business set-aside A legal requirement that firms receiving government grants or contracts allocate a certain percentage of their purchases of supplies and services to businesses owned or controlled by members of minority groups.

In *City of Richmond v. J. A. Croson Co.* (1989) and *Adarand Constructors v. Pena* (1995), the Supreme Court put many affirmative action policies in constitutional jeopardy. The *Croson* case dealt with a minority business set-aside program for municipal construction contracts established by the city of Richmond, Virginia. A **minority business set-aside** is a legal requirement that firms receiving government grants or contracts allocate a certain percentage of their purchases of supplies and services to businesses owned or controlled by members of minority groups. Even though African Americans constituted half of Richmond's population, less than 1 percent of city government construction dollars had typically gone to minority-owned firms. In light of this history, the city council passed an ordinance requiring that prime contractors who were awarded city construction contracts over the following five years must subcontract at least 30 percent of the dollar amount of their contracts to one or more minority-business enterprises. The ordinance allowed waivers when contractors could prove that the requirements of the ordinance could not be achieved.

Richmond's minority business set-aside program soon became the target of litigation. J. A. Croson Co., a contracting company whose bid for a city project was rejected for failing to meet the minority set-aside, filed suit against the ordinance, charging that it was unconstitutional. The U.S. Supreme Court ruled that Richmond's set-aside ordinance unconstitutionally violated the Equal Protection Clause of the Fourteenth Amendment because it denied certain persons the opportunity to compete for a fixed percentage of city contracts based solely on their race.

The most significant aspect of the *Croson* decision was that the Court applied strict judicial scrutiny to race-conscious efforts to remedy the effects of past discrimination. For years, the Court had applied the standard of strict judicial scrutiny to government restrictions on measures that disadvantaged individuals based on their race or citizenship status. In *Croson*, the Court served notice that it would also apply strict scrutiny to programs designed to correct the effects of past discrimination.

The Court's majority opinion declared that although minority set-aside programs can be justified as a remedy for discrimination in some instances, the Richmond city council failed to demonstrate a specific history of discrimination in the city's construction industry sufficient to justify a race-based program of relief. The mere fact that few city construction contracts had gone to minority firms was not sufficient evidence to prove discrimination either by the city government or in the city's construction industry. Instead of comparing the number of city contracts going to minority businesses with the proportion of minority citizens in Richmond, the Court ruled that the city council should have compared contracts with the proportion of minority-owned enterprises in the city's construction industry. Perhaps Richmond had few minority-owned construction companies. Instead of racial discrimination, the lack of minority-owned businesses might have reflected differences in educational opportunities or career choices by members of minority groups.

The Court also held that Richmond's set-aside program was constitutionally unacceptable because it was not narrowly tailored to achieve any goal except "outright racial balancing." The plan gave absolute preference to minority entrepreneurs from anywhere in the country, not just the Richmond area. Furthermore, the Court said, the program made no effort to determine whether particular minority businesspersons seeking a racial preference had themselves suffered the effects of discrimination.[52]

Adarand Constructors v. Pena involved a discrimination lawsuit by Adarand Constructors, a Colorado construction company, against the federal Department of Transportation (DOT). Adarand's low bid on a contract to build highway guardrails was rejected in favor of a higher bid by Gonzales Construction Company, which was certified by the DOT as a small business controlled by "socially and economically disadvantaged individuals." The DOT, which gave additional compensation to prime contractors who subcontracted with socially and economically disadvantaged companies, assumed that businesses that are 51 percent owned by individuals who are "black, Hispanic, Asian Pacific, Subcontinent Asian, and Native American" were socially and economically disadvantaged. The prime contractor for the job stipulated that Adarand would have received the bid were it not for the financial incentive given by the DOT for using a company that is certified as socially and economically disadvantaged.

The Supreme Court ordered the *Adarand* case returned to the trial court for reconsideration in light of the standard of strict judicial scrutiny. All racial classifications, whether imposed by state and local governments or the federal government, must serve a compelling government interest and must be narrowly tailored to further that interest. The goal of remedying the effects of past discrimination may be sufficient justification, the Court said, but only when a clear history of specific discrimination can be demonstrated. Statistics showing racial disparities in hiring and promotion are not sufficient to prove discrimination as long as an employer can produce evidence that employment practices resulting in a racial imbalance are justified by legitimate business necessity, such as the absence of qualified minority workers. Furthermore, any affirmative action plan designed to address the problem must be narrowly tailored to achieve that end.[53]

The Supreme Court first dealt with affirmative action in college admissions in *Regents of the University of California v. Bakke* (1978). Allan Bakke, a white male, sued the university after he was denied admission to medical school. The university had a minority admissions program in which it set aside 16 of 100 places each year for minority applicants. Because he was not allowed to compete for any of the slots reserved for minority applicants, Bakke charged that he was the victim of illegal racial discrimination and the Court agreed. The Court ordered the college to admit Bakke, saying that a numerical quota for minority admissions violated the Equal Protection Clause of the Fourteenth Amendment. The Court added, however, that race and ethnicity could be considered as one of several factors in admissions decisions as a "plus factor" in an individualized admissions process.[54]

The Supreme Court reaffirmed the *Bakke* precedent in Barbara Grutter's lawsuit against the University of Michigan Law School. The Court ruled that the university, which is a government agency, could consider race in its admissions program because the government has a compelling interest in promoting racial and ethnic diversity in higher education. The law school's admissions process was constitutional, the Court held, because it considered race and ethnicity as only one of numerous factors in the admissions process and did not establish a quota system for minority applicants. Consequently, Ms. Grutter lost her case.[55]

The Supreme Court's position on affirmative action in college admissions may not stand for long. The vote in the Michigan Law School Case was 5–4, with Justice Sandra Day O'Connor in the majority. When O'Connor retired in 2006, President George W. Bush nominated Samuel Alito to replace her and he was confirmed by the U.S. Senate. Justice Alito has aligned himself with the four justices on the losing side in the Michigan Law School Case in at least one other case involving employment law, suggesting that the Court will eventually overturn its position in both *Bakke* and the Michigan Law School Case.[56]

Making Civil Rights Policy

The Constitution is the most important contextual factor affecting civil rights policymaking, just as it is for civil liberties. Affirmative action, school integration, voting rights, and other civil rights concerns are constitutional issues. Consequently, civil rights policies reflect the parameters of constitutional law.

The policy preferences of federal judges affect civil rights policymaking. Liberal judges are more likely than conservative judges to rule in favor of women and members of minority groups. In contrast, conservative judges are hesitant to expand constitutional rights. The appointment of relatively more conservative justices by recent Republican presidents has created a Supreme Court majority almost as skeptical of racial, ethnic, and gender preferences as it is racial, ethnic, and gender discrimination. Because the current Court is closely divided on a number of civil rights issues, including affirmative action, the retirement of one or two justices could have a major policy impact, depending, of course, on the judicial philosophy of their replacements.

Civil rights policymaking is also affected by the presence of organized groups concerned with civil rights issues. For example, the adoption of policies favorable to gay and lesbian rights coincides with the appearance of gay rights organizations, such as the Human Rights Campaign. Laws protecting gay and lesbian rights are least common in the South, where conservative Christian groups opposed to gay and lesbian rights are influential.

Party control of Congress and the White House influences civil rights policy. Groups favoring women's rights, affirmative action, voting rights, and gay and lesbian rights have more influence in the Democratic Party than they do in the GOP. Presidents Reagan, George H. W. Bush, and George W. Bush, for example, appointed relatively conservative justices whose rulings on school integration, legislative redistricting, and affirmative action have been generally conservative. At the state level, Republican legislatures and governors are less likely to enact affirmative action laws and measures outlawing discrimination against gay men and lesbians than are their Democratic counterparts.

Public opinion is another important element of the environment for civil rights policymaking. Survey research shows that Americans have grown more tolerant of racial and cultural diversity. As recently as the 1940s, a majority of white

Americans supported racial segregation and discrimination, both in principle and in practice. By the 1970s, support for overt discrimination had virtually vanished. Today, polls find that large majorities of Americans of all races and both genders oppose discrimination.[57] Nonetheless, whites and African Americans do not see eye to eye on the rate of minority progress. A recent public opinion survey found that 61 percent of African Americans say that there has been "no real progress for blacks in the last few years," compared with 31 percent of white Americans who take that position.[58]

Agenda Setting

Individuals, groups, political parties, and the media all participate in setting the agenda for civil rights policymaking. Susan B. Anthony, for example, was a leader of the movement for women's suffrage. Dr. Martin Luther King, Jr., was the foremost spokesperson for civil rights for African Americans during the 1960s. Linda Brown advanced the cause of civil rights issues by participating in a lawsuit.

A number of groups help set the agenda for civil rights issues. The NAACP Legal Defense Fund, Mexican American Legal Defense and Education Fund (MALDEF), the National Organization for Women (NOW), and other groups raise civil rights issues by supporting lawsuits as test cases. Large national membership organizations, such as NOW, the NAACP, and the League of United Latin American Citizens (LULAC), lobby elected officials at the state and national level to address their policy concerns. Groups gather signatures to put their pet policy issues on the ballot in states with the **initiative process,** which is a procedure available in some states and cities whereby citizens can propose the adoption of a policy measure by gathering a prerequisite number of signatures. Voters must then approve the measure before it can take effect. After the Supreme Court upheld the University of Michigan Law School's affirmative action program, Barbara Grutter and other opponents of racial preferences gathered signatures to put the issue on the ballot and won. In November 2006, Michigan voters approved an amendment to the state constitution to prohibit state agencies and institutions from operating affirmative action programs that grant preferences based on race, color, ethnicity, national origin, or gender.[59]

Initiative process A procedure available in some states and cities whereby citizens can propose the adoption of a policy measure by gathering a prerequisite number of signatures. Voters must then approve the measure before it can take effect.

Political parties often promote civil rights causes. The modern Democratic Party has adopted platforms supporting school integration, affirmative action, women's rights, equal employment opportunities, and gay and lesbian rights. All of these positions reflect alliances between the party and various interest groups and blocs of voters. African American, Latino, female, and gay and lesbian voters are a major part of the base of the Democratic Party. Although the Republican Party favors equal opportunity and opposes discrimination based on race, ethnicity, or gender, the GOP is generally against affirmative action and opposes gay and lesbian rights. The Republican position reflects the views of the middle-income whites who compose the core of GOP voters, as well as the conservative Christian groups that ally with the party.

Because of Title IX, high schools, colleges, and universities have expanded athletic opportunities for women.

The media play a role in setting the agenda for civil rights. News reports and media coverage of political demonstrations highlight issues that might otherwise receive relatively little notice. During the 1960s, for example, media coverage of political demonstrations in favor of black civil rights and the violent reaction to those demonstrations helped mobilize northern white public opinion in favor of the protesters.

Policy Formulation, Adoption, and Legitimation

Civil rights policy formulation, adoption, and legitimation may involve action by the president, Congress, the bureaucracy, local governments, private individuals, corporations, and the courts. Civil rights policies often take the form of legislation or executive orders. The ADA, for example, is a federal law, passed by Congress and signed by the president. State and local governments adopt affirmative action plans, such as Richmond's minority business set-aside plan. Colleges and universities formulate and adopt admissions policies. Civil rights policies may sometimes take the form of executive orders. President Truman, for example, issued an executive order to racially integrate the armed forces. The battle over civil rights policies does not end with policy adoption, however, as the various political actors involved in civil rights policymaking battle over policy legitimacy. Consider the issues of affirmative action. Although the principle of nondiscrimination is now widely accepted, many Americans oppose affirmative action as reverse discrimination.

Court decisions set the boundaries for civil rights policymaking for other branches of government. Legislatures and executives considering affirmative action policies must take into account the *Croson* and *Adarand* rulings or risk the possibility of an expensive court challenge that they will likely lose. After the *Adarand* ruling, for example, the government issued new guidelines for federal affirmative action programs designed to conform to the Court's decision.

Judicial decisions are not necessarily the last word in civil rights policymaking, especially when the courts base their rulings on the interpretation of statutory law. Congress, after all, can rewrite laws to overcome judicial objections. In 1984, for example, the Supreme Court severely restricted the impact of federal laws prohibiting discrimination on the basis of gender, race, age, or disability by institutions receiving federal funds. The Court ruled that the law prohibited discrimination only by the *direct* recipient of the money.[60] Thus, if a university's chemistry department received federal funds but its athletic department did not, the latter would not be covered. Congress responded to the Court's decision by rewriting the law (and overriding President Reagan's veto in the process). Because athletic programs receive little if any federal money, most college athletic departments did not take Title IX seriously until after Congress rewrote the law. In theory, a college or university that fails to comply with Title IX in athletics could lose federal funding for student scholarships and research grants.

Policy Implementation, Evaluation, and Change

The implementation of civil rights policy falls to the executive branch of the national government, lower federal courts, state and local governments, individuals, and private businesses. Under the provisions of the VRA, for example, the Justice Department reviews changes in election laws and procedures proposed by state and local governments in covered jurisdictions. The implementation of school desegregation policy takes place under the supervision of federal district judges.

Interest groups, individuals, and their attorneys play a major role in civil rights policy implementation by suing and threatening to sue. Civil rights groups file suit, for example, to challenge legislative districts they believe violate the VRA. Individuals who think that they have been denied a job or promotion because of illegal bias can sue as well. In practice, many companies devise hiring and promotion procedures with the goal of protecting themselves against discrimination lawsuits.

Consider the implementation of Title IX. Congress voted to prohibit discrimination on the basis of gender without specifying how that prohibition would apply to college athletic programs. In fact, southern conservatives added Title IX to the measure, hoping Congress would defeat the entire bill rather than enact legislation

In 2008, Congress passed, and President Bush signed, legislation to expand protections for people with disabilities by overturning several recent Supreme Court decisions that had narrowed the standard used to determine whether an individual was disabled.

to prohibit discrimination on the basis of gender. They were wrong; the legislation passed anyway. The details of implementation of Title IX were left to the federal bureaucracy, universities, and the courts. In practice, each university takes steps to implement Title IX based on federal court decisions, guidelines set by the Department of Education, and the resources at hand. Individuals and groups who believe that a university has failed adequately to implement the law can file suit, asking a federal court to issue an **injunction,** that is, a court order, directing the university to take additional steps to comply with the law. People can also ask a court to award financial damages.

Injunction A court order.

The evaluation of civil rights policies involves both factual analyses and analyses based on values. Consider the impact of the elimination of affirmative action in university admissions after the passage of Proposition 209 in California, which was a state ballot measure passed in 1996 that was designed to eliminate affirmative action in the state by banning preferential treatment of women and minorities in public hiring, contracting, and education. The number of African American and Latino students admitted to law school at the University of California, Berkeley, fell after the adoption of the measure. The critics of Proposition 209 worry that the state's best colleges and universities will have student bodies composed almost entirely of white and Asian students. In contrast, other observers believe that ending affirmative action helps well-qualified African American and Latino students who are admitted to the best schools because no one will question whether they really belong. Minority students who are not as well prepared will benefit as well because they will not be placed in situations where they cannot effectively compete.

Cold War The period of international tension between the United States and the Soviet Union lasting from the late 1940s through the late 1980s.

Civil rights policies change as the context for policymaking changes. World War II and the Cold War provided the context for advances in African American civil rights in the 1950s and 1960s. Laws mandating racial discrimination in the United States were difficult to defend after the United States fought a war against Nazi Germany, a regime that asserted the racial superiority of its people. Moreover, an argument in favor of the *Brown* decision was that ending school segregation enhanced the image of the United States in its Cold War competition with the Soviet Union. The **Cold War** was a period of international tension between the United States and the Soviet Union lasting from the late 1940s through the late 1980s.

WHAT WE HAVE LEARNED

1. **What is the constitutional basis for civil rights in America, including both the U.S. Constitution and state constitutions?**

The most important provisions in the U.S. Constitution dealing with civil rights are the Fourteenth Amendment, which includes the Equal Protection Clause, and the Fifteenth Amendment, which protects the right to vote from abridgement on account of "race, color, or previous condition of servitude." Many state constitutions include civil rights protections as well.

2. **How does the Equal Protection Clause affect African American civil rights, immigrant rights, women's rights, and gay and lesbian rights?**

The Supreme Court has ruled that policy distinctions among persons based on their race, ethnicity, and citizenship status are suspect classifications, which are distinctions among persons that must be justified on the basis of a compelling government interest. Government need only demonstrate some "reasonable basis" in order to justify public policies that distinguish among persons on the basis of such factors as relative wealth, physical ability, marital status, residency, or sexual orientation. As for gender, the Court has ruled that the government must offer an "exceedingly persuasive justification" that gender-based distinctions are necessary to achieve some "important governmental objective."

The Equal Protection Clause initially had little effect on African American civil rights. States adopted Jim Crow laws and the Supreme Court endorsed them in *Plessy v. Ferguson* and other cases. Eventually, the Court overturned the *Plessy* decision in *Brown v. Board of Education*, ruling that separate-but-equal, the standard adopted in *Plessy* to satisfy the Equal Protection Clause, was a contradiction in terms. Implementation of *Brown* was slow and unsteady. Even today, many minority youngsters attend schools where children of color make up the overwhelming majority of the student body. *Brown v. Board of Education* prohibited racial discrimination in assigning children to public schools. What was less clear after *Brown* was whether the Equal Protection Clause required the side-by-side instruction of students of different races in the same schools and classrooms. During the 1970s, the Supreme Court ordered school districts to take race into account in assigning students to schools in order to increase racial integration. Since the 1980s, the Supreme Court has abandoned efforts to compel the racial integration of public schools in favor of a stance that requires local officials to ignore race in making school assignment decisions.

The Equal Protection Clause also affects groups other than African Americans. The Supreme Court has struck down most state laws treating noncitizens differently than citizens. The Supreme Court has invalidated most distinctions based on gender with the exception of the exclusion of women from having to register for possible military service. The Supreme Court applied the protections of the Equal Protection Clause to gay men and lesbians for the first time in the case of *Romer v. Evans*, which struck down a Colorado ballot voter initiative that repealed all laws protecting gay men and lesbians from discrimination and prohibited their future enactment. Gay and lesbian rights groups hope that the Supreme Court will eventually rule that limiting marriage rights to opposite-sex couples violates the Equal Protection Clause.

3. **What is the history of voting rights in America, both for women and African Americans?**

States initially limited suffrage to white male property owners. Property qualifications were dropped in the nineteenth century and women won the right to vote in the early twentieth century. The struggle for African American voting rights was more difficult despite the adoption of the Fifteenth Amendment after the Civil War. Tests of understanding, literacy tests, the white primary, grandfather clauses, and poll taxes were all used to disfranchise African Americans. All of these and other restrictions on minority voting rights eventually fell because of court rulings, a constitutional amendment to outlaw the poll tax, and the passage of the Voting Rights Act.

4. **What steps has government taken to protect women and minorities from discrimination?**

In *Shelley v. Kraemer* the Supreme Court ruled that racially restrictive covenants are unenforceable. The Civil Rights Act of 1964 outlawed discrimination based on race, religion, color, sex, or national origin in hotels, restaurants, gas stations, and other public accommodations. The ADA protects disabled persons against discrimination and eliminates barriers to their full participation in American society. The Civil Rights Act of 1991 dealt with hiring practices that are not overtly discriminatory but which nonetheless limit employment opportunities for women and minorities. In recent years, however, the Supreme Court has interpreted civil rights laws narrowly, making it more difficult for women and minorities to prove discrimination. The Court has also held that state and local civil rights laws must be balanced against individual rights.

5. **To what extent are colleges, universities, and employers legally able to use affirmative action to increase enrollment and employment of women and minorities?**

An affirmative action program is a program designed to ensure equal opportunities in employment and college admissions for racial minorities and women. The Supreme Court applies strict judicial scrutiny to affirmative action programs, which means that those programs must be justified by a compelling government interest and be narrowly tailored to further that interest. The Court struck down affirmative action programs dealing with minority business set-asides and government contracts in *Croson* and *Adarand Contractors*.

As for college and university admissions, the Court ruled quotas unconstitutional, but said that race and ethnicity could be considered as one of several factors in admissions decisions as a "plus factor" in an individualized admissions process. In the *University of Michigan Law School Case*, the Court ruled that the university had a compelling interest in promoting racial and ethnic diversity in higher education. It upheld the law school's admissions program because the university considered race and ethnicity as part of an individualized admissions process without having a quota system for minority students.

6. **How is civil rights policy made?**

The Constitution is the most important contextual factor affecting civil rights policymaking, just as it is for civil liberties. The policy preferences of federal judges affect civil rights policymaking. A number of interest groups are involved in civil rights policymaking, including the NAACP and LULAC. Public opinion is important as well. Individuals, groups, political parties, and the media all participate in setting the agenda for civil rights policymaking. Civil rights policy formulation, adoption, and legitimation may involve action by the president, Congress, the bureaucracy, local governments, private individuals, corporations, interest groups, and the courts. The implementation of civil rights policy falls to the executive branch of the national government, lower federal courts, state and local governments, individuals, and private businesses. The evaluation of civil rights policies involves both factual analyses and analyses based on values. Civil rights policies change as the context for policymaking changes.

KEY TERMS

affirmative action programs
Americans with Disabilities Act (ADA)
civil rights
Cold War
disfranchisement
Equal Protection Clause
grandfather clause
initiative process
injunction
Interstate Commerce Clause
Jim Crow laws
literacy test
majority-minority districts
minority business set-aside
poll tax
primary election
racially restrictive covenants
referendum
separate-but-equal
statutory law
strict judicial scrutiny
suffrage
suspect classifications
test case
test of understanding
Voting Rights Act (VRA)
white primary

NOTES

1. Pam Belluck, "Massachusetts Rejects Bill to Eliminate Gay Marriage," *New York Times*, September 15, 2005, available at www.nytimes.com.
2. "Surveying the Land," *Advocate*, August 2009, p. 57.
3. Mike O'Sullivan, "San Francisco Gay Marriage Court Case Could Have National Impact," *Voice of America*, January 13, 2010, available at www1.voanews.com.
4. Randall T. Shepherd, "Second Wind for the State Bill of Rights," in David J. Bodenhammer and James W. Ely, Jr., *The Bill of Rights in Modern America* (Bloomington, IN: Indiana University Press, 2008), p. 251.
5. Elder Witt, *The Supreme Court and Individual Rights*, 2nd ed. (Washington, DC: Congressional Quarterly Press, 1988), pp. 223–226.

6. *Plessy v. Ferguson*, 163 U.S. 537 (1896).
7. *Cumming v. Richmond County Board of Education*, 175 U.S. 528 (1899).
8. *Gong Lum v. Rice*, 275 U.S. 78 (1927).
9. *Missouri ex rel Gaines v. Canada*, 305 U.S. 337 (1938).
10. *Sweatt v. Painter*, 399 U.S. 629 (1950).
11. *McLaurin v. Oklahoma State Regents*, 339 U.S. 637 (1950).
12. *Brown v. Board of Education of Topeka*, 347 U.S. 483 (1954).
13. *Brown v. Board of Education of Topeka*, 349 U.S. 294 (1955).
14. Quoted in Harrell R. Rodgers, Jr., and Charles S. Bullock III, *Law and Social Change* (New York: McGraw-Hill, 1972), p. 71.
15. Gerald Rosenberg, "Substituting Symbol for Substance: What Did *Brown* Really Accomplish?" *P.S. Political Science and Politics*, April 2004, p. 205.
16. *Alexander v. Holmes County Board of Education*, 396 U.S. 19 (1969).
17. Rosenberg, "Substituting Symbol for Substance," p. 206.
18. Raymond Wolters, *Race and Education 1954–2007* (Columbia, MO: University of Missouri Press, 2008), p. 302.
19. Martha Minow, *In* Brown's *Wake: Legacies of America's Education Landmark* (New York: Oxford University Press, 2010), pp. 6–7.
20. *Swann v. Charlotte-Mecklenburg Board of Education*, 402 U.S. 1 (1971).
21. *Keyes v. School District #1, Denver, Colorado*, 413 U.S. 189 (1973).
22. *Missouri v. Jenkins*, 515 U.S. 70 (1995).
23. *Parents Involved in Community Schools v. Seattle School District No. 1*, 551 U.S. 701 (2007).
24. Dana Goldstein, "On MLK Day, Some Thoughts on Segregated Schools, Arne Duncan, and President Obama," January 17, 2011, available at www.danagoldstein.net.
25. "School Segregation on the Rise," *Harvard Gazette News*, July 19, 2001, available at www.new.harvard.edu/gazette.
26. *In re Griffiths*, 413 U.S. 717 (1973); *Examining Board of Engineers, Architects and Surveyors v. de Otero*, 426 U.S. 572 (1976); *Bernal v. Fainter*, 467 U.S. 216 (1984).
27. Henry Weinstein, "Airport Screener Curb Is Rejected," *Los Angeles Times*, November 16, 2002, available at www.latimes.com.
28. *Bradwell v. Illinois*, 16 Wall 130 (1873).
29. Philippa Smith, "The Virginia Military Institute Case," in Sibyl A. Schwarzenbach and Patricia Smith, eds., *Women and the Constitution: History, Interpretation, and Practice* (New York: Columbia University Press, 2003), p. 343.
30. *United States v. Virginia*, 518 U.S. 515 (1996).
31. *Rostker v. Goldberg*, 453 U.S. 57 (1981).
32. *Romer v. Evans*, 517 U.S. 620 (1996).
33. *Smith v. Allwright*, 321 U.S. 649 (1944).
34. *Guinn v. United States*, 238 U.S. 347 (1915).
35. *Louisiana v. United States*, 380 U.S. 145 (1965).
36. *Harper v. State Board of Elections*, 383 U.S. 663 (1966).
37. *Shaw v. Reno*, 509 U.S. 630 (1993) and *Miller v. Johnson*, 515 U.S. 900 (1995).
38. Abigail Thenstrom, *Voting Rights—and Wrongs: The Elusive Quest for Racially Fair Elections* (Washington, DC: American Enterprise Institute, 2009), p. 202.
39. *Northwest Austin Municipal Utility District Number One v. Holder*, 557 U.S. (2009).
40. Quoted in Alfred H. Kelley and Winfred A. Harbison, *The American Constitution: Its Origins and Development* (New York: Norton, 1970), p. 460.
41. Quoted in Witt, *The Supreme Court and Individual Rights*, p. 247.
42. *Civil Rights Cases*, 109 U.S. 3 (1883).
43. *Buchanan v. Warley*, 245 U.S. 60 (1917).
44. *Shelley v. Kraemer*, 334 U.S. 1 (1948).
45. *Jones v. Alfred H. Meyer Co.*, 392 U.S. 409 (1968).
46. *Heart of Atlanta Motel v. United States*, 379 U.S. 241; and *Katzenbach v. McClung*, 379 U.S. 294 (1964).
47. *Patterson v. McLean Credit Union*, 491 U.S. 164 (1989).
48. *St. Mary's Honor Center v. Hicks*, 509 U.S. 502 (1993).
49. *Boy Scouts of America et al. v. Dale*, 530 U.S. 640 (2000).
50. *Hurley v. Irish-American Gay, Lesbian, and Bisexual Group of Boston*, 515 U.S. 557 (1993).
51. *Grutter v. Bollinger*, 539 U.S. 306 (2003).
52. *City of Richmond v. J. A. Croson Co.*, 488 U.S. 469 (1989).
53. *Adarand Constructors v. Pena*, 515 U.S. 200 (1995).
54. *Regents of the University of California v. Bakke*, 438 U.S. 265 (1978).
55. *Grutter v. Bollinger*, 539 U.S. 306 (2003).
56. *Ricci v. DeStefano*, No. 07-1428 (2009).
57. Gallup, "Race Relations," available at www.gallup.com.
58. The Pew Center for the People and the Press, "The Black and White of Public Opinion," October 2005, available at www.people-press.org.
59. Peter Schmidt, "Michigan Overwhelmingly Adopts Ban on Affirmative-Action Preferences," *Chronicle of Higher Education*, November 17, 2006, p. A23.
60. *Grove City College v. Bell*, 465 U.S. 555 (1984).

Chapter 17

Foreign and Defense Policy

CHAPTER OUTLINE

WHAT WE WILL LEARN

After studying Chapter 17, students should be able to answer the following questions:

1. What are the governmental and nongovernmental political actors that make up the international community?
2. What are the primary goals of American foreign and defense policy?
3. How does the United States attempt to achieve its foreign and defense policy goals?
4. What is the history of American foreign and defense policy?
5. How do the foreign policies of the George W. Bush administration and the Barack Obama administration differ?
6. What are the basic elements of American defense policy?
7. How is American foreign and defense policy made?

The United States and its allies believe that Iran is trying to build a nuclear weapon. Iran has been acquiring the raw materials, building the parts, and developing the expertise necessary to construct nuclear weapons. Under the terms of the Nuclear Non-Proliferation Treaty, Iran has the right to develop nuclear energy for peaceful purposes but not to build nuclear weapons. Although the government of Iran insists that its only goal is the peaceful development of nuclear energy, the United States and its allies are skeptical because Iran is a major oil producer without the need of alternative energy sources. Furthermore, the Iranian government has generally failed to cooperate with the International Atomic Energy Agency (IAEA), denying it access to nuclear sites and refusing to answer questions about the suspected link between Iran's nuclear program and the Iranian military.

Rogue state A nation that threatens world peace by sponsoring international terrorism and promoting the spread of weapons of mass destruction.

Weapons of mass destruction (WMD) Nuclear, chemical, and biological weapons that are designed to inflict widespread military and civilian casualties.

The United States and its allies believe that a nuclear Iran would threaten world peace. The United States considers Iran to be a **rogue state,** which is a nation that threatens world peace by sponsoring international terrorism and promoting the spread of weapons of mass destruction. **Weapons of mass destruction (WMD)** are nuclear, chemical, and biological weapons that are designed to inflict widespread military and civilian casualties. Iran supports international terrorism by providing arms and money to Hezbollah, an Islamic organization based in Lebanon that has carried out terrorist attacks against Israel. American policymakers worry that an Iran armed with nuclear weapons would bully its neighbors, perhaps setting off regional arms races with other nations rushing to acquire nuclear weapons themselves to counter the Iranian threat. The Iranians might even use a nuclear weapon against the United States or its allies. Mahmoud Almadinejad, the president of Iran, has ominously said that Israel should be "wiped off the map."

The United States and its allies have several options for dealing with the Iranian nuclear threat, but none of the alternatives appear likely to be effective. First, the nations opposed to Iran's nuclear program could impose economic sanctions against Iran by limiting trade and other economic activity with the country. The goal of trade restrictions is to create enough economic hardship in Iran that the nation's people pressure the government to change its behavior. For international economic sanctions to work, all of the world's major trading nations must participate; however, both Russia and China are reluctant to join the effort. Moreover, Iran is not a democracy that responds readily to public pressure. In fact, the Iranian government has shown that it is willing to use deadly force against citizens protesting its decisions.[1]

Second, the United States and its allies could seek to engage the government of Iran diplomatically with the goal of convincing the nation's leaders that Iran would be better off politically, economically, and militarily if it were perceived as a member in good standing of the international community rather than a rogue state. If Iran were to renounce nuclear weapons and the support of terror groups, it could normalize relationships with the United States and improve its economy through trade. For this strategy to work, however, the Iranian leadership has to be open to changing its relationship with the rest of the world. In 2009, the Obama administration attempted to open a dialogue with the Iranian government aimed at convincing Iran to get out of the terror business, but the talks went nowhere.[2]

Finally, the United States or Israel (because it feels directly threatened by the prospect of an Iranian nuclear weapon) could launch missile strikes against Iran aimed at destroying its nuclear capacity before it is able to construct a weapon. The strikes might prove ineffective, however, because Iran has scattered its nuclear facilities at various sites around the country. Some of them are deep underground and some may be unknown to western intelligence. Furthermore, Iran could retaliate by disrupting oil shipments through the Persian Gulf, seriously damaging the economies of the nations of Western Europe and the United States.

The threat of nuclear weapons development in Iran is a major foreign and defense policy challenge for the United States. The United States went to war against Iraq to defuse a threat that in retrospect was less serious than the threats posed by the Iranians. Can the United States and its allies convince Iran to abandon its nuclear ambitions through negotiations? Will Iran respond to the threat of economic sanctions by abandoning its nuclear program? Does the United States have a realistic military option for dealing with Iran? If all else fails, will the United States simply have to learn to live with a nuclear Iran?

Foreign policy Public policy that concerns the United States' relationship to the international political environment.

Defense policy Public policy that concerns the armed forces of the United States.

These questions introduce Chapter 17 on the foreign and defense policies of the United States. **Foreign policy** is public policy that concerns the relationship of the United States to the international political environment. **Defense policy** is public policy that concerns the armed forces of the United States. The chapter begins with a description of the international environment, considering both governmental and nongovernmental international political actors. It lists the goals of American foreign policy and identifies the resources for achieving those

The United States and its allies believe that a nuclear Iran would threaten world peace. Mahmoud Ahmadinejad, pictured above, is the president of Iran.

goals. The chapter traces the history of American foreign and defense policy. It then examines the current foreign policy and the current defense policy of the United States. Finally, the chapter discusses how foreign and defense policies are made.

The International Community

Nation-state A political community occupying a definite territory that has an organized government.

Postindustrial societies Nations whose economies are increasingly based on services, research, and information rather than heavy industry.

Diplomatic relations A system of official contacts between two nations in which the countries exchange ambassadors and other diplomatic personnel and operate embassies in each other's country.

United Nations (UN) An international organization founded in 1945 as a diplomatic forum to resolve conflicts among the world's nations.

World Health Organization (WHO) An international organization created to control disease worldwide.

Since the seventeenth century, the nation-state has been the basic unit of the international community. A **nation-state** is a political community that occupies a definite territory and has an organized government. Other nations recognize its independence and respect the right of its government to exercise authority within its boundaries free from external interference. Today, more than 190 countries comprise the world community of nations.[3]

Political scientists divide the world's nations into three groups based on their level of economic development. The United States, Canada, Japan, and the countries of Western Europe are **postindustrial societies,** which are nations whose economies are increasingly based on services, research, and information rather than heavy industry. India, China, South Korea, Brazil, and a number of other countries are modernizing industrial states that are emerging as important economic powers. Finally, many of the countries of Asia, Africa, and Latin America are pre-industrial states with an average standard of living well below that found in postindustrial societies.[4]

The United States has diplomatic relations with almost all of the world's nations. The term **diplomatic relations** refers to a system of official contacts between two nations in which the countries exchange ambassadors and other diplomatic personnel and operate embassies in each other's country. Iran, Cuba, and North Korea are among the few nations with which the United States does not have formal diplomatic ties.

In addition to the governments of the world, more than a hundred transnational (or multinational) organizations are active on the international scene. The best known of these is the **United Nations (UN),** which is an international organization founded in 1945 as a diplomatic forum to resolve conflicts among the world's nations. In practice, the UN has not always been effective at maintaining the peace. The UN Security Council, which is the organization charged with maintaining peace and security among nations, has frequently been unable to act because each of its five permanent members (Russia, China, Britain, France, and the United States) has a veto on its actions. For example, the Security Council has been unable to persuade Iran to give up its nuclear weapons program at least in part because the permanent members disagree on how best to approach the problem.

Some of the UN's most important accomplishments have come in the areas of disaster relief, refugee relocation, agricultural development, loans for developing nations, and health programs. The UN has several agencies that carry out these and other tasks, including the **World Health Organization (WHO),** which is an international organization created to control disease worldwide. The WHO is a world clearinghouse for medical and scientific information. It sets international standards for drugs and vaccines and, on government request, helps fight disease in any country. The WHO is in the forefront of the battle against the spread of AIDS in the developing world.

The UN and its affiliated agencies are funded through dues and assessments charged to member nations. The amount of each nation's contribution depends, in general, on the strength of the nation's economy. Although every nation, even small and very poor nations, must support the work of the UN financially, the United States has the largest assessment because the American economy is the world's largest. As a result, the United States is also the UN's most influential member. Nonetheless, the United States has often been highly critical of some UN procedures, especially those associated with budgeting. Congress has sometimes made payment of American dues contingent on the UN agreeing to internal reforms to improve its operations.[5]

North Atlantic Treaty Organization (NATO) A military alliance consisting of the United States, Canada, and most European democracies.

A number of other international organizations are important to American foreign and defense policies. The **North Atlantic Treaty Organization (NATO)** is a military alliance consisting of the United States, Canada, and most European democracies. The United States and its allies formed NATO after World War II to defend against the threat of a Soviet attack in Western Europe. With the collapse of the Soviet Union, NATO has expanded to include some of the nations that were once part of the Soviet bloc: Albania, Poland, Hungary, the Czech Republic, Bulgaria, Croatia, Estonia, Latvia, Lithuania, Romania, Slovakia, and Slovenia. The United States, Canada, and the established democracies of Western Europe hope that the inclusion of these nations in the NATO alliance will strengthen their commitment to democratic institutions and capitalist economic structures. In the meantime, NATO has changed its military focus to take account of the changing international environment by creating a multinational force that can be deployed quickly. The United States wants NATO to become a global security organization that is capable either of taking military action or providing humanitarian relief anywhere in the world.

World Trade Organization (WTO) An international organization that administers trade laws, and provides a forum for settling trade disputes among nations.

Tariffs Taxes on imported goods.

The **World Trade Organization (WTO)** is an international organization that administers trade laws, and provides a forum for settling trade disputes among nations. It promotes international trade by sponsoring negotiations to reduce **tariffs,** which are taxes on imported goods, and other barriers to trade. The WTO also arbitrates disputes over trade among the 145 member nations. For example, the WTO has sponsored negotiations to allow developing countries to make generic versions of lifesaving drugs for their own use and for export to countries too poor either to make the drugs themselves or purchase them from pharmaceutical companies. Wealthy nations, led by the United States, want to sharply limit the number of diseases covered by the drugs in order to protect the intellectual property rights of pharmaceutical companies. In contrast, developing nations, such as Brazil, China, and India, argue that governments should have the right to determine which diseases constitute public health crises in their countries.[6]

International Monetary Fund (IMF) An international organization created to promote economic stability worldwide.

Nongovernmental organizations (NGOs) International organizations committed to the promotion of a particular set of issues.

The **International Monetary Fund (IMF)** is an international organization created to promote economic stability worldwide. It provides loans to nations facing economic crises, usually on the condition that they adopt and implement reforms designed to bring long-term economic stability. In 2008, for example, the IMF loaned Iceland more than $2 billion to stabilize that country's banking system hard hit by the world financial crisis.

Nongovernmental organizations (NGOs) are international organizations committed to the promotion of a particular set of issues. Greenpeace, Friends of the Earth, World Wide Fund for Nature, and the Nature Conservancy are NGOs that address environmental issues. Save the Children is an NGO concerned with the welfare of children. NGOs vary in their relationship to the international community. NGOs such as the International Red Cross and Doctors Without Borders work in partnership with national governments to assist the victims of natural disasters or political turmoil. Other NGOs lobby national governments over policy issues such as the effort to ban the importation of genetically modified foods. Some NGOs encourage consumers to boycott retailers who sell goods produced under exploitative working conditions in developing countries. They organize protests at international meetings of the WTO to push for the incorporation of health and safety conditions in international trade agreements.[7] Meanwhile, with the collapse of the Soviet Union, al Qaeda and other international terrorist organizations have emerged as the principal opponents to the United States in the world.[8]

In 2011, U.S. Navy SEALs killed al Qaeda leader Osama bin Laden in a raid on a secret compound in Pakistan.

The Goals of American Foreign and Defense Policy

Cold War The period of international tension between the United States and the Soviet Union lasting from the late 1940s through the late 1980s.

The United States has consistently pursued three foreign and defense policy goals throughout its history: national security, economic prosperity, and the projection of American values abroad.[9] The foremost goal of American foreign and defense policies is national security. A basic aim of the foreign policy of any nation is to preserve its sovereignty and protect its territorial integrity. No nation wants to be overrun by a foreign power or dominated by another nation. During the **Cold War,** which was the period of international tension between the United States and the Soviet Union lasting from the late 1940s through the late 1980s, American foreign policy was premised on the goal of protecting the nation from communist aggression. Although the United States is today the world's foremost military power, it still has national security concerns. The terrorist attacks of September 11, 2001, demonstrated the vulnerability of the United States to terrorism. Although Iran is not capable of mounting a direct attack on the United States, it could threaten American interests in the Middle East. It could also give or sell nuclear weapons to terrorist groups.

National prosperity is another goal of American foreign and defense policy. This goal includes encouraging free markets, promoting international trade, and protecting American economic interests and investments abroad. Because the American economy is closely entwined with the global economy, it is essential to the nation's economic health that the United States has access both to foreign suppliers of goods and services and to foreign markets for American products. The nation's military involvement in the Persian Gulf, for example, has been motivated at least in part by a U.S. desire to protect access to the region's oil fields.

International trade has grown increasingly important to the U.S. economy. Trade now accounts for 25 percent of the nation's output of goods and services compared to only 11 percent in 1970. The United States exported $1.6 trillion worth of goods and services in 2009 while importing $1.9 trillion worth. Canada is the United States' most important trading partner, followed, in order of importance, by China, Mexico, Japan, and Germany.[10]

Trade is controversial in the United States because it produces winners and losers. Consumers benefit from trade because they have the opportunity to purchase a broad range of goods at competitive prices. American manufacturers of medical instruments, farm equipment, pharmaceuticals, oil drilling equipment, and electronics benefit because they sell their products abroad. In contrast, inefficient small farmers, old steel mills, and the nation's clothing and textile manufacturers suffer because they do not compete effectively against international competition. Furthermore, some liberal groups in the United States oppose trade because they believe it rewards international corporations that exploit low-wage workers in developing countries and leads to environmental degradation around the globe.

North American Free Trade Agreement (NAFTA) An international accord among the United States, Mexico, and Canada to lower trade barriers among the three nations.

Recent administrations of both political parties have favored the growth of trade because they believe that the economic gains from trade outweigh the costs. President Bill Clinton won congressional support for the **North American Free Trade Agreement (NAFTA),** which was an international accord among the United States, Mexico, and Canada to lower trade barriers among the three nations, despite the opposition of a majority of the members of his own political party. The George W. Bush administration negotiated the Central America Free Trade Agreement (CAFTA) with Nicaragua, Honduras, Costa Rica, El Salvador, and Guatemala to phase out tariffs among participating nations on manufactured goods, agricultural commodities, chemicals, and construction equipment.

A final general policy goal of American foreign and defense policy is the promotion of American ideas and ideals abroad. Historically, American policymakers have justified military interventions as efforts to protect freedom and promote democracy. Many of the nation's foreign policies today are designed to further the causes of democracy, free-market capitalism, and human rights. For years, the United States has attempted to isolate Cuba economically and diplomatically in hopes of either driving the Castro regime out of power or forcing Castro to bring democracy and free-market capitalism to the island.

Spreading democracy was at the center of the foreign policy of the George W. Bush administration. When American forces failed to uncover WMD in Iraq, President Bush offered the promotion of democracy as the new justification for the invasion. Democracies are stronger economically and more stable politically than undemocratic governments, he declared. Consequently, their residents have few incentives to join terrorist organizations. Bush also endorsed the theory of the **democratic peace,** which is the concept that democracies do not wage war against other democracies.[11]

Democratic peace The concept that democracies do not wage war against other democracies.

Critics of the Bush administration warn that an emphasis on democratization is unrealistic, naïve, and counterproductive. Implanting democracy in countries without a democratic tradition may be impossible because people may be unwilling to make the compromises necessary for democracy to work. The various tribal and religious factions in Iraq fought with each other despite the introduction of democracy after the fall of Saddam. Furthermore, democracy may result in the election of governments hostile to American interests. In much of the Arab world, free elections would likely produce the selection of distinctly anti-American Islamic regimes. Finally, American pressure to democratize may alienate allies in the war on terror. Consider the dilemma posed to the Obama administration by the popular uprising in Egypt against the government of Hosni Mubarak. Even though Mubarak was a brutal dictator, his government worked closely with the United States in the war on terror. The United States welcomes the emergence of democracy in Egypt, but it is questionable whether a democratic government in Egypt will be as friendly to the interests of the United States as was the Mubarak government.

THE MEANS FOR ACHIEVING FOREIGN AND DEFENSE POLICY GOALS

The United States pursues its foreign and defense policy goals through military, economic, cultural, and diplomatic means. Since the end of World War II, the U.S. armed forces have intervened militarily in various countries around the world. The United States has also given military assistance in the form of arms and advisors to friendly governments fighting against forces hostile to the interests of the United States. For example, the United States has provided military aid to the government of Columbia to assist it in its war against guerrilla forces supported by international narcotics traffickers. After September 11, 2001, the United States supplied military aid, including American advisors, to the government of the Philippines to assist in the war against insurgent forces, which may have ties to al Qaeda.

Besides the actual use of military force, the United States has pursued its policy goals by forming defense alliances and transferring military hardware to other nations. Since the end of World War II, the United States has participated in a number of defense alliances, including NATO and SEATO (the Southeast Asia Treaty Organization). America is also the world's major distributor of weapons, accounting for 68 percent of weapons sales worldwide in 2008. Italy and Russia were second and third. The United Arab Emirates, Morocco, Taiwan, India, Iraq, Saudi Arabia, Egypt, South Korea, and Brazil are among the major purchasers of American arms.[12] Some international arms sales are private transactions between American firms and foreign governments. Most sales, however, are government-to-government transactions in which the U.S. Department of Defense acts as a purchasing agent for a foreign government wanting to buy American-made weapons.

The United States attempts to achieve foreign policy goals through economic means, such as trade and foreign aid. Trade can be used to improve international relations. For example, one method the United States employed to improve relations with China was to open the door to trade. In contrast, America has erected trade barriers against foreign governments it wishes to pressure or punish. For example, the United States attempts to isolate Cuba and North Korea economically. Trade sanctions could also be employed against Iran.

The United States uses foreign aid to achieve foreign policy goals. Although the United States is the world's largest donor, its level of giving as a share of national income is among the lowest among developed nations, less than half that of European countries.[13] The size of the foreign aid budget is relatively small, less than 1 percent of the federal budget, and most of the money goes to further the nation's foreign policy aims. In 2008, the primary recipients of U.S. foreign aid were, in order of importance, Iraq, Afghanistan, Israel, Egypt, and Colombia.[14] Each nation is important to American foreign policy. The United States is trying to build effective governments in Iraq and Afghanistan while American forces fight wars in those countries. Israel and Egypt are countries critical to Middle Eastern peace. Meanwhile, the United States assists Colombia in its war against drug traffickers and terrorists.

Foreign policy goals can sometimes be realized through cultural means, including the promotion of tourism and student exchanges, goodwill tours, and international athletic events. For example, the process of improving relations between the United States and China in the 1970s was facilitated by cultural exchanges. In fact, one of the first contacts between the two nations was the visit of an American table tennis team to China—"ping-pong diplomacy," it was called. The Olympic Games, meanwhile, are not just a sporting event but also a forum for nations to make political statements. The United States boycotted the 1980 Moscow Olympics to protest the Soviet invasion of Afghanistan. The Soviet Union returned the favor in 1984 by staying home when the games were held in Los Angeles.

Diplomacy The process by which nations carry on political relations with each other.

Finally, foreign policy goals can be achieved through **diplomacy,** which is the process by which nations carry on political relations with each other. Ambassadors and other embassy officials stationed abroad provide an ongoing link between governments. The UN, which is headquartered in New York City, offers a forum in which the world's nations can make diplomatic contacts, including countries that may not have diplomatic relations with one another. Diplomacy can also be pursued through special negotiations or summit meetings among national leaders.

The History of American Foreign and Defense Policy

American foreign policy is best understood within the context of its historical development.

From Isolationism to Internationalism

Isolationism The view that the United States should stay out of the affairs of other nations.

Monroe Doctrine A declaration of American foreign policy opposing any European intervention in the Western Hemisphere and affirming the American intention to refrain from interfering in European affairs.

For almost a century, the principal theme of American foreign policy toward Europe was **isolationism,** which is the view that the United States should minimize its interactions with other nations. In his farewell address in 1796, retiring President George Washington warned the nation to avoid "entangling alliances" with other countries. President James Monroe articulated the policy in his **Monroe Doctrine** of 1823, which was a declaration of American foreign policy opposing any European intervention in the Western Hemisphere and affirming the American intention to refrain from interfering in European affairs. The United States would stay out of European affairs; the Europeans must stay out of American affairs. Isolationism also had its practical side. The United States was far from a world power in the early nineteenth century. Americans devoted their energies to subduing and developing North America and did not welcome European interference. The American policy of isolationism had an aspect of arrogance in that the country wanted to avoid soiling itself by making alliances with colonial powers. Instead, the United States would serve as a moral example for them. Finally, isolationism contained an element of hypocrisy because it did not apply to American actions in the Western Hemisphere. The United States reserved for itself the right to interfere in the affairs of the nations of the Americas.

And interfere it did. America fought a war with Mexico in order to annex the area that is now California, Arizona, and New Mexico. President Theodore Roosevelt intervened in Colombia to create the nation of Panama so the United States could build a canal. In the twentieth century, America intervened militarily in several Latin American nations, including Cuba, El Salvador, Nicaragua, the Dominican Republic, Grenada, and Panama. The United States was involved indirectly in the political affairs of many other countries in the hemisphere, including Chile, Honduras, Venezuela, Guatemala, Ecuador, Brazil, and Guyana.

The United States began to break out of its isolationism toward nations outside the Western Hemisphere in the 1890s. The treaty that ended the Spanish-American War awarded the United States a colonial empire extending beyond this hemisphere to Guam and the Philippines. Furthermore, America had developed trading interests around the world that it wanted to protect. Eventually, World War I thrust the United States to the forefront of international affairs.

Between the two world wars, the United States once again turned inward. Part of the explanation for the return to isolationism was that President Woodrow Wilson (1913–1921), the wartime chief executive, had oversold World War I as "the war to end all wars" and "the war to make the world safe for democracy." The idealism faded in the midst of bloody war, and the international political haggling after the war disillusioned many Americans. Another reason for the focus on domestic affairs was the Great Depression. Americans looked inward as they sought to cope with the economic crisis.

By 1945, America's romance with isolationism had ended. Because of improved technology, isolationism was more difficult, if not impossible, to achieve. Modern communications and transportation had shrunk the world. More important, the United States emerged from World War II as a great power, militarily and economically. It was the only nation with nuclear weapons and the only major industrial country whose economic foundations had not been battered by war. With important military, political, and economic interests around the globe, the United States could no longer afford isolationism.

The Cold War and the Policy of Containment

The relationship between the United States and the Soviet Union was the dominant element of American foreign policy after World War II. Even though the United States and the Soviet Union had been wartime allies, the two nations began a bitter struggle for dominance in the international arena in the late 1940s. In the eyes of most Americans, the Soviets were determined to expand their control into Eastern Europe and Southeast Asia. In contrast, the Soviets regarded American actions, particularly Central Intelligence Agency (CIA) activities in Eastern Europe, as a threat to their national security.

The Cold War was an ideological and political struggle. It pitted communism against capitalism, and dictatorship against democracy. The leaders of both the United States and the Soviet Union pictured the international competition as a contest between different ways of life, one representing good and the other representing evil. The Cold War was also a bipolar (two-sided) struggle between the world's two remaining military superpowers. The other great powers of the prewar era—Germany, France, the United Kingdom, and Japan—had either been destroyed or weakened by the war. That left a political vacuum into which the war's survivors, the United States and the Soviet Union, sought to enter. As one observer phrased it, they were like two scorpions trapped in a jar. Tension and conflict were probably inevitable.

Truman Doctrine The foreign policy put forward by President Harry Truman calling for American support for all free peoples resisting communist aggression by internal or outside forces.

Containment The American policy of keeping the Soviet Union from expanding its sphere of control.

Balance of power A system of political alignments in which peace and security may be maintained among rival groups of nations.

Marshall Plan An American program that provided billions of dollars to the countries of Western Europe to rebuild their economies after World War II.

Sputnik The world's first satellite, launched by the Soviet Union.

President Harry Truman (1946–1953) first articulated America's response to the Soviet Union and the spread of communism. The **Truman Doctrine** was the foreign policy put forward by President Harry Truman calling for American support for all free peoples resisting communist aggression by internal or outside forces. In particular, Truman asked Congress to appropriate money for military and economic aid to Greece and Turkey to strengthen them against local communist insurgencies. Congress complied with the president's request.

The Truman Doctrine was part of the strategy of **containment,** which was the American policy of keeping the Soviet Union from expanding its sphere of control. The United States adopted the policy of containment for essentially the same reason it entered World War I and World War II—to preserve the balance of power in Europe and Asia. A **balance of power** is a system of political alignments in which peace and security may be maintained among rival groups of nations. America's leaders recognized that any nation controlling all of Europe and Asia would command more industrial power than the United States.[15] The United States had to intervene militarily in World War I and World War II to prevent rival powers from becoming stronger than the United States.

The policy of containment included several aspects. First, the United States gave economic assistance to nations threatened by communist subversion. The **Marshall Plan,** for example, was an American program that provided billions of dollars to the countries of Western Europe to rebuild their economies after World War II. The United States also adopted programs giving technical and economic aid to developing nations. Second, the United States devoted substantial resources to national defense, including the development of its nuclear forces. Finally, America offered military assistance to nations threatened by communism. Not only did the United States send weapons and financial aid to foreign countries, such as Greece and Turkey, but at times it also committed American fighting forces abroad in countries such as Korea and Vietnam.

In the early 1950s, the Cold War entered a new phase. Before then, the struggle between the United States and the Soviet Union had been waged on the perimeters of Soviet influence—Eastern Europe, Berlin, China, Indochina, and Korea. In the 1950s, Nikita Khrushchev, an imaginative new Soviet leader, adopted a different tactic. The Soviets leapfrogged the old lines to push their cause into Cuba, Egypt, the Congo, Indonesia, and elsewhere in the developing world, well behind the American wall of containment. Furthermore, the Soviets had developed nuclear weapons and, with the launch of the ***Sputnik*** satellite in 1957, demonstrated that they were ahead of the United States in missile technology.

The Cuban missile crisis of 1962 was the climactic event of the Cold War. Despite launching the world's first satellite, the Soviet Union remained clearly inferior to the United States in nuclear weaponry. To close the gap, Khrushchev decided to install missiles in Cuba, just 90 miles from American soil. When the United States discovered the Soviet move, President John Kennedy responded with a naval blockade. The stage was set for a nuclear confrontation, but the Soviets backed down, withdrawing their missiles. The two nations were eyeball-to-eyeball on the brink of nuclear war, said Secretary of State Dean Rusk, and the Soviets blinked.

The Cuban missile crisis brought the United States and the Soviet Union to the brink of war.

Détente

Détente A period of improved communications and visible efforts to relieve tensions between the two superpowers.

Convergence theory The view that communism and capitalism were evolving in similar ways, or converging.

The Cuban missile crisis may have had a sobering effect on the leaders of the United States and the Soviet Union. In the late 1960s and early 1970s, the two superpowers entered an era of improved relations known as **Détente,** which was a period of improved communications and visible efforts to relieve tensions between the two superpowers. The United States and Soviet Union increased trade and cultural relations, and exchanged scientific information in such fields as cancer research, weather forecasting, and space exploration. Some observers promoted a **convergence theory,** the view that communism and capitalism were evolving in similar ways, or converging. As communism and capitalism became more alike they would no longer be a threat to one another.[16]

Perhaps the most important aspect of Détente was arms control. Both the United States and the Soviet Union found advantage in slowing the arms race. Arms control saved money and, perhaps, reduced the probability of nuclear war. It was also good domestic politics, certainly in the United States and probably in the Soviet Union as well.

During the 1960s and 1970s, the United States and the Soviet Union agreed on a number of important arms-control measures. In 1963, the two superpowers and Great Britain signed a treaty prohibiting the aboveground testing of nuclear

Nuclear Non-Proliferation Treaty An international agreement designed to prevent the spread of nuclear weapons.

weapons. Subsequently, the United States and the Soviet Union agreed to ban nuclear weapons from the ocean floor. In 1968, they signed the **Nuclear Non-Proliferation Treaty,** which is an international agreement designed to prevent the spread of nuclear weapons. Under terms of the treaty, the five nations that then possessed nuclear weapons (the United States, the Soviet Union, China, France, and Great Britain) agreed not to deliver nuclear weapons or weapons technology to other nations; non-nuclear countries agreed not to seek or develop nuclear weapons. All of the world's nations, including Iran, are parties to the Nuclear Non-Proliferation Treaty except for Cuba, Israel, India, and Pakistan. North Korea signed the treaty but subsequently withdrew after the United States accused it of having a weapons program.[17] Iran stands accused of violating the treaty. Although North Korea is no longer a party to the treaty, the international community is in general agreement that a nuclear North Korea would be a threat to world peace.

In 1969, the United States and the Soviet Union began the Strategic Arms Limitation Talks (SALT), a series of negotiations designed to control nuclear weapons, delivery systems, and related offensive and defensive weapons systems. In 1972, the two nations agreed to the Anti-Ballistic Missile (ABM) Treaty to limit the deployment of ABM systems, which are designed to destroy enemy missiles carrying nuclear weapons. The treaty also established a five-year moratorium on the placement of additional land- and sea-based missiles.

Ten years later, a second round of negotiations, known as SALT II, produced another arms agreement, setting limits on weapons, missiles, and long-range bombers. The SALT II treaty, however, never came to a vote in the U.S. Senate. Treaty opponents, including then presidential candidate Ronald Reagan, argued that the United States had given up too much. Furthermore, Détente was ending as a result of the Soviet invasion of Afghanistan and the beginning of a substantial American military buildup.

In retrospect, Détente was probably overrated by a world eager to find signs of peace in a nuclear age. Similarly, convergence theory was more wishful thinking than it was an accurate assessment of reality. The United States and the Soviet Union had vastly different historical, cultural, political, and economic backgrounds. Each nation had interests around the globe and those interests sometimes clashed. Détente was a period of better communications between the superpowers that eased tensions, but it was naive to expect Détente to bring an end to international conflict.

American Foreign Policy in the 1970s: Recognition of Limits

During the 1970s, the administrations of Presidents Richard Nixon, Gerald Ford, and Jimmy Carter attempted to adapt American foreign policy to the realities of a changing, more complex world and adjust to what they saw as the long-term decline of American economic and military power. Nixon and Henry Kissinger, who was chief foreign policy advisor to both Presidents Nixon and Ford, spoke of the end of the postwar world and emphasized what they called a realistic foreign policy, designed to control America's descent into an uncertain future. The Nixon-Ford-Kissinger foreign policy sought to maintain American interests and commitments abroad but

Nixon Doctrine A corollary to the policy of containment that declared that if the United States would help small nations threatened by communist aggression with economic and military aid, those countries must play a major role in their own defense.

at a reduced cost. The cornerstone of this policy was the **Nixon Doctrine,** which was a corollary to the policy of containment. Although the United States would help small nations threatened by communist aggression with economic and military aid, those countries must play a major role in their own defense.

Foreign policy during the Carter administration also reflected an understanding that the international system had changed since the 1950s. Carter's restrained response to the hostage crisis in Iran showed that the president recognized the limits of American power. The Panama Canal Treaty, which provided for the eventual return of sovereignty over the canal to the government of Panama, represented an accommodation to the concerns of Latin America.

The Carter administration's foreign policy stressed the importance of human rights. Carter declared that American trade, aid, and alliances would be based at least in part on the way other governments treated their own citizens. The policy had both an idealistic and a practical side. In the aftermath of the Vietnam War, Carter wanted to return an air of morality to American foreign policy. The United States would have a "foreign policy as good as the American people," Carter promised. From a practical standpoint, the president hoped to pressure repressive noncommunist governments to reform their policies. Carter recognized that dictatorships are politically unstable. They invite subversion, increasing opportunities for communist influence.

Carter's critics argued that the principle of human rights was too simplistic a doctrine on which to base a global foreign policy strategy. What if American security interests and human rights conflict? Would the administration sacrifice United States defense interests in South Korea, for example, in the name of human rights? The answer turned out to be no, leaving the Carter administration open to charges of hypocrisy. Furthermore, many observers believed that the policy reflected an arrogant attitude toward the rest of the world. It seemed that Carter had adopted the role of a missionary, helping the poor abroad and bringing American values to those who suffer in the dark.[18]

American Foreign Policy in the 1980s: A Resurgent America

Reagan Doctrine A corollary to the policy of containment enunciated by President Reagan calling for the United States to offer military aid to groups attempting to overthrow communist governments anywhere in the world.

When Ronald Reagan became president, he promised an end to the self-doubt and decline that had infected United States foreign policy in the 1970s. The problem, Reagan charged, lay not with America but with its leaders. Reagan spoke optimistically of a resurgent United States, which he called, quoting Abraham Lincoln, "the last, best hope of man on earth." In contrast, he branded the Soviet Union "the evil empire."

Reagan based his foreign policy on firm opposition to communism. He regarded world politics as a bipolar rivalry between the United States and the Soviet Union, and he left no doubt who the bad guys were. The Soviet leaders, Reagan declared, reserved for themselves the right "to lie, to cheat, to commit any crime." To meet the challenge, Reagan called for a resolute national will and a military buildup.

The centerpiece of the president's foreign policy was known as the **Reagan Doctrine,** which was a corollary to the policy of containment enunciated by

President Reagan calling for the United States to offer military aid to groups attempting to overthrow communist governments anywhere in the world. Reagan offered military assistance to "liberation forces" in Nicaragua, Afghanistan, and Angola. In this fashion, Reagan aimed to increase the cost to the Soviet Union for what the president considered to be its policy of exporting revolution. Reagan hoped that the Soviets would eventually have to choose between reducing their commitments abroad and economic collapse at home. Rejecting the Carter emphasis on human rights, Reagan offered practically unconditional support to anticommunist governments, even those that were undemocratic.

During his first term in office, Reagan rejected the idea that the United States should adapt its policies to a changing international environment. Reagan asked Congress for a substantial increase in defense spending and began to flex American military muscle abroad. Reagan ordered an invasion of the Caribbean country of Grenada to overthrow a government friendly to Cuba. He directed air strikes against the North African nation of Libya in retaliation for that country's alleged support of terrorism. He ordered American naval vessels to escort Kuwaiti oil tankers through the Persian Gulf, protecting them from attacks by Iran.

By the mid-1980s, however, the key feature of American foreign policy was once again caution. In a number of crisis situations, the Reagan administration responded with restraint. The United States reacted to an apparently accidental Iraqi missile attack against the *U.S.S. Stark*, an American naval vessel, by taking no action. (In those days, the United States and Iraqi President Saddam Hussein were friends.) Similarly, the administration responded to a terrorist bombing in Beirut, Lebanon, that killed more than 200 marines by withdrawing American forces. Although the White House often talked tough, the substance of Reagan's foreign policies increasingly resembled the policies of the 1970s that Reagan had so roundly criticized. On arms control, for example, the Reagan administration generally adhered to the weapons limits set by SALT II even though the treaty was never ratified. Furthermore, by the mid-1980s, the United States and the Soviet Union were engaged in serious negotiations aimed at arms control and arms reductions. As for the Reagan Doctrine, the administration continued to support the Contras in Nicaragua and other anticommunist forces, but it changed its policy of unconditional support for anticommunist dictators. In both the Philippines and Haiti, the administration backed local efforts to oust unpopular dictators in favor of reform-minded democratic governments.

Several factors were behind the modifications in President Reagan's foreign policy focus. First, Congress was unwilling to support all of the president's foreign policy initiatives. Congress consistently refused to give the Contras as much aid as Reagan requested. By Reagan's second term, Congress's willingness to fund the president's military buildup had evaporated. Second, public opinion did not support all aspects of Reagan's foreign policies. Although the president's vision of an America standing tall was popular, surveys found substantial opposition to American military involvement in Nicaragua and other trouble spots. Many Americans feared a confrontation with the Soviet Union. Also, polls taken in the mid-1980s showed that a majority of Americans believed the United States was spending enough money for defense. Finally, firsthand experience in dealing with the realities of international affairs forced Reagan to modify his foreign policy focus. Once in office, President Reagan found that dealing with terrorism and hostage taking was as difficult for him as it had been for President Carter.[19]

The End of the Cold War

In the late 1980s, a new Soviet leader, Mikhail Gorbachev, recognized that the Soviet system was failing. Although the Soviet Union was a military superpower, its economy was a shambles. Gorbachev reasoned that economic reforms would not succeed unless some of the enormous human and material resources devoted to the Soviet military could be diverted to the domestic economy. In order to make this shift in priorities possible, Gorbachev proposed "New Thinking" in foreign and defense policy to ease tensions with the West and reduce Soviet commitments abroad. Gorbachev declared that the Soviet Union would not intervene militarily in the internal affairs of other nations and ordered the withdrawal of Soviet military units from Afghanistan where they had been fighting a protracted guerrilla war against anticommunist rebels. Gorbachev also announced significant reductions in Soviet defense spending and called for the negotiation of arms control and arms reduction treaties with the United States.

The new direction in Soviet foreign policy led to a change in the status of Eastern Europe. For decades after the end of World War II, the Soviet Union held the nations of Eastern Europe as political satellites, intervening politically and militarily to ensure communist party rule. The primary purpose of the policy was to maintain a buffer between the Soviet Union and Western Europe, which in modern times has been the main source of invasion against Russia. Gorbachev decided, however, that the Soviet Union could no longer afford to maintain satellites. He ordered Soviet forces to withdraw from Eastern Europe and encouraged the nations of the region to adopt political and economic reforms.

Although the opening of the Berlin Wall may have been the single most dramatic development, nearly every nation in the region underwent major change. Without the backing of the Soviet military, one-party communist regimes in one country after another collapsed under popular pressure to be replaced by reform governments promising democratic elections, individual freedom, and fewer economic controls. In fact, most of the nations of Eastern Europe adopted more extensive economic and political reforms than were then in place in the Soviet Union.[20]

In the meantime, the Soviet Union began to break up. Many of the Republics that comprised the Soviet Union had different histories and cultures than Russia, the largest Soviet republic, and resented Russian domination. When given the opportunity for political change, a number of Soviet republics, including Lithuania, Estonia, Belarus, Georgia, and the Ukraine, declared their independence from Russian control. In late 1991, Russia and some of the other republics dissolved the Soviet Union. With the dissolution of the Soviet Union, leadership passed from Gorbachev to Boris Yeltsin, the president of the Russian Republic, and the heads of the other republics.

The disintegration of the Soviet Union ended the Cold War. Russia and the other Republics that once composed the Soviet Union lacked the resources or the desire to continue the conflict with the West, focusing instead on creating new economic and political institutions. In exchange for its retreat from its external empire, Russia sought access to the global economy. In particular, Yeltsin requested western economic aid and investment.

The end of the Cold War changed the basic premise of American foreign and defense policy. From the late 1940s until the early 1990s, the overriding purpose of U.S. policy was to prevail against a perceived threat to the nation's survival presented by international communism and the Soviet Union. The collapse of the Soviet Union left the United States as the world's single dominant military superpower. After the collapse of the Soviet Union, developing nations in Latin America, Africa, Asia, and Eastern Europe turned to the American model of political and economic development. During the Cold War era, authoritarian communism and capitalist democracy competed for the allegiance of non-aligned countries. During the 1990s, military governments and one-party governments around the world were replaced through the electoral process. Even Russia turned to democracy. Meanwhile, Russia, China, and other countries that had once been part of the communist bloc opened their economies to international trade and investment, creating a **global economy,** which is the integration of national economies into a world economic system in which companies compete worldwide for suppliers and markets.

Global economy The integration of national economies into a world economic system in which companies compete worldwide for suppliers and markets.

9/11 and the War on Terror

The war on terror began on September 11, 2001, when terrorists took over four American passenger airplanes. They flew two of them into the World Trade Center towers in New York City and a third into the Pentagon in Washington, DC. A fourth plane crashed in Pennsylvania after passengers fought back against the hijackers. The events of 9/11, as the date is popularly known, changed the environment for American foreign and defense policy by demonstrating that the United States was vulnerable to attack despite its status as the world's sole superpower. No nation could match American military might, but international terror organizations such as al Qaeda could inflict significant casualties and seriously disrupt the world economy.

The war on terror raises a number of important issues for American policymakers to address:

- **Fighting international terrorism.** Terror organizations do not have home countries. The challenge for the U.S. armed forces is to find and root out terrorist organizations before they can strike against Western interests. After 9/11, the United States and its allies invaded Afghanistan to overthrow the Taliban government because it was either unwilling or unable to expel the al Qaeda terrorist forces operating from Afghan soil. Allied forces easily forced the Taliban from power, but most Taliban and al Qaeda fighters escaped in rugged, lawless territory along the Afghan-Pakistani border. The Taliban soon regrouped and launched an insurgency against the new Afghan government and allied forces. In 2010, the American military commander in the region warned that the war was in danger of being lost. President Obama ordered an additional 30,000 troops to the region, bringing the total American force commitment to nearly 100,000.

- **Controlling the spread of weapons of mass destruction (WMD).** In 2003, President George W. Bush ordered U.S. forces to invade Iraq and overthrow the government of Saddam Hussein even though Iraq had had nothing to do with 9/11. Bush believed that Iraq had WMD and worried that Saddam would share them with enemies of the United States. Al Qaeda with a nuclear weapon would be a potential catastrophe. As it turned out, Iraq did not have WMD. Moreover, the United States soon became embroiled in a protracted war against insurgents.

Failed state
A nation-state whose government no longer effectively functions and has lost control of a significant portion of its territory.

- **Preventing the development of failed states.** A **failed state** is a nation-state whose government no longer effectively functions and has lost control of a significant portion of its territory. Failed states can become havens for terrorist groups, may threaten regional security, and may disrupt regional economies. The United States has not yet pulled out of Iraq and Afghanistan because American policymakers worry that they might become failed states if American forces leave before their governments are ready.
- **Limiting regional conflicts.** The United States has an interest in resolving regional conflicts in the Middle East, Southeast Asia, Africa, and elsewhere because they disrupt regional economies and provide opportunities for terror groups to establish footholds.
- **Dealing with rogue states.** Rogue states, such as Iran and North Korea, are a threat to world peace because they sponsor international terrorism and threaten to spread WMD.

American Foreign Policy

American policymakers generally agree that the United States must be closely engaged in world affairs not just to protect its economic interests abroad but also to guard the American homeland against assault by terrorist groups or rogue states. Policymakers also concur that the United States should exert leadership in international affairs because it is the world's foremost military and economic power. As former secretary of state Madeleine Albright phrased it, the United States is the world's "indispensable nation" in that its participation is essential to solving the world's military, economic, and humanitarian problems.[21] Policymakers disagree, however, on how closely the United States should work with its allies and the other nations of the world.

Some policymakers believe that the United States should follow a unilateralist approach to achieving its foreign policy goals, acting alone if necessary. The advocates of the unilateralist approach argue that the United States should cooperate with international agreements only so far as they benefit America. Because the United States has the world's most powerful military and largest economy, it can assert itself internationally. Other nations will have no choice but to accept the leadership of the United States and adapt to American preferences.[22]

President George W. Bush pursued a unilateralist foreign policy, at least during his first term. Bush justified attacking Iraq without UN support because the United States believed that Saddam Hussein had WMD that he could give to terrorists who could then use them to kill tens of thousands of Americans. "When it comes to our security," said Bush, "we really don't need anybody's permission."[23] Similarly, the Bush administration rejected a series of global agreements that enjoyed overwhelming international support, including the Global Warming Treaty, Biological Diversity Treaty, Land Mine Ban Treaty, and the International Criminal Court. The United States refused to ratify the **Global Warming Treaty,** which is an international agreement to reduce the worldwide emissions of carbon dioxide and other greenhouse gases, because it believed that the treaty put too much of the burden for reducing emissions on the United States. It rejected the Biological Diversity Treaty because it argued that the agreement did not go far enough to protect the patent rights of bioengineering companies. The United States opposed the Land Mine Treaty because it claimed that it needed land mines to protect American troops in South Korea. The United States rejected the International Criminal Court Treaty because it did not want Americans subject to international criminal court prosecution.

Global Warming Treaty An international agreement to reduce the worldwide emissions of carbon dioxide and other greenhouse gases.

Other policymakers believe that the United States should take an internationalist approach to achieving its foreign policy goals by working in close concert with the global community. After World War II, the United States and its allies established the UN, NATO, the IMF, and other international institutions to keep the peace, deter aggression, and promote economic development. The advocates of an internationalist approach to American foreign policy believe that the United States should work with these institutions and with its allies to address the problems of international terrorism, nuclear proliferation, and rogue states.

President Obama favors an internationalist foreign policy, reversing many of the policies of the George W. Bush administration. The themes of the Obama administration are partnership, engagement, and common interests with other nations. President Obama has made it clear that the United States will approach international issues from a perspective of cooperation with other countries—not just with America's traditional allies in Western Europe and Japan, but also with emerging global powers such as China, India, Russia, Brazil, Turkey, Indonesia, and South Africa. The Obama administration has also been trying to engage countries with whom the United States has had poor relations, especially in the Muslim world, including Syria and even Iran. Furthermore, President Obama delivered an address in Cairo, Egypt, during his first year in office in which he discussed the various issues of contention between the United States and the Muslim world and spoke of the need for dialogue and understanding.[24]

WHAT IS YOUR OPINION?

If necessary, should the United States act on its own to achieve its foreign policy and defense goals, even if its allies disagree with the action?

American Defense Policy

The nineteenth-century military strategist Karl von Clausewitz once described war as "diplomacy by other means." He meant that defense concerns and foreign policy issues are closely related. Foreign policy goals determine defense strategies. Military capabilities, meanwhile, influence a nation's foreign policy by expanding or limiting the options available to policymakers.

Defense Spending

Gross domestic product (GDP) The value of goods and services produced by a nation's economy in a year, excluding transactions with foreign countries.

Figure 17.1 depicts U.S. defense spending from 1950 through 2010 as a percentage of the **gross domestic product (GDP),** which is the total value of goods and services produced by a nation's economy in a year, excluding transactions with foreign countries. In general, defense spending increases during wartime and falls during peacetime. Defense expenditures peaked relative to the size of the economy during the Korean War in the early 1950s and the Vietnam War in the late 1960s. After the end of both the Korean and Vietnam conflicts, defense spending fell. The only exception to the pattern of rising defense spending during wartime and falling defense expenditures during peacetime occurred during the early 1980s when President Reagan proposed, and Congress passed, the largest peacetime increase in military spending in the nation's history. Defense spending fell again in the 1990s after the collapse of the Soviet Union and the end of the Cold War. Since 9/11, defense

President Obama delivered an address in Cairo, Egypt, during his first year in office in which he discussed the various issues of contention between the United States and the western world and spoke of the need for dialogue and understanding.

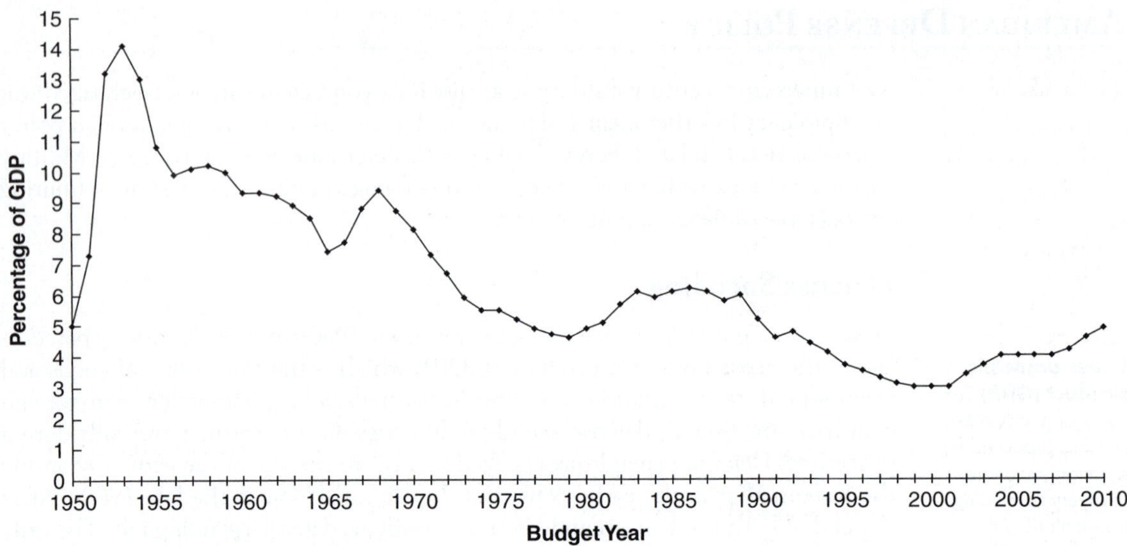

FIGURE 17.1 Defense Spending as Percentage of GDP.
Source: Office of Management and Budget.

expenditures have increased as Congress and the president fund the war on terror as well as military operations in Afghanistan and Iraq.

Defense Forces and Strategy

Strategic forces Nuclear forces.

Conventional forces Non-nuclear forces.

Mutual assured destruction (MAD) The belief that the United States and the Soviet Union would be deterred from launching a nuclear assault against each other for fear of being destroyed in a general nuclear war.

America's defense strategy is based on **strategic (*nuclear*) forces** and **conventional (*non-nuclear*) forces.**

Strategic Forces The United States has 5,000 nuclear weapons.[25] More than half are currently active and deployed, ready to be carried to their targets through a variety of delivery systems. The Air Force can deliver at least 320 nuclear missiles by plane—B-52s or B-2s. The Navy has more than 2,000 nuclear missiles on submarines, with at least a third of the subs on patrol at any one time. The Army has 1,450 nuclear weapons configured for cruise missile delivery. Other missiles sit in silos located in 12 states and 6 European countries, ready for launch.[26] In late 2010 and early 2011, the United States and Russia ratified the New Strategic Arms Reduction Treaty (START) that reduces the number of deployed nuclear weapons in each country to 1,500 to 2,200 while lowering the number of delivery vehicles to a figure between 500 and 1,100.[27] President Obama believes that the United States can maintain its security despite the reductions by relying more heavily on missile defense and by improving the reliability and accuracy of its remaining missiles.[28]

Many defense theorists believe that nuclear weapons promoted world peace during the Cold War because no national leader acting rationally would risk initiating a nuclear holocaust. This concept was formalized in the doctrine of **mutual assured destruction (MAD),** which was the belief that the United States and the

Around the World

Nuclear Weapons in Pakistan

Pakistan became a nuclear power in 1998 when it successfully tested several nuclear weapons. International observers believe that it has as many as 100 nuclear devices.* Pakistan has also purchased or developed medium-range ballistic missiles that are capable of striking cities in neighboring India.

Pakistan developed nuclear weapons to achieve military parity with India and to gain international prestige as a nuclear power. Pakistan and India are longstanding enemies, having fought three wars since 1948. The two nations remain locked in a bitter dispute over control of the border region of Kashmir. Pakistan began a nuclear program in the early 1970s to match India's nuclear program and to offset India's advantage in conventional weapons. By developing nuclear weapons, Pakistan hopes to establish itself as a regional power and to claim leadership of the Muslim world as the first Muslim nation to have the bomb.

The United States opposes Pakistan's nuclear weapons program because of the danger that the next war between Pakistan and India will be a nuclear war and because of the fear that Pakistani nuclear weapons may fall into the hands of terrorists. The government of Pakistan is unstable and senior officials in the Pakistani military are known for being sympathetic with the former Taliban government of Afghanistan and with Osama bin Laden. The United States responded to Pakistan's nuclear tests in 1998 by imposing economic sanctions in hopes of convincing the Pakistani government that the price of nuclear weapons was too high, but Pakistan refused to change course. After September 11, 2001, the United States lifted the sanctions in exchange for Pakistani cooperation in the war against the Taliban government of Afghanistan and the fight against Osama bin Laden's terrorist network.†

QUESTIONS

1. Does Pakistan having nuclear weapons make war between Pakistan and India more likely or less likely? Explain the reasoning behind your answer.
2. Is the United States hypocritical to oppose nuclear weapons in Pakistan, considering that the United States is the world's foremost nuclear power?
3. Is a nuclear Pakistan a threat to world peace? Why or why not?

*Joby Warrick, "Nuclear Experts Say Pakistan May Be Building 4th Plutonium Reactor," *Washington Post,* February 9, 2011, available at www.washingtonpost.com.

†Farzana Shaikh, "Pakistan's Nuclear Bomb: Beyond the Non-Proliferation Regime," *International Affairs* 78 (January 2002): 29–48.

Nuclear winter The concept that a nuclear war would throw so much dust and debris into the atmosphere as to produce a long period of darkness and cold, destroying agriculture and killing millions of people.

Soviet Union would be deterred from launching a nuclear assault against each other for fear of being destroyed in a general nuclear war. In the 1980s, scientists developed the concept of a nuclear winter to describe the impact of a nuclear exchange on the planet. **Nuclear winter** is the concept that a nuclear war would throw so much dust and debris into the atmosphere as to produce a long period of darkness and cold, destroying agriculture and killing millions of people.[29] The concept of nuclear winter implies that a nuclear war would be unwinnable. Even if one country were able to destroy the other country without suffering a single retaliatory strike, the environmental damage from the nuclear attack would be catastrophic to the entire planet, including the country that won the nuclear war. The threat of nuclear winter also underscores the importance of preventing regional nuclear wars, such as a nuclear exchange between Pakistan and India, because of their threat to the global environment.

Deterrence The ability of a nation to prevent an attack against itself or its allies by threat of massive retaliation.

Massive retaliation The concept that the United States will strike back against an aggressor with overwhelming force.

Deterrence was the organizing principle of American defense policy during the Cold War. It was the ability of a nation to prevent an attack against itself or its allies by threat of **massive retaliation,** which is the concept that the United States will strike back against an aggressor with overwhelming force. American leaders often explained the concept of deterrence with the phrase "peace through strength." By preparing for war, the United States would ensure the peace. Weaker nations would be deterred from attacking the United States because America enjoyed military superiority. In the meantime, the United States and the Soviet Union would be deterred from attacking each other because both countries possessed nuclear arsenals capable of destroying the other. Deterrence worked to prevent nuclear war during the Cold War because both the United States and the Soviet Union believed that the other side had an effective second-strike capability. The Soviet Union did not dare launch an attack against the United States (and vice versa) because Soviet leaders believed that enough American nuclear forces would survive the initial Soviet strike to destroy their country.

Deterrence is an imperfect defense strategy in the post-Cold War world because of rogue states and, especially, terrorist organizations. Although deterrence continues to be an effective defense strategy against the threat of attack by Russia or China, some defense analysts believe that deterrence may be ineffective against rogue states whose leaders are sometimes prone to engage in high risk behavior. Terrorist organizations, meanwhile, are unlikely to be deterred by threat of massive retaliation because they lack a home base that the United States could attack.[30]

Military preemption The defense policy that declares that the United States will attack nations or groups that represent a potential threat to the security of the United States.

President George W. Bush responded to the terrorist attacks of September 11, 2001, by announcing that the United States had adopted the policy of **military preemption,** which is the defense policy that declares that the United States will attack nations or groups that represent a potential threat to the security of the United States. Under certain circumstances, military preemption could even involve the United States using nuclear weapons against a potential enemy threat. President Bush justified the policy of military preemption as follows:

> Given the goals of rogue states and terrorists, the United States can no longer solely rely on a reactive posture as we have in the past. The inability to deter a potential attacker, the immediacy of today's threats, and the magnitude of potential harm that could be caused by our adversaries' choice of weapons, do not permit that option. We cannot let our enemies strike first.[31]

The American attack against Iraq to overthrow the regime of Saddam Hussein was the first application of the doctrine of military preemption. The United States went to war not because Iraq posed an immediate threat to national security, but because of the possibility that Iraq could give weapons of mass destruction to terrorists. "The people of the United States will not live at the mercy of an outlaw regime that threatens the peace with weapons of mass murder," said Bush.

The policy of military preemption is controversial, especially against rogue states. Critics question the assertion that deterrence is ineffective against rogue states. The leaders of Iran, North Korea, and other enemies of the United States

The United States based its invasion of Iraq on the doctrine of military preemption.

are not suicidal. Overwhelming military force deters rogue states as effectively as it does other nations. Just because American policymakers may not always understand Iranian or North Korean politics does not mean that those nations or their leaders behave irrationally.[32] Saddam Hussein was an evil dictator, but was he really an immediate threat to the United States? Critics also warn that the consistent application of the doctrine of military preemption would involve the United States in perpetual war. Iran and North Korea have greater weapons capability than Iraq had. Does the United States plan to go to war against those nations just as it did Iraq? Finally, the critics of military preemption worry that other nations will use the doctrine to justify attacking their neighbors.[33]

Conventional Forces For decades, the United States maintained a large standing army in order to defend against a possible conventional arms attack by the Soviet Union in Western Europe. More than 2 million men and women served in the U.S. armed forces through the 1980s. After the end of the Cold War, the United States scaled back its conventional forces, cutting the size of its armed forces sharply in the early 1990s. With the dissolution of the Soviet Union, the chances of great armies clashing on the scale of World War II were remote. The United States instead was more likely to be embroiled in **asymmetrical warfare,** which is a conflict in which the military capabilities of the two belligerents differ significantly, such as the current conflict in Afghanistan. Nonetheless, the United States kept the basic structure of a large military intact, with 1.4 million troops in uniform. Pentagon planners believed that substantial military forces were still needed to fulfill the mission of fighting

Asymmetrical warfare A conflict in which the military capabilities of the two belligerents differ significantly.

regional wars, promoting regional stability, keeping the peace, and participating in humanitarian relief efforts.

Donald Rumsfeld, the secretary of defense in the George W. Bush administration from 2001 through the end of 2006, advocated restructuring the U.S. military. He believed that the U.S. armed forces could accomplish their mission by relying on speed, mobility, and firepower rather than a large army, as was characteristic of twentieth-century warfare.[34] Rumsfeld put his theory into action in Afghanistan, where American airpower, including an unmanned aircraft called the Predator, defeated Taliban and al Qaeda forces by using precision weapons operating at extremely long range, with targeting information gathered on the ground, in the air, and from space. American troops on the ground initially served as spotters for airpower and acted as liaison to local Afghan militia. The United States employed a similar strategy in Iraq, using highly mobile ground forces to slice through Iraqi defenses by use of overwhelming firepower, much of it delivered by air.

Rumsfeld's critics believe that the United States still needs substantial conventional forces and that, in fact, the U.S. military is too small. Although firepower and mobility enabled the United States to defeat the Taliban and the Iraqi army in short order, American forces were insufficient to stabilize either nation. As a result, the United States and its allies remained embroiled in protracted warfare against insurgent forces in both Afghanistan and Iraq years after the initial invasion.

Making Foreign and Defense Policy

International events are the most important environmental factors affecting foreign and defense policymaking. During the Cold War, American foreign and defense policies were formulated, adopted, legitimized, implemented, and evaluated in light of the perceived threat of international communism. The Cold War shaped international diplomacy, alliances, defense budgets, and defense strategy. Today, the most important event for shaping American foreign and defense policy was the terrorist attack of September 11, 2001.

Survey research shows that although most Americans support an active role for the United States in world affairs, the general public is more cautious about American involvement abroad than are policy leaders in government, the media, business, and academia. For example, the general public is less supportive of foreign aid and immigration than are policy leaders. The public is also less willing than policy leaders to endorse the use of the U.S. armed forces to defend American interests abroad.[35]

Agenda Setting

Events, public opinion, the media, interest groups, Congress, and the president all play a role in setting the agenda for foreign and defense policymaking. Some issues become important items on the policy agenda because of media coverage of dramatic international events, such as the bombing of Pearl Harbor, the launch of *Sputnik*, or 9/11. Events affect the agenda for foreign and defense policymaking because

GETTING INVOLVED

America in the Eyes of the World

What do people in other countries think about the United States? Do they love America or hate it? Do they fear it or respect it? Are they envious or admiring? The class project is to interview international students and other foreign nationals about the perceptions held by people in their home countries about the United States. Note that the assignment is not to ask international students *their* opinion about the United States because they may be uncomfortable expressing anything other than positive points of view. Instead, class members should ask international students about the attitudes of people back home in their country. International students who are part of the class can take the lead, interviewing their friends and helping American students understand the information they receive.

The interviews should focus on the following subject areas:

- **Culture.** How influential is American culture (television, films, music, etc.) in your country? Do people admire American culture or does it offend them? Do they worry that American culture will overwhelm their own culture?
- **Economics.** Do people in your country believe that they benefit from the economic power of the United States or do they think that they are hurt economically by the United States?
- **Foreign policy.** What do people in your country think about American foreign policy? Do they consider the United States to be a force for good or do they believe the United States acts unfairly in its own interest? Do they think that the United States is a bully? Has the election of Barack Obama had an effect on how people think about the United States?

After the interviews are complete, the instructor will ask the students to discuss what they learned from the activity. In which of the three areas (culture, economics, and foreign policy) were attitudes about the United States the most positive? In which area were they the least positive? How did points of view vary from region to region? Finally, why do people from other nations think as they do about the United States?

of their impact on public opinion. When the Soviet Union launched the *Sputnik* satellite, for example, the American scientific and educational communities became alarmed that the United States was falling behind the Soviet Union in science education and space technology.

Many interest groups participate in foreign and defense policymaking. Dozens of corporations and their employee unions lobby on behalf of weapons systems in which they have a financial interest. Corporate and trade groups focus on trade policy, either seeking protection from foreign competition or working against restrictive trade policies that could threaten their import or export businesses. Environmental groups emphasize international environmental issues, such as global warming and resource conservation. Ethnic groups—African Americans, Mexican Americans, Cuban Americans, Greek Americans, Chinese Americans, Arab Americans, and Jewish Americans—take an interest in foreign policies affecting regions of the world that are of particular interest to them. The American Jewish community, for example, is concerned about policy toward Israel and the Arab world. Likewise, Cuban Americans focus on U.S. policy toward Cuba.

Historically, the president has taken the lead in foreign and defense policy matters.[36] In 1947, for instance, the Truman administration convinced congressional leaders that U.S. aid for Greece and Turkey was essential to American security. During the 1960s and 1970s, a series of presidents and a procession of Department of State and Pentagon spokespersons worked to persuade Congress and the nation of the importance of American intervention in Vietnam. After 9/11, President George W. Bush announced a new American policy of military preemption, and focused the world's attention on the goal of disarming Iraq. Bush used his second inaugural address to emphasize that democratization had become the principal goal of American foreign policy.

Bipartisanship A close cooperation and general agreement between the two major political parties in dealing with foreign policy matters.

During the Cold War, presidents could generally count on bipartisan support for foreign policy issues. **Bipartisanship** is the close cooperation and general agreement between the two major political parties in dealing with foreign policy matters. Democrats and Republicans alike agreed that Soviet expansion was the primary threat to American interests and that deterrence and containment were the appropriate strategy to counter the threat. Congressional consensus on foreign policy and defense policy issues has become much less frequent since the end of the Cold War.[37] Consider the controversy over the war in Iraq. When the president ordered the U.S. military to invade Iraq to overthrow Saddam Hussein, Congress offered support and voted to provide additional money to fund the war and help rebuild Iraq. As the situation in Iraq worsened and public opinion began to turn against the war, individual members of Congress spoke out against administration policies and congressional committees initiated investigations of the Iraqi prisoner abuse scandal at Abu Ghraib Prison, and over allegations the Halliburton and other private contractors had overcharged the U.S. government for work performed in Iraq. After Democrats won control of Congress in the 2006 election, congressional opposition to the war increased. Although Congress continued to fund operations, Democratic leaders spoke out against the war and attempted to enact legislation to force the Bush administration to set a timetable for withdrawing American forces.

Policy Formulation, Adoption, and Legitimation

The president and Congress share constitutional authority to formulate and adopt foreign and defense policy. The president negotiates treaties, but the Senate must ratify them. The president has the power of diplomatic recognition, but the Senate must confirm ambassadorial appointments. The president can request money for foreign aid and defense, but Congress must appropriate the funds. The president is commander-in-chief of the armed forces, but Congress declares war. Congress also has the constitutional authority to raise and support armies and a navy.

The president often initiates foreign and defense policies, with Congress acting to modify or, occasionally, reject policies formulated in the executive branch. This division of labor has developed for a number of reasons. First, the executive branch is better equipped to deal with international crises than the legislative branch. The executive branch is unitary, under the authority of a single person, the president. In contrast, Congress is a bicameral institution that often seems to speak with

535 separate voices, the sum total of members of the House and Senate. Whereas the president can respond quickly to international events and speak with one voice, Congress often reacts slowly and without unity.

Second, the president has an advantage in that secret national security information from the Central Intelligence Agency (CIA), military, Federal Bureau of Investigation (FBI), and diplomatic corps flows directly to the White House. The president can keep Congress in the dark about foreign and defense developments or can release information selectively to support policies. President Bush, for example, justified the invasion of Iraq by declaring that the U.S. government had proof that Iraq had WMD.

Third, the general public expects the president to lead in foreign and defense policymaking. As a rule, the public is neither well informed nor particularly attentive to foreign affairs. In times of international crisis, Americans tend to rally around the president. Presidents typically enjoy a surge of popularity for roughly a 30-day period following the visible use of military force.[38] Immediately after 9/11, for example, the percentage of Americans who told survey researchers that they approved of President Bush's performance in office leaped from 51 percent in early September to 90 percent later in the month. Bush's approval rating stayed well above the 60 percent level for more than a year, significantly strengthening the president's hand on foreign and defense policy issues.[39]

Finally, the president has often had considerable influence on foreign and defense policymaking because Congress has allowed it. Many members of Congress are not interested in overall foreign policy and defense strategy. Congress as an institution is decentralized, addressing the parts of policy but rarely the big picture. Individual members focus primarily on the big issues that gain national attention, such as the war in Iraq, or with issues of primary importance to their constituents, such as Department of Defense decisions on closing military bases or the purchase of weapons systems manufactured in their states and districts.

The nature of the president's role in foreign and defense policymaking depends on the individual officeholder. Presidents with a special interest and experience in foreign policy may take personal charge of foreign and defense policymaking. Richard Nixon and George H. W. Bush, two presidents with extensive foreign policy experience and expertise, immersed themselves in the details of the nation's foreign policies. In contrast, Ronald Reagan entered office with almost no foreign policy experience and apparently little interest in the subject. He relied heavily on aides and advisors for foreign policy advice.

Some foreign and defense policies can be adopted in the executive branch alone, but most require congressional action as well. Foreign aid and defense budgets must journey through the regular appropriations process. The Senate must ratify treaties and confirm appointments. In practice, Congress more frequently modifies than blocks executive-branch initiatives in foreign and defense policy. The Senate, for example, ratified the Panama Canal Treaty after tacking on 24 amendments, reservations, conditions, and understandings.

In general, Congress is more likely to support presidential initiatives in foreign and defense policy when the president's party controls Congress, when the president enjoys a relatively high approval rating, and during times of international crisis. After 9/11, President George W. Bush benefited from an atmosphere of international crisis and strong public support on foreign and defense policy issues. Furthermore, the Republican Party controlled the House and the Senate during the first few months of 2000 and then again after the 2002 election. As a result, Bush won congressional support for his proposals concerning homeland security, defense spending, trade, and the invasion of Iraq. Congress also granted the president authority to negotiate trade agreements that would not be subject to congressional amendment. Even after the situation in Iraq soured and public opinion began to turn against administration policy, congressional criticism of the administration was muted until 2007 because Republican legislative leaders did not want to challenge a president from their party. After Democrats won a majority in Congress in the 2006 election, however, Bush faced a Congress hostile to his administration's foreign and defense policies, especially in Iraq.

Presidents take the lead in foreign and defense policy legitimation, frequently with an address directly to the American people. For example, when President George W. Bush decided to order the invasion of Iraq, he explained and justified his action in a televised address from the White House. Presidents are usually successful in building initial support for a policy because they frame the issue in terms of national defense and support for the troops. In 2003, when the war in Iraq began, 75 percent of the public supported the decision to overthrow the government of Saddam Hussein. Over time, however, foreign and defense policies can lose their legitimacy, especially if things go badly. By 2010, public support for the war in Iraq had fallen below 40 percent.[40]

Policy Implementation, Evaluation, and Change

The executive branch is primarily responsible for the implementation of foreign policy. The Department of State, Department of Defense, and CIA are prominently involved, but many other agencies and departments play a role as well. The Department of Agriculture, for example, promotes the sale of American agricultural products abroad. The Department of Education administers student-exchange programs.

Foreign and defense policies may not always be implemented the way the president and Congress originally intended or expected. Bureaucrats sometimes have priorities of their own. Also, large bureaucracies tend to develop standard operating procedures (SOPs) that they follow in performing their tasks regardless of whether they conform to the goals of the original policy.

The government has no systematic, ongoing mechanism for evaluating foreign and defense policies. Congress monitors expenditures, but often limits its policy oversight to high-profile issues, such as the war in Iraq, or issues that impact the home districts of members, such as the decision by the Pentagon to close a local military base. Scandals also receive considerable attention as well. Other efforts at evaluation take place in the executive branch, in academia, and by the news media.

In general, foreign and defense policies are probably more difficult to evaluate than policies in other areas. It is not always possible to determine whether policy goals have been met. In the absence of war, for example, any evaluation of the effectiveness of particular defense strategies has to be at least somewhat speculative. Another problem is that many of the details of policy implementation are secret. Only now, years after the events took place, is information available so that historians can begin to intelligently evaluate American foreign policy in the years immediately following World War II.

Foreign and defense policies change because of changes in the policymaking environment and because of policy evaluation. After the collapse of the Soviet Union, for example, the United States policy of containment was no longer necessary, and the focus of the U.S. defense policy changed from defending against the Soviet Union to preparing for asymmetrical warfare against guerrilla forces and terrorist organizations. American policymakers also change course because of the perception that previous policy approaches have failed. After the failure to find WMD in Iraq, for example, the United States will be reluctant to act preemptively against another country unless proof of a threat is overwhelming.

WHAT WE HAVE LEARNED

1. **What are the governmental and nongovernmental political actors that make up the international community?**

   The nation-state is the basic unit of the international community. In addition to the governments of the world, more than a hundred transnational (or multinational) organizations are active on the international stage, including the United Nations (UN) and its various components, such as the WHO. Nongovernmental organizations, including Greenpeace, International Red Cross, and even terror organizations, are important international political actors as well.

2. **What are the primary goals of American foreign and defense policy?**

   The United States has consistently pursued three foreign and defense policy goals throughout its history: national security, economic prosperity, and the projection of American values abroad. American foreign and defense policies are aimed at protecting national security interests against foreign enemies, promoting trade, and spreading American values abroad, including democracy, human rights, and free-market capitalism.

3. **How does the United States attempt to achieve its foreign and defense policy goals?**

   The United States pursues its foreign and defense policy goals through military, economic, cultural, and diplomatic means. In addition to the actual use of force, the United States forms defense alliances and transfers military hardware to other countries. It promotes trade with other nations and uses foreign aid to win international backing for its goals. Foreign policy goals can sometimes be realized through cultural means. Finally, foreign policy goals can be achieved through diplomacy.

4. **What is the history of American foreign and defense policy?**

   For almost a century, the principal theme of American foreign policy was isolationism. Although World War I thrust the United States to the forefront of international affairs, it turned inward again between the wars. Not until World War II did the United States permanently end its flirtation with isolationism. The relationship between the United States and the Soviet Union was the dominant element of American foreign policy after World War II as the two nations were locked in the Cold War from the late 1940s until the collapse of the Soviet Union in 1991. The primary strategy of the United States for dealing with the Soviet Union was known as containment, which was the American policy of keeping the Soviet Union from expanding its sphere of control. The late 1960s and early 1970s was a period of improved relations known as Détente, but it ended when the Soviet Union invaded Afghanistan in 1979. The Nixon, Ford, and Carter administrations attempted to adapt American foreign policy to the realities of a more complex world and adjust to what they saw as the long-term decline of American economic and military power. In contrast, President Reagan, at least initially, sought to restore American power with a military buildup. He also offered aid to groups attempting to overthrow communist governments around the world. The collapse of the Soviet Union ended the Cold War and left the United States as the world's only superpower. The events of 9/11 changed the environment for American foreign and defense policy by demonstrating that the United States is vulnerable to attack despite its status as the world's sole superpower. The war on terror raises a number of important issues for American policymakers, including controlling the spread of WMD, preventing failed states, limiting regional conflicts, dealing with rogue states, and fighting international terrorism.

5. **How do the foreign policies of the George W. Bush administration and the Barack Obama administration differ?**

American policymakers generally agree that the United States must be fully engaged in world affairs, but they disagree on how closely the United States should work with its allies and the other nations of the world. The George W. Bush administration followed a unilateralist approach to achieving its foreign policy goals. The United States invaded Iraq without much international support and rejected a series of international agreements that were endorsed by most other nations. In contrast, the Obama administration has taken an internationalist approach, reversing many of the decisions of the Bush administration. The foreign policy themes of the Obama administration are partnership, engagement, and common interests with other nations.

6. **What are the basic elements of American defense policy?**

In general, defense spending increases during wartime and falls during peacetime. Since 9/11, defense expenditures have increased as Congress and the president fund the war on terror as well as military operations in Afghanistan and Iraq. America's defense strategy is based on strategic (nuclear) and conventional (non-nuclear) forces. Many defense theorists believe that nuclear weapons promoted world peace during the Cold War because no national leader acting rationally would risk nuclear war for fear of nuclear retaliation—the concept of MAD—or that a nuclear exchange would cause catastrophic climate change—the concept of nuclear winter. Deterrence was the organizing principle of American defense policy during the Cold War, but it is an imperfect strategy today because of rogue states and, especially, terrorist organizations. Terrorists have no home country to be attacked in retaliation and may be willing to die for their cause. Since the end of the Cold War, the United States has restructured its conventional forces to move away from the prospect of fighting a large standing army, preparing instead for the challenges of asymmetrical warfare by focusing on speed, mobility, and firepower.

7. **How is American foreign and defense policy made?**

International events are the most important environmental factors affecting foreign and defense policymaking. Events, public opinion, the media, interest groups, Congress, and the president all play a role in setting the agenda for foreign and defense policymaking. The president and Congress share constitutional authority to formulate and adopt foreign and defense policy. Presidents take the lead in foreign and defense policy legitimation. The executive branch is primarily responsible for the implementation of foreign policy. The government has no systematic, ongoing mechanism for evaluating foreign and defense policies. Finally, foreign and defense policies change because of changes in the policymaking environment and because of policy evaluation.

KEY TERMS

asymmetrical warfare
balance of power
bipartisanship
Cold War
containment
conventional forces
convergence theory
defense policy
democratic peace
Détente
deterrence
diplomacy
diplomatic relations
failed state
foreign policy
global economy
Global Warming Treaty
gross domestic product (GDP)
International Monetary Fund (IMF)
isolationism
Marshall Plan
massive retaliation
military preemption
Monroe Doctrine
mutual assured destruction (MAD)
nation-state
Nixon Doctrine
nongovernmental organizations (NGOs)
North American Free Trade Agreement (NAFTA)
North Atlantic Treaty Organization (NATO)
Nuclear Non-Proliferation Treaty
nuclear winter
postindustrial societies
Reagan Doctrine
rogue state
Sputnik
strategic forces
tariffs
Truman Doctrine
United Nations (UN)
weapons of mass destruction (WMD)
World Health Organization (WHO)
World Trade Organization (WTO)

NOTES

1. Borzou Daragahi, "Clinton Offers New Tactic in Iran Sanctions," *San Francisco Chronicle*, February 10, 2010, available at www.sfgate.com.
2. Peter Beinart, "Shrinking the War on Terrorism," *Time*, December 14, 2009, pp. 42–45.
3. Marcus Franda, *The United Nations in the Twenty-First Century: Management and Reform Processes in a Troubled Organization* (Lanham, MD: Rowman & Littlefield, 2006), p. 1.
4. Robert Cooper, *The Postmodern State and the World Order* (London, UK: Demos, 2000), p. 22.
5. Courtney B. Smith, *Politics and Process at the United Nations: The Global Dance* (Boulder, CO: Lynne Rienner, 2006), p. 28.
6. Elizabeth Becker, "Trade Talks Fail to Agree on Drugs for Poor Nations," *New York Times*, December 21, 2002, available at www.nytimes.com.
7. Jonathan P. Doh and Hildy Teegan, *Globalization and NGOs: Transforming Business, Government, and Society* (Westport, CT: Praeger, 2003), pp. 3–9, 206–219.
8. Michael E. Brown, ed., *Grave New World: Security Challenges in the 21st Century* (Washington, DC: Georgetown University Press, 2003), p. 307.

9. Terry L. Deibel, *Foreign Affairs Strategy: Logic for American Statecraft* (New York: Cambridge University Press, 2007), p. 271.
10. U.S. Census Bureau, "International Trade in Goods and Services," available at www.census/foreign-trade.gov.
11. Marvin Zonis, "The 'Democracy Doctrine' of President George W. Bush," in Stanley A. Renshon and Peter Suedfeld, eds., *Understanding the Bush Doctrine: Psychology and Strategy in an Age of Terrorism* (New York: Routledge, 2007), p. 232.
12. Thom Shanker, "Despite Slump, U.S. Role as Top Arms Supplier Grows," *New York Times*, September 7, 2009, available at www.nytimes.com.
13. Celia W. Dugger, "U.S. Challenged to Increase Aid to Africa," *New York Times*, June 5, 2005, available at www.nytimes.com.
14. U.S. Census Bureau, "U.S. Government Foreign Grants and Credits by Country: 2000–2008," *2011 Statistical Abstract*, available at www.census.gov.
15. George F. Kennan, *American Diplomacy 1900–1950* (New York: New American Library, 1951), p. 10.
16. Philip J. Allen, ed., *Pitirim A. Sorokin in Review* (Durham, NC: Duke University Press, 1963).
17. "Treaty on the Non-Proliferation of Nuclear Weapons," available at www.un.org.
18. Stanley Hoffman, "Requiem," *Foreign Policy* 42 (Spring 1981): 3–26.
19. Robert J. Lieber, "*Eagle* Revisited: A Reconsideration of the Reagan Era in U.S. Foreign Policy," *Washington Quarterly*, Summer 1989, pp. 115–126.
20. Coil D. Blacker, "The New United States-Soviet Detente," *Current History* 88 (October 1989): 321–325, 357–359.
21. Robert J. Lieber, *Eagle Rules? Foreign Policy and American Primacy in the Twenty-First Century* (Upper Saddle River, NJ: Pearson, 2002), pp. 5–6.
22. Stanley A. Renshon, "The Bush Doctrine Reconsidered," in Renshon and Suedfeld, eds., *Understanding the Bush Doctrine*, p. 2.
23. Quoted in G. John Ikenberry, "Is American Multilateralism in Decline?" *Perspectives on Politics* 1 (September 2003): 534.
24. Peter Beinart, "Shrinking the War on Terrorism," *Time*, December 14, 2009, pp. 42–45.
25. *Time*, September 27, 2010, p. 39.
26. Isaiah Wilson III, "What Weapons Do They Have and What Can They Do?" *PS: Political Science & Politics*, July 2007, p. 473.
27. Michael A. Fletcher and Philip P. Pan, "U.S. and Russia to Reduce Arsenals," *Washington Post*, July 7, 2009, available at www.washingtonpost.com.
28. David E. Sanger and Thom Shanker, "White House Is Rethinking Nuclear Policy," *New York Times*, February 28, 2010, available at www.nytimes.com.
29. Deborah MacKenzie, "'Nuclear Winter' May Kill More than Nuclear War," *New Scientist*, March 1, 2007, available at www.newscientist.com.
30. Willie Curtis, "Illusionary Promises and Strategic Reality: Rethinking the Implications of Strategic Deterrence in a Post 9/11 World," in Renshon and Suedfeld, eds., *Understanding the Bush Doctrine*, pp. 133–143.
31. George W. Bush, "The National Security Strategy of the United States of America," available at www.whitehouse.gov.
32. Steven Mufson, "Rogue States: A Real Threat?" *Washington Post National Weekly Edition*, June 12, 2000, p. 15.
33. John Dumbrell, "The Bush Doctrine," in George C. Edwards III and Philip John Davies, *New Challenges for the American Presidency* (New York: Longman, 2004), pp. 232–234.
34. Thomas E. Ricks, "A New Way of War," *Washington Post National Weekly Edition*, December 10–16, 2001, p. 6.
35. Richard Morin, "A Gap in Worldviews," *Washington Post National Weekly Edition*, April 19, 1999, p. 34.
36. Cecil V. Crabb, Jr., Glenn J. Antizzo, and Leila E. Serieddine, *Congress and the Foreign Policy Process* (Baton Rouge, LA: Louisiana State University Press, 2000), p. 189.
37. Robert S. Litwak, *Regime Change: U.S. Strategy Through the Prism of 9/11* (Baltimore, MD: Johns Hopkins University Press, 2007), p. 48.
38. Richard J. Stoll, "The Sound of the Guns," *American Politics Quarterly* 15 (April 1987): 223–237.
39. Jeffrey M. Jones, "Bush's High Approval Ratings Among Most Sustained for Presidents," *Gallup Poll Monthly*, November 2001, p. 32.
40. "Iraq," Gallup, available at www.gallup.com.

The Declaration of Independence

In Congress, July 4, 1776

The unanimous Declaration of the thirteen united States of America.

When in the Course of human events, it becomes necessary for one people to dissolve the political bands which have connected them with another, and to assume among the Powers of the earth, the separate and equal station to which the Laws of Nature and of Nature's God entitle them, a decent respect to the opinions of mankind requires that they should declare the causes which impel them to the separation.

We hold these truths to be self-evident, that all men are created equal, that they are endowed by their Creator with certain unalienable Rights, that among these are Life, Liberty and the pursuit of Happiness. That to secure these rights, Governments are instituted among Men, deriving their just powers from the consent of the governed. That whenever any Form of Government becomes destructive of these ends, it is the Right of the People to alter or to abolish it, and to institute new Government, laying its foundation on such principles and organizing its powers in such form, as to them shall seem most likely to effect their Safety and Happiness. Prudence, indeed, will dictate that Governments long established should not be changed for light and transient causes; and accordingly all experience hath shown, that mankind are more disposed to suffer, while evils are sufferable, than to right themselves by abolishing the forms to which they are accustomed. But when a long train of abuses and usurpations, pursuing invariably the same Object evinces a design to reduce them under absolute Despotism, it is their right, it is their duty, to throw off such Government, and to provide new Guards for their future security.—Such has been the patient sufferance of these Colonies; and such is now the necessity which constrains them to alter their former Systems of Government. The history of the present King of Great Britain is a history of repeated injuries and usurpations, all having in direct object the establishment of an absolute Tyranny over these States. To prove this, let Facts be submitted to a candid world.

He has refused his Assent to Laws, the most wholesome and necessary for the public good.

He has forbidden his Governors to pass Laws of immediate and pressing importance, unless suspended in their operation till his Assent should be obtained; and when so suspended, he has utterly neglected to attend to them.

He has refused to pass other Laws for the accommodation of large districts of people, unless those people would relinquish the right of Representation in the Legislature, a right inestimable to them and formidable to tyrants only.

He has called together legislative bodies at places unusual, uncomfortable, and distant from the depository of their Public Records, for the sole purpose of fatiguing them into compliance with his measures.

He has dissolved Representative Houses repeatedly, for opposing with manly firmness his invasions on the rights of the people.

He has refused for a long time, after such dissolutions, to cause others to be elected; whereby the Legislative Powers, incapable of Annihilation, have returned to the People at large for their exercise; the State remaining in the mean time exposed to all the dangers of invasion from without, and convulsions within.

He has endeavoured to prevent the population of these States; for that purpose obstructing the Laws for Naturalization of Foreigners; refusing to pass others to encourage their migrations hither, and raising the conditions of new Appropriations of Lands.

He has obstructed the Administration of Justice, by refusing his Assent to Laws for establishing Judiciary Powers.

He has made Judges dependent on his Will alone, for the tenure of their offices, and the amount and payment of their salaries.

He has erected a multitude of New Offices, and sent hither swarms of Officers to harass our people, and eat out their substance.

He has kept among us, in times of peace, Standing Armies without the Consent of our legislatures.

He has affected to render the Military independent of and superior to the Civil Power.

He has combined with others to subject us to a jurisdiction foreign to our constitution, and unacknowledged by our laws; giving his Assent to their acts of pretended Legislation:

For quartering large bodies of armed troops among us:

For protecting them, by a mock Trial, from Punishment for any Murders which they should commit on the inhabitants of these States:

For cutting off our Trade with all parts of the world:

For imposing taxes on us without our Consent;

For depriving us in many cases, of the benefits of Trial by Jury:

For transporting us beyond Seas to be tried for pretended offences:

For abolishing the free System of English Laws in a neighbouring Province, establishing therein an Arbitrary government, and enlarging its Boundaries so as to render it at once an example and fit instrument for introducing the same absolute rule into these Colonies:

For taking away our Charters, abolishing our most valuable Laws, and altering fundamentally the Forms of our Governments:

For suspending our own Legislature, and declaring themselves invested with Power to legislate for us in all cases whatsoever.

He has abdicated Government here, by declaring us out of his Protection and waging War against us.

He has plundered our seas, ravaged our Coasts, burnt our towns, and destroyed the lives of our people.

He is at this time transporting large armies of foreign mercenaries to compleat the works of death, desolation and tyranny, already begun with circumstances of Cruelty & perfidy scarcely paralleled in the most barbarous ages, and totally unworthy the Head of a civilized nation.

He has constrained our fellow Citizens taken Captive on the high Seas to bear Arms against their Country, to become the executioners of their friends and Brethren, or to fall themselves by their Hands.

He has excited domestic insurrections amongst us, and has endeavoured to bring on the inhabitants of our frontiers, the merciless Indian Savages, whose known rule of warfare, is an undistinguished destruction of all ages, sexes and conditions.

In every stage of these Oppressions We have Petitioned for Redress in the most humble terms: Our repeated Petitions have been answered only by repeated injury. A Prince, whose character is thus marked by every act which may define a Tyrant, is unfit to be the ruler of a free people.

Nor have we been wanting in attentions to our British brethren. We have warned them from time to time of attempts by their legislature to extend an unwarrantable jurisdiction over us. We have reminded them of the circumstances of our emigration and settlement here. We have appealed to their native justice and magnanimity, and we have conjured them by the ties of our common kindred to disavow these usurpations which, would inevitably interrupt our connections and correspondence. They too have been deaf to the voice of justice and of consanguinity. We must, therefore, acquiesce in the necessity, which denounces our Separation, and hold them, as we hold the rest of mankind, Enemies in War, in Peace Friends.

We, therefore, the Representatives of the United States of America, in General Congress, Assembled, appealing to the Supreme Judge of the world for the rectitude of our intentions, do, in the Name, and by authority of the good People of these Colonies, solemnly publish and declare, That these United Colonies are, and of Right ought to be Free and Independent States; that they are Absolved from all Allegiance to the British Crown, and that all political connection between them and the State of Great Britain, is and ought to be totally dissolved; and that as Free and Independent States, they have full Power to levy War, conclude Peace, contract Alliances, establish Commerce, and to do all other Acts and Things which Independent States may of right do. And for the support of this Declaration, with a firm reliance of the Protection of Divine Providence, we mutually pledge to each other our Lives, our Fortunes and our sacred Honor.

The Constitution of the United States of America

We the people of the United States, in Order to form a more perfect Union, establish justice, insure domestic Tranquility, provide for the common defence, promote the general Welfare, and secure the Blessings of Liberty to ourselves and our Posterity, do ordain and establish this Constitution for the United States of America.

Article I

Section 1.

All legislative Powers herein granted shall be vested in a Congress of the United States, which shall consist of a Senate and House of Representatives.

Section 2.

The House of Representatives shall be composed of Members chosen every second Year by the People of the several States, and the Electors in each State shall have the Qualifications requisite for Electors of the most numerous Branch of the State Legislature.

No person shall be a Representative who shall not have attained to the Age of twenty five Years, and been seven Years a Citizen of the United States, and who shall not, when elected, be an Inhabitant of that State in which he shall be chosen.

Representatives and direct Taxes shall be apportioned among the several States which may be included within this Union, according to their respective Numbers, which shall be determined by adding to the whole Number of free Persons, including those bound to Service for a Term of Years, and excluding Indians not taxed, three fifths of all other Persons.* The actual Enumeration shall be made within three years after the first Meeting of the Congress of the United States, and within every subsequent Term of ten Years, in such Manner as they shall by Law direct. The Number of Representatives shall not exceed one for every thirty Thousand, but each State shall have at Least one Representative; and until such enumeration shall be made, the State of New Hampshire shall be entitled to chuse three, Massachusetts eight, Rhode-Island and Providence Plantations one, Connecticut five, New-York six, New Jersey four, Pennsylvania eight, Delaware one, Maryland six, Virginia ten, North Carolina five, South Carolina five, and Georgia three.

When vacancies happen in the Representation from any State, the Executive Authority thereof shall issue Writs of Election to fill such Vacancies.

The House of Representatives shall chuse their Speaker and other Officers; and shall have the sole Power of Impeachment.

Section 3.

The Senate of the United States shall be composed of two Senators from each State, chosen by the Legislature thereof, for six Years; and each Senator shall have one Vote.

Immediately after they shall be assembled in Consequence of the first Election, they shall be divided as equally as many be into three Classes. The Seats of the Senators of the first Class shall be vacated at the Expiration of the second Year, of the second Class at the Expiration of the fourth Year, and of the third Class at the Expiration of the sixth Year, so that one third may be chosen every second Year; and if Vacancies happen by Resignation, or otherwise, during the Recess of the Legislature of any State, the Executive thereof may make temporary Appointments until the next Meeting of the Legislature, which shall then fill such Vacancies.†

No Person shall be a Senator who shall not have attained to the Age of thirty Years, and been nine Years a Citizen of the United States, and who shall not, when elected, be an Inhabitant of that State in which he shall be chosen.

The Vice President of the United States shall be President of the Senate, but shall have no Vote, unless they be equally divided.

The Senate shall chuse their other Officers, and also a President pro tempore, in the Absence of the Vice President, or when he shall exercise the Office of the President of the United States.

The Senate shall have the sole Power to try all impeachments. When sitting for that Purpose, they shall be on Oath or

* "Other Persons" being black slaves. Modified by Amendment XIV, Section 2.

†Provisions changed by Amendment XVII.

Affirmation. When the President of the United States is tried, the Chief Justice shall preside: And no person shall be convicted without the Concurrence of two thirds of the Members present.

Judgment in Cases of Impeachment shall not extend further than to removal from Office, and disqualification to hold and enjoy any Office of honor, Trust or Profit under the United States; but the Party convicted shall nevertheless be liable and subject to Indictment, Trial, Judgment and Punishment, according to Law.

Section 4.

The Times, Places and Manner of holding Elections for Senators and Representatives, shall be prescribed in each State by the Legislature thereof; but the Congress may at any time by Law make or alter such Regulations, except as to the Places of chusing Senators.

The Congress shall assemble at least once in every Year, and such Meeting shall be on the first Monday in December, unless they shall by Law appoint a different Day.*

Section 5.

Each House shall be the Judge of the Elections, Returns and Qualifications of its own Members, and a Majority of each shall constitute a Quorum to do Business; but a smaller number may adjourn from day to day, and may be authorized to compel the Attendance of absent Members, in such Manner, and under such Penalties as each House may provide.

Each House may determine the Rules of its Proceedings, punish its Members for disorderly Behaviour, and, with the Concurrence of two thirds, expel a Member.

Each House shall keep a Journal of its Proceedings, and from time to time publish the same, excepting such Parts as may in their Judgment require Secrecy; and the Yeas and Nays of the Members of either House on any question shall, at the Desire of one fifth of those Present, be entered on the Journal.

Neither House, during the Session of Congress, shall, without the Consent of the other, adjourn for more than three days, nor to any other Place than that in which the two Houses shall be sitting.

Section 6.

The Senators and Representatives shall receive a Compensation for their Services, to be ascertained by Law, and paid out of the Treasury of the United States. They shall in all Cases, except Treason, Felony and Breach of the Peace, be privileged from arrest during their Attendance at the Session of their respective Houses, and in going to and returning from the same; and for any Speech or Debate in either House, they shall not be questioned in any other Place.

No Senator or Representative shall, during the Time for which he was elected, be appointed to any civil Office under the Authority of the United States, which shall have been created, or the Emoluments whereof shall have been encreased, during such time; and no Person holding any Office under the United States shall be a Member of either House during his Continuance in Office.

Section 7.

All Bills for raising Revenue shall originate in the House of Representatives; but the Senate may propose or concur with Amendments as on other Bills.

Every Bill which shall have passed the House of Representatives and the Senate, shall, before it become a Law, be presented to the President of the United States; If he approve he shall sign it, but if not he shall return it, with his Objections, to that House in which it shall have originated, who shall enter the Objections at large on their Journal, and proceed to reconsider it. If after such Reconsideration two thirds of that House shall agree to pass the Bill, it shall be sent, together with the Objections, to the other House, by which it shall likewise be reconsidered, and if approved by two thirds of that House, it shall become a Law. But in all such Cases the Votes of both Houses shall be determined by Yeas and Nays, and the Names of the Persons voting for and against the Bill shall be entered on the Journal of each House respectively. If any Bill shall not be returned by the President within ten Days (Sundays excepted) after it shall have been presented to him, the Same shall be a Law, in like Manner as if he had signed it, unless the Congress by their Adjournment prevent its Return, in which Case it shall not be a Law.

Every Order, Resolution, or Vote to which the Concurrence of the Senate and House of Representatives may be necessary (except on a question of Adjournment) shall be presented to the President of the United States; and before the Same shall take Effect, shall be approved by him, or being disapproved by him, shall be repassed by two thirds of the Senate and House of Representatives, according to the Rules and Limitations prescribed in the Case of a Bill.

Section 8.

The Congress shall have Power To lay and collect Taxes, Duties, Imposts and Excises, to pay the Debts and provide for the common Defence and general Welfare of the United States; but all Duties, Imposts and Excises shall be uniform throughout the United States;

To borrow Money on the credit of the United States;

To regulate Commerce with foreign Nations, and among the several States, and with the Indian Tribes;

To establish a uniform Rule of Naturalization, and uniform Laws on the subject of Bankruptcies throughout the United States;

To coin Money, regulate the Value thereof, and of foreign Coin, and fix the Standard of Weights and Measures;

To provide for the Punishment of counterfeiting the Securities and current Coin of the United States;

To establish Post offices and post Roads;

*Provisions changed by Amendment XX, Section 2.

To promote the Progress of Science and useful Arts, by securing for limited Times to Authors and Inventors the exclusive Right to their respective Writings and Discoveries;

To constitute Tribunals inferior to the supreme Court;

To define and punish Piracies and Felonies committed on the high Seas, and Offences against the Law of Nations;

To declare War, grant Letters of Marque and Reprisal, and make Rules concerning Captures on Land and Water;

To raise and support Armies, but no Appropriation of Money to that Use shall be for a longer Term than two Years;

To provide and maintain a Navy;

To make Rules for the Government and Regulation of the land and naval Forces;

To provide for calling forth the Militia to execute the Laws of the Union, suppress Insurrections and repel Invasions;

To provide for organizing, arming, and disciplining, the Militia, and for governing such Part of them as may be employed in the Service of the United States, reserving to the States respectively, the Appointment of the Officers, and the Authority of training the Militia according to the discipline prescribed by Congress;

To exercise exclusive Legislation in all Cases whatsoever, over such District (not exceeding ten Miles square) as may, by Cession of particular States, and the Acceptance of Congress, become the Seat of Government of the United States, and to exercise like Authority over all Places purchased by the Consent of the Legislature of the State in which the Same shall be, for the Erection of Forts, Magazines, Arsenals, dock-Yards, and other needful Buildings;—And

To make all Laws which shall be necessary and proper for carrying into Execution the foregoing Powers, and all other Powers vested by this Constitution in the Government of the United States, or in any Department or Officer thereof.

Section 9.

The Migration or Importation of such Persons as any of the States now existing shall think proper to admit, shall not be prohibited by the Congress prior to the Year one thousand eight hundred and eight, but a Tax, or duty may be imposed on such Importation, not exceeding ten dollars for each Person.

The privilege of the Writ of Habeas Corpus shall not be suspended, unless when in Cases of Rebellion or Invasion the public Safety may require it.

No Bill of Attainder or ex post facto Law shall be passed.

No Capitation, or other direct, Tax shall be laid, unless in Proportion to the Census or Enumeration herein before directed to be taken.

No Tax or Duty shall be laid on Articles exported from any State.

No Preference shall be given by any Regulation of Commerce or Revenue to the Ports of one State over those of another; nor shall Vessels bound to, or from, one State, be obliged to enter, clear, or pay Duties in another.

No Money shall be drawn from the Treasury, but in Consequence of Appropriations made by Law; and a regular Statement and Account of the Receipts and Expenditures of all public Money shall be published from time to time.

No Title of Nobility shall be granted by the United States: And no Person holding any Office of Profit or Trust under them, shall, without the Consent of the Congress, accept of any present, Emolument, Office, or Title, of any kind whatever, from any King, Prince, or foreign State.

Section 10.

No State shall enter into any Treaty, Alliance, or Confederation; grant Letters of Marque and Reprisal; coin Money; emit Bills of Credit; make any Thing but gold and silver Coin a Tender in Payment of Debts; pass any Bill of Attainder, ex post facto Law, or Law impairing the Obligation of Contracts, or grant any Title of Nobility.

No State shall, without the Consent of the Congress, lay any Imposts or Duties on Imports or Exports, except what may be absolutely necessary for executing its inspection Laws: and the net Produce of all Duties and Imposts, laid by any State on Imports or Exports, shall be for the Use of the Treasury of the United States; and all such Laws shall be subject to the Revision and Control of the Congress.

No State shall, without the Consent of Congress, lay any Duty of Tonnage, keep Troops, or Ships of War in time of Peace, enter into any Agreement or Compact with another State, or with a foreign Power, or engage in War, unless actually invaded, or in such imminent Danger as will not admit of delay.

Article II

Section 1.

The executive Power shall be vested in a President of the United States of America. He shall hold his Office during the Term of four Years, and, together with the Vice President, chosen for the same Term, be elected, as follows:

Each State shall appoint, in such Manner as the Legislature thereof may direct, a Number of Electors, equal to the whole Number of Senators and Representatives to which the State may be entitled in the Congress; but no Senator or Representative, or Person holding an Office of Trust or Profit under the United States, shall be appointed an Elector.

The Electors shall meet in their respective States, and vote by Ballot for two Persons, of whom one at least shall not be an Inhabitant of the same State with themselves. And they shall make a List of all the Persons voted for, and of the Number of Votes for each; which List they shall sign and certify, and transmit sealed to the Seat of the Government of the United States, directed to the President of the Senate. The President of the Senate shall, in the Presence of the Senate and House of Representatives, open all the Certificates, and the Votes shall then be counted. The Person having the greatest Number of

Votes shall be the President, if such Number be a Majority of the whole Number of Electors appointed; and if there be more than one who have such Majority, and have an equal Number of Votes, then the House of Representatives shall immediately chuse by Ballot one of them for President; and if no Person have a Majority, then from the five highest on the List the said House shall in like Manner chuse the President. But in chusing the President, the Votes shall be taken by States, the Representation from each State having one Vote; a quorum for this Purpose shall consist of a Member or Members from two thirds of the States, and a Majority of all the States shall be necessary to a Choice. In every Case, after the Choice of the President, the Person having the greatest Number of Votes of the Electors shall be the Vice President. But if there should remain two or more who have equal Votes, the Senate shall chuse from them by Ballot the Vice President.*

The Congress may determine the Time of chusing the Electors, and the Day on which they shall give their Votes; which Day shall be the same throughout the United States.

No Person except a natural born Citizen, or a Citizen of the United States, at the time of the Adoption of this Constitution, shall be eligible to the Office of President; neither shall any Person be eligible to that Office who shall not have attained to the Age of thirty five Years, and been fourteen Years a Resident within the United States.

In Case of the Removal of the President from Office, or of his Death, Resignation, or Inability to discharge the Powers and Duties of the said Office, the Same shall devolve on the Vice President, and the Congress may by Law provide for the Case of Removal, Death, Resignation or Inability, both of the President and Vice President, declaring what Officer shall then act as President, and such Officer shall act accordingly, until the Disability be removed, or a President shall be elected.

The President shall, at stated Times, receive for his Services, a Compensation, which shall neither be encreased nor diminished during the Period for which he shall have been elected, and he shall not receive within that Period any other Emolument from the United States, or any of them.

Before he enter on the Execution of his Office, he shall take the following Oath or Affirmation:—"I do solemnly swear (or affirm) that I will faithfully execute the Office of President of the United States, and will to the best of my Ability, preserve, protect and defend the Constitution of the United States."

Section 2.

The President shall be Commander in Chief of the Army and Navy of the United States, and of the Militia of the several States, when called into the actual Service of the United States; he may require the Opinion, in writing, of the principal Officer in each of the executive Departments, upon any Subject relating to the Duties of their respective Offices, and he shall have Power to grant Reprieves and Pardons for Offences against the United States, except in Cases of Impeachment.

He shall have Power, by and with the Advice and Consent of the Senate, to make Treaties, provided two thirds of the Senators present concur; and he shall nominate, and by and with the Advice and Consent of the Senate, shall appoint Ambassadors, other public Ministers and Consuls, Judges of the supreme Court, and all other Officers of the United States, whose Appointments are not herein otherwise provided for, and which shall be established by Law: but the Congress may by Law vest the Appointment of such inferior Officers, as they think proper in the President alone, in the Courts of Law, or in the Heads of Departments.

The President shall have Power to fill up all Vacancies that may happen during the Recess of the Senate, by granting Commissions which shall expire at the end of their next Session.

Section 3.

He shall from time to time give to the Congress Information of the State of the Union, and recommend to their Consideration such Measures as he shall judge necessary and expedient; he may, on extraordinary occasions, convene both Houses, or either of them, and in Case of Disagreement between them, with Respect to the Time of Adjournment, he may adjourn them to such Time as he shall think proper; he shall receive Ambassadors and other public Ministers; he shall take Care that the Laws be faithfully executed, and shall Commission all the Officers of the United States.

Section 4.

The President, Vice President and all civil Officers of the United States, shall be removed from Office on Impeachment for, and Conviction of, Treason, Bribery, or other high Crimes and Misdemeanors.

Article III

Section 1.

The judicial Power of the United States, shall be vested in one supreme Court, and in such inferior Courts as the Congress may from time to time ordain and establish. The Judges, both of the supreme and inferior Courts, shall hold their Offices during good Behaviour, and shall, at stated Times, receive for their Services, a Compensation, which shall not be diminished during their Continuance in Office.

Section 2.

The judicial Power shall extend to all Cases in Law and Equity, arising under this Constitution, the Laws of the United States, and Treaties made, or which shall be made, under their Authority;—to all Cases affecting Ambassadors, other public Ministers and Consuls;—to all cases of admiralty and maritime

---

* Provisions superseded by Amendment XII.

Jurisdiction;—to Controversies to which the United States shall be a Party;—to Controversies between two or more States;—between a State and Citizens of another State;—between Citizens of different States;—between Citizens of the same State claiming Lands under Grants of different States, and between a State, or the Citizens thereof, and foreign States, Citizens or Subjects.*

In all Cases affecting Ambassadors, other public Ministers and Consuls, and those in which a State shall be Party, the supreme Court shall have original Jurisdiction. In all the other Cases before mentioned, the supreme Court shall have appellate Jurisdiction, both as to Law and Fact, with such Exceptions, and under such Regulations as the Congress shall make.

The Trial of all Crimes, except in Cases of Impeachment, shall be by Jury; and such Trial shall be held in the State where the said Crimes shall have been committed, but when not committed within any State, the Trial shall be at such Place or Places as the Congress may by law have directed.

Section 3.

Treason against the United States, shall consist only in levying War against them, or in adhering to their Enemies, giving them Aid and Comfort. No person shall be convicted of Treason unless on the Testimony of two Witnesses to the same overt Act, or on Confession in open Court.

The Congress shall have Power to declare the Punishment of Treason, but no Attainder of Treason shall work Corruption of Blood, or Forfeiture except during the Life of the Person attained.

Article IV

Section 1.

Full Faith and Credit shall be given in each State to the public Acts, Records, and judicial Proceedings of every other State. And the Congress may by general Laws prescribe the Manner in which such Acts, Records and Proceedings shall be proved, and the Effect thereof.

Section 2.

The Citizens of each State shall be entitled to all Privileges and Immunities of Citizens in the several States.

A Person charged in any State with Treason, Felony, or other Crime, who shall flee from Justice, and be found in another State, shall on Demand of the executive Authority of the State from which he fled, be delivered up, to be removed to the State having Jurisdiction of the Crime.

No Person held to Service or Labour in one State, under the Laws thereof, escaping into another, shall, in Consequence of any Law or Regulation therein, be discharged from such Service or Labour, but shall be delivered up on Claim of the Party to whom such Service or Labour may be due.

Section 3.

New States may be admitted by the Congress into this Union; but no new State shall be formed or erected within the Jurisdiction of any other State; nor any State be formed by the Junction of two or more States, or Parts of States, without the Consent of the Legislatures of the States concerned as well as of the Congress.

The Congress shall have Power to dispose of and make all needful Rules and Regulations respecting the Territory or other Property belonging to the United States; and nothing in this Constitution shall be so construed as to Prejudice any Claims of the United States, or of any particular State.

Section 4.

The United States shall guarantee to every State in this Union a Republican Form of Government, and shall protect each of them against Invasion; and on Application of the Legislature, or of the Executive (when the Legislature cannot be convened) against domestic Violence.

Article V

The Congress, whenever two thirds of both Houses shall deem it necessary, shall propose Amendments to this Constitution, or, on the Application of the Legislatures of two thirds of the several States, shall call a Convention for proposing Amendments, which, in either Case, shall be valid to all Intents and Purposes, as Part of this Constitution, when ratified by the Legislatures of three fourths of the several states, or by Conventions in three fourths thereof, as the one or the other Mode of Ratification may be proposed by the Congress; Provided that no Amendment which may be made prior to the Year One thousand eight hundred and eight shall in any Manner affect the first and fourth Clauses in the Ninth Section of the first Article; and that no State, without its Consent, shall be deprived of its equal Suffrage in the Senate.

Article VI

All Debts contracted and Engagements entered into, before the Adoption of this Constitution, shall be as valid against the United States under this Constitution, as under the Confederation.

This Constitution, and the Laws of the United States which shall be made in Pursuance thereof; and all Treaties made, or which shall be made, under the Authority of the United States, shall be the supreme Law of the Land; and the Judges in every State shall be bound thereby, any Thing in the Constitution or Laws of any State to the Contrary notwithstanding.

The Senators and Representatives before mentioned, and the Members of the several State Legislatures and all executive

*Clause changed by Amendment XI.

and judicial Officers, both of the United States and of the several States, shall be bound by Oath or Affirmation to support this Constitution; but no religious Test shall ever be required as a Qualification to any Office or public Trust under the United States.

Article VII

The Ratification of the Conventions of nine States shall be sufficient for the Establishment of this Constitution between the States so ratifying the Same.

Done in Convention by the Unanimous Consent of the States present the Seventeenth Day of September in the Year of our Lord one thousand seven hundred and Eighty seven and of the Independence of the United States of America the Twelfth.* In Witness whereof We have hereunto subscribed our Names.

---

*The Constitution was submitted on September 17, 1787, by the Constitutional Convention, was ratified by the conventions of several states at various dates up to May 29, 1790, and became effective on March 4, 1789.

Amendments to the Constitution

(The First Ten Amendments Form the Bill of Rights)

Amendment I [1791]

Congress shall make no law respecting an establishment of religion, or prohibiting the free exercise thereof; or abridging the freedom of speech, or of the press, or the right of the people peaceably to assemble, and to petition the Government for a redress of grievances.

Amendment II [1791]

A well regulated Militia being necessary to the security of a free State, the right of the people to keep and bear Arms, shall not be infringed.

Amendment III [1791]

No Soldier shall, in time of peace, be quartered in any house, without the consent of the Owner, nor in time of war, but in a manner to be prescribed by law.

Amendment IV [1791]

The right of the people to be secure in their persons, houses, papers, and effects, against unreasonable searches and seizures, shall not be violated, and no Warrants shall issue, but upon probable cause, supported by Oath or affirmation, and particularly describing the place to be searched, and the persons or things to be seized.

Amendment V [1791]

No person shall be held to answer for a capital or otherwise infamous crime, unless on a presentment or indictment of a Grand Jury, except in cases arising in the land or naval forces, or in the Militia, when in actual service in time of War or public danger; nor shall any person be subject for the same offence to be twice put in jeopardy of life or limb; nor shall be compelled in any criminal case to be a witness against himself, nor be deprived of life, liberty, or property, witshout due process of law; nor shall private property be taken for public use, without just compensation.

Amendment VI [1791]

In all criminal prosecutions, the accused shall enjoy the right to a speedy and public trial, by an impartial jury of the State and district wherein the crime shall have been committed, which district shall have been previously ascertained by law, and to be informed of the nature and cause of the accusation; to be confronted with the witnesses against him; to have compulsory process for obtaining witnesses in his favor, and to have the Assistance of Counsel for his defence.

Amendment VII [1791]

In Suits at common law, where the value in controversy shall exceed twenty dollars, the right of trial by jury shall be preserved, and no fact tried by a jury, shall be otherwise reexamined in any court of the United States, than according to the rules of the common law.

Amendment VIII [1791]

Excessive bail shall not be required, nor excessive fines imposed, nor cruel and unusual punishments inflicted.

Amendment IX [1791]

The enumeration in the Constitution, of certain rights, shall not be construed to deny or disparage others retained by the people.

Amendment X [1791]

The powers not delegated to the United States by the Constitution, nor prohibited by it to the States, are reserved to the States respectively, or to the people.

Amendment XI [1798]

The Judicial power of the United States shall not be construed to extend to any suit in law or equity, commenced or prosecuted against one of the United States by Citizens of another State, or by Citizens of Subjects of any Foreign State.

Amendment XII [1804]

The Electors shall meet in their respective states and vote by ballot for President and Vice-President, one of whom, at least, shall not be an inhabitant of the same state with themselves; they shall name in their ballots the person voted for as President, and in distinct ballots the person voted for as Vice-President, and they shall make distinct lists of all persons voted for as President, and of all persons voted for as Vice-President, and of the number of votes for each, which lists they shall sign and certify, and transmit sealed to the seat of the government of the United States, directed to the President of the Senate;—The President of the Senate shall, in the presence of the Senate and House of Representatives, open all the certificates and the votes shall then be counted;—The person having the greatest number of votes for President, shall be the President, if such number be a majority of the whole number of Electors appointed; and if no person have such majority, then from the persons having the highest numbers not exceeding three on the list of those voted for as President, the House of Representatives shall choose immediately, by ballot, the President. But in choosing the President, the votes shall be taken by states, the representation from each state having one vote; a quorum for this purpose shall consist of a member or members from two-thirds of the states, and a majority of all the states shall be necessary to a choice. And if the House of Representatives shall not choose a President whenever the right of choice shall devolve upon them, before the fourth day of March next following, then the Vice-President shall act as President, as in the case of the death or other constitutional disability of the President.—The person having the greatest number of votes as Vice-President, shall be the Vice-President, if such number be a majority of the whole number of Electors appointed, and if no person have a majority, then from the two highest numbers on the list, the Senate shall choose the Vice-President; a quorum for the purpose shall consist of two-thirds of the whole number of Senators, and a majority of the whole number shall be necessary to a choice. But no person constitutionally ineligible to the office of President shall be eligible to that of Vice-President of the United States.

Amendment XIII [1865]

Section 1.

Neither slavery nor involuntary servitude, except as a punishment for crime whereof the party shall have been duly convicted, shall exist within the United States, or any place subject to their jurisdiction.

Section 2.

Congress shall have power to enforce this article by appropriate legislation.

Amendment XIV [1868]

Section 1.

All persons born or naturalized in the United States, and subject to the jurisdiction thereof, are citizens of the United States and the State wherein they reside. No State shall make or enforce any law which shall abridge the privileges or immunities of citizens of the United States; nor shall any State deprive any person of life, liberty, or property, without due process of law; nor deny to any person within its jurisdiction the equal protection of the laws.

Section 2.

Representatives shall be apportioned among the several States according to their respective numbers, counting the whole number of persons in each State, excluding Indians not taxed. But when the right to vote at any election for the choice of electors for President and Vice President of the United States, Representatives in Congress, the Executive and Judicial officers of a State, or the members of the Legislature thereof, is denied to any of the male inhabitants of such State being twenty-one years of age, and citizens of the United States or in any way abridged, except for participation in rebellion or other crime, the basis of representation therein shall be reduced in the proportion which the number of such male citizens shall bear to the whole number of male citizens twenty-one years of age in such State.

Section 3.

No person shall be a Senator or Representative in Congress, or elector of President and Vice President, or hold any office, civil or military, under the United States or under any State, who, having previously taken an oath, as a member of Congress, or as an officer of the United States, or as a member of any State legislature or as an executive or judicial officer of any State to support the Constitution of the United States, shall have engaged in insurrection or rebellion against the same, or given aid or comfort to the enemies thereof. But Congress may by a vote of two-thirds of each House, remove such disability.

Section 4.

The validity of the public debt of the United States, authorized by law, including debts incurred for payment of pensions and bounties for services in suppressing insurrection or rebellion, shall not be questioned. But neither the United States nor any State shall assume or pay any debt or obligation incurred in aid of insurrection or rebellion against the United States, or any claim for the loss or emancipation of any slave; but all such debts, obligations and claims shall be held illegal and void.

Section 5.

The Congress shall have the power to enforce, by appropriate legislation, the provisions of this article.

Amendment XV [1870]

Section 1.

The right of citizens of the United States to vote shall not be denied or abridged by the United States or by any State on account of race, color, or previous condition of servitude.

Section 2.

The Congress shall have power to enforce this article by appropriate legislation.

Amendment XVI [1913]

The Congress shall have power to lay and collect taxes on incomes, from whatever source derived, without apportionment among the several States, and without regard to any census or enumeration.

Amendment XVII [1913]

The Senate of the United States shall be composed of two Senators from each State, elected by the people thereof, for six years; and each Senator shall have one vote. The electors in each State shall have the qualifications requisite for electors of the most numerous branch of the State legislatures.

When vacancies happen in the representation of any State in the Senate, the executive authority of such State shall issue writs of election to fill such vacancies: *Provided*, That the legislature of any State may empower the executive thereof to make temporary appointments until the people fill the vacancies by election as the legislature may direct.

This amendment shall not be so construed as to affect the election or term of any Senator chosen before it becomes valid as part of the Constitution.

Amendment XVIII [1919]

Section 1.

After one year from the ratification of this article the manufacture, sale, or transportation of intoxicating liquors within, the importation thereof into, or the exportation thereof from the United States and all territory subject to the jurisdiction thereof for beverage purposes is hereby prohibited.

Section 2.

The Congress and the several States shall have concurrent power to enforce this article by appropriate legislation.

Section 3.

This article shall be inoperative unless it shall have been ratified as an amendment to the Constitution by the legislatures of the several States, as provided in the Constitution, within seven years from the date of the submission hereof to the States by the Congress.

Amendment XIX [1920]

The right of citizens of the United States to vote shall not be denied or abridged by the United States or by any State on account of sex.

Congress shall have power to enforce this article by appropriate legislation.

Amendment XX [1933]

Section 1.

The terms of the President and Vice President shall end at noon on the 20th day of January, and the terms of Senators and Representatives at noon on the 3d day of January, of the years in which such terms would have ended if this article had not been ratified; and the terms of their successors shall then begin.

Section 2.

The Congress shall assemble at least once in every year, and such meeting shall begin at noon on the 3d day of January, unless they shall by law appoint a different day.

Section 3.

If, at the time fixed for the beginning of the term of the President, the President elect shall have died, the Vice President elect shall become President. If a President shall not have been chosen before the time fixed for the beginning of his term, or if the President elect shall have failed to qualify, then the Vice President elect shall act as President until a President shall have qualified; and the Congress may by law provide for the case wherein neither a President elect nor a Vice President elect shall have qualified, declaring who shall then act as President, or the manner in which one who is to act shall be selected, and such person shall act accordingly until a President or Vice President shall have qualified.

Section 4.

The Congress may by law provide for the case of the death of any of the persons from whom the House of Representatives may choose a President whenever the right of choice shall have devolved upon them, and for the case of the death of any of the persons from whom the Senate may choose a Vice-President whenever the right of choice shall have devolved upon them.

Section 5.

Sections 1 and 2 shall take effect on the 15th day of October following the ratification of this article.

Section 6.

This article shall be inoperative unless it shall have been ratified as an amendment to the Constitution by the legislatures of three-fourths of the several States within seven years from the date of its submission.

Amendment XXI [1933]

Section 1.

The eighteenth article of amendment to the Constitution of the United States is hereby repealed.

Section 2.

The transportation or importation into any State, Territory, or possession of the United States for delivery or use therein of intoxicating liquors, in violation of the laws thereof, is hereby prohibited.

Section 3.

This article shall be inoperative unless it shall have been ratified as an amendment to the Constitution by conventions in the several States, as provided in the Constitution, within seven years from the date of the submission hereof to the States by the Congress.

Amendment XXII [1951]

Section 1.

No person shall be elected to the office of the President more than twice, and no person who has held the office of President, or acted as President, for more than two years of a term to which some other person was elected President shall be elected to the office of the President more than once. But this Article shall not apply to any person holding the office of President when this Article was proposed by the Congress, and shall not prevent any person who may be holding the office of President or acting as President, during the term within which this Article becomes operative from holding the office of President or acting as President during the remainder of such term.

Amendment XXIII [1961]

Section 1.

The District constituting the seat of Government of the United States shall appoint in such manner as the Congress may direct:

A number of electors of President and Vice President equal to the whole number of Senators and Representatives in Congress to which the District would be entitled if it were a State, but in no event more than the least populous State; they shall be in addition to those appointed by the States, but they shall be considered, for the purposes of the election of President and Vice President, to be electors appointed by a State; and they shall meet in the District and perform such duties as provided by the twelfth article of Amendment.

Section 2.

The Congress shall have power to enforce this article by appropriate legislation.

Amendment XXIV [1964]

Section 1.

The right of citizens of the United States to vote in any primary or other election for President or Vice President, for electors for President or Vice President, or for Senator or Representative in Congress, shall not be denied or abridged by the United States or any State by reason of failure to pay any poll tax or other tax.

Section 2.

The Congress shall have the power to enforce this article by appropriate legislation.

Amendment XXV [1967]

Section 1.

In case of the removal of the President from office or his death or resignation, the Vice President shall become President.

Section 2.

Whenever there is a vacancy in the office of the Vice President, the President shall nominate a Vice President who shall take the office upon confirmation by a majority vote of both houses of Congress.

Section 3.

Whenever the President transmits to the President pro tempore of the Senate and the Speaker of the House of Representatives his written declaration that he is unable to discharge the powers and duties of his office, and until he transmits to them a written declaration to the contrary, such powers and duties shall be discharged by the Vice President as Acting President.

Section 4.

Whenever the Vice President and a majority of either the principal officers of the executive departments or of such other body as Congress may by law provide, transmit to the President pro tempore of the Senate and the Speaker of the House of Representatives their written declaration that the President is unable to discharge the powers and duties of his office, the Vice President shall immediately assume the powers and duties of the office as Acting President.

Thereafter, when the President transmits to the President pro tempore of the Senate and the Speaker of the House of Representatives his written declaration that no inability exists, he shall resume the powers and duties of his office unless the Vice President and a majority of either the principal officers of the executive department or of such other body as Congress may by law provide, transmit within four days to the President pro tempore of the Senate and the Speaker of the House of Representatives their written declaration that the President is unable to discharge the powers and duties of his office. Thereupon Congress shall decide the issue, assembling within 48 hours for that purpose if not in session. If the Congress, within 21 days after receipt of the latter written declaration, or, if Congress is not in session, within 21 days after Congress is required to assemble, determines by two-thirds vote of both houses that the President is unable to discharge the powers and duties of his office, the Vice President shall continue to discharge the same as Acting President; otherwise, the President shall resume the powers and duties of his office.

Amendment XXVI [1971]

Section 1.

The right of citizens of the United States, who are 18 years of age or older, to vote shall not be denied or abridged by the United States or any state on account of age.

Section 2.

The Congress shall have the power to enforce this article by appropriate legislation.

Amendment XXVII [1992]

No law varying the compensation for the service of Senators and Representatives shall take effect until an election of Representatives shall have intervened.

Choosing the President

Election Year	Elected to Office			
	President	Party	Vice President	Party
1789	George Washington		John Adams	Parties not yet established
1792	George Washington		John Adams	Federalist
1796	John Adams	Federalist	Thomas Jefferson	Democratic-Republican
1800	Thomas Jefferson	Democratic-Republican	Aaron Burr	Democratic-Republican
1804	Thomas Jefferson	Democratic-Republican	George Clinton	Democratic-Republican
1808	James Madison	Democratic-Republican	George Clinton	Democratic-Republican
1812	James Madison	Democratic-Republican	Elbridge Gerry	Democratic-Republican
1816	James Monroe	Democratic-Republican	Daniel D. Tompkins	Democratic-Republican
1820	James Monroe	Democratic-Republican	Daniel D. Tompkins	Democratic-Republican
1824	John Quincy Adams Elected by House of Representatives because no candidate received a majority of electoral votes.	National Republican	John C. Calhoun	Democratic
1828	Andrew Jackson	Democratic	John C. Calhoun	Democratic
1832	Andrew Jackson	Democratic	Martin Van Buren	Democratic

Major Opponents		**Electoral Vote**		**Popular Vote**
For President	Party			
		Washington Adams	69 34	Electors selected by state legislatures
George Clinton	Democratic-Republican	Washington Adams Clinton	132 77 50	Electors selected by state legislatures
Thomas Pinckney Aaron Burr	Federalist Democratic-Republican	Adams Jefferson Pinckney	71 68 59	Electors selected by state legislatures
John Adams Charles Cotesworth Pinckney	Federalist Federalist	Jefferson Adams	73 65	Electors selected by state legislatures
Charles Cotesworth Pinckney	Federalist	Jefferson Pinckney	162 14	Electors selected by state legislatures
Charles Cotesworth Pinckney George Clinton	Federalist Eastern Republican	Madison Pinckney	122 47	Electors selected by state legislatures
De Witt Clinton	Democratic-Republican (antiwar faction) and Federalist	Madison Clinton	128 89	Electors selected by state legislatures
Rufus King	Federalist	Monroe King	183 34	Electors selected by state legislatures
		Monroe John Quincy Adams	231 1	Electors selected by state legislatures
Andrew Jackson Henry Clay William H. Crawford	Democratic Democratic-Republican Democratic-Republican	Adams Jackson Clay Crawford	84 99 37 41	113,122 151,271 47,531 40,856
John Quincy Adams	National Republican	Jackson Adams	178 83	642,553 500,897
Henry Clay William Wirt	National Republican Anti-Masonic	Jackson Clay Wirt Floyd	219 49 7 11	701,780 482,205 100,715 Delegates chosen by South Carolina legislature

Election Year	Elected to Office			
	President	Party	Vice President	Party
1836	Martin Van Buren	Democratic	Richard M. Johnson First and only vice president elected by Senate (1837), having failed to receive a majority of electoral votes.	Democratic
1840	William Henry Harrison Died in 1841; succeeded by John Tyler.	Whig	John Tyler Assumed presidency in 1841; vice president's office was left vacant.	Whig
1844	James K. Polk	Democratic	George M. Dallas	Democratic
1848	Zachary Taylor Died in 1850; succeeded by Millard Fillmore.	Whig	Millard Fillmore Assumed presidency in 1850; vice president's office was left vacant.	Whig
1852	Franklin Pierce	Democratic	William R. King	Democratic
1856	James Buchanan	Democratic	John C. Breckenridge	Democratic
1860	Abraham Lincoln	Republican	Hannibal Hamlin	Republican
1864	Abraham Lincoln Died in 1865; succeeded by Andrew Johnson.	National Union/ Republican	Andrew Johnson Assumed presidency in 1865; vice president's office was left vacant.	National Union/ Republican
1868	Ulysses S. Grant	Republican	Schuyler Colfax	Republican
1872	Ulysses S. Grant	Republican	Henry Wilson	Republican

Major Opponents		**Electoral Vote**		**Popular Vote**
For Presidsent	Party			
Daniel Webster Hugh L. White William Henry Harrison	Whig Whig Anti-Masonic	Van Buren Harrison White Webster Mangum	170 73 26 14 11	764,176 550,816 146,107 41,201 Delegates chosen by South Carolina legislature
Martin Van Buren James G. Birney	Democratic Liberty	Harrison Van Buren	234 60	1,274,624 1,127,781
Henry Clay James G. Birney	Whig Liberty	Polk Clay Birney	170 105 —	1,338,464 1,300,097 62,300
Lewis Cass Martin Van Buren	Democratic Free-Soil	Taylor Cass Van Buren	163 127 —	1,360,967 1,222,342 291,263
Winfield Scott John P. Hale	Whig Free-Soil	Pierce Scott Hale	254 42 —	1,601,117 1,385,453 155,825
John C. Fremont Millard Fillmore	Republican American (Know-Nothing)	Buchanan Fremont Fillmore	174 114 8	1,832,955 1,339,932 871,731
John Bell Stephen A. Douglas John C. Breckinridge	Constitutional Union Democratic Democratic	Lincoln Breckinridge Douglas Bell	180 72 12 39	1,865,593 848,356 1,382,713 592,906
George B. McClennan	Democratic	Lincoln McClennan Eleven secessionist states did not participate.	212 21	2,218,388 1,812,807
Horatio Seymour	Democratic	Grant Seymour Texas, Mississippi, and Virginia did not participate.	286 80	3,598,235 2,706,829
Horace Greeley Charles O'Connor James Black	Democratic and Liberal Republican Democratic Temperance	Grant Greeley Greeley died before the Electoral College met. His electoral votes were divided among the four minor candidates.	286 80	3,598,235 2,834,761

Election Year	Elected to Office			
	President	Party	Vice President	Party
1876	Rutherford B. Hayes Contested result settled by special election commission in favor of Hayes.	Republican	William A. Wheeler	Republican
1880	James A. Garfield Died in 1881; succeeded by Chester A. Arthur.	Republican	Chester A. Arthur Assumed presidency in 1881; vice president's office was left vacant	Republican
1884	Grover Cleveland	Democratic	Thomas A. Hendricks	Democratic
1888	Benjamin Harrison	Republican	Levi P. Morton	Republican
1892	Grover Cleveland	Democratic	Adlai Stevenson	Democratic
1896	William McKinley	Republican	Garret A. Hobart	Republican
1900	William McKinley Died in 1901; succeeded by Theodore Roosevelt.	Republican	Theodore Roosevelt Assumed presidency in 1901; vice president's office was left vacant	Republican
1904	Theodore Roosevelt	Republican	Charles W. Fairbanks	Republican
1908	William Howard Taft	Republican	James S. Sherman	Republican
1912	Woodrow Wilson	Democratic	Thomas R. Marshall	Democratic

Major Opponents		**Electoral Vote**		**Popular Vote**
For President	Party			
Samuel J. Tilden Peter Cooper Green Clay Smith	Democratic Greenback Prohibition	Hayes Tilden Cooper	185 184 —	4,034,311 4,288,546 75,973
Winfield S. Hancock James B. Weaver Neal Dow	Democratic Greenback Prohibition	Garfield Hancock Weaver	214 155 —	4,446,158 4,444,260 305,997
James G. Blaine John P. St. John Benjamin F. Butler	Republican Prohibition Greenback	Cleveland Blaine Butler St. John	219 182 — —	4,874,621 4,848,936 175,096 147,482
Grover Cleveland Clinton B. Fisk Alson J. Streeter	Democratic Prohibition Union Labor	Harrison Cleveland	233 168	5,447,129 5,537,857
Benjamin Harrison James B. Weaver John Bidwell	Republican Populist Prohibition	Cleveland Harrison Weaver	277 145 22	5,555,426 5,182,600 1,029,846
William Jennings Bryan Joshua Levering John M. Palmer	Democratic, Populist, and National Silver Republican Prohibition National Democratic	McKinley Bryan	271 176	7,102,246 6,492,559
William Jennings Bryan Wharton Barker Eugene V. Debs John G. Woolley	Democratic and Fusion Populist Anti-Fusion Populist Social Democratic Prohibition	McKinley Bryan Woolley Debs	292 155 — —	7,218,039 6,358,345 209,004 86,935
Alton B. Parker Eugene V. Debs Silas C. Swallow	Democratic Socialist Prohibition	Roosevelt Parker Debs Swallow	336 140 — —	7,626,593 5,082,898 402,489 258,596
William Jennings Bryan Eugene V. Debs Eugene W. Chafin	Democratic Socialist Prohibition	Taft Bryan Debs Chafin	321 162 — —	7,676,258 6,406,801 420,380 252,821
William Howard Taft Theodore Roosevelt Eugene V. Debs Eugene W. Chafin	Republican Progressive (Bull Moose) Socialist Prohibition	Wilson Roosevelt Taft	435 88 8	6,296,547 4,118,571 3,486,720

Election Year	Elected to Office			
	President	Party	Vice President	Party
1916	Woodrow Wilson	Democratic	Thomas R. Marshall	Democratic
1920	Warren G. Harding Died in 1923; succeeded by Calvin Coolidge	Republican	Calvin Coolidge Assumed presidency in 1923; vice president's office was left vacant	Republican
1924	Calvin Coolidge	Republican	Charles G. Dawes	Republican
1928	Herbert C. Hoover	Republican	Charles Curtis	Republican
1932	Franklin D. Roosevelt	Democratic	John N. Garner	Democratic
1936	Franklin D. Roosevelt	Democratic	John N. Garner	Democratic
1940	Franklin D. Roosevelt	Democratic	Henry A. Wallace	Democratic
1944	Franklin D. Roosevelt Died in 1945; succeeded by Harry S. Truman	Democratic	Harry S. Truman Assumed presidency in 1945; vice president's office was left vacant	Democratic
1948	Harry S. Truman	Democratic	Alben W. Barkley	Democratic
1952	Dwight D. Eisenhower	Republican	Richard M. Nixon	Republican
1956	Dwight D. Eisenhower	Republican	Richard M. Nixon	Republican
1960	John F. Kennedy Died in 1963; succeeded by Lyndon B. Johnson	Democratic	Lyndon B. Johnson Assumed presidency in 1963; vice president's office was left vacant	Democratic
1964	Lyndon B. Johnson	Democratic	Hubert H. Humphrey	Democratic
1968	Richard M. Nixon	Republican	Spiro T. Agnew	Republican

Major Opponents		Electoral Vote		Popular Vote
For President	Party			
Charles E. Hughes Allen L. Benson J. Frank Hanly Charles W. Fairbanks	Republican Socialist Prohibition Republican	Wilson Hughes	277 254	9,127,695 8,533,507
James M. Cox Eugene V. Debs	Democratic Socialist	Harding Cox Debs	404 127 —	16,133,314 9,140,884 913,664
John W. Davis Robert M. LaFollette	Democratic Progressive	Coolidge Davis LaFollette	382 136 13	15,717,553 8,386,169 4,184,050
Alfred E. Smith Norman Thomas	Democratic Socialist	Hoover Smith	444 87	21,391,993 15,016,169
Herbert C. Hoover Norman Thomas	Republican Socialist	Roosevelt Hoover	472 59	22,809,638 15,758,901
Alfred M. Landon William Lemke	Republican Union	Roosevelt Landon	523 8	27,752,869 16,674,665
Wendell L. Wilkie	Republican	Roosevelt Wilkie	449 82	27,263,448 22,336,260
Thomas E. Dewey	Republican	Roosevelt Dewey	432 99	25,611,936 22,013,372
Thomas E. Dewey J. Strom Thurmond Henry A. Wallace	Republican States' Rights Democratic Progressive	Truman Dewey Thurmond Wallace	303 189 39 —	24,105,182 21,970,065 1,169,063 1,157,326
Adlai E. Stevenson	Democratic	Eisenhower Stevenson	442 89	33,936,137 27,314,649
Adlai E. Stevenson	Democratic	Eisenhower Stevenson	457 73	35,585,245 26,030,172
Richard M. Nixon	Republican	Kennedy Nixon Byrd (Ind. Dem.)	303 219 15 —	34,227,096 34,108,546
Barry M. Goldwater	Republican	Johnson Goldwater	486 52	43,126,584 27,177,838
Hubert H. Humphrey George C. Wallace	Democratic American Independent	Nixon Humphrey Wallace	301 191 46	31,770,237 31,270,533 9,906,141

Election Year	Elected to Office			
	President	Party	Vice President	Party
1972	Richard M. Nixon Resigned in 1974; succeeded by Gerald R. Ford	Republican	Spiro T. Agnew Resigned in 1974; replaced by Gerald R. Ford, who was in turn replaced by Nelson Rockefeller	Republican
1976	Jimmy Carter	Democratic	Walter Mondale	Democratic
1980	Ronald Reagan	Republican	George Bush	Republican
1984	Ronald Reagan	Republican	George Bush	Republican
1988	George H. Bush	Republican	J. Danforth Quayle	Republican
1992	Bill Clinton	Democratic	Albert Gore, Jr.	Democratic
1996	Bill Clinton	Democratic	Albert Gore, Jr.	Democratic
2000	George W. Bush	Republican	Richard Cheney	Republican
2004	George W. Bush	Republican	Richard Cheney	Republican
2008	Barack Obama	Democratic	Joseph Biden	Democratic

Major Opponents		**Electoral Vote**		**Popular Vote**
For President	Party			
George S. McGovern	Democratic	Nixon	520	46,740,323
		McGovern	17	28,901,598
		Hospers (Va.)	1	—
Gerald R. Ford	Republican	Carter	297	40,830,763
Eugene McCarthy	Independent	Ford	240	39,147,793
		McCarthy	—	756,631
Jimmy Carter	Democratic	Reagan	489	43,899,248
John B. Anderson	Independent	Carter	49	35,481,435
Ed Clark	Libertarian	Anderson	—	5,719,437
Walter Mondale	Democratic	Reagan	525	54,451,521
David Bergland	Libertarian	Mondale	13	37,565,334
Michael Dukakis	Democratic	Bush	426	47,946,422
		Dukakis	112	41,016,429
George Bush	Republican	Clinton	370	44,908,233
H. Ross Perot	Independent	Bush	168	39,102,282
		Perot	—	19,217,213
Robert Dole	Republican	Clinton	379	45,590,703
H. Ross Perot	Independent	Dole	159	37,816,307
		Perot	—	7,866,284
Al Gore	Democratic	Bush	271	50,456,141
Ralph Nader	Green	Gore	266	50,996,039
Patrick Buchanan	Reform	Nader	—	2,882,807
		Buchanan	—	448,868
John Kerry	Democratic	Bush	286	62,028,194
Ralph Nader	Green	Kerry	252	59,027,612
Michael Badnarik	Libertarian	Nader	—	460,650
		Badnarik	—	396,888
John McCain	Republican	Obama	365	69,456,897
Ralph Nader	Green	McCain	173	59,934,814
		Nader	—	

Glossary

24-hour news cycle: The round-the-clock reporting of news. (Ch. 6)

527 committee: Organization created to influence the outcomes of elections by raising and spending money that candidates and political parties cannot raise and spend legally. (Chs. 7 and 9)

AARP (formerly the American Association of Retired Persons): An interest group representing the concerns of older Americans. (Chs. 7 and 14)

Ability to pay theory of taxation: An approach to government finance that holds that taxes should be based on an individual's ability to pay. (Ch. 14)

Absolute monarchy: A country ruled by one person, usually a king or queen. (Ch. 1)

Access: The opportunity to communicate directly with legislators and other government officials in hopes of influencing the details of policy. (Chs. 7 and 8)

Advocacy groups: Organizations created to seek benefits on behalf of groups of persons who are in some way incapacitated or otherwise unable to represent their own interests. (Ch. 7)

Affirm: Uphold the decision of a lower court. (Ch. 13)

Affirmative action programs: Programs designed to ensure equal opportunities in employment and college admissions for racial minorities and women. (Chs. 4, 7, and 16)

Agenda setting: The process through which problems become matters of public concern and government action. (Intro)

Agents of socialization: The factors that contribute to political socialization by shaping formal and informal learning. (Ch. 4)

Air war: Campaign activities that involve the media, including television, radio, and the Internet. (Ch. 9)

American Bar Association (ABA): An interest group representing the concerns of lawyers. (Ch. 7)

American Civil Liberties Union (ACLU): A group organized to protect the rights of individuals as outlined in the U.S. Constitution. (Ch. 7)

American Federation of Labor-Congress of Industrial Organizations (AFL-CIO): An American union federation. (Ch. 7)

American Indian Movement (AIM): A group representing the views of Native Americans. (Ch. 7)

American Medical Association (AMA): An interest group representing the concerns of physicians. (Ch. 7)

Americans with Disabilities Act (ADA): A federal law intended to end discrimination against persons with disabilities and to eliminate barriers preventing their full participation in American society through imposing a broad range of federal mandates. (Intro, Chs. 3 and 16)

***Amicus curiae* or friend of the court briefs:** Written legal arguments presented by parties not directly involved in the case. (Chs. 13 and 15)

Anti-clericalism: A movement that opposes the institutional power of religion, as well as the church's involvement in all aspects of public and political life. (Ch. 7)

Antifederalists: Americans opposed to the ratification of the Constitution of 1787 because they thought it gave too much power to the national government. (Ch. 2)

Appeal: The taking of a case from a lower court to a higher court by the losing party in a lower court decision. (Ch. 13)

Apportionment: The allocation of legislative seats among the states. (Ch. 9)

Appropriation bill: A legislative authorization to spend money for particular purposes. (Ch. 10)

Appropriations process: The procedure through which Congress legislatively provides money for a particular purpose. (Ch. 14)

Articles of impeachment: A document listing the impeachable offenses that the House believes the president committed. (Ch. 11)

Asymmetrical warfare: A conflict in which the military capabilities of the two belligerents differ significantly. (Ch. 17)

At-large election: A method for choosing public officials in which the citizens of an entire political subdivision, such as a state, vote to select officeholders. (Ch. 9)

Attack journalism: An approach to news reporting in which journalists take an adversarial attitude toward candidates and elected officials. (Ch. 6)

Authorization process: The procedure through which Congress legislatively establishes a program, defines its general purpose, devises procedures for its operation, specifies an agency to implement the program, and indicates an approximate level of funding for the program (but does *not* actually provide money). (Ch. 14)

Baby-boom generation: The exceptionally large number of Americans born after the end of World War II. (Chs. 1 and 14)

Balance of power: A system of political alignments in which peace and security may be maintained among rival groups of nations. (Ch. 17)

Balance the ticket: An attempt to select a candidate for vice president who will appeal to different groups of voters than the presidential nominee. (Ch. 9)

Balanced budget: Budget receipts that equal budget expenditures. (Ch. 14)

Base voters: Rock solid Republicans or hardcore Democrats who are firmly committed to voting for their party's nominee. (Ch. 9)

Battleground states: Swing states in which the relative strength of the two major party presidential candidates is close enough so that either candidate could conceivably carry the state. (Ch. 9)

Biased question: A survey question that produces results tilted to one side or another. (Ch. 4)

Biased sample: A sample that tends to produce results that do not reflect the true characteristics of the universe because it is unrepresentative of the universe. (Ch. 4)

Bicameral legislature: Legislature with two chambers. (Chs. 2 and 10)

Bill: A proposed law. (Ch. 10)

Bill of attainder: A law declaring a person or a group of persons guilty of a crime and providing for punishment without benefit of a judicial proceeding. (Ch. 2)

Bill of Rights: A constitutional document guaranteeing individual rights and liberties. The first ten amendments to the U.S. Constitution constitute the U.S. Bill of Rights. (Chs. 2 and 15)

Bipartisan Campaign Reform Act (BCRA): A campaign finance reform law designed to limit the political influence of big money campaign contributors. (Ch. 9)

Bipartisanship: A close cooperation and general agreement between the two major political parties in dealing with foreign policy matters. (Ch. 17)

Blanket primary: A primary election system that allows voters to select candidates without regard for party affiliation. (Ch. 9)

Block grant program: A federal grant program that provides money for a program in a broad, general policy area, such as childcare or job training. (Ch. 3)

Blue states: Democratic states. (Ch. 9)

Broadcast media: Television and radio. (Ch. 6)

Budget deficit: The amount by which annual budget expenditures exceed annual budget revenues. (Ch. 14)

Budget surplus: The sum by which annual budget revenues exceed annual budget expenditures. (Ch. 14)

Bundling: A procedure in which an interest group gathers checks from individual supporters made out to the campaigns of targeted candidates. The group then passes the checks along to the candidates. (Ch. 7)

Cabinet departments: The major administrative units of the federal government that have responsibility for the conduct of a wide range of government operations. (Ch. 12)

Cap and trade: An approach to pollution control in which the government sets a limit on the amount of emissions allowed (the cap) and then permits companies to buy and sell emissions allowances (the trade). (Ch. 12)

Capital punishment: The death penalty. (Chs. 13 and 15)

Capitalism: An economic system characterized by individual and corporate ownership of the means of production, and a market economy based on the supply and demand of goods and services. (Ch. 1)

Captured agencies: Agencies that work to benefit the economic interests they regulate rather than serving the public interest. (Ch. 12)

Card check: A method of union authorization that allows union organizers to collect employee signatures on authorization forms instead of holding a secret ballot election. (Ch. 7)

Categorical grant program: A federal grant program that provides funds to state and local governments for a narrowly defined purpose, such as removing asbestos from school buildings or acquiring land for outdoor recreation. (Ch. 3)

Caucus method of delegate selection: A procedure for choosing national party convention delegates that involves party voters participating in a series of precinct and district or county political meetings. (Ch. 9)

Cause groups: Organizations whose members care intensely about a single issue or small group of related issues. (Ch. 7)

Central Intelligence Agency (CIA): The federal agency that gathers and evaluates foreign intelligence information in the interest of national security. (Ch. 12)

***Certiorari* or Cert:** The technical term for the Supreme Court's decision to hear arguments and make a ruling in a case. (Ch. 13)

Chamber of Commerce: A business federation representing the interests of more than 3 million businesses of all sizes, sectors, and regions. (Ch. 7)

Charter schools: Publicly funded but privately managed schools that operate under the terms of a formal contract, or charter, with the state. (Ch. 3)

Checks and balances: The overlapping of the powers of the branches of government, designed to ensure that public officials limit the authority of one another. (Ch. 2)

Chief executive: The head of the executive branch of government. (Ch. 11)

Chief of state: The official head of government. (Ch. 11)

Citizen groups: Organizations created to support government policies that they believe will benefit the public at large. (Ch. 7)

Civil case: A legal dispute concerning a private conflict between two parties—individuals, corporations, or government agencies. (Ch. 13)

Civil liberties: The protection of the individual from the unrestricted power of government. (Chs. 4, 13, and 15)

Civil rights: The protection of the individual from arbitrary or discriminatory acts by government or by other individuals based on an individual's group status, such as race or gender. (Chs. 13 and 16)

Civilian supremacy of the armed forces: The concept that the armed forces should be under the direct control of civilian authorities. (Ch. 11)

Closed primary: An election system that limits primary election participation to registered party members. (Ch. 9)

Closed rule: A rule that prohibits floor consideration of amendments on the House floor. (Ch. 10)

Cloture: The procedure for ending a filibuster. (Ch. 10)

Club for Growth: A cause group that favors a low tax and limited government agenda. (Ch. 7)

Coattail effect: The political phenomenon in which a strong candidate for one office gives a boost to fellow party members on the same ballot seeking other offices. (Ch. 9)

Cold War: The period of international tension between the United States and the Soviet Union lasting from the late 1940s through the late 1980s. (Chs. 16 and 17)

Collective bargaining: A negotiation between an employer and a union representing employees over the terms and conditions of employment. (Ch. 12)

Commerce Clause: The constitutional provision giving Congress authority to "regulate commerce . . . among the several states." (Ch. 3)

Common Cause: A group organized to work for campaign finance reform and other good government causes. (Ch. 7)

Compulsory voting: The legal requirement that citizens participate in national elections. (Ch. 5)

Concurrent powers: The powers of government that are jointly exercised by the national government and state governments. (Ch. 3)

Concurring opinion: A judicial statement that agrees with the Court's ruling but disagrees with the reasoning of the majority opinion. (Ch. 13)

Confederation: A league of nearly independent states, similar to the United Nations today. (Ch. 2)

Conferees: The members of a conference committee. (Ch. 10)

Conference: A closed meeting of the justices of the Supreme Court. (Ch. 13)

Conference committee: A special congressional committee created to negotiate differences on similar pieces of legislation passed by the House and Senate. (Ch. 10)

Conference report: A revised bill produced by a conference committee. (Ch. 10)

Conservatism: The political philosophy that government power undermines the development of the individual and diminishes society as a whole. (Ch. 4)

Constituency: The district from which an officeholder is elected. (Ch. 4)

Constituency service: The actions of members of Congress and their staffs while attending to the individual, particular needs of constituents. (Ch. 10)

Constituents: The people an officeholder represents. (Ch. 4)

Constitution: The fundamental law by which a state or nation is organized and governed, and to which ordinary legislation must conform. (Ch. 2)

Constitutional amendment: A formal, written change or addition to the nation's governing document. (Ch. 2)

Constitutional law: Law that involves the interpretation and application of the Constitution. (Ch. 13)

Constitutional monarchy: A country in which the powers of the ruler are limited to those granted under the constitution and the laws of the nation. (Ch. 1)

Consumer price index (CPI): A measure of inflation that is based on the changing cost of goods and services. (Ch. 14)

Containment: The American policy of keeping the Soviet Union from expanding its sphere of control. (Ch. 17)

Conventional forces: Non-nuclear forces. (Ch. 17)

Convergence theory: The view that communism and capitalism were evolving in similar ways, or converging. (Ch. 17)

Corporation for Public Broadcasting: A government agency chartered and funded by the U.S. government with the goal of promoting public broadcasting. (Ch. 6)

Cost-benefit analysis: An evaluation of a proposed policy or regulation based on a comparison of its expected benefits and anticipated costs. (Ch. 12)

Cost-of-living adjustment (COLA): An increase in the size of a payment to compensate for the effects of inflation. (Ch. 14)

Criminal case: A legal dispute dealing with an alleged violation of a penal law. (Ch. 13)

Defense of Marriage Act (DOMA): A federal law stipulating that each state may choose either to recognize or not recognize same-sex marriages performed in other states. (Ch. 3)

Defense policy: Public policy that concerns the armed forces of the United States. (Ch. 17)

Delegated *or* enumerated powers: The powers explicitly granted to the national government by the Constitution. (Ch. 3)

Democracy: A system of government in which ultimate political authority is vested in the people. (Chs. 1 and 2)

Democratic peace: The concept that democracies do not wage war against other democracies. (Ch. 17)

Depression: A severe and prolonged economic slump characterized by decreased business activity and high unemployment. (Ch. 14)

Détente: A period of improved communications and visible efforts to relieve tensions between the two superpowers. (Ch. 17)

Deterrence: The ability of a nation to prevent an attack against itself or its allies by threat of massive retaliation. (Ch. 17)

Developing countries: Nations with relatively low levels of per capita income. (Ch. 1)

Diplomacy: The process by which nations carry on political relations with each other. (Ch. 17)

Diplomatic relations: A system of official contacts between two nations in which the countries exchange ambassadors and other diplomatic personnel and operate embassies in each other's country. (Ch. 17)

Direct democracy: A political system in which the citizens vote directly on matters of public concern. (Ch. 2)

Discharge petition: A procedure whereby a majority of the members of the House of Representatives can force a committee to report a bill to the floor of the House. (Ch. 10)

Discretionary spending: Budgetary expenditures that are not mandated by law or contract. (Ch. 14)

Disfranchisement: The denial of voting rights. (Ch. 16)

Dissenting opinion: A judicial statement that disagrees with the decision of the court's majority. (Ch. 13)

District election: A method for choosing public officials that divides a political subdivision, such as a state, into geographic areas called districts; each district elects one official. (Ch. 9)

Divided government: The phenomenon of one political party controlling the legislative branch of government while the other holds the executive branch. (Ch. 8)

Doctrine of natural rights: The belief that individual rights transcend the power of government. (Ch. 2)

Double jeopardy: The government trying a criminal defendant a second time for the same offense after an acquittal in an earlier prosecution. (Ch. 15)

Due Process Clause: The constitutional provision that declares that no state shall "deprive any person of life, liberty, or property, without due process of law." (Ch. 3)

Due process of law: The constitutional principle holding that government must follow fair and regular procedures in actions that could lead to an individual's suffering loss of life, liberty, or property. (Chs. 2 and 15)

Earmarks: Provisions that direct funds to be spent for particular purposes. (Ch. 14)

Earned Income Tax Credit (EITC): A federal program designed to give cash assistance to low-income working families by refunding some or all of the taxes they pay and, if their wages are low, giving them an additional refund. (Ch. 14)

Election campaign: An attempt to get information to voters that will persuade them to elect a candidate or not elect a candidate's opponent. (Ch. 9)

Electoral College: The system established in the Constitution for indirect election of the president and vice president. (Chs. 8 and 9)

Electors: Individuals selected in each state officially to cast that state's electoral votes. (Ch. 9)

EMILY's List: A PAC whose goal is the election of pro-choice Democratic women to office. (Ch. 7)

Entitlement program: A government program providing benefits to all persons qualified to receive them under law. (Ch. 14)

Environmental Protection Agency (EPA): The federal agency responsible for enforcing the nation's environmental laws. (Ch. 12)

Equal Employment Opportunity Commission (EEOC): An agency that investigates and rules on charges of employment discrimination. (Ch. 12)

Equal Protection Clause: A provision found in the Fourteenth Amendment of the U.S. Constitution that declares that "No State shall . . . deny to any person within its jurisdiction the equal protection of the laws." (Chs. 2, 3, 13, and 16)

Equal-time rule: An FCC regulation requiring broadcasters to provide an equivalent opportunity to all political candidates competing for the same office. (Ch. 6)

Estate tax: A tax levied on the value of an inheritance. (Ch. 14)

European Union (EU): An economic and political union of 27 member states, mostly in Europe. (Ch. 14)

***Ex post facto* law:** A retroactive criminal statute that operates to the disadvantage of accused persons. (Ch. 2)

Exclusionary rule: The judicial doctrine stating that when the police violate an individual's constitutional rights, the evidence obtained as a result of police misconduct or error cannot be used against the defendant in a criminal prosecution. (Chs. 13 and 15)

Excise taxes: Taxes levied on the manufacture, transportation, sale, or consumption of a particular item or set of related items. (Chs. 3 and 14)

Executive agreement: An international understanding between the president and foreign nations that does not require Senate ratification. (Ch. 11)

Executive Office of the President: The group of White House offices and agencies that develop and implement the president's policies and programs. (Ch. 11)

Executive order: A directive issued by the president to an administrative agency or executive department. (Ch. 11)

Executive power: The power to enforce laws. (Chs. 2 and 3)

Exit polls: Surveys based on random samples of voters leaving the polling place. (Chs. 8 and 9)

External political efficacy: The assessment of an individual's view of government responsiveness to his or her concerns. (Ch. 4)

Extradition: The return from one state to another of a person accused of a crime. (Ch. 3)

Factions: Special interests who seek their own good at the expense of the common good. (Ch. 2)

Failed state: A nation-state whose government no longer effectively functions and has lost control of a significant portion of its territory. (Ch. 17)

Fairness Doctrine: An FCC regulation requiring broadcasters to present controversial issues of public importance and to cover them in an honest, equal, and balanced manner. (Ch. 6)

Federal Communications Commission (FCC): An agency that regulates interstate and international radio, television, telephone, telegraph, and satellite communications, as well as licensing radio and television stations. (Ch. 12)

Federal Deposit Insurance Corporation (FDIC): A federal agency established to insure depositors' accounts in banks and thrift institutions. (Ch. 12)

Federal Election Commission (FEC): The agency that enforces federal campaign finance laws. (Ch. 12)

Federal grant program: A program through which the national government gives money to state and local governments to spend in accordance with set standards and conditions. (Ch. 3)

Federal mandate: A legal requirement placed on a state or local government by the national government requiring certain policy actions. (Ch. 3)

Federal Open Market Committee (FOMC): A committee of the Federal Reserve that meets eight times a year to review the economy and adjust monetary policy to achieve its goals. (Ch. 14)

Federal preemption of state authority: An act of Congress adopting regulatory policies that overrule state policies in a particular regulatory area. (Ch. 3)

Federal Reserve System (Fed): The central banking system of the United States with authority to establish banking policies and influence the amount of credit available in the economy. (Ch. 14)

Federal Trade Commission (FTC): An agency that regulates business competition, including enforcement of laws against monopolies and the protection of consumers from deceptive trade practices. (Ch. 12)

***Federalist Papers*:** Series of essays written by James Madison, Alexander Hamilton, and John Jay to advocate the ratification of the Constitution of 1787. (Ch. 2)

Federalists: Americans who supported the ratification of the Constitution of 1787. (Ch. 2)

Federation *or* **federal system:** A political system that divides power between a central government, with authority over the whole nation, and a series of state governments. (Chs. 2, 3, and 9)

Filibuster: An attempt to defeat a measure in the Senate through prolonged debate. (Ch. 10)

Fire-alarm oversight: An indirect system of congressional surveillance of bureaucratic administration characterized by rules, procedures, and informal practices that enable individual citizens and organized interest groups to examine administrative decisions, charge agencies with violating legislative goals, and seek remedies from agencies, courts, and the Congress itself. (Ch. 12)

Fiscal policy: The use of government spending and taxation for the purpose of achieving economic goals. (Ch. 14)

Fiscal year (FY): Budget year. (Ch. 14)

Flat tax: An income tax that assesses the same percentage tax rate on all income levels above a personal exemption while allowing few, if any, deductions. (Ch. 14)

Floor: The full House or full Senate taking official action. (Ch. 10)

Foreign policy: Public policy that concerns the United States' relationship to the international political environment. (Ch. 17)

Formula grant program: A grant program that awards funding on the basis of a formula established by Congress. (Ch. 3)

Framing: The process by which a communication source, such as a news organization, defines and constructs a political issue or public controversy. (Ch. 6)

Franking privilege: Free postage provided to members of Congress. (Ch. 10)

Free-rider barrier to group membership: The concept that individuals will have little incentive to join a group and contribute resources to it if the group's benefits go to members and nonmembers alike. (Ch. 7)

Friendly incumbent rule: A policy whereby an interest group will back any incumbent who is generally supportive of the group's policy preferences, without regard for the party or policy views of the challenger. (Ch. 7)

Frostbelt: The Northeast and Midwest regions of the United States. (Chs. 1 and 7)

Full Faith and Credit Clause: The constitutional provision requiring that states recognize the official acts of other states, such as marriages, divorces, adoptions, court orders, and other legal decisions. (Ch. 3)

Fundamental right: A constitutional right that is so important that government cannot restrict it unless it can demonstrate a compelling or overriding public interest for so doing. (Ch. 15)

Gender gap: Differences in party identification and political attitudes between men and women. (Chs. 4 and 8)

General election: An election to fill state and national offices held in November of even-numbered years. (Ch. 9)

Gerrymandering: The drawing of legislative district lines for political advantage. (Ch. 9)

Global economy: The integration of national economies into a world economic system in which companies compete worldwide for suppliers and markets. (Chs. 1 and 17)

Global warming: The gradual warming of Earth's atmosphere, reportedly caused by the burning of fossil fuels and industrial pollutants. (Intro, Chs. 4 and 12)

Global Warming Treaty: An international agreement to reduce the worldwide emissions of carbon dioxide and other greenhouse gases. (Ch. 17)

Governing party: The political party or party coalition holding the reins of government in a democracy. (Ch. 8)

Government: The institution with authority to set policy for society. (Intro)

Government program: A system of projects or services intended to meet a public need. (Intro)

Grand Old Party (GOP): A nickname for the Republican Party. (Ch. 8)

Grandfather clause: A provision that exempted those persons whose grandfathers had been eligible to vote at some earlier date from tests of understanding, literacy tests, and other difficult-to-achieve voter qualification requirements. (Ch. 16)

Great Society: The legislative program of President Lyndon Johnson. (Ch. 11)

Gross domestic product (GDP): The value of goods and services produced by a nation's economy in a year, excluding transactions with foreign countries. (Intro, Chs. 1, 14, and 17)

Ground war: Campaign activities featuring direct contact between campaign workers and citizens, such as door-to-door canvassing and personal telephone contacts. (Ch. 9)

Hard money: Funds that are raised subject to federal campaign contribution and expenditure limitations. (Ch. 9)

Hatch Act: A measure designed to restrict the political activities of federal employees to voting and the private expression of views. (Ch. 12)

Hate crimes law: A legislative measure that increases penalties for persons convicted of offenses, motivated by prejudice based on race, religion, national origin, gender, or sexual orientation. (Ch. 15)

Honeymoon effect: The tendency of a president to enjoy a high level of public support during the early stages of an administration. (Ch. 11)

House Majority Leader: The second ranking figure in the majority party in the House. (Ch. 10)

House Rules Committee: A standing committee that determines the rules under which a specific bill can be debated, amended, and considered on the House floor. (Ch. 10)

Human Rights Campaign (HRC): A cause group formed to promote the cause of gay and lesbian rights. (Ch. 7)

Impeach: To formally accuse. (Ch. 10)

Impeachment: The process in which an executive or judicial official is formally accused of an offense that could warrant removal from office. (Ch. 11)

Implied powers: The powers of Congress not explicitly mentioned in the Constitution but derived by implication from the delegated powers. (Ch. 3)

***In forma pauperis*:** The process whereby an indigent litigant can file an appeal of a case to the Supreme Court without paying the usual fees. (Ch. 13)

Income redistribution: The government taking items of value, especially money, from some groups of people and then giving items of value, either in cash or services, to other groups of people. (Ch. 14)

Income tax: A tax levied on personal income.

Incumbent: Current officeholder. (Ch. 6)

Independent executive agencies: Executive branch agencies that are not part of any of the 15 cabinet-level departments. (Ch. 12)

Independent expenditures: Money spent in support of a candidate but not coordinated with the candidate's campaign. (Ch. 9)

Independent regulatory commission: An agency outside the major executive departments that is charged with the regulation of important aspects of the economy. (Ch. 12)

Inflation: A decline in a currency's purchasing power. (Ch. 14)

Inherent powers: Those powers vested in the national government, particularly in the area of foreign and defense policy, which do not depend on any specific grant of authority by the Constitution, but rather exist because the United States is a sovereign nation. (Ch. 11)

Initiative process: A procedure available in some states and cities whereby citizens can propose the adoption of a policy measure by gathering a prerequisite number of signatures. Voters must then approve the measure before it can take effect. (Ch. 16)

Injunction: A court order. (Ch. 16)

Inner cabinet: The four cabinet officials—the secretary of state, secretary of defense, secretary of the treasury, and the attorney general—that are considered the most important because of the critical nature of the issues that their departments address. (Ch. 12)

Interest group: An organization of people who join together voluntarily on the basis of some interest they share for the purpose of influencing policy. (Ch. 7)

Internal political efficacy: The assessment by an individual of his or her personal ability to influence the policymaking process. (Ch. 4)

International Monetary Fund (IMF): An international organization created to promote economic stability worldwide. (Chs. 14 and 17)

Interstate Commerce Clause: The constitutional provision giving Congress authority to "regulate commerce . . . among the several states." (Ch. 16)

Invisible primary: The period between the time when candidates announce their intention to run for the presidency and the actual delegate selection begins. (Ch. 9)

Isolationism: The view that the United States should stay out of the affairs of other nations. (Ch. 17)

Issue network: A group of political actors that is concerned with some aspect of public policy. (Ch. 12)

Issue ownership: The concept that the public considers one political party more competent at addressing a particular issue than the other political party. (Ch. 9)

Jim Crow laws: Legal provisions requiring the social segregation of African Americans in separate and generally unequal facilities. (Chs. 13 and 16)

Joint committee: A committee that includes members from both houses of Congress. (Ch. 10)

Judicial activism: The charge that judges are going beyond their authority by making the law and not just interpreting it. (Ch. 13)

Judicial power: The power to interpret laws. (Chs. 2 and 3)

Judicial restraint: The concept that judges should defer to the policymaking judgment of the legislative and executive branches of government unless their actions clearly violate the law or the Constitution. (Ch. 13)

Judicial review: The power of courts to declare unconstitutional the actions of the other branches and units of government. (Chs. 2 and 13)

Jurisdiction: The authority of a court to hear a case. (Chs. 2 and 13)

Killer amendment: An amendment designed to make a measure so unattractive that it will lack enough support to pass. (Ch. 10)

Lame duck: An official whose influence is diminished because the official either cannot or will not seek reelection. (Ch. 11)

League of United Latin American Citizens (LULAC): A Latino interest group. (Ch. 7)

Left wing: Liberal. (Ch. 4)

Legal brief: Written legal argument. (Ch. 13)

Legislative markup: The process in which legislators go over a measure line-by-line, revising, amending, or rewriting it. (Ch. 10)

Legislative power: The power to make laws. (Chs. 2 and 3)

Libel: False written statements that lower a person's reputation or expose a person to hatred, contempt, or ridicule. (Ch. 15)

Liberalism: The political philosophy that favors the use of government power to foster the development of the individual and promote the welfare of society. (Ch. 4)

Limited government: The constitutional principle that government does not have unrestricted authority over individuals. (Ch. 2)

Literacy test: A legal requirement that citizens must demonstrate the ability to read and write before they can register to vote. (Ch. 16)

Lobbying: The communication of information by a representative of an interest group to a government official for the purpose of influencing a policy decision. (Ch. 7)

Logrolling: An arrangement in which two or more members of Congress agree in advance to support each other's favored legislation. (Ch. 10)

Loose construction: A doctrine of constitutional interpretation holding that the document should be interpreted broadly. (Ch. 13)

Louisiana Purchase: The acquisition from France of a vast expanse of land stretching from New Orleans north to the Dakotas. (Ch. 11)

Majority opinion: The official written statement of the Supreme Court that explains and justifies its ruling and serves as a guideline for lower courts when similar legal issues arise in the future. (Ch. 13)

Majority-minority districts: Legislative districts whose population was more than 50 percent African American and Latino. (Chs. 9 and 16)

Mandatory spending: Budgetary expenditures that are mandated by law, including entitlements and contractual commitments made in previous years. (Ch. 14)

Margin of error *or* sample error: A statistical term that refers to the accuracy of a survey. (Ch. 4)

Marshall Plan: An American program that provided billions of dollars to the countries of Western Europe to rebuild their economies after World War II. (Ch. 17)

Massive retaliation: The concept that the United States will strike back against an aggressor with overwhelming force. (Ch. 17)

Matching funds requirement: A legislative provision that the national government will provide grant money for a particular activity only on the condition that the state or local government involved supplies a certain percentage of the total money required for the project or program. (Ch. 3)

Means-tested program: A government program that provides benefits to recipients based on their financial need. (Ch. 14)

Medicaid: A federal health insurance program for low-income persons, people with disabilities, and elderly people who are impoverished. (Chs. 1, 2, 3, 10, and 14)

Medicare: A federal health insurance program for people 65 and older. (Chs. 1, 7, 10, and 14)

Military preemption: The defense policy that declares that the United States will attack nations or groups that represent a potential threat to the security of the United States. (Ch. 17)

Minimum wage: The lowest hourly wage that an employer can legally pay covered workers. (Ch. 7)

Minority business set-aside: A legal requirement that firms receiving government grants or contracts allocate a certain percentage of their purchases of supplies and services to businesses owned or controlled by members of minority groups. (Ch. 16)

Miranda warning: The requirement that police inform suspects of their rights before questioning them. (Ch. 15)

Mixed economy: An economic system that combines private ownership with extensive governmental intervention. (Ch. 1)

Monetary policy: The control of the money supply for the purpose of achieving economic goals. (Ch. 14)

Monroe Doctrine: A declaration of American foreign policy opposing any European intervention in the Western Hemisphere and affirming the American intention to refrain from interfering in European affairs. (Ch. 17)

Mothers Against Drunk Driving (MADD): A cause group that supports the reform of laws dealing with drunk driving. (Ch. 7)

Multiparty system: The division of voter loyalties among three or more major political parties. (Ch. 8)

Multiple referral of legislation: The practice of assigning legislation to more than one committee. (Ch. 10)

Mutual assured destruction (MAD): The belief that the United States and the Soviet Union would be deterred from launching a nuclear assault against each other for fear of being destroyed in a general nuclear war. (Ch. 17)

NARAL Pro-Choice America: A cause group that supports abortion rights. (Ch. 7)

Nation-state: A political community occupying a definite territory that has an organized government. (Ch. 17)

National Aeronautics and Space Administration (NASA): The federal agency in charge of the space program. (Ch. 12)

National Association for the Advancement of Colored People (NAACP): An interest group organized to represent the concerns of African Americans. (Ch. 7)

National debt: The accumulated indebtedness of the federal government. (Ch. 14)

National Endowment for the Arts (NEA): A federal agency created to nurture cultural expression and promote appreciation of the arts. (Ch. 12)

National Organization for Women (NOW): A cause group organized to promote women's rights. (Ch. 7)

National Public Radio (NPR): A nonprofit membership organization of radio stations. (Ch. 6)

National Railroad Passenger Service Corporation (AMTRAK): A federal agency that operates inter-city passenger railway traffic. (Ch. 12)

National Rifle Association (NRA): An interest group organized to defend the rights of gun owners and defeat efforts at gun control. (Ch. 7)

National Right to Life Committee: A cause group that is opposed to abortion. (Ch. 7)

National Science Foundation (NSF): A federal agency established to encourage scientific advances and improvements in science education. (Ch. 12)

National Security Council (NSC): The agency in the Executive Office of the President that advises the chief executive on matters involving national security. (Ch. 11)

National Supremacy Clause: The constitutional provision that declares that the Constitution and laws of the United States take precedence over the constitutions and laws of the states. (Ch. 3)

National Voter Registration Act (NVRA): A federal law designed to make it easier for citizens to register to vote by requiring states to allow mail registration and provide an opportunity for people to register when applying for or renewing driver's licenses, as well as when visiting federal, state, or local agencies, such as welfare offices. (Ch. 5)

Necessary and Proper Clause or Elastic Clause: The Constitutional provision found in Article I, Section 8, that declares that "[Congress shall have the power] to make all laws which shall be necessary and proper for carrying into execution the foregoing powers, and all other powers vested by this Constitution in the government of the United States, or in any department or office thereof." It is the basis for much of the legislation passed by Congress because it gives Congress the means to exercise its delegated authority. (Ch. 3)

New Deal: The legislative package of reform measures proposed by President Franklin Roosevelt for dealing with the Great Depression. (Chs. 3, 11, and 13)

New media: A term used to refer to alternative media sources, such as the Internet, cable television, and satellite radio. (Ch. 6)

Nixon Doctrine: A corollary to the policy of containment that declared that if the United States would help small nations threatened by communist aggression with economic and military aid, those countries must play a major role in their own defense. (Ch. 17)

No Child Left Behind (NCLB): A federal law that requires state governments and local school districts to institute basic skills testing as a condition for receiving federal aid. (Ch. 3)

Nongermane amendments: Amendments which are unrelated to the subject matter of the original measure. (Ch. 10)

Nongovernmental organizations (NGOs): International organizations committed to the promotion of a particular set of issues. (Ch. 17)

North American Free Trade Agreement (NAFTA): An international accord among the United States, Mexico, and Canada to lower trade barriers among the three nations. (Chs. 1 and 17)

North Atlantic Treaty Organization (NATO): A military alliance consisting of the United States, Canada, and most European democracies. (Ch. 17)

Nuclear Non-Proliferation Treaty: An international agreement designed to prevent the spread of nuclear weapons. (Ch. 17)

Nuclear winter: The concept that a nuclear war would throw so much dust and debris into the atmosphere as to produce a long period of darkness and cold, destroying agriculture and killing millions of people. (Ch. 17)

Nullification: A constitutional theory that gives an individual state the right to declare null and void any law passed by the U.S. Congress which the state deems unacceptable and unconstitutional. (Ch. 3)

Objective journalism: A style of news reporting that focuses on facts rather than opinion, and presents all sides of controversial issues. (Ch. 6)

Office of Management and Budget (OMB): An agency that assists the president in preparing the budget. (Ch. 11)

Omnibus bills: Complex, highly detailed legislative proposals covering one or more subjects or programs. (Ch. 10)

One person, one vote: The judicial ruling that the Equal Protection Clause of the Fourteenth Amendment to the U.S. Constitution requires legislative districts to be apportioned on the basis of population. (Ch. 9)

Open primary: An election system that allows voters to pick the party primary of their choice without regard to their party affiliation. (Ch. 9)

Open rule: A rule that opens a measure to amendment on the House floor without restriction. (Ch. 10)

Opposition party: The political party out of power in a democracy. (Ch. 8)

Original jurisdiction: The set of cases a court may hear as a trial court. (Ch. 13)

Pardon: An executive action that frees an accused or convicted person from all penalties for an offense. (Ch. 11)

Parental choice: An educational reform aimed at improving the quality of schools by allowing parents to select the school their children will attend. (Ch. 15)

Parliament: The British legislature. (Ch. 2)

Parliamentary system: A system of government in which political power is concentrated in a legislative body and a cabinet headed by a prime minister. (Ch. 2)

Party caucus: All of the party members of a chamber meeting as a group. (Ch. 10)

Party era: A period of time characterized by a degree of uniformity in the nature of political party competition. (Ch. 8)

Party platform: A statement of party principles and issue positions. (Chs. 8 and 9)

Party realignment: A change in the underlying party loyalties of voters that ends one party era and begins another. (Ch. 8)

PAYGO: A pay-as-you-go budget rule that requires that any tax cut or spending increase be offset by tax increases or spending cuts elsewhere in the budget. (Ch. 14)

Peace Corps: The agency that administers an American foreign aid program under which volunteers travel to developing nations to teach skills and help improve living standards. (Ch. 12)

Per capita: Per person. (Ch. 1)

***Per curiam* opinion:** An unsigned written opinion issued by the Supreme Court. (Ch. 13)

Plurality election system: A method for choosing public officials that awards office to the candidate with the most votes. (Ch. 8)

Pocket veto: The action of a president allowing a measure to die without signature after Congress has adjourned. (Ch. 10)

Policy adoption: The official decision of a government body to accept a particular policy and put it into effect. (Intro)

Policy change: The modification of policy goals and means in light of new information or shifting political environments. (Intro)

Policy evaluation: The assessment of policy. (Intro)

Policy formulation: The development of strategies for dealing with the problems on the policy agenda. (Intro)

Policy implementation: The stage of the policy process in which policies are carried out. (Intro)

Policy legitimation: The actions taken by government officials and others to ensure that most citizens regard the policy as a legal and appropriate government response to a problem. (Intro)

Policymaking process: A logical sequence of activities affecting the development of public policies. (Intro)

Political action committee (PAC): An organization created to raise and distribute money in election campaigns. (Chs. 7 and 9)

Political culture: The widely held, deeply rooted political values of a society. (Ch. 1)

Political efficacy: The extent to which individuals believe they can influence the policymaking process. (Chs. 4 and 5)

Political elites: Persons that exercise a major influence on the policymaking process. (Ch. 4)

Political left: Liberalism. (Ch. 4)

Political legitimacy: The popular acceptance of a government and its officials as rightful authorities in the exercise of power. (Chs. 4 and 9)

Political movement: A group of people that wants to convince other citizens and/or government officials to take action on issues that are important to the group. (Ch. 5)

Political participation: An activity that has the intent or effect of influencing government action. (Ch. 5)

Political party: An organization that seeks political power. (Ch. 8)

Political right: Conservatism. (Ch. 4)

Political socialization: The process whereby individuals acquire political knowledge, attitudes, and beliefs. (Ch. 4)

Politics: The process that determines who shall occupy the roles of leadership in government and how the power of government shall be exercised. (Intro)

Poll tax: A tax levied on the right to vote. (Ch. 16)

Pork barrel spending: Expenditures to fund local projects that are not critically important from a national perspective. (Chs. 9 and 14)

Postindustrial societies: Nations whose economies are increasingly based on services, research, and information rather than heavy industry. (Ch. 17)

Poverty threshold: The amount of money an individual or family needs to purchase basic necessities, such as food, clothing, healthcare, shelter, and transportation. (Ch. 1)

Power of the purse: The authority to raise and spend money. (Chs. 2 and 3)

Presidential preference primary: An election in which party voters cast ballots for the presidential candidate they favor and in so doing help determine the number of national convention delegates that candidate will receive. (Ch. 9)

Presidential signing statement: A pronouncement issued by the president at the time a bill passed by Congress is signed into law. (Ch. 11)

President's cabinet: A body that includes the executive department heads and other senior officials chosen by the president, such as the U.S. ambassador to the United Nations. (Ch. 12)

Primary election: An intra-party election held to select party candidates for the general-election ballot. (Chs. 9 and 16)

Print media: Newspapers and magazines. (Ch. 6)

Prior restraint: Government action to prevent the publication or broadcast of objectionable material. (Ch. 15)

Private sector: Privately owned segment of the economy. (Ch. 1)

Privatization: A process that involves the government contracting with private business to implement government programs. (Ch. 14)

Privileges and Immunities Clause: The constitutional provision prohibiting state governments from discriminating against the citizens of other states. (Ch. 3)

Probable cause: The reasonable suspicion based on evidence that a particular search will uncover contraband. (Ch. 15)

Progressive tax: A levy that taxes people earning higher incomes at a higher rate than it does individuals making less money. (Ch. 14)

Project grant program: A grant program that requires state and local governments to compete for available federal money. (Ch. 3)

Proportional representation (PR): An election system that awards legislative seats to each party approximately equal to its popular voting strength. (Chs. 8 and 9)

Proportional tax: A levy that taxes all persons at the same percentage rate, regardless of income. (Ch. 14)

Prospective voting: The concept that voters evaluate the incumbent officeholder and the incumbent's party based on their expectations of future developments. (Ch. 9)

Public Broadcasting Service (PBS): A nonprofit private media corporation that is jointly owned by hundreds of member television stations throughout the United States. (Ch. 6)

Public policy: What government officials choose to do or not to do about public problems. (Intro)

Public sector: Governmentally owned segment of the economy. (Ch. 1)

Quasi-governmental company: A private, profit-seeking corporation created by Congress to serve a public purpose. (Ch. 12)

Racial profiling: The practice of a police officer targeting individuals as suspected criminals on the basis of their race or ethnicity. (Ch. 1)

Racially restrictive covenants: Private deed restrictions that prohibited property owners from selling or leasing property to African Americans or other minorities. (Ch. 16)

Rally effect: The tendency of the general public to express support for the incumbent president during a time of international threat. (Ch. 11)

Random sample: An unbiased sample in which each member of a universe has an equal likelihood of being included. (Ch. 4)

Ranking member: The leader of the minority party on a committee. (Ch. 10)

Reagan Doctrine: A corollary to the policy of containment enunciated by President Reagan calling for the United States to offer military aid to groups attempting to overthrow communist governments anywhere in the world. (Ch. 17)

Reapportionment: The reallocation of legislative seats. (Ch. 9)

Recession: An economic slowdown characterized by declining economic output and rising unemployment. (Chs. 1, 3, and 14)

Reconstruction: The process whereby the states that had seceded during the Civil War were reorganized and reestablished in the Union. (Ch. 11)

Red states: Republican states. (Ch. 9)

Redistricting: The process through which the boundaries of legislative districts are redrawn to reflect population movement. (Ch. 9)

Referendum: An election in which state voters can approve or reject a state law or constitutional amendment. (Ch. 16)

Regressive tax: A levy whose burden falls more heavily on lower-income groups than on wealthy taxpayers. (Ch. 14)

Regulatory negotiation: A structured process by which representatives of the interests that would be substantially impacted by a rule work with government officials to negotiate agreement on the terms of the rule. (Ch. 12)

Religious left: Individuals who hold liberal views because of their religious beliefs. (Chs. 4 and 7)

Religious right: Individuals who hold conservative views because of their religious beliefs. (Chs. 4 and 7)

Remand: Return a case to a lower court. (Ch. 13)

Representative democracy *or* republic: A political system in which citizens elect representatives to make policy decisions on their behalf. (Chs. 2 and 3)

Reprieve: An executive action that delays punishment for a crime. (Ch. 11)

Republican in name only (RINO): An accusation that a Republican candidate or elected official is insufficiently conservative to merit the support of party activists. (Ch. 8)

Reserved *or* residual powers: The powers of government left to the states. (Ch. 3)

Resolution: A legislative statement of opinion on a certain matter. (Ch. 10)

Retrospective voting: The concept that voters choose candidates based on their perception of an incumbent candidate's past performance in office or the performance of the incumbent party. (Ch. 9)

Rider: A provision, unlikely to become law on its own merits, which is attached to an important measure so that it will ride through the legislative process. (Ch. 10)

Right wing: Conservative. (Ch. 4)

Right-to-work laws: Statutes that prohibit union membership as a condition of employment. (Ch. 7)

Rogue state: A nation that threatens world peace by sponsoring international terrorism and promoting the spread of weapons of mass destruction. (Ch. 17)

Rose garden strategy: A campaign approach in which an incumbent president attempts to appear presidential rather than political. (Ch. 9)

Rule: A legally binding regulation. (Ch. 12)

Rule of Four: Decision process used by the Supreme Court to determine which cases to consider on appeal, holding that the Court will hear a case if four of the nine justices agree to the review. (Ch. 13)

Rule of law: The constitutional principle that holds that the discretion of public officials in dealing with individuals is limited by the law. (Ch. 2)

Rulemaking: A regulatory process used by government agencies to enact legally binding regulations. (Ch. 12)

Runoff: An election between the two candidates receiving the most votes when no candidate wins a majority in an initial election. (Ch. 9)

Sales tax: A levy on the retail sale of taxable items. (Ch. 14)

Sample: A subset or part of a universe. (Ch. 4)

School Lunch Program: A federal program that provides free or reduced-cost lunches to children from poor families. (Ch. 3)

Securities and Exchange Commission (SEC): An agency that regulates the sale of stocks and bonds as well as investment and holding companies. (Ch. 12)

Selective incorporation of the Bill of Rights against the states: The process through which the U.S. Supreme Court interpreted the Due Process Clause of the Fourteenth Amendment of the U.S. Constitution to apply most of the provisions of the national Bill of Rights to the states. (Chs. 2 and 15)

Senate Majority Leader: The head of the majority party in the Senate and that chamber's most important figure. (Ch. 10)

Senate president pro tempore: The official presiding officer in the Senate in the vice president's absence. (Ch. 10)

Senatorial courtesy: The custom that senators have a veto on the nomination of judges to staff district courts located in their states. (Ch. 13)

Seniority: Length of service. (Ch. 10)

Separate-but-equal: The judicial doctrine holding that separate facilities for whites and African Americans satisfy the equal protection requirement of the Fourteenth Amendment. (Ch. 16)

Separation of powers: The division of political power among executive, legislative, and judicial branches of government. (Chs. 2, 5, and 8)

Shield law: A statute that protects journalists from being forced to disclose confidential information in a legal proceeding. (Ch. 6)

Sierra Club: An environmental organization. (Ch. 7)

Signaling role: A term that refers to the media's accepted responsibility to alert the public to important developments as they happen. (Ch. 6)

Slander: False spoken statements that lower a person's reputation or expose a person to hatred, contempt, or ridicule. (Ch. 15)

Small Business Administration (SBA): The federal agency established to make loans to small businesses and assist them in obtaining government contracts. (Ch. 12)

Social Security: A federal pension and disability insurance program funded through a payroll tax on workers and their employers. (Chs. 1, 7, 11, and 14)

Social Security Administration (SSA): The federal agency that operates the Social Security system. (Ch. 12)

Socialism: An economic system characterized by governmental ownership of the means of production and control of the distribution of goods and services. (Ch. 1)

Soft money: The name given to funds that are raised by political parties which are not subject to federal campaign finance regulations. (Ch. 9)

Sound bite: A short phrase taken from a candidate's speech by the news media for use on newscasts. (Ch. 6)

Sovereign immunity: The legal concept that individuals cannot sue the government without the government's permission. (Ch. 13)

Sovereignty: The authority of a state to exercise its legitimate powers within its boundaries, free from external interference. (Ch. 2)

Speaker of the House: The presiding officer in the House of Representatives and the leader of the majority party in that chamber. (Ch. 10)

Special or select committee: A committee established for a limited time only. (Ch. 10)

Split ticket ballot: Voters casting their ballots for the candidates of two or more political parties. (Ch. 9)

Spoils system: The method of hiring government employees from among the friends, relatives, and supporters of elected officeholders. (Ch. 12)

***Sputnik*:** The world's first satellite, launched by the Soviet Union. (Ch. 17)

Standard of living: A term that refers to the goods and services affordable by and available to the residents of a nation. (Ch. 1)

Standing committee: A permanent legislative committee with authority to draft legislation in a particular policy area or areas. (Ch. 10)

State Children's Health Insurance Program (SCHIP): A federal program designed to provide health insurance to children from low-income families whose parents are not poor enough to qualify for Medicaid. (Ch. 2)

States' rights: An interpretation of the Constitution that favors limiting the authority of the federal government while expanding the powers of the states. (Chs. 3 and 13)

Statutory law: Law that is written by a legislature, rather than constitutional law. (Chs. 12, 13, and 16)

Straight ticket ballot: Voters selecting the entire slate of candidates of one party only. (Ch. 9)

Strategic forces: Nuclear forces. (Ch. 17)

Strict construction: The doctrine of constitutional interpretation holding that the document should be interpreted narrowly. (Ch. 13)

Strict judicial scrutiny: The judicial decision rule holding that the Supreme Court will find a government policy unconstitutional unless the government can demonstrate a compelling interest justifying the action. (Ch. 16)

Structured rules: Rules that specify which amendments are allowed and under what conditions, the time available for debate, and/or the method of voting on amendments. (Ch. 10)

Subgovernment or **iron triangle:** A cozy, three-sided relationship among government agencies, interest groups, and key members of Congress in which all parties benefit. (Ch. 12)

Subsidy: A financial incentive given by government to an individual or a business interest to accomplish a public objective. (Ch. 14)

Suffrage: The right to vote. (Ch. 16)

Sunbelt: Southern and Western regions of the United States. (Chs. 1 and 7)

Super delegates: Democratic Party officials and officeholders selected to attend the national party convention on the basis of the offices they hold. (Ch. 9)

Super majority: A voting margin which is greater than a simple majority. (Chs. 2 and 10)

Superpower: A country powerful enough to influence events throughout the world. (Ch. 1)

Supplemental Nutrition Assistance Program (SNAP): A federal program (once called the Food Stamp program) that provides vouchers to low-income families and individuals that can be used to purchase food from grocery stores. (Chs. 3 and 14)

Supplemental Security Income (SSI): A federal program that provides money to low-income people who are elderly, blind, or disabled who do not qualify for Social Security benefits. (Ch. 14)

Survey research: The measurement of public opinion. (Ch. 4)

Suspect classifications: Policy distinctions among persons based on their race, ethnicity, and citizenship status. (Ch. 16)

Swing voters: Citizens who could vote for either the Democratic or the Republican nominee. (Ch. 9)

Table: Postpone consideration of a legislative measure. (Ch. 10)

Tariffs: Taxes on imported goods. (Chs. 3 and 17)

Tax credit: An expenditure that reduces an individual's tax liability by the amount of the credit. (Ch. 14)

Tax deduction: An expenditure that can be subtracted from a taxpayer's gross income before figuring the tax owed. (Ch. 14)

Tax exemption: The exclusion of some types of income from taxation. (Ch. 14)

Tax preference: A tax deduction or exclusion that allows individuals to pay less tax than they would otherwise. (Ch. 14)

Tea Party movement: A loose network of conservative activists organized to protest high taxes, excessive government spending, and big government in general. (Chs. 5, 7, and 8)

Temporary Assistance to Needy Families (TANF): A federal program that provides temporary financial assistance and work opportunities to needy families. (Ch. 14)

Tennessee Valley Authority (TVA): A federal agency established to promote the development of the Tennessee River and its tributaries. (Ch. 12)

Term limitation: The movement to restrict the number of terms public officials may serve. (Ch. 10)

Test case: A lawsuit initiated to assess the constitutionality of a legislative or executive act. (Chs. 13, 15, and 16)

Test of understanding: A legal requirement that citizens must accurately explain a passage in the United States or state constitution before they can register to vote. (Ch. 16)

Third party: A minor party in a two-party system. (Ch. 8)

Trade associations: Organizations representing the interests of firms and professionals in the same general field. (Ch. 7)

Trial: The formal examination of a judicial dispute in accordance with law before a single judge. (Ch. 13)

Truman Doctrine: The foreign policy put forward by President Harry Truman calling for American support for all free peoples resisting communist aggression by internal or outside forces. (Ch. 17)

Two-party system: The division of voter loyalties between two major political parties, resulting in the near exclusion of minor parties from seriously competing for a share of political power. (Ch. 8)

Tyranny of the majority: The abuse of the minority by the majority. (Ch. 2)

Unanimous consent agreement (UCA): A formal understanding on procedures for conducting business in the Senate that requires the acceptance of every member of the chamber. (Ch. 10)

Unfunded mandate: A requirement imposed by Congress on state or local governments without providing federal funding to cover its cost. (Ch. 3)

Unicameral legislature: Legislature with one chamber. (Ch. 2)

Unitary government: A governmental system in which political authority is concentrated in a single national government. (Ch. 2)

United Nations (UN): An international organization founded in 1945 as a diplomatic forum to resolve conflicts among the world's nations. (Ch. 17)

Universe: The population researchers wish to study. (Ch. 4)

U.S. Postal Service (USPS): A government corporation responsible for mail service. (Ch. 12)

Value added tax (VAT): A tax on the estimated market value added to a product or material at each stage of its manufacture or distribution, which is ultimately passed on to the consumer. (Ch. 14)

Veto: An action by the chief executive refusing to approve a measure passed by the legislature. (Ch. 10)

Voter mobilization: The process of motivating citizens to vote. (Ch. 5)

Voting age population (VAP): The number of U.S. residents who are 18 years of age or older. (Ch. 5)

Voting eligible population (VEP): The number of U.S. residents who are legally qualified to vote. (Ch. 5)

Voting Rights Act (VRA): A federal law designed to protect the voting rights of racial and ethnic minorities. (Chs. 7, 9, and 16)

War Powers Act: A law limiting the president's ability to commit American armed forces to combat abroad without consultation with Congress and congressional approval. (Ch. 11)

Warrant: An official authorization issued by a judicial officer. (Ch. 15)

Watergate: A scandal that involved the abuse of presidential power by President Richard Nixon and members of his administration that led to his resignation in 1974. (Ch. 6)

Weapons of mass destruction (WMD): Nuclear, chemical, and biological weapons that are designed to inflict widespread military and civilian casualties. (Chs. 11 and 17)

Welfare programs: Government programs that provide benefits to individuals based on their economic status. (Ch. 14)

Welfare state: A government that takes responsibility for the welfare of its citizens through programs in public health, public housing, old-age pensions, unemployment compensation, and the like. (Ch. 14)

Whips: Assistant floor leaders in Congress. (Ch. 10)

Whistleblowers: Workers who report wrongdoing or mismanagement. (Ch. 12)

White primary: An electoral system used in the South to prevent the participation of African Americans in the Democratic primary. (Ch. 16)

World Health Organization (WHO): An international organization created to control disease worldwide. (Ch. 17)

World Trade Organization (WTO): An international organization that administers trade laws, and provides a forum for settling trade disputes among nations. (Ch. 17)

Writ of *Habeas corpus*: A court order requiring that government authorities either release a person held in custody or demonstrate that the person is detained in accordance with law. (Chs. 2 and 13)

Writ of *Mandamus*: A court order directing a public official to perform a specific act or duty. (Ch. 2)

Zone of acquiescence: The range of policy options acceptable to the public on a particular issue. (Ch. 4)

Photo Credits

4: Gary C. Caskey/UPI/Landov; 8: Bob Daemmrich/The Image Works; 17: Al Crespo/Sipa press; 20: Rob Crandall/The Image Works; 22: Paul Saloma/AP Photo; 35: David Bacon/The Image Works; 38: Bob Daemmrich/The Image Works; 40: Roger Violett/The Image Works; 45: J. Berry/The Image Works; 60: David Young Wolff/PhotoEdit; 64: Owen Franken/Corbis; 67: Marilyn Humphness/The Image Works; 69: Danny Moloshok/AP Photos; 78: Bettmann/Corbis; 81: Masterfile; 83: James Leynse/Corbis; 90: Bettmann/Corbis; 92: Brent Jones; 100: Melanie Stetson/The Image Works; 110: Marjorie Cortera/The Image Works; 112: Bob Daemmrich/The Image Works; 116: Ken Cedeno/Corbis; 119: Chris Fitzgerald/The Image Works; 121: Bob Daemmrich Photography; 129: Monika Graff/The Image Works; 130: Larry Downing/Corbis; 136: David Zalubowski/AP Photo; 137: Scott Applewhite/AP Photo; 144: Robert Wallis/Corbis; 147: Joe Skipper/Reuters/Corbis; 151: Richard B. Levine/newcom.com; 153: Kenneth Lambert/AP Photo; 159: Tim Lynch/age fotostock; 167: AP Photo; 173: Larry Smith/Corbis; 175: zumapress/news.com; 183: Judy Dehaas/AP Photo; 189: Tim Mueller/AP Photo; 198: Michael Maloney/Corbis; 204: Rick Friedman/Corbis; 208: Ramin Talaie/Corbis; 213: Chris Fitzgerald/The Image Works; 217: Justin Lane/Corbis; 235: Michael Reynolds/Corbis; 238: Taylor Jones/Corbis; 241: Michael Reynolds/Corbis; 244: AP Photo; 254: Ron Sachs/Getty Images; 258: AP Photo; 262: Corbis; 269: Ed Fischer/Cartoon Stock; 271: Elliott Erwitt/Magnum; 274: The Franklin D. Roosevelt Library; 278: AP Photo; 281: AP Photo; 284: UPI/news.com; 292: Pete Souza/Corbis; 305: Caro/Top Foto/The Image Works; 311: AP Photo; 317: AP Photo; 320: Peter Hvizdak/The Image Works; 331: AP Photo; 336: Najlah Feanny/Corbis; 344: Bettmann/Corbis; 349: Supreme Court Historical Society; 361: AP Photo; 369: Cherry Himmelstein/Corbis; 376: Susan Lapides; 385: Wasserman/Boston Globe/TMS International; 386: Topfoto/The Image Works; 390: AP Photo; 406: AP Photo; 407: news.com; 409: William Campbell/Sygma/Corbis; 418: Ramin Talaie/Corbis; 425: Jeff Danziger/the Christian Science Monitor; 434: Jim West/The Image Works; 438: AP Photo; 441: VMI Photo; 444: Hulton Archive/Getty Images; 458: Bob Daemmrich/PhotoEdit; 465: Ramin Talaie/Corbis; 468: AP Photo; 475: Bettmann/Corbis; 483: Pete Souza/Corbis; 487: Jeffrey Alexander/The Image Works.

Index

PRACTICE TESTS

NOTE: The first number in parenthesis after each question stem indicates the "What We Will Learn" question associated with the particular multiple-choice question. The second is the page number(s) in the text addressed in the question. For example, multiple-choice question 1 deals with material covered in the first "What We Will Learn" questions. The information is found on p. 2 of the text.

Introduction: Government, Politics, and the Policymaking Process

Circle the correct answer.

1. How does government affect individuals? (1) (pp. 2–3)

   (A) Through taxes and fees
   (B) By providing services
   (C) Through regulations
   (D) All of the above

2. Taxes and fees collected by all levels of government combined represent what proportion of the nation's GDP? (1) (p. 2)

   (A) 5 percent
   (B) 15 percent
   (C) 25 percent
   (D) 35 percent

3. The institution with authority to set policy for society is known as which of the following? (2) (p. 4)

   (A) Politics
   (B) Government
   (C) Public policy
   (D) Gross domestic policy (GDP)

4. Congress, the president, the Federal Communications Commission, and the Supreme Court are all part of which of the following institutions? (2) (p. 4)

   (A) Government
   (B) Politics
   (C) Policymaking environment
   (D) Public policy

5. The process that determines who shall occupy the roles of leadership in government and how the power of government shall be exercised is a definition of which of the following? (2) (p. 4)

   (A) Politics
   (B) Political science
   (C) Government
   (D) Public policy

6. Which of the following terms is defined as the actions government officials choose to do or not to do about public problems? (3) (p. 5)

   (A) Politics
   (B) Government
   (C) Political science
   (D) Public policy

7. A city council refuses to enact an ordinance (local law) designed to regulate smoking in public places. Is this decision an example of a public policy? (3) (p. 5)

   (A) No. Public policies require the adoption of a policy and the city council rejected the policy proposal.
   (B) No. This proposal would have violated the ADA.
   (C) Yes. This is an example of a public policy because it would have regulated public places.
   (D) Yes. A public policy is what government officials choose to do or *not* to do about public problems.

8. Is the ADA an example of a public policy? (3) (p. 5)

   (A) Yes, because it is what government officials choose to do about the problem of discrimination against people with disabilities
   (B) Yes, because it was not done secretly
   (C) Yes, because it affects a lot of people
   (D) No, because it does not involve an election

9. Which of the following is *not* an example of a public policy? (3) (p. 5)

   (A) The refusal of the U.S. government to grant diplomatic recognition to the nation of Cuba
   (B) The decision of CBS News to name Katie Couric as the anchor of its network evening news
   (C) The decision of Federal Communications Commission (FCC) to adopt a rule concerning the joint ownership of a newspaper, television, and radio station in the same market
   (D) The decision of the U.S. Senate to confirm a presidential appointment to the Fifth Circuit Court of Appeals

10. The factors that determine the problems that government will address, the set of policy alternatives that decision-makers will consider, and the resources available for addressing the problem are known as which of the following? (3) (p. 5)

    (A) Agenda setting
    (B) Policymaking process
    (C) The context of policymaking
    (D) Politics

11. Which of the following is part of the context of policymaking? (3) (pp. 5–6)

    (A) Which political party controls Congress and the White House
    (B) The state of the nation's economy
    (C) The U.S. Constitution
    (D) All of the above

12. The process through which problems become matters of public concern and government action is a definition of which of the following terms? (3) (p. 6)
    (A) Policy adoption
    (B) Policy implementation
    (C) Agenda setting
    (D) Policy formulation

13. The development of strategies for dealing with the problems on the official policy agenda is a definition for which of the following? (3) (p. 7)
    (A) Policy formulation
    (B) Policy adoption
    (C) Policy implementation
    (D) Policy evaluation

14. The official decision of a government body to accept a particular policy and put it into effect is a definition for which of the following? (3) (p. 7)
    (A) Policy evaluation
    (B) Policy formulation
    (C) Policy implementation
    (D) Policy adoption

15. Which of the following is an example of policy adoption? (3) (pp. 7–8)
    (A) Congress passes the ADA and the president signs the measure into law.
    (B) The Supreme Court rules that state laws requiring racial segregation in public schools are unconstitutional.
    (C) The president issues an executive order prohibiting the use of torture in the questioning of suspected terrorists.
    (D) All of the above are correct answers.

16. The actions taken by government officials and others to ensure that most citizens regard a policy as a legal and appropriate government response to a problem is the definition of which of the following terms? (3) (p. 8)
    (A) Policy formulation
    (B) Policy adoption
    (C) Policy legitimation
    (D) Policy evaluation

17. The stage of the policy process in which policies are carried out is a definition for which of the following? (3) (p. 9)
    (A) Agenda setting
    (B) Policy adoption
    (C) Policy evaluation
    (D) Policy implementation

18. The EEOC files suit against a business accused of failing to be accessible to people with disabilities. This action illustrates which of the following stages of the policymaking process? (3) (p. 9)
    (A) Policy implementation
    (B) Agenda setting
    (C) Policy adoption
    (D) Policy formulation

19. The assessment of policy is a definition of which of the following? (3) (p. 9)
    (A) Policy implementation
    (B) Policy evaluation
    (C) Policy change
    (D) Policy legitimation

20. The modification of policy goals and means in light of new information or shifting political environments is the definition of which of the following? (3) (p. 10)
    (A) Policy implementation
    (B) Policy evaluation
    (C) Policy change
    (D) Policy legitimation

Chapter 1: A Changing America in a Changing World

Circle the correct answer.

1. What is racial profiling? (1) (p. 13)
   (A) The practice of a police officer targeting individuals as suspected criminals based on their race or ethnicity.
   (B) The practice of giving preference to racial and ethnic minorities in college and university admissions.
   (C) The practice of giving preference to racial and ethnic minorities in hiring.
   (D) None of the above are correct answers.

2. Which of the following statements is true about the baby-boom generation? (2) (p. 13)
   (A) The baby-boom generation is smaller than preceding or succeeding generations.
   (B) The baby-boom generation retired just before 2000.
   (C) The baby-boom generation was born after World War II.
   (D) None of the above are correct answers.

3. Which of the following countries is *not* an important source of recent immigration to the United States? (2) (p. 15)
   (A) Mexico
   (B) China
   (C) Great Britain
   (D) India

4. Demographers expect which of the following racial/ethnic groups will grow most rapidly in the years ahead? (2) (p. 16)
   (A) Latinos
   (B) Whites
   (C) African Americans
   (D) Asian Americans

5. After the 2010 Census, Texas gained seats in the U.S. House of Representatives. Knowing that fact, which of the following statements must therefore be true? (2) (p. 17)
   (A) Texas is the most populous state in the nation.
   (B) The population of Texas increased at a faster rate in the 2000s than did the population of the United States as a whole.
   (C) Texas is in the Sunbelt.
   (D) All of the above are correct answers.

6. The term *superpower* accurately describes which of the following nations today? (3) (p. 19)
   (A) Russia
   (B) China
   (C) United States
   (D) All of the above

7. Which of the following nations spends the most money on its military? (3) (p. 19)
   (A) United States
   (B) China
   (C) Russia
   (D) India

8. Which of the following nations has the largest economy? (3) (p. 19)
   (A) China
   (B) Russia
   (C) India
   (D) United States

9. The integration of national economies into a world economic system in which companies compete worldwide for suppliers and markets is the definition for which of the following terms? (4) (p. 21)
   (A) Capitalism
   (B) Socialism
   (C) Democracy
   (D) Global economy

10. Which of the following countries was *not* part of the North America Free Trade Agreement (NAFTA)? (4) (p. 21)
    (A) United States
    (B) Mexico
    (C) Canada
    (D) El Salvador

11. How have low-skilled workers been affected by the global economy? (4) (p. 21)
    (A) They have been harmed because global competition has led to price increases for many of the products that they purchase.
    (B) They have been harmed because American companies cannot afford to pay high wages to low-skill workers and still compete effectively against foreign competitors with lower wage costs.
    (C) They have been helped because the number of good jobs available to low-skill workers has increased.
    (D) All of the above are correct answers.

12. Which of the following statements is true about income distribution in the United States? (5) (pp. 22–23)
    (A) Since 1980, the proportion of national income received by the wealthiest fifth of the population has increased.
    (B) Since 1980, the proportion of income received by the poorest fifth of the population has fallen.
    (C) The income gap between the wealthiest and poorest families has been increasing.
    (D) All of the above are correct answers.

13. Median household income in the United States is highest for which of the following groups? (5) (p. 23)

(A) Asian Americans
(B) Whites
(C) African Americans
(D) Latinos

14. Which of the following statements is true? (5) (pp. 23–24)

(A) Household income is higher in the South than it is in any other region.
(B) On average, women earn more than men.
(C) The average income for people living in metropolitan areas is lower than it is for people living outside metropolitan areas.
(D) None of the above are correct answers.

15. How is the official poverty threshold determined? (5) (p. 24)

(A) The poverty threshold is set at 30 percent of average household income. Anyone earning less than 30 percent of the average is considered poor.
(B) The official poverty rate was set in 1950 at $8,000 and changes each year based on the inflation rate.
(C) The poverty threshold is based on the amount of money an individual or family needs to purchase basic necessities.
(D) People declare whether they are poor based on their perception of their ability to buy the things they need.

16. The poverty rate is highest for which of the following racial/ethnic groups? (5) (pp. 24–25)

(A) Asian Americans
(B) Whites
(C) African Americans
(D) Latinos

17. Which of the following statements is true about healthcare insurance coverage in America? (5) (p. 25)

(A) Government programs, primarily Medicare and Medicaid, cover more people than insurance through employers.
(B) Citizens are more likely to have health insurance than are noncitizens.
(C) African Americans and Latinos are more likely to have health insurance coverage than are whites.
(D) All of the above are correct answers.

18. Which of the following terms is defined as "the widely held, deeply rooted political values of a society?" (6) (p. 26)

(A) Socialism
(B) Political culture
(C) Democracy
(D) Capitalism

19. A system of government in which ultimate political authority is vested in the people is the definition of which of the following terms? (6) (p. 26)

(A) Mixed economy
(B) Political culture
(C) Democracy
(D) Capitalism

20. According to Robert A. Dahl, which of the following is a criterion of democracy? (6) (pp. 26–27)

(A) Citizens have the right to form political parties and organize groups.
(B) All businesses and industry are privately owned.
(C) All citizens enjoy a minimum standard of living, including access to healthcare.
(D) All of the above are correct answers.

21. Why do political scientists consider Saudi Arabia to be an absolute monarchy? (6) (p. 27)

(A) Saudi Arabia is ruled by one person—King Abdullah.
(B) Religion is very important in Saudi Arabia.
(C) Women do not have the right to vote in Saudi Arabia.
(D) The Saudi economy is dominated by the oil industry.

22. Which of the following is characteristic of a democracy? (6) (pp. 26–27)

(A) People have the right to criticize the government.
(B) People have the right to join unions and other interest groups.
(C) People have the right to run against current officeholders.
(D) All of the above are correct answers.

23. An economic system characterized by individual and corporate ownership of the means of production, and a market economy based on the supply and demand of goods and services, is a definition of which of the following? (6) (p. 27)

(A) Socialism
(B) Capitalism
(C) Democracy
(D) Mixed economy

24. In Country A, the government owns and operates business and industry. It makes decisions about the production and distribution of goods and services in the public interest without regard for the profit motive. Which of the following terms best describes Country A? (6) (pp. 27–28)

(A) Democracy
(B) Mixed economy
(C) Socialism
(D) Capitalism

25. In Country A, most business and industry are privately owned, but they are subject to extensive regulation. Which of the following terms best describes Country A? (6) (p. 28)

(A) Mixed economy
(B) Socialism
(C) Constitutional monarchy
(D) Democracy

Chapter 2: The American Constitution

Circle the correct answer.

1. The fundamental law by which a state or nation is organized and governed, and to which ordinary legislation must conform, is the definition of which of the following? (1) (p. 33)

   (A) Bicameralism (B) Separation of powers
   (C) Constitution (D) Federalism

2. What does "power of the purse" mean? (1) (p. 34)

   (A) Control of the finances of government
   (B) Control of the armed forces
   (C) Control of foreign relations
   (D) Control of the power to appoint public officials

3. Which of the following was *not* a criticism of the Articles of Confederation? (1) (pp. 35–36)

   (A) The Articles were too difficult to amend.
   (B) The Articles gave too much power to the president.
   (C) The Articles failed to give the national government adequate authority to raise revenue.
   (D) The Articles failed to give the national government adequate authority to regulate commerce.

4. The political thought of John Locke had the most influence over which of the following documents? (2) (p. 36)

   (A) Articles of Confederation
   (B) Declaration of Independence
   (C) Constitution of 1787
   (D) Fourteenth Amendment

5. In 2009, voters in Switzerland voted to approve a ban on the construction of minarets, which are spires next to mosques from which the call to prayer is issued. The Swiss vote is an example of which of the following? (3) (p. 38)

   (A) Representative democracy
   (B) Republic
   (C) Confederation
   (D) Direct democracy

6. Suppose that the majority of the people of a particular political district adhere to the same religion. The majority uses its control of government to adopt policies that limit public office to members of that religion and seriously disadvantage people who do not share their belief. The framers of the U.S. Constitution would use which of the following terms or phrases to describe that situation? (3) (p. 38)

   (A) Tyranny of the majority
   (B) Representative democracy
   (C) Direct democracy
   (D) Separation of powers with checks and balances

7. The voters in Country A elect legislators who make policy decisions on their behalf. Which of the following terms best describes Country A? (3) (pp. 38–39)

   (A) Federalism
   (B) Direct democracy
   (C) Unitary government
   (D) Representative democracy

8. The political thought of Baron de Montesquieu is associated most closely with which of the following constitutional principles? (4) (p. 39)

   (A) Bill of Rights
   (B) Separation of powers
   (C) Federalism
   (D) Due process of law

9. According to James Madison, what constitutional principle was designed to prevent the concentration of power in the hands of one government official or set of officials? (4) (p. 39)

   (A) Separation of powers with checks and balances
   (B) *Federalist Papers*
   (C) Tyranny of the majority
   (D) Bill of Rights

10. The president nominates Person A to the U.S. Supreme Court, but the Senate rejects the nomination. This scenario is an example of which of the following? (4) (p. 41)

    (A) Federalism
    (B) Bicameralism
    (C) Checks and balances
    (D) Tyranny of the majority

11. Which of the following statements is true of the British parliamentary system? (4) (p. 41)

    (A) It is undemocratic because it does not have separation of powers.
    (B) The House of Lords and the House of Commons are equally powerful.
    (C) The prime minister is chosen by majority vote of the House of Commons.
    (D) All of the above are correct answers.

12. Why did the framers of the Constitution divide Congress into two chambers? (4) (pp. 41–42)

    (A) They wanted to ensure that the executive branch would be the dominant branch of government.
    (B) They wanted to prevent the legislative branch from becoming too powerful.
    (C) They wanted to prevent the judicial branch from becoming too powerful.
    (D) They wanted to strengthen the legislative branch.

13. A political system that divides power between a central government, with authority over the whole nation, and a series of state governments is known as which of the following? (4) (p. 43)

    (A) Unitary government
    (B) Confederation
    (C) Federal system
    (D) Authoritarian government

14. Congress passes a law that criminalizes past actions that were taken before the law was passed. This law would be an example of which of the following? (5) (p. 45)
    (A) *Ex post facto* law
    (B) Bill of attainder
    (C) *Habeas corpus*
    (D) Separation of powers

15. The Constitution guarantees accused persons the right to a speedy, public trial by an impartial jury, the right to confront witnesses, and the right to legal counsel. These provisions embody which of the following constitutional principles? (5) (p. 45)
    (A) Separation of powers
    (B) Tyranny of the majority
    (C) Checks and balances
    (D) Due process of law

16. The constitutional principle that government does not have unrestricted authority over individuals is the definition for which of the following terms? (5) (p. 46)
    (A) Limited government
    (B) Due process of law
    (C) Separation of powers
    (D) Bicameralism

17. The first ten amendments to the Constitution are known as which of the following? (5) (p. 46)
    (A) Declaration of Independence
    (B) Articles of Confederation
    (C) Bill of Rights
    (D) Bill of attainder

18. Do the provisions of the Bill of Rights apply to state governments? (5) (p. 47)
    (A) No. The Bill of Rights applies only to the actions of the federal government.
    (B) Yes. The Supreme Court has ruled that the entire Bill of Rights applies to state governments as well as the national government.
    (C) Yes. The Supreme Court has ruled that the Bill of Rights applies to the states but not to the national government.
    (D) Yes, for the most part. The Supreme Court has ruled that most of the provisions of the Bill of Rights apply to the states.

19. The selective incorporation of the Bill of Rights to the states is based on which of the following constitutional provisions? (5) (p. 47)
    (A) The Due Process Clause of the Fourteenth Amendment
    (B) The Equal Protection Clause of the Fourteenth Amendment
    (C) The Privileges and Immunities Clause of the Fourteenth Amendment
    (D) The Thirteenth Amendment

20. Which of the following is a means through which the Constitution changes? (6) (pp. 48–49)
    (A) Practice and experience
    (B) Constitutional amendment
    (C) Judicial interpretation
    (D) All of the above

21. Which of the following is a step in the process of amending the Constitution? (6) (p. 48)
    (A) The House votes to propose the amendment by majority vote.
    (B) The Senate votes to propose the amendment by majority vote.
    (C) The president signs the proposed amendment.
    (D) Three-fourths of the states ratify the proposed amendment.

22. Which of the following procedures for proposing or ratifying constitutional amendments has never been used? (6) (p. 48)
    (A) A constitutional convention called by the states proposes an amendment.
    (B) The House and Senate propose an amendment by a two-thirds vote.
    (C) Three-fourths of state legislatures ratify a constitutional amendment.
    (D) Three-fourths of specially called state conventions ratify a constitutional amendment.

23. Which of the following branches of government has the role of interpreting the meaning of the Constitution? (6) (p. 49)
    (A) Legislative branch
    (B) Judicial branch
    (C) Executive branch
    (D) All three branches play an equal role.

24. What was the significance of *Marbury v. Madison*? (6) (pp. 49–50)
    (A) It was the first case in which the U.S. Supreme Court declared an act of Congress unconstitutional.
    (B) The U.S. Supreme Court ruled that racial segregation was constitutional.
    (C) The U.S. Supreme Court ruled that state laws requiring racially segregated schools were unconstitutional.
    (D) The U.S. Supreme Court ruled that federal law takes precedence over state law.

25. In which of the following ways does the Constitution affect policymaking? (7) (pp. 51–53)
    (A) Policies change rapidly, sometimes without sufficient deliberation.
    (B) A narrow majority, 50 percent plus one, can almost always force through major changes over the objections of the minority.
    (C) Government is sometimes unable to adopt solutions to problems when no consensus exists in the nation as to the direction that should be taken.
    (D) All of the above are correct answers.

Chapter 3: The Federal System

Circle the correct answer.

1. Which of the following arguments best supports the adoption of federal education programs and initiatives such as No Child Left Behind and Race to the Top? (1) (pp. 58–59)
   (A) Federal officials understand the policy preferences of local residents better than do state officials.
   (B) Federal programs offer local officials more flexibility in the implementation of education programs than do state programs.
   (C) Only the federal government has the financial resources necessary to achieve educational goals.
   (D) All of the above are correct answers.

2. A political system that divides power between a central government with authority over the whole nation and a series of state governments is known as which of the following? (2) (p. 59)
   (A) Federal system of government
   (B) Confederation
   (C) Unitary government
   (D) Republic

3. Article I, Section 8, of the U.S. Constitution declares that Congress has the authority to coin money. Coining money is an example of which of the following? (2) (p. 60)
   (A) Delegated powers
   (B) Implied powers
   (C) Checks and balances
   (D) Concurrent powers

4. Which of the following branches of government has the most extensive list of delegated powers? (2) (p. 60)
   (A) Judicial branch
   (B) Legislative branch
   (C) Executive branch
   (D) State governments

5. Which of the following is true about Congress? (2) (pp. 60–61)
   (A) The Constitution vests legislative power in Congress.
   (B) Congress has the power of the purse.
   (C) The Constitution delegates certain powers to Congress in Article I, Section 8.
   (D) All of the above are correct answers.

6. Which of the following statements is accurate about the powers of Congress? (2) (pp. 60–61)
   (A) Congress can exercise any power it wishes to exercise because it is a sovereign body.
   (B) Congress can exercise any power except those powers prohibited by the U.S. Constitution.
   (C) Congress can exercise only those powers delegated to it by the U.S. Constitution or implied through the application of the Necessary and Proper Clause.
   (D) Congress can exercise only those powers given to it in the Bill of Rights.

7. In Article I, Section 8, the Constitution grants Congress authority to "regulate commerce among the several states." Congress passes legislation establishing regulations for interstate trucking, including safety standards for trucks and drivers. Which of the following constitutional provisions or principles gives Congress the authority to set standards for trucks and truck drivers? (2) (pp. 61–62)
   (A) National Supremacy Clause
   (B) Implied powers
   (C) Concurrent powers
   (D) Equal Protection Clause

8. The Elastic Clause is another name for which of the following constitutional provisions? (2) (p. 61)
   (A) National Supremacy Clause
   (B) Equal Protection Clause
   (C) Necessary and Proper Clause
   (D) Commerce Clause

9. The Constitution delegates which of the following powers to the president? (2) (p. 62)
   (A) The power to regulate commerce among the states
   (B) The power to command the armed forces
   (C) The power to declare war
   (D) All of the above

10. Suppose Congress passes a law which conflicts with the state constitution of Georgia. Which takes precedence—the U.S. law or the Georgia Constitution? (2) (pp. 62–63)
    (A) The Georgia Constitution because of the Tenth Amendment
    (B) The Georgia Constitution because all constitutions take precedence over all laws
    (C) The U.S. law because of the delegated powers
    (D) The U.S. law because of the National Supremacy Clause

11. Race to the Top requires that states eliminate barriers to the expansion of charter schools in order to continue receiving federal funds. This requirement is an example of which of the following? (2) (p. 63)
    (A) Federal mandate
    (B) Matching funds requirement
    (C) Federal preemption of state authority
    (D) Project grant

12. Congress passes legislation prohibiting states from regulating cellular telephone rates. The action is an example of which of the following? (2) (p. 63)
    (A) Federal mandate
    (B) Matching funds requirement
    (C) Federal preemption of state authority
    (D) Nullification

13. Mr. and Mrs. Brown are residents of Louisiana. They fly to Nevada and get divorced. Are they legally divorced in the eyes of the state of Louisiana? Why or why not? (3) (p. 64)

(A) They are not divorced. Because they were married in Louisiana, they must get divorced in Louisiana.
(B) They are not divorced because the Defense of Marriage Act declares that states are not required to recognize divorces granted in other states.
(C) They are divorced because the Privileges and Immunities Clause requires states to honor the official actions of other states.
(D) They are divorced because the Full Faith and Credit Clause forces states to honor the official actions of other states.

14. A person wanted for a crime in New York flees to Florida where he is arrested. The procedure for returning the accused person to New York to face criminal charges is known as which of the following? (3) (p. 65)

(A) Full Faith and Credit
(B) Privileges and Immunities
(C) Extradition
(D) Delegated powers

15. The Tenth Amendment is the constitutional basis for which of the following? (3) (p. 65)

(A) Reserved powers
(B) Delegated powers
(C) Implied powers
(D) Concurrent powers

16. Both state governments and the national government have the constitutional authority to tax and spend. Therefore, the power to tax and spend is an example of which of the following? (3) (p. 65)

(A) Reserved powers
(B) Delegated powers
(C) Implied powers
(D) Concurrent powers

17. Which of the following statements would be most likely to come from an advocate of a strong national government as opposed to a supporter of states' rights? (4) (pp. 65–66)

(A) National control makes for better public policies.
(B) The Constitution is a compact among the states, and the powers of the national government should be narrowly interpreted.
(C) The powers of the national government should be closely limited to the delegated powers.
(D) All of the above are correct answers.

18. Would states' rights advocates favor or oppose the Race to the Top? (4) (pp. 65–66)

(A) They would favor the law because it provides federal money to support state education programs.
(B) They would favor the law because a Democratic president was behind the initiative.
(C) They would oppose the law because it increased federal involvement in education policy, which is traditionally an area of state responsibility.
(D) They would oppose the law because it didn't provide enough money to support public education.

19. Which of the following was part of the Supreme Court's ruling in *McCulloch v. Maryland*? (5) (pp. 66–68)

(A) The Supreme Court ruled that Congress lacked the constitutional authority to charter a bank.
(B) The Supreme Court ruled that the powers of Congress were limited to the delegated powers.
(C) The Supreme Court upheld the Maryland tax on the bank.
(D) None of the above are correct answers.

20. Which of the following constitutional provisions has played the most prominent role in the modern expansion of federal government authority? (5) (p. 68)

(A) Equal Protection Clause
(B) Full Faith and Credit Clause
(C) Privileges and Immunities Clause
(D) Commerce Clause

21. A federal grant program that provides funds to state and local governments for a fairly narrow, specific purpose is known as which of the following? (6) (p. 71)

(A) Block grant
(B) Formula grant
(C) Categorical grant
(D) Project grant

22. A federal grant program that provides money for a program in a broad, general policy area, such as childcare or job training, is known as which of the following? (6) (p. 71)

(A) Block grant
(B) Formula grant
(C) Categorical grant
(D) Project grant

23. A grant program that requires state and local governments to compete for available federal money is known as which of the following? (6) (p. 72)

(A) Block grant
(B) Formula grant
(C) Categorical grant
(D) Project grant

24. A grant program that awards funding on the basis of a formula established by Congress is known as which of the following? (6) (p. 72)

(A) Block grant
(B) Formula grant
(C) Categorical grant
(D) Project grant

25. In order to qualify for a federal grant, a unit of local government is required to spend a certain amount of its own money on the activity supported by the grant. This is an example of which of the following? (6) (p. 72)

(A) Matching funds requirement
(B) Federal preemption of state authority
(C) Appropriations process
(D) Nullification

Chapter 4: Public Opinion

Circle the correct answer.

1. The process whereby individuals acquire political attitudes, knowledge, and beliefs is known as which of the following? (1) (p. 78)

   (A) Political efficacy
   (B) Political socialization
   (C) Political trust
   (D) Political science

2. Which of the following statements about the socialization process is *not* true? (1) (pp. 79–83)

   (A) Political socialization ends when individuals reach their early 20s.
   (B) Young children typically identify with the same political party as their parents.
   (C) Schools historically have taught the children of immigrants to be patriotic Americans and they continue to play that role today.
   (D) Personal involvement in religious organizations is associated with political participation.

3. Which of the following agents of socialization plays the most important role in shaping the party identification of youngsters? (1) (p. 80)

   (A) Family
   (B) School
   (C) Peers
   (D) Media

4. A team of political scientists wants to measure the attitudes of college students toward politics and government. The universe for the study would be which of the following? (2) (p. 84)

   (A) The group of individuals who are actually interviewed for the study
   (B) All college-age adults
   (C) All college students
   (D) All Americans

5. A professionally administered survey has a margin of error of plus or minus 3 percentage points. Assume that the sample was properly drawn and carefully conducted. How often will a sample differ from the universe by more than 3 percentage points, merely on the basis of chance? (2) (p. 85)

   (A) Never. If the sample is truly random, it will never differ by more than the margin of error.
   (B) One time in 20. Even a perfectly drawn sample will by chance be outside the margin of error 5 percent of the time.
   (C) Three percent of the time. The margin of error indicates the error factor built into a survey.
   (D) One time in five. A well-conducted survey will be wrong 20 percent of the time.

6. A public opinion poll taken a month before the election has a margin of error of 3 percentage points. The poll shows Candidate A ahead of Candidate B by 46 percent to 44 percent with the rest undecided. What is the best analysis of the result of the poll? (2) (p. 85)

   (A) Candidate A is ahead by at least 2 percentage points but may actually be ahead by 5 percentage points.
   (B) Candidate A is ahead but it is impossible to know by how much.
   (C) Candidate B is actually ahead because Candidate A did not reach the 50 percent support level.
   (D) The candidates are in a statistical tie because the difference in their support is within the margin of error.

7. A major Internet provider regularly conducts online polls about current issues, such as healthcare reform, the war in Afghanistan, and immigration reform. Sometimes tens of thousands of people participate. Would the results of these polls be accurate? (2) (p. 85)

   (A) Yes. The sample size is large and everyone has a chance to participate.
   (B) No. The sample size is too small.
   (C) No. The sample size is too large.
   (D) Probably not. It is unlikely that the sample is a representative sample of the universe.

8. Why did the *Literary Digest* poll fail to correctly predict the outcome of the 1936 presidential election? (2) (p. 86)

   (A) The sample size was too small.
   (B) The sample size was too large.
   (C) The sample was biased because it included only people with telephones and automobiles.
   (D) The questions were biased because they were slanted in favor of the Republican candidate.

9. A survey conducted October 1, more than a month before the election, shows Candidate A with 55 percent support and Candidate B with 40 percent. The margin of error is 4 percentage points. What is the best evaluation of the survey? (2) (pp. 88–89)

   (A) Candidate A is ahead today but surveys can't predict the future.
   (B) Neither candidate is ahead because the survey is within the margin of error.
   (C) Candidate A will win by a 15 percentage point margin.
   (D) Candidate A will win by a margin of 11 to 19 percentage points.

10. Which of the following statements about interest in and knowledge about government and politics is true? (3) (pp. 90–91)

   (A) People who are interested and informed are more likely to vote than people who are not.
   (B) Republicans as a group are better informed than Democrats.
   (C) Over the last decade, interest in politics and government has increased.
   (D) All of the above are correct answers.

11. Which of the following groups of Americans is the best informed and most interested in politics and government? (3) (p. 91)

(A) Younger women
(B) Younger men
(C) Older women
(D) Older men

12. On which of the following questions would you expect a survey to find the highest level of public support? (4) (pp. 91–92)

(A) The public library should include all books, including books advocating racism and atheism.
(B) People should enjoy freedom of speech regardless of their political views.
(C) A college professor who condones the terror attack of September 11, 2001, should be allowed to teach at a public university.
(D) The Ku Klux Klan should be allowed to hold a rally in the city park.

13. Which of the following groups would you expect to express the highest level of support for civil liberties? (4) (p. 93)

(A) Low-income people
(B) Political elites, that is, people who exercise influence on the policy process
(C) People who seldom if ever vote
(D) Recent immigrants

14. The popular acceptance of a government and its officials as rightful authorities in the exercise of power is a good definition of which of the following? (5) (p. 94)

(A) Political efficacy
(B) Political tolerance
(C) Political legitimacy
(D) Opinion leaders

15. Which of the following would likely be a result of a low level of political legitimacy in a society? (5) (p. 94)

(A) Election turnout would be high.
(B) Most people would voluntarily obey laws and regulations.
(C) People wanting to bring about political change would turn to the electoral system rather than violence.
(D) None of the above are correct answers.

16. The extent to which individuals believe they can influence the policymaking process is a definition of which of the following? (6) (p. 94)

(A) Political efficacy
(B) Political legitimacy
(C) Political trust
(D) Public opinion

17. Which of the following statements reflects a high level of internal political efficacy? (6) (pp. 94–95)

(A) "I don't believe that government officials care what I think."
(B) "I have a good understanding of how government works."
(C) "I think that most of the people running the government are crooks."
(D) "Sometimes politics and government seem so complicated that a person like me can't really understand what's going on."

18. An individual's assessment of the government's responsiveness to his or her concerns is a definition of which of the following terms? (6) (p. 95)

(A) Political trust
(B) External political efficacy
(C) Internal political efficacy
(D) Political legitimacy

19. Which of the following positions would most likely be taken by a conservative? (7) (pp. 95–96)

(A) "Government has a responsibility to ensure that all Americans have access to affordable healthcare."
(B) "Government should act aggressively to adopt regulations to slow global warming."
(C) "Government has a responsibility to protect the unborn by limiting access to abortion."
(D) "Government should address the problem of homelessness by providing more public housing."

20. Which of the following statements reflects a liberal ideology? (7) (pp. 95–96)

(A) The government that governs least governs best.
(B) Government regulations often do more harm than good.
(C) The government has no business telling women that they must carry a fetus to term.
(D) Churches and private charities do a better job than the government at solving social problems.

21. Which of the following terms is *not* synonymous with the other terms in the list? (7) (p. 95)

(A) Political left
(B) Conservative
(C) Right wing
(D) Political right

22. The range of policy options acceptable to the public on a particular issue is the definition for which of the following concepts? (8) (p. 102)

(A) Zones of acquiescence
(B) Latent opinion
(C) Political efficacy
(D) Political legitimacy

Chapter 5: Political Participation

Circle the correct answer.

1. Which of the following is a goal of the Tea Party Movement? (1) p. 109)
   (A) Reducing government spending
   (B) Reducing government regulation
   (C) Reducing taxes
   (D) All of the above are correct.

2. Which of the following is the most common form of political participation? (1) (p. 109)
   (A) Contributing money to candidates
   (B) Joining an interest group
   (C) Contacting an elected official
   (D) Voting

3. For which election will turnout be higher *as a proportion of eligible voters*—a presidential election or a local election for mayor? (1) (p. 110)
   (A) The presidential election because interest will probably be greater in that contest.
   (B) The presidential election because more people are eligible to vote for president than are eligible to vote for mayor.
   (C) The local election for mayor because local officials have a more direct impact on the lives of ordinary people.
   (D) Turnout will be the same for each type of election.

4. Which of the following is a form of political participation? (1) (pp. 109–111)
   (A) Sending an e-mail message to a local official about a problem
   (B) Giving money to a candidate for a school board election
   (C) Putting up a yard sign to support a candidate for the state legislature
   (D) All of the above

5. Which of the following is a reasonable explanation why more people vote than volunteer to work in a political campaign? (2) (p. 111)
   (A) Voting requires less time and effort than volunteer work.
   (B) Voting has a greater impact on the outcome of an election than volunteer work.
   (C) Most political campaigns don't want volunteer help because they prefer to rely on professional campaign consultants.
   (D) None of the above are correct answers.

6. Is political efficacy related to political participation? (2) (p. 112)
   (A) No. People vote out of civic duty regardless of other factors.
   (B) Yes. People who think they can impact government policies are more likely to participate than are other people.
   (C) Yes. People who express a high level of trust in public officials are more likely to vote than people who do not trust the government to do what is right.
   (D) No. One vote seldom impacts the outcome of an election.

7. The process of motivating people to vote is known as which of the following? (2) (p. 112)
   (A) Political efficacy
   (B) Political participation
   (C) Voter mobilization
   (D) Straight ticket voting

8. Which of the following play(s) a positive role in voter mobilization? (2) (pp. 113 and 115)
   (A) Political parties
   (B) Interest groups
   (C) Individual contacts
   (D) All of the above

9. Why is the voting age population (VAP) an imperfect database to measure voter participation? (3) (p. 113)
   (A) The census has a fairly accurate count of the population, but measures of the population by age group are imprecise.
   (B) Voter turnout numbers are often inaccurate.
   (C) The VAP includes large numbers of people who are not eligible to vote, including noncitizens and people who are incarcerated.
   (D) All of the above are correct answers.

10. Which of the following groups of people are included in the voting age population (VAP) database but not the voting eligible (VEP) database? (3) (p. 113)
    (A) Prison inmates
    (B) Illegal aliens
    (C) People who are mentally incapacitated
    (D) All of the above

11. Which of the following statements best describes recent trends in voter turnout? (3) (pp. 113–114)
    (A) Voter turnout in presidential elections has increased in each of the last three presidential elections.
    (B) Voter turnout in presidential elections has been falling consistently since the early 1960s.
    (C) Voter turnout in presidential elections has been rising consistently since the early 1960s.
    (D) Voter turnout in presidential elections has fallen in each of the last three presidential elections.

12. How does voter turnout in the United States compare with turnout in other democracies? (4) (pp. 114–115)
    (A) Turnout in the United States is relatively low.
    (B) Turnout in the United States is relatively high.
    (C) Turnout in the United States is average.
    (D) Turnout in the United States is relatively high for national elections, but low for state elections.

13. Which of the following factors accounts for the United States having a lower voter turnout rate than in many other democracies? (4) (pp. 114–116)

(A) American political parties are relatively weak.
(B) The United States has a relatively cumbersome voter registration system.
(C) American labor unions are relatively weak.
(D) All of the above are correct answers.

14. Which of the following statements about compulsory voting in Australia is true? (4) (p. 117)

(A) People who do not vote in Australia can go to jail for as much as a year.
(B) Voter turnout in Australia is much higher than it is in the United States.
(C) Political scientists believe that compulsory voting in Australia harms working class parties because it weakens the advantage labor unions enjoy in turning out their vote.
(D) None of the above are correct answers.

15. Would you expect the average voter turnout rate to be higher for people earning $80,000 a year or for those making $30,000 a year? (5) (pp. 116–117)

(A) Turnout would be greater for the higher income group.
(B) Turnout would be greater for the lower income group.
(C) Turnout would be the same for both groups.
(D) Turnout would be greater for the higher income group in all elections but presidential elections where the turnout rate would be the same.

16. What is the relationship between age and political participation? (5) (p. 118)

(A) Participation rates fall as people age.
(B) Participation rates increase as people age.
(C) Participation rates increase as people age until individuals reach old age and then participation rates turn downward.
(D) Participation increases through middle age and then gradually declines throughout the last half of the individual life span.

17. For which of the following age groups would you expect the voting participation rate to be the lowest? (5) (p. 118)

(A) People in their twenties
(B) People in their thirties
(C) People in their forties
(D) People in the fifties

18. Which of the following groups is the least represented in all areas of political participation compared with the other groups? (5) (pp. 118–119)

(A) Latinos
(B) Whites
(C) African Americans
(D) The groups participate at roughly the same rate.

19. Voter turnout increased for which of the following racial/ethnic groups in 2008 compared with 2004? (5) (p. 118)

(A) Turnout increased for all groups in roughly the same proportion.
(B) Turnout increased for whites and African Americans but declined for other groups.
(C) Turnout increased for African Americans while holding steady for all other groups.
(D) Turnout increased for African Americans, Asian Americans, and Latinos but not for whites.

20. Which of the following groups is most seriously impacted by state laws that disqualify individuals with serious criminal offenses from voting? (5) (p. 119)

(A) White women
(B) Latino males
(C) African American males
(D) White males

21. Compared with men, women are more likely to do which of the following? (5) (p. 120)

(A) Vote
(B) Give money to candidates
(C) Join a political group
(D) There are no differences in participation rates between men and women.

22. Which of the following statements is true according to research on political participation? (6) (p. 120)

(A) Low voter turnout tends to benefit the Republicans because groups that support the Republican Party are more likely to vote in a low turnout election.
(B) Bad weather typically benefits the Democrats because Democrats have a better GOTV organization.
(C) Most nonvoters would have voted Democratic had they actually voted.
(D) None of the above are correct answers.

23. Political activists are more likely than the population as a whole to favor which of the following policies? (6) (p. 122)

(A) Programs that benefit minority groups
(B) Programs that assist the poor
(C) Increased spending for public services
(D) None of the above

24. Which of the following was the primary goal of the National Voter Registration Act? (7) (p. 123)

(A) Prevent voter fraud by tightening voter registration requirements
(B) Make it easier for citizens to register to vote
(C) Ensure that ballots are counted fairly in hopes of preventing election controversies such as the Florida recount of 2000
(D) Establish uniform requirements for electronic voting machines

Chapter 6: The News Media

Circle the correct answer.

1. Which of the following media outlets is owned by the U.S. government? (1) (p. 129)
   (A) *New York Times*
   (B) CBS Evening News
   (C) National Public Radio
   (D) None of the above

2. Which of the following is a set of radio stations? (1) (p. 129)
   (A) NPR
   (B) PBS
   (C) Corporation for Public Broadcasting
   (D) None of the above

3. Which of the following is a set of television stations? (1) (p. 129)
   (A) NPR
   (B) PBS
   (C) Corporation for Public Broadcasting
   (D) None of the above

4. Clear Channel Communication is most closely associated with which of the following? (1) (p. 130)
   (A) Newspapers
   (B) Internet
   (C) Radio stations
   (D) Cable television

5. Cross-media ownership refers to which of the following? (1) (p.130)
   (A) A corporation owning several different types of media outlets
   (B) A corporation owning a chain of television stations in more than one city
   (C) A corporation owning multiple radio stations in the same city
   (D) A newspaper jointly owned by several corporations

6. Which of the following has (have) been suffering from a loss of viewers or readers? (1) (pp. 130–131)
   (A) Daily newspapers
   (B) Network evening news shows
   (C) Newsmagazines
   (D) All of the above

7. Which of the following would be characterized as new media? (1) (pp. 131–132)
   (A) *Time* magazine
   (B) CBS television
   (C) *Chicago Tribune*
   (D) None of the above

8. A blog would be characterized as which of the following? (1) (p. 131)
   (A) Print media
   (B) Attack journalism
   (C) New media
   (D) All of the above

9. Which of the following media sources was more important in 2008 than it was in 2000? (1) (p. 131)
   (A) Newpapers
   (B) Online
   (C) Radio
   (D) Television

10. Which of the following provisions of the Constitution guarantees freedom of the press? (2) (p. 133)
    (A) First Amendment
    (B) Second Amendment
    (C) Fifth Amendment
    (D) Fifteenth Amendment

11. Which of the following agencies has the authority to regulate the broadcast media that use the public airwaves? (2) (p. 134)
    (A) Corporation for Public Broadcasting
    (B) National Public Radio
    (C) Public Broadcasting Service
    (D) Federal Communication Commission

12. Which of the following media outlets is *not* regulated by the FCC? (2) (p. 134)
    (A) UHF television
    (B) Cable television
    (C) AM radio
    (D) FM radio

13. An FCC regulation requiring broadcasters to provide an equivalent opportunity to opposing political candidates competing for the same office is a definition of which of the following terms? (2) (p. 134)
    (A) Objective journalism
    (B) Equal-time rule
    (C) Fairness Doctrine
    (D) Attack journalism

14. A major newspaper carries a series of articles discussing the backgrounds and issue orientations of all the major candidates running for the presidency. The paper's decision to cover all of the candidates and not just its favorite candidate can be explained by which of the following? (2) (p. 134)
    (A) The Fairness Doctrine requires that all candidates be covered.
    (B) The equal-time rule requires that all candidates be covered.
    (C) The newspaper is voluntarily practicing objective journalism.
    (D) The newspaper is following guidelines established by the FCC.

15. A television network carries a press conference by the president who is running for reelection. Will the network be required to give the challenger an equal amount of coverage? (2) (p. 134)
   (A) No. The equal-time rule exempts news coverage.
   (B) Yes. The Fairness Doctrine requires it.
   (C) Yes. The equal-time rule requires it.
   (D) No. The television networks are not subject to FCC regulation.

16. What is the purpose of a shield law? (2) (p. 135)
   (A) To protect journalists from being sued for negative reporting
   (B) To protect journalists from being forced to disclose confidential information in a legal proceeding
   (C) To protect journalists from being charged with violating FCC indecency standards
   (D) None of the above

17. Arbitron ratings are the basis for setting advertising rates for which of the following media outlets? (3) (p. 135)
   (A) Radio
   (B) Television
   (C) Newspapers
   (D) Internet

18. Nielsen ratings are the basis for setting advertising rates for which of the following media outlets? (3) (p. 135)
   (A) Radio
   (B) Television
   (C) Newspapers
   (D) Internet

19. "Read my lips: No new taxes." This is an example of which of the following? (3) (p. 137)
   (A) Objective journalism
   (B) Attack journalism
   (C) Equal-time rule
   (D) Sound bite

20. Which of the following groups is most likely to distrust the media and believe that the media are biased? (4) (p. 139)
   (A) People who identify with the Democratic Party
   (B) People who say they are independent
   (C) People who identify with the Republican Party
   (D) The three groups above are equally likely to distrust the media and believe they are biased.

21. Which of the following statements most accurately describes media coverage of the 2008 presidential election? (4) (p. 139)
   (A) Most media coverage of the McCain campaign was negative whereas coverage of the Obama campaign was balanced.
   (B) Most media coverage of the Obama campaign was negative whereas coverage of the McCain campaign was balanced.
   (C) Coverage of both the Obama and the McCain campaign was negative.
   (D) Coverage of both the Obama and the McCain campaign was balanced.

22. In 2008, a Republican was more likely than a Democrat to regularly watch which of the follow news sources? (4) (p. 139)
   (A) MSNBC
   (B) CNN
   (C) Fox
   (D) Democrats and Republicans have similar viewing habits.

23. "The media have a responsibility to report the news as it happens." This statement best reflects which of the following concepts? (5) (p. 138)
   (A) Attack journalism
   (B) Objective journalism
   (C) Framing
   (D) Signaling role

24. Which of the following is best defined as a term that refers to the accepted responsibility of the media to alert the public to important developments as they happen? (5) (p. 140)
   (A) Attack journalism
   (B) Objective journalism
   (C) Framing
   (D) Signaling role

25. Which of the following terms is best defined as the process by which a communication source, such as a news organization, defines and constructs a political issue or public controversy? (5) (p. 140)
   (A) Attack journalism
   (B) Objective journalism
   (C) Framing
   (D) Signaling role

Chapter 7: Interest Groups

Circle the correct answer.

1. "I don't see any point in joining the neighborhood civic association. My $25 annual dues aren't enough to make much difference. At any rate, I will benefit from the association's activities whether I am a member or not." The above statement reflects which of the following concepts? (1) (p. 145)

   (A) Friendly Incumbent Rule
   (B) Free-rider barrier to group membership
   (C) Material incentives to group membership
   (D) Purposive incentives to group membership

2. Eric joined the American Legion because he enjoys hanging out at the legion hall with his buddies. This action illustrates which of the following concepts? (1) (pp. 145–146)

   (A) Free-rider barrier to group membership
   (B) Material incentive for joining a group
   (C) Purposive incentive for joining a group
   (D) Solidary incentive for joining a group

3. Which of the following is an example of a purposive incentive for joining an interest group? (1) (pp. 145–146)

   (A) Lee joins Greenpeace because he feels strongly about protecting the environment.
   (B) Diego joins the NRA because he wants to enroll his sons in NRA gun safety classes.
   (C) Luisa joins the American Federation of Teachers because many of her fellow teachers belong and she enjoys spending time with her friends.
   (D) None of the above are correct answers.

4. Which of the following organizations is a business federation representing the interests of businesses of all sizes, sectors, and regions? (2) (p. 146)

   (A) National Federation of Independent Businesses
   (B) AFL-CIO
   (C) U.S. Chamber of Commerce
   (D) NAACP

5. Which of the following organizations would be most likely to favor legislation to allow drilling off the California coast and the East Coast? (2) (pp. 146–147)

   (A) Chamber of Commerce
   (B) AFL-CIO
   (C) Exxon Mobil
   (D) AARP

6. Which of the following organizations would be most likely to favor enactment of the Employee Free Choice Act, which provides for card check? (2) (p. 148)

   (A) Chamber of Commerce
   (B) AFL-CIO
   (C) Club for Growth
   (D) LULAC

7. Which of the following statements is true about organized labor? (2) (pp. 147–149)

   (A) The percentage of the workforce that belongs to labor unions has been in decline for years.
   (B) Wal-Mart, the nation's largest employer, has successfully resisted unionization efforts.
   (C) Organized labor is stronger in the Frostbelt and weaker in the Sunbelt.
   (D) All of the above are correct answers.

8. Which of the following organizations would be most likely to favor increasing the minimum wage? (2) (pp. 147–149)

   (A) Chamber of Commerce
   (B) American Farm Bureau
   (C) AFL-CIO
   (D) AARP

9. Which of the following organizations would be most likely to favor affirmative action in college and university admissions? (2) (pp. 149–151)

   (A) NAACP (B) AFL-CIO
   (C) AARP (D) Sierra Club

10. Which of the following organizations would be most likely to celebrate Earth Day? (2) (pp. 152–153)

    (A) NARAL Pro-Choice America
    (B) Sierra Club
    (C) Human Rights Campaign
    (D) Common Cause

11. Which of the following pairs of organizations would be most likely to be on the opposite sides of the issue of abortion? (2) (p. 153)

    (A) Right to Life and NARAL Pro-Choice America
    (B) Chamber of Commerce and the AFL-CIO
    (C) Club for Growth and the NRA
    (D) Sierra Club and NOW

12. Which of the following organizations would be most likely to endorse a Democratic candidate for president in the next election? (3) (p. 154)

    (A) Right to Life
    (B) Chamber of Commerce
    (C) NRA
    (D) NARAL Pro-Choice America

13. What are Political Action Committees (PACs)? (3) (p. 155)

    (A) They are organizations representing the interests of firms and professionals in the same general field.
    (B) They are organizations whose members care intensely about a single issue or small group of related issues.
    (C) They are organizations created to raise and distribute money in election campaigns.
    (D) They are organizations created to seek benefits on behalf of groups of persons who are in some way incapacitated or otherwise unable to represent their own interests.

14. Why do PACs associated with lawyers typically support Democratic candidates? (3) (p. 155)

(A) Lawyers oppose Republican efforts to enact lawsuit reform.
(B) Most lawyers are pro-choice and that is a Democratic position.
(C) Lawyers always back the party that holds the presidency because they hope to be nominated to judicial positions.
(D) All of the above are correct.

15. PACs associated with which of the following tend to give most of their campaign contributions to incumbent members of Congress of both political parties? (3) (p. 155)

(A) Business groups
(B) Labor unions
(C) NRA
(D) Cause groups

16. Which of the following candidates would you expect to benefit the most from PAC contributions? (3) (p. 156)

(A) A Republican challenger
(B) A Democratic challenger
(C) A candidate from either party running for an open seat
(D) An incumbent from either party running for reelection

17. A PAC representing Interest Group A contributed to Congressman B's reelection campaign even though the congressman sides with the interest group's issue positions only about 60 percent of the time. The PAC is acting in accordance with which of the following principles? (3) (p. 155)

(A) Friendly Incumbent Rule
(B) Free-rider barrier to group membership
(C) Bundling
(D) Material incentive to group membership

18. An interest group that engages in bundling is doing which of the following? (3) (p. 156)

(A) Lobbying more than one member of Congress at the same time
(B) Joining forces with other interest groups to lobby on behalf of the same cause
(C) Gathering checks from individual supporters made out to a particular candidate and then giving the checks to the candidate in a bundle
(D) Giving money to more than one candidate for the same office

19. An organization created by individuals and groups to influence the outcomes of elections by raising and spending money that candidates and political parties cannot legally raise is known by which of the following names? (3) (p. 156)

(A) Political action committee
(B) Interest group
(C) Political party
(D) 527 committee

20. Which of the following statements about lobbying and lobbyists is true? (3) (p. 158)

(A) Groups lobby the legislative branch of government but not the executive branch.
(B) Interest group lobbyists frequently focus on the details of legislation rather than votes on final passage.
(C) Former members of Congress are prohibited by law from becoming lobbyists.
(D) None of the above are correct answers.

21. What is the best assessment of the relationship between campaign contributions and interest group lobbying? (3) (p. 157)

(A) Money buys votes. Members of Congress vote for the causes supported by the groups that give them the most money.
(B) Money buys access. Members of Congress are willing to meet with lobbyists representing groups that provide them with campaign contributions.
(C) Money and lobbying are unrelated. Members of Congress are open to consider all views regardless of political contributions.
(D) Because of campaign finance regulations, interest groups are prohibited from contributing money to help members of Congress run for reelection.

22. Which of the following organizations specializes in the use of litigation to achieve its goals rather than employing litigation as one of a number of approaches to achieving influence? (3) (p. 159)

(A) Chamber of Commerce
(B) American Bar Association
(C) ACLU
(D) NRA

23. Which of the following types of interest groups is typically allied with the Republican Party? (4) (p. 161)

(A) Organized labor
(B) Environmental organizations
(C) African American rights groups
(D) Anti-tax groups

24. Which of the following types of interest groups is typically allied with the Democratic Party? (4) (p. 161)

(A) Business groups
(B) Abortion rights organizations
(C) Conservative Christian organizations
(D) None of the above

25. Which of the following factors contributes positively to the strength of an interest group? (4) (pp. 161–162)

(A) Public opinion support for the group's goals
(B) An alliance with the political party that controls Congress and the White House
(C) No or only weak opposition from other interest groups
(D) All of the above

Chapter 8: Political Parties

Circle the correct answer.

1. Which of the following terms is best defined as a group of individuals who join together to seek government office in order to make public policy? (1) (p. 167)

   (A) Interest group
   (B) Political action committee
   (C) Issue network
   (D) Political party

2. The Green, Reform, and Libertarian Parties are examples of which of the following? (1) (p. 168)

   (A) Interest groups
   (B) Party eras
   (C) Third parties
   (D) Political action committees

3. Which of the following is *not* a reason why the United States has a two-party system rather than a multiparty system? (1) (pp. 168–169)

   (A) The plurality election system awards office to the candidate with the most votes, leaving candidates who finish a strong second or third with nothing.
   (B) The Electoral College awards electoral votes only to candidates who win the most votes in each state.
   (C) The United States is not deeply divided along social and political lines.
   (D) Federal law limits the number of parties on the ballot to two.

4. An election system that awards office to the candidate with the most votes is known by which of the following terms? (1) (p. 168)

   (A) Proportional representation
   (B) Party realignment
   (C) Plurality election system
   (D) Two-party system

5. Which of the following statements is true about Israel but is *not* true about the United States? (1) (p. 169)

   (A) If a political party gets 10 percent of the vote, it will get 10 percent of the seats in the national legislature.
   (B) Candidates for the national legislature run from geographical areas called districts.
   (C) Nearly all of the members of the national legislature are members of one of two major political parties.
   (D) Voters may be reluctant to vote for a smaller party because they do not want to "throw their vote away" on a party that has no chance to gain representation.

6. Which of the following statements is true about party fundraising? (2) (p. 170–171)

   (A) The Democratic Party has historically raised more money than the Republican Party.
   (B) The Republican Party closed the fundraising gap with the Democrats in 2006 and especially 2008.
   (C) The Republican Party has caught up with the Democrats because of Internet fundraising.
   (D) None of the above are correct answers.

7. Which of the following candidates would be most likely to benefit from financial support from the national party organization? (2) (p. 171)

   (A) A powerful committee chair facing only token opposition
   (B) A candidate for an open seat locked in a close contest
   (C) A challenger taken on an entrenched incumbent who will be very difficult to defeat
   (D) A member of Congress running for reelection unopposed

8. Which of the following is a period of time characterized by a degree of uniformity in the nature of political party competition? (3) (p. 173)

   (A) Plurality election system
   (B) Party realignment
   (C) Party era
   (D) Proportional representation

9. A change in the underlying party loyalties of voters that ends one party era and begins another is known by which of the following terms? (3) (p. 173)

   (A) Plurality election system
   (B) Party realignment
   (C) Proportional representation
   (D) Divided government

10. Which of the following statements about Republican Party strength after the 2010 election is correct? (4) (p. 174)

    (A) Republicans held a majority of seats in the U.S. House of Representatives.
    (B) Republicans held a majority of seats in the U.S. Senate.
    (C) The president was a Republican.
    (D) None of the above

11. Which of the following statements about party identification is accurate? (4) (p. 174)

    (A) Democrats outnumber Republicans by a ratio of two-to-one.
    (B) Republicans outnumber Democrats by a ratio of two-to-one.
    (C) Democrats hold a narrow advantage in party ID.
    (D) Republicans hold a narrow advantage in party ID.

12. Among which of the following income groups would you expect the Republican candidate for president to do best in the next presidential election? (5) (p. 174)

(A) People making less than $30,000 a year
(B) People making between $30,000 and $60,000 a year
(C) People making between $100,000 and $150,000 a year
(D) People making more than $200,000 a year

13. Which of the following groups would be *least* likely to give a majority of its votes to the Democratic candidate for president in the next election? (5) (pp. 174–175)

(A) Asian Americans
(B) African Americans
(C) Whites
(D) Latinos

14. Which of the following groups of Latinos is *least* supportive of Democratic candidates? (5) (p. 175)

(A) Cuban Americans
(B) Mexican Americans
(C) Puerto Ricans
(D) All of the above groups typically support Democratic candidates.

15. Which of the following statements is true about the groups that support each of the two major political parties? (5) (pp. 174–176)

(A) Men are more likely than women to vote Democratic.
(B) The more education one has, the more likely that person is to vote Republican.
(C) White voters are more likely than non-white voters to support Republican candidates.
(D) None of the above are correct answers.

16. Which of the following statements is true about voter preferences? (5) (p. 176)

(A) Gay and lesbian voters tend to vote Republican.
(B) Married voters tend to vote Democratic.
(C) Women are more likely to vote Republican than are men.
(D) None of the above are correct answers.

17. The Republican Party is strongest in which of the following regions? (5) (pp. 176–177)

(A) South
(B) West Coast
(C) Midwest
(D) Northeast

18. Which of the following groups tends to vote Democratic? (5) (pp. 174–177)

(A) People who call themselves conservative
(B) Gays and lesbians
(C) People living in small towns and rural areas
(D) Men

19. Which of the following groups tend to vote Republican? (5) (pp. 174–178)

(A) People who attend religious services on a weekly basis
(B) Women
(C) People living in inner-city areas
(D) Jews

20. Which of the following groups would be the most supportive of Democratic candidates? (5) (pp. 177–178)

(A) Catholics
(B) White evangelical Protestants
(C) Jews
(D) Members of mainline Protestant denominations

21. The Republican Party takes which of the following issue positions? (6) (pp. 178–180)

(A) Opposition to all tax increases
(B) Opposition to abortion
(C) Opposition to gay marriage
(D) All of the above

22. The Democratic Party favors which of the following issue positions? (6) (pp. 178–180)

(A) Support for Israel
(B) Healthcare reform
(C) Immigration reform
(D) All of the above

23. The Republican Party favors which of the following public policies? (6) (pp. 178–180)

(A) Embryonic stem cell research
(B) Energy exploration in the Arctic National Wildlife Preserve
(C) Affirmative action
(D) All of the above

24. Which political party was the governing party of American national government after the 2008 election? (7) (p. 180)

(A) The Republican Party because the president was a Republican
(B) The Democratic Party because opinion polls showed a majority of Americans identified with the Democratic Party
(C) The Democratic Party because it held majorities in both houses of Congress and held the presidency
(D) The Republican Party because it held majorities in both houses of Congress and held the presidency

25. Political Party A controls both houses of Congress while Political Party B holds the presidency. This situation is an example of which of the following? (7) (p. 181)

(A) Divided government
(B) Responsible parties
(C) Proportional representation
(D) Realignment

Chapter 9: Elections

Circle the correct answer.

1. Luisa Cangelosi voted for the Republican candidate for president, the Democratic candidate for the U.S. Senate, and the Democratic candidate for the U.S. House. Ms. Cangelosi did which of the following? (1) (p. 188)
   (A) Violated the Voting Rights Act
   (B) Voted in a presidential preference primary
   (C) Voted a split ticket ballot
   (D) Voted in a primary election

2. State A limits primary voting to people who are registered party members. State A has which of the following? (1) (p. 189)
   (A) A closed primary
   (B) An open primary
   (C) A blanket primary
   (D) A presidential preference primary

3. Which of the following elections is *not* conducted statewide at large in most states? (2) (p. 190)
   (A) Election for governor
   (B) Election for U.S. House
   (C) Election for U.S. Senate
   (D) Election for president

4. How often does reapportionment take place? (2) (p. 190)
   (A) Every ten years after the U.S. Census is taken
   (B) Every four years to coincide with the presidential election
   (C) Whenever population changes by more than 10 percent
   (D) None of the above

5. *Baker v. Carr* (1962) and *Wesberry v. Sanders* (1964) dealt with which of the following issues? (2) (p. 190)
   (A) Gerrymandering
   (B) Reapportionment
   (C) Redistricting
   (D) Voting Rights Act

6. Why did state legislatures, especially in the South, increase the number of congressional districts that were likely to elect African Americans to Congress after the 1990 Census? (2) (pp. 191–192)
   (A) Most state legislatures were controlled by the Democratic Party and the Democrats wanted to increase minority representation in Congress.
   (B) The population of African Americans increased rapidly in the 1980s.
   (C) The legislatures were attempting to comply with the Voting Rights Act (VRA).
   (D) All of the above are correct answers.

7. Which of the following statements about the Voting Rights Act (VRA) is true? (2) (pp. 191–192)
   (A) The VRA prohibits gerrymandering.
   (B) The pre-clearance provision of the VRA does not apply to the entire country.
   (C) The VRA only protects the voting rights of African Americans.
   (D) All of the above are correct answers.

8. Which of the following statements is true about the role of money in political campaigns? (3) (pp. 193–197)
   (A) All presidential candidates accept federal funding for their campaigns because it saves them the time and trouble of fundraising.
   (B) Advertising, especially television advertising, is the single largest expenditure in most campaign budgets.
   (C) Candidates who provide most of their own campaign money usually win because they do not have to spend time fundraising.
   (D) All of the above are correct answers.

9. Which of the following is an organization created by an individual or group to influence the outcomes of elections by raising and spending money that candidates and political parties cannot raise legally? (3) (p. 196)
   (A) Interest group
   (B) PAC
   (C) 527 committee
   (D) Political party

10. A newspaper reports that the incumbent president running for reelection is using a "rose garden strategy." What is a rose garden strategy? (3) (p. 199)
    (A) The president stresses domestic issues, such as the economy.
    (B) The president focuses on the positive.
    (C) The president runs an aggressive campaign, attacking the qualifications of the opposing candidate.
    (D) The president tries to appear presidential rather than political.

11. Which of the following statements about negative campaigning is true? (3) (pp. 199–200)
    (A) Negative campaigning is relatively new in American politics.
    (B) Political scientists agree that negative campaigning decreases voter turnout.
    (C) Political scientists agree that negative campaigning almost never works.
    (D) None of the above are correct answers.

12. Which of the following is an example of the air war in a political campaign? (3) (p. 200)

    (A) Volunteers go door-to-door registering voters.
    (B) Volunteers call campaign supporters and encourage them to go vote.
    (C) The campaign purchases time on cable television stations to run political advertisements.
    (D) All of the above are correct answers.

13. Which of the following reasons helps explain why most incumbent members of the U.S. House are reelected? (4) (p. 201)

    (A) They usually have more money than their challengers.
    (B) They are usually better known than their challengers.
    (C) Many congressional districts are safe for one party or the other.
    (D) All of the above are correct answers.

14. In 2008, a voter was drawn to the polls out of excitement for the candidacy of Barack Obama and decided to vote for the other Democratic candidates as well. This action illustrates which of the following concepts? (4) (p. 202)

    (A) Coattail effect
    (B) Retrospective voting
    (C) Rose garden strategy
    (D) Split ticket ballot

15. How were the delegates to the 2008 Republican National Convention chosen? (5) (pp. 205–206)

    (A) They were chosen by the Congress.
    (B) They were chosen by the Electoral College.
    (C) They were chosen by each state party, either through a presidential preference primary or a party caucus.
    (D) They were chosen in a national primary election.

16. Which of the following plays the most important role in selecting the presidential nominees of the Democratic and Republican parties? (5) (pp. 207–209)

    (A) Party activists and party voters
    (B) Party bosses
    (C) Each party's congressional delegation
    (D) Independent voters

17. Why is doing well in the Iowa Caucus and the New Hampshire Primary important for candidates seeking their party's nomination for president? (5) (pp. 210–211)

    (A) Candidates who do well in both states benefit from large numbers of convention delegates.
    (B) Candidates who do well in both states benefit from a large amount of favorable publicity.
    (C) Candidates who do well in both states benefit from a large number of electoral votes.
    (D) All of the above are correct answers.

18. Which of the following statements about presidential electors is true? (5) (p. 215)

    (A) They choose the party's presidential nominee at the national party convention.
    (B) They are elected officials, including members of Congress and state legislatures.
    (C) They are individuals chosen by the state parties to cast the state's electoral votes.
    (D) They select the president by a two-thirds vote.

19. Alabama elects seven members of the House. How many electoral votes does Alabama have? (5) (p. 215)

    (A) Seven
    (B) Eight
    (C) Nine
    (D) Eleven

20. Assume for the purpose of this question that a Democrat, a Republican, and a major independent candidate are running for president. In California, the Democrat gets 45 percent of the vote, the Republican gets 40 percent, and the independent receives the rest. How many of California's electoral votes will the Democratic candidate receive? (5) (p. 215)

    (A) All of them
    (B) 45 percent of them
    (C) None of them
    (D) It depends on the outcome of the runoff between the Democrat and the Republican, the two top finishers.

21. Under which of the following circumstances would Candidate A win the 2012 presidential election? (5) (pp. 214–216)

    (A) Candidate A wins a majority of the popular vote nationwide.
    (B) Candidate A carries more states than any other candidate.
    (C) Candidate A wins a plurality of the popular vote nationwide.
    (D) Candidate A wins a majority of the electoral vote.

22. Which of the following is considered a Red State? (5) (p. 218)

    (A) New York
    (B) California
    (C) Texas
    (D) Illinois

23. Which of the following factors affect the outcome of presidential elections? (6) (pp. 224–226)

    (A) The state of the economy
    (B) The incumbent president's approval rating in the months before the election
    (C) The length of time the president's party has held the White House
    (D) All of the above

Chapter 10: Congress

Circle the correct answer.

1. Which of the following statements about the constitutional roles of the House and Senate is correct? (1) (pp. 235–236)
   (A) Legislation to raise taxes must originate in the House.
   (B) The Senate is solely responsible for ratifying constitutional amendments by a two-thirds vote.
   (C) The Senate is solely responsible for confirming presidential appointments by a two-thirds vote.
   (D) The House is solely responsible for confirming a presidential nomination to fill a vacancy in the office of vice president.

2. Which of the following statements better describes the House than it does the Senate? (1) (p. 236)
   (A) It makes most decisions strictly by majority vote.
   (B) It has a tradition as a great debating society where members enjoy broad freedom to voice their points of view.
   (C) It is an individualistic body where one member has considerable influence on the legislative process.
   (D) All of the above are correct answers.

3. Which of the following statements better describes the Senate than it does the House? (1) (p. 236)
   (A) Every member stands for reelection every two years.
   (B) It is known as a great debating society.
   (C) Members of this chamber sometimes run for seats in the other chamber.
   (D) None of the above are correct answers.

4. The office of Congresswoman Martinez helps a district resident resolve a problem with the Social Security Administration. The action was an example of which of the following? (2) (p. 240)
   (A) Filibuster
   (B) Logrolling
   (C) Party-line vote
   (D) Constituency service

5. How did constituency pressure affect the vote on healthcare reform? (2) (pp. 239–240)
   (A) Many Republican members of Congress voted in favor of healthcare reform because polls showed strong support for the bill among independents.
   (B) Every Republican member of Congress voted against healthcare reform because polls showed strong opposition to the bill among Republicans, especially party activists.
   (C) Every Democratic member of Congress voted in favor of healthcare reform because polls showed strong opposition to the bill among Republicans, and Democrats enjoy making Republican voters angry.
   (D) Constituency attitudes about healthcare reform had no effect on congressional votes on the measure.

6. Which of the following statements about congressional turnover is *not* true? (2) (pp. 240–242)
   (A) Most members of Congress are reelected.
   (B) The reelection rate for House members is higher than it is for senators.
   (C) Congress experiences significant turnover because term limits restrict members of the House and Senate to no more than 12 consecutive years in office.
   (D) Voters typically express a higher level of approval for their representative in Congress than they do for the institution as a whole.

7. According to the Constitution, which of the following officials is the "President of the Senate"? (3) (p. 243)
   (A) Speaker of the House
   (B) Senate president pro tempore
   (C) Senate Majority Leader
   (D) Vice president

8. In practice, which of the following officials is the most important leader in the U.S. Senate? (3) (p. 243)
   (A) Speaker of the House
   (B) Senate president pro tempore
   (C) Senate Majority Leader
   (D) Vice president

9. Which of the following officials is the most important leader in the U.S. House? (3) (p. 243)
   (A) Speaker of the House
   (B) Senate president pro tempore
   (C) Senate Majority Leader
   (D) Vice president

10. How is the Senate Majority Leader selected? (3) (p. 243)
    (A) By vote of the members of the majority party in the Senate
    (B) By popular vote in a national election
    (C) By the president
    (D) By being the longest served member of the majority party in the Senate

11. In which chamber of Congress does the minority leadership have the most influence and why? (3) (p. 246)
    (A) In the House, because the rules of the House require a two-thirds vote to approve most measures and that ensures that the two parties must work together
    (B) In the Senate, because the rules of the Senate give the minority substantial power to delay or defeat legislation, forcing the majority to work with the minority
    (C) In the House, because the Speaker of the House is independent of the two political parties
    (D) In the Senate, because the detailed work of the chamber takes place in committee

12. In 2011, the Republican Party was the majority party in the House, the Democratic Party was the majority Party in the Senate, and a Democrat, Barack Obama, occupied the White House. Was the chair of the House Ways and Means Committee a Democrat or Republican? How do you know? (3) (p. 249)
    (A) The chair could have been a Democrat or Republican depending on which member of the committee had the most seniority.
    (B) The chair was a Democrat because the president was a Democrat.
    (C) The chair was a Republican because Republicans were the majority party in the House.
    (D) The chair could have been a Democrat or a Republican depending on which member of the committee won a vote of the committee membership.

13. When the Democratic Party is the majority party in the House, how are committee chairs chosen in the House? (3) (p. 250)
    (A) By the president
    (B) By the Speaker
    (C) By majority vote of committee members
    (D) By majority vote of the party caucus

14. Why do major legislative measures often take the form of omnibus bills, which are complex, highly detailed legislative proposals covering one or more subjects or programs? (4) (p. 250)
    (A) Complex problems require complex solutions.
    (B) Government is so big that legislation must deal with a broad range of policy areas.
    (C) Congress is in session only part of the year and omnibus bills enable it to get more done in a short period of time.
    (D) Congressional leaders assemble omnibus bills in order to attract as much support as possible.

15. Which of the following individuals has the authority to introduce a bill in the U.S. Senate? (4) (p. 251)
    (A) A senator
    (B) A member of the House
    (C) The president
    (D) All of the above

16. How does multiple referral of legislation affect the power of the leadership? (4) (pp. 254–255)
    (A) It diminishes the power of the leadership because the fate of a bill is in the hands of two or more committee chairs, giving the chairs more power than they would otherwise have.
    (B) It has no effect on the power of the leadership, but it delays passage of legislation by increasing the steps of the legislative process.
    (C) It diminishes the power of the leadership because a conference committee has to resolve differences among the committees.
    (D) It enhances the power of the leadership because the leadership can devise referral arrangements that enhance policy goals and set timetables for committee consideration of multiple referred bills.

17. The detailed work of Congress takes place at which point in the legislative process? (4) (p. 255)
    (A) On the floor
    (B) In committee
    (C) In conference committee
    (D) In the Rules Committee

18. Legislative markup occurs at which stage of the legislative process? (4) (p. 255)
    (A) On the floor
    (B) In committee
    (C) In conference committee
    (D) In the Rules Committee

19. What is the purpose of a discharge petition? (4) (pp. 255–256)
    (A) It is the process that is used to end a filibuster.
    (B) It is a demand that a member of Congress be expelled for misconduct.
    (C) It is a procedure used to force a committee to report a bill to the floor of the House.
    (D) It is the beginning of the impeachment process.

20. What is the purpose of a closed rule? (4) (p. 256)
    (A) It prohibits consideration of amendments to a bill on the floor of the House.
    (B) It is a procedure for ending a filibuster.
    (C) It is a means of coordinating the work of committees when a bill is multiple referred.
    (D) It is a procedure used to force a committee to report a bill to the floor of the House.

21. An amendment designed to make a measure so unattractive that it will lack enough support to pass is known as which of the following? (4) (pp. 257–258)
    (A) Discharge petition
    (B) Nongermane amendment
    (C) Killer amendment
    (D) Cloture petition

22. The opponents of a bill in the Senate have resorted to a filibuster to block it. How many votes will the measure's supporters need to invoke cloture and end the filibuster? (4) (p. 259)
    (A) 51
    (B) 67
    (C) 60
    (D) 40

23. A conference committee agrees on a conference report. It passes the House, but it fails to pass the Senate. What is the status of the bill? (4) (pp. 260–261)
    (A) The measure goes to the president.
    (B) The measure is dead unless the Senate reconsiders it and passes it.
    (C) The House votes again on the measure and if it passes again, it goes to the president.
    (D) The president convenes a reconciliation committee involving the leadership of both the House and Senate.

Chapter 11: The Presidency

Circle the correct answer.

1. After winning reelection in 2004, President George W. Bush was a lame duck. What does that phrase mean? (1) (p. 270)

   (A) President Bush was unpopular.
   (B) President Bush was ineligible to run for reelection.
   (C) President Bush had to deal with a Congress controlled by the opposition party.
   (D) President Bush was facing impeachment charges.

2. Which of the following is *not* part of the impeachment process? (1) (p. 270)

   (A) The House drafts articles of impeachment.
   (B) The House votes to impeach the president by majority vote.
   (C) The Chief Justice presides over an impeachment trial in the Senate.
   (D) The Senate votes to remove the president by majority vote.

3. Which of the following presidents was impeached and removed from office? (1) (pp. 271–273)

   (A) Andrew Johnson
   (B) Richard Nixon
   (C) Bill Clinton
   (D) None of the above

4. What happens if the vice president resigns or dies in office? (1) (p. 274)

   (A) The Speaker of the House becomes vice president.
   (B) The president appoints another vice president subject to confirmation by the House and Senate.
   (C) The Senate president pro temp becomes vice president.
   (D) The office remains vacant until the next election.

5. Which of the following statements about the vice presidency is true? (1) (pp. 275–276)

   (A) The vice president votes in the Senate only to break a tie.
   (B) The policymaking influence of the vice president today is significantly greater than it was 50 years ago.
   (C) In case of presidential disability, the vice president can become acting president.
   (D) All of the above are correct answers.

6. Who is the chief of state of American government? (2) (p. 276)

   (A) The president
   (B) The Senate president pro tempore
   (C) The Speaker of the House
   (D) The chief justice of the United States

7. The United States does not currently have diplomatic relations with Cuba. What would be the process for the United States officially to recognize the government of Cuba? (2) (p. 276)

   (A) Official recognition would be granted through the legislative process. Congress would pass legislation subject to a presidential veto.
   (B) The process of recognition would require a popular vote of the American people.
   (C) The president grants diplomatic recognition.
   (D) Congress grants diplomatic recognition.

8. What is the difference between an executive agreement and a treaty? (2) (p. 277)

   (A) Executive agreements do not require Senate ratification.
   (B) Treaties are more numerous than executive agreements.
   (C) The president negotiates treaties but members of Congress negotiate executive agreements.
   (D) None of the above are correct answers.

9. Which of the following statements about the War Powers Act is true? (2) (p. 279)

   (A) It only applies to officially declared wars.
   (B) It requires the president to consult with Congress whenever possible before committing American forces to combat.
   (C) It has proved to be an effective check on the president's authority as commander-in-chief.
   (D) None of the above are correct answers.

10. What constitutional authority does the president have over the Supreme Court? (2) (p. 280)

    (A) The president can fill vacancies by appointment subject to Senate confirmation.
    (B) The president can veto Supreme Court rulings subject to possible override by the Court.
    (C) The president can initiate removal proceedings against justices.
    (D) None of the above are correct answers.

11. Which of the following statements about executive orders is true? (2) (pp. 281–282)

    (A) The president can issue executive orders without congressional approval.
    (B) Congress can override an executive order legislatively, subject to possible presidential veto.
    (C) The Supreme Court can overturn an executive order on constitutional grounds.
    (D) All of the above are correct answers.

12. A pronouncement issued by the president at the time a bill passed by Congress is signed into law is known as which of the following? (2) (p. 282)

(A) A veto statement
(B) The State of the Union address
(C) A presidential signing statement
(D) An executive order

13. Which branch of American national government was more important in the nineteenth century? (3) (p. 283)

(A) Legislative branch
(B) Executive branch
(C) Judicial branch
(D) The three branches were equally influential.

14. Many political scientists believe that the era of the modern presidency began with the administration of which of the following presidents? (3) (p. 284)

(A) Franklin Roosevelt
(B) Theodore Roosevelt
(C) Abraham Lincoln
(D) Woodrow Wilson

15. The New Deal is associated with which of the following presidents? (3) (p. 284)

(A) Theodore Roosevelt
(B) Franklyn Roosevelt
(C) Harry Truman
(D) John Kennedy

16. Which of the following presidential appointments does *not* require Senate confirmation? (4) (p. 285)

(A) A cabinet secretary
(B) A federal judge
(C) An ambassador
(D) A member of the White House staff

17. Which of the following agencies is part of the Executive Office of the President? (4) (p. 286)

(A) Department of Justice
(B) Federal Communication Commission (FCC)
(C) Office of Management and Budget (OMB)
(D) All of the above

18. Which of the following political scientists analyzes presidential performance based on the personality traits of the president? (5) (pp. 289–290)

(A) Samuel Kernell
(B) Richard Neustadt
(C) Fred I. Greenstein
(D) James David Barber

19. Which of the following political scientists analyzes presidential performance based on leadership style? (5) (p. 291)

(A) Samuel Kernell
(B) Richard Neustadt
(C) Fred I. Greenstein
(D) James David Barber

20. Which of the following political scientists analyzes presidential performance based on the chief executive's skill as a political bargainer and coalition builder? (5) (pp. 291–293)

(A) Samuel Kernell
(B) Richard Neustadt
(C) Fred I. Greenstein
(D) James David Barber

21. Which of the following is an example of a unilateral tool of presidential power that does not require congressional approval? (5) (p. 294)

(A) Executive agreements
(B) Recess appointments
(C) Signing statements
(D) All of the above

22. When a president first takes office, public opinion polls typically indicate that the president enjoys a high approval rating. Which of the following terms describes this phenomenon? (6) (pp. 294–295)

(A) Honeymoon effect
(B) Two-presidencies thesis
(C) Coattail effect
(D) Rally effect

23. President George W. Bush's approval rating soared after September 11, 2001. Which of the following terms would political scientists use to describe that phenomenon? (6) (p. 295)

(A) Two-presidencies thesis
(B) Coattail effect
(C) Honeymoon effect
(D) Rally effect

24. In which of the following ways does a president benefit from having Congress controlled by the same political party? (7) (pp. 297–298)

(A) A Congress controlled by the same party is more likely to investigate administration actions than a Congress controlled by the opposition party.
(B) A Congress controlled by the same party is more likely to pass bills the administration favors than a Congress controlled by the opposition party.
(C) A Congress controlled by the same party is more likely to override presidential vetoes than a Congress controlled by the opposition party.
(D) All of the above are correct answers.

25. Whereas President Clinton issued no vetoes in 1993 and 1994, he issued numerous vetoes every year from 1995 through the end of his presidency in 2001. What is the best explanation for this pattern of veto issuance? (7) (pp. 297–298)

(A) President Clinton was less popular in the latter years of his administration.
(B) President Clinton was more popular in the latter years of his administration.
(C) Democrats controlled Congress in 1993–1994; Republicans were in the majority for the rest of the Clinton administration.
(D) The economy was stronger from 1995–2001 than it was in 1993 and 1994.

Chapter 12: The Federal Bureaucracy

Circle the correct answer.

1. How did the Department of Defense, Federal Communication Commission, Postal Service, and other federal agencies come into existence? (1) (p. 306)
   (A) The president created them by executive order.
   (B) The Constitution established them.
   (C) They were established by court order.
   (D) Congress and the president created them through the legislative process.

2. Which of the following is *not* a cabinet department? (1) (p. 306)
   (A) Environmental Protection Agency (EPA)
   (B) Department of Homeland Security
   (C) Department of Defense
   (D) Department of Justice

3. Which of the following cabinet departments has the largest number of civilian employees? (1) (p. 306)
   (A) Department of Homeland Security
   (B) Department of Defense
   (C) Department of Education
   (D) Department of Justice

4. The attorney general heads which of the following departments? (1) (p. 306)
   (A) Department of Homeland Security
   (B) Department of Defense
   (C) Department of Justice
   (D) Department of State

5. Which of the following is *not* part of the inner cabinet? (1) (p. 308)
   (A) Secretary of state
   (B) Secretary of homeland security
   (C) Secretary of defense
   (D) Attorney general

6. Which of the following is *not* an example of an independent executive agency? (1) (p. 308)
   (A) Peace Corps
   (B) CIA
   (C) FCC
   (D) NASA

7. A college student who wanted to assist people in developing countries would volunteer for which of the following agencies? (1) (p. 308)
   (A) Peace Corps
   (B) CIA
   (C) AMTRAK
   (D) NASA

8. Which of the following is *not* an example of a government corporation? (1) (pp. 308–309)
   (A) AMTRAK
   (B) CIA
   (C) Postal Service
   (D) FDIC

9. Which of the following agencies is expected to be self-financing? (1) (pp. 308–309)
   (A) FEMA
   (B) EPA
   (C) FDIC
   (D) Peace Corps

10. Which of the following agencies regulates business competition, including enforcement of laws against monopolies and the protection of consumers from deceptive trade practices? (1) (p. 310)
    (A) FCC
    (B) FTC
    (C) SEC
    (D) EPA

11. Which of the following agencies regulates interstate and international radio, television, telephone, telegraph, and satellite communications, as well as licensing radio, and television stations? (1) (p. 310)
    (A) FCC
    (B) FTC
    (C) SEC
    (D) EPA

12. The president has the authority to remove all but which one of the following government officials? (1) (p. 310)
    (A) Attorney general
    (B) EPA administrator
    (C) SEC commissioner
    (D) Secretary of transportation

13. Which of the following agencies is an example of a quasi-government company? (1) (pp. 310–311)
    (A) Postal Service
    (B) SEC
    (C) AMTRAK
    (D) Fannie Mae

14. The spoils system involved which of the following? (2) (p. 313)
    (A) Hiring friends, relatives, and political supporters to work for the government
    (B) Giving government contracts to companies owned by friends, relatives, and political supporters
    (C) Contracting out with private companies to implement government programs
    (D) Forbidding government employees from engaging in political activities

15. The Hatch Act deals with which of the following federal personnel issues? (2) (p. 314)
    (A) Collective bargaining
    (B) Protecting federal workers from being forced by their bosses to work for particular candidates and parties
    (C) Whistleblower protection
    (D) Right to strike

16. Which of the following rights do federal employees enjoy? (2) (p. 314)

    (A) The right to form unions
    (B) The right to vote for candidates of their choice
    (C) The right to bargain collectively over issues other than pay and benefits
    (D) All of the above

17. Are private companies legally obligated to follow rules adopted by regulatory agencies? (3) (p. 315)

    (A) No. Only Congress has the authority to enact legally binding regulations.
    (B) Yes, but only if the rules are ratified by Congress.
    (C) Yes. Rules are legally binding.
    (D) No, although many businesses follow them voluntarily.

18. Suppose the Department of Labor adopts a rule that a majority of the members of Congress oppose. What steps, if any, can Congress take to reverse the rule? (3) (p. 316)

    (A) Congress lacks the authority to overturn the rule.
    (B) Congress can pass legislation to reverse the rule, but it would either require presidential approval or Congress would have to vote to override a veto.
    (C) Congress can ask the Supreme Court to overturn the rule.
    (D) Congress can do nothing, but the president can veto the rule.

19. Suppose the president disagrees with the policy initiatives of a federal agency. What can the president do to exert control? (4) (pp. 316–319)

    (A) The president can ask Congress to cut the agency's budget.
    (B) The president can appoint administrators to head the agency that agree with the president's policy position.
    (C) The president can ask Congress to reorganize the agency.
    (D) All of the above are correct answers.

20. Suppose that a majority of the members of Congress disagree with the policy initiatives of a federal agency. What actions can Congress take to exert control? (4) (p. 319)

    (A) Congress can cut the agency's budget.
    (B) Congress can change the legislation under which the agency operates.
    (C) Congress can reorganize the agency or merge it with another agency.
    (D) All of the above are correct answers.

21. Which of the following is an example of fire-alarm oversight? (4) (p. 319)

    (A) Congress conducts periodic review of an agency's operation.
    (B) The president conducts periodic review of an agency's operation.
    (C) Congress responds to well-publicized complaints about an agency's performance.
    (D) All of the above are correct answers.

22. An agency that is accused of working too closely with the interest groups it is supposed to be regulating is known as which of the following? (4) (p. 320)

    (A) Issue network
    (B) Captured agency
    (C) Independent regulatory commission
    (D) Iron triangle

23. Which of the following political actors is *not* part of a subgovernment or iron triangle? (5) (pp. 322–323)

    (A) President
    (B) Congress
    (C) Interest group
    (D) Government agency

24. Which of the following is a group of political actors that is concerned with some aspect of public policy? (5) (p. 324)

    (A) Issue network
    (B) Captured agency
    (C) Independent regulatory commission
    (D) Iron triangle

25. Which of the following factors has contributed to an increase in the importance of issue networks and a decline in the significance of subgovernments? (5) (p. 324)

    (A) Committee chairs in Congress are less influential now than in the past.
    (B) Interest groups are more numerous now than in the past.
    (C) New issues have arisen that are not dominated by a single interest group.
    (D) All of the above are correct answers.

Chapter 13: The Federal Courts

Circle the correct answer.

1. The power of the courts to declare unconstitutional the actions of the other branches and units of government is known as which of the following? (1) (p. 330)
   (A) Loose construction
   (B) Judicial review
   (C) Strict construction
   (D) Civil liberties

2. Which of the following statements most closely reflects the philosophy of loose construction of the Constitution? (1) (p. 331)
   (A) Judges should interpret the Constitution broadly to allow it to change with the times.
   (B) Judges should recognize that their role is to interpret the law rather than make the law.
   (C) Judges should stick to the literal meaning of the Constitution.
   (D) Judges should closely follow the intent of the framers of the Constitution.

3. An interpretation of the Constitution that favors limiting the authority of the national government while expanding the powers of the states is known as which of the following? (1) (pp. 332–333)
   (A) Strict construction
   (B) Loose construction
   (C) States' rights
   (D) Judicial review

4. The Supreme Court claimed the power of judicial review in which of the following cases? (2) (p. 332)
   (A) *Marbury v. Madison*
   (B) *McCulloch v. Maryland*
   (C) *Brown v. Board of Education*
   (D) *Plessy v. Ferguson*

5. The agenda of the modern Supreme Court (since 1937) has focused on which of the following sets of issue areas? (2) (p. 333)
   (A) Civil liberties and civil rights
   (B) Foreign and defense policy
   (C) Regulatory policy
   (D) Social welfare policy

6. Which of the following federal courts is exclusively a trial court? (3) (p. 336)
   (A) District court
   (B) Courts of appeal
   (C) Supreme Court
   (D) None of the above

7. The taking of a case from a lower court to a higher court by the losing party in a lower court decision is known as which of the following? (3) (p. 337)
   (A) Test case
   (B) Judicial review
   (C) Trial
   (D) Appeal

8. How are U.S. district judges selected? (4) (p. 338)
   (A) They are career civil servants, chosen through a merit hiring process.
   (B) They are appointed by the president subject to confirmation by the Senate.
   (C) They are elected by the voters in the states where they serve.
   (D) They are appointed by the president subject to confirmation by the House and Senate.

9. Which of the following statements most accurately describes the principle of senatorial courtesy? (4) (p. 338)
   (A) The Senate almost always confirms the president's district court nominees.
   (B) Senators will always confirm judicial nominees who have the support of the senators from their home states.
   (C) Senators have a veto on the confirmation of district judge nominees from their states.
   (D) Senators agree not to filibuster judicial nominations.

10. A liberal judge is more likely than a conservative judge to take which of the following policy actions? (4) (p. 338)
    (A) To rule in favor of the government and against criminal defendants
    (B) To rule in favor of workers and against corporate interests
    (C) To rule in favor of state governments in federalism disputes with the federal government
    (D) All of the above

11. What is the term of office of a federal district judge? (4) (p. 338)
    (A) 2 years
    (B) 4 years
    (C) 6 years
    (D) Life, with "good behavior"

12. The "nuclear option" involved which of the following actions? (5) (p. 341)
    (A) An attempt to increase the size of the Supreme Court
    (B) An effort to amend the Constitution to restrict the president's authority as commander-in-chief
    (C) An effort to eliminate the Senate filibuster for judicial nominees
    (D) An attempt to limit the jurisdiction of the Supreme Court to prevent it from hearing abortion cases

13. A corporation is unhappy with a regulatory ruling made by the Federal Trade Commission (FTC). Does the corporation have the right of appeal? (5) (p. 341)

   (A) The decisions of regulatory commissions can be appealed to the U.S. Courts of Appeals.
   (B) The decisions of regulatory commissions can be appealed to the U.S. Supreme Court.
   (C) The decisions of regulatory commissions can be appealed to the U.S. District Courts.
   (D) The decisions of regulatory commissions cannot be appealed, but Congress can rewrite the law on which the decision was based.

14. According to the U.S. Constitution, how many justices serve on the Supreme Court? (6) (p. 342)

   (A) 7
   (B) 9
   (C) 11
   (D) The Constitution says nothing about the size of the Supreme Court.

15. The Supreme Court decides a case by a unanimous vote. Who writes the majority opinion? (6) (p. 342)

   (A) The chief justice
   (B) The most senior justice
   (C) Either the chief justice writes the opinion or assigns it to another justice
   (D) A randomly assigned justice

16. Suppose that Congress passes controversial legislation that some people believe is unconstitutional. When, if ever, will the Supreme Court address the issue? (6) (pp. 342–343)

   (A) The Supreme Court will decide the issue when and if it accepts a case that involves a challenge to the constitutionality of the legislation.
   (B) The Supreme Court reviews legislation passed by Congress before it takes effect.
   (C) The Supreme Court will only review the legislation if Congress requests a review.
   (D) Never.

17. Why was *Brown v. Board of Education* an example of a test case? (6) (p. 346)

   (A) The Supreme Court reversed an earlier decision (the *Plessy Case*) when it decided *Brown*.
   (B) The case was prepared, presented, and financed by an interest group.
   (C) An interest group submitted a legal brief that discussed issues raised by the case.
   (D) *Brown* is considered a landmark decision in constitutional law.

18. How many justices must agree before the Supreme Court agrees to hear a case on appeal? (6) (p. 346)

   (A) Three
   (B) Four
   (C) Five
   (D) Nine

19. What is a friend of the court brief? (6) (p. 347)

   (A) An opinion written by a member of a court who agrees with the court's ruling but disagrees with the reasoning behind it
   (B) A judicial order directing the government either to release someone in custody or to justify why the person is being held
   (C) A court case that is supported financially by an interest group
   (D) A brief submitted by an interest group not directly involved in a case that is attempting to influence the outcome of the case

20. A Supreme Court justice agrees with the outcome of a case but disagrees with the legal reasoning presented in the majority opinion. Which of the following actions would the justice take? (6) (pp. 348–349)

   (A) File a friend of the court brief.
   (B) Write a concurring opinion.
   (C) Write a majority opinion.
   (D) Write a dissenting opinion.

21. What is a dissenting opinion? (6) (p. 348)

   (A) It is a legal brief written by an interest group attempting to influence the outcome of a case.
   (B) It is an opinion written by a justice on the Supreme Court who agrees with the outcome of a case but disagrees with the reasoning contained in the majority opinion.
   (C) It is an opinion written by a justice of the Supreme Court that disagrees with the majority ruling on a case.
   (D) It is a document written by an interest group that disagrees with a ruling issued by the Supreme Court.

22. Assuming that the Supreme Court is fully staffed and that every justice participates in a decision, how many justices must agree to decide the outcome of a case? (6) (p. 349)

   (A) Four
   (B) Five
   (C) Six
   (D) Nine

23. Suppose that a majority of the members of the Supreme Court believe that a recent action by the president violates the Constitution. What can they do? (7) (p. 352)

   (A) They can do nothing until a case arises that involves the issue and the case is appealed to the Supreme Court.
   (B) Nothing. The Supreme Court can review the acts of Congress but not the actions of the president.
   (C) The Supreme Court can issue an opinion declaring the president's action unconstitutional.
   (D) The Supreme Court can invite parties to file a challenge against the president's action.

Chapter 14: Economic Policymaking

Circle the correct answer.

1. A financial incentive given by government to an individual or a business interest to accomplish a public objective is known by which of the following terms? (1) (p. 363)
   (A) Entitlement
   (B) Welfare program
   (C) Subsidy
   (D) Progressive taxation

2. "The nation is suffering a severe economic slump. Many companies have gone out of business and unemployment is at a record high." That statement describes which of the following? (1) (p. 364)
   (A) Inflation
   (B) Recession
   (C) Depression
   (D) Supply-side economics

3. "Prices just keep going up. It sure seems like a dollar doesn't go as far these days as it used to." The above statement describes which of the following? (1) (p. 364)
   (A) Inflation
   (B) Recession
   (C) Depression
   (D) Supply-side economics

4. Which of the following is the most important tax source of revenue for the U.S. government? (2) (p. 365)
   (A) Sales taxes
   (B) Payroll taxes
   (C) Corporate income taxes
   (D) Individual income taxes

5. An individual has a net income of $100,000, including $10,000 of income that is tax exempt. What is the individual's taxable income? (2) (p. 367)
   (A) $100,000
   (B) $90,000
   (C) $10,000
   (D) It depends on the individual's tax bracket.

6. Payroll taxes help fund which of the following programs? (2) (p. 368)
   (A) Social Security
   (B) Medicaid
   (C) School Lunch Program
   (D) All of the above

7. Federal taxes on gasoline, tires, and airplane tickets are examples of which of the following? (2) (p. 368)
   (A) Progressive taxes
   (B) Excise taxes
   (C) Payroll taxes
   (D) Tax preferences

8. The federal income tax is an example of which of the following? (3) (p. 370)
   (A) Progressive tax
   (B) Regressive tax
   (C) Proportional tax
   (D) Excise tax

9. Which of the following taxes can be justified on the basis of the ability to pay theory of taxation? (3) (p. 371)
   (A) Excise taxes on tobacco and alcohol
   (B) Payroll taxes to support Social Security and Medicare
   (C) Individual income tax
   (D) Excise taxes on tires and gasoline

10. An income tax that assesses the same percentage tax rate on all income levels above a personal exemption while allowing few if any deductions is a definition of which of the following? (3) (pp. 371–372)
    (A) Progressive tax
    (B) Value added tax (VAT)
    (C) Excise tax
    (D) Flat tax

11. Assume that federal government revenues are $2.5 trillion and expenditures are $3 trillion. Which of the following statements is accurate? (4) (p. 374)
    (A) The budget is balanced.
    (B) The government ran a surplus of $0.5 trillion.
    (C) The government ran a deficit of $0.5 trillion.
    (D) The national debt is $0.5 trillion.

12. How does a deficit of $400 billion affect the national debt? (4) (p. 374)
    (A) It has no impact on the national debt.
    (B) It increases the national debt by $400 billion.
    (C) It decreases the national debt by $400 billion.
    (D) The national debt is $400 billion.

13. Why does a recession increase the size of a budget deficit? (4) (p. 374)
    (A) Individual income tax collections fall because people who have lost their jobs make less money on which to pay taxes.
    (B) Corporate income tax collections fall because corporations make smaller profits or even lose money.
    (C) Spending increases because more people qualify for welfare benefits.
    (D) All of the above are correct answers.

14. Which of the following is *not* one of the top five major expenditure categories in the federal budget? (5) (p. 377)
    (A) Foreign aid
    (B) Social Security
    (C) National defense
    (D) Healthcare

15. Which of the following is an element of healthcare reform adopted in 2010? (5) (pp. 379–380)

(A) An expansion of Medicaid coverage
(B) A requirement that everyone not otherwise covered by health insurance purchase a policy
(C) Higher taxes on upper-income individuals and families
(D) All of the above

16. Which of the following is a factor negatively affecting the future of the Social Security program? (5) (p. 381)

(A) The cost of prescription drugs is rising rapidly.
(B) The baby-boom generation is beginning to retire.
(C) The number of people receiving welfare benefits is less now than during the 1990s.
(D) All of the above are correct answers.

17. Is Social Security a means-tested program? (5) (pp. 380–382)

(A) No, because eligibility does not depend on income
(B) No, because it is funded by a special tax rather than general revenues
(C) Yes, because everyone who meets certain criteria is eligible
(D) Yes, because the program is jointly administered by the national government and the states

18. Is Social Security an entitlement program? (6) (p. 385)

(A) No, because eligibility does not depend on income
(B) No, because implementation of the program does not involve the states
(C) Yes, because it provides benefits to everyone qualified to receive them under the law
(D) Yes, because it has a dedicated source of tax revenue supporting it (the payroll tax)

19. Which of the following terms is best described in the following sentence: "Congress can only spend a dollar if it saves a dollar elsewhere"? (6) (p. 386)

(A) Privatization
(B) Discretionary spending
(C) Pork barrel spending
(D) PAYGO

20. "Budgetary expenditures that are not mandated by law or contract" is the definition for which of the following terms? (6) (p. 387)

(A) Privatization
(B) Discretionary spending
(C) Pork barrel spending
(D) PAYGO

21. Which of the following is primarily responsible for setting monetary policy? (7) (p. 389)

(A) Fed
(B) Office of Management and Budget
(C) Department of the Treasury
(D) Congress

22. The Federal Open Market Committee (FOMC) makes decisions that directly impact which of the following? (7) (p. 389)

(A) Tax rates
(B) Fiscal policy
(C) Interest rates
(D) Social Security

23. The Fed took which of the following actions in response to the deepening recession in late 2008? (7) (pp. 389–390)

(A) Loaned banks money
(B) Increased interest rates
(C) Raised taxes
(D) All of the above

24. An appropriation bill includes $600,000 to fund a water storage tower in Ada, Oklahoma, a town of 16,000 residents. This provision is an example of which of the following? (8) (p. 392)

(A) Entitlement
(B) Means-tested program
(C) Privatization
(D) Earmark

25. Which of the following units of government is *least* involved in the adoption of economic policies? (8) (pp. 390–393)

(A) Congress
(B) Supreme Court
(C) President
(D) Fed

Chapter 15: Civil Liberties

Circle the correct answer.

1. The protection of the individual from the unrestricted power of government is the definition for which of the following? (1) (p. 400)
   (A) Selective incorporation of the Bill of Rights
   (B) Fundamental rights
   (C) Civil rights
   (D) Civil liberties

2. Where is the Bill of Rights found? (1) (p. 401)
   (A) It is the first ten amendments to the Constitution.
   (B) It is found in Article I, Section 8, of the Constitution.
   (C) It is part of the Declaration of Independence.
   (D) It is part of the Articles of Confederation.

3. The Bill of Rights initially restricted the power of which of the following levels of government? (1) (p. 401)
   (A) Neither the national government nor state governments
   (B) Both the national government and state governments
   (C) The national government but not state governments
   (D) State governments but not the national government

4. The selective incorporation of the Bill of Rights against the states is based on which of the following? (1) (p. 401)
   (A) Due Process Clause of the Fourteenth Amendment
   (B) First Amendment
   (C) Equal Protection Clause of the Fourteenth Amendment
   (D) Thirteenth Amendment

5. Your son who works at a local construction company was fired because his boss disagreed with him over a bumper sticker for a presidential candidate. Does your son have any legal recourse under the U.S. Constitution or federal law? (1) (p. 401)
   (A) Yes, he can sue for his job back based on his boss violating his freedom of expression.
   (B) No, he cannot sue because the First Amendment protects freedom of speech and bumper stickers are not speech.
   (C) No. The First Amendment does not apply to private employers.
   (D) Yes. Your son can sue his former boss for age discrimination.

6. Which of the following statements is true about the fundamental rights protected by the Bill of Rights? (1) (pp. 401–402)
   (A) They are absolute and may never be abridged by the government.
   (B) They can be abridged but only when the government can demonstrate a plausible justification.
   (C) They are guidelines, but government officials can abridge them when they determine it is in the public interest.
   (D) They cannot be abridged unless the government can demonstrate a compelling or overriding public interest for so doing.

7. Opponents of state aid to church-related schools believe that it violates which of the following provisions of the Constitution? (2) (p. 404)
   (A) The freedom of religion clause in the First Amendment
   (B) The establishment of religion clause in the First Amendment
   (C) The freedom of expression clause in the First Amendment
   (D) The freedom of assembly clause in the First Amendment

8. Disputes over school prayer are based on which of the following provisions of the U.S. Constitution? (2) (p. 405)
   (A) The freedom of religion clause in the First Amendment
   (B) The establishment of religion clause in the First Amendment
   (C) The freedom of expression clause in the First Amendment
   (D) The freedom of assembly clause in the First Amendment

9. *Engel v. Vitale* dealt with which of the following issues? (2) (p. 405)
   (A) Abortion
   (B) Freedom of religion
   (C) Freedom of speech
   (D) Establishment of religion

10. A dispute over a local law aimed at preventing a religious group from passing out literature door-to-door would involve which of the following constitutional provisions? (2) (p. 406)
    (A) The freedom of religion clause in the First Amendment
    (B) The establishment of religion clause in the First Amendment
    (C) The freedom of expression clause in the First Amendment
    (D) The freedom of assembly clause in the First Amendment

11. In some countries, people who criticize government officials are put in jail for not supporting the government. What provision of the U.S. Constitution protects individuals who criticize the government? (3) (p. 408)
    (A) The freedom of religion clause in the First Amendment
    (B) The establishment of religion clause in the First Amendment
    (C) The freedom of expression clause in the First Amendment
    (D) The freedom of assembly clause in the First Amendment

12. Which of the following is an example of a hate crime? (3) (p. 410)

(A) A group of young Latino and African American men break into the home of an Asian family. While robbing the family, they use racial/ethnic slurs, threatening the Asian family with violence if they don't move out of the neighborhood.
(B) A woman publishes a newsletter in which she attacks homosexuals as "godless pagans who spread disease."
(C) A white man who is fleeing from the scene of a crime shoots and wounds a police officer who is African American.
(D) All of the above are correct answers.

13. Which of the following elements is *not* part of the official definition of legal obscenity? (4) (pp. 411–412)

(A) The work depicts sexual conduct.
(B) The work contains extreme violence.
(C) The work appeals to an excessive interest in sex.
(D) The work taken as a whole lacks serious literary, artistic, political, or scientific value.

14. A supermarket tabloid newspaper prints a story stating that a prominent U.S. senator is having an affair with a married woman. It names both parties. As it turns out, the accusation is false. Both the senator and the woman sue the newspaper for defamation. Which of them is more likely to win? (4) (p. 412)

(A) Neither can win a lawsuit because the First Amendment protects the newspaper's right to publish.
(B) The senator and the woman are equally likely to win because the courts treat all parties the same.
(C) The senator is more likely to win because he has more to lose than the woman, who is just an ordinary citizen.
(D) The woman is more likely to win because the standard to prove defamation is lower for an ordinary citizen than it is for a public figure.

15. In 2008, the U.S. Supreme Court ruled that a District of Columbia ban against gun ownership violated which of the following constitutional provisions? (5) (p. 413)

(A) Fifth Amendment
(B) First Amendment
(C) Second Amendment
(D) Fourth Amendment

16. Which of the following statements is true regarding a right to privacy? (6) (p. 413)

(A) The First Amendment guarantees people the right to personal privacy.
(B) The Supreme Court has interpreted various provisions of the Bill of Rights to create "zones of privacy."
(C) A right to privacy is the basis for *Engel v. Vitale*.
(D) All of the above are correct answers.

17. *Roe v. Wade* was based on which of the following constitutional principles? (6) (p. 414)

(A) A constitutional right to privacy
(B) The Equal Protection Clause of the Fourteenth Amendment
(C) The Establishment Clause of the First Amendment
(D) The Free Exercise Clause of the First Amendment

18. The constitutional principle that government cannot deprive someone of life, liberty, or property without following fair and regular procedures is known as which of the following? (7) (p. 415)

(A) Selective incorporation
(B) Parental choice
(C) Exclusionary rule
(D) Due process of law

19. What is the rationale for the exclusionary rule? (7) (pp. 416–417)

(A) If the evidence proves a defendant's guilt, then the evidence should be used against the defendant regardless of how the evidence was obtained.
(B) If the government is allowed to use evidence that was obtained illegally, then the government has no incentive to follow the law in collecting evidence.
(C) Defendants should be informed of their rights so they can knowingly choose to exercise them or not to exercise them.
(D) All of the above are correct answers.

20. *Boumediene v. Bush* dealt with which of the following issues? (8) (p. 423)

(A) Exclusionary rule
(B) Freedom of religion
(C) The rights of terror suspects held at Guantánamo
(D) Abortion rights

21. Why was President Obama initially unable to keep his promise to close the prison at Guantánamo Bay, Cuba? (8) (p. 423)

(A) The Supreme Court ruled that Guantánamo had to remain open.
(B) Congress ordered the release of prisoners held at Guantánamo.
(C) Neither foreign countries nor American communities were willing to accept the transfer of prisoners.
(D) All of the above are correct answers.

22. Which of the following would be most likely to initiate a test case to influence civil liberties policy? (9) (p. 425)

(A) Congress
(B) President
(C) Supreme Court
(D) Interest group

Chapter 16: Civil Rights

Circle the correct answer.

1. Which of the following constitutional provisions has the greatest impact on civil rights policymaking? (1) (p. 434)
   (A) Equal Protection Clause of the Fourteenth Amendment
   (B) First Amendment
   (C) Second Amendment
   (D) Due Process Clause of the Fourteenth Amendment

2. Which of the following constitutional amendments deals with voting rights? (1) (p. 434)
   (A) First Amendment
   (B) Thirteenth Amendment
   (C) Fourteenth Amendment
   (D) Fifteenth Amendment

3. Which of the following is *not* a suspect classification? (1) (p. 435)
   (A) Race
   (B) Sexual orientation
   (C) Ethnicity
   (D) National origin

4. Under what circumstances, if any, can the government treat people of different races or ethnicities differently? (2) (p. 435)
   (A) The government must demonstrate an overriding public interest in making the distinction and prove that it is achieving that public interest in the least restrictive way possible.
   (B) The government must have a reasonable basis for making the distinction.
   (C) The government must prove that the distinction is necessary to achieve an important governmental objective.
   (D) The government must treat all persons identically. The Constitution is color blind.

5. Suppose the government reinstates the military draft, but only drafts men and not women. Would it be possible for the government to adopt the policy constitutionally? (2) (p. 435)
   (A) Yes, but it would have to demonstrate a rational basis for making the distinction.
   (B) Yes, but it would have to offer an "exceedingly persuasive justification" to make the distinction.
   (C) Yes, but it would have to demonstrate a compelling government interest in making the distinction.
   (D) No. Because of the Equal Protection Clause, any draft would have to include both men and women.

6. The judicial decision rule holding that the Supreme Court will find a government policy unconstitutional unless the government can demonstrate a compelling interest justifying the action is known as which of the following? (2) (p. 435)
   (A) Strict judicial scrutiny
   (B) Separate but equal
   (C) Civil liberties
   (D) Civil rights

7. The doctrine of separate but equal concerned what issue? (2) (p. 436)
   (A) Separation of powers with checks and balances
   (B) Affirmative action
   (C) Voting rights for African Americans
   (D) Whether laws requiring separate facilities for whites and blacks satisfy the Equal Protection Clause

8. Which of the following statements about *Brown v. Board of Education* is true? (2) (pp. 437–438)
   (A) It dealt with racially restrictive covenants.
   (B) It overturned *Plessy v. Ferguson*, at least as it applied to public education.
   (C) It was a voting rights case.
   (D) It involved affirmative action policies in education.

9. Which of the following statements most closely reflects the current status of constitutional law concerning school integration? (2) (p. 439)
   (A) School officials can assign students of different races to different schools if those schools are equal quality.
   (B) School officials must ensure that all students are assigned to schools that are racially mixed.
   (C) School officials must ignore race in making school assignments.
   (D) School officials can consider race as a "plus factor" among several criteria in making school assignments.

10. A state university decides to limit graduate student enrollment in its space physics program to American citizens, excluding noncitizens. Is such an action constitutional? (2) (pp. 440–441)
   (A) Yes, if the university can demonstrate a compelling governmental interest in making the distinction between citizens and noncitizens.
   (B) Yes, if the university can state a rational basis for the distinction.
   (C) Yes. Noncitizens are not protected by the Constitution.
   (D) No. The Constitution prohibits distinctions based on citizenship status. Everyone must be treated equally.

16. "Because the United States is the world's only superpower, it can assert itself internationally and other nations will have no choice but to go along." The above statement most closely reflects which of the following approaches to foreign policy? (5) (p. 481)

(A) Isolationist approach
(B) Internationalist approach
(C) Multinational approach
(D) Unilateralist approach

17. Which of the following is an argument offered by those people who believe that the United States should take an internationalist approach to foreign policy? (5) (p. 482)

(A) The United States should act in its own best interests rather than compromising with other nations.
(B) As the world's most powerful nation, the United States does not have to accommodate the interests of other countries.
(C) The United States needs the support of other nations if it hopes to accomplish its foreign policy goals.
(D) All of the above are correct answers.

18. Which of the following presidents is associated with a unilateralist foreign policy? (5) (p. 482)

(A) George W. Bush
(B) Barack Obama
(C) Franklin Roosevelt
(D) All of the above

19. Which of the following statements is true about American defense spending? (6) (pp. 483–484)

(A) In general, defense spending rises during wartime and falls during peacetime.
(B) As a percentage of GDP, defense spending is greater today than at any time since World War II.
(C) Defense spending has been falling in recent years despite the war on terror and wars in Afghanistan and Iraq.
(D) All of the above are correct answers.

20. Tanks, personnel carriers, aircraft carriers, and so on, are examples of which of the following? (6) (pp. 484–487)

(A) Don't ask, don't tell
(B) Conventional forces
(C) Strategic forces
(D) Mutual assured destruction (MAD)

21. "The Soviet leaders did not dare launch a nuclear attack against the United States because the American counterattack would have destroyed the Soviet Union and vice versa." The above statement is an expression of which of the following? (6) (pp. 484–485)

(A) Military preemption
(B) Isolationism
(C) Mutual assured destruction (MAD)
(D) Nuclear winter

22. "The United States needs to attack Iran to eliminate its nuclear capacity before it has the opportunity to attack us or provide WMD to terrorists." The above statement is an expression of which of the following concepts? (6) (p. 486)

(A) Nuclear winter
(B) Mutual assured destruction (MAD)
(C) Deterrence
(D) Military preemption

23. Which president is most closely associated with the concept of military preemption? (6) (p. 486)

(A) Richard Nixon
(B) George W. Bush
(C) Bill Clinton
(D) Ronald Reagan

24. Which of the following officials has historically taken the lead in American foreign and defense policymaking? (7) (p. 490)

(A) President
(B) Speaker of the House
(C) Chief Justice of the United States
(D) Secretary of defense

25. Which of the following statements best describes bipartisanship? (7) (p. 490)

(A) Congress and the president work closely together.
(B) The House and Senate work closely together.
(C) Republicans and Democrats work closely together.
(D) The United States and Russia work closely together.

ANSWERS TO PRACTICE TEST QUESTIONS

Introduction: Government, Politics, and the Policymaking Process

1. D
2. C
3. B
4. A
5. A
6. D
7. D
8. A
9. B
10. C
11. D
12. C
13. A
14. D
15. D
16. C
17. D
18. A
19. B
20. C

Chapter 1: A Changing America in a Changing World

1. A
2. C
3. C
4. A
5. B
6. C
7. A
8. D
9. D
10. D
11. B
12. D
13. A
14. D
15. C
16. C
17. B
18. B
19. C
20. A
21. A
22. D
23. B
24. C
25. A

Chapter 2: The American Constitution

1. C
2. A
3. B
4. B
5. D
6. A
7. D
8. B
9. A
10. C
11. C
12. B
13. C
14. A
15. D
16. A
17. C
18. D
19. A
20. D
21. D
22. A
23. B
24. A
25. C

Chapter 3: The Federal System

1. C
2. A
3. A
4. B
5. B
6. C
7. B
8. C
9. B
10. D
11. A
12. C
13. D
14. C
15. A
16. D
17. A
18. C
19. D
20. D
21. C
22. A
23. D
24. B
25. A

Chapter 4: Public Opinion

1. B
2. A
3. A
4. C
5. B
6. D
7. D
8. C
9. A
10. D
11. D
12. B
13. B
14. C
15. D
16. A
17. B
18. B
19. C
20. C
21. A
22. A

Chapter 5: Political Participation

1. D
2. D
3. A
4. D
5. A
6. B
7. C
8. D
9. C
10. D
11. A
12. A
13. D
14. B
15. A
16. C
17. A
18. A
19. D
20. C
21. A
22. A
23. D
24. B

Chapter 6: The News Media

1. D
2. A
3. B
4. C
5. A
6. D
7. D
8. C
9. B
10. A
11. D
12. B
13. B
14. C
15. A
16. B
17. A
18. B
19. D
20. C
21. A
22. C
23. B
24. D
25. C

Chapter 7: Interest Groups

1. B
2. D
3. A
4. C
5. C
6. B
7. D
8. C
9. A
10. B
11. A
12. D
13. C
14. A
15. A
16. D
17. A
18. C
19. D
20. B
21. B
22. C
23. D
24. B
25. D

Chapter 8: Political Parties

1. D
2. C
3. D
4. C
5. A
6. D
7. B
8. C
9. B
10. A
11. C
12. D
13. C
14. A
15. C
16. D
17. A
18. B
19. A
20. C
21. D
22. D
23. B
24. C
25. A

Chapter 9: Elections

1. C
2. A
3. B
4. A
5. B
6. C
7. B
8. B
9. C
10. D
11. D
12. C
13. D
14. A
15. C
16. A
17. B
18. C
19. C
20. A
21. D
22. C
23. D

Chapter 10: Congress

1. A
2. A
3. B
4. D
5. B
6. C
7. D
8. C
9. A
10. A
11. B
12. C
13. D
14. D
15. A
16. D
17. B
18. B
19. C
20. A
21. C
22. C
23. B

Chapter 11: The Presidency

1. B
2. D
3. D
4. B
5. D
6. A
7. C
8. A
9. B
10. A
11. D
12. C
13. A
14. A
15. B
16. D
17. C
18. D
19. C
20. B
21. D
22. A
23. D
24. B
25. C

Chapter 12: The Federal Bureaucracy

1. D
2. A
3. B
4. C
5. B
6. C
7. A
8. B
9. C
10. B
11. A
12. C
13. D
14. A
15. B
16. D
17. C
18. B
19. D
20. D
21. C
22. B
23. A
24. A
25. D

Chapter 13: The Federal Courts

1. B
2. A
3. C
4. A
5. A
6. A
7. D
8. B
9. C
10. B
11. D
12. C
13. A
14. D
15. C
16. A
17. B
18. B
19. D
20. B
21. C
22. B
23. A

Chapter 14: Economic Policymaking

1. C
2. C
3. A
4. D
5. B
6. A
7. B
8. A
9. C
10. D
11. C
12. B
13. D
14. A
15. D
16. B
17. A
18. C
19. D
20. B
21. A
22. C
23. A
24. D
25. B

Chapter 15: Civil Liberties

1. D
2. A
3. C
4. A
5. C
6. D
7. B
8. B
9. D
10. A
11. C
12. A
13. B
14. D
15. C
16. B
17. A
18. D
19. B
20. C
21. C
22. D

Chapter 16: Civil Rights

1. A
2. D
3. B
4. A
5. B
6. A
7. D
8. B
9. C
10. A
11. C
12. B
13. A
14. C
15. D
16. D
17. B
18. A
19. B
20. C
21. C
22. B

Chapter 17: Foreign and Defense Policy

1. A
2. C
3. D
4. B
5. C
6. D
7. A
8. B
9. C
10. B
11. D
12. B
13. B
14. C
15. A
16. D
17. C
18. A
19. A
20. B
21. C
22. D
23. B
24. A
25. C